IMAGES of America

Ohio River Images

Cincinnati to Louisville in the Packet Boat Era

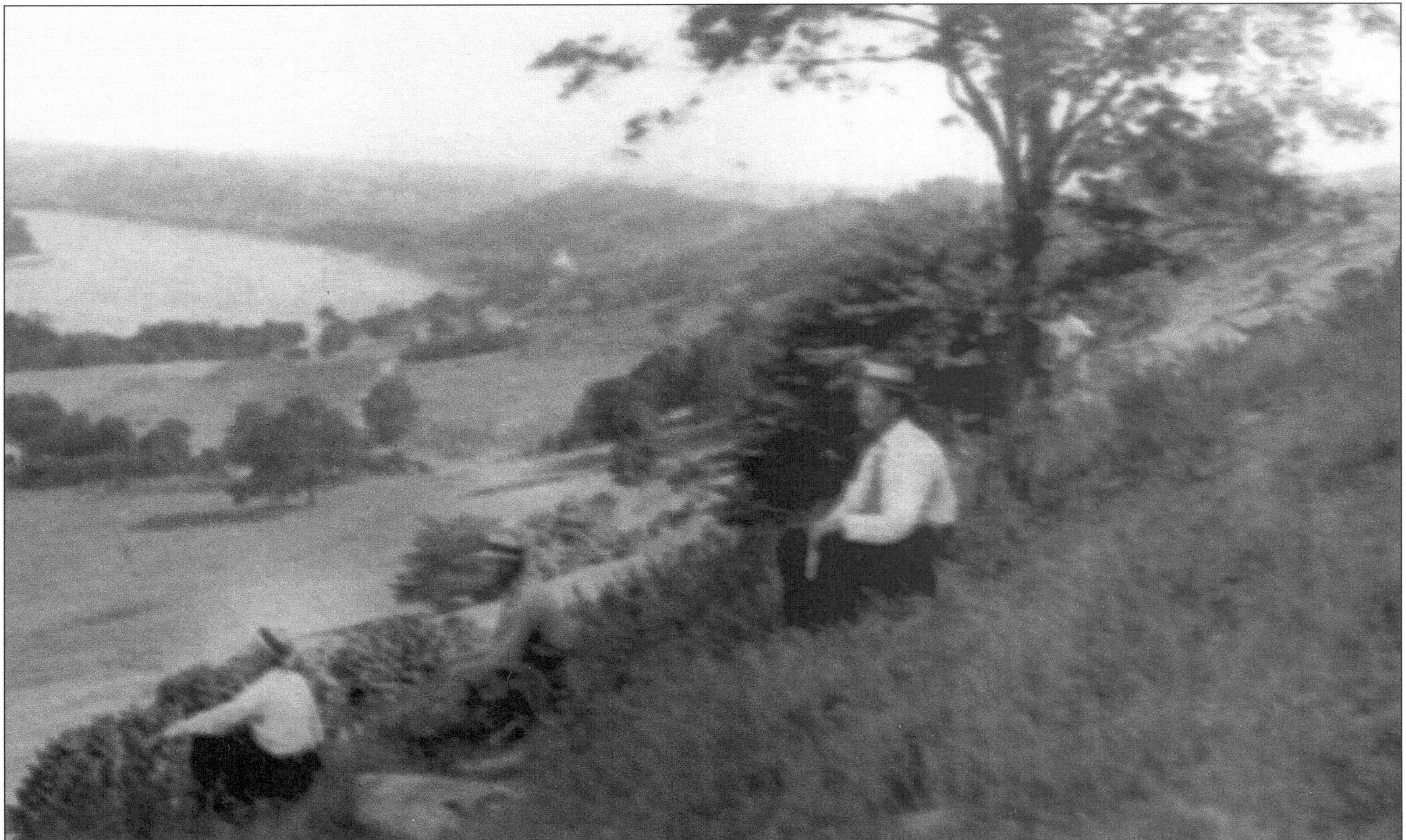

A lazy summer afternoon on the hillside above Buckeye Landing, below Rising Sun, Indiana, is captured on film. This is a portion of a 36-inch long photograph probably taken shortly after 1900. The men are unidentified. (North 02.)

IMAGES
of America

OHIO RIVER IMAGES

CINCINNATI TO LOUISVILLE IN THE PACKET BOAT ERA

Russell G. Ryle

ARCADIA

ISBN 0-7385-0739-3

Published by Arcadia Publishing,
an imprint of Tempus Publishing, Inc.
3047 N. Lincoln Ave., Suite 410
Chicago, IL 60657

Printed in Great Britain.

Library of Congress Catalog Card Number: 00-105899

For all general information contact Arcadia Publishing at:
Telephone 843-853-2070
Fax 843-853-0044
E-Mail sales@arcadiapublishing.com

For customer service and orders:
Toll-Free 1-888-313-2665

Visit us on the internet at http://www.arcadiapublishing.com

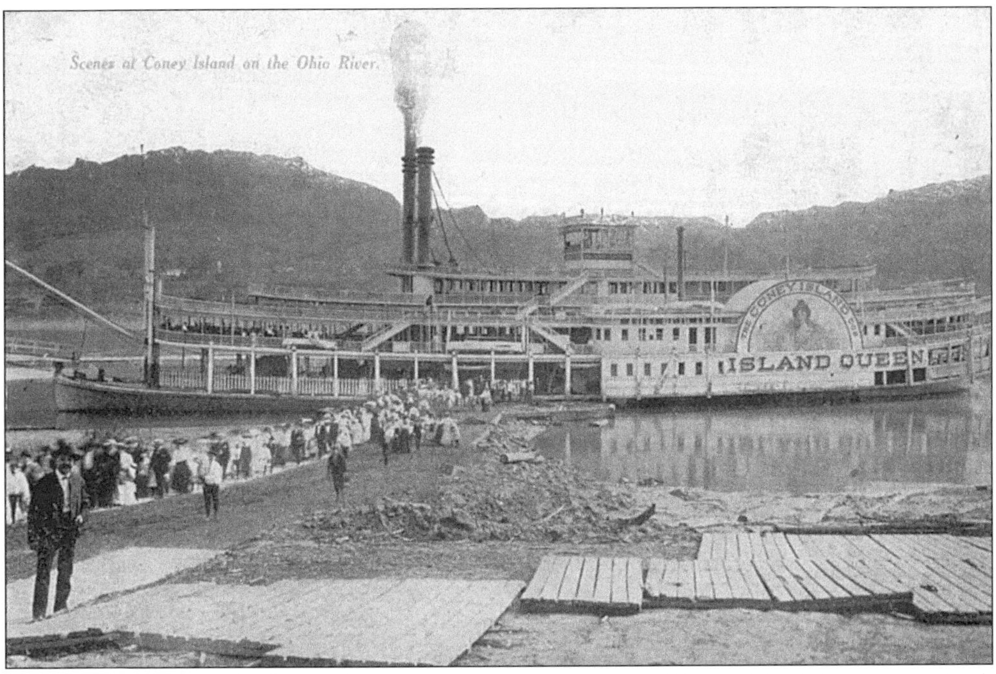

The *Str. Island Queen* discharges her cargo of excursion riders at Coney Island Amusement Park just above Cincinnati, Ohio, on a warm summer weekend afternoon. Wood planks, like those in the foreground, have been laid across the shallow mud from the permanent dock to the boat. The low, summertime water level of the river prevents this big boat from getting any closer to shore. (North 03.)

Contents

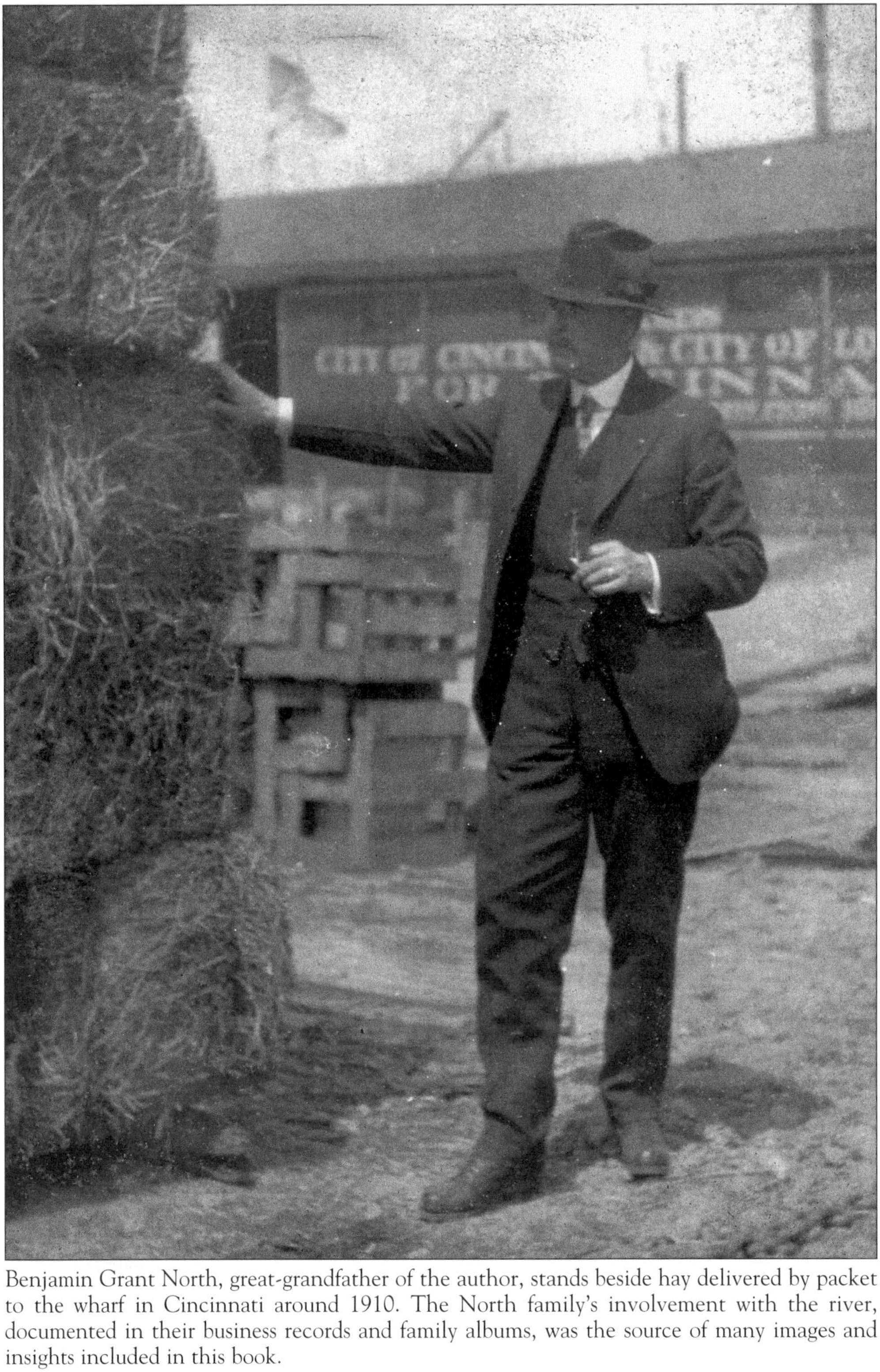

Benjamin Grant North, great-grandfather of the author, stands beside hay delivered by packet to the wharf in Cincinnati around 1910. The North family's involvement with the river, documented in their business records and family albums, was the source of many images and insights included in this book.

INTRODUCTION

What was it like to live, work, play, and travel along the Ohio River in the early part of the twentieth century? What was the look and feel of the towns and villages along its shores in the days before the private car, superhighway, television, and computer? The images that follow will give the reader insight into life along the river in the packet era. They also document the gradual change towards more modern times, and what the river is like today.

During this period man attempted to tame the Ohio River by building dams, guaranteeing a minimum 9-foot navigable water depth year round. Channels were improved and marked. The risks of steamboat travel were reduced. However, man could not completely control nature. Periodic spring floods stopped commerce. Winter ice destroyed everything caught in its cold grip when the ice was forced downriver by warming rains.

River trade slowly moved away from the hauling of small cargoes and daily travel. The last packets were finally and permanently tied to the shore in the early 1930s, a casualty of hard economic times and technical progress. River traffic shifted its focus towards bulk cargoes moved by large tows of barges from city to city, for the most part bypassing the small towns and landings. People living along the river shore no longer relied upon it for their daily travel and commerce. The river became a scenic neighbor, drawing visitors to cities, towns, and villages along its banks.

Today, a few excursion boats can still offer an approximation of what is was like to travel on the Ohio River when it was the water highway over which most in the area traveled and traded. Sit quietly along its shore, and you will hear and feel a sample of bygone times. It is the author's hope that the images that follow will leave the reader with a sense of what it was like to grow up along the river's banks, listening to the stories told by those that lived the packet era.

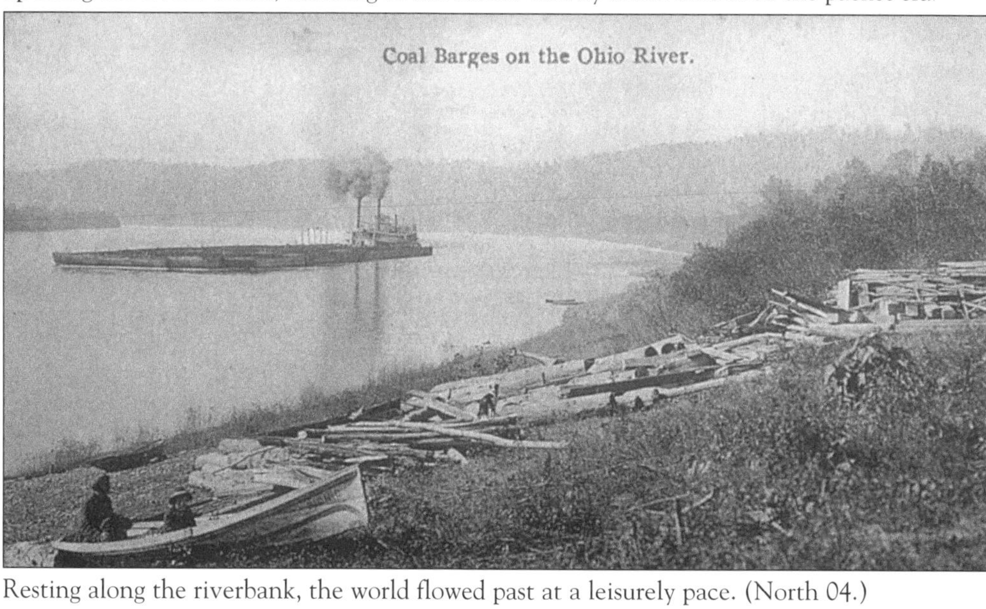

Resting along the riverbank, the world flowed past at a leisurely pace. (North 04.)

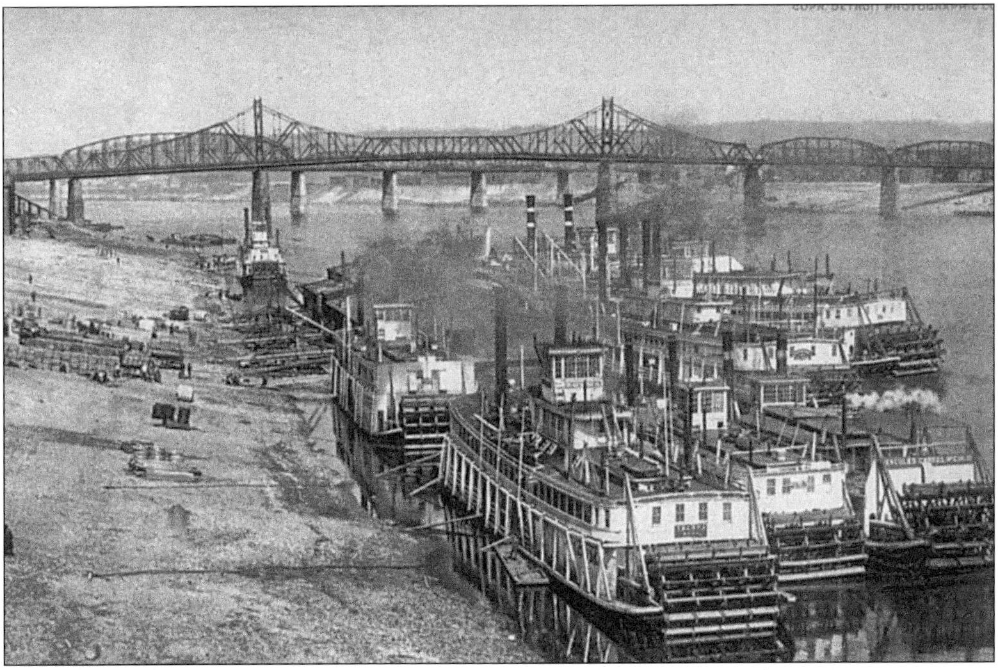

The wharf at Cincinnati, Ohio was a busy destination for passengers and cargoes.

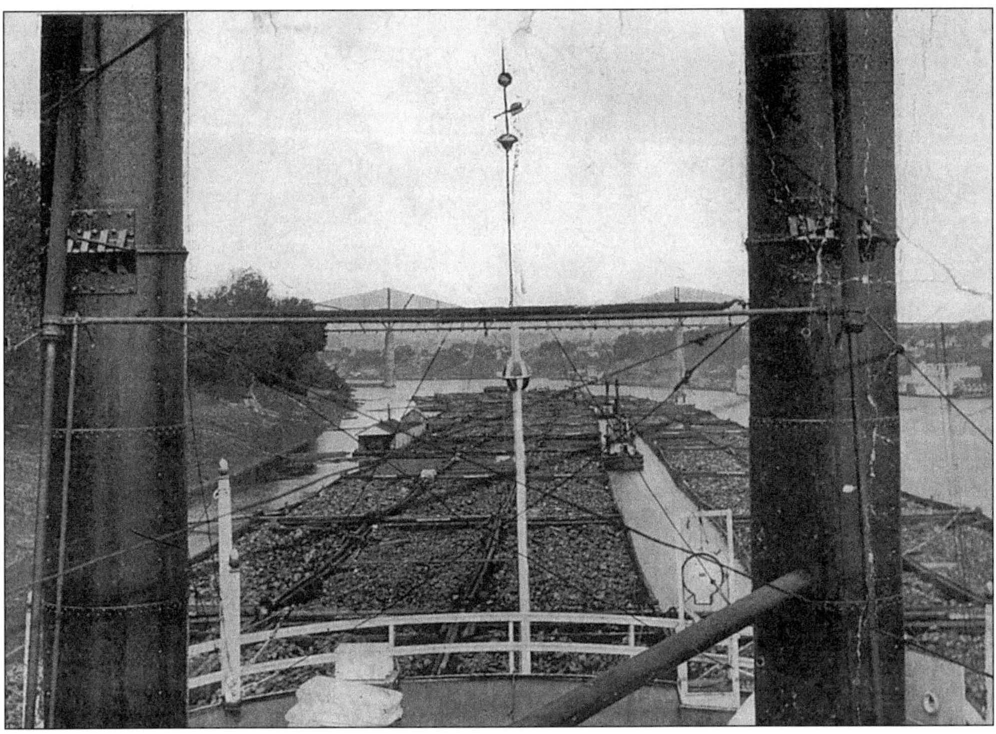

A pilot's-eye view of the world is pictured above.

One

Boats of the Packet Era

The river was home to several types of boats, each serving a specific function. Packets and towboats moved people and cargoes the length of the river. Smaller packets or "local boats" made slower, shorter runs to nearby cities and towns. Ferries and launches carried people, carriages, and cargoes across the river between towns on the opposite shore. Numerous houseboats, launches, yawls, and skiffs also met the needs of the people living along the river's banks.

The packets were steam-powered, wood-hulled boats of two general styles. Large side-wheel packets were valued for their speed, maneuverability, and ability to haul large numbers of passengers and cargo. They were the preferred vessels on the longer, regularly scheduled daily runs. Smaller side or stern wheel packets were used on the shorter routes. They also worked the longer routes when the water level was too low for the bigger packets to operate.

The basic design of these boats evolved over the previous 80 years as experience and better engineering greatly reduced the risk of boiler explosion. Wood remained the material of choice until its unavailability and cost became prohibitive during World War I. Gradually, the working life of a packet was expanded from a few years to as long as a few decades.

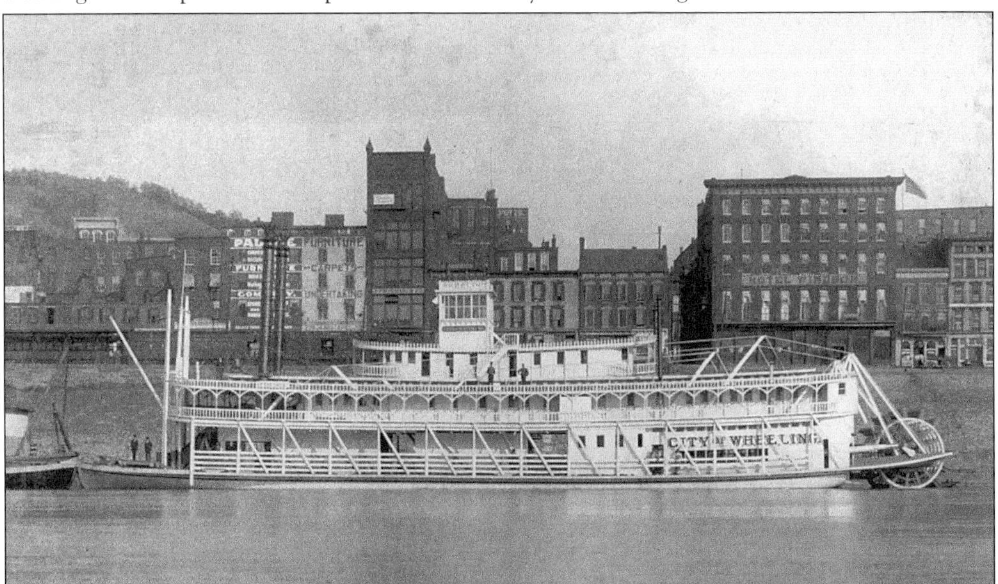

The *Str. City of Wheeling* is here tied to the wharf at the Cincinnati public landing. This style of shallow-draft, sternwheel packet could operate in lower summer water levels, as seen in this photograph. Until the system of locks and dams was completed in 1929, navigation was frequently halted by low water in the summer months. (North 05.)

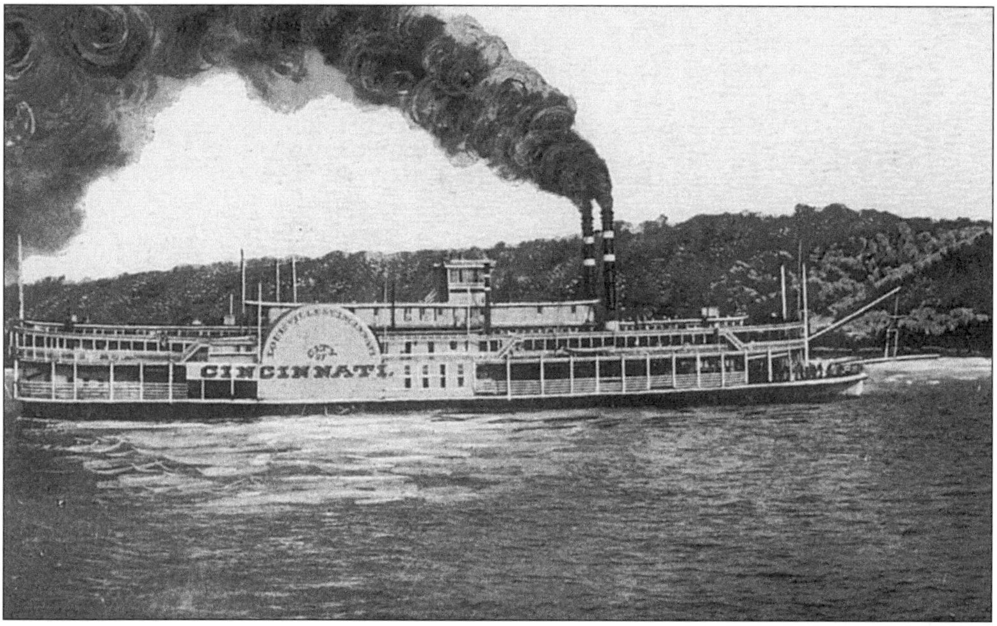

The *Str. City of Cincinnati* was operated by the Louisville and Cincinnati Packet Company. Known as the "mail line," this company dominated the Cincinnati to Louisville river route from just after the Civil War until packet service was suspended in 1933. (North 06.)

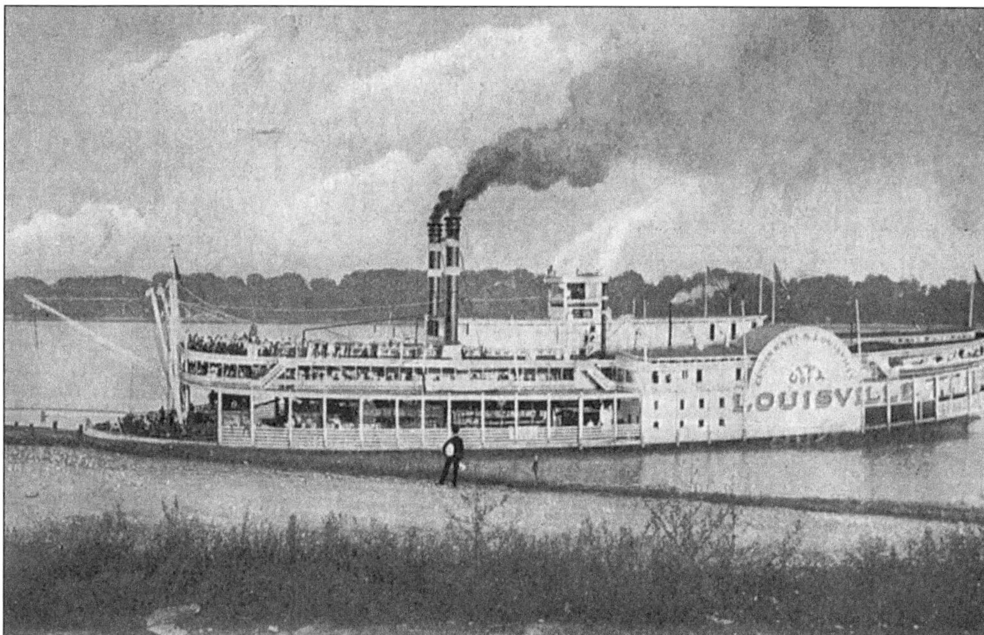

Str. City of Louisville, sister ship to the *Cincinnati*, was known as "the big boat." She set speed records for the route that were never bettered. Both boats were relatively deep draft, side-wheelers that carried large loads of passengers and freight.

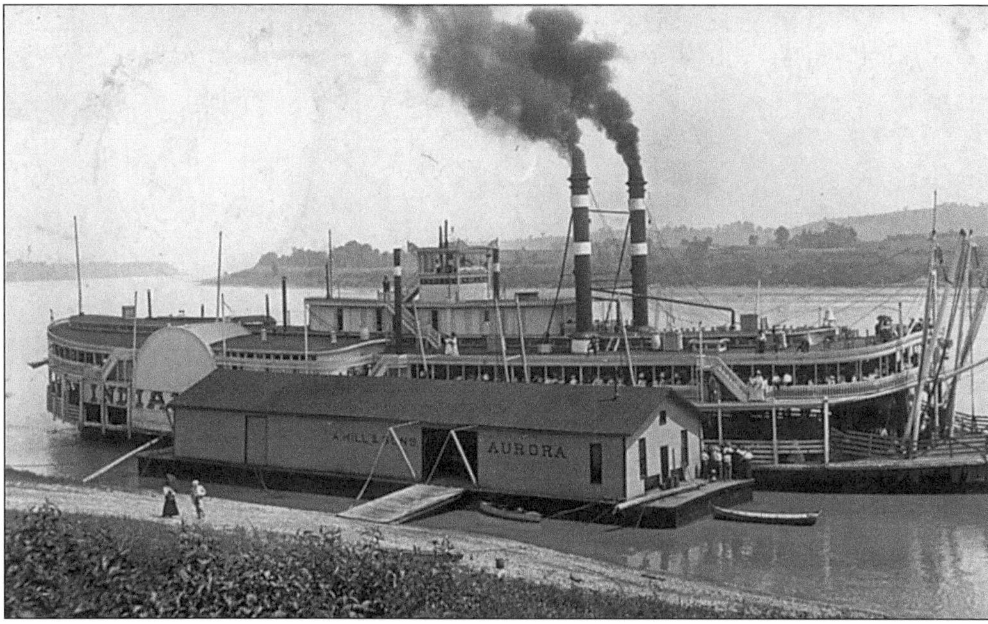

Str. Indiana was a smaller, slower side-wheel boat operated by the Louisville and Cincinnati Packet Company on the Cincinnati to Louisville route in lower water stages. Above, she is landed facing downriver at the Aurora, Indiana wharfboat during summer low water. Boats usually land facing upstream into the current, giving the pilots better control; however, a careful "straight in" approach was needed to keep from hitting bottom in the conditions shown above. (North 07.)

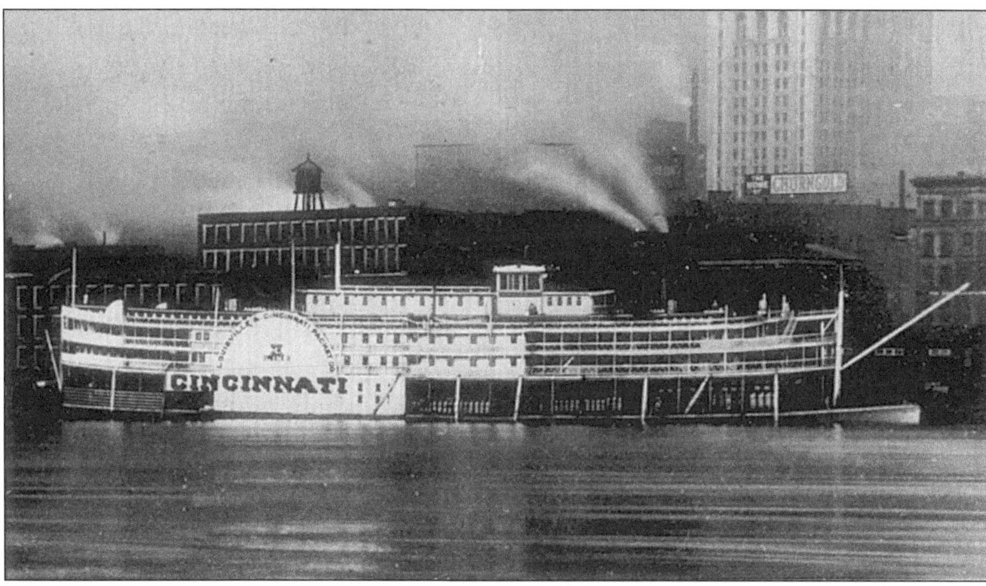

The *Str. Cincinnati* was photographed here when she was placed in service in 1924. She was a steel-hulled boat built to replace the earlier wood-hulled city boats that had been destroyed in the great ice of 1918. Sold in 1933 when pulled from packet service, she was renamed *Str. President* and given a completely different top structure. She later became an excursion boat, and then a gambling boat, with heavy modifications. Converted to diesel power in 1978, she is the last big side-wheel packet hull left. (North 08.)

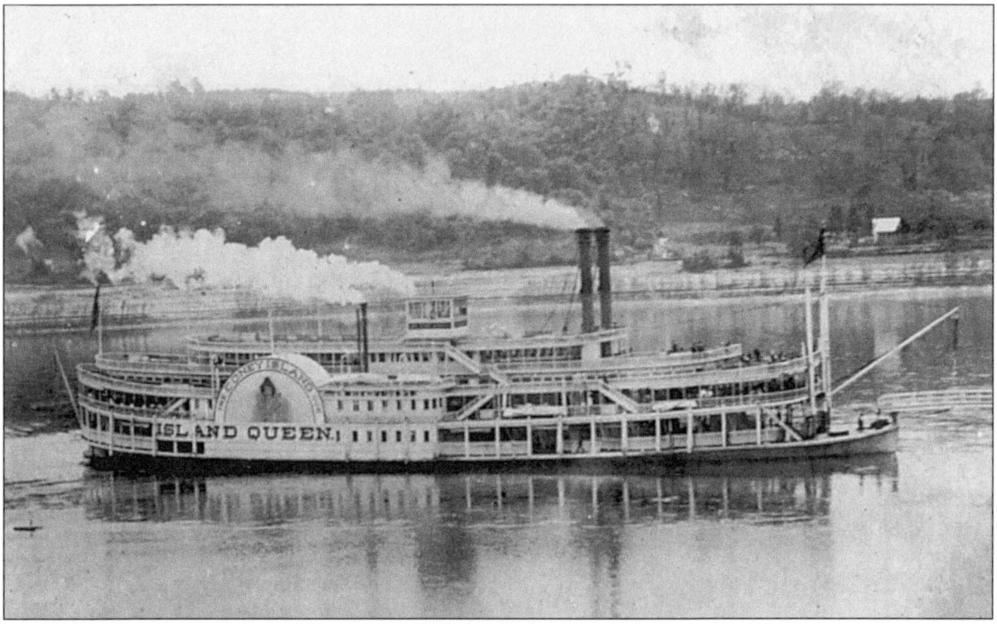

The *Str. Island Queen (1st)* arrives here in Rising Sun to pick up a day cruise. Owned by the Coney Island Company, her primary trade was the hauling of guests from the Cincinnati Public Landing to the amusement park six miles upriver. The company's boats also earned their keep by making charter cruises in the area. (North 09.)

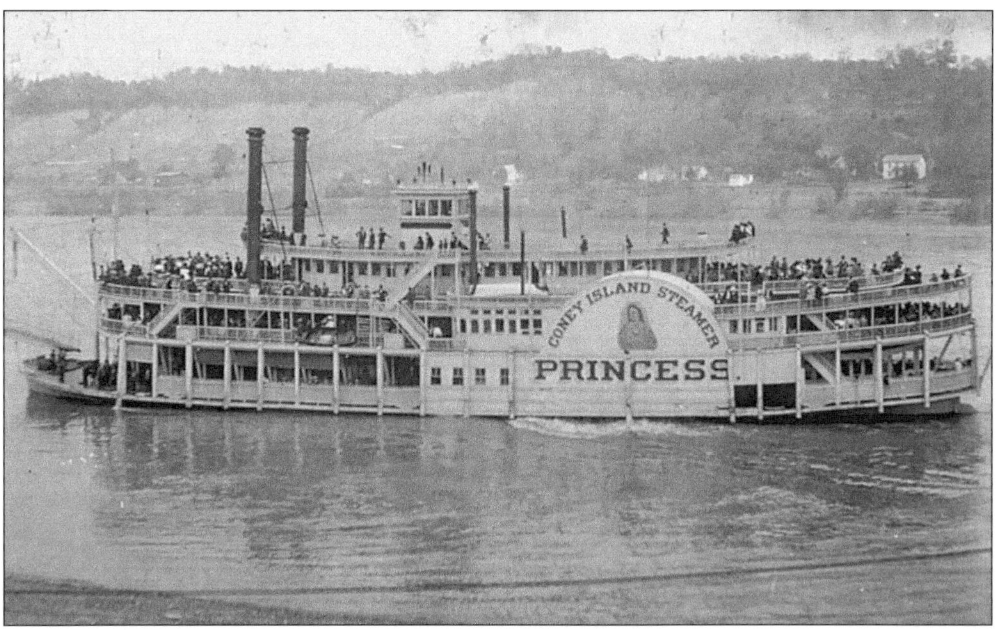

The *Str. Princess* is loaded with a charter group departing Rising Sun. Also owned by the Coney Island Company, she was somewhat smaller than the *Island Queen*. She could operate in shallower water, offering summer season service to the park. (North 10.)

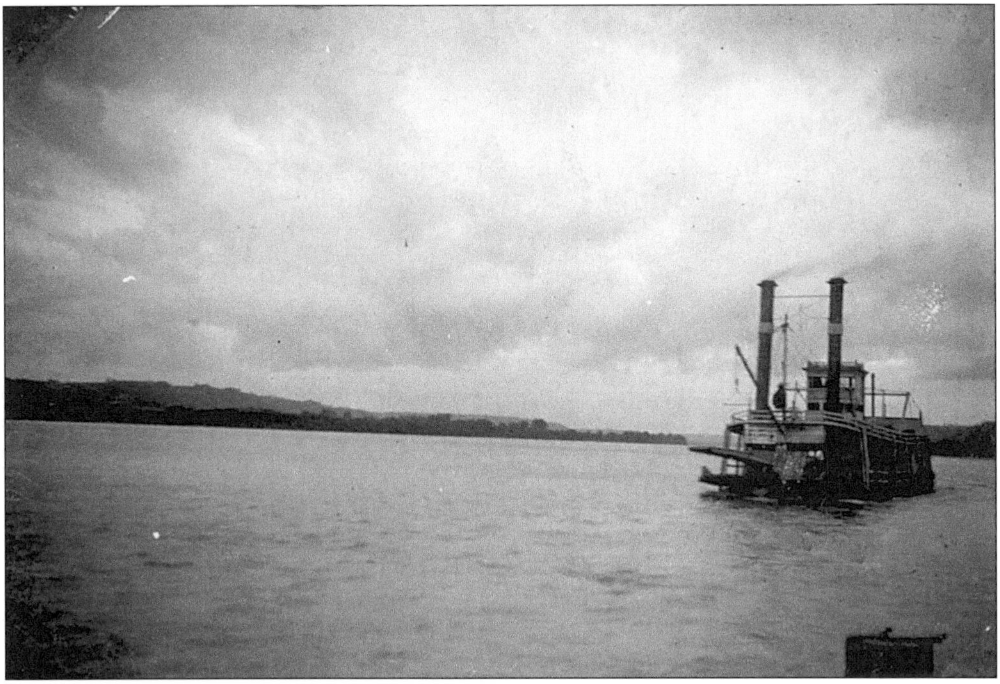

The *Str. Hattie Brown* is shown approaching Vevay on high water on a spring evening. A small, sternwheel local boat, she operated from Madison to Vevay.

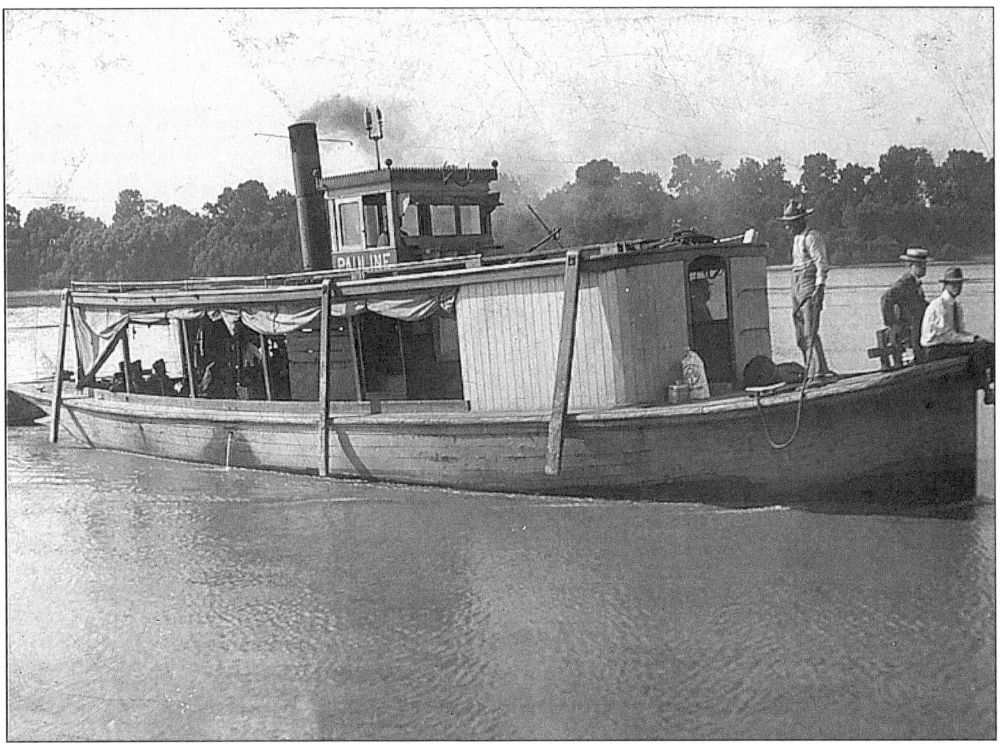

The steam-powered launch *Pauline* carried people and mail between Petersburg, Kentucky, and Lawrenceburg, Indiana. (North 11.)

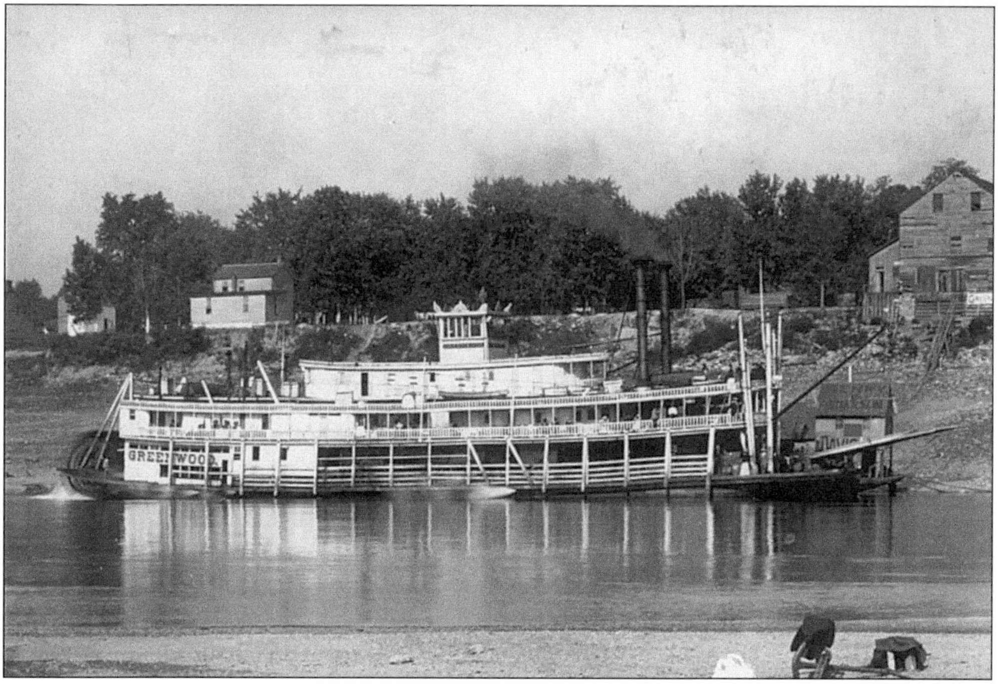

The *Str. Greenwood* is shown arriving at Rising Sun, Indiana, on a very low summer water level. She occasionally operated the Cincinnati to Louisville route when the bigger, faster side-wheelers were forced to the bank by low water. Operated by the Green Lines, who later would operate the *Str. Delta Queen*, her usual route was upriver from Cincinnati, Ohio, to Charleston, West Virginia. (North 12.)

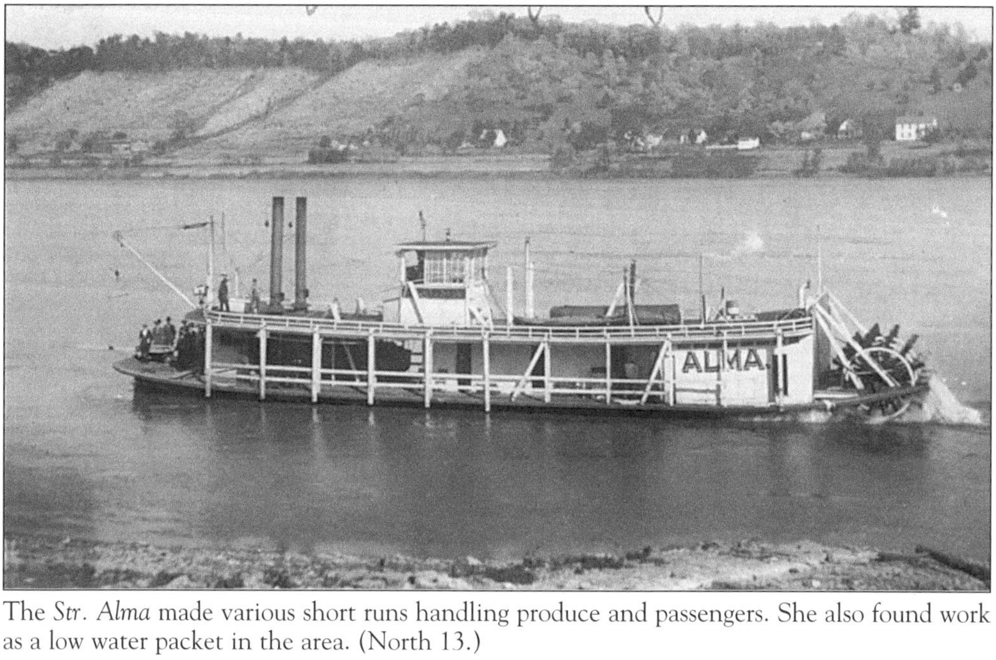

The *Str. Alma* made various short runs handling produce and passengers. She also found work as a low water packet in the area. (North 13.)

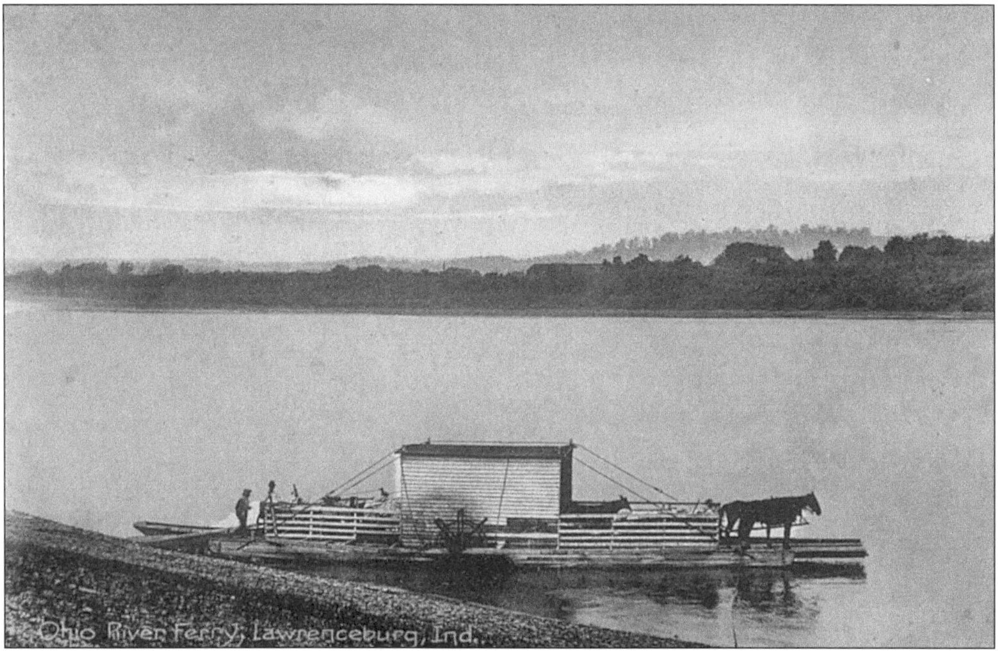

This is a horse or mule-powered ferry based in Lawrenceburg, Indiana, that was designed to carry people and wagons across the river. The animals walked on a tread that powered its side wheels. This gives real meaning to the term "horsepower."

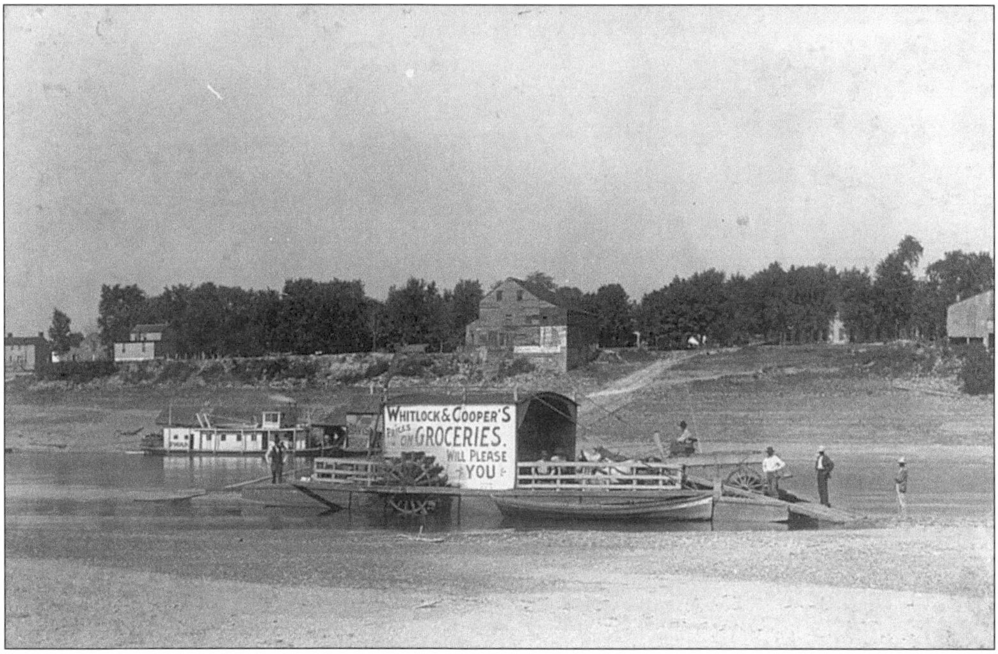

This horse-powered ferry on the Rising Sun, Indiana, to Rabbit Hash, Kentucky route, is shown pulled up to the riverbed that has been exposed by very low summer water conditions on the Kentucky shore. *Str. Lola*, docked at the Rising Sun, Indiana wharfboat in the background, was another small local sternwheel boat used for short runs. (North 14.)

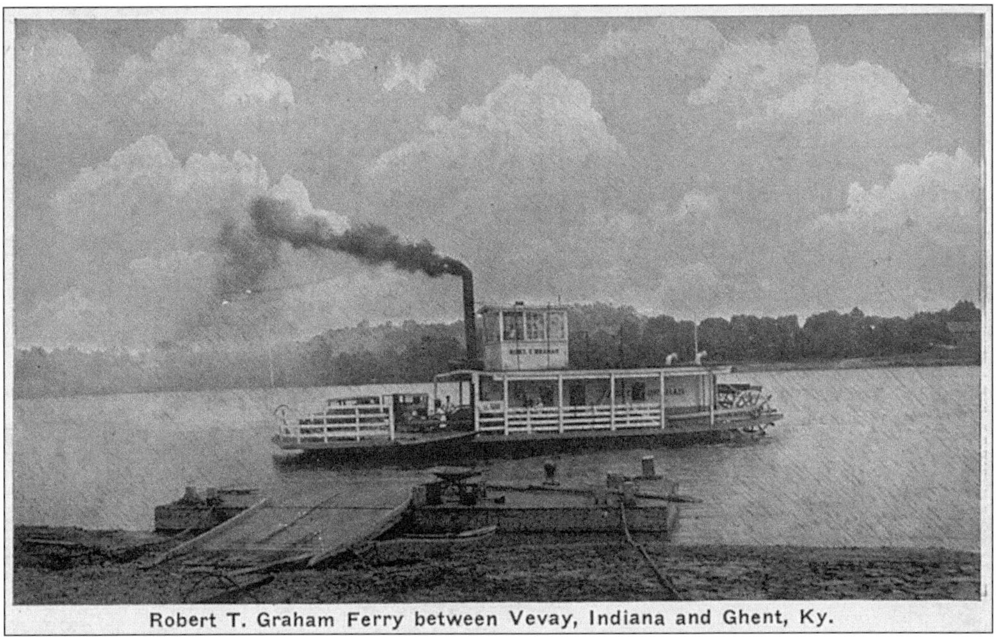

The ferry *Robert T. Graham* departs Vevay, Indiana, for Ghent, Kentucky. A steam-powered, sternwheel, side-loading ferry, she was lost in the ice of 1942. (North 15.)

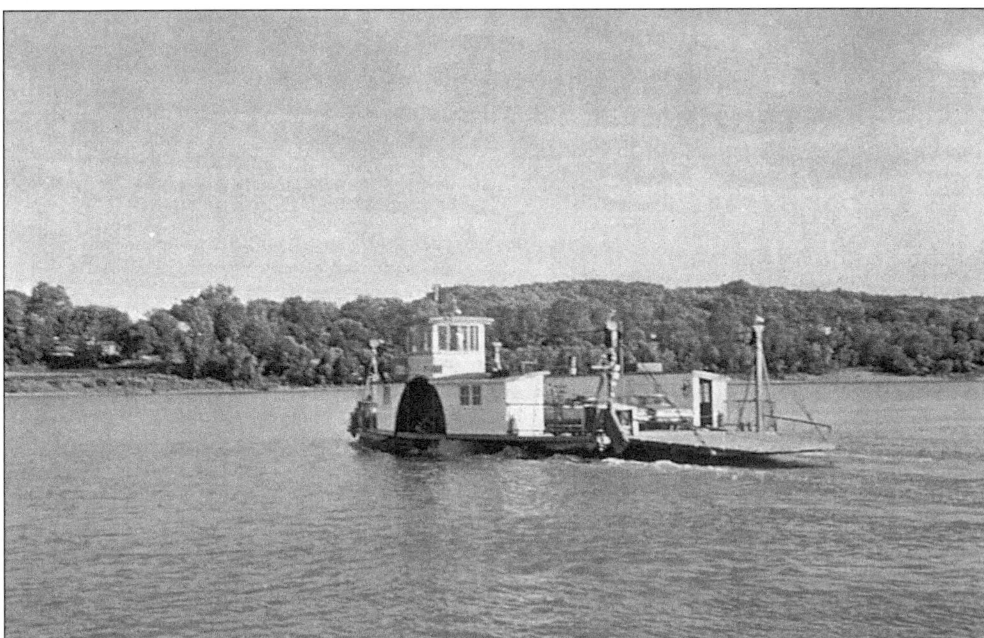

Here, the ferry *Martha A. Graham* returns to the Vevay, Indiana landing. She replaced the *Robert* shown above. An end-loading, diesel-powered, side-wheel ferry, she could hold up to six vehicles.

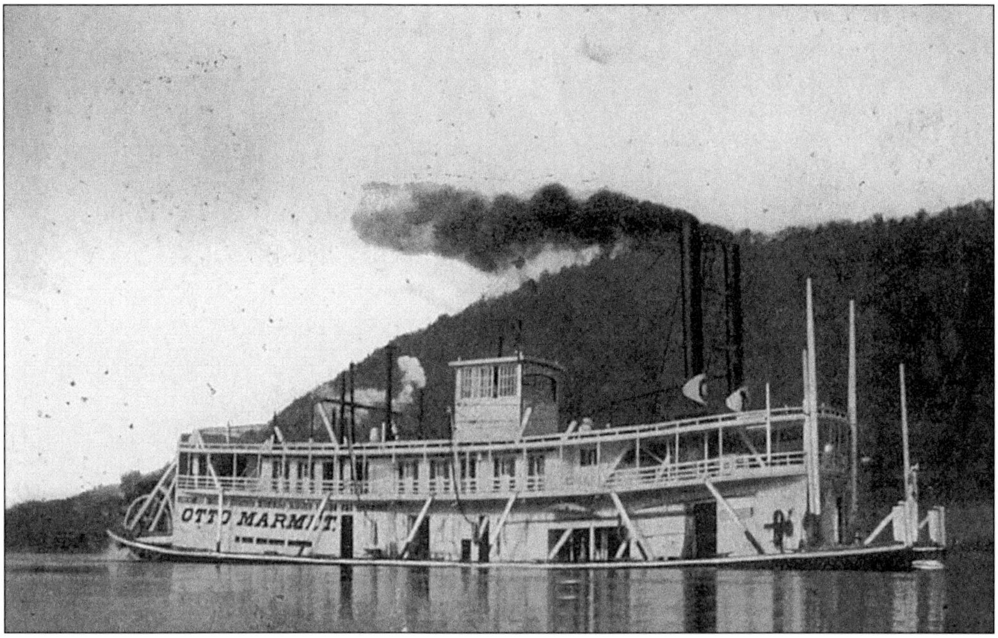

The Raymond Street Coal Company of Cincinnati operated the *Str. Otto Marmet*. A sternwheel steam towboat, she delivered coal barges to towns along the river. (North 16.)

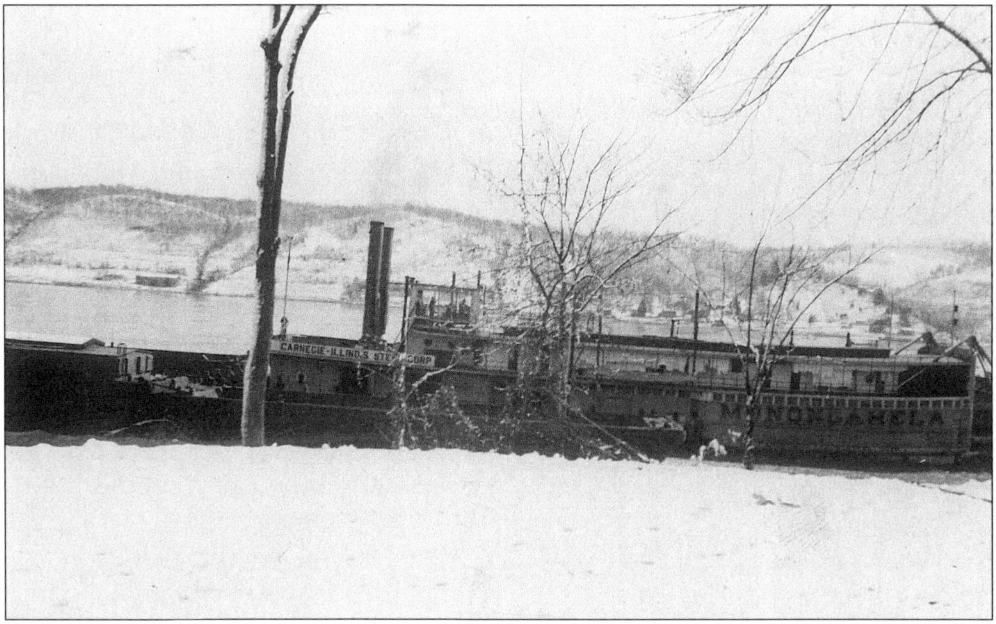
Str. *Monongahelia*, operated by the Carnegie Steel Corporation of Pittsburgh, Pennsylvania, was a steel-hulled, steam-powered, sternwheeler towboat. She is shown above pushing a tow of steel barges upriver past Rising Sun, Indiana. Towboats and barges have been the dominant configuration of commercial traffic on the Ohio River since the 1930s.

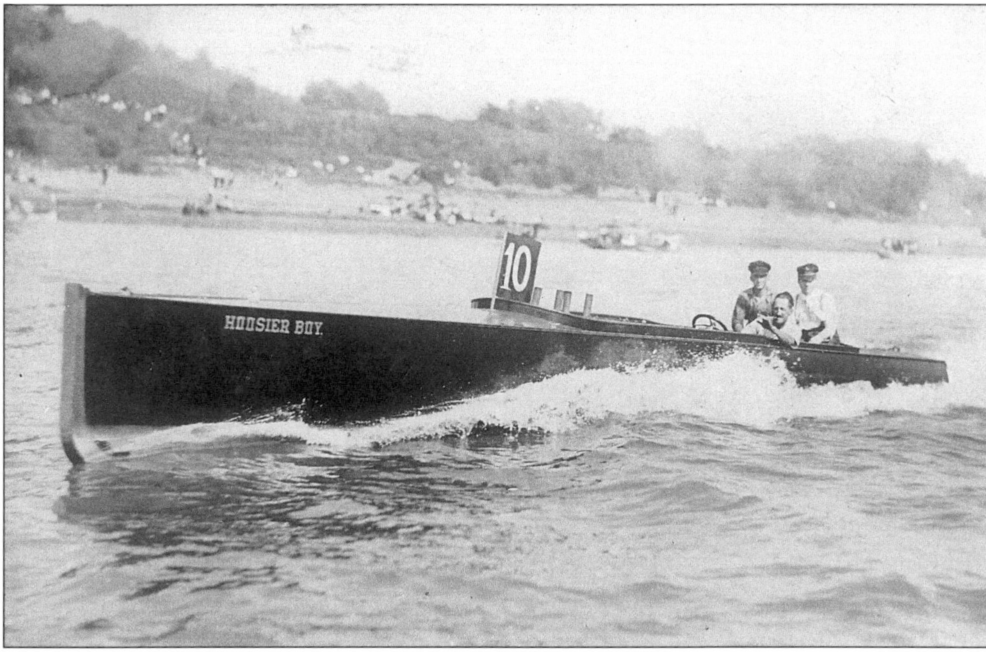

Hoosier Boy was the name carried by a series of record setting speedboats built and driven by J.W. Whitlock of Rising Sun, Indiana. The hull shown above, powered by a 75 horsepower Buffalo Speed Engine, dominated match racing around 1910. (North 17.)

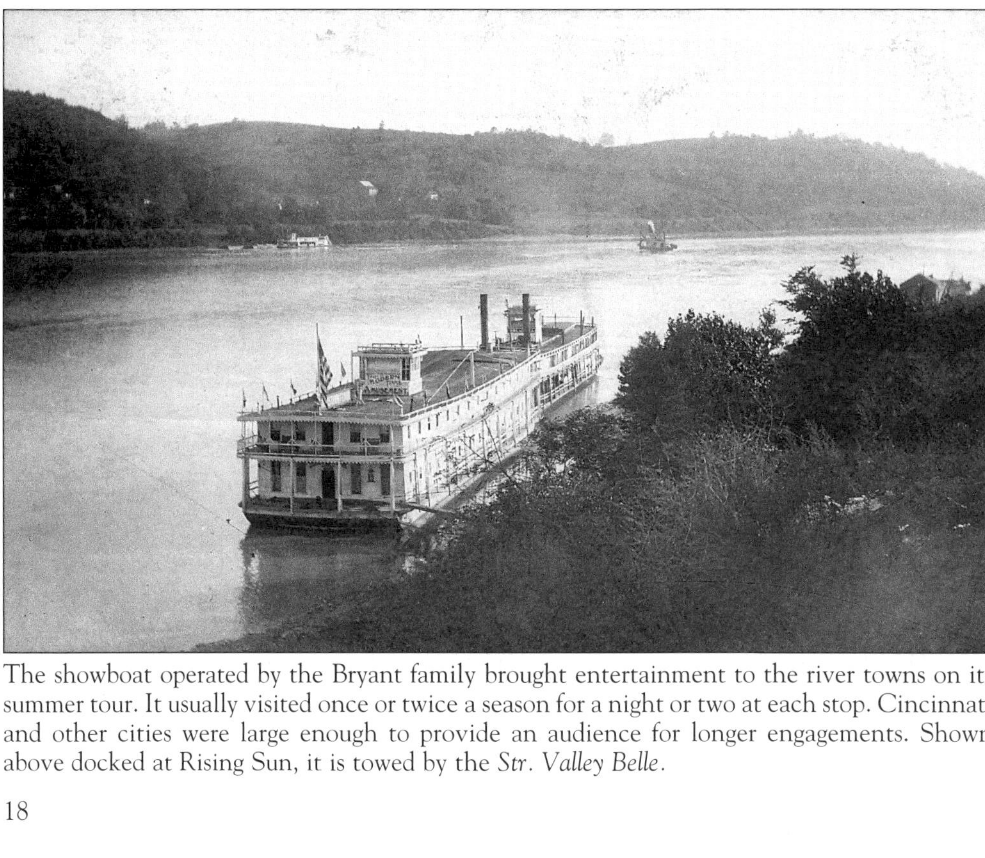

The showboat operated by the Bryant family brought entertainment to the river towns on its summer tour. It usually visited once or twice a season for a night or two at each stop. Cincinnati and other cities were large enough to provide an audience for longer engagements. Shown above docked at Rising Sun, it is towed by the *Str. Valley Belle*.

Two

Cities and Towns Along the Way

Cincinnati, Ohio, the "Queen City of the West," began as a fort in the days of the Northwest Territory. It rapidly developed into a large city by the early 1800s. It served as the hub through which settlers passed into new lands in Indiana and other points west. It was a regional commercial center of manufacturing and shipping, spreading out over seven hills rising above the river valley. Farm products headed east, by rail or boat, passed across its wharf.

Between Cincinnati and Louisville, numerous landings, villages, and towns lined the river. Traveling by road between these towns for any great distance was a time-consuming journey. Dirt or gravel roads, winding along the river valley or climbing steep hills heading away from the river, made for slow travel whatever the distance. The river was the most practical way to transport frieght. It was also the quickest way to get between points along its shore.

These settlements were some of the oldest in the states bordering the river. Early settlers turned the virgin forests along the river into fertile fields prior to 1820. Lawrenceburg, Rising Sun, and Vevay were three of the ten largest cities in Indiana until the 1830s. However, their stature and size was eclipsed by cities established away from the river, as rail and road transportation improved prior to the Civil War. They remained vibrant communities, sustained by the fertile fields of the river valley, throughout the packet era.

Louisville predates Cincinnati, growing from a small, early settlement on the Kentucky shore adjacent to the "Falls of the Ohio." Early cargoes headed west down the Ohio River had to be unloaded and carried around the falls. Its wharf and surrounding warehouses made up the other regional hub for area agricultural goods headed to the south and west.

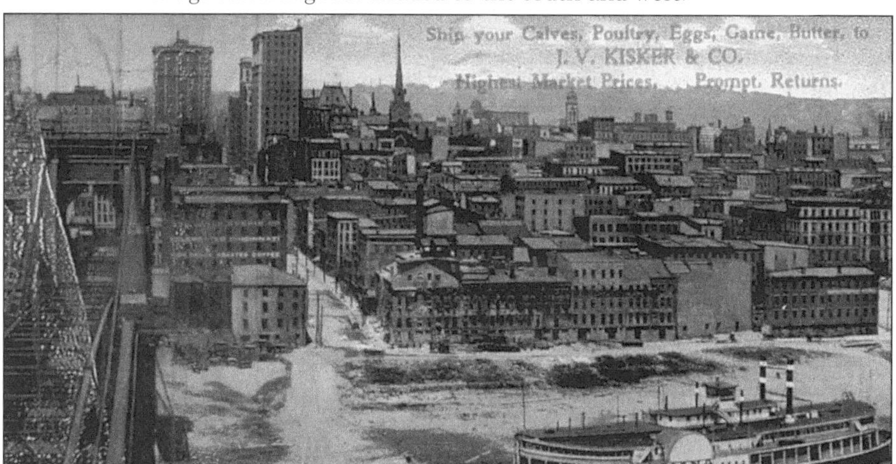

The Cincinnati, Ohio commercial district, adjacent to the public landing, is seen here from the tower of the suspension bridge on the Kentucky shore. This is an advertising card sent by a wholesale buyer of farm products to the North Brothers in 1910. (North 18.)

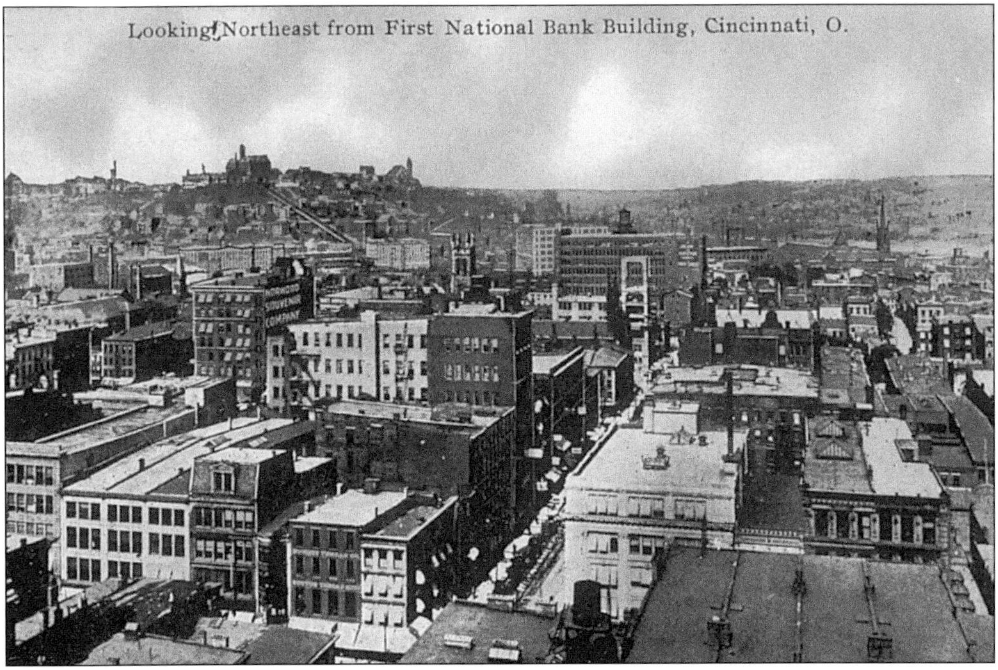

Here, Cincinnati, Ohio, spreads out along the Ohio River below Mount Adams about 1914. The public landing is off to the right from this view. The business and commercial district spread out away from the river over more than one hundred city blocks.

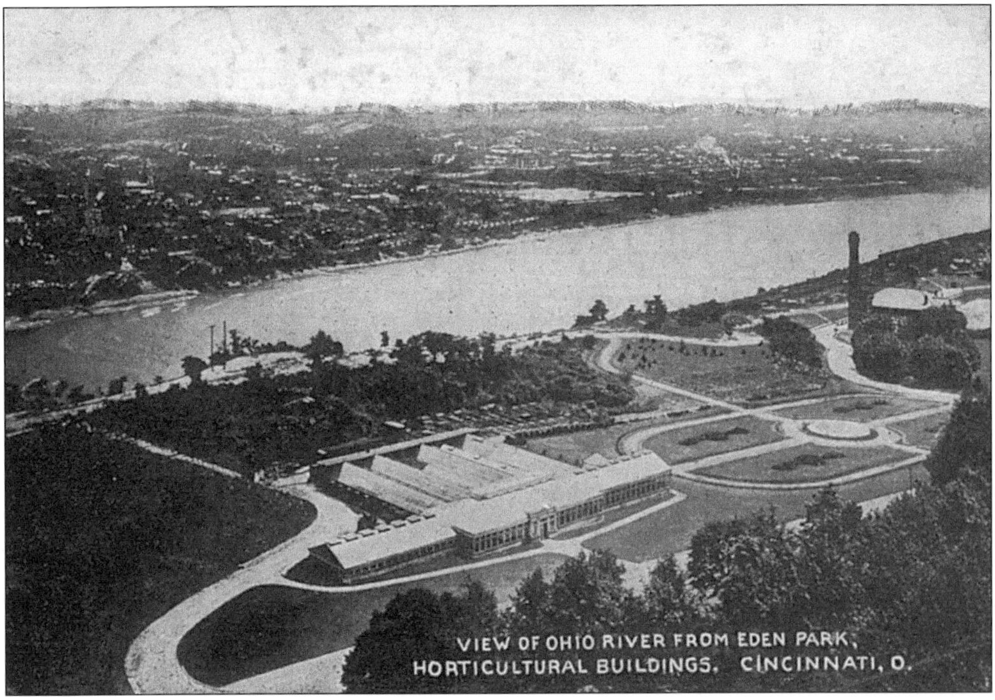

This view of the Ohio River from Eden Park shows Dayton, Kentucky, on the Kentucky shore.

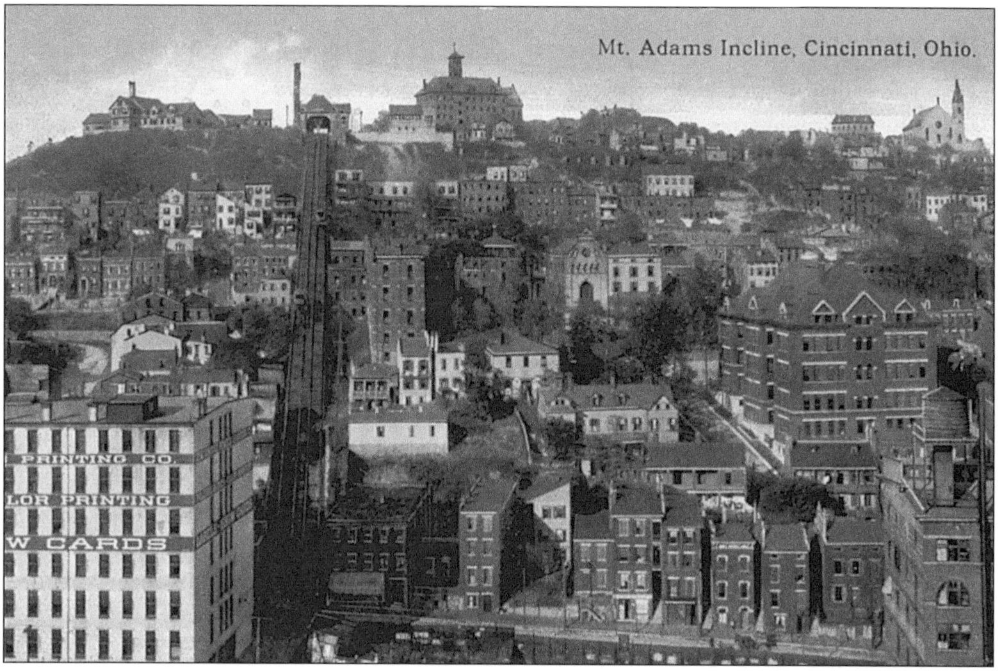

Cincinnati was spread out over seven hills along the Mill Creek Valley and Ohio River. The Mount Adams Incline was used to move streetcars to the top of one hill. The hilltops were valued as residential areas. Inclines were used to provide trolley service to the downtown.

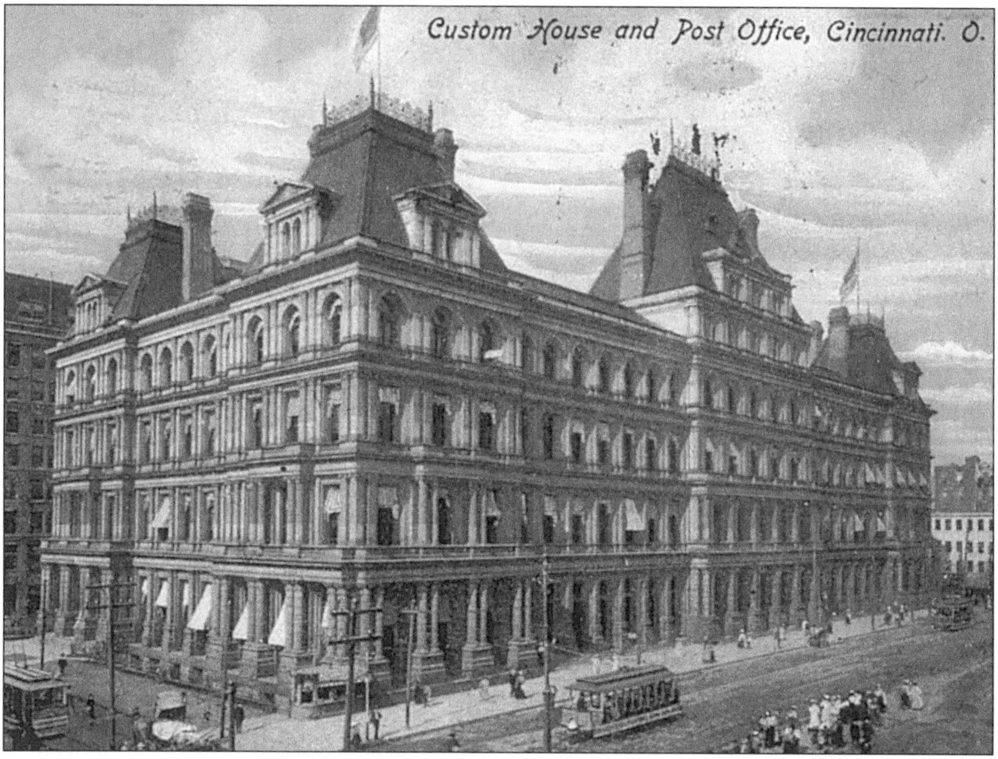

Downtown Cincinnati was a busy regional center of trade and commerce.

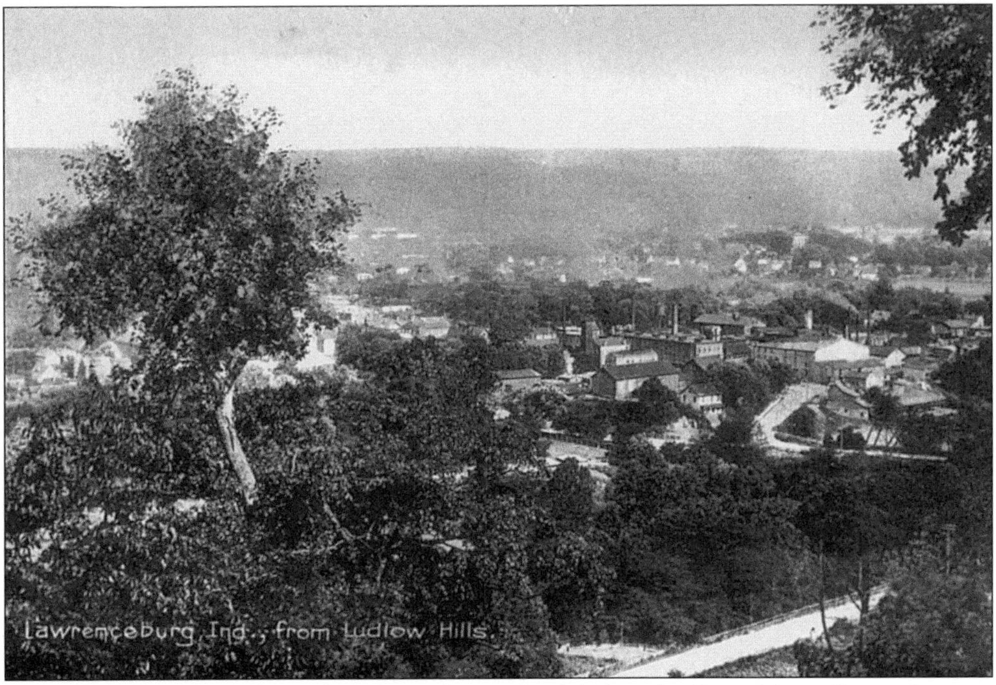

Lawrenceburg, Indiana, lies in broad river bottomlands below the Great Miami River. Artesian wells provide pure water to its spirit distilleries.

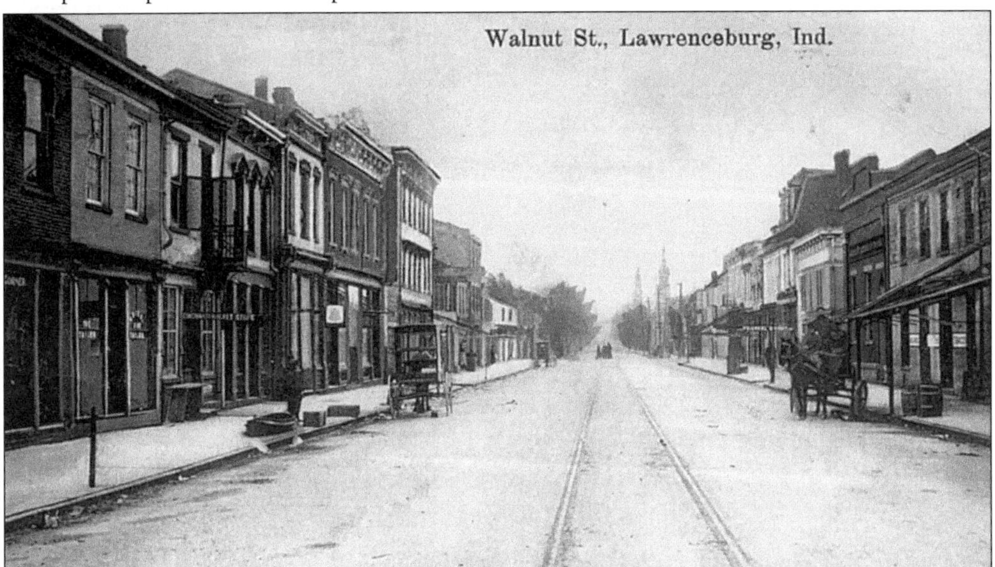

Walnut Street in Lawrenceburg, Indiana, is pictured here. The railroad tracks ran down the center of the street. Railroad tracks extended to Aurora, but then left the river valley as they proceeded west, leaving towns downriver without service. Madison, Indiana, and Carrollton, Kentucky, both had spur lines that reached their commercial areas. However, there was no regularly scheduled rail passenger service competing with the packet boats in most towns and villages. The passenger trade on the river would not be diminished until private cars and better roads became widely available in the 1920s.

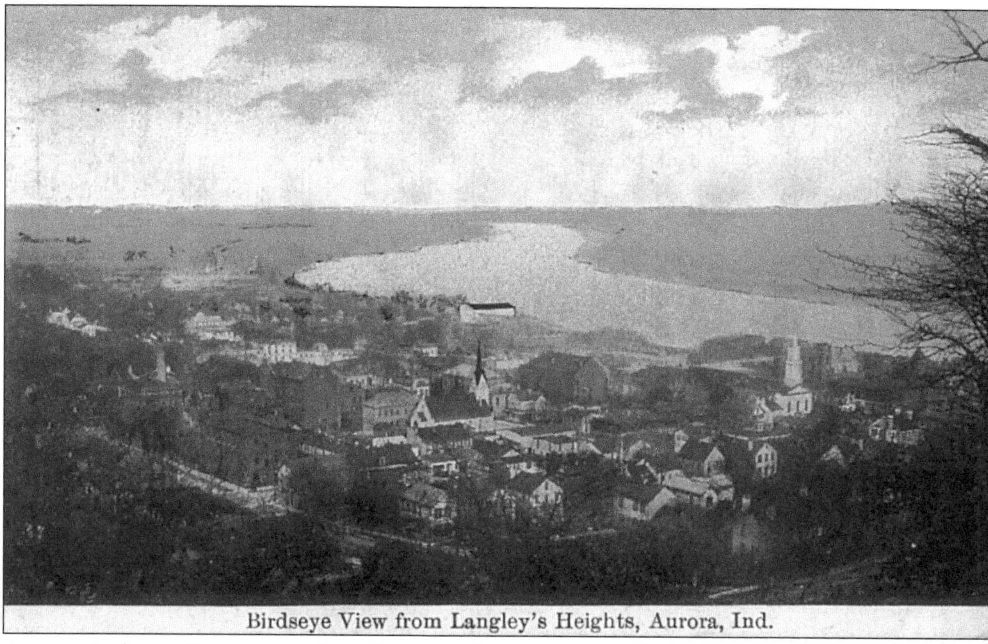

Aurora, Indiana, downstream from Lawrenceburg, was a smaller town of businesses and houses. Spreading away from the river along Hogan Creek, it was easily flooded.

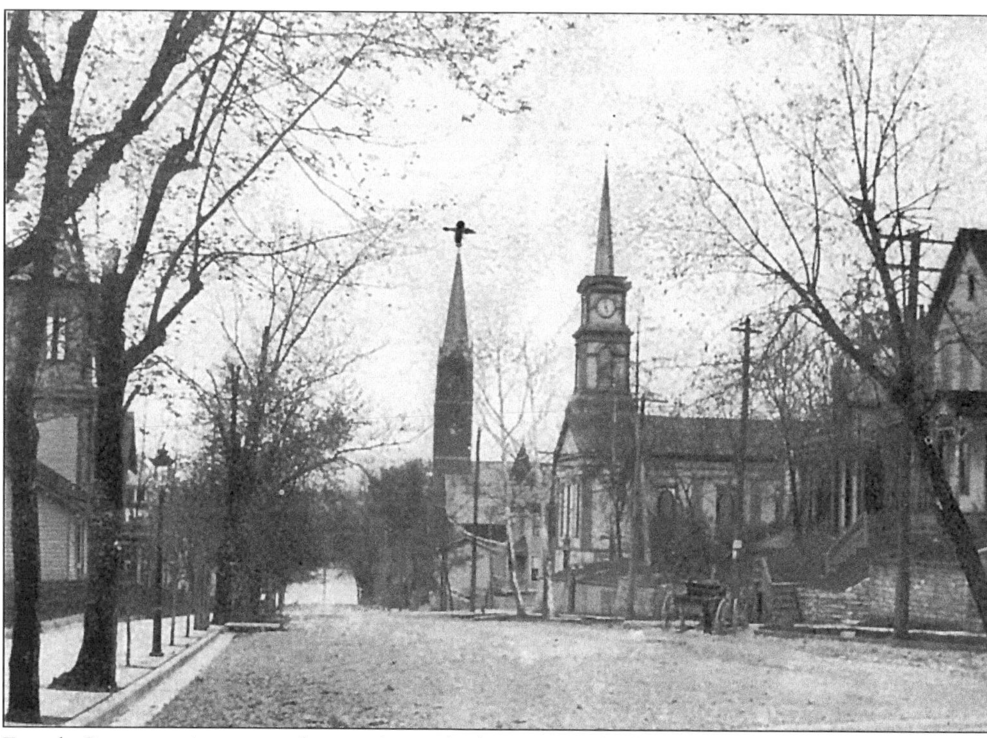

Fourth Street in Aurora is shown above, looking towards the river. Located at the mouth of Hogan Creek on relatively low ground, the Aurora downtown area flooded easily. Fourth Street climbed the hillside, providing a place for homes and churches safe from flooding.

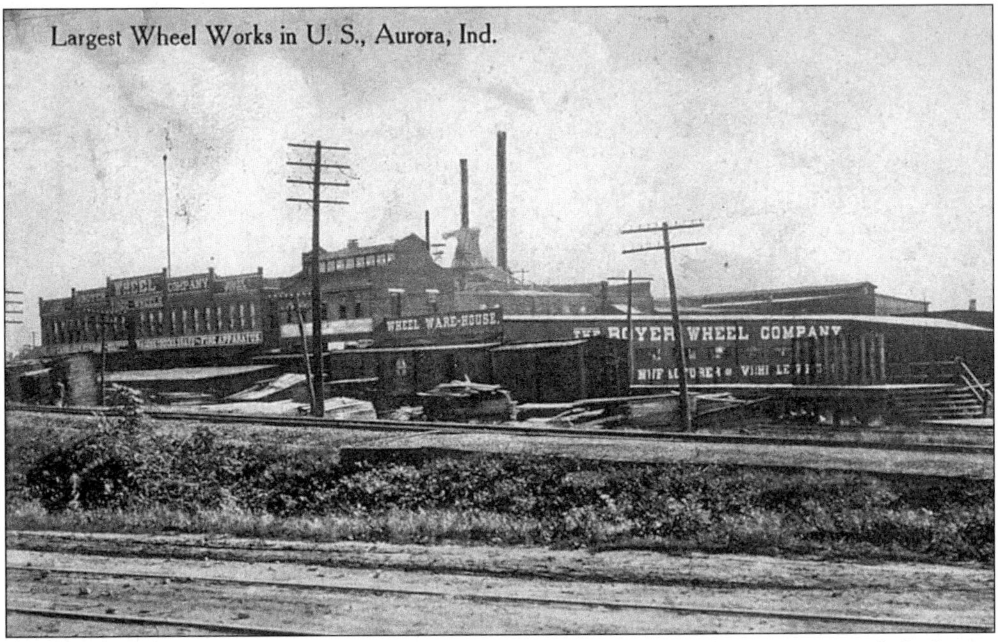

One of the main Baltimore and Ohio rail lines, running west from Cincinnati towards St. Louis, passed through Aurora before climbing out of the river valley away from the river. Chairs and caskets were also manufactured in Aurora, but primarily shipped by rail.

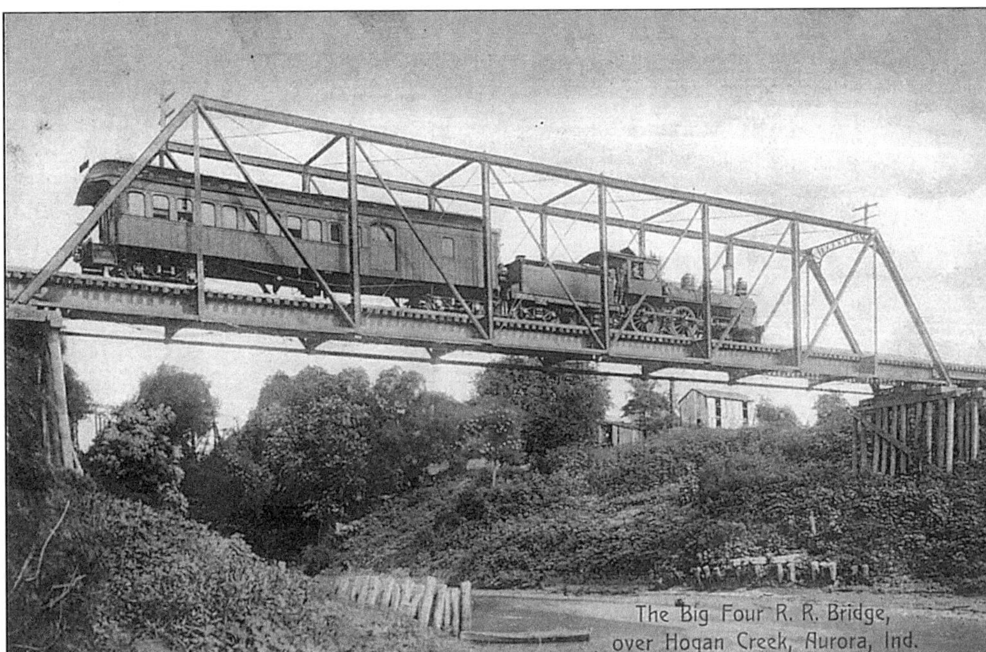

Local passenger service east to Lawrenceburg and Cincinnati was also available in Aurora. However, people wishing to reach towns below Aurora on the river had to rely on packets or horse-drawn vehicles.

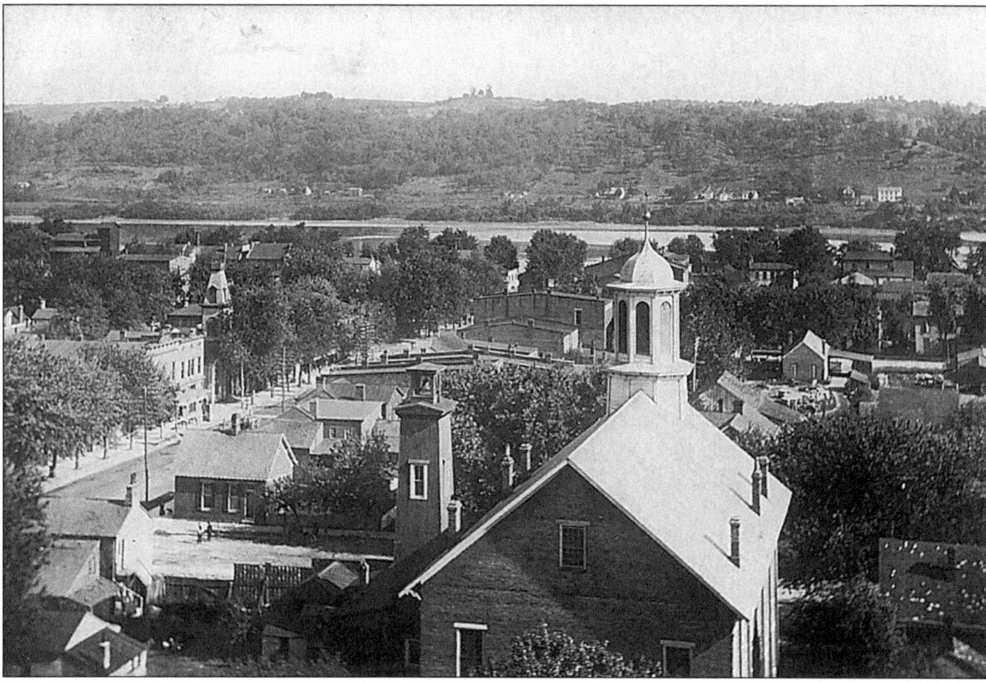

Rising Sun, Indiana, grew from a few cabins in 1812 to one of the ten largest cities in Indiana by 1830. Built upon the second bank back from the normal water level of the Ohio River, it was much less prone to flooding than most other towns between Cincinnati and Louisville. It was the mercantile center for a large farming area. (North 19.)

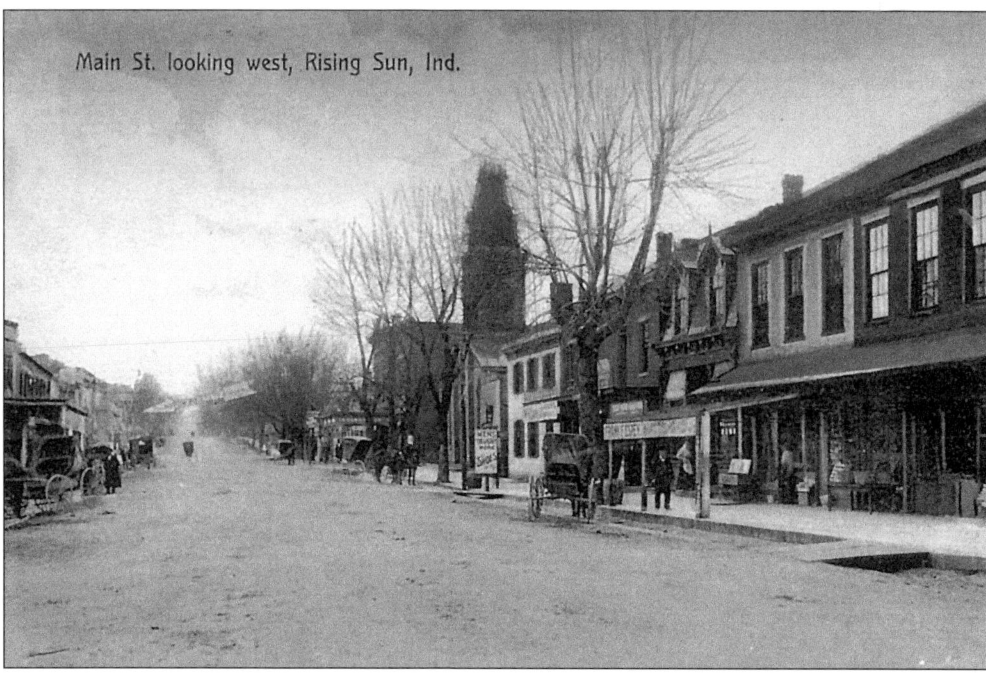

Looking away from the river, the business district shows the activity of the era. Farm families came to town to shop and visit with family and friends.

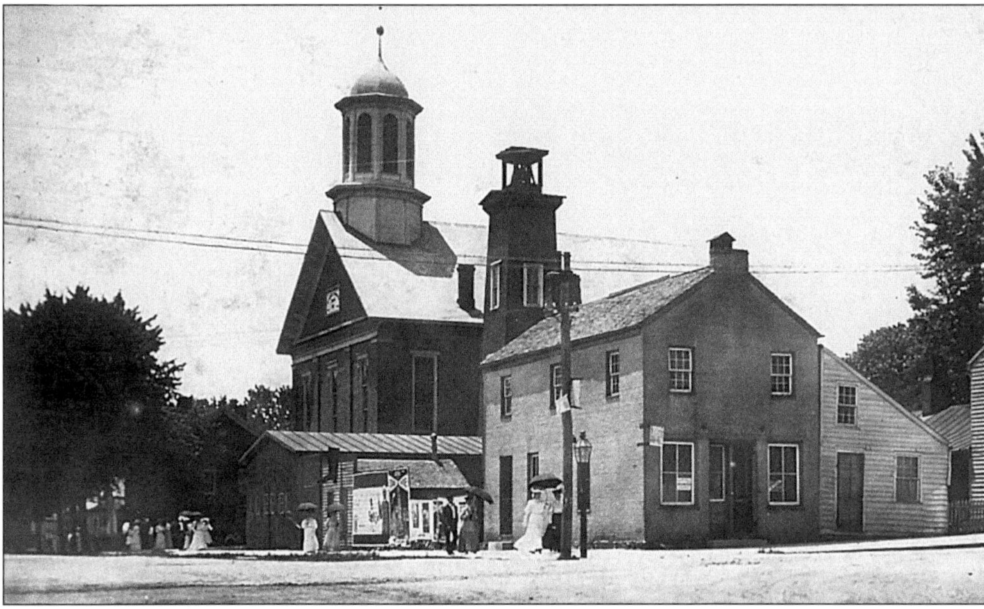

This view shows Walnut and Main Streets in Rising Sun, Indiana. The photograph was probably taken on a Sunday after church. The Methodist Church shown in the center left still stands. The smaller building and home at right are gone, replaced by a municipal building that also housed the volunteer fire department sometime after World War I.

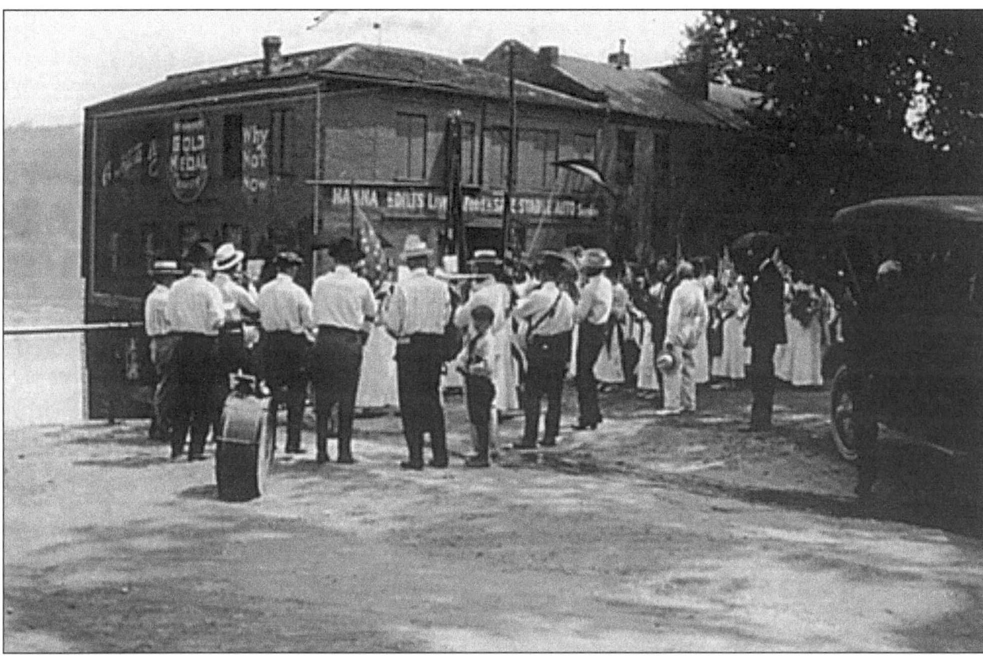

Here, the community band performs on a summer day at the intersection of Front and Main Streets in Rising Sun, Indiana. The river is visible at left behind the buildings. Local bands and sports teams were a major part of social activities in the early part of the 1900s.

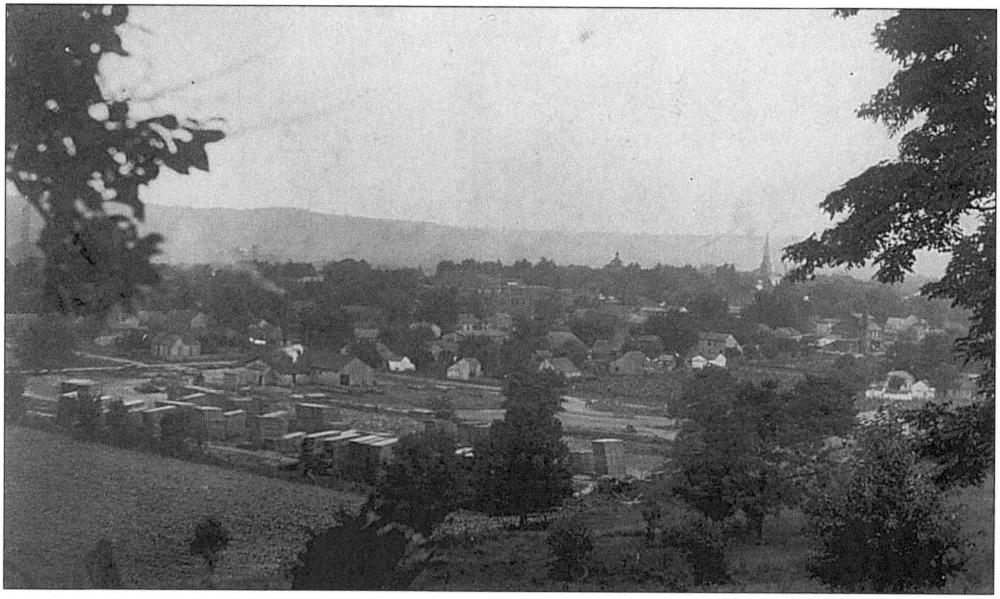

Vevay, Indiana, is seen here from the high ridge of the river valley with the Kentucky hills in the background. The river meanders through a broad valley between Cincinnati and Louisville. Usually, it flows near the hills on one side of the valley, leaving a broad, fertile river bottom on the other. Early settlers west of Cincinnati were first attracted to the richness of these lands, and left the less fertile, harder-to-reach lands beyond the river valley for those that followed later. Vevay was first settled about 1810 at a relatively high point in the valley that was less prone to flooding than Patriot, Florence, Markland, and other smaller settlements nearby.

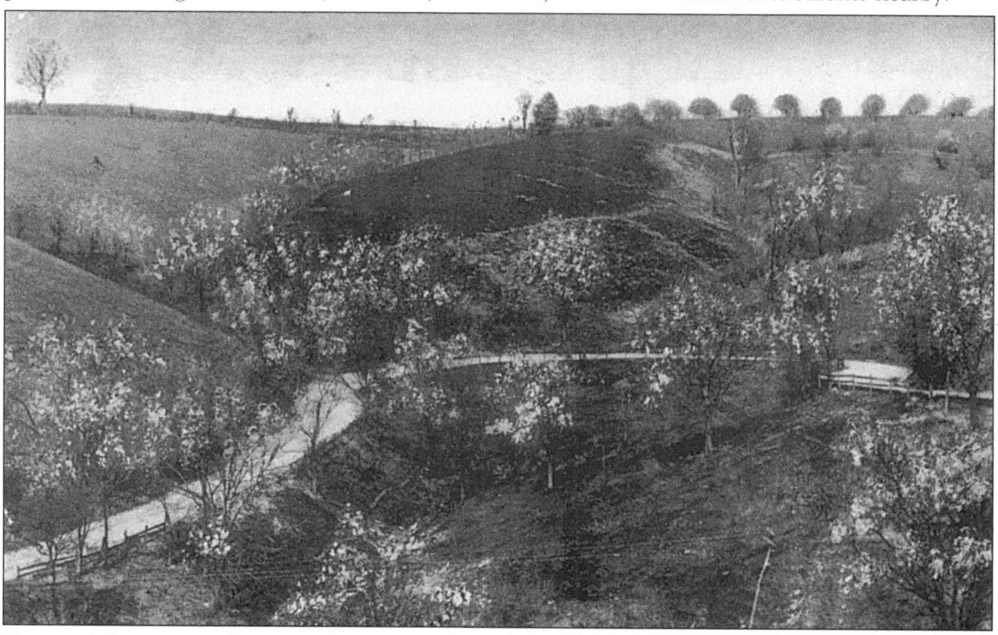

Steep roads are seen here winding away from the river at Vevay. Southeastern Indiana was originally very densely forested. Once the land away from the river was cleared, it was not nearly as productive, lacking the renewal of nutrients from periodic flooding. Crops had to be brought to the river for shipment down these steep slopes.

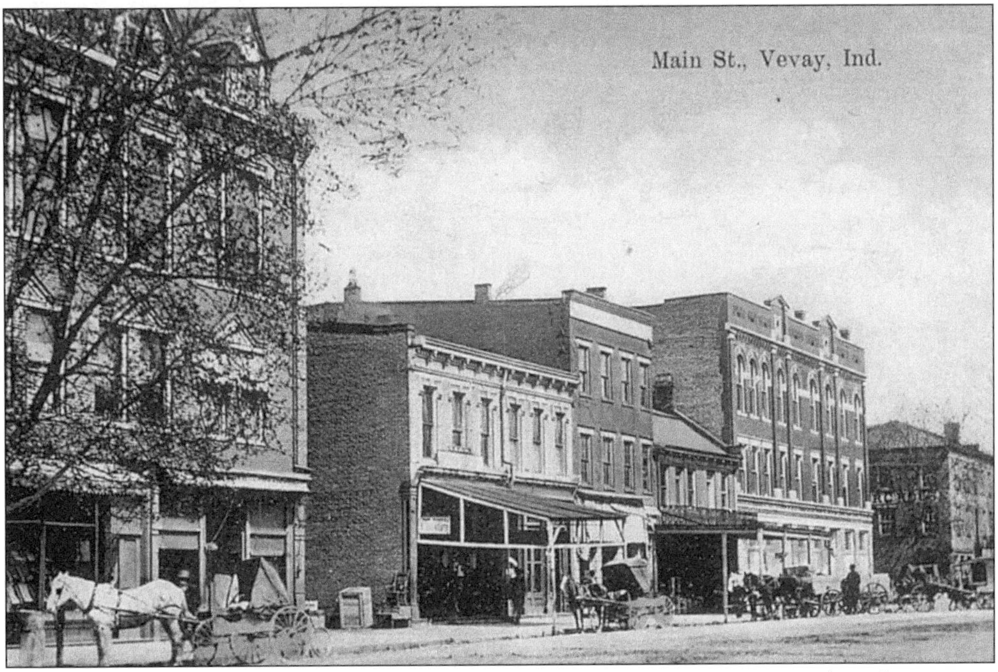

This photo of downtown Vevay, Indiana, shows it to be a prosperous regional market center. Horse-drawn wagons were the basic mode of land transportation until private cars became common in the 1920s. Things change a little slower in these river towns. Many of the buildings shown above, and in other pictures in this chapter, still stand today. (North 20.)

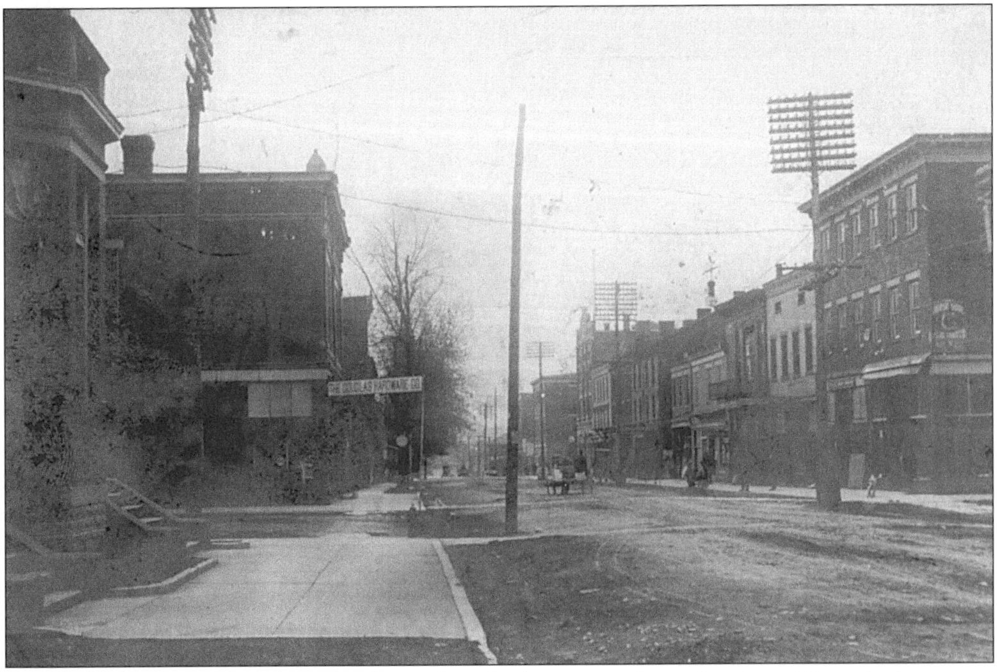

Ferry Street, in Vevay, Indiana, is shown here looking away from the river. The telephone and telegraph had arrived by the early 1900s to the area. Rural Free Delivery mail service was in place by 1905.

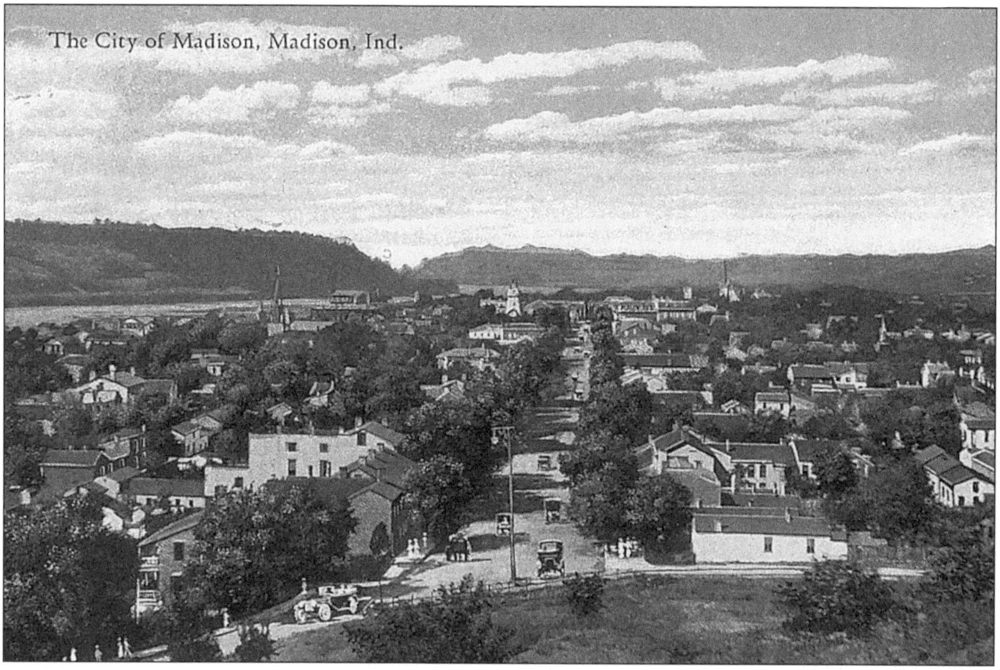

Madison, Indiana, spreads out on low river bottom lands below high hills. Although rail service existed between Madison and Indianapolis prior to the Civil War, most farm produce and manufactured goods were shipped by river.

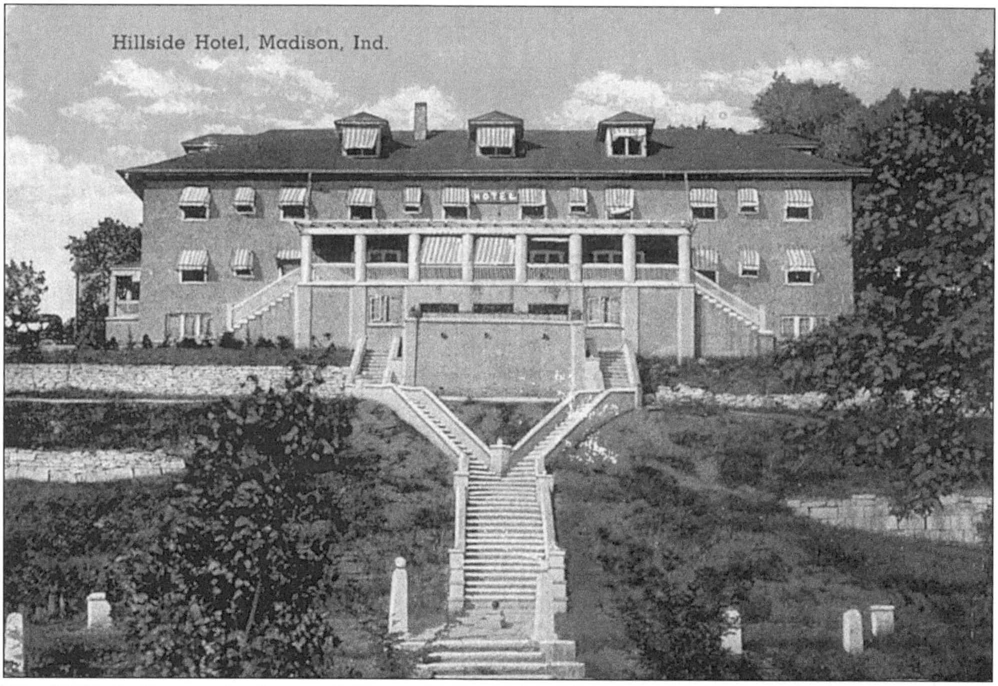

The Hillside Inn sat high on a hill overlooking the Ohio River Valley on the eastern edge of Madison. It was a thriving tourist stop for people wishing to enjoy the river valley. This building burned on a very cold night in 1963. The fire department was unable to save it.

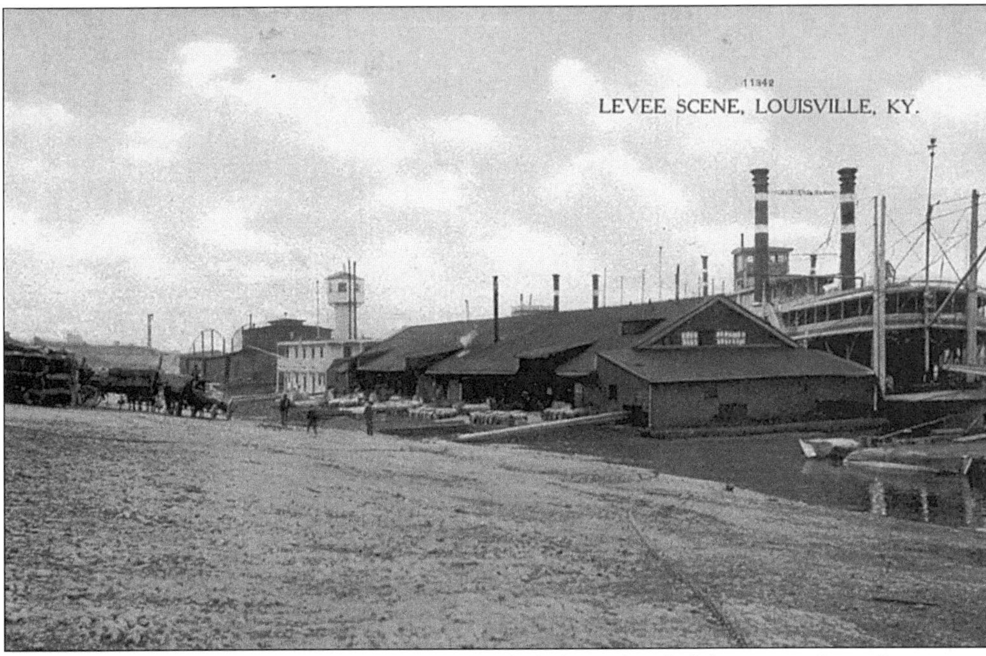

The wharf in Louisville was the destination for daily boats headed downriver from Cincinnati. Cargoes would be transferred to boats headed downriver below Louisville. The *Str. City of Louisville* is shown beside the wharfboat preparing to return upriver to Cincinnati.

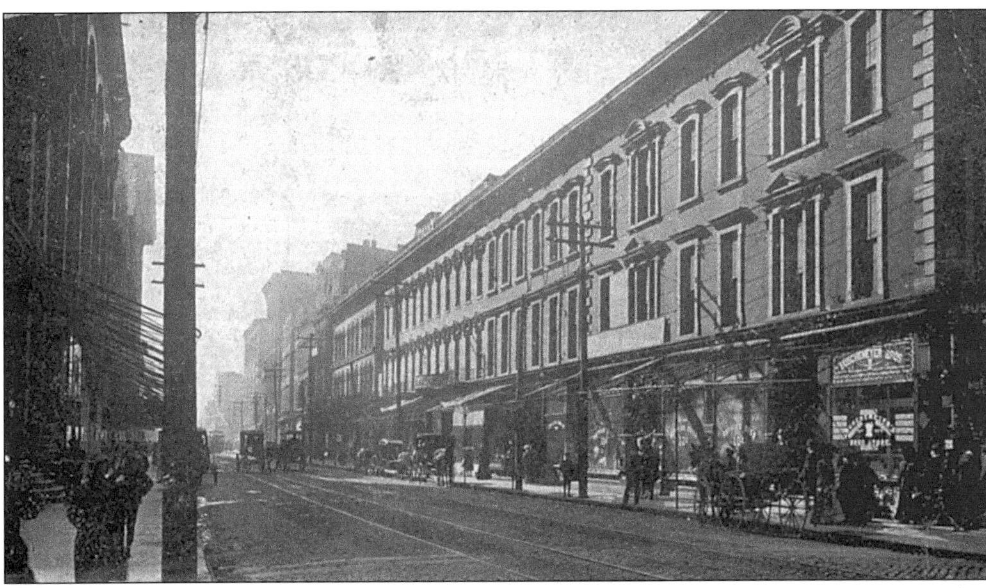

The Louisville, Kentucky business district, inland from the public landing, was comprised of somewhat smaller buildings than those in Cincinnati. River-related commerce directly and indirectly generated business activity throughout Louisville.

Three

CINCINNATI TO LOUSIVILLE BY PACKET

The Cincinnati and Louisville Packet Company maintained a daily schedule between Cincinnati and Louisville, with stops at most towns along the way. The speed and size of their boats enabled them to make the trip in 8 to 14 hours, depending upon river conditions. A boat would depart each city in early morning. They would usually meet at Vevay or thereabouts to exchange passengers wishing to return to their port of origin. City residents routinely made these "meet the boat" trips as a pleasure cruise, especially on summer weekends.
The boats would then continue on, arriving at their destination city around dark.

The images in this chapter follow a journey from Cincinnati to Louisville around 1910 along a pilot's chart of the river of that era. Notations as to all the creeks, landings, towns, and villages accompany the charts. The images illustrate many stops and sites along the way.

Steamboat travel is a slow, steady journey. The sounds of the river can often be heard over the rhythmic, soft hiss of steam and splash of the wheel. There is a fresh green smell to the fog of the morning and the evening mist. The day moves along at a peaceful, steady pace as the shore glides past.

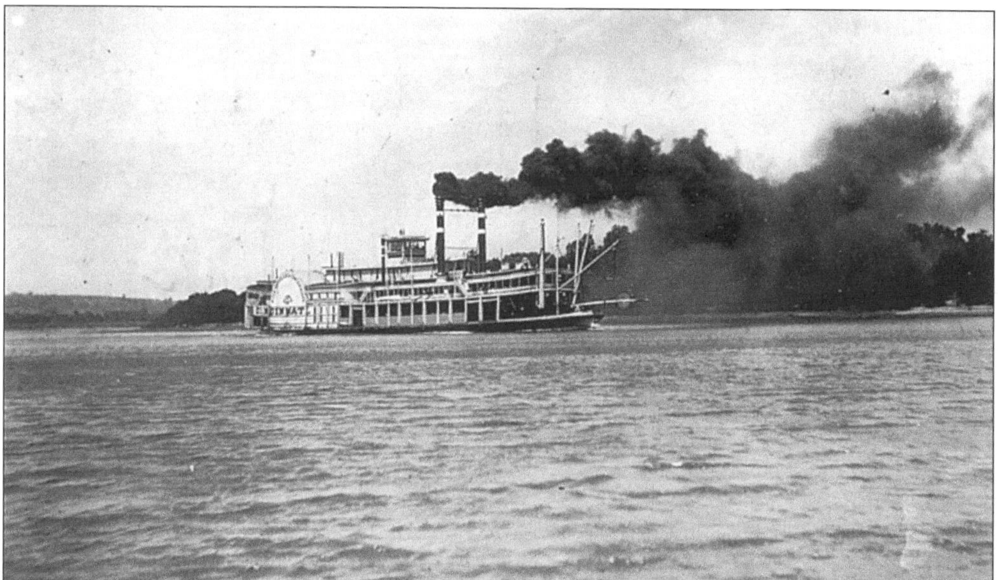

Here, the *Str. City of Cincinnati* is headed downriver below Cincinnati on a daily run to Louisville. This photograph was taken on a windy spring day when the water level in the river was higher than usual. These conditions would make for difficult landings at stops along the way, but also resulted in a faster run and arrival before dark in Louisville. (North 21.)

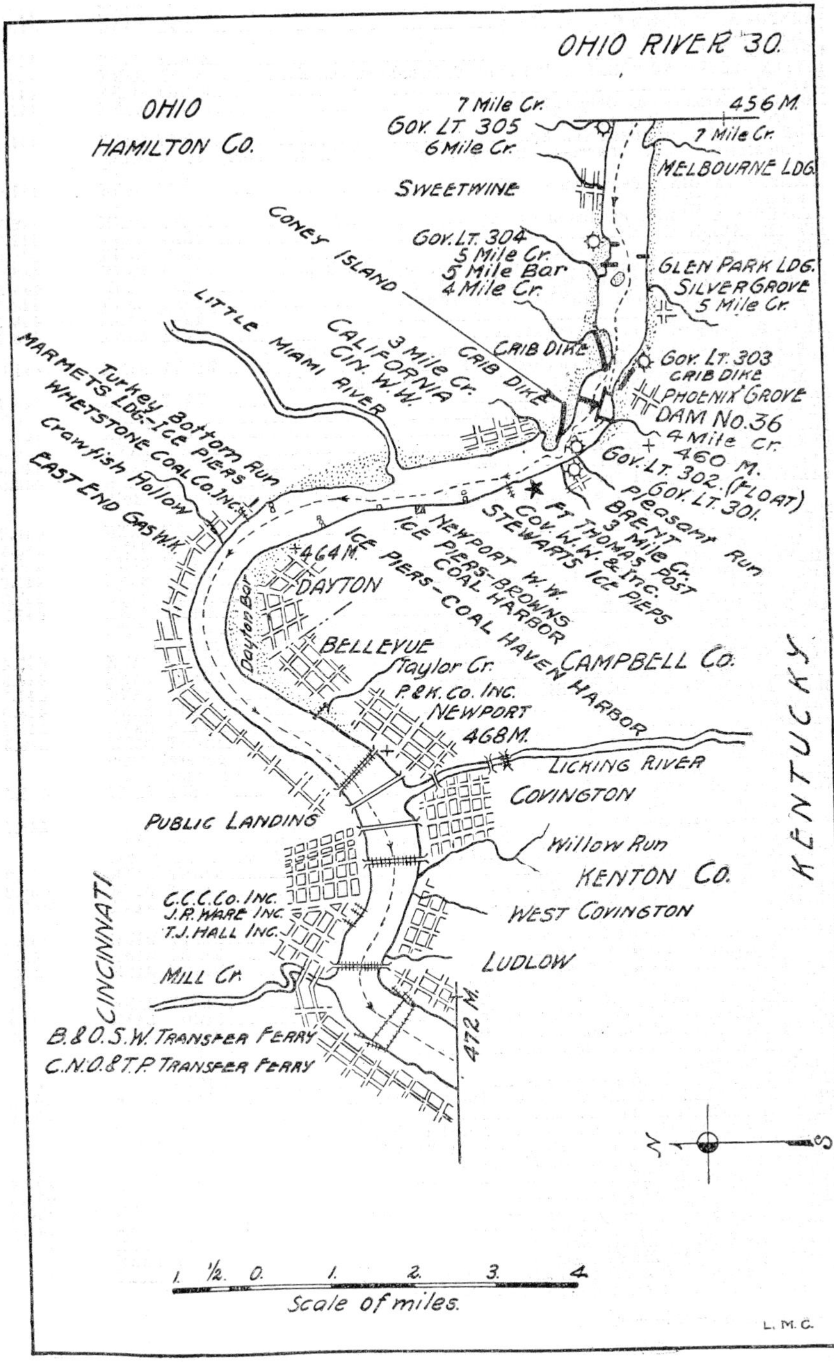
OHIO RIVER 30.
OHIO
HAMILTON CO.
7 Mile Cr.
GOV. LT. 305
6 Mile Cr.
456 M.
7 Mile Cr.
MELBOURNE LDG.
SWEETWINE
CONEY ISLAND
GOV. LT. 304
5 Mile Cr.
5 Mile Bar
4 Mile Cr.
GLEN PARK LDG.
SILVER GROVE
5 Mile Cr.
LITTLE MIAMI RIVER
CALIFORNIA
CIN. W.W.
3 Mile Cr.
CRIB DIKE
CRIB DIKE
GOV. LT. 303
CRIB DIKE
PHOENIX GROVE
DAM No. 36
4 Mile Cr.
460 M.
GOV. LT. 302 (FLOAT)
GOV. LT. 301.
Pleasant Run
BRENT
3 Mile Cr.
FT THOMAS POST
COV. W.W. & Inc.
STEWARTS ICE PIERS
Turkey Bottom Run
MARMETS LDG.-ICE PIERS
WHETSTONE COAL CO. INC.
Crawfish Hollow
EAST END GAS WK.
464 M.
DAYTON
Dayton Bar
NEWPORT W.W.
ICE PIERS-BROWNS
COAL HARBOR
ICE PIERS-COAL HAVEN HARBOR
BELLEVUE
Taylor Cr.
P. & K. Co. INC.
NEWPORT
468 M.
CAMPBELL CO.
KENTUCKY
LICKING RIVER
COVINGTON
PUBLIC LANDING
Willow Run
KENTON CO.
C.C.C. Co. INC.
J.R. WARE INC.
T.J. HALL INC.
WEST COVINGTON
CINCINNATI
LUDLOW
MILL Cr.
472 M.
B. & O. S.W. TRANSFER FERRY
C.N.O. & T.P. TRANSFER FERRY
N
S
1. ½. 0. 1. 2. 3. 4.
Scale of miles.
L. M. C.

Chart No. 30.

		Miles below Pittsburgh.
SEVEN MILE OHIO CREEK	RIGHT BANK	456.0
305. NINE MILE BAR LIGHT No. 1. Color White	RIGHT BANK	456.0
SEVEN MILE KENTUCKY CREEK	LEFT BANK	456.2
MELBOURNE LANDING, Campbell Co., Ky. (337)	LEFT BANK	456.4
Road to Melbourne Station, C. & O. R. R.		
SIX MILE OHIO CREEK	RIGHT BANK	457.0
SWEETWINE, Hamilton Co., Ohio	RIGHT BANK	457.0
Electric line: New Richmond-Cincinnati, Ohio.		
304. FIVE MILE BAR LIGHT. Color White	RIGHT BANK	457.5
STONE DIKE (low) from	RIGHT BANK	457.5
STONE DIKE (low) from	LEFT BANK	457.6
HEAD OF FIVE MILE BAR. Least depth, 2–3 feet, in cut	RIGHT BANK	457.6
STONE DIKE (low) from	RIGHT BANK	457.7
GLEN PARK LANDING, Campbell Co., Ky	LEFT BANK	457.8
Road to Glen Park Station, C. & O. R. R.		
FIVE MILE OHIO CREEK	RIGHT BANK	457.9
SILVER GROVE, Campbell Co., Ky. (19)	LEFT BANK	457.9
FIVE MILE KENTUCKY CREEK	LEFT BANK	458.0
FOUR MILE OHIO CREEK	RIGHT BANK	458.6
UPPER END OF UPPER FOUR MILE CRIB DIKE	RIGHT BANK	458.6
Sometimes known as Campbells Dike.		
UPPER END OF KENTUCKY FOUR MILE CRIB DIKE	LEFT BANK	459.1
Sometimes known as Gander Dike. Least depth, upper end, 2.9 feet.		
PHOENIX GROVE STATION, C. & O. R. R	LEFT BANK	459.1
OHIO RIVER DAM No. 36		459.2
Under construction, 1922. When completed, lock on left bank; length, 600 feet; width, 110 feet; width of navigable pass, 700 feet. Special care necessary in passing dam while under construction. After completion note the directions and caution as in case of Dam No. 2, p. 27.		
FOUR MILE KENTUCKY CREEK	LEFT BANK	459.7
LOWER FOUR MILE CRIB DIKE	RIGHT BANK	459.8
(Coney Island Pleasure Resort.) Electric lines: New Richmond-Cincinnati, Ohio; Bethel, Batavia, Georgetown, and Ripley, Ohio. Least water, foot of dike, about 3 feet. Channel usually near dike, but occasionally crosses to Woodhouse Chute, on Kentucky shore.		
PLEASANT RUN	LEFT BANK	460.2
301. FOUR MILE BAR LIGHT. Color White	LEFT BANK	460.3
BRENT, Campbell Co., Ky. (319). Railroad: C. & O. R. R	LEFT BANK	460.3
THREE MILE KENTUCKY CREEK	LEFT BANK	460.4
THREE MILE OHIO CREEK	RIGHT BANK	460.6
CALIFORNIA, Hamilton Co., Ohio	RIGHT BANK	461.0
Now a part of Cincinnati, Ohio. Electric lines to Cincinnati, New Richmond, Bethel, Batavia, Georgetown, and Ripley, Ohio.		
CINCINNATI WATERWORKS PUMPING STATION	RIGHT BANK	461.4
FORT THOMAS (U. S. post), Ky., on bluff	LEFT BANK	461.5
COVINGTON WATERWORKS PUMPING STATION AND INCLINE	LEFT BANK	461.5
ICE PIERS, STEWARTS LANDING	LEFT BANK	461.8
NEWPORT WATERWORKS PUMPING STATION	LEFT BANK	462.3
LITTLE MIAMI RIVER. See Tributary streams	RIGHT BANK	462.6
ICE PIERS, BROWNS COAL HARBOR	LEFT BANK	462.8
ICE PIERS, COAL HAVEN HARBOR	LEFT BANK	463.5
ICE PIERS, MARMETS LANDING, Carrel St., Cincinnati, Ohio	RIGHT BANK	463.9
HEAD OF DAYTON BAR	LEFT BANK	464.6
EAST END GAS WORKS	RIGHT BANK	465.0
FOOT OF BERRY STREET, Dayton, Campbell Co., Ky. (7,646)	LEFT BANK	466.1
FOOT OF TAYLOR AVENUE, Bellevue, Campbell Co., Ky. (7,379)	LEFT BANK	467.0
TAYLOR CREEK	LEFT BANK	467.4
LOUISVILLE & NASHVILLE RAILWAY AND HIGHWAY BRIDGE		467.9
Channel span, 490 feet; height, 102 feet.		
FOOT OF MONMOUTH STREET, Newport, Campbell Co., Ky. (30,309)	LEFT BANK	468.0
Bellevue, adjoining Newport on the east, had (1910) a population of 6,683, and Dayton, next east of Bellevue, had the same year a population of 6,979. Railroads: L. & N. and C. & O.		
NEWPORT & CINCINNATI HIGHWAY BRIDGE		468.2
Channel span, 502 feet; height, 102.4 feet and 108 feet.		
PUBLIC LANDING, Cincinnati, Ohio (401,247)	RIGHT BANK	468.5
Industries include banking, insurance, and manufacturing of all kinds. Railroads: Pennsylvania lines, N. Y. Central lines, B. & O., C. & O., L. & N., N. & W., Cincinnati Southern, C., H. & D., Chi., Cin. & Lou., and allied lines. Electric interurban lines, north, east, and west. Miami and Erie Canal in outskirts of city has no direct connection with the Ohio River.		
LICKING RIVER	LEFT BANK	468.6
This stream includes the main Licking and two principal branches, the North and South Forks. See Tributary streams.		
COVINGTON & CINCINNATI HIGHWAY SUSPENSION BRIDGE		468.7
Channel span, 1,004 feet; height, 92 feet and 101.5 feet.		
FOOT OF WASHINGTON STREET, Covington, Kenton Co., Ky. (57,121)	LEFT BANK	469.0
Railroads: L. & N. and C. & O.		
CHESAPEAKE & OHIO RAILWAY AND HIGHWAY BRIDGE		469.3
Channel span, 524 feet; height, 105.3 feet.		
WEST COVINGTON, Kenton Co., Ky	LEFT BANK	470.0
CINCINNATI SOUTHERN RAILWAY BRIDGE		470.7
Channel span, 500 feet; height, 101.5 feet.		
MOUTH OF MILL CREEK	RIGHT BANK	470.8
LUDLOW, Kenton Co., Ky. (4,582)	LEFT BANK	471.1

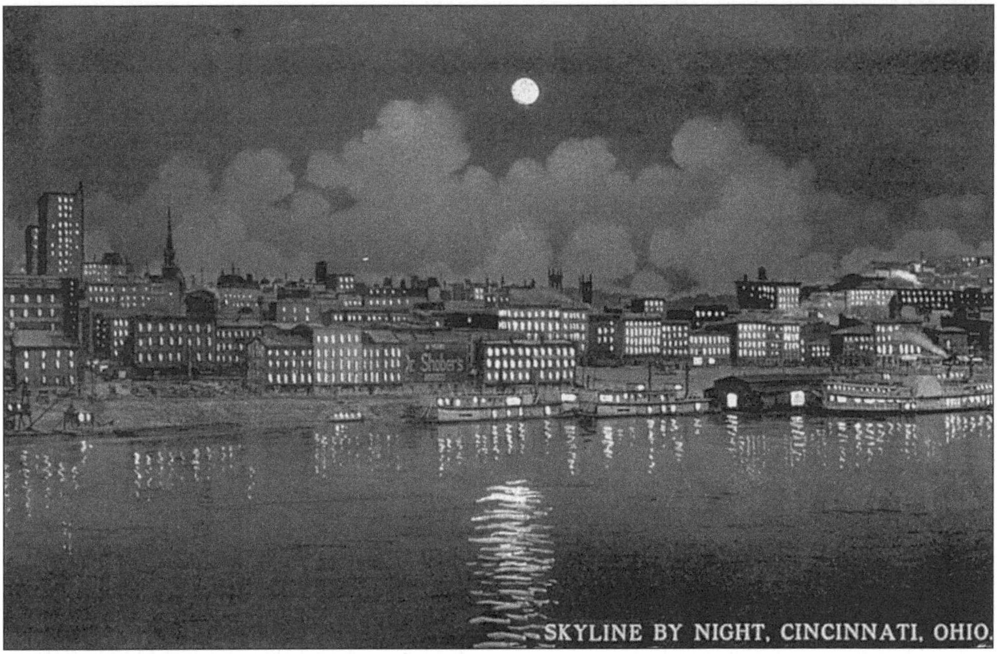

Activity slows but does not stop in the darkness before the dawn of another busy day. The *Str. Indiana* is loading cargo at the wharfboat, while two other packets lay downriver along the cobblestone wharf. Steamboats were usually landed facing upstream, even if that meant making a 180-degree turn midstream. The pilots had much better control over the boat facing into the current.

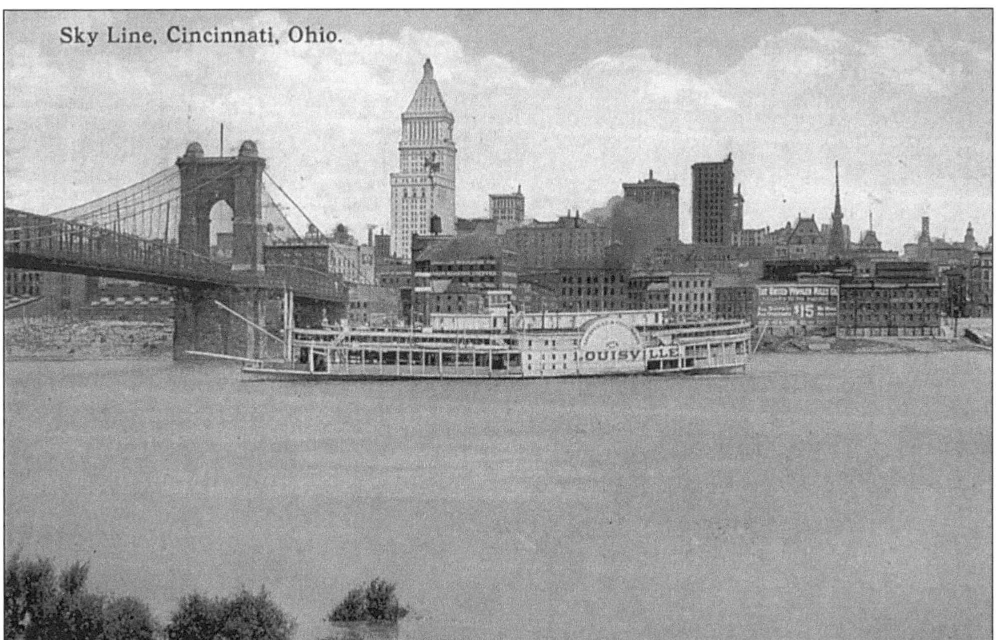

The Cincinnati and Louisville Packet Company's *Str. City of Louisville* is shown shortly after her early morning departure from the public landing en route to Louisville. After slowly backing away from the landing in a broad arc, she has rounded out to pass under the suspension bridge.

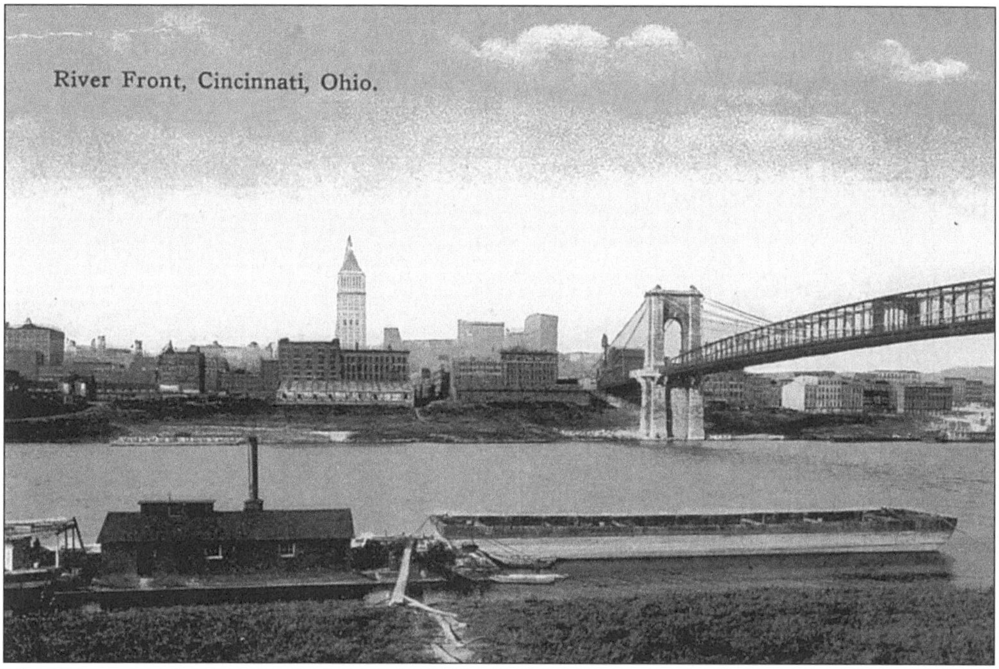

The Cincinnati harbor, just below the suspension bridge, is seen here from the Kentucky shore.

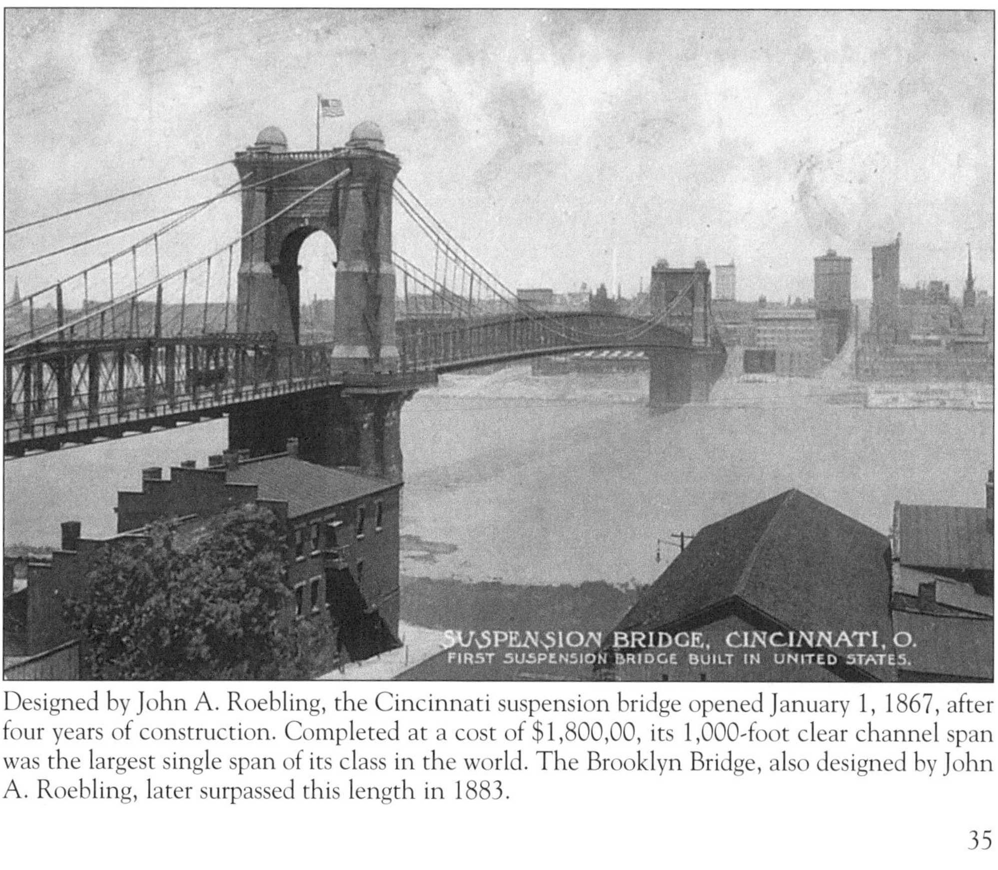

Designed by John A. Roebling, the Cincinnati suspension bridge opened January 1, 1867, after four years of construction. Completed at a cost of $1,800,00, its 1,000-foot clear channel span was the largest single span of its class in the world. The Brooklyn Bridge, also designed by John A. Roebling, later surpassed this length in 1883.

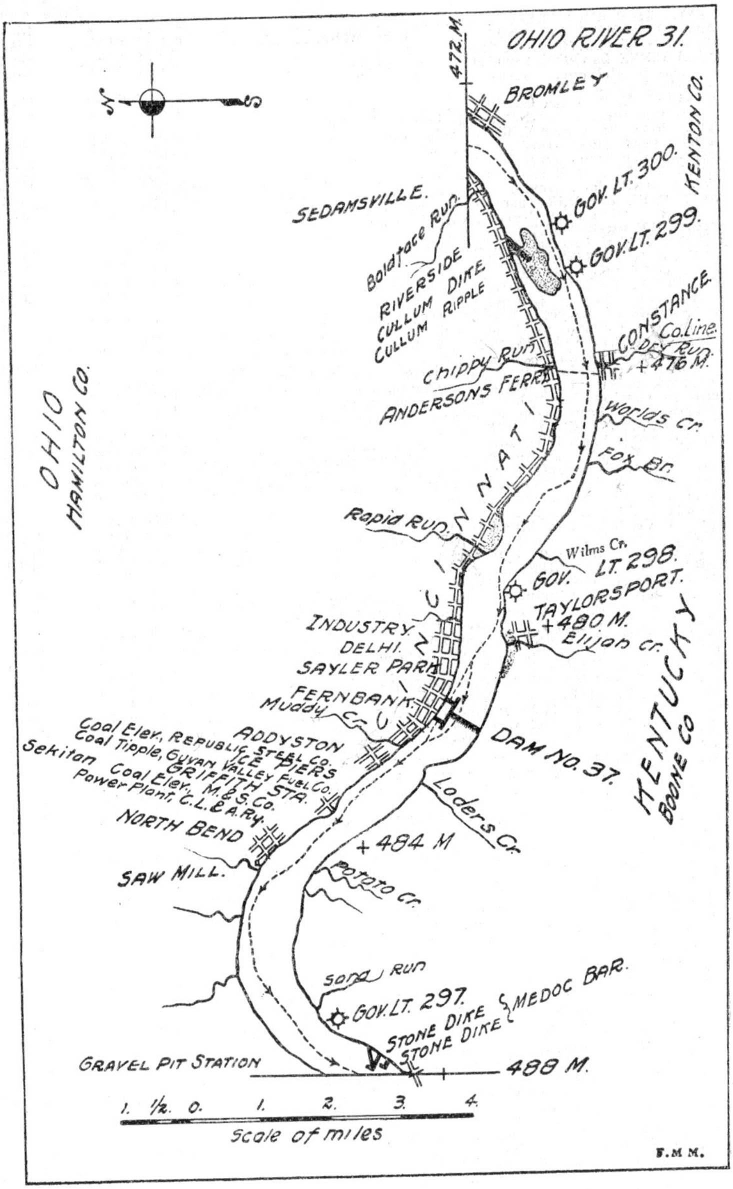
OHIO RIVER 31.
472 M.
BROMLEY
KENTON CO.
SEDAMSVILLE.
Boldface Run
GOV. LT. 300.
GOV. LT. 299.
RIVERSIDE
CULLUM DIKE
CULLUM RIPPLE
CONSTANCE
Co. Line
Dry Run
+476 M.
Chippy Run
ANDERSONS FERRY
Worlds Cr.
OHIO
HAMILTON CO.
Fox Br.
CINCINNATI
Rapid Run
Wilms Cr.
GOV. LT. 298.
TAYLORSPORT.
+480 M.
Elijah Cr.
INDUSTRY
DELHI
SAYLER PARK
KENTUCKY
BOONE CO
FERNBANK
Muddy Cr.
ADDYSTON
Coal Elev., REPUBLIC STEEL Co.
Coal Tipple, Guyan Valley Fuel Co.
ICE PIERS
Sekitan
GRIFFITH STA.
Coal Elev. M. & S. Co.
Power Plant, C. L. & A. Ry.
DAM No. 37.
Loders Cr.
NORTH BEND
+484 M
SAW MILL.
Potato Cr.
Sand Run
MEDOC BAR.
GOV. LT. 297.
STONE DIKE
STONE DIKE
GRAVEL PIT STATION
488 M.
1. 1/2. 0. 1. 2. 3. 4.
Scale of miles
F. M. M.

Chart No. 31.

		Miles below Pittsburgh.
BROMLEY, Kenton Co., Ky. (736)	**LEFT BANK**	**472.2**
Electric cars to Covington and Cincinnati.		
SEDAMSVILLE, Hamilton Co., Ohio (suburb of Cincinnati)	**RIGHT BANK**	**472.3**
BOLD FACE RUN	**RIGHT BANK**	**472.4**
FLEISCHMANNS DISTILLERY	**RIGHT BANK**	**472.8**
RIVERSIDE, Hamilton Co., Ohio (suburb of Cincinnati)	**RIGHT BANK**	**473.5**
Electric cars to Cincinnati-Andersons Ferry.		
HEAD OF CULLUM DIKE (stone and piling) from	**RIGHT BANK**	**473.7**
Channel near left bank. Least water, at head, 3.4 feet, open river.		
300. CULLUM RIPPLE LIGHT No. 4. Color White	**LEFT BANK**	**473.9**
299. CULLUM RIPPLE LIGHT No. 2. Color White	**LEFT BANK**	**474.5**
CHIPPY RUN	**RIGHT BANK**	**475.8**
ANDERSONS FERRY, Hamilton Co., Ohio	**RIGHT BANK**	**475.9**
Suburb of Cincinnati, Ohio. C. L. & A. electric line to Lawrenceburg and Aurora, Ind.; Harrison, Ohio, and intermediate points. Railroads: B. & O. S. W., to Louisville, St. Louis, etc. Ferry to Constance, Ky.		
DRY RUN and CONSTANCE, Ky	**LEFT BANK**	**475.9**
WORLDS CREEK	**LEFT BANK**	**476.6**
FOX BRANCH	**LEFT BANK**	**477.3**
RAPID RUN	**RIGHT BANK**	**479.0**
298. RAPID RUN LIGHT. Color White	**LEFT BANK**	**479.3**
WILMS CREEK	**LEFT BANK**	**479.4**
INDUSTRY, Hamilton Co., Ohio (suburb of Cincinnati)	**RIGHT BANK**	**480.0**
Electric cars: Cincinnati, Ohio; Lawrenceburg and Aurora, Ind.		
TAYLORSPORT, Boone Co., Ky. (161)	**LEFT BANK**	**480.0**
ELIJAH CREEK	**LEFT BANK**	**480.3**
DELHI, Hamilton Co., Ohio (suburb of Cincinnati)	**RIGHT BANK**	**480.3**
Electric cars: Cincinnati, Ohio; Lawrenceburg and Aurora, Ind.; and Harrison, Ohio. Railroads: B. & O. S. W., C. C. C. & St. L. Ferry to Taylorsport, Ky.		
SAYLER PARK (Home City), Hamilton Co., Ohio (suburb of Cincinnati)	**RIGHT BANK**	**480.7**
Electric cars: Cincinnati, Ohio; Lawrenceburg and Aurora, Ind.; and Harrison, Ohio. Railroads: B. & O. S. W. and C. C. C. & St. L.		
OHIO RIVER DAM No. 37		**481.3**
Lock on right bank. Length, 600 feet; width, 110 feet; width of navigable pass, 900 feet. Note directions and caution as in case of Dam No. 2, p. 27.		
FERNBANK, Hamilton Co., Ohio (suburb of Cincinnati)	**RIGHT BANK**	**481.7**
Electric cars: Cincinnati, Ohio; Lawrenceburg and Aurora, Ind.; and Harrison, Ohio. Railroads: B. & O. S. W. and C. C. C. & St. L.		
MUDDY CREEK—Corporation Line Cincinnati, Ohio	**RIGHT BANK**	**482.3**
ADDYSTON, Hamilton Co., Ohio (1,448)	**RIGHT BANK**	**482.5**
Industries: Republic Steel Co., manufacturing cast-iron water pipe, etc. Electric cars: Cincinnati, Ohio; Lawrenceburg and Aurora, Ind.; and Harrison, Ohio. Railroads: B. & O. S. W. and C. C. C. & St. L.		
LODERS CREEK	**LEFT BANK**	**482.5**
COAL ELEVATORS, Republic Steel Co	**RIGHT BANK**	**482.7**
ICE PIERS, Guyan Valley Fuel Co	**RIGHT BANK**	**483.1**
COAL TIPPLE, Guyan Valley Fuel Co	**RIGHT BANK**	**483.2**
GRIFFITH STATION, Hamilton Co., Ohio	**RIGHT BANK**	**483.8**
Electric cars: Cincinnati, Ohio; Lawrenceburg and Aurora, Ind.; and Harrison, Ohio. Railroads: B. & O. S. W. and C. C. C. & St. L.		
SEKITAN, P. O., Hamilton Co., Ohio (1,100)	**RIGHT BANK**	**484.1**
COAL ELEVATOR, MARMET & SMITH CO	**RIGHT BANK**	**484.1**
POWER PLANT, C. L. & A. Electric Street R. R. Co	**RIGHT BANK**	**484.2**
NORTH BEND, Hamilton Co., Ohio (597)	**RIGHT BANK**	**484.5**
Electric lines: Cincinnati, Ohio; Lawrenceburg and Aurora, Ind.; and Harrison, Ohio. Railroads: B. & O. S. W. and C. C. C. & St. L.		
POTATO CREEK	**LEFT BANK**	**484.7**
SAWMILL, North Bend, Ohio	**RIGHT BANK**	**484.7**
SAND RUN	**LEFT BANK**	**486.2**
297–a. PIKE PEAK LIGHT. Color White	**RIGHT BANK**	**486.2**
297. MEDOC BAR LIGHT No. 4. Color White	**LEFT BANK**	**486.8**
RIPRAP STONE DIKE (low)	**LEFT BANK**	**487.4**
Channel to right of dike. Least depth, 3.7 feet, near upper dike, open river.		
RIPRAP STONE DIKE (low)	**LEFT BANK**	**487.7**
GRAVEL PIT STATION (B. & O. S. W. R. R.)	**RIGHT BANK**	**488.0**

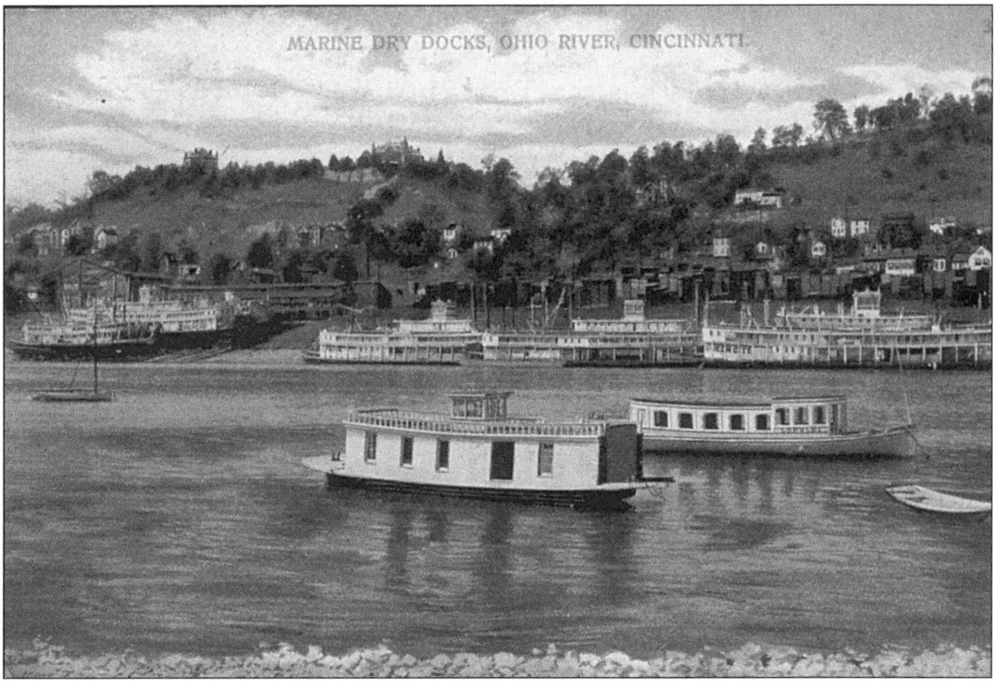

The Cincinnati dry dock was a primary facility used to maintain boats and barges in the Cincinnati area. Wood-hulled packets regularly needed repairs and maintenance. Several boats and barges could be routinely found here pulled out of the water. Privately owned small boats, as seen in the foreground along the Kentucky shore, were plentiful along the river.

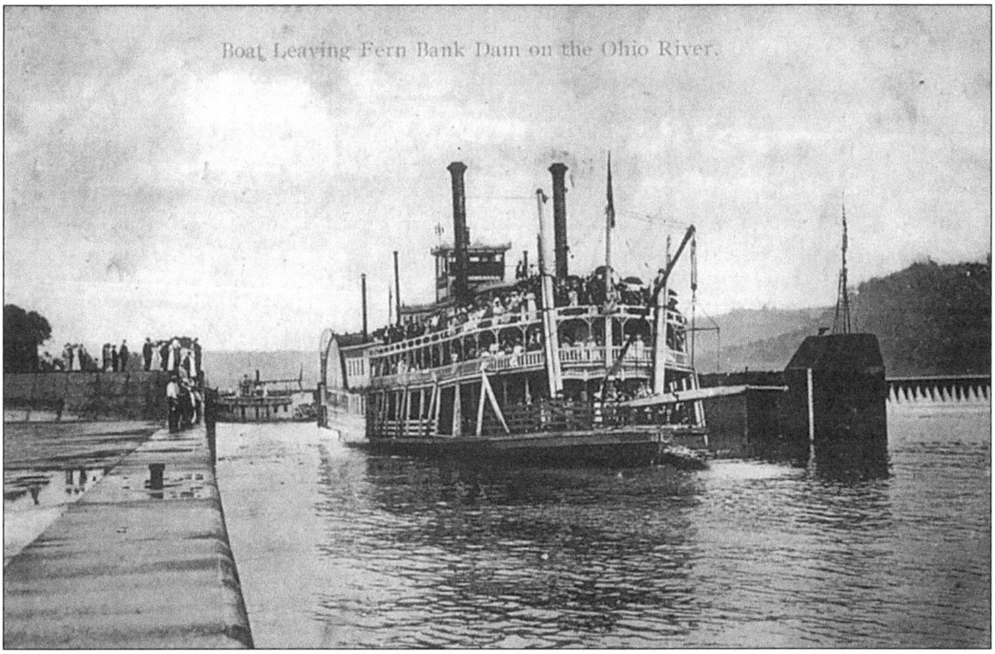

Packets locked through Fernbank Dam below Cincinnati after 1911. Fernbank Dam maintained a nine-foot water level in the Cincinnati harbor, alleviating low, summer water conditions. (North 22.)

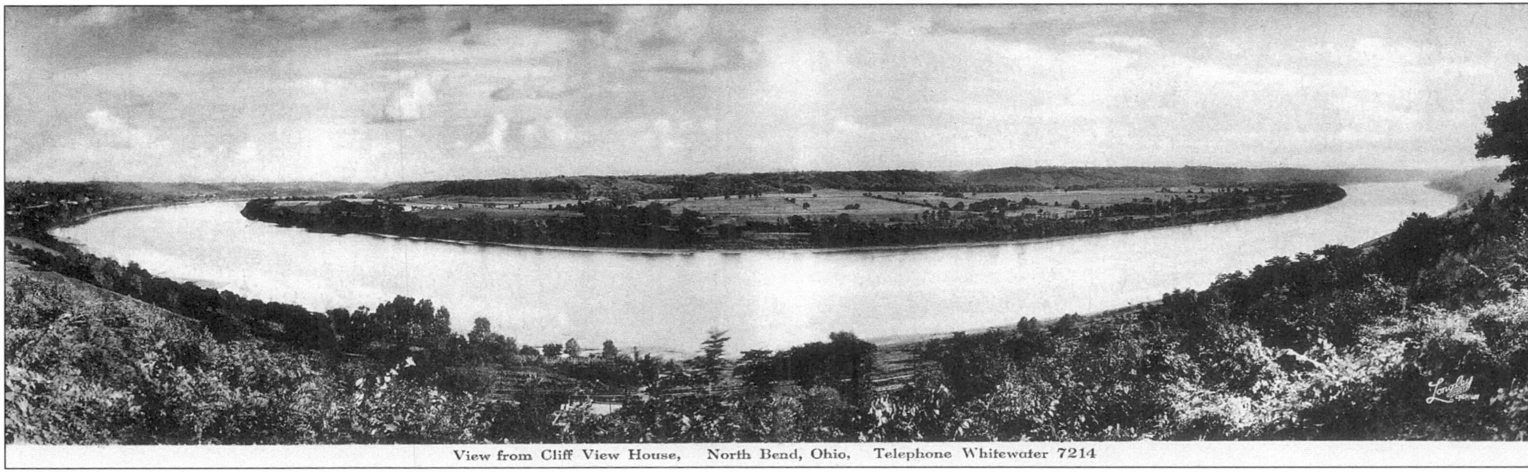

The beauty of the Ohio River as it sweeps through a broad area between the Ohio and Kentucky hills below Cincinnati is captured in summer. Once away from the cities and towns, river travel is a tranquil and quiet passage through farms and forests. The soft, rhythmic sounds made by the boat steadily moving upon the water are only broken by sounds from animals and people along the shore.

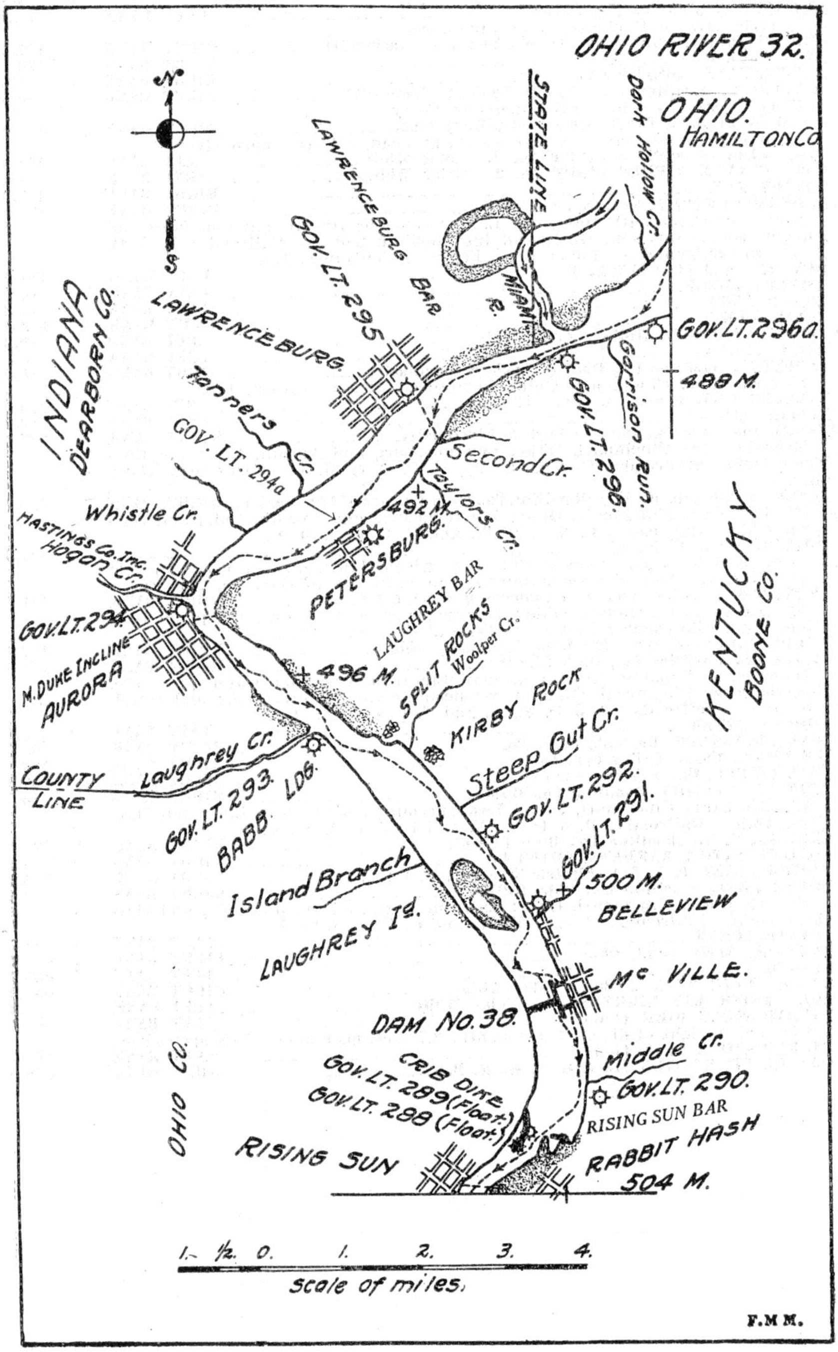
OHIO RIVER 32.
N
S
OHIO.
HAMILTON Co.
STATE LINE
Dark Hollow Cr.
LAWRENCEBURG BAR
GOV. LT. 295
MIAMI R.
GOV. LT. 296a.
Garrison Run.
488 M.
GOV. LT. 296.
LAWRENCEBURG
INDIANA
DEARBORN CO.
Tanners Cr.
GOV. LT. 294a
Second Cr.
Taylors Cr.
492 M.
Whistle Cr.
HASTINGS Co. Inc.
Hogan Cr.
PETERSBURG.
KENTUCKY
BOONE CO.
LAUGHREY BAR
GOV. LT. 294
M. DUKE INCLINE
AURORA
SPLIT ROCKS
Woolper Cr.
496 M.
KIRBY ROCK
Steep Gut Cr.
COUNTY LINE
Laughrey Cr.
GOV. LT. 293.
BABB LDG.
GOV. LT. 292.
GOV. LT. 291.
Island Branch
500 M.
BELLEVIEW
LAUGHREY Id.
Mc VILLE.
DAM No. 38.
CRIB DIKE
Middle Cr.
GOV. LT. 289 (Float)
GOV. LT. 288 (Float)
GOV. LT. 290.
RISING SUN BAR
OHIO CO.
RISING SUN
RABBIT HASH
504 M.
1. ½. 0. 1. 2. 3. 4.
scale of miles.
F.M.M.

Chart No. 32.

Miles below Pittsburgh.

DARK HOLLOW CREEK — RIGHT BANK — 488.2

296a. MEDOC BAR LIGHT No. 2. Color White — LEFT BANK — 488.3

GARRISON RUN — LEFT BANK — 488.9

296. BIG MIAMI LIGHT. Color White — LEFT BANK — 489.4

MIAMI RIVER — RIGHT BANK — 489.4

At the mouth of the Miami a high bar extends half way across the Ohio. Channel lies along the left bank, deep water at all stages. State line, Ohio-Indiana, right bank of Miami at mouth. (For Miami River, see Tributary streams.)

HEAD OF LAWRENCEBURG BAR — RIGHT BANK — 491.0

Channel crosses to left bank. Least depth, near head, 2.5 feet, open river.

295. LAWRENCEBURG LIGHT. Color White, Red Front — RIGHT BANK — 491.1

LAWRENCEBURG, county seat of Dearborn Co., Ind. (3,466) — RIGHT BANK — 491.1

Principal industries: Flouring mills, cooperage, chair factory, carriage works, manufacture of veneers, saws and cutlery, shoes and coffins, banking and general merchandising. Railroads: B. & O. S. W. R. R. and C., C. C. & St. L. Electric line to Cincinnati, Ohio, and Aurora, Ind. Ferry to Kentucky shore.

SECOND or FERRY CREEK — LEFT BANK — 491.3

TAYLORS CREEK — LEFT BANK — 491.7

TANNERS CREEK — RIGHT BANK — 493.0

PETERSBURG, Boone Co., Ky. (331) — LEFT BANK — 493.0

Principal industries: Flour mills and general merchandise.

294-a. PETERSBURG LIGHT. Color White; flash every 2 seconds — LEFT BANK — 493.0

WHISTLE CREEK — RIGHT BANK — 493.9

HOGAN CREEK — RIGHT BANK — 494.7

M. DUKE INCLINE (below Hogan Creek) — RIGHT BANK — 494.7

294. AURORA LIGHT. Color White, Red Front — RIGHT BANK — 494.8

AURORA, Dearborn Co., Ind. (4,299) — RIGHT BANK — 494.8

Principal industries: Flour mills, manufacture of furniture, shoes, coffins, foundry and machine shop, cooperage, carriage works, tool works, creamery, coal elevator, banking and general merchandise. Railroad: B. & O. S. W. Electric line: Lawrenceburg-Cincinnati. Stage to Rising Sun, Ind., ferry to Kentucky shore.

LAUGHREY BAR — LEFT BANK — 496.2

LAUGHREY CREEK — RIGHT BANK — 496.6

Lower portion of creek navigable at ordinary stages.

293. LAUGHREY CREEK LIGHT. Color White — RIGHT BANK — 496.7

BABB LANDING, Ohio Co., Ind — RIGHT BANK — 496.8

SPLIT ROCKS — LEFT BANK — 497.3

WOOLPER CREEK — LEFT BANK — 497.7

KIRBY ROCK — LEFT BANK — 497.9

A fantastic formation of natural cemented gravel.

STEEP GUT CREEK — LEFT BANK — 498.5

292. LAUGHREY ISLAND LIGHT No. 4. Color White — LEFT BANK — 499.1

ISLAND BRANCH — RIGHT BANK — 499.2

HEAD OF LAUGHREY ISLAND — RIGHT BANK — 499.2

Channel near left bank. Least depth at low water, a little below U. S. Light No. 292, 3 feet, open river.

291. LAUGHREY ISLAND LIGHT No. 2. Color White — LEFT BANK — 500.2

Channel crosses toward right bank and then returns. Least depth, at foot of island, 2.7 feet, open river.

BELLEVIEW, Boone Co., Ky. (120) — LEFT BANK — 500.7

OHIO RIVER DAM No. 38 — 501.3

Under construction, 1922. When completed, lock on left bank; length, 600 feet; width, 110 feet; width of navigable pass, 700 feet. Special care necessary in passing dam while under construction. After completion note the directions and caution as in case of Dam No. 2, p. 27.

MAXVILLE (or Moville), Boone Co., Ky — LEFT BANK — 501.3

Ferry to Indiana shore.

MIDDLE CREEK — LEFT BANK — 502.4

290. MIDDLE CREEK LIGHT. Color White — LEFT BANK — 502.6

Channel crosses toward right bank.

HEAD OF CRIB DIKE — RIGHT BANK — 503.2

Channel between dike and Rising Sun Bar. Least depth, near head of bar, 4.2 feet, open river. (N. B.—Not safe to run Kentucky shore except at high stages.)

289. RISING SUN FLOAT LIGHT No. 7. Color White — RIGHT OF CHANNEL — 503.5

During low water stages, on dike at mid-length.

288. RISING SUN FLOAT LIGHT No. 5. Color White — RIGHT OF CHANNEL — 503.7

During low water stages, at end of dike.

RABBIT HASH, Boone Co., Ky. (24) — LEFT BANK — 504.0

Ferry to Rising Sun.

RISING SUN, county seat of Ohio Co., Ind. (1,411) — RIGHT BANK — 504.0

Stage to Aurora, Ind. Ferry to Rabbit Hash, Ky.

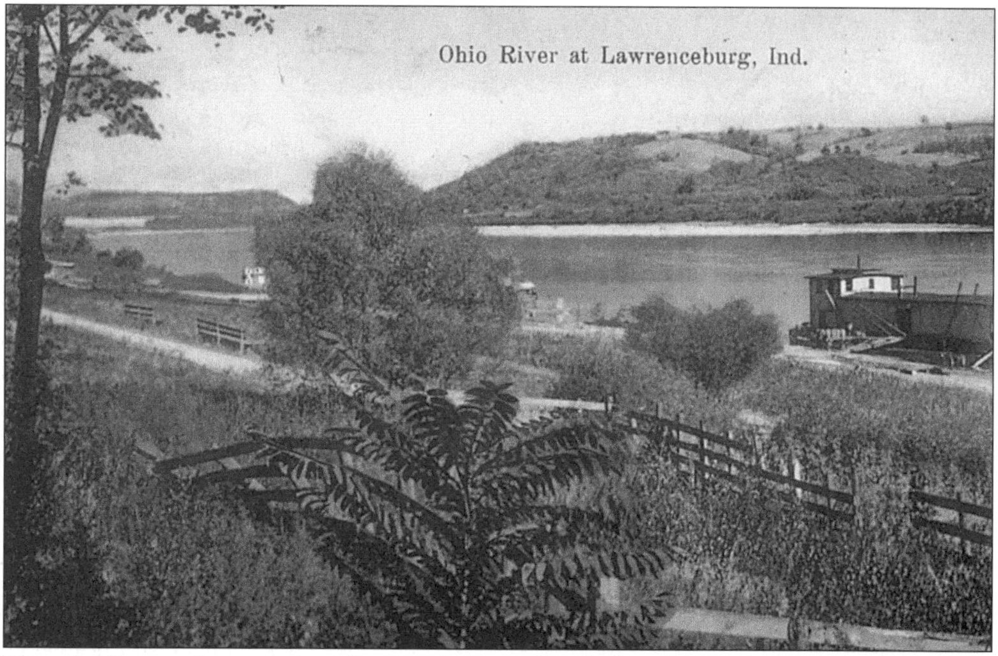

The wharfboat at Lawrenceburg lies just below a big shallow bar at the mouth of the Great Miami River near the Ohio and Indiana border. Landing a boat at Lawrenceburg could be a challenge in either low or high water. The river quickly grew in width at Lawrenceburg, flooding out over the broad, low, Indiana shore.

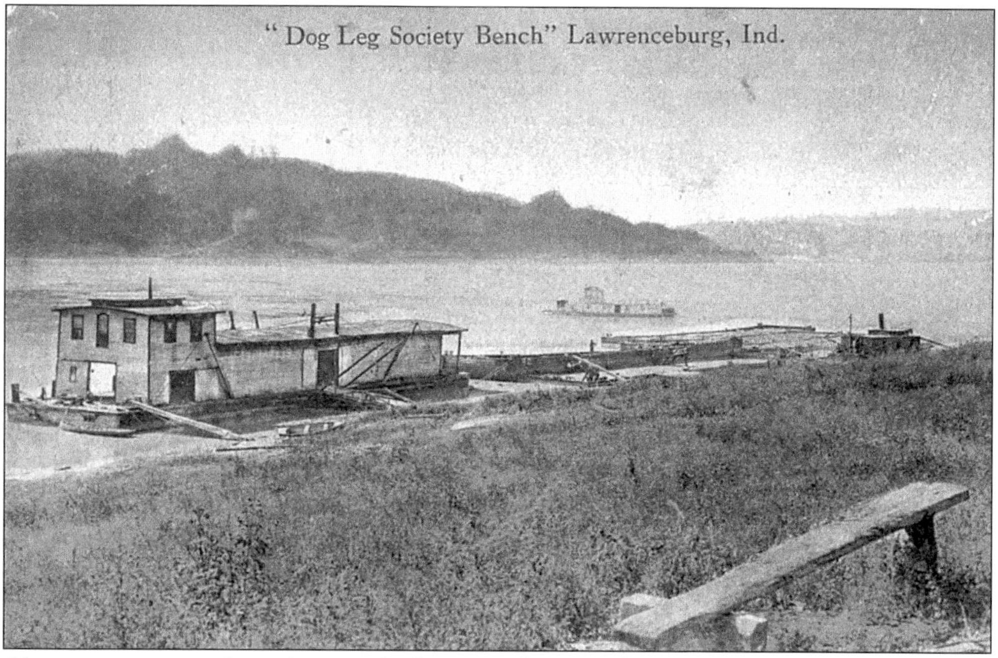

Almost every town along the river had a spot where residents could sit and enjoy the river. Most were community gathering places for local news and gossip as the river flowed by.

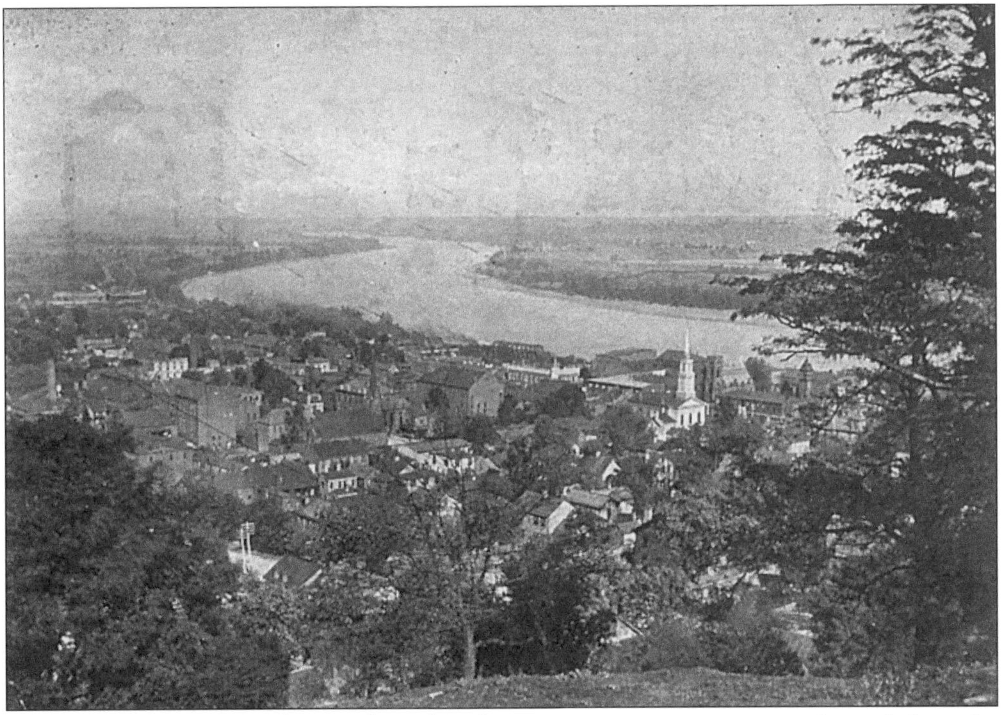

The river below Lawrenceburg makes a broad, sweeping turn into a narrow channel along the Indiana shore at Aurora. The town itself lies in the Hogan Creek valley and in the surrounding hills. Aurora had relatively little land along the river that did not easily flood.

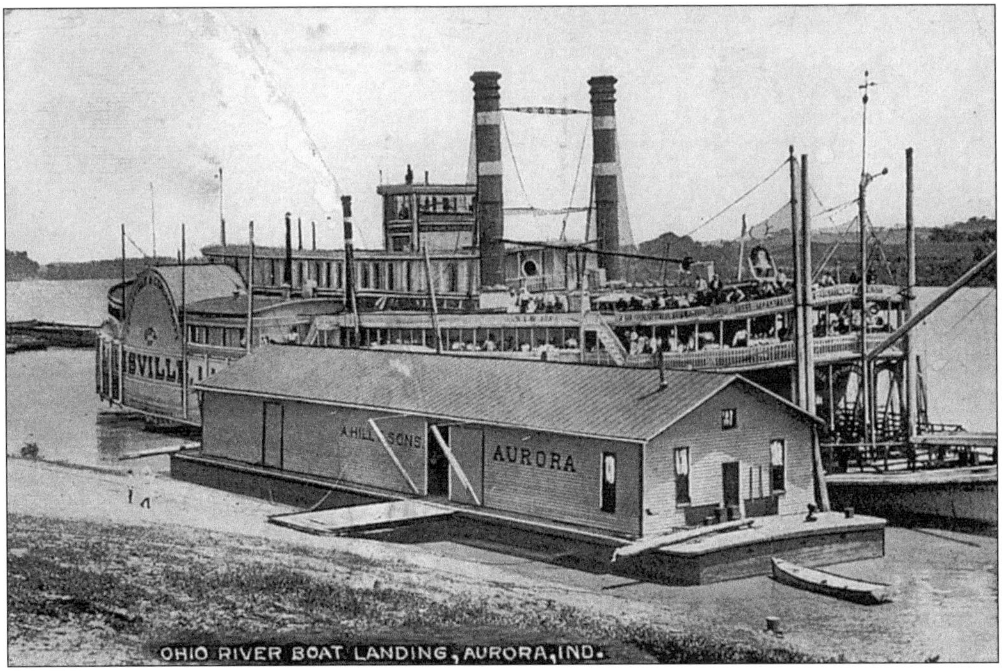

Str. City of Louisville, the "big boat," is here landed facing downstream at Aurora during low water. It is now mid-morning on our run to Louisville. (North 23.)

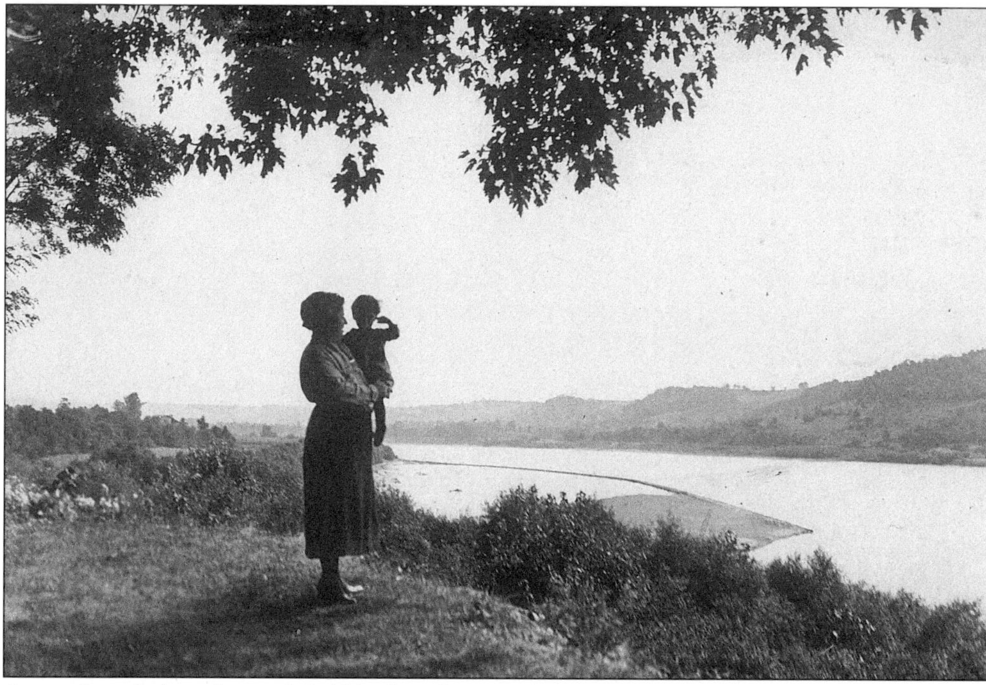

An unidentified mother and child look at the river from the upper riverbank at about Fourth and Front Streets in Rising Sun, Indiana, on a summer afternoon. The water level, or stage, is very low, exposing the man-made crib dike just above Rising Sun. The Rising Sun bar is exposed above the water level at center right. The government built this crib dike in the late 1800s to force an increased water level into a narrow channel along the Kentucky shore above Rising Sun. Prior to its construction, river navigation was often halted at this point due to low water.

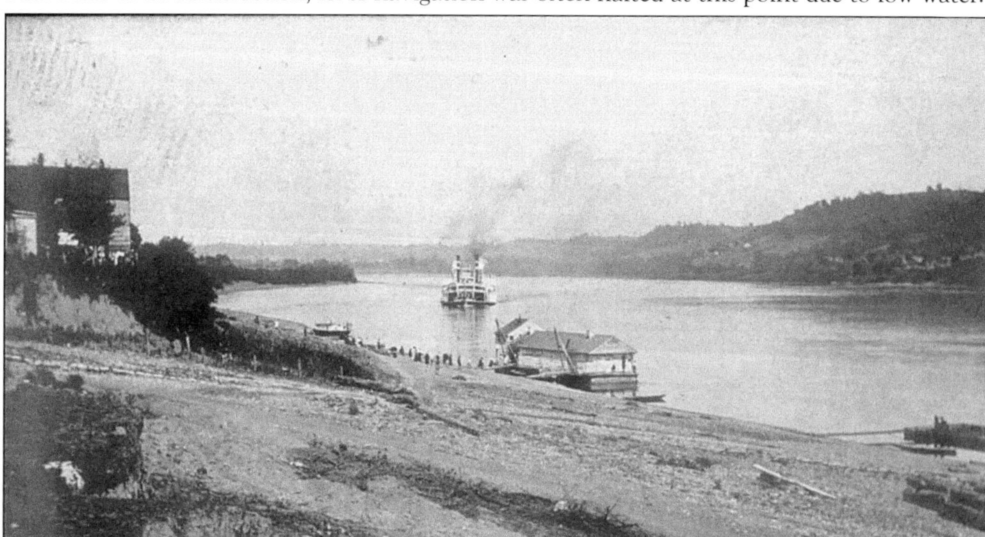

The arrival of the daily packet from Cincinnati in Rising Sun in late morning drew a group of people to meet friends, go aboard for points downriver, or just to watch. The river is a little low in this picture, as you can see the top of the Rising Sun dike just behind the steamboat. It looks like the pilot is going to bring her straight into the wharfboat, pointing downriver.

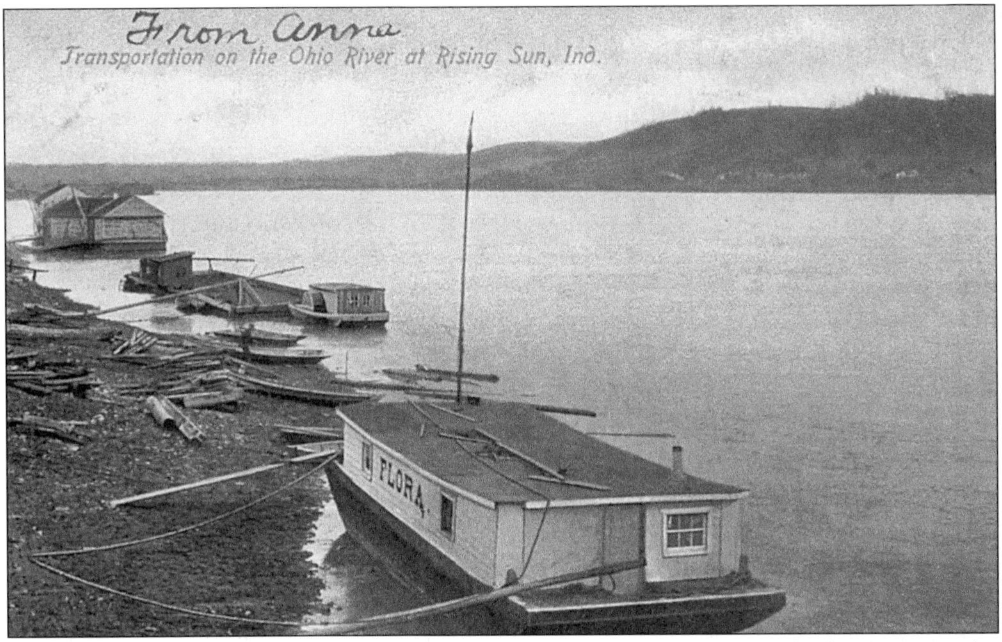

The floating photography studio of Hubert M. Flora visited Rising Sun and other towns in the area, taking pictures of the river and its people. Residing in Madison, Indiana—where he also maintained a studio—Mr. Flora left a legacy of river pictures, some of which can be found on cards in this book.

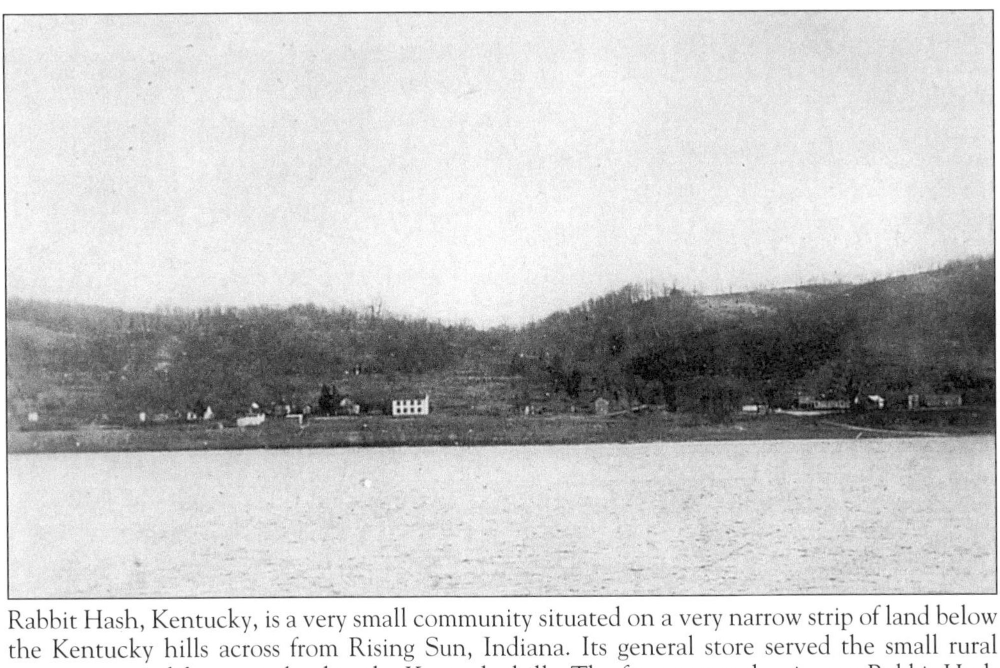

Rabbit Hash, Kentucky, is a very small community situated on a very narrow strip of land below the Kentucky hills across from Rising Sun, Indiana. Its general store served the small rural community and farmers inland in the Kentucky hills. The ferry across the river to Rabbit Hash from Rising Sun was the only ferry between Aurora, 7 miles upriver, and Warsaw, 23 miles downriver.

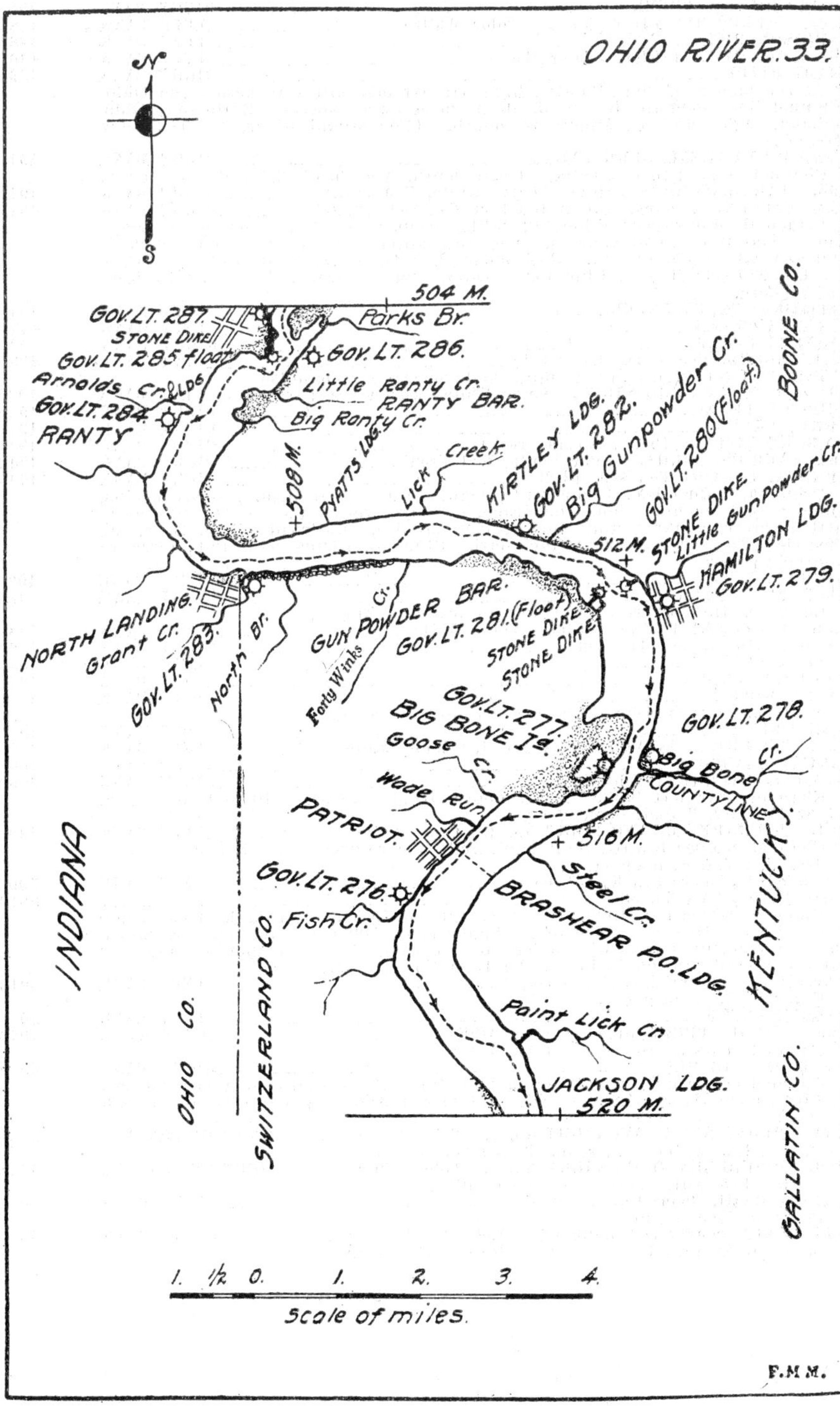
OHIO RIVER 33.
N
S
504 M.
GOV. LT. 287.
STONE DIKE
Parks Br.
GOV. LT. 285 float
GOV. LT. 286.
Arnolds Cr. & LDG
Little Ranty Cr.
RANTY BAR.
GOV. LT. 284.
RANTY
Big Ranty Cr.
508 M.
PYATTS LDG.
Lick Creek
KIRTLEY LDG.
GOV. LT. 282.
Big Gunpowder Cr.
GOV. LT. 280 (Float)
BOONE CO.
STONE DIKE
Little Gun Powder Cr.
512 M.
HAMILTON LDG.
GOV. LT. 279.
NORTH LANDING
Grant Cr.
GOV. LT. 283.
North Br.
GUN POWDER BAR.
Cr.
Forty Winks
GOV. LT. 281 (Float)
STONE DIKE
STONE DIKE
GOV. LT. 277.
BIG BONE Id.
GOV. LT. 278.
Goose Cr.
Big Bone Cr.
COUNTY LINE
Wade Run
PATRIOT.
516 M.
GOV. LT. 276.
Fish Cr.
Steel Cr.
BRASHEAR P.O. LDG.
INDIANA
KENTUCKY.
OHIO CO.
SWITZERLAND CO.
Paint Lick Cr.
JACKSON LDG.
520 M.
GALLATIN CO.
1. 1/2 0. 1. 2. 3. 4.
Scale of miles.
F.M.M.

Chart No. 33.

		Miles below Pittsburgh.
PARKS BRANCH	**LEFT BANK**	**504.0**
287. RISING SUN LIGHT No. 3. Color Red	**RIGHT BANK**	**504.1**
Channel crosses to left bank. Least depth on Middle Bar, 3 feet, open river.		
HEAD OF STONE and PILE DIKE curving from	**RIGHT BANK**	**504.3**
286. RABBIT HASH LIGHT. Color White	**LEFT BANK**	**504.4**
285. RISING SUN FLOAT LIGHT No. 1. Color White	**RIGHT OF CHANNEL**	**504.4**
Over foot of dike. In low stages on lower end of dike.		
LITTLE RANTY CREEK	**LEFT BANK**	**505.3**
A gravel bar extends between the Ranty Creeks. Channel to right of bar. Least water, 3.3 feet, open river.		
RANTY BAR, head	**LEFT BANK**	**505.3**
BIG RANTY CREEK	**LEFT BANK**	**505.6**
ARNOLDS CREEK and LANDING, Ind	**RIGHT BANK**	**505.8**
284. RANTY BAR LIGHT. Color White	**RIGHT BANK**	**505.9**
Channel from this point follows close to right bank.		
RANTY, IND	**RIGHT BANK**	**505.9**
NORTH LANDING, Ohio Co., Ind. (77)	**RIGHT BANK**	**507.3**
GRANT CREEK	**RIGHT BANK**	**507.5**
283. NORTH LIGHT. Color White	**RIGHT BANK**	**507.5**
NORTH BRANCH	**RIGHT BANK**	**508.0**
PYATTS LANDING, Boone Co., Ky	**LEFT BANK**	**508.3**
LICK CREEK	**LEFT BANK**	**509.6**
FORTY WINKS CREEK	**RIGHT BANK**	**509.6**
KIRTLEY LANDING, Boone Co., Ky	**LEFT BANK**	**510.2**
HEAD OF GUNPOWDER BAR	**RIGHT BANK**	**510.4**
Channel to left of bar.		
282. GUNPOWDER LIGHT No. 4. Color White	**LEFT BANK**	**510.8**
BIG GUNPOWDER CREEK	**LEFT BANK**	**511.2**
281. GUNPOWDER FLOAT LIGHT No. 1. Color White	**RIGHT OF CHANNEL**	**511.9**
End of small stone and pile dike from right bank.		
STONE and PILE DIKE	**RIGHT BANK**	**512.1**
280. GUNPOWDER FLOAT LIGHT No. 2, end of dike. Color White.	**LEFT OF CHANNEL**	**512.2**
STONE DIKE	**LEFT BANK**	**512.2**
LITTLE GUNPOWDER or LANDING CREEK	**LEFT BANK**	**512.3**
279. HAMILTON LANDING LIGHT. Color White	**LEFT BANK**	**512.6**
Hamilton, Boone Co., Ky. (83). Industries: General merchandising.		
HEAD OF BIG BONE BAR or ISLAND	**RIGHT BANK**	**514.3**
Channel past bar lies near left bank, with good depth of water.		
278. BIG BONE LIGHT No. 2. Color White	**LEFT BANK**	**514.4**
277. BIG BONE LIGHT No. 1, on island. Color White	**RIGHT OF CHANNEL**	**514.6**
BIG BONE CREEK	**LEFT BANK**	**514.6**
GOOSE CREEK and LANDING	**RIGHT BANK**	**516.1**
STEEL CREEK	**LEFT BANK**	**516.3**
WADE RUN	**RIGHT BANK**	**516.5**
PATRIOT, Switzerland Co., Ind. (289)	**RIGHT BANK**	**516.8**
Ferry to Brashear post office landing.		
LANDING for Brashear post office, Gallatin Co., Ky	**LEFT BANK**	**516.8**
276. PATRIOT BEND LIGHT. Color White	**RIGHT BANK**	**517.3**
FISH CREEK	**RIGHT BANK**	**517.4**
PAINT LICK CREEK	**LEFT BANK**	**519.0**
JACKSON LANDING, Gallatin Co., Ky	**LEFT BANK**	**519.7**

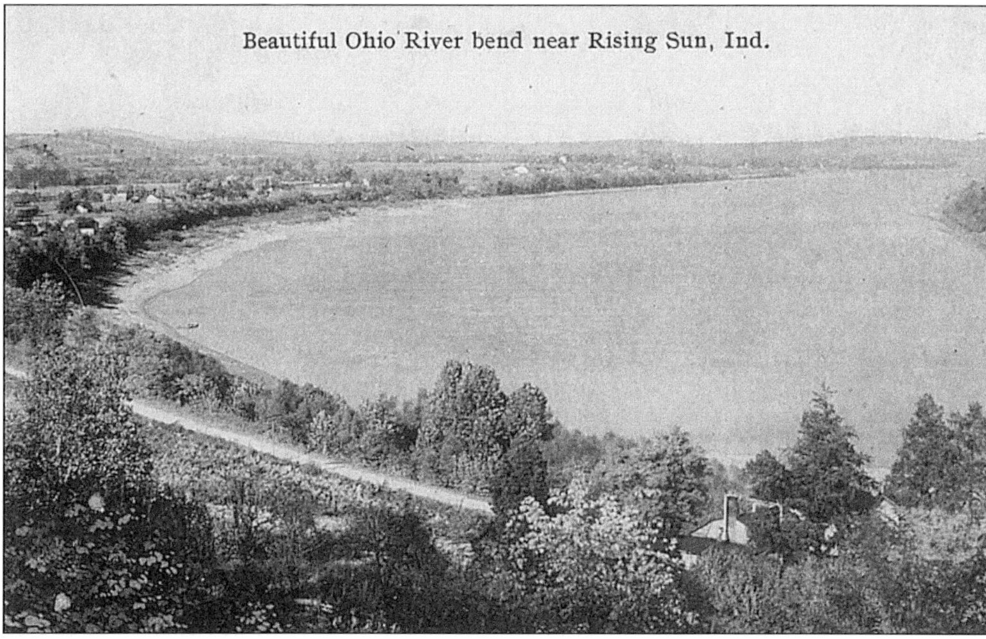

Below Rising Sun, the river sweeps into a broad bend at the mouth of Arnold's Creek. This card is from the 1920s, after the ice of 1918 destroyed the coal yard at Buckeye Landing. It would have been situated in the left center of the photograph, in the trees just above the low, flat riverbed that is exposed along the Indiana shore by the low stage of the river.

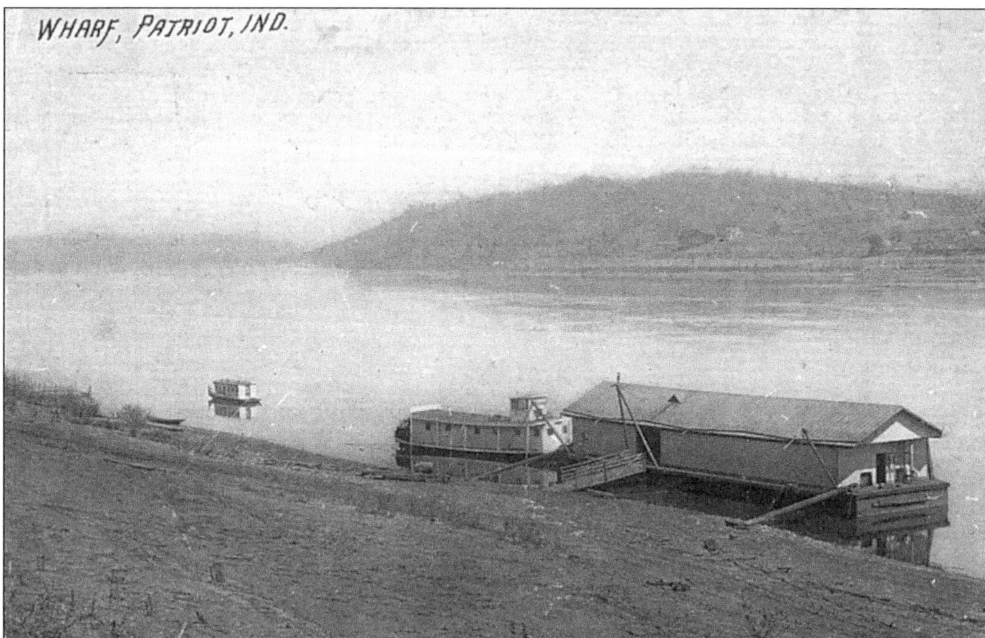

Patriot, Indiana, is situated on low-lying river bottoms on the Indiana shore. It was easily flooded by high water. The small, sternwheeler boat at the wharf is unidentified. The smaller boat at left was probably someone's home, or "shanty boat" as they were called. It was not uncommon for people to live on the water.

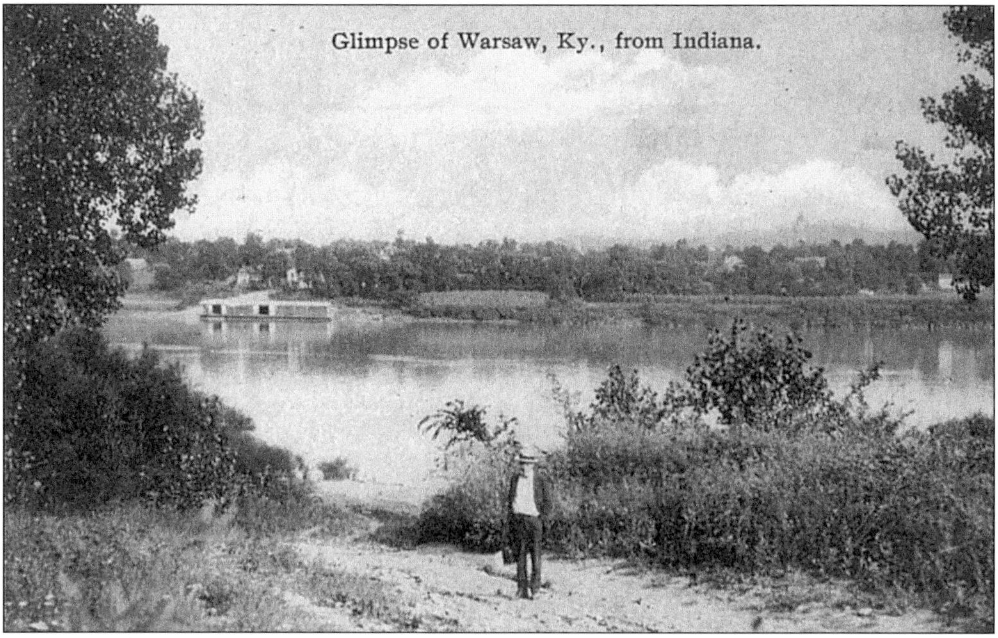

Warsaw, Kentucky, with its wharfboat on the adjacent shore, is here viewed from the Indiana side just above Florence, Indiana. A rural farming community, it was smaller than Carrollton, located downriver, and lacked its regional market activities. The man in the foreground is unidentified.

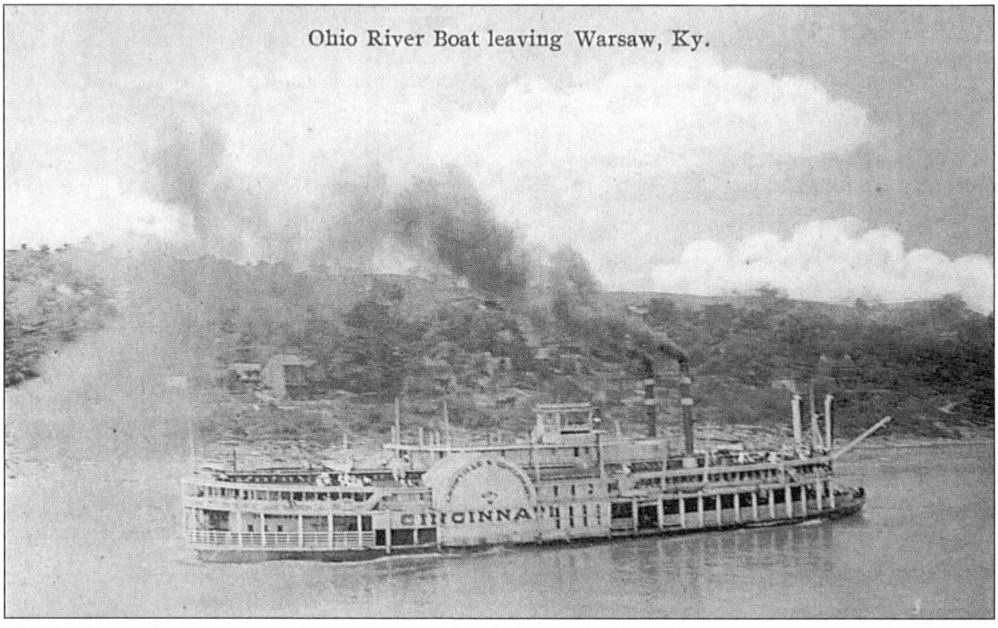

The Indiana shore opposite Warsaw is visible behind the *Str. City of Cincinnati* as she departs Warsaw upriver for Cincinnati. The river channel runs right up against the Indiana hills just below Gunpowder Bar, leaving only land for a road and a few buildings on the Indiana shore.

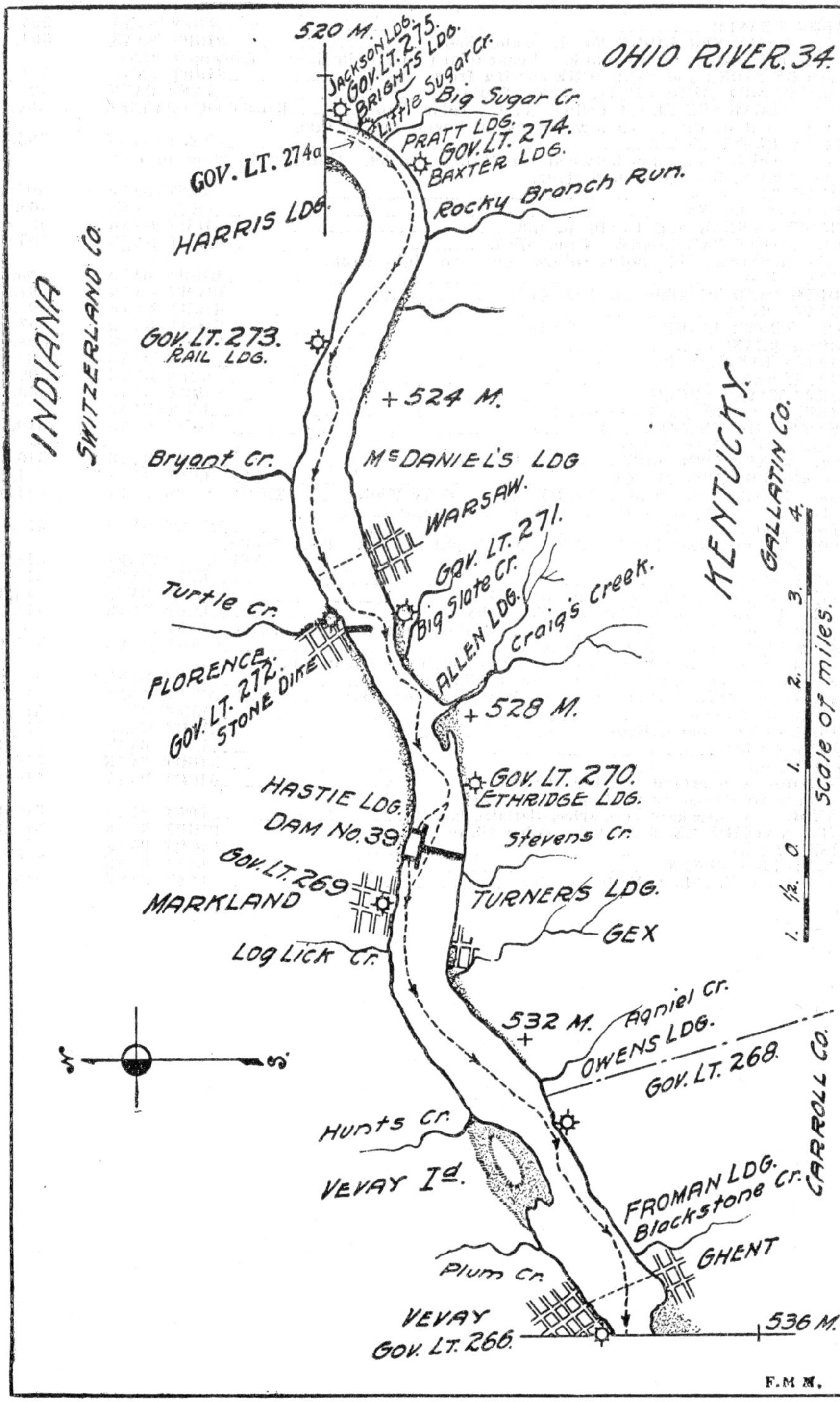
OHIO RIVER. 34.
520 M.
JACKSON LDG.
GOV. LT. 275.
BRIGHTS LDG.
Little Sugar Cr.
Big Sugar Cr.
PRATT LDG.
GOV. LT. 274.
BAXTER LDG.
GOV. LT. 274a
HARRIS LDG.
Rocky Branch Run.
INDIANA
SWITZERLAND CO.
GOV. LT. 273.
RAIL LDG.
+ 524 M.
Bryant Cr.
McDANIEL'S LDG
WARSAW.
GOV. LT. 271.
Big Slate Cr.
ALLEN LDG.
Craig's Creek.
KENTUCKY
GALLATIN CO.
Turtle Cr.
FLORENCE
GOV. LT. 272.
STONE DIKE
+ 528 M.
GOV. LT. 270.
ETHRIDGE LDG.
HASTIE LDG.
DAM No. 39
Stevens Cr.
GOV. LT. 269
MARKLAND
TURNER'S LDG.
GEX
Log Lick Cr.
Scale of miles.
1. ½. 0. 1. 2. 3. 4.
532 M.
Agniel Cr.
OWENS LDG.
GOV. LT. 268.
CARROLL CO.
Hunts Cr.
VEVAY Id.
FROMAN LDG.
Blackstone Cr.
GHENT
Plum Cr.
VEVAY
GOV. LT. 266.
536 M.
F. M. M.

Chart No. 34.

Miles below Pittsburgh.

275. JACKSON LANDING LIGHT. Color White	LEFT BANK	519.8
BRIGHTS LANDING, Gallatin Co., Ky	LEFT BANK	520.3
LITTLE SUGAR CREEK	LEFT BANK	520.5
274–a. SUGAR CREEK LIGHT. Color White	LEFT BANK	520.5
BIG SUGAR CREEK	LEFT BANK	520.7
PRATT LANDING, Gallatin Co., Ky	LEFT BANK	520.7
HARRIS LANDING, Switzerland Co., Ind	RIGHT BANK	520.8
274. BAXTER LANDING LIGHT. Color White	LEFT BANK	521.1
ROCKY BRANCH RUN (or JOHNSONS BRANCH)	LEFT BANK	522.0
273. RAIL LANDING LIGHT. Color White	RIGHT BANK	523.5
McDANIELS LANDING, Gallatin Co., Ky	LEFT BANK	524.8
BRYANT CREEK	RIGHT BANK	525.0
WARSAW, county seat, Gallatin Co., Ky. (800)	LEFT BANK	525.9
Established in 1831 and first known as Fredericksburg. Industries: Flouring mills, tobacco packing and shipping, machine shops, furniture manufacturing, and general merchandising. Connection by wagon road, 9 miles, to L. & N. R. R. at Sparta, Ky. Ferry to right bank.		
272. FLORENCE LIGHT. Color White, Red Front	RIGHT BANK	526.2
TURTLE CREEK	RIGHT BANK	526.3
FLORENCE, Switzerland Co., Ind. (253)	RIGHT BANK	526.3
By wagon road, via Warsaw, about 10 miles to railroad at Sparta, Ky.		
271. WARSAW BAR LIGHT. Color White	LEFT BANK	526.4
WARSAW DIKE, riprap	RIGHT BANK	526.5
Top about 4 feet above low water; channel to left.		
BIG SLATE CREEK	LEFT BANK	526.7
ALLEN LANDING, Gallatin Co., Ky	LEFT BANK	527.4
CRAIGS CREEK	LEFT BANK	527.7
270. ETHRIDGE LANDING LIGHT. Color White	LEFT BANK	528.8
HASTIE LANDING, Switzerland Co., Ind	RIGHT BANK	529.3
OHIO RIVER DAM No. 39		529.6
Lock on right bank; length, 600 feet; width, 110 feet; width of navigable pass, 800 feet. Note the directions and caution given as in case of Dam No. 2, p. 27.		
STEVENS CREEK	LEFT BANK	529.8
TURNERS LANDING, Gallatin Co., Ky	LEFT BANK	530.2
269. MARKLAND LIGHT. Color White, Red Front	RIGHT BANK	530.3
MARKLAND, Switzerland Co., Ind. (213)	RIGHT BANK	530.3
Industries: General merchandising. Wagon road via Warsaw to L. & N. R. R. at Sparta, Ky., about 13 miles. By wagon road to Madison, Ind., about 24.5 miles.		
LOG LICK CREEK	RIGHT BANK	530.8
GEX, Gallatin Co., Ky. (30)†	LEFT BANK	530.8
HUNTS CREEK	RIGHT BANK	532.5
AGNIEL CREEK	LEFT BANK	532.9
VEVAY ISLAND, head	RIGHT BANK	533.0
Channel to left of island. Good depth of water.		
OWENS LANDING, Gallatin Co., Ky	LEFT BANK	533.0
268. VEVAY ISLAND LIGHT. Color White	LEFT BANK	533.1
PLUM CREEK	RIGHT BANK	534.0
FROMAN LANDING, Carroll Co., Ky	LEFT BANK	534.3
BLACKSTONE CREEK	LEFT BANK	534.9
GHENT, Carroll Co., Ky. (438)	LEFT BANK	535.2
Ferry to Vevay, Ind.; wagon road, 10 miles, to L. & N. R. R., Sanders, Ky.		
VEVAY, Switzerland Co., Ind. (1,175)	RIGHT BANK	535.2
Ferry to Ghent, Ky., and thence wagon road, 10 miles, to Sanders, Ky. Also wagon road, 19.5 miles, to Penna. R. R. at Madison, Ind.		
VEVAY BAR, head	LEFT BANK	535.7
266. VEVAY BAR LIGHT. Color White	RIGHT BANK	535.8

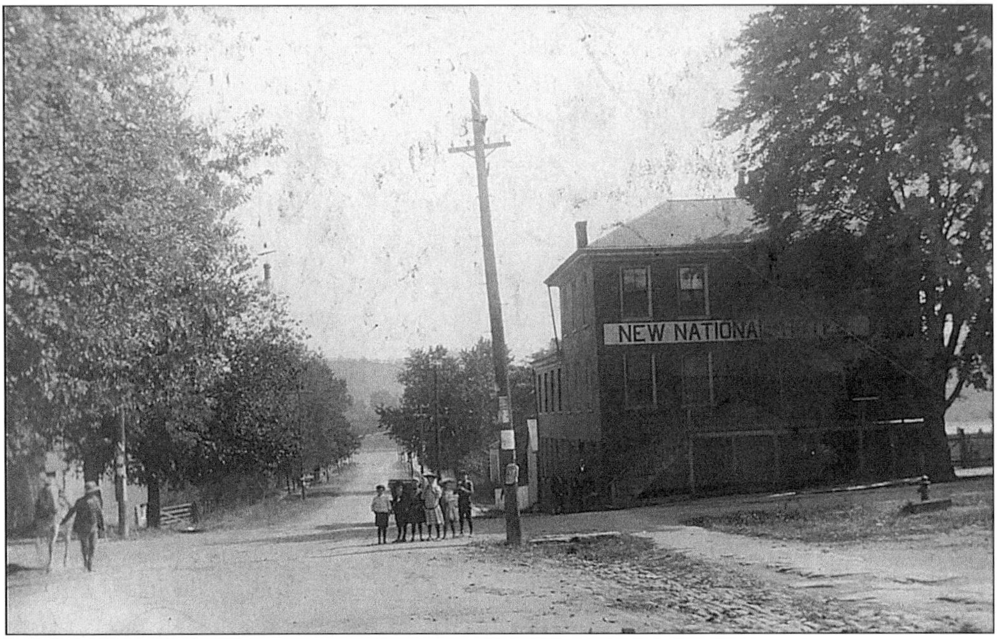

Vevay, Indiana, was situated on a second bank above the water level. Ferry Street connected the riverfront with the main business district. The people standing in the center of this picture are on the top of this second elevation.

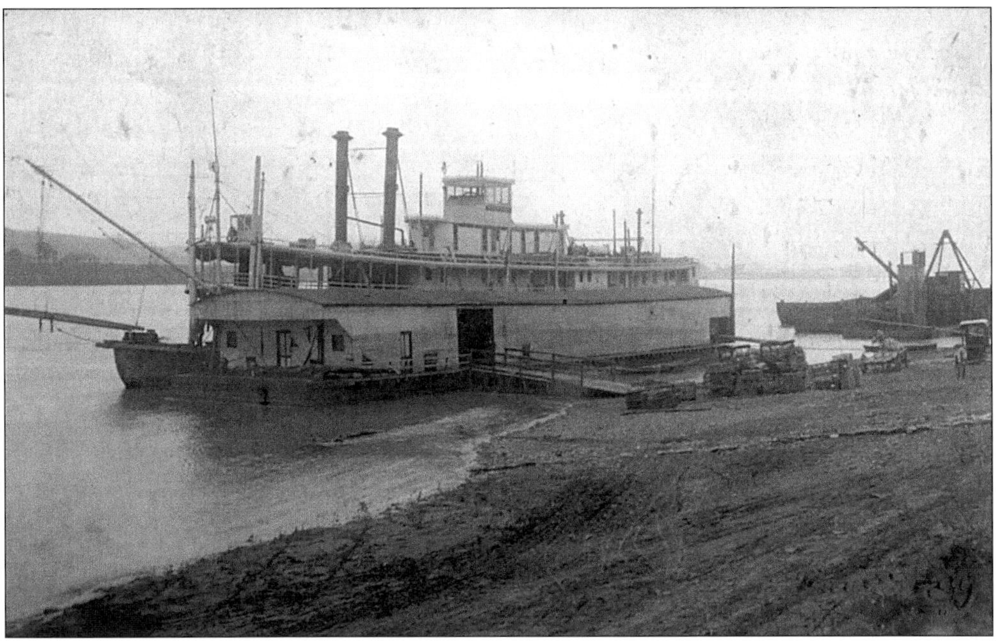

The landing and wharfboat in Vevay, Indiana, are pictured here. A steamboat, facing upriver, is alongside. Although not identified by name, she looks like possibly the sternwheeler *Str. Kentucky*. The barges and apparatus at right are delivering coal to Vevay.

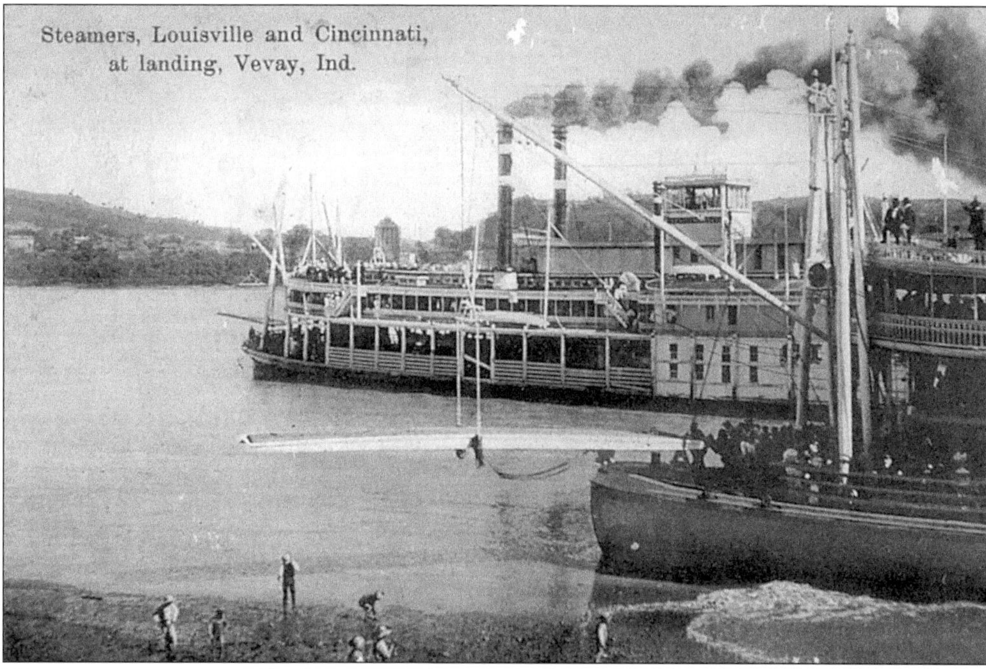

The *Str. City of Louisville* departs upriver for Cincinnati, while the *Str. City of Cincinnati* remains dockside at Vevay. It is now early afternoon, and the boats that left port at dawn have met to exchange passengers near the mid-point of their trip.

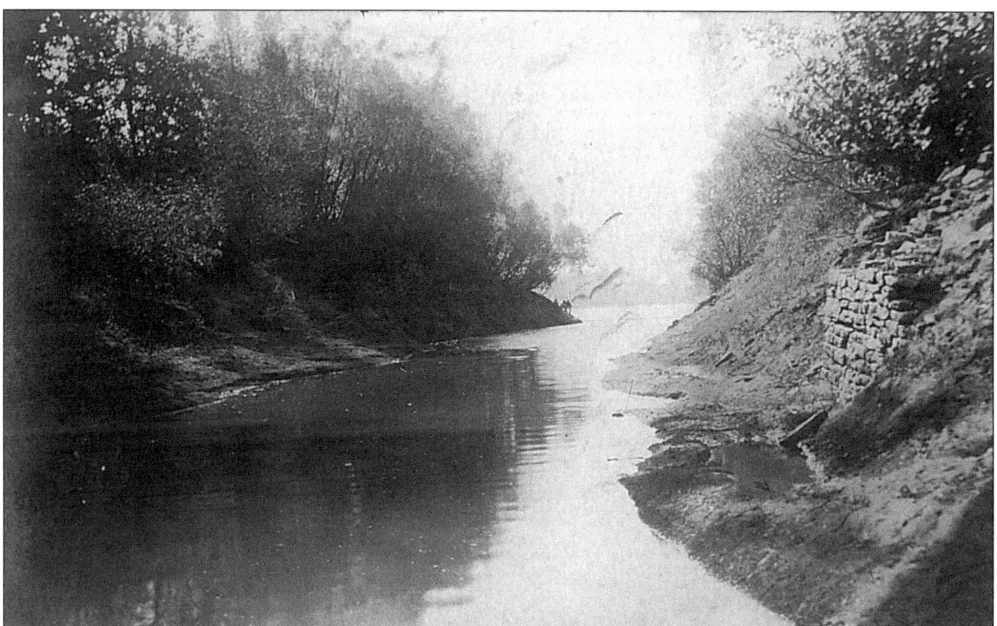

Indian Creek, just below Vevay, Indiana, quietly empties into the Ohio River on a warm summer day. Creeks like this drain highlands and creek valleys along the river, generating massive torrents of water during heavy rains.

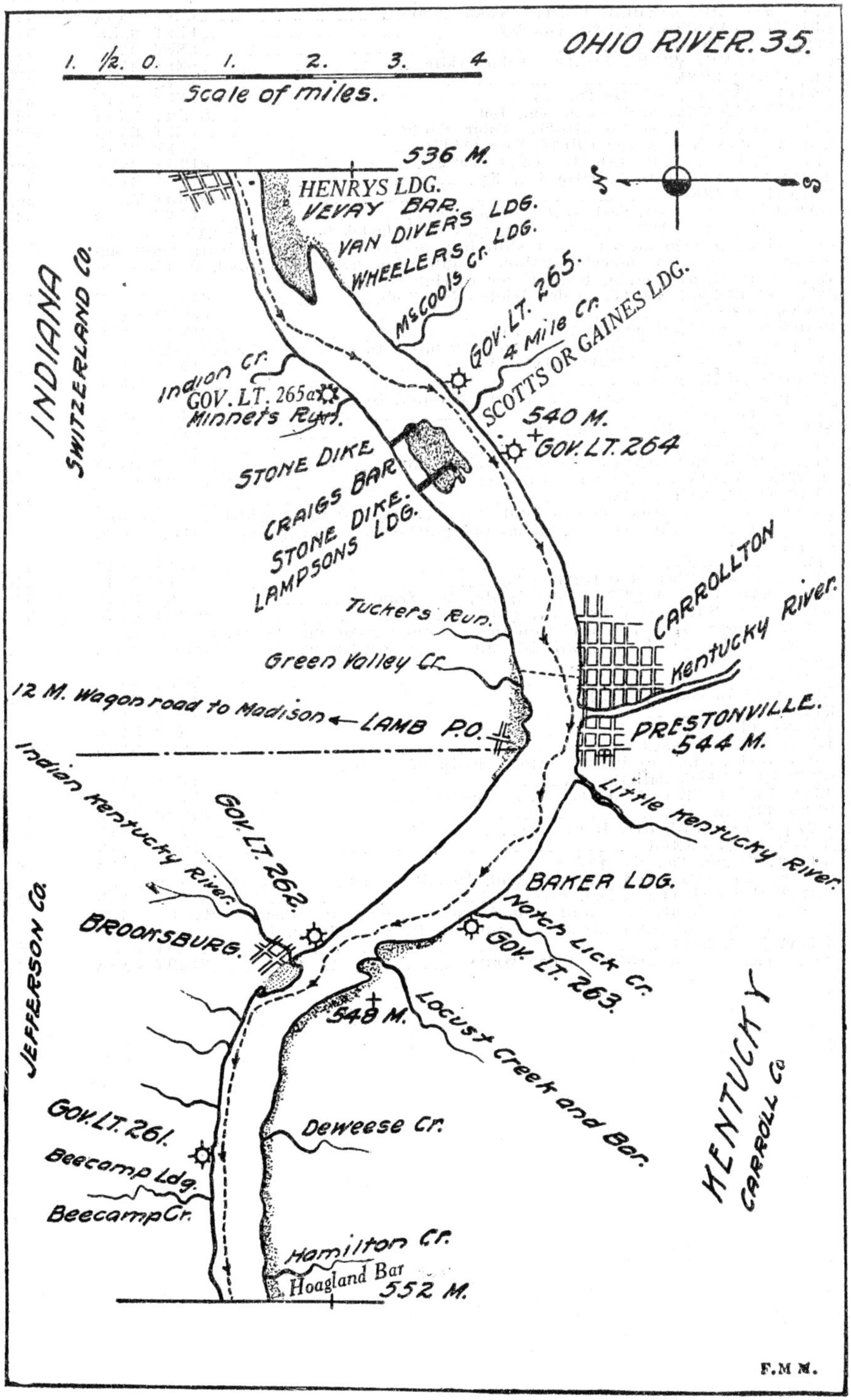

OHIO RIVER. 35.
1. ½. 0. 1. 2. 3. 4
Scale of miles.
536 M.
HENRYS LDG.
VEVAY BAR.
VAN DIVERS LDG.
WHEELERS LDG.
McCools Cr.
GOV. LT. 265.
4 Mile Cr.
SCOTTS OR GAINES LDG.
INDIANA
SWITZERLAND CO.
Indian Cr.
GOV. LT. 265a
Minnets Run.
540 M.
GOV. LT. 264
STONE DIKE
CRAIGS BAR
STONE DIKE.
LAMPSONS LDG.
CARROLLTON
Kentucky River.
Tuckers Run.
Green Valley Cr.
12 M. Wagon road to Madison
LAMB P.O.
PRESTONVILLE.
544 M.
Little Kentucky River.
Indian Kentucky River.
GOV. LT. 262.
BAKER LDG.
JEFFERSON CO.
BROOKSBURG.
Notch Lick Cr.
GOV. LT. 263.
548 M.
Locust Creek and Bar.
KENTUCKY
CARROLL Co
GOV. LT. 261.
Beecamp Ldg.
BeecampCr.
Deweese Cr.
Hamilton Cr.
Hoagland Bar
552 M.
F.M M.

Chart No. 35.

		Miles below Pittsburgh.
HENRYS LANDING, Carroll Co., Ky	**LEFT BANK**	**536.5**
VAN DIVERS LANDING, Carroll Co., Ky	**LEFT BANK**	**537.3**
WHEELERS LANDING, Carroll Co., Ky	**LEFT BANK**	**537.8**
INDIAN CREEK	**RIGHT BANK**	**538.0**
McCOOLS CREEK	**LEFT BANK**	**538.4**
265–a. MINNET RUN LIGHT. Color White	**RIGHT BANK**	**538.6**
MINNETS RUN	**RIGHT BANK**	**438.6**
HEAD OF CRAIGS BAR	**RIGHT BANK**	**539.1**
Channel to left of bar and dike, with least depth, near foot, 4 feet, open river.		
STONE DIKE (upper) from	**RIGHT BANK**	**539.2**
265. CRAIG BAR LIGHT No. 4. Color White	**LEFT BANK**	**539.2**
FOUR MILE CREEK	**LEFT BANK**	**539.6**
STONE DIKE (lower) from	**RIGHT BANK**	**539.8**
SCOTTS or GAINES LANDING, Carroll Co., Ky	**LEFT BANK**	**539.9**
LAMPSONS LANDING, Switzerland Co., Ind	**RIGHT BANK**	**539.9**
264. CRAIG BAR LIGHT No. 2. Color White	**LEFT BANK**	**540.2**
TUCKERS RUN	**RIGHT BANK**	**542.5**
CARROLLTON, Carroll Co., Ky., upper landing	**LEFT BANK**	**543.0**
GREEN VALLEY CREEK	**RIGHT BANK**	**543.3**
CARROLLTON, Carroll Co., Ky. (2,281), lower landing	**LEFT BANK**	**543.4**
County seat Carroll Co. Carrollton is connected by a branch 8 miles in length with Worthville on the main line of the L. & N. R. R. There is a ferry to the right bank of the Ohio, and a highway bridge crossing the Kentucky River to Prestonville. Principal industries: Furniture factory, tobacco re-handling and shipping, sawmills, brick manufacturing, banking, and general merchandising.		
KENTUCKY RIVER	**LEFT BANK**	**543.4**
For Kentucky River, see Tributary streams.		
PRESTONVILLE, Carroll Co., Ky. (131)	**LEFT BANK**	**543.6**
LAMB, post office, Switzerland Co., Ind. (34)	**RIGHT BANK**	**544.0**
Wagon road to Madison, Ind., 12 miles.		
LITTLE KENTUCKY RIVER	**LEFT BANK**	**544.3**
BAKER LANDING, Carroll Co., Ky	**LEFT BANK**	**545.6**
NOTCH LICK CREEK	**LEFT BANK**	**546.3**
263. NOTCH LICK LIGHT. Color White	**LEFT BANK**	**546.4**
LOCUST CREEK	**LEFT BANK**	**547.4**
262. LOCUST CREEK BAR LIGHT. Color White	**RIGHT BANK**	**548.0**
INDIAN KENTUCKY RIVER	**RIGHT BANK**	**548.2**
BROOKSBURG, Jefferson Co., Ind. (117)	**RIGHT BANK**	**548.3**
Principal industries: General merchandise. Wagon road to Madison, Ind., 7 miles.		
DEWEESE CREEK	**LEFT BANK**	**550.1**
261. BEECAMP LANDING LIGHT. Color White	**RIGHT BANK**	**550.4**
BEECAMP CREEK	**RIGHT BANK**	**550.8**
HAMILTON CREEK	**LEFT BANK**	**551.7**
HEAD OF HOAGLAND BAR	**LEFT BANK**	**551.7**

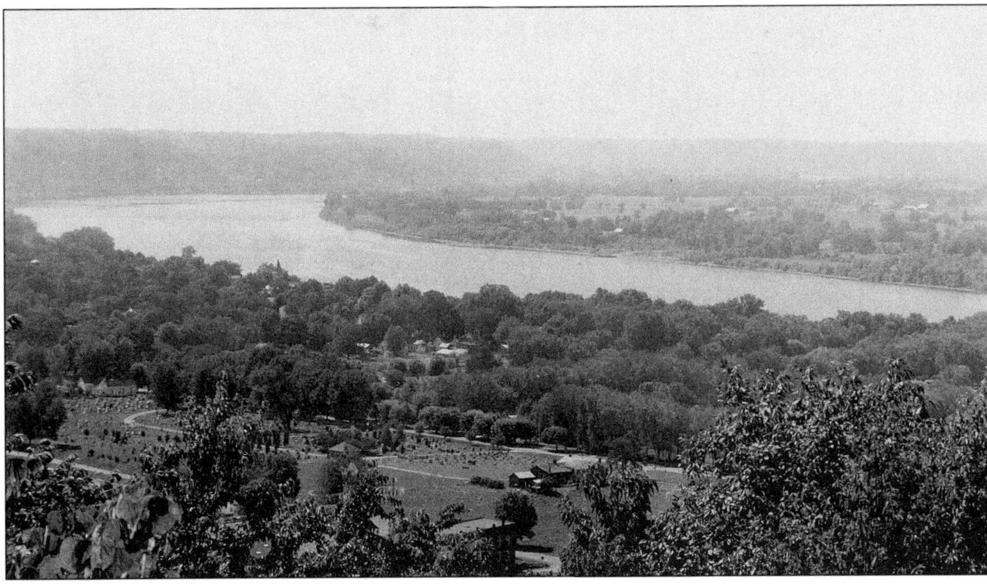

Carrollton, Kentucky, lies below a high bluff overlooking the Ohio River, just above the mouth of the Kentucky River. Settled prior to 1800 as early travelers pushed north and west out of Kentucky, it did not develop a commercial base like towns upriver on the Indiana shore due to its relatively isolated location.

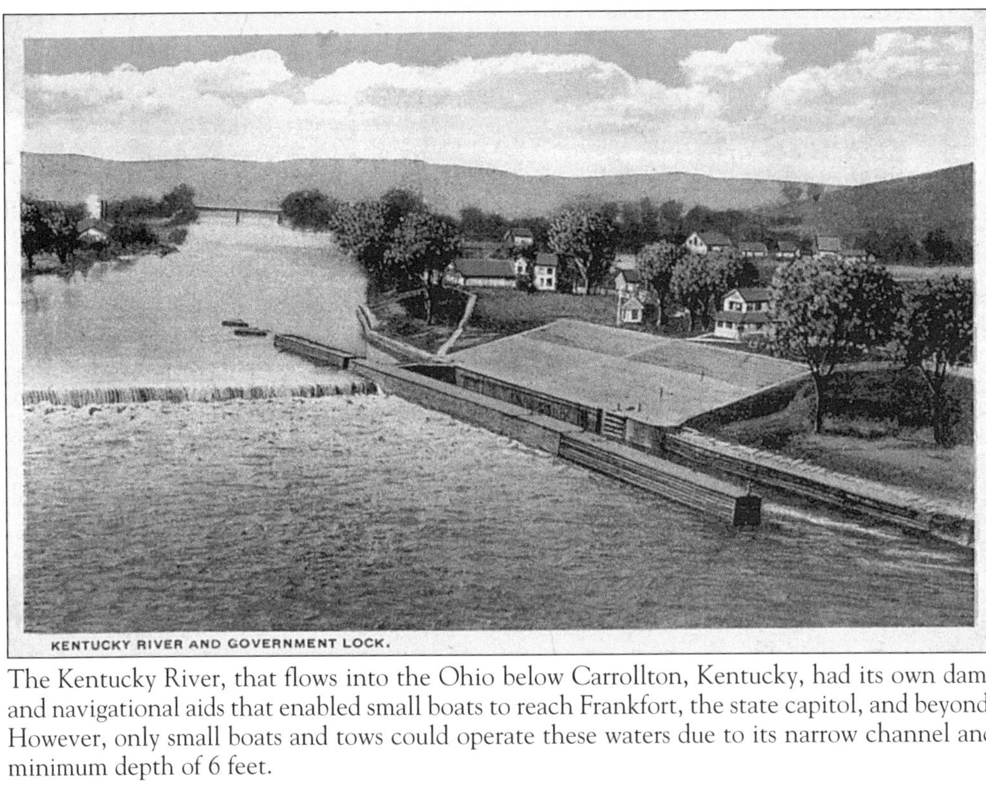

The Kentucky River, that flows into the Ohio below Carrollton, Kentucky, had its own dams and navigational aids that enabled small boats to reach Frankfort, the state capitol, and beyond. However, only small boats and tows could operate these waters due to its narrow channel and minimum depth of 6 feet.

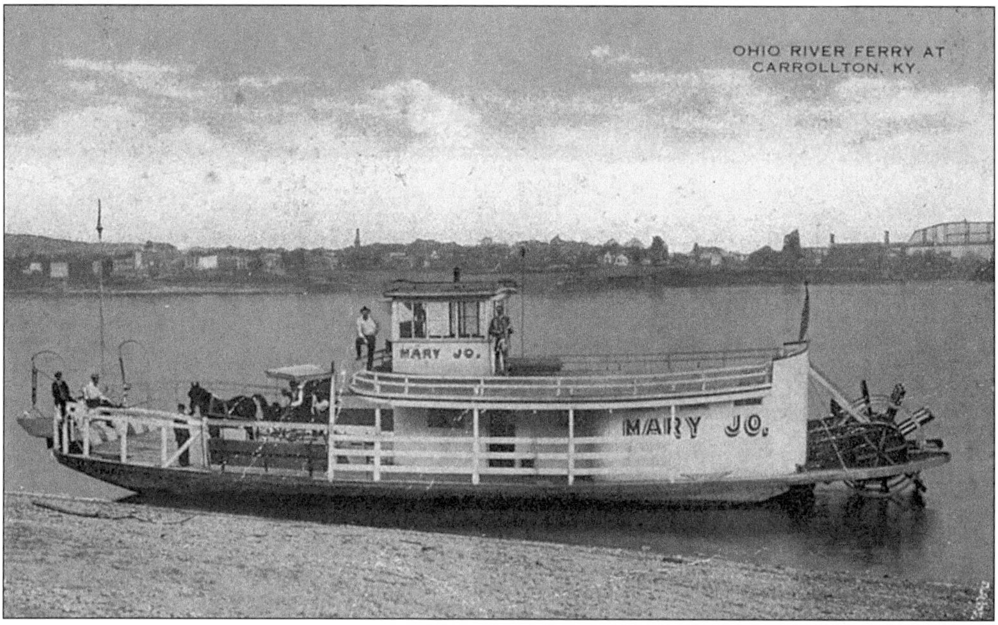

The gas motor-powered, side-loading, sternwheeler ferry *Mary Jo* ran from Carrollton, Kentucky, to Lamb, Indiana, on the Indiana shore. At far right, on the Kentucky shore, you can see the highway bridge across the mouth of the Kentucky River. This picture dates from the 1920s.

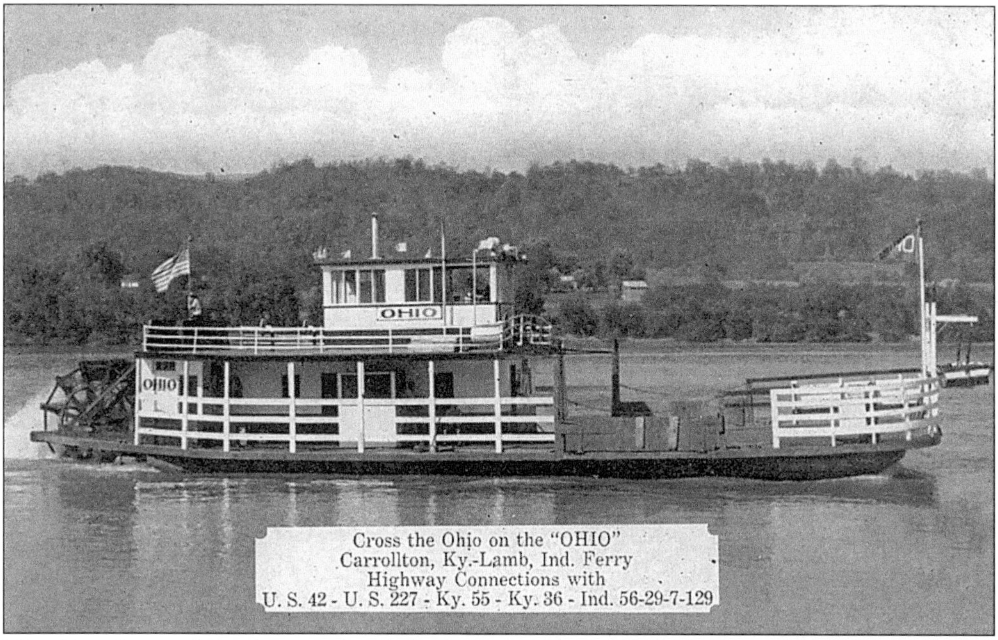

The *Ohio* shown above later replaced the *Mary Jo*. This steel-hulled, gas engine-powered, side-loading ferry combined the older side-loading design with relatively modern construction materials and power.

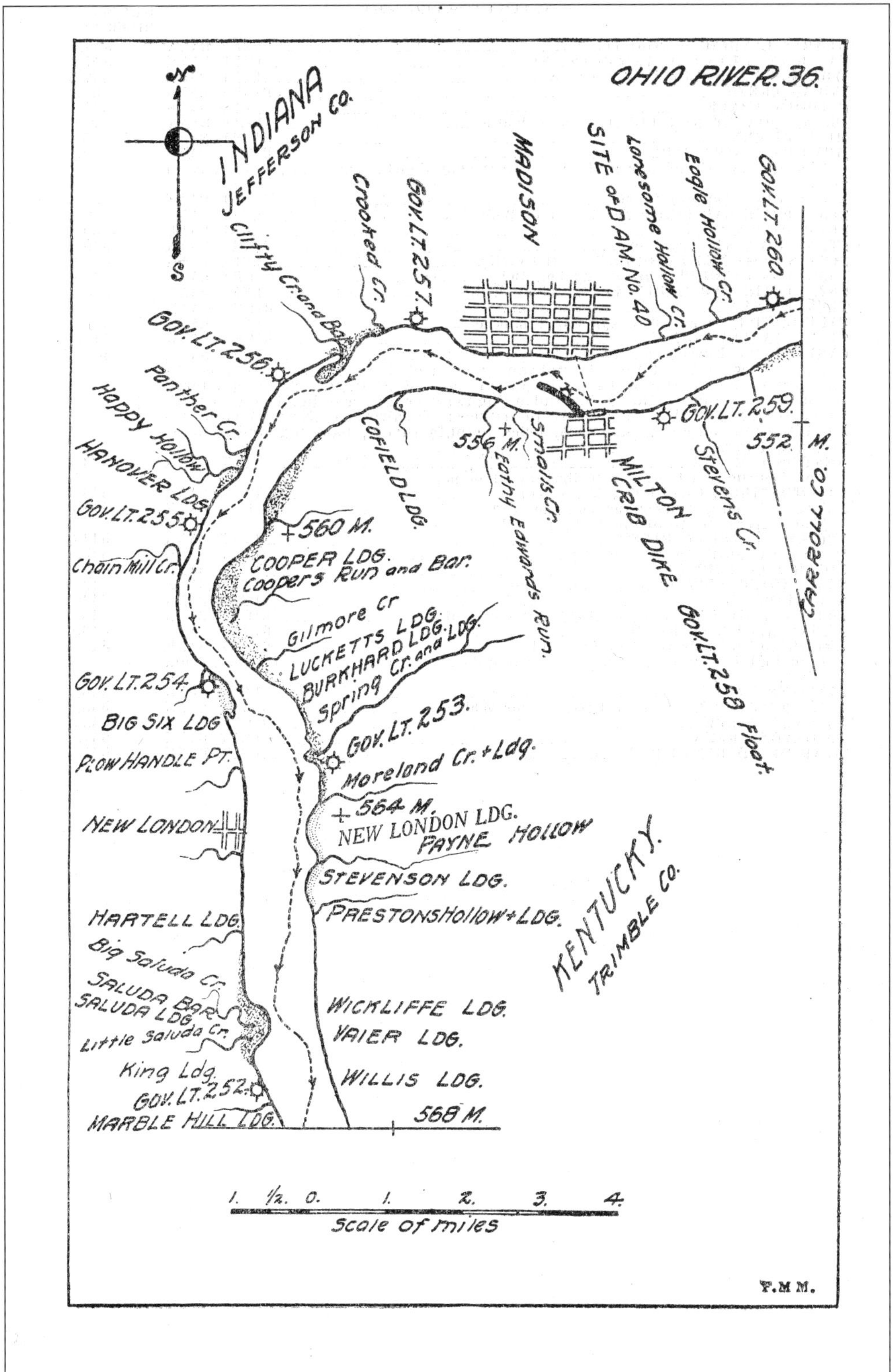

OHIO RIVER. 36.
INDIANA
JEFFERSON CO.
MADISON
SITE of DAM. No. 40
Lonesome Hollow Cr.
Eagle Hollow Cr.
GOV. LT. 260
GOV. LT. 257.
Crooked Cr.
Clifty Cr. and Bar
GOV. LT. 256.
Panther Cr.
Happy Hollow
HANOVER LDG.
GOV. LT. 255
Chain Mill Cr.
COFIELD LDG.
556 M.
Smalls Cr.
Eathy Edwards Run.
MILTON
CRIB DIKE
GOV. LT. 259.
552 M.
Stevens Cr.
CARROLL CO.
GOV. LT. 258 Float.
560 M.
COOPER LDG.
Coopers Run and Bar.
Gilmore Cr
LUCKETTS LDG.
BURKHARD LDG.
Spring Cr. and LDG.
GOV. LT. 254.
BIG SIX LDG
PLOW HANDLE PT.
GOV. LT. 253.
Moreland Cr. + Ldg.
564 M.
NEW LONDON
NEW LONDON LDG.
PAYNE HOLLOW
STEVENSON LDG.
PRESTONS Hollow + LDG.
KENTUCKY.
TRIMBLE CO.
HARTELL LDG.
Big Saluda Cr.
SALUDA BAR
SALUDA LDG.
Little Saluda Cr.
King Ldg.
GOV. LT. 252.
MARBLE HILL LDG.
WICKLIFFE LDG.
VAIER LDG.
WILLIS LDG.
568 M.
1. 1/2. 0. 1. 2. 3. 4.
Scale of miles
F.M.M.

Chart No. 36.

		Miles below Pittsburgh.
260. HOAGLAND LIGHT. Color White	RIGHT BANK	552.3
EAGLE HOLLOW CREEK	RIGHT BANK	553.1
OHIO RIVER DAM No. 40		553.6

Approval of dam postponed. If constructed, lock will be on right bank; length, 600 feet; width, 110 feet; width of navigable pass, 700 feet. (NOTE.—Should this dam be constructed special care must be used in passing the dam while under construction. After completion, note directions and caution as in case of Dam No. 2, p. 27.)

STEVENS CREEK	LEFT BANK	553.7
LONESOME HOLLOW CREEK	RIGHT BANK	553.9
259. RICHWOOD LIGHT. Color White	LEFT BANK	554.0
MILTON, Trimble Co., Ky. (320)	LEFT BANK	554.9

Established by act of Virginia in 1789. Ferry to Madison, Ind. Wagon road, 20.5 miles, to L. & N. R. R. at Worthville, and 19 miles to Sulphur, via Bedford, county seat of Trimble County.

MADISON CRIB DIKE, head curving from	LEFT BANK	555.0

Good depth of water past dike, with Louisville dam up. Channel to right.

258. MADISON DIKE FLOAT LIGHT. Color White	LEFT OF CHANNEL	555.2
MADISON, Jefferson Co., Ind. (6,711)	RIGHT BANK	555.5

Principal industries: Shipyard, sawmills, banking and general merchandising. Railroads: P. C. C. & St. L. to North Vernon and beyond. At North Vernon, connections with B. & O. S. W. and C. C. C. & St. L. Rys.

SMALLS CREEK	LEFT BANK	555.9
EATHY EDWARDS RUN	LEFT BANK	556.1
257. CLIFTY CREEK LIGHT No. 3. Color White	RIGHT BANK	557.2
CROOKED CREEK and BAR	RIGHT BANK	557.5
CLIFTY CREEK and BAR	RIGHT BANK	557.8
COFIELD LANDING, Trimble Co., Ky	LEFT BANK	558.0
256. CLIFTY CREEK LIGHT No. 1. Color White	RIGHT BANK	558.5
PANTHER CREEK	RIGHT BANK	559.2
HAPPY HOLLOW	RIGHT BANK	559.6
HANOVER LANDING, Jefferson Co., Ind	RIGHT BANK	560.0
255. COOPER BAR LIGHT No. 3. Color White	RIGHT BANK	560.0
CHAIN MILL CREEK	RIGHT BANK	560.5
COOPER LANDING, Trimble Co., Ky	LEFT BANK	560.8
254. COOPER BAR LIGHT No. 1. Color White	RIGHT BANK	561.6
COOPERS RUN and BAR	LEFT BANK	561.6
BIG SIX LANDING, Jefferson Co., Ind	RIGHT BANK	561.6
GILMORE CREEK	LEFT BANK	561.9
LUCKETTS LANDING, Trimble Co., Ky	LEFT BANK	563.0
BURKHARD LANDING, Trimble Co., Ky	LEFT BANK	563.2
SPRING CREEK LANDING, Trimble Co., Ky	LEFT BANK	563.2
SPRING CREEK	LEFT BANK	563.2
PLOW HANDLE POINT	RIGHT BANK	563.2
253. SPRING CREEK LIGHT. Color White	LEFT BANK	563.3
MORELAND CREEK and LANDING	LEFT BANK	563.8
NEW LONDON LANDING, Trimble Co., Ky	LEFT BANK	564.3
NEW LONDON, Ind	RIGHT BANK	564.3
PAYNE HOLLOW	LEFT BANK	564.5
STEVENSON LANDING, Trimble Co., Ky	LEFT BANK	564.7
PRESTONS HOLLOW and LANDING, Trimble Co., Ky	LEFT BANK	565.2
HARTELL LANDING, Jefferson Co., Ind	RIGHT BANK	565.3
WICKLIFFE LANDING, Trimble Co., Ky	LEFT BANK	566.3
VAIER LANDING, Trimble Co., Ky	LEFT BANK	566.7
SALUDA BAR and LANDING, Ind	RIGHT BANK	566.7
BIG SALUDA CREEK	RIGHT BANK	566.7
LITTLE SALUDA CREEK	RIGHT BANK	566.8
WILLOW ISLAND, or TOWHEAD	LEFT OF CHANNEL	599.6
WILLIS LANDING, Trimble Co., Ky	LEFT BANK	567.5
MARBLE HILL LANDING, Jefferson Co., Ind. (114)	RIGHT BANK	567.7

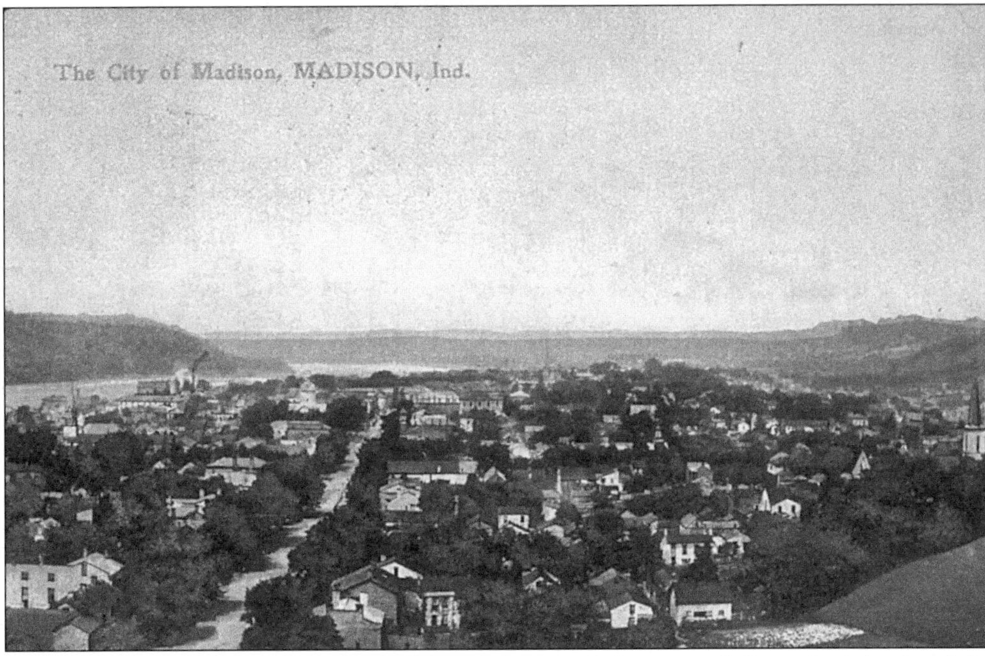

Madison, Indiana, lies in a broad and flat river bottom, below steep hills on both banks of the river. This view looks downriver from the Hillside Inn location shown earlier in Chapter Two. Between Madison and Louisville, towns and villages become less frequent as the river winds between steep hills through less populated farmland.

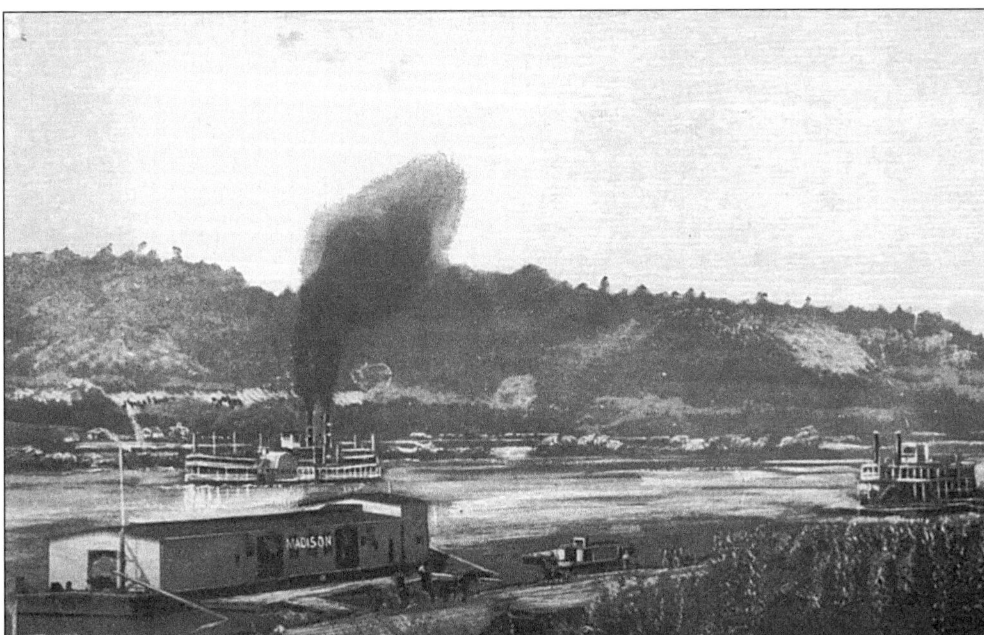

The wharfboat at Madison was located just below the present location of its highway bridge. Madison was built on somewhat higher ground at the base of the Indiana hills.

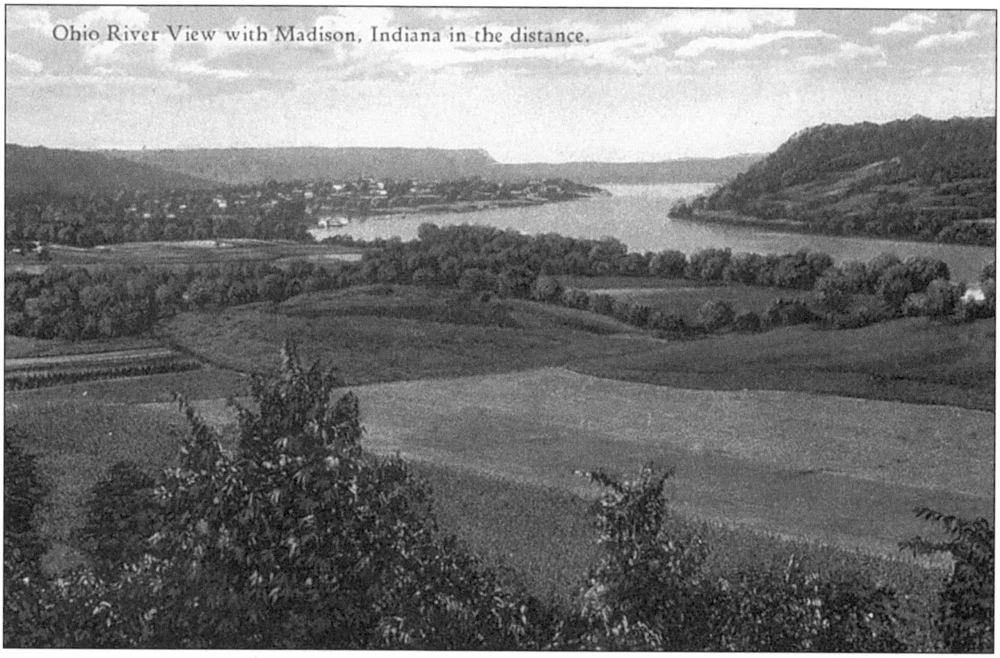

The Ohio River below Madison flows through high Kentucky hills, leaving broad, flat farmlands under the high bluffs in which the town of Hanover, Indiana, is located.

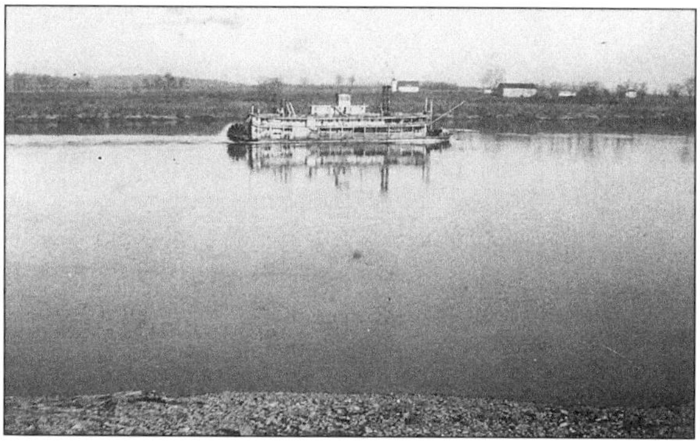

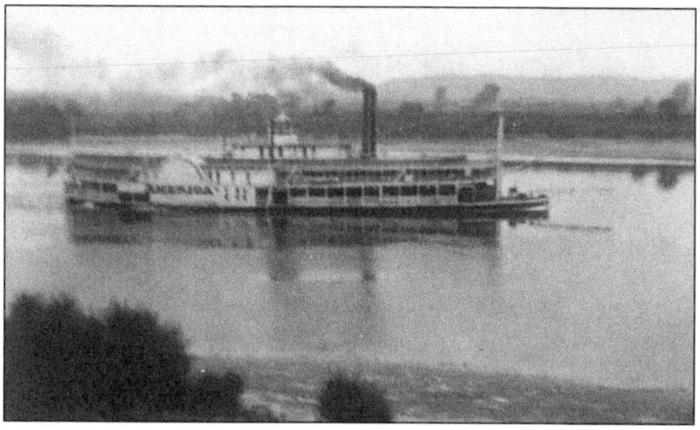

The two images above, of boats plying the Ohio River on a calm summer afternoon, are from the North family album. The sternwheeler at top is unidentified. The side-wheeler is the excursion boat *America*. Both are operating on a low, summertime stage of water.

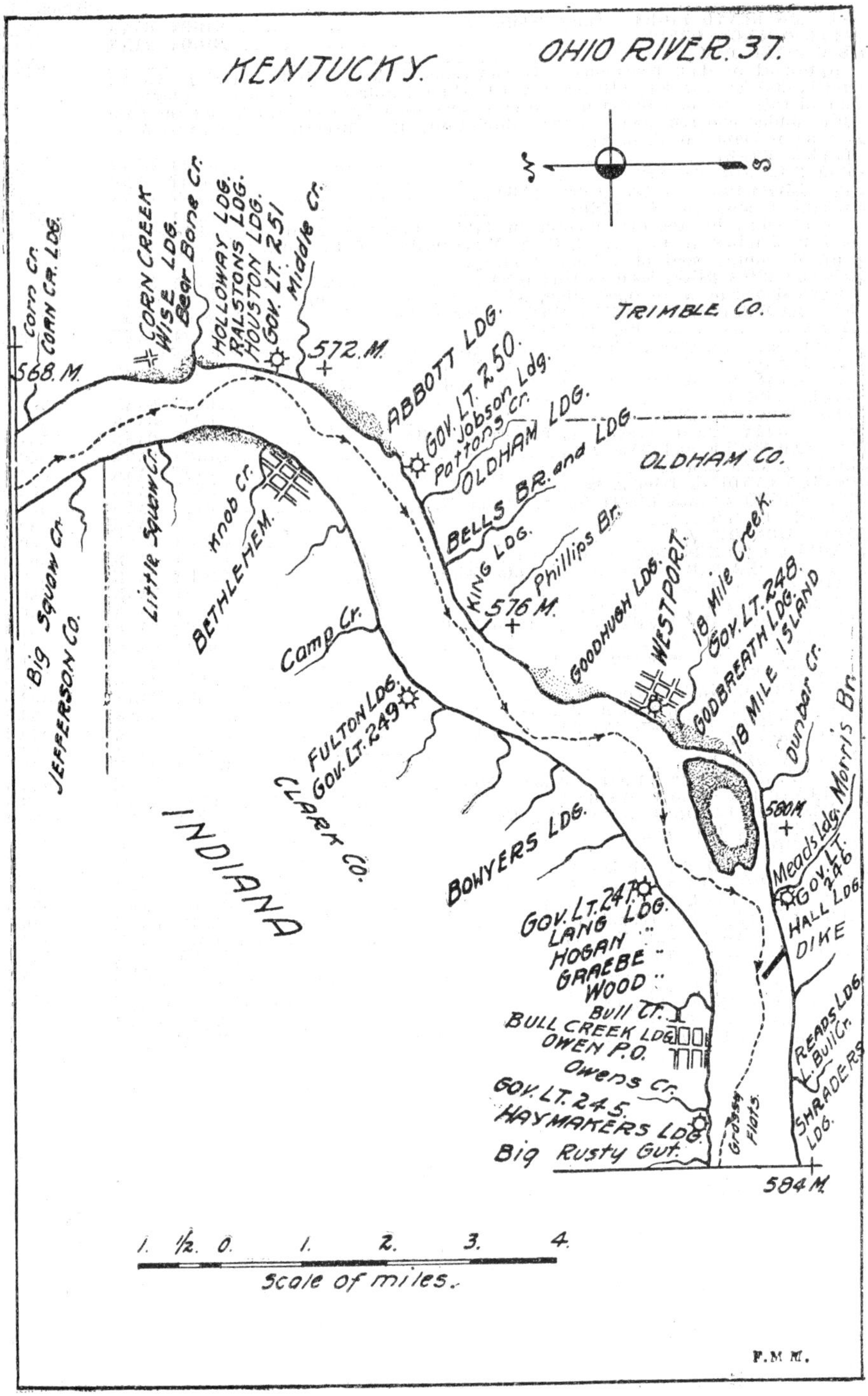

KENTUCKY.
OHIO RIVER. 37.
TRIMBLE CO.
OLDHAM CO.
JEFFERSON CO.
CLARK CO.
INDIANA
Corn Cr.
CORN CR. LDG.
568. M.
CORN CREEK
WISE LDG.
Bear Bone Cr.
HOLLOWAY LDG.
RALSTON LDG.
HOUSTON LDG.
GOV. LT. 251
Middle Cr.
572. M.
ABBOTT LDG.
GOV. LT. 250.
Jobson Ldg.
Pattons Cr.
OLDHAM LDG.
BELLS BR. and LDG.
KING LDG.
Phillips Br.
576 M.
GOODHUGH LDG.
WESTPORT.
18 Mile Creek.
GOV. LT. 248.
GODBREATH LDG.
18 MILE ISLAND
Dunbar Cr.
Morris Br.
580 M.
Mead's Ldg.
GOV. LT. 246
HALL LDG.
DIKE
READS LDG.
L. Bull Cr.
SHRADERS LDG.
584 M.
Big Squaw Cr.
Little Squaw Cr.
Knob Cr.
BETHLEHEM.
Camp Cr.
FULTON LDG.
GOV. LT. 249
BOWYERS LDG.
GOV. LT. 247
LANG LDG.
HOGAN "
GRAEBE "
WOOD "
Bull Cr.
BULL CREEK LDG.
OWEN P.O.
Owens Cr.
GOV. LT. 245.
HAYMAKERS LDG.
Big Rusty Gut.
Grassy Flats.
1. ½. 0. 1. 2. 3. 4.
Scale of miles.
F.M.M.

Chart No. 37.

		Miles below Pittsburgh.
CORN CREEK and LANDING	LEFT BANK	568.2
BIG SQUAW CREEK	RIGHT BANK	568.6
LITTLE SQUAW CREEK	RIGHT BANK	569.2
WISE LANDING, Corn Creek post office, Trimble Co., Ky	LEFT BANK	570.0
BEAR BONE CREEK	LEFT BANK	570.3
HOLLOWAY LANDING, Trimble Co., Ky	LEFT BANK	570.9
RALSTONS LANDING, Trimble Co., Ky	LEFT BANK	571.3
HOUSTON LANDING, Trimble Co., Ky	LEFT BANK	571.4
251. BETHLEHEM REACH LIGHT. Color White	LEFT BANK	571.4
MIDDLE CREEK	LEFT BANK	571.6
KNOB CREEK	RIGHT BANK	571.6
BETHLEHEM, Clark Co., Ind. (132)†	RIGHT BANK	572.1
ABBOTT LANDING, Trimble Co., Ky	LEFT BANK	572.1
250. JOBSON LANDING LIGHT. Color White	LEFT BANK	573.6
JOBSON LANDING, Trimble Co., Ky	LEFT BANK	573.6
PATTONS CREEK, county line	LEFT BANK	573.8
OLDHAM LANDING, Oldham Co., Ky. (35)†	LEFT BANK	573.9
Formerly Oldhamsburg. Wagon road via Westport, 12 miles to La Grange, county seat, on the L. & N. R. R.		
BELLS LANDING, Oldham Co., Ky	LEFT BANK	574.5
BELLS BRANCH	LEFT BANK	574.6
KING LANDING, Oldham Co., Ky	LEFT BANK	575.5
PHILLIPS BRANCH	LEFT BANK	575.5
CAMP CREEK	RIGHT BANK	575.8
FULTON LANDING, Clark Co., Ind	RIGHT BANK	576.0
249. FULTON LIGHT. Color White	RIGHT BANK	576.0
GOODHUGH LANDING, Ky	LEFT BANK	576.2
WESTPORT, Oldham Co., Ky. (317)	LEFT BANK	577.8
Former county seat of Oldham County. Wagon road, 8 miles to La Grange, on L. & N. R. R.		
248. WESTPORT LIGHT. Color White	LEFT BANK	577.9
BOWYERS LANDING, Clark Co., Ind	RIGHT BANK	577.9
EIGHTEEN MILE CREEK	LEFT BANK	578.2
GODBREATH LANDING, Oldham Co., Ky	LEFT BANK	578.6
HEAD OF EIGHTEEN MILE ISLAND	LEFT OF CHANNEL	578.8
Channel to right of island. Good water with Louisville Dam up. Least water, open river, 5.3 feet, near foot of island.		
DUNBAR CREEK (behind island)	LEFT BANK	579.5
247. EIGHTEEN MILE ISLAND DAYMARK No. 1. Color White	RIGHT BANK	579.9
LANG LANDING, Clark Co., Ind	RIGHT BANK	580.1
HOGAN LANDING, Clark Co., Ind	RIGHT BANK	580.2
FOOT OF EIGHTEEN MILE ISLAND	LEFT OF CHANNEL	580.4
MORRIS BRANCH	LEFT BANK	580.9
246. EIGHTEEN MILE ISLAND LIGHT No. 2. Color White	LEFT BANK	580.9
GRAEBE LANDING, Clark Co., Ind	RIGHT BANK	581.3
GRASSY FLATS DIKE	LEFT BANK	581.4
Dike shows about 1,000 feet long, much leveled down. Channel to right. Good water with Louisville Dam up. Least water, open river, 5.4 feet, near foot of flats.		
WOOD LANDING, Clark Co., Ind	RIGHT BANK	581.7
HALL LANDING, Oldham Co., Ky	LEFT BANK	582.1
BULL CREEK LANDING (Owen post office), Clark Co., Ind	RIGHT BANK	582.2
Formerly known as a Herculaneum.		
READS LANDING, Oldham Co., Ky	LEFT BANK	582.3
LITTLE BULL CREEK	LEFT BANK	583.0
OWENS CREEK	RIGHT BANK	583.3
SHRADERS LANDING, Oldham Co., Ky	LEFT BANK	583.3
HAYMAKERS LANDING, Clark Co., Ind	RIGHT BANK	583.6
245. GRASSY FLATS LIGHT No. 1. Color White	RIGHT BANK	583.6
BIG RUSTY GUT	RIGHT BANK	583.9

11194°—22——7

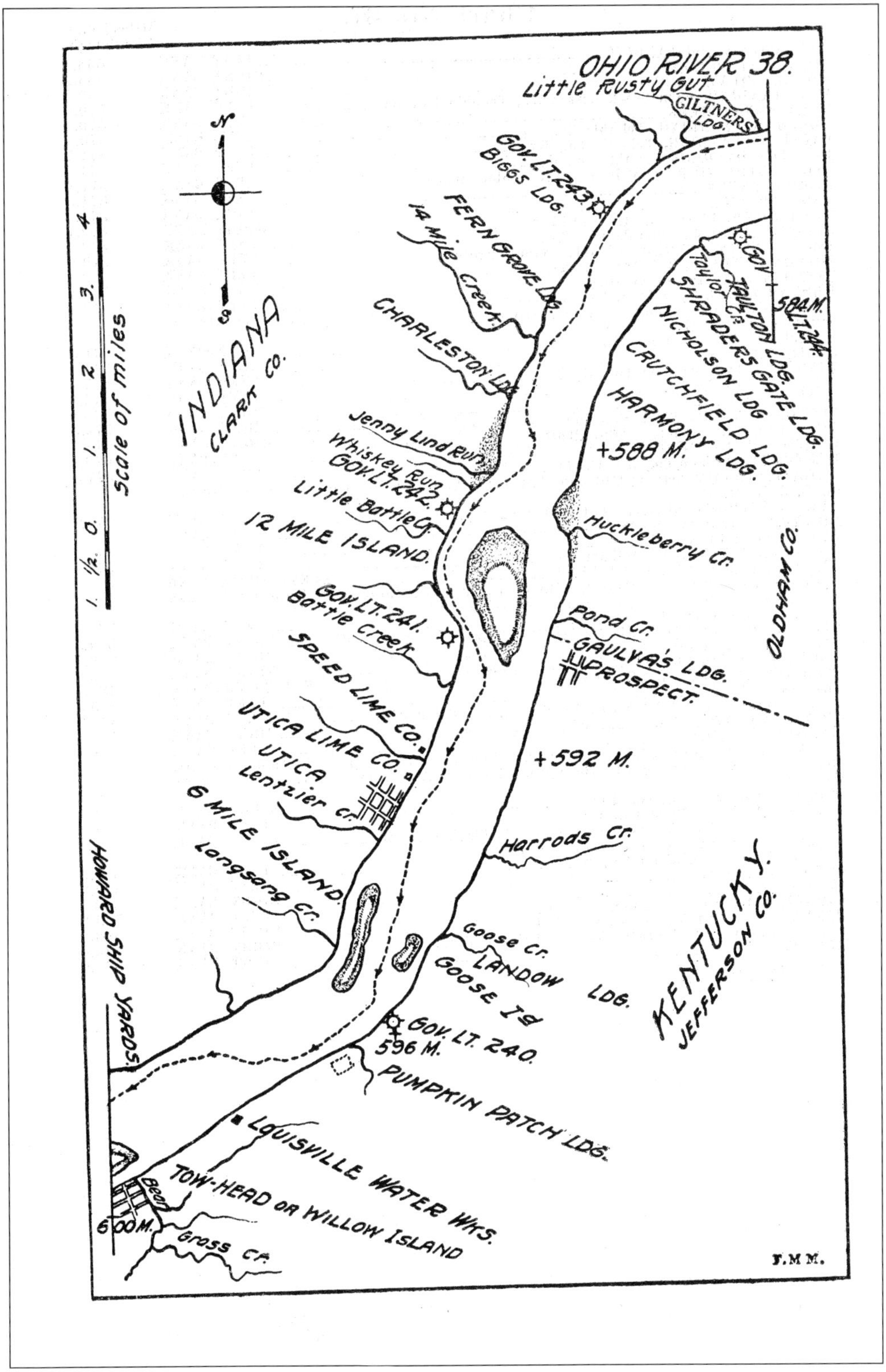

OHIO RIVER 38.
Little Rusty Gut
GILTNERS LDG.
GOV. LT. 243
BIGGS LDG.
FERN GROVE LDG.
14 Mile Creek
CHARLESTON LDG.
INDIANA
CLARK CO.
Scale of miles
1. 1/2. 0. 1. 2. 3. 4
N
S
Jenny Lind Run
Whiskey Run
GOV. LT. 242.
Little Battle Cr.
12 MILE ISLAND.
GOV. LT. 241.
Battle Creek
SPEED LIME CO.
UTICA LIME CO.
UTICA
Lentzier Cr.
6 MILE ISLAND
Longsang Cr.
HOWARD SHIP YARDS.
GOV.
TAULTON LDG.
Taylor Cr.
SHRADERS GATE LDG.
NICHOLSON LDG
CRUTCHFIELD LDG.
HARMONY LDG.
584 M.
LT. 244
+588 M.
Huckleberry Cr.
OLDHAM CO.
Pond Cr.
GAULVA'S LDG.
PROSPECT.
+592 M.
Harrods Cr.
KENTUCKY.
JEFFERSON CO.
Goose Cr.
LANDOW LDG.
GOOSE ID
GOV. LT. 240.
596 M.
PUMPKIN PATCH LDG.
LOUISVILLE WATER WKS.
TOW-HEAD OR WILLOW ISLAND
Beargrass
600 M.
Gross Cr.
F.M.M.

Chart No. 38.

		Miles below Pittsburgh.
244. GRASSY FLATS DAYMARK No. 2. Color White	LEFT BANK	584.2
LITTLE RUSTY GUT	RIGHT BANK	584.2
GILTNERS LANDING, Clark Co., Ind	RIGHT BANK	584.2
TAULTON LANDING, Oldham Co., Ky	LEFT BANK	584.8
TAYLOR CREEK	LEFT BANK	584.9
243. BEGGS LANDING LIGHT. Color White	RIGHT BANK	585.4
SHRADERS GATE LANDING, Oldham Co., Ky	LEFT BANK	585.5
NICHOLSON LANDING, Oldham Co., Ky	LEFT BANK	585.8
CRUTCHFIELD LANDING, Oldham Co., Ky	LEFT BANK	586.5
FERN GROVE LANDING, Clark Co., Ind	RIGHT BANK	586.6
FOURTEEN MILE CREEK	RIGHT BANK	586.9
HARMONY LANDING, Oldham Co., Ky	LEFT BANK	587.1
CHARLESTON LANDING, Clark Co., Ind	RIGHT BANK	587.6
JENNY LIND RUN	RIGHT BANK	588.5
HUCKLEBERRY CREEK	LEFT BANK	588.6
WHISKEY RUN	RIGHT BANK	588.9
242. TWELVE MILE ISLAND LIGHT No. 3. Color White	RIGHT BANK	589.3
HEAD OF TWELVE MILE ISLAND	LEFT OF CHANNEL	589.3
Channel to right of island. Good water with Louisville Dam up.		
LITTLE BATTLE CREEK	RIGHT BANK	589.4
POND CREEK	LEFT BANK	590.2
241. TWELVE MILE ISLAND LIGHT No. 1. Color White	RIGHT BANK	590.4
GAULVA'S LANDING (Prospect post office), Jefferson Co., Ky. (31)	LEFT BANK	590.4
Terminus of a branch line L. & N. R. R. to Louisville, Ky.		
FOOT OF TWELVE MILE ISLAND	LEFT OF CHANNEL	591.3
BATTLE CREEK	RIGHT BANK	591.5
SPEED LIME CO.'S PLANT	RIGHT BANK	592.5
UTICA LIME CO.'S PLANT	RIGHT BANK	592.7
UTICA, Clark Co., Ind. (426)†	RIGHT BANK	593.2
Principal industries: Manufacturing of building lime. Wagon road 6 miles to Jeffersonville, Ind.		
HARRODS CREEK	LEFT BANK	593.3
LENTZIER CREEK	RIGHT BANK	593.7
HEAD OF SIX MILE ISLAND	RIGHT OF CHANNEL	594.3
Channel to left of island. Good water with Louisville Dam up.		
GOOSE CREEK	LEFT BANK	594.4
GOOSE ISLAND, near	LEFT BANK	594.8
Channel between Goose and Six Mile Island; good water.		
LANDOW LANDING, Jefferson Co., Ky	LEFT BANK	594.8
LANGSANG CREEK	RIGHT BANK	595.2
240. SIX MILE ISLAND LIGHT. Color White	LEFT BANK	596.0
PUMPKIN PATCH COAL LANDING, opposite foot of island	LEFT BANK	596.6
LOUISVILLE WATERWORKS	LEFT BANK	598.1
HOWARDS' SHIPYARDS, upper Jeffersonville	RIGHT BANK	599.4
WILLOW ISLAND, or TOWHEAD	LEFT OF CHANNEL	599.6
Channel to right of island.		
BEAR GRASS CREEK	LEFT BANK	599.6
Discharging into back channel, behind island. The creek's mouth has been diverted in recent years.		

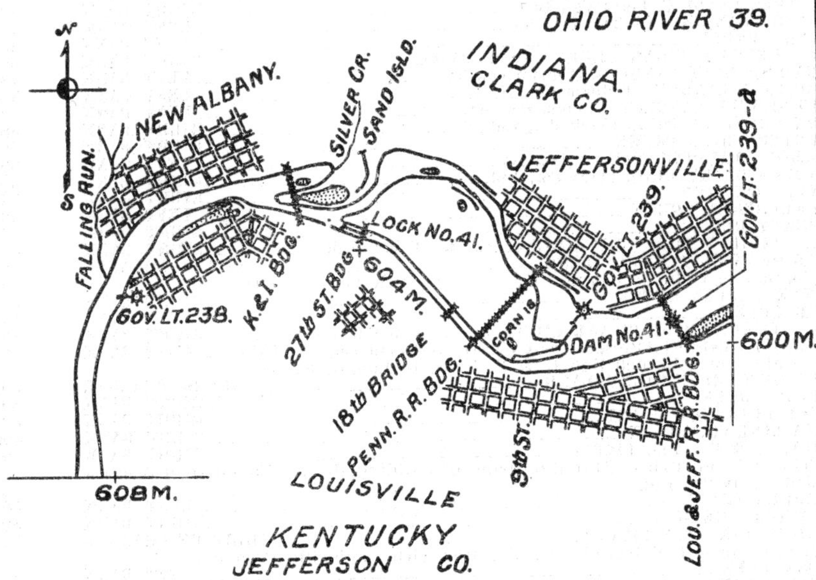

OHIO RIVER FALLS

LOUISVILLE KY.

Louisville in its early days owed its importance largely to its location at the "Falls of the Ohio," where for much of the year it was necessary to break bulk for all cargoes. The falls had a length of about 3 miles with a total extreme fall of 25-1/4 feet. A canal around the falls was projected about 1825 and opened to navigation 1830-31, under the name of the Louisville and Portland Canal. This work was enlarged and new and larger locks were completed in 1872. The United States, which had been a large stock-holder in the original company, took over the canal and its appurtenances in 1874, reducing the canal tolls from 50 to 5 cents per ton; in 1880 the canal was made free of tolls and has since so remained.

An additional lock, 600 feet long and 110 feet wide, has been constructed and the canal has been widened to 200 feet.

1 1/2 0 1 2 3

Scale of miles

Chart No. 39.

Miles below Pittsburgh.

JEFFERSONVILLE, Clark Co., Ind. (10,098) (ferry landing)--------RIGHT BANK 600.4
Principal industries: Shipbuilding, banking, and general merchandise. The United States maintains a quartermaster depot here and the southern penitentiary of Indiana is also situated in Jeffersonville. Railroals: P. C. C. & St. L., B. & O. S. W. (from North Vernon), and C. C. C. & St. L. Ferry to Louisville, Ky.

LOUISVILLE AND JEFFERSONVILLE BRIDGE—C. C. C. & St. L. R. R.------------ 600.5
Channel span, 538 feet; height, 92.8 feet.

239-a. OHIO FALLS DAYMARK. Color White------------------------------ 600.5
(Shown from Louisville and Jeffersonville Bridge.)

LOUISVILLE, Jefferson Co., Ky. (234,891). Public landing---------LEFT BANK 601.6
The metropolis of Kentucky; widely varied business interests in manufacturing, banking, insurance, tobacco, and general merchandise. Railroads: L. & N., I. C., Southern, B. & O. S. W., P. C. C. & St. L., C. C. C. & St. L., C. & O., L. M. A. & C., L. H. & St. L. Ferries to Jeffersonville and New Albany, Ind.

239. OHIO FALLS LIGHT. Color Red------------------------RIGHT BANK 601.6

DAM No. 41, OHIO RIVER. Part movable and part fixed. Length, 5,247 feet.

INDIANA CHUTE CHANNEL.
Length, 2⅝ miles; width, 400 feet. Navigable by heavy-draft boats at stages 11.5 feet or more upper canal gage.

ENTRANCE TO LOUISVILLE AND PORTLAND CANAL-----------------LEFT BANK 601.9
Length, including locks and lower entrance, 2½ miles. Width at upper entrance, 400 feet, reducing to 86.5 feet throughout the canal.
N. B.—Permit to enter canal must be obtained from the canal office at head of canal, Louisville, Ky.

FOOT OF NINTH STREET, LOUISVILLE, KY----------------------LEFT BANK 602.0

OHIO FALLS BRIDGE-- 602.5
P. C. C. & St. L. R. R. Channel span, 620 feet; height, 95.4 feet.

EIGHTEENTH STREET BRIDGE over canal--------------------------------- 602.8

TWENTY-SEVENTH STREET BRIDGE over canal----------------------------- 604.0
LOUISVILLE AND PORTLAND CANAL LOCKS.—Heads of locks. Locks, now in use, 2, each 80 feet wide and 350 feet long. Depth on lower miter sill at extreme low water, 4 feet. A new lock 110 feet wide and 600 feet long now under construction. This lock will supplement those now in use and is designated as No. 41 of the Ohio River series.
Portland, at the foot of canal on left bank, was laid out as a separate town in 1814, but is now a part of Louisville.

KENTUCKY AND INDIANA BRIDGE-- 604.5
Channel span, 600 feet; height, 106 feet.

PORTLAND DIKE, extending from left bank, head--------------------------- 604.7
Keep over toward the right; the channel crosses toward right (Indiana) shore.

NEW ALBANY, county seat of Floyd Co., Ind. (22,992)-------------RIGHT BANK 604.9
Principal industries: Rolling mills, saw and veneer mills, boat building, iron, steel, and wood, and light manufacturing; fertilizer plant; also banking and general merchandising. Railroads: P. C. C. & St. L.; B. & O. S. W.; Southern (L. & St. L. Div.); Chicago, Ind. & Louisville. Electric lines both local and to Louisville via K. and I. Bridge.

LOOSE STONE DIKE--LEFT BANK 606.1

LOOSE STONE DIKE--LEFT BANK 606.2

FALLING RUN; high rock bar at mouth and below-----------------RIGHT BANK 606.2

238. FALLING RUN LIGHT. Color White-----------------------LEFT BANK 606.3

LOOSE STONE DIKE--LEFT BANK 606.4

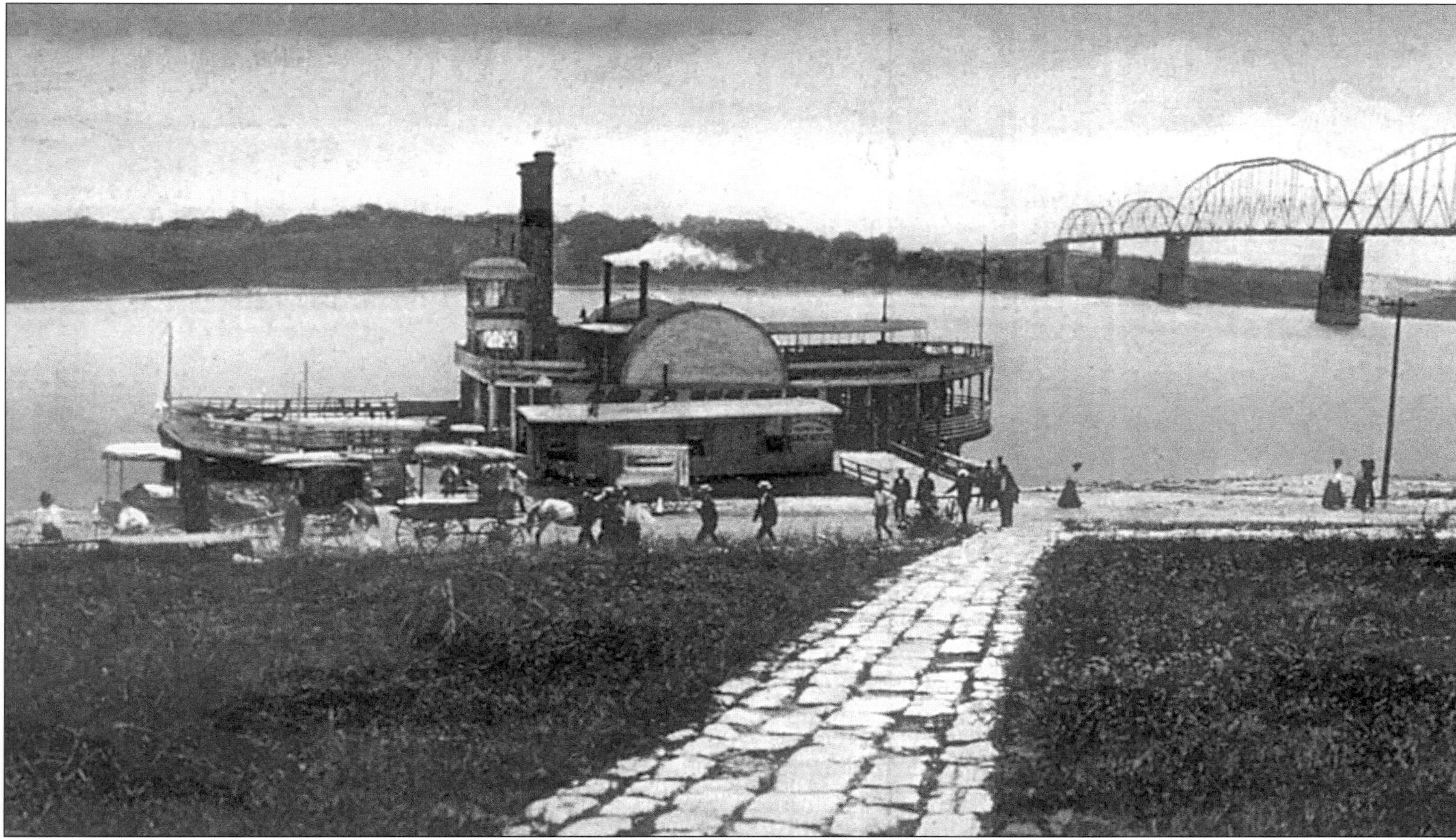

Ferry boats were the primary transports for people and vehicles from Jeffersonville, on the Indiana shore, across the river to Louisville. This view shows the cobblestone ferry landing just above the Big Four Railroad Bridge. The wood-hulled, side-loading, steam-powered ferry *W.C. Hite* is shown working at the landing.

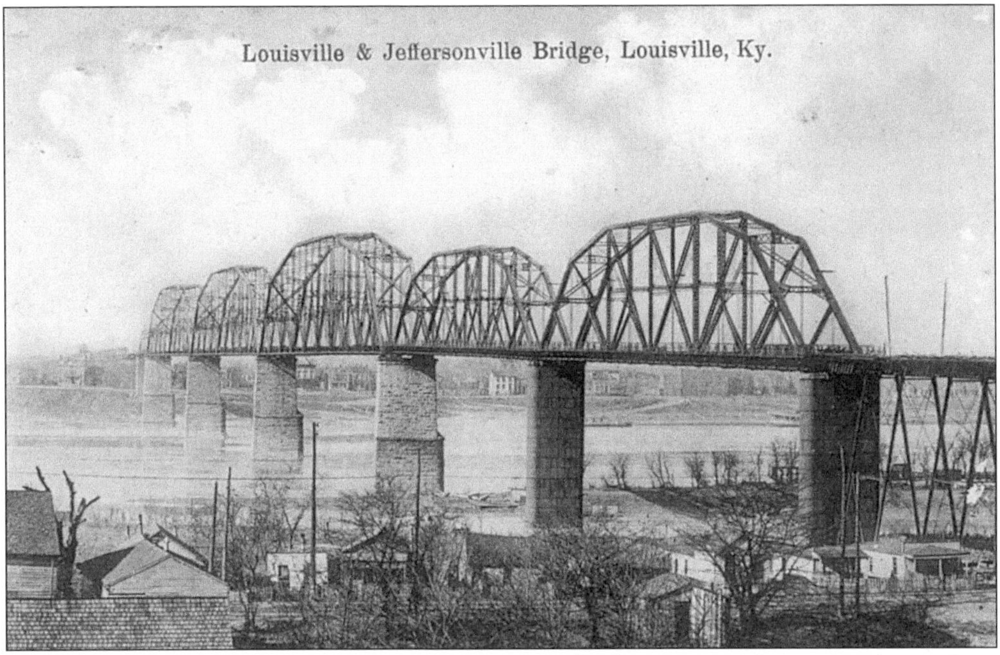

Pictured is the first bridge to be run entering Louisville from upriver. It presented steamboat pilots with a 538-foot navigable pass under the center span. A residential area along the river in Jeffersonville, Indiana, is visible in the foreground.

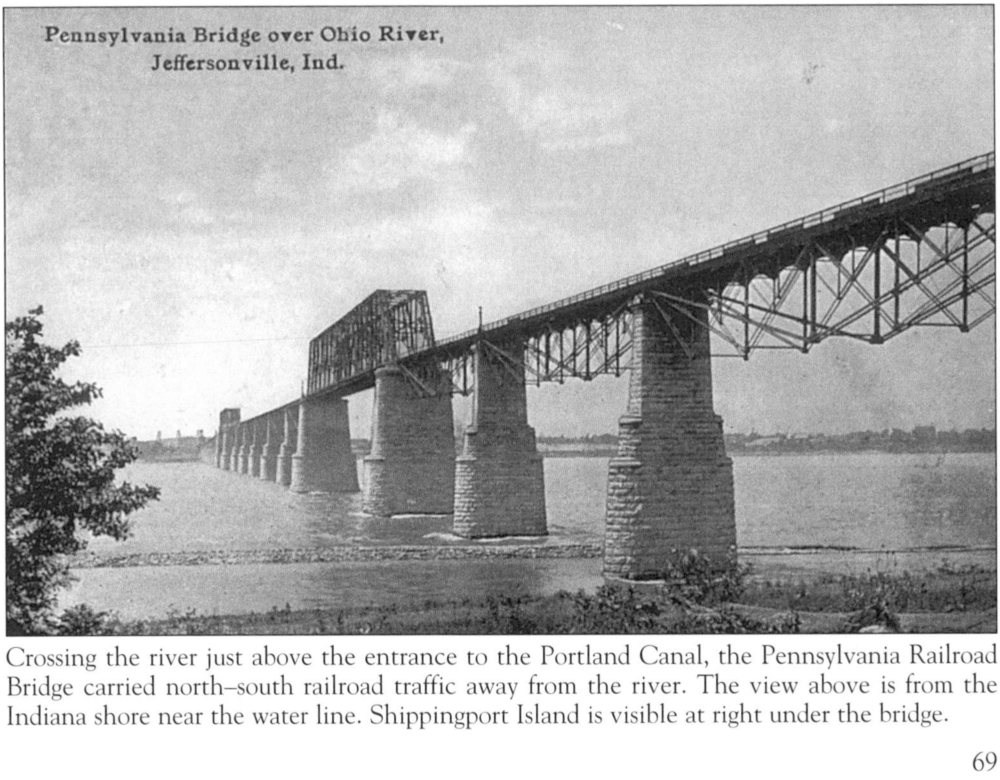

Crossing the river just above the entrance to the Portland Canal, the Pennsylvania Railroad Bridge carried north–south railroad traffic away from the river. The view above is from the Indiana shore near the water line. Shippingport Island is visible at right under the bridge.

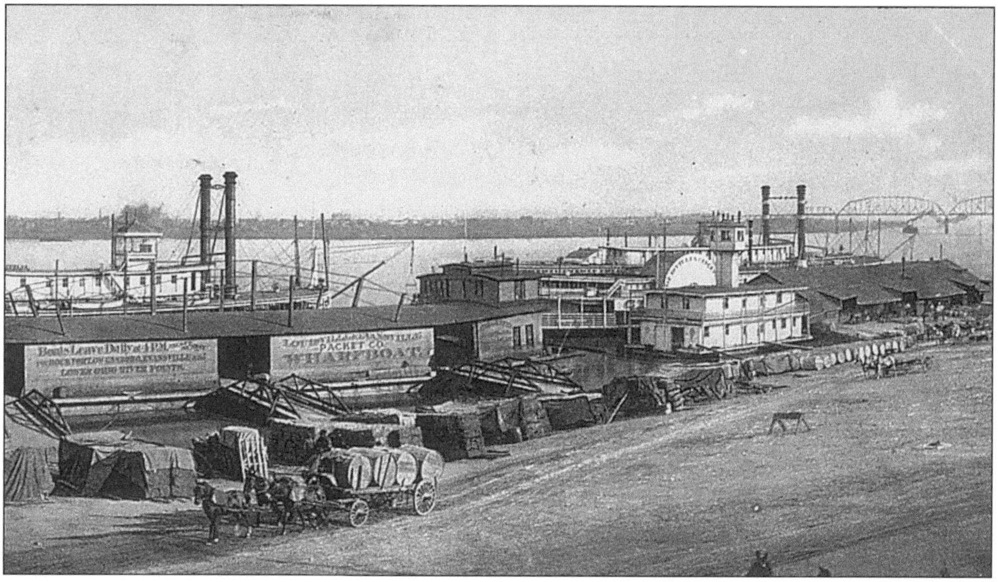

The wharf at Louisville, Kentucky, just above the entrance to the Portland Canal, bustles with activity. The *Str. City of Cincinnati* lays at the wharfboat in the center right of the photo, just above the uniquely-styled Coast Guard Life Saving Station.

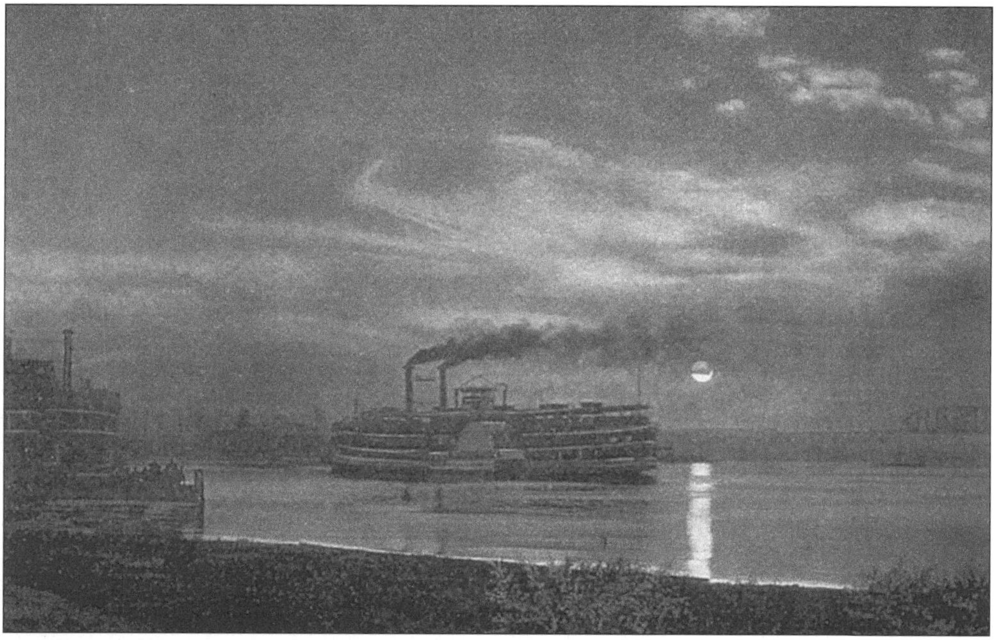

A twilight arrival at Louisville ends a long day's journey from Cincinnati. It could also be the end of a fun day of riding the river for passengers who left Louisville that morning, and changed over to the boat going in the opposite direction. The Louisville and Cincinnati packet that came down that day is tied to the wharfboat. An unidentified excursion steamer approaches to land.

Four

CARGOES AND COMMERCE

The Ohio River was the transportation method of choice for people and cargoes along the river. Farm goods going to market made up the bulk of what was sent from the smaller towns and villages to the bigger cities. Manufactured goods, and other products not produced locally, came back by river to area homes and stores. Coal was delivered by barge to local coal yards to power local businesses and small manufacturing firms. It was also the primary fuel of choice for winter heat.

The North family albums provide the following chronicle of river trade. Brothers Ira L. and Benjamin G. North operated a wharfboat, warehouse, and general store at North's Landing, Indiana, below Rising Sun, from 1894 till 1918. With brother-in-law J.O. Hamilton, they also operated a coal yard upriver at Buckeye Landing. Damage caused by the ice of 1918 effectively closed all businesses.

It was not always an easy or lucrative business. Under-capitalized small operators came and went. River floods and freezes periodically threatened. It was not an easy way to make money. The passenger and local produce business moved off of the water by the 1930s. Bulk cargoes, that were carried in larger tows of steel barges pushed by the towboats of a few companies, were left to see river commerce into modern times.

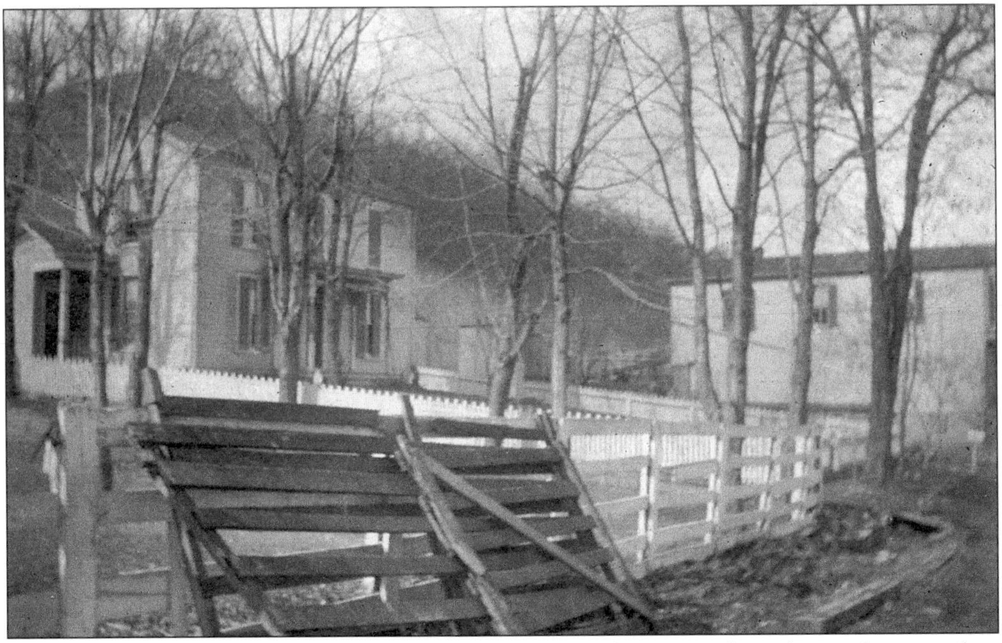

The North family home on the left and the North General Store on the right are shown as they were about 1900. The North family first settled in the area about 1816, establishing a store in the 1850s at what would become North's Landing near the mouth of Grant's Creek.

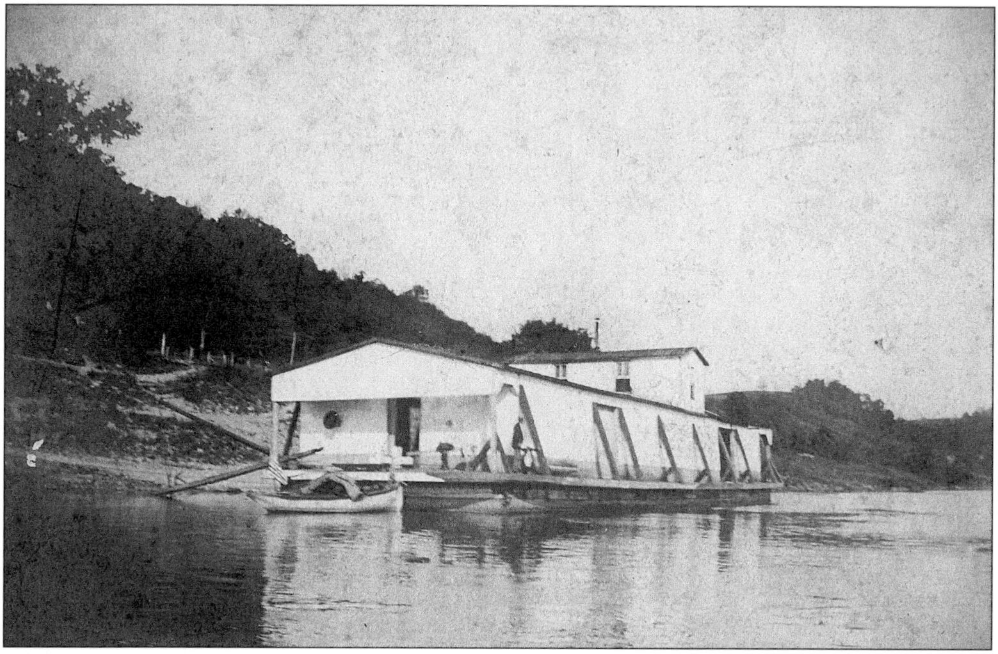

Here, the wharfboat at North's Landing, Indiana, rides a low, summer water level. Wharfboats were used so the packets could dock to exchange cargoes and passengers without running aground. The North Store is in the trees at the upper left. (North 24.)

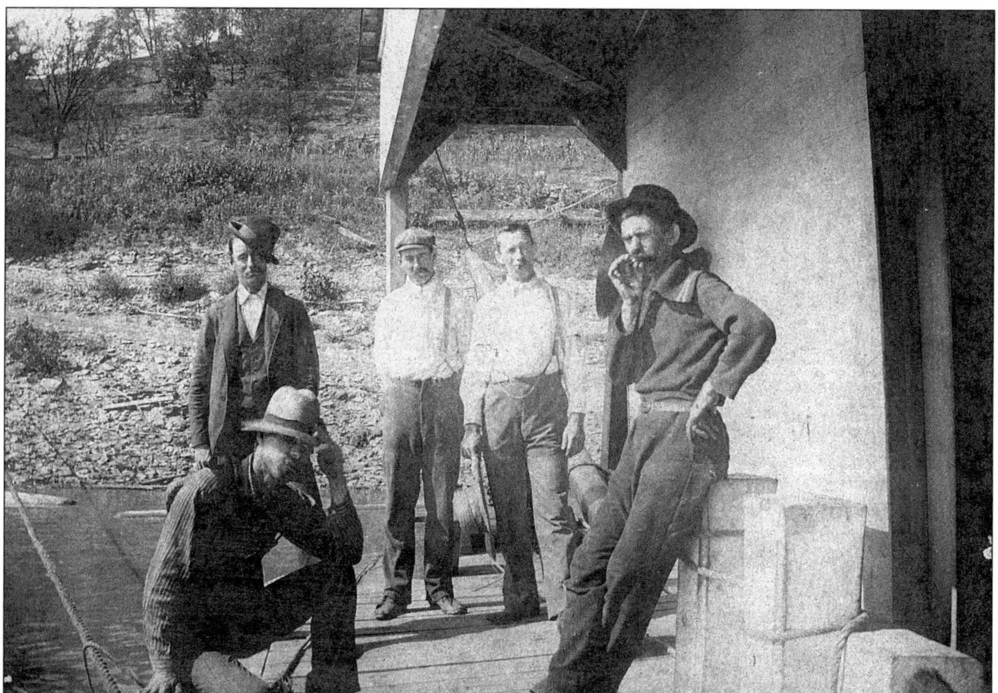

Ira L. North is shown standing in a suit, while Benjamin Grant North and John O. Hamilton stand in their shirtsleeves behind. The other two gentlemen are unidentified. The picture was taken on the wharfboat, probably the same time as the top view, sometime around 1900.

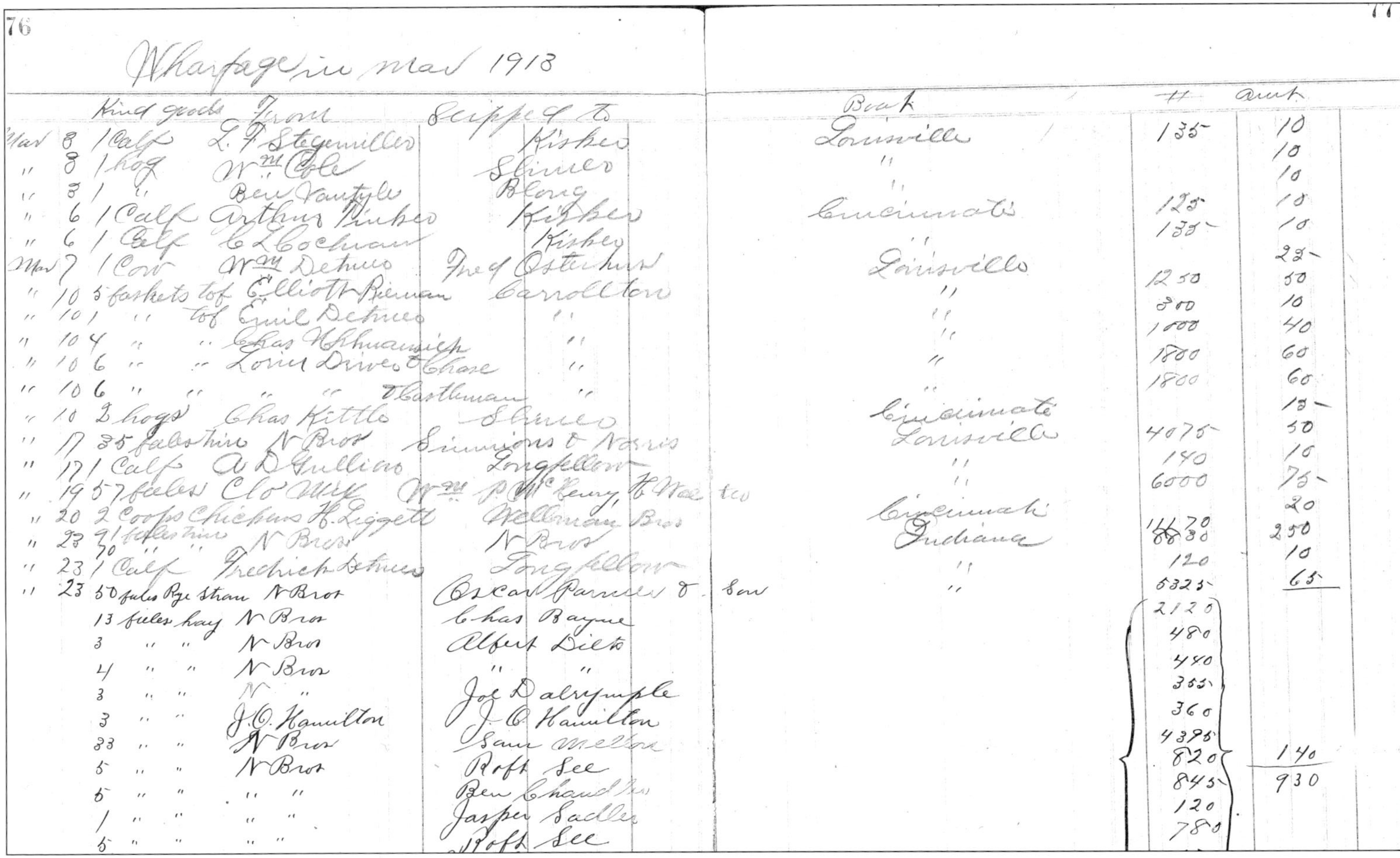

Wharfage in Mar 1913

Date	Kind goods	From	Shipped to	Boat	#	Amt
Mar 8	1 Calf	L. F. Stegemiller	Kisker	Louisville	135	10
" 8	1 hog	Wm Cole	Slimer	"		10
" 8	1 "	Ben Vantyle	Blong	"		10
" 6	1 Calf	Arthur Pinker	Kisker	Cincinnati	125	10
" 6	1 Calf	C L Cochran	Kisker	"	135	10
Mar 7	1 Cow	Wm Detmer	Fred Ostenhus	Louisville		25
" 10	5 baskets tof	Elliott Rieman	Carrollton	"	1250	50
" 10	1 " tof	Emil Detmer	"	"	300	10
" 10	4 " "	Chas [illegible]	"	"	1000	40
" 10	6 " "	Louis Drives & Chase	"	"	1800	60
" 10	6 " "	" " [illegible]	"	"	1800	60
" 10	2 hogs	Chas Kittle	Slimer	Cincinnati		15
" 17	35 [illegible]	N Bros	Simmons & Norris	Louisville	4075	50
" 17	1 Calf	A D Gullion	Longfellow	"	140	10
" 19	57 bales	Clo Mfg	Wm P McHenry & [illegible]	"	6000	75
" 20	2 Coops Chickens	H. Liggett	Wellman Bros	Cincinnati		20
" 23	91 [illegible]	N Bros	N Bros	Indiana	11170 8830	250
" 23	1 Calf	Frederick Detmer	Longfellow	"	120	10
" 23	50 bales Rye straw	N Bros	Oscar Parmer & Son	"	5325	65
	13 bales hay	N Bros	Chas Bayne		2120	
	3 " "	N Bros	Albert Dilts		480	
	4 " "	N Bros	" "		440	
	3 " "	N "	Joe Dalrymple		355	
	3 " "	J.C. Hamilton	J C Hamilton		360	
	33 " "	N Bros	Sam Mellon		4395	
	5 " "	N Bros	Robt Lee		820	140
	5 " "	" "	Ben Chandler		845	930
	1 " "	" "	Jasper Sadler		120	
	5 " "	" "	Robt Lee		780	

A page from the North's Landing Wharfboat "Wharfage Book" shows cargoes shipped during March, 1913. The fees collected are noted at right.

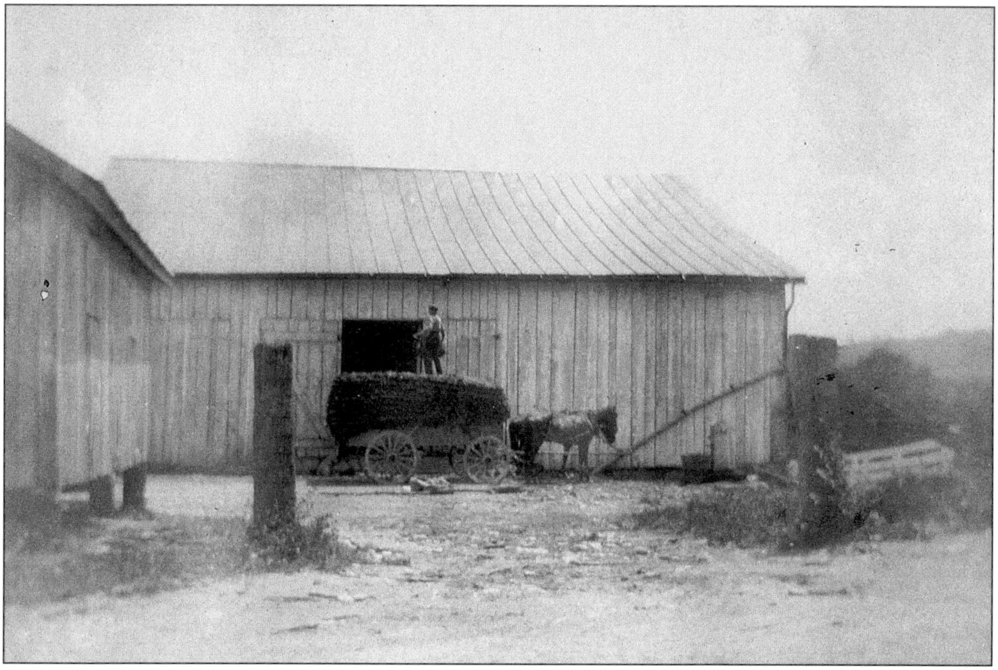

Tobacco was cured (dried) by hanging cut stalks in barns. It was then stripped by removing the leaves from the stalks, and tied into small groups or "hands" for shipment. The wagon above is loading stripped "hands" of tobacco from the barn adjacent to the North Brothers Store.

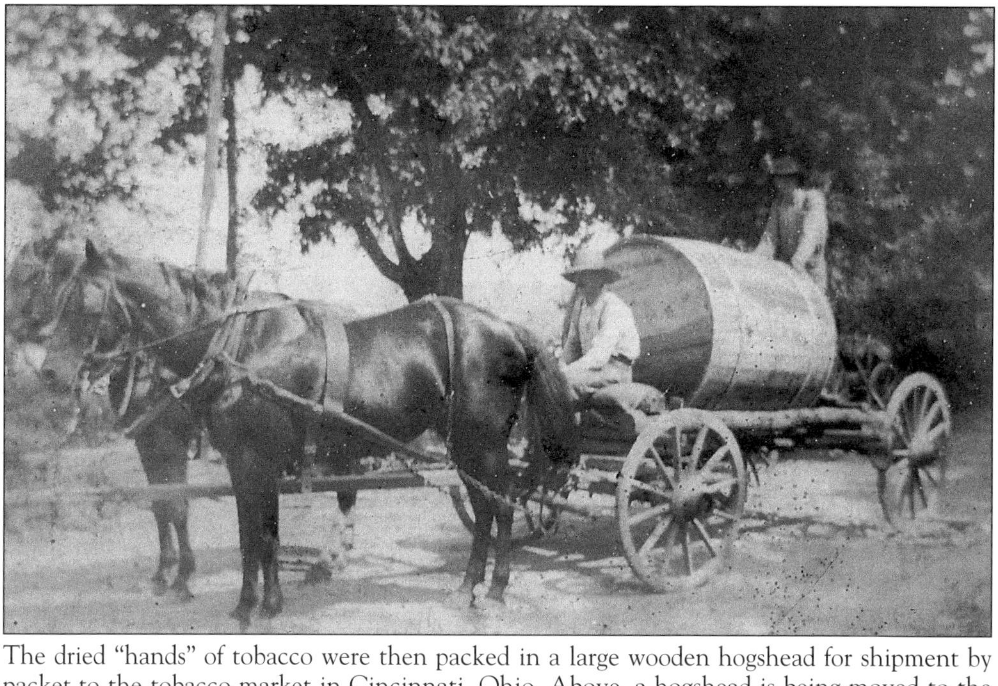

The dried "hands" of tobacco were then packed in a large wooden hogshead for shipment by packet to the tobacco market in Cincinnati, Ohio. Above, a hogshead is being moved to the wharfboat by Jeff and Daisy, horses owned and driven by J.O. Hamilton. Harry Stegemiller rides on the rear of the wagon. This picture was taken at North's Landing.

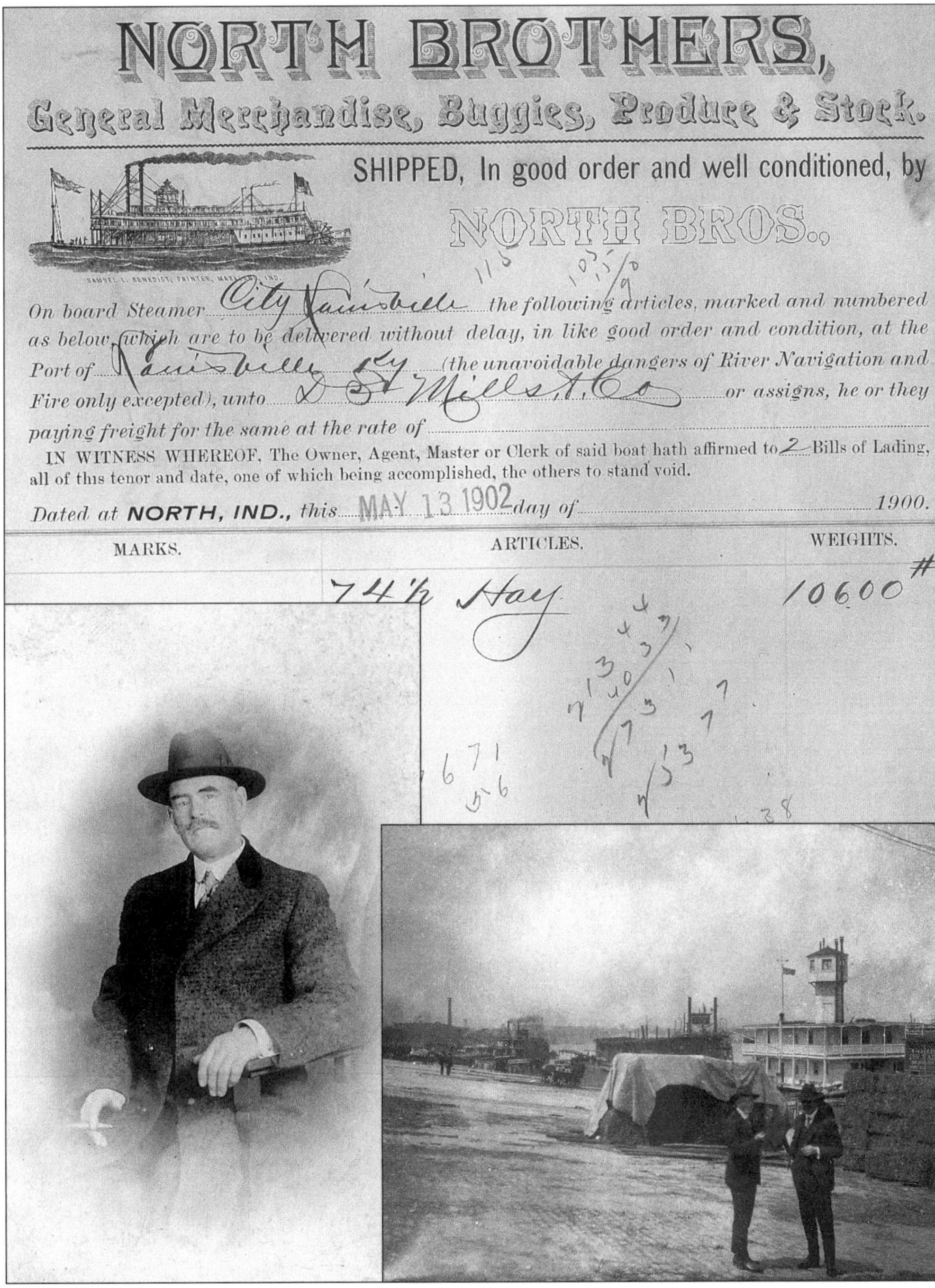

NORTH BROTHERS,

General Merchandise, Buggies, Produce & Stock.

SHIPPED, In good order and well conditioned, by

NORTH BROS.,

SAMUEL L. BENEDICT, PAINTER, MADISON, IND.

On board Steamer City Louisville *the following articles, marked and numbered as below, which are to be delivered without delay, in like good order and condition, at the Port of* Louisville Ky *(the unavoidable dangers of River Navigation and Fire only excepted), unto* D. H. Mills & Co *or assigns, he or they paying freight for the same at the rate of*

IN WITNESS WHEREOF, The Owner, Agent, Master or Clerk of said boat hath affirmed to 2 Bills of Lading, all of this tenor and date, one of which being accomplished, the others to stand void.

Dated at **NORTH, IND.,** *this* MAY 13 1902 *day of* 1900.

MARKS.	ARTICLES.	WEIGHTS.
	74½ Hay	10600#

This is a Bill of Landing for hay shipped by the North Brothers to market in Louisville, Kentucky, on the *Str. City of Louisville*. It carries the official name for the post office, which had been changed to North, Indiana, in 1894. The inserted picture on the left is a business post card that Benjamin used to solicit business as a hay merchant. The picture at right shows Benjamin standing next to hay delivered by packet for sale on the wharf at Louisville, Kentucky.

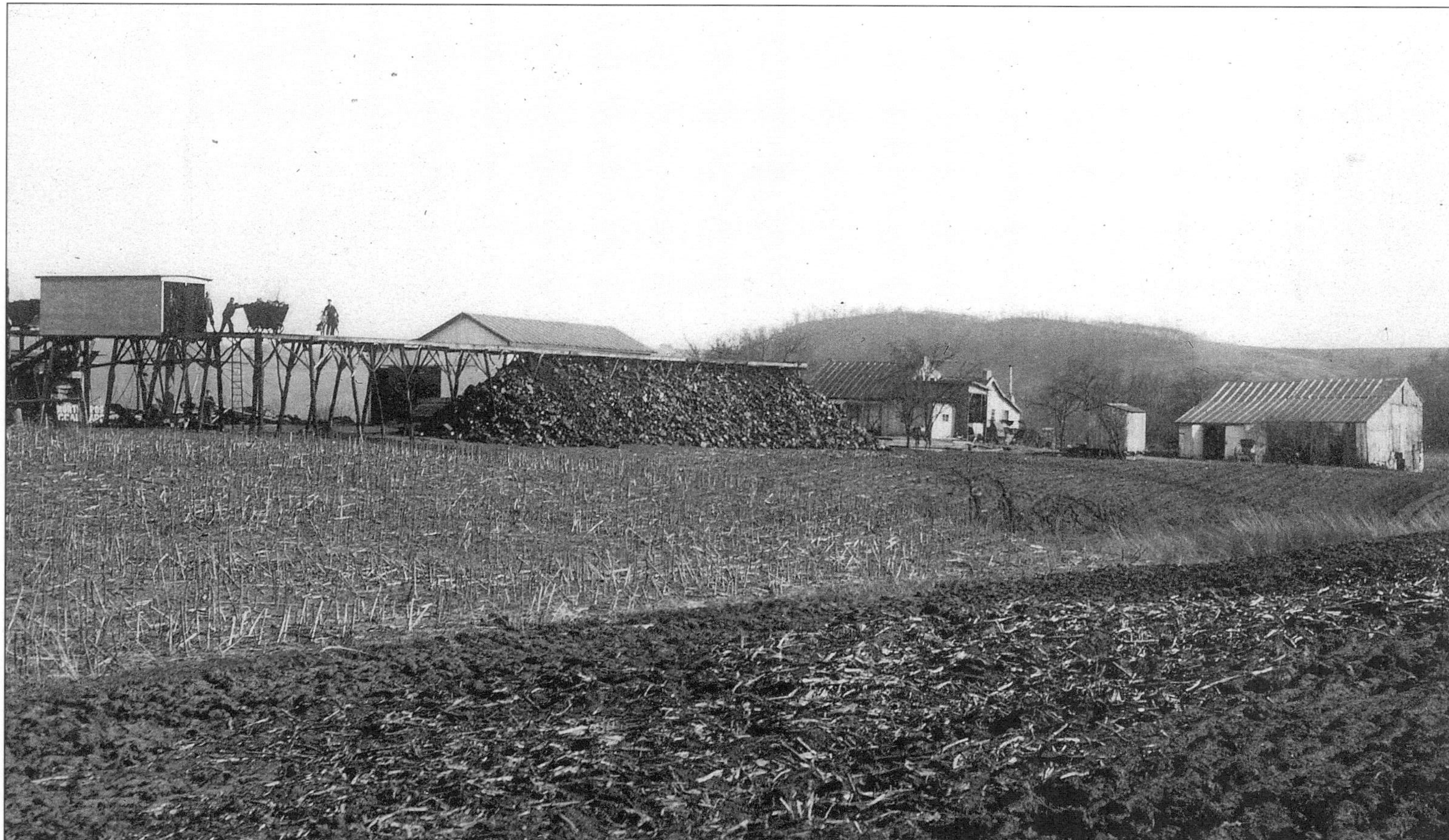

The coal yard at Buckeye Landing, Indiana, operated by the North Brothers, included two barns for holding hay and straw that would be shipped by packet to Cincinnati or Louisville. The Norths actually combined two businesses at this location. A wharfboat was not needed here. The depth of the water permitted barges bringing coal in, and boats hauling hay and straw out, to land directly on shore.

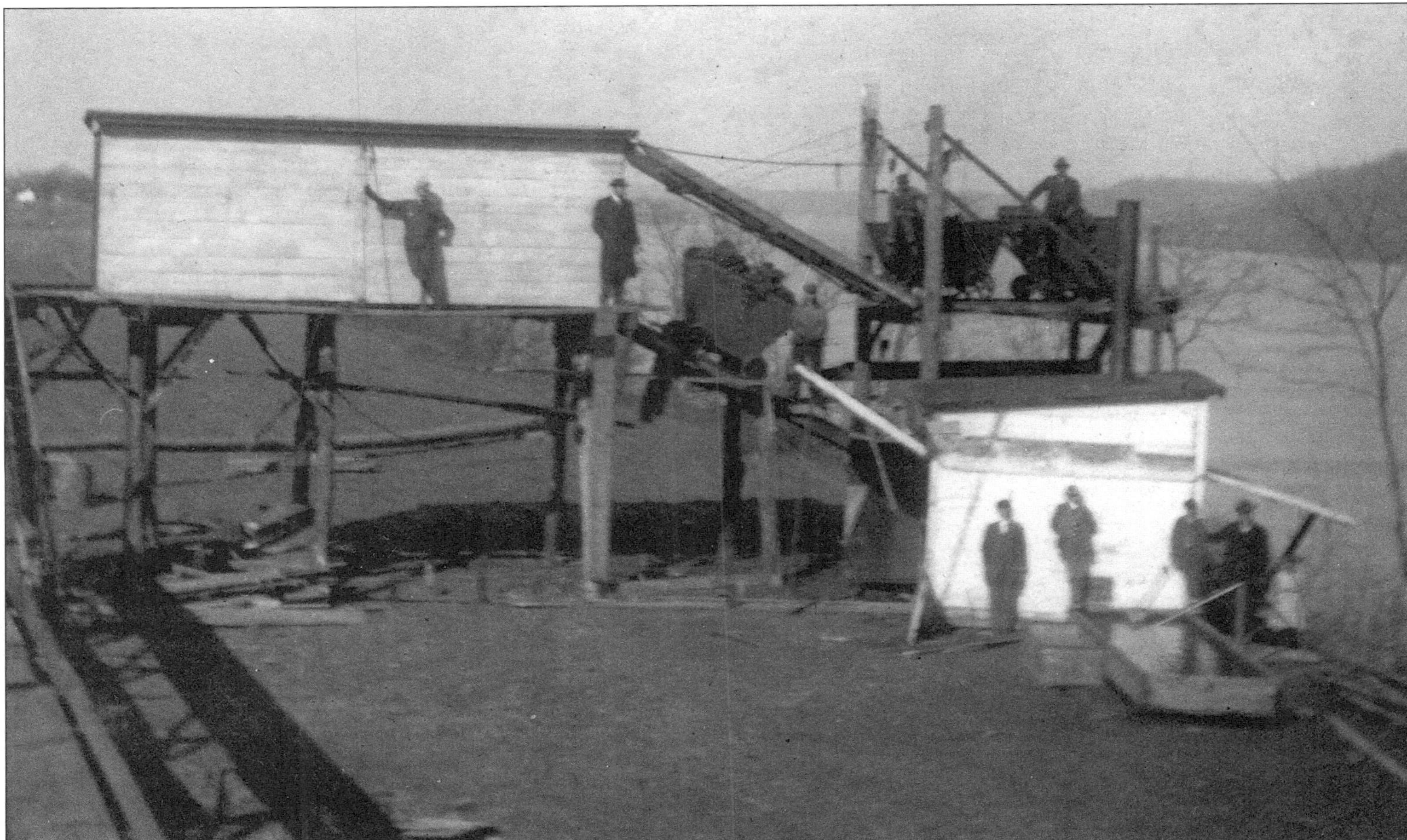

The crew at Buckeye Landing pose atop the coal incline above. The coal pile is out of this view at the bottom left. The inclined track running to the river runs out of the white shed at right.

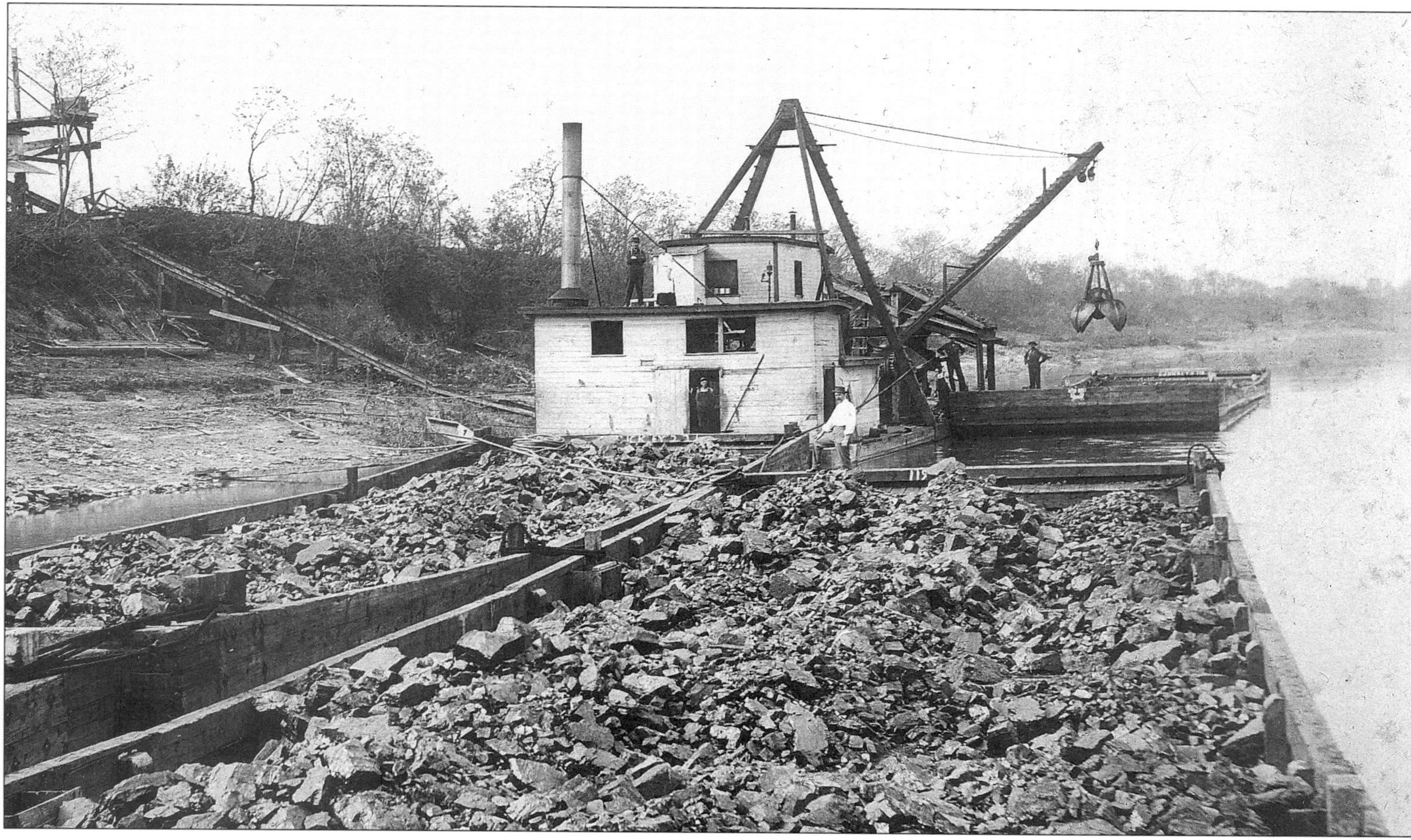

A steam-powered, clamshell crane, or "coal digger" as they were called, is unloading a tow of coal barges at Buckeye Landing. Coal purchased from wholesalers upriver was shipped to local dealers' yards in tows of barges that included this device to aid in unloading. Benjamin North, wearing a white shirt and standing on the coal barge behind the "coal digger," inspects his purchased coal.

FORWARDED BY

NORTH BROTHERS

GENERAL MERCHANDISE, COAL, PRODUCE & STOCK

HAY and STRAW a Specialty

From BUCKEYE LANDING, IND.

R. R. 2, North, Ind. ______________________ *19* ____

____

____

____

We ship you to-day ______________________________
which please sell to the best advantage and send account sales and net proceeds for the same to
______________________, *P. O.* ______________________ *Ind.*

____

____

Yours respectfully,

NORTH BROTHERS

The invoice above was used to ship farm goods from Buckeye Landing by packet. The address should have read "R.R. # 2, Rising Sun, Indiana." However, many people who had lived in the area for years continued to address items to North, Indiana, long after its post office closed in 1919.

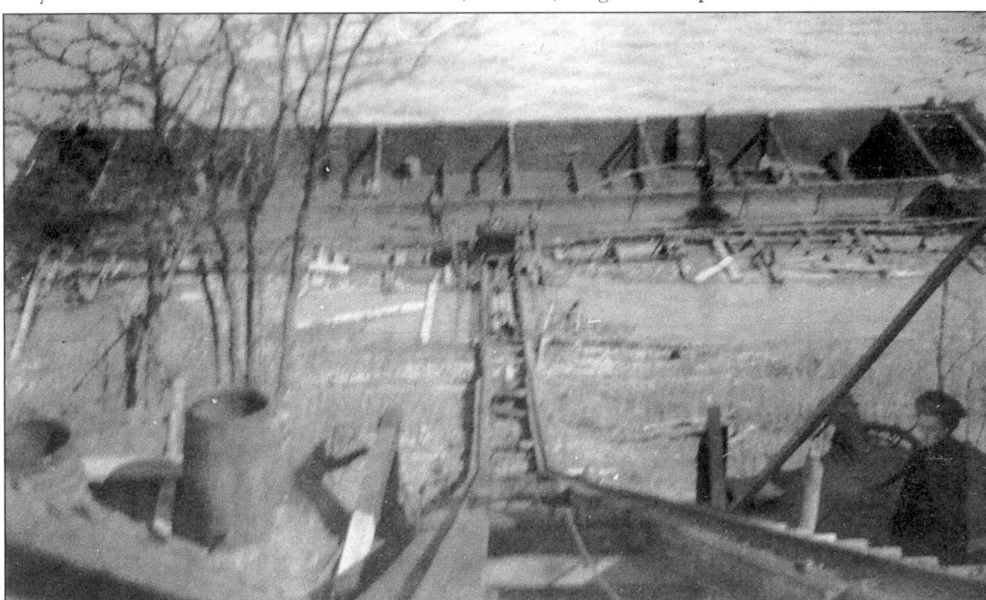

Here is the view from the top of the incline looking down upon a barge tied at dockside in Buckeye Landing. Coal was removed from the barges into carts for its trip up the bank to the coal yard. The visible cable running down the center of the incline cart track pulls the loaded cart to the top, where it was manually pushed out the tracks over the coal pile and dumped.

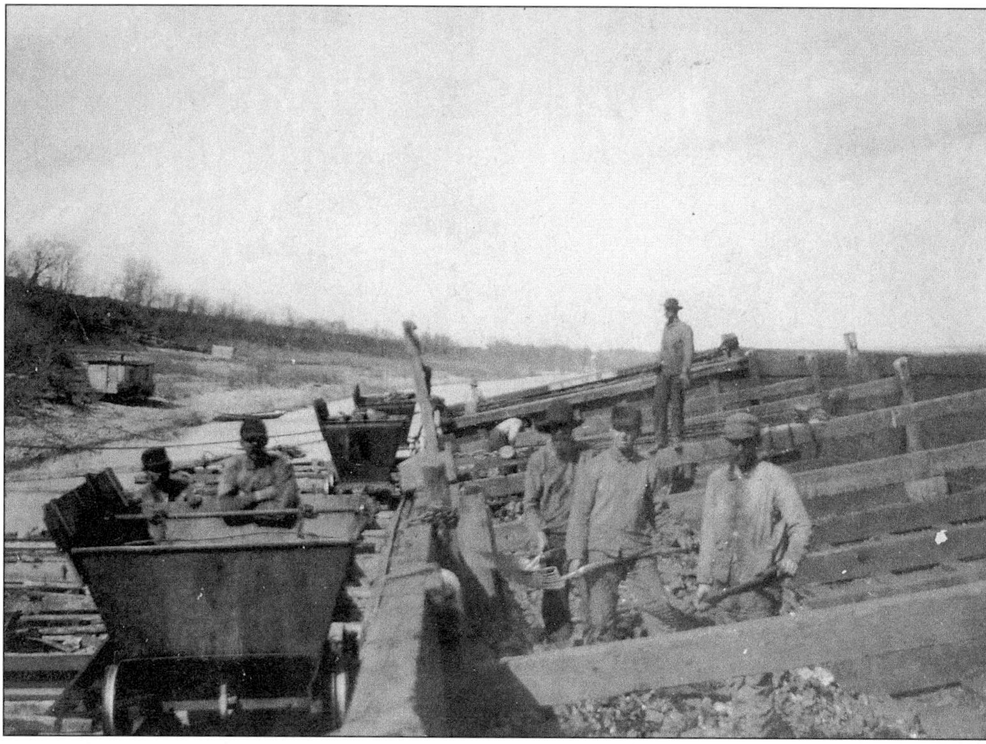

Pictured is a gang of day laborers, who are getting the last few chunks of coal out of the barges a shovelful at a time.

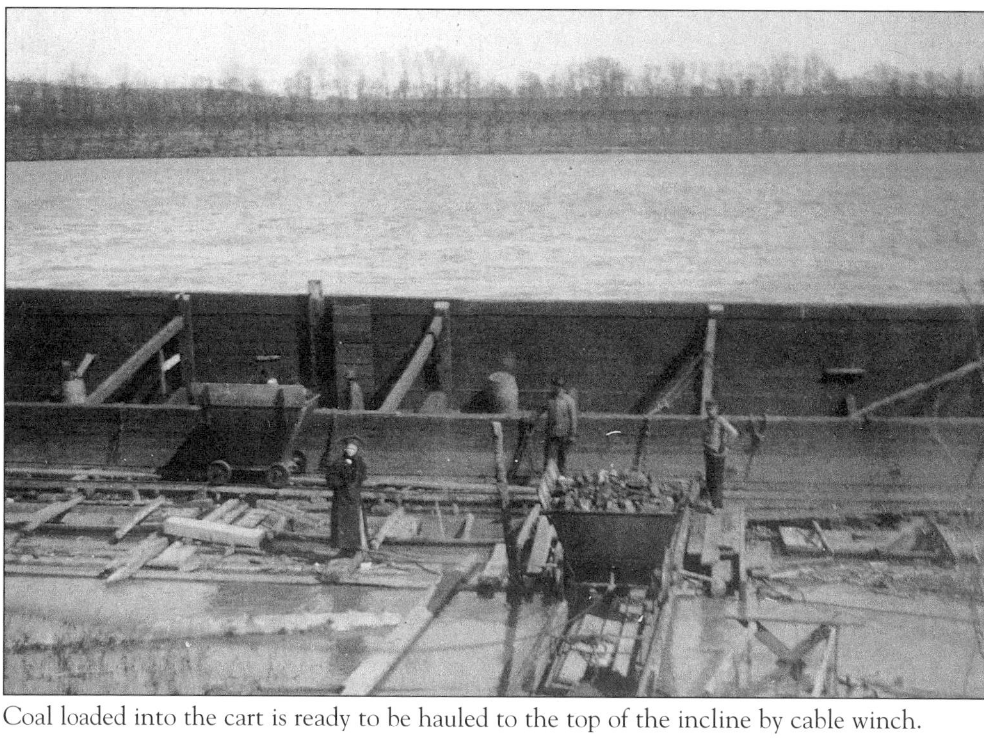

Coal loaded into the cart is ready to be hauled to the top of the incline by cable winch.

Five
Fun on the River

The river has always provided recreation to residents along its banks. During the early days of the twentieth century, excursion boats came frequently to river towns. Various civic and social groups would cruise to adjacent towns, or just spend a lazy afternoon or evening away from shore. Showboats brought melodramas and vaudeville entertainment to towns in the time before movies, television, and radio.

Fishing served the practical purpose of providing food for the table, but the river also provided fish for the pleasure of catching. Others found their attention captured by the challenge of developing new ways to speed across the water. On summer evenings, a walk along the shore was a favorite pastime of the young and the young of heart. This you can still enjoy today. The following pictures give you a glimpse of some of the other pastimes that have been lost or changed over time.

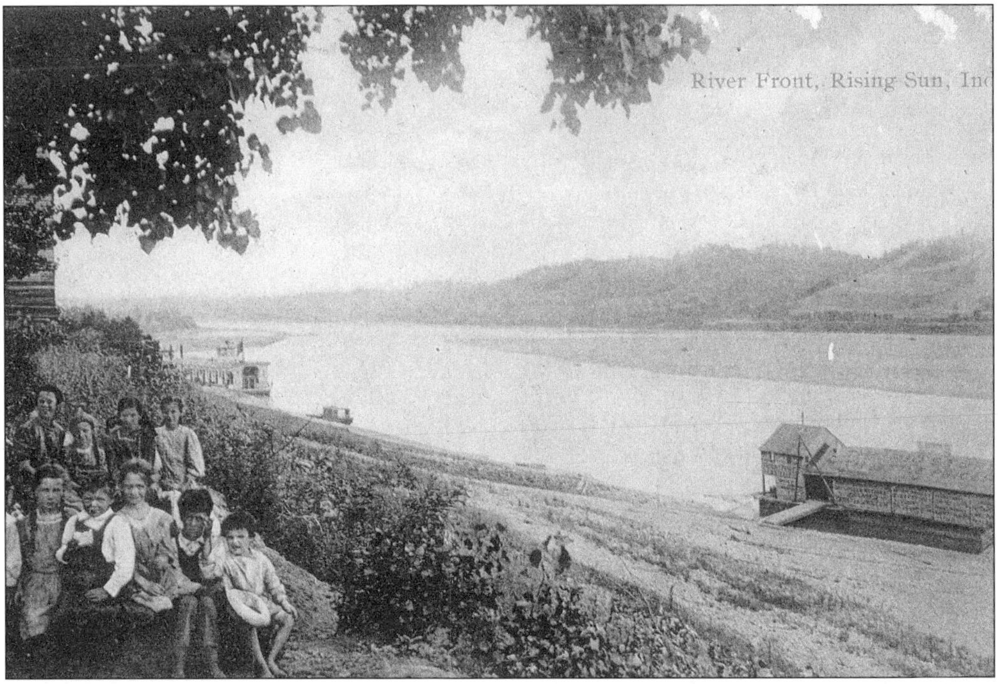

This photograph shows some local children on a lazy summer afternoon on the riverbank above the landing at Rising Sun, Indiana. The Bryant Family's showboat is tied up above the wharfboat in the center left of the photo. The riverbank was a favorite play area for kids growing up in a riverside town. This day, they also possibly dreamed of getting a ticket to that night's stage show. (North 25.)

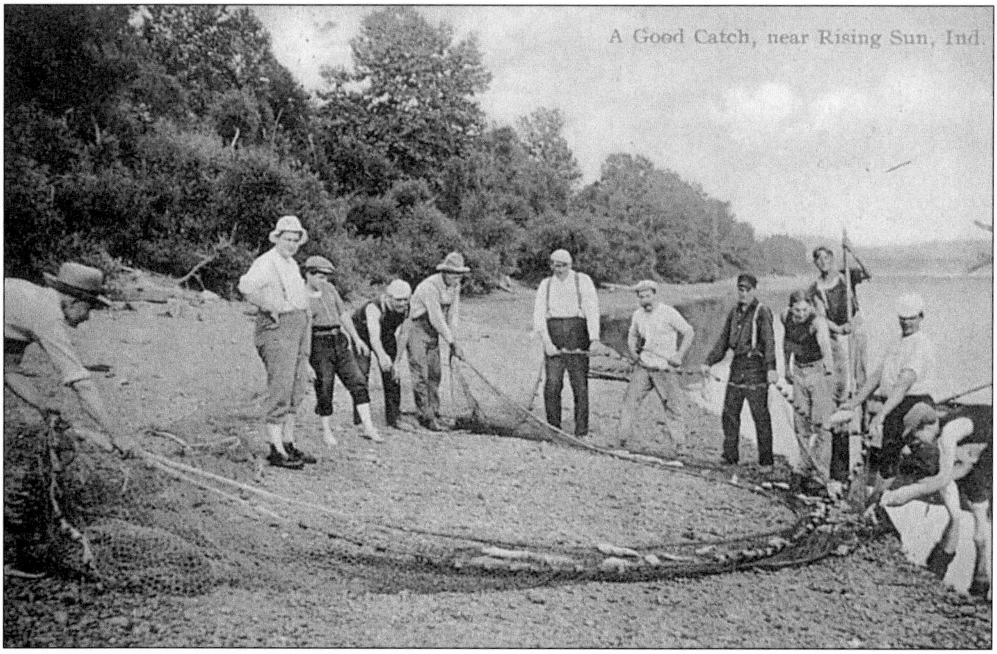

Fishing in the river was both a commercial enterprise and a recreational pastime. Above, a group of men examine their catch from a large seine net. (North 26.)

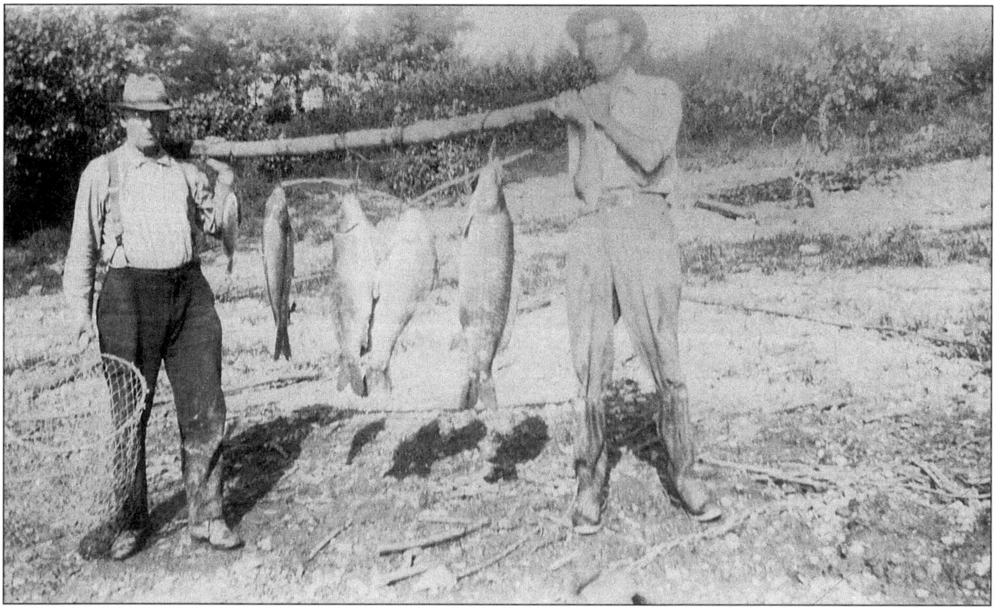
Ira L. North and friend Edgar Pendry proudly display a group of large channel catfish taken from the river near North's Landing, Indiana.

The author's grandmother and fishing companion, Pearl North Stegemiller, daughter of Benjamin Grant North, poses with her catch out of Bells Branch, a tributary stream flowing into Laughery Creek. Laughery Creek enters the Ohio River between Aurora and Rising Sun, Indiana. Ma Pearl taught the author this very important skill while sharing stories about growing up at North's Landing around the general store, and later river experiences while raising a family in Rising Sun, Indiana.

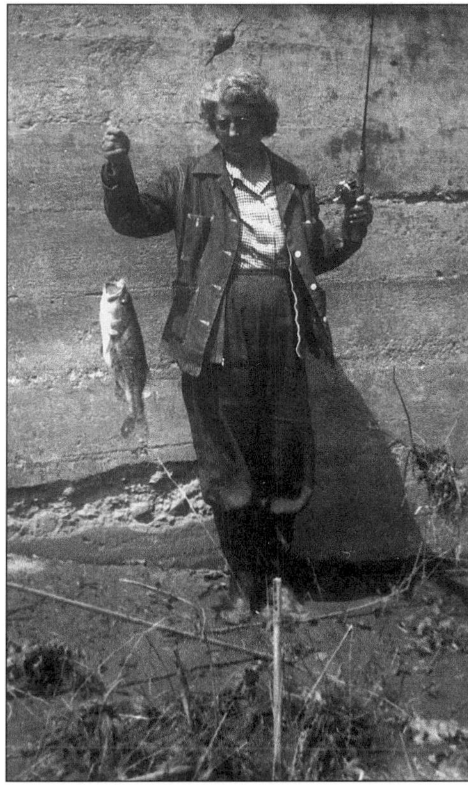

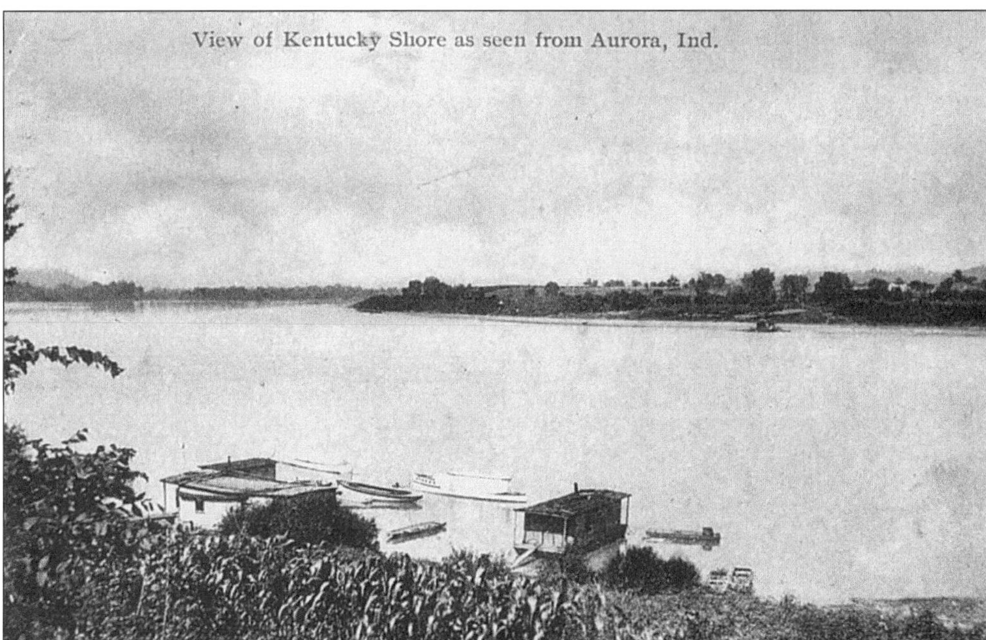

Houseboats ride along shore below the Aurora, Indiana ferry landing. The diesel-powered, end-loading, side-wheeled ferry is visible along the Kentucky shore at the right. These "shanty" boats were the permanent homes of some families.

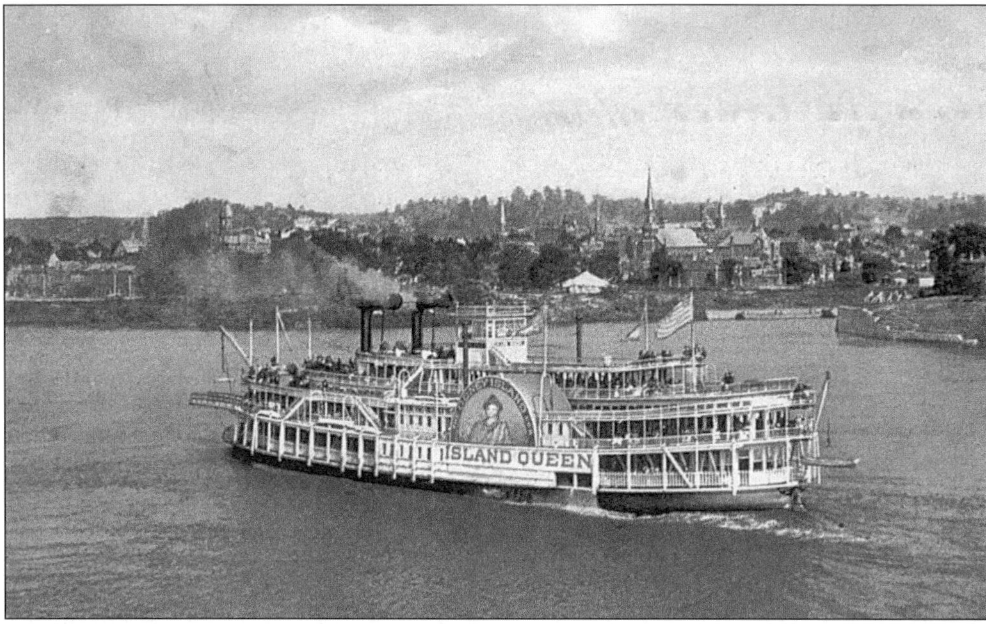

The *Str. Island Queen (1st)* is loaded with visitors headed 6 miles upriver from the Cincinnati public landing to the Coney Island Amusement Park. This picture was probably taken from the Cincinnati Suspension Bridge just after the boat pulled away from the public landing. The mouth of the Licking River is visible on the Kentucky shore behind the boat. Newport, Kentucky, is the city to the left of the Licking River.

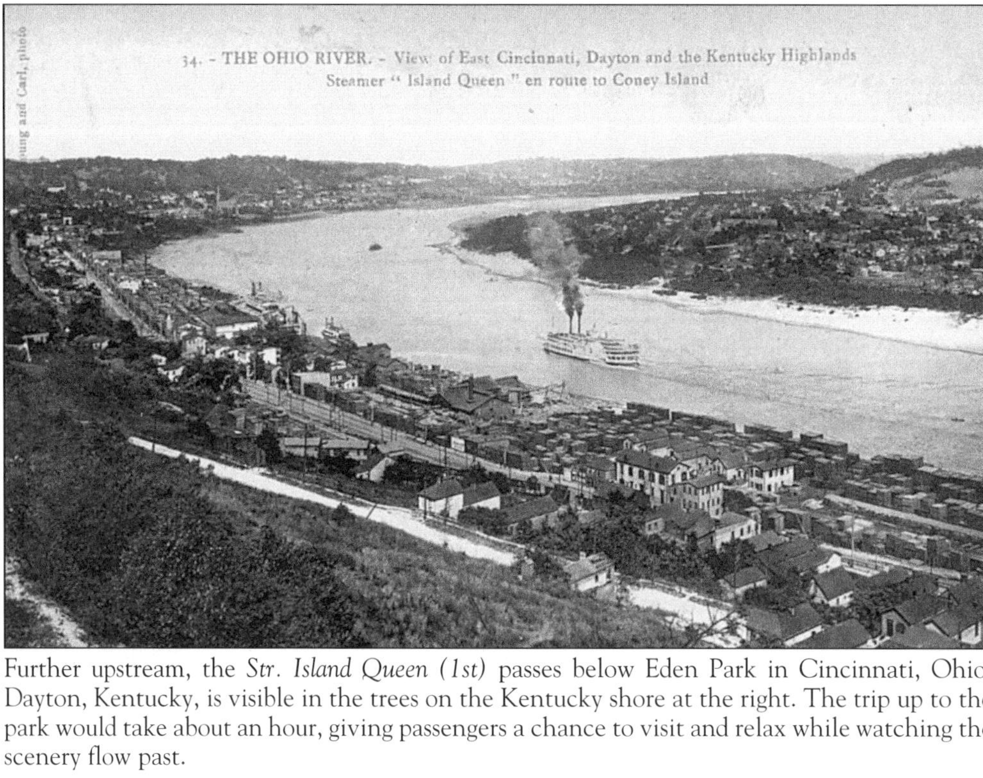

Further upstream, the *Str. Island Queen (1st)* passes below Eden Park in Cincinnati, Ohio. Dayton, Kentucky, is visible in the trees on the Kentucky shore at the right. The trip up to the park would take about an hour, giving passengers a chance to visit and relax while watching the scenery flow past.

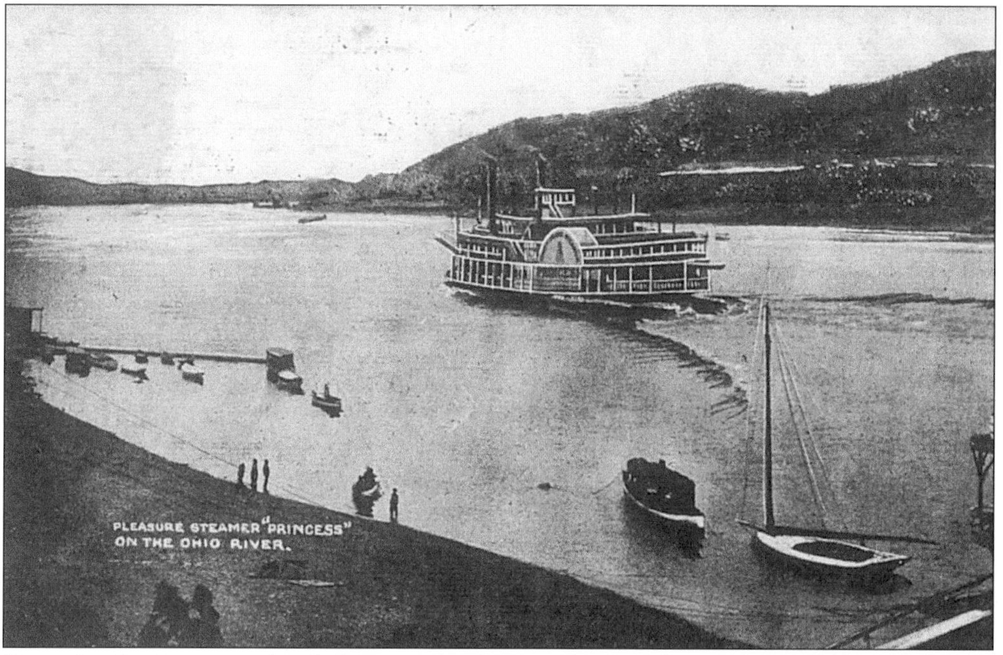

Here, the *Str. Princess* is headed upriver for Coney Island. Taken close to the riverbank, this picture shows examples of the small pleasure crafts of the day. The river level appears low on this day. The larger *Str. Island Queen (1st)* possibly would not have had sufficient water to make the trip, or she could have been off to another town on a charter trip.

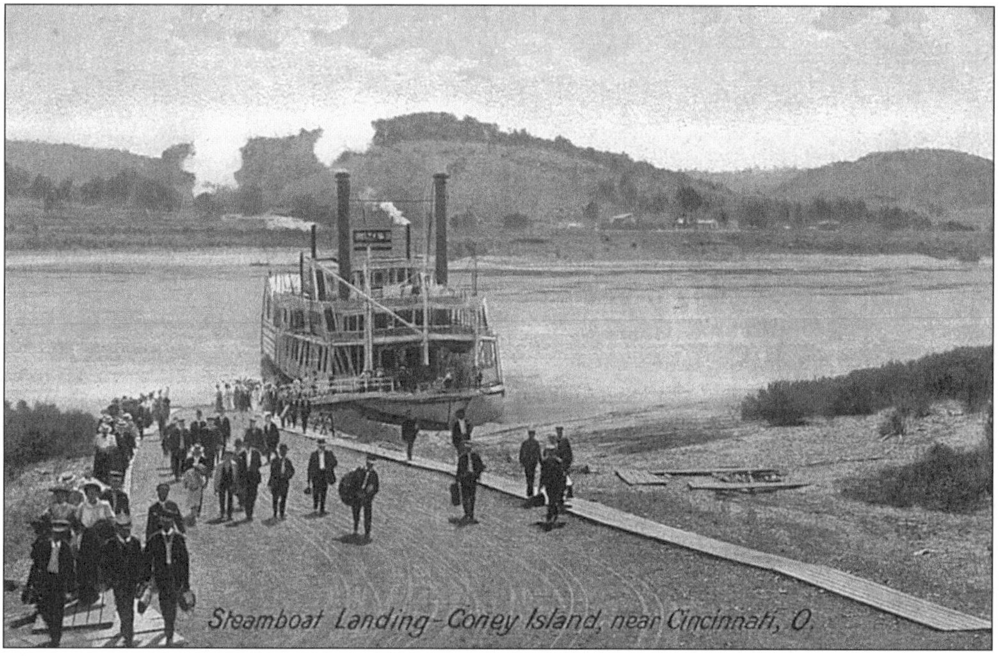

The *Str. Princess* is pictured at the landing adjacent to the Coney Island Amusement Park, discharging passengers headed for a day of fun. The river stage was high enough on this day to permit the *Princess* to land almost directly against the paved landing.

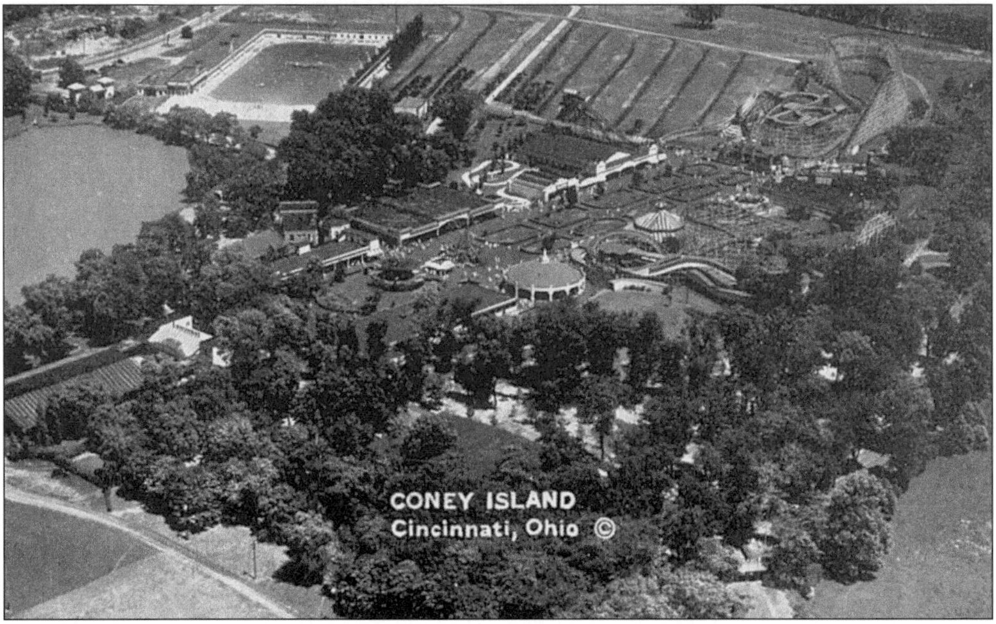

The Coney Island Amusement Park was located about 9 miles upriver from Cincinnati Public Landing. Lake Como is in the center left, with rides, midway, and picnic grounds spreading into the trees at right. Frequently flooded by both rivers due to its low location, it operated into the 1960s, and was eventually bought by the company that built King's Island Amusement Park inland away from the river. Many of its classic rides, including the carousel and wooden roller coaster, the "Racer," still operate today.

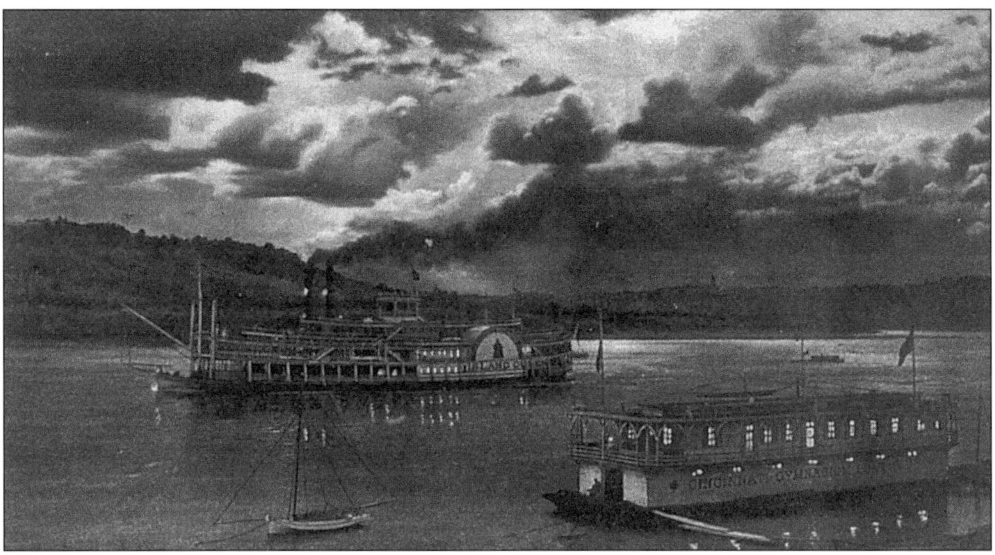

The *Str. Island Queen (1st)*, pictured above Cincinnati, is headed home for the night. The quiet peace of a moonlit night sparked many a romance.

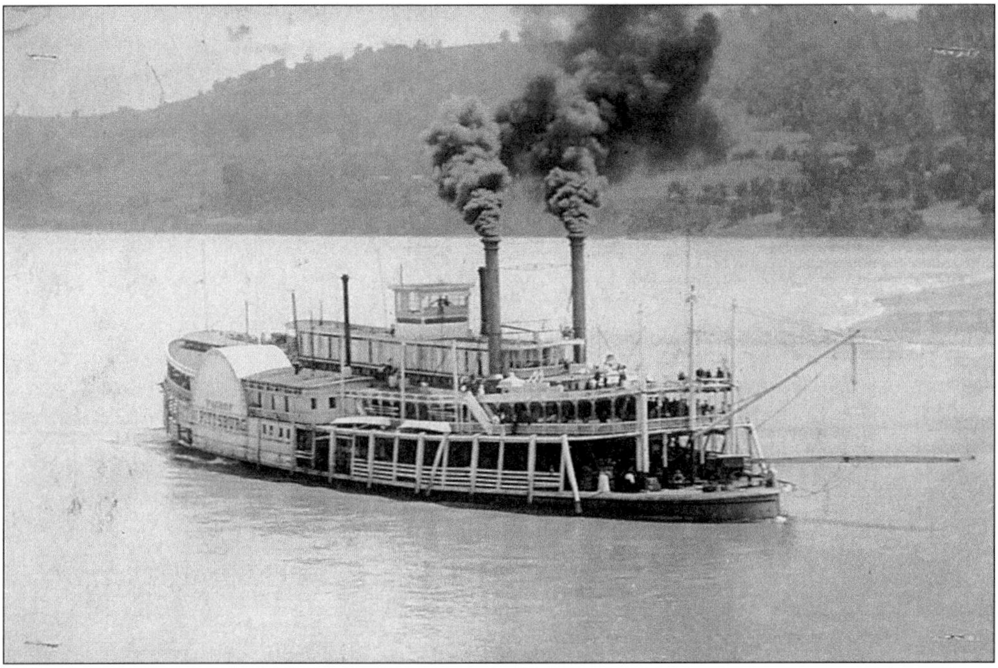

Other steamboats worked the excursion business between Cincinnati and Louisville. Above, the *Str. Pittsburgh* returns a group to the landing at Rising Sun, Indiana. She worked the entire length of the river in her career. (North 27.)

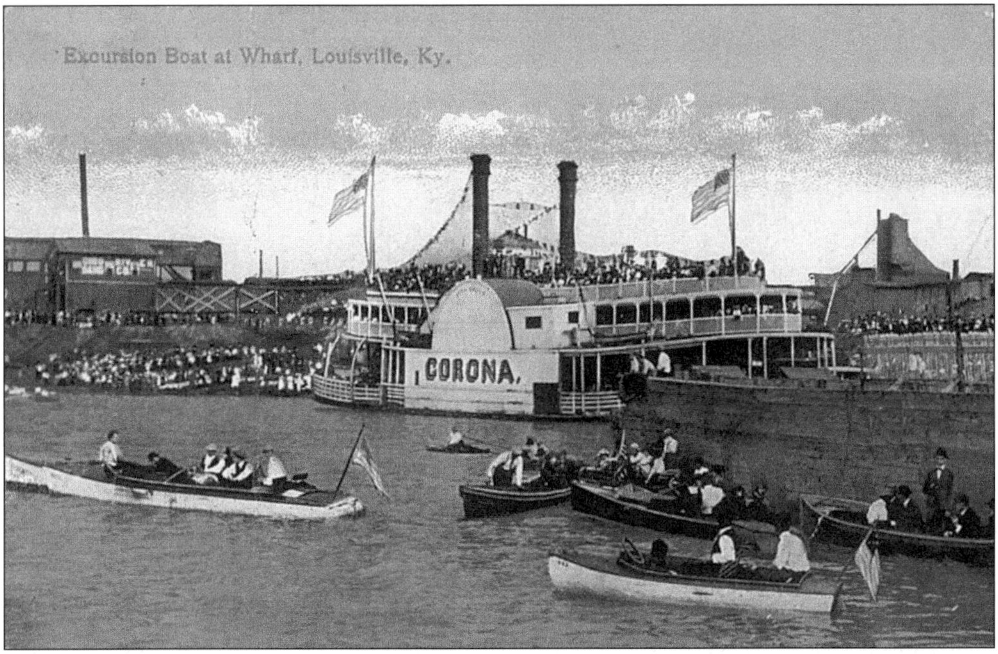

The Louisville and Jeffersonville Ferry Company rebuilt its ferry *W.C. Hite* as an excursion boat in 1914, and renamed it *Str. Corona*. Much smaller than most excursion boats of the era, she worked the Louisville area for years until dismantled.

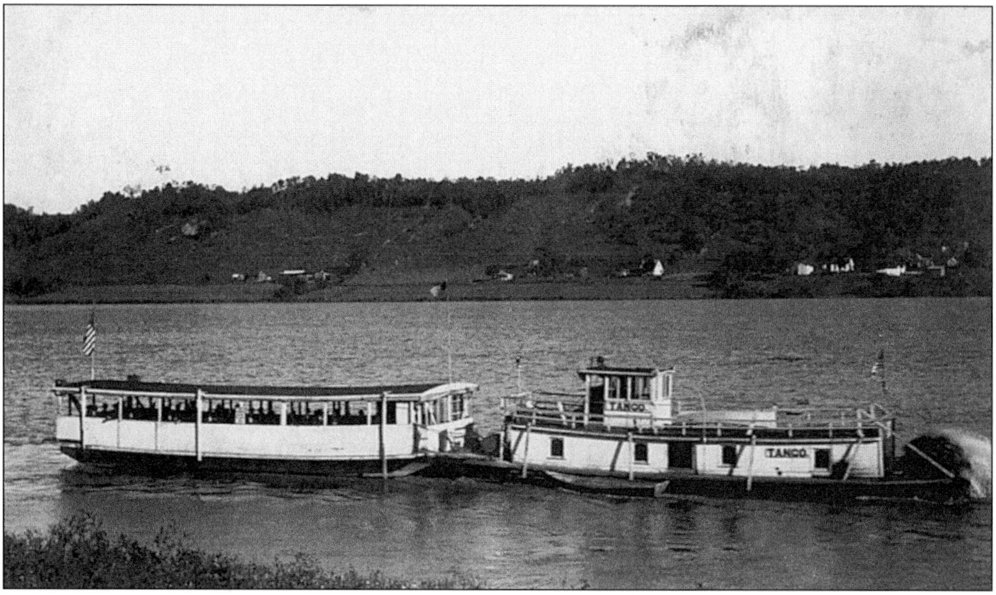

Excursion business continued into later years. Here, the sternwheel, diesel-powered *Tango* pushes a passenger barge upriver, departing Rising Sun, Indiana. (North 28.)

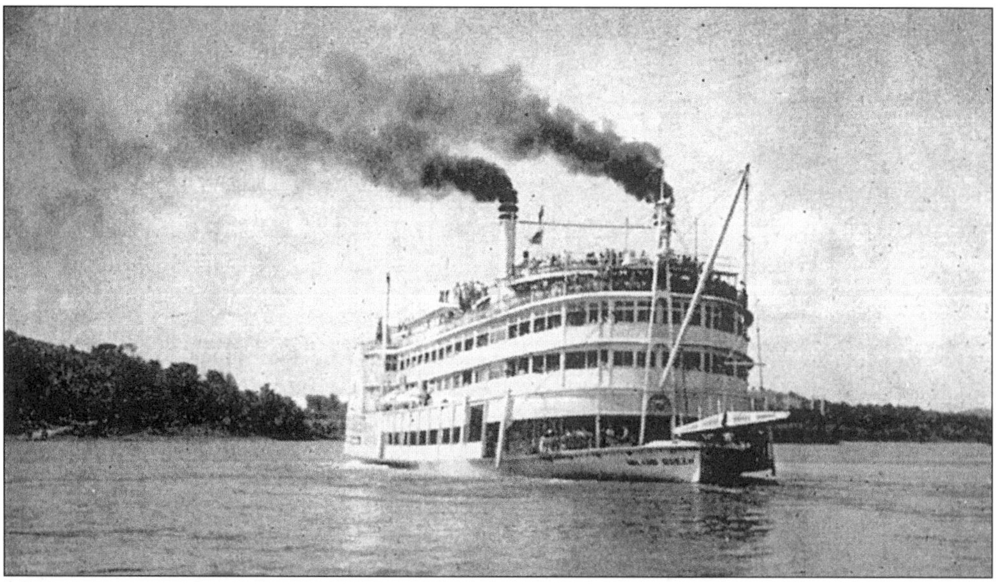
Str. Island Queen (2nd) carries a charter group to Lawrenceburg, Indiana around 1940. When the *Str. Island Queen (1st)* was lost in Cincinnati to fire on November 4, 1932, *Str. Island Queen (2nd)* was built to continue service to Coney Island Amusement Park. One of the last big side-wheeled, steam-powered boats, she was constructed on a steel hull. She was also lost to fire on September 9, 1947, while docked in Pittsburgh, Pennsylvania. She had been on a tramping run upriver, giving excursions in various towns. (North 29.)

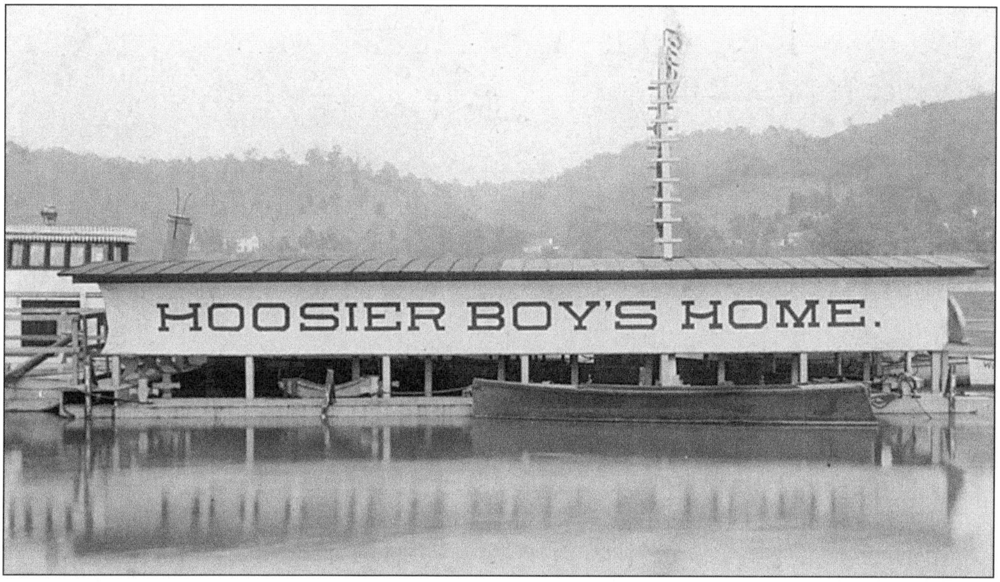

J.W. "Row" Whitlock's hobby and passion was speed on the water. A successful manufacturer and inventor from Rising Sun, Indiana, he developed and raced wood-hulled speedboats from about 1909 into the 1920s. Several versions of his *Hoosier Boy* gradually re-defined the speed records for this class of boat throughout the era. "Row" experimented with various hull designs and engines, always looking for the next mile per hour of speed. (North 30.)

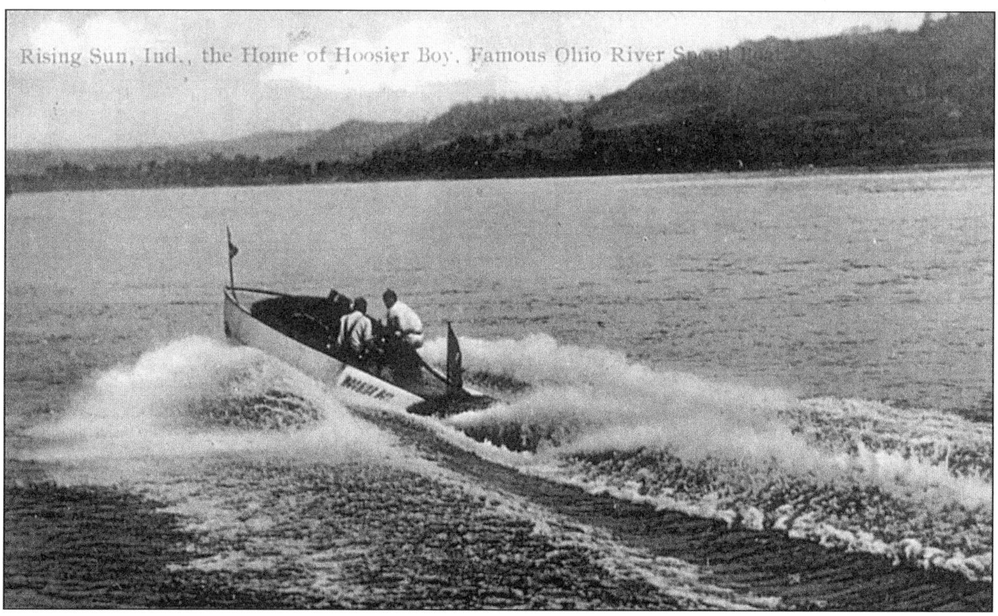

Early versions of the *Hoosier Boy* attained an unheard-of speed of 23 to 25 miles per hour by 1910. "Row" regularly entered and won match races on the Ohio River and other nearby venues during the pre-World War I era. The hull above begins to show some evolution away from typical craft of the era. (North 31.)

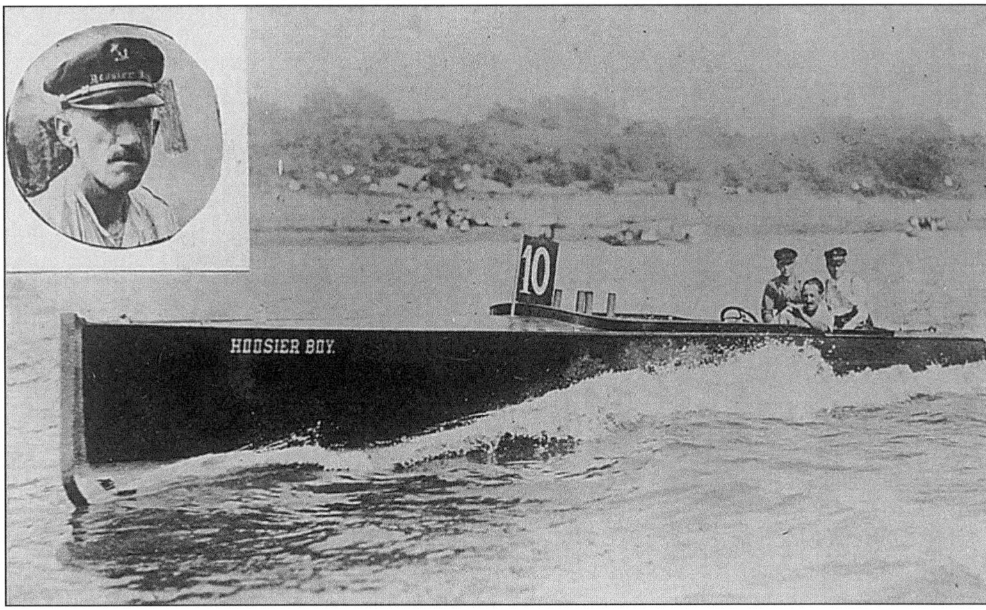

Here is another version of the *Hoosier Boy* with Row's profile in the upper left portion of the photo. This hull design, powered by a 75 horsepower Buffalo Speed Engine, is very pointed in the bow. The engine is set further back for balance and to reduce drag. (North 32.)

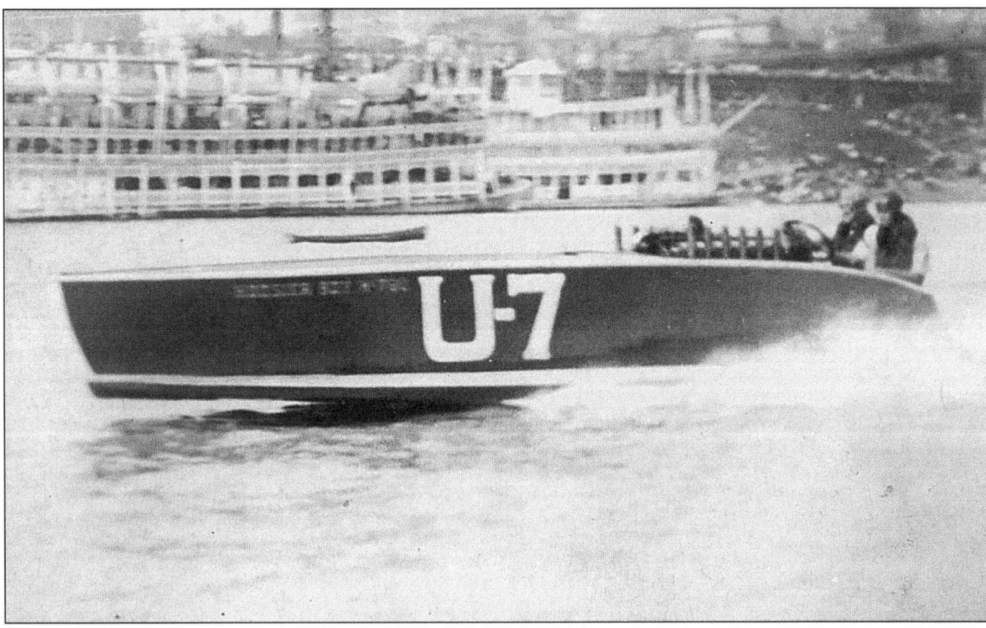

On October 9, 1924, just prior to the opening of the dams on the Ohio River between Cincinnati and Louisville, the *Hoosier Boy* made a round trip from Cincinnati to Louisville in 267 minutes and 49 seconds. This works out to an average speed of a few seconds slower than 60 miles per hour. This record has never been beaten. Dams since built on the river have prevented later attempts. This picture was taken in Louisville, Kentucky, but probably not during the record run. (North 33.)

Six

"THE BIG ICE" THAT CLEARED THE RIVER

Ice, even more than high water, was the most feared and respected force of nature to be faced by people who made their living from the river. A long, cold, frigid winter would diminish the amount of precipitation and run-off from melting snow that maintained the water level in the Ohio River. This would lead to very low water levels, especially before the system of navigational dams was completed in 1929.

What would start as a thin skin of ice on the still water would quickly thicken, sometimes freezing all the way to the bottom of the river in low spots. Water expands as it freezes, and as the ice thickens, it places enormous pressure on any hulls and structures it encases. Heavy, prolonged ice, especially when followed by a rapid warming of temperatures and accompanying heavy rain, was a recipe for disaster. This scenario was the fate of the river, the packet boats, and all else in the path of the ice in the winter of 1917–1918.

The following images chronicle the beauty of the river in winter that masks these powerful, destructive forces. When spring finally came in 1918, the valley was never again the same.

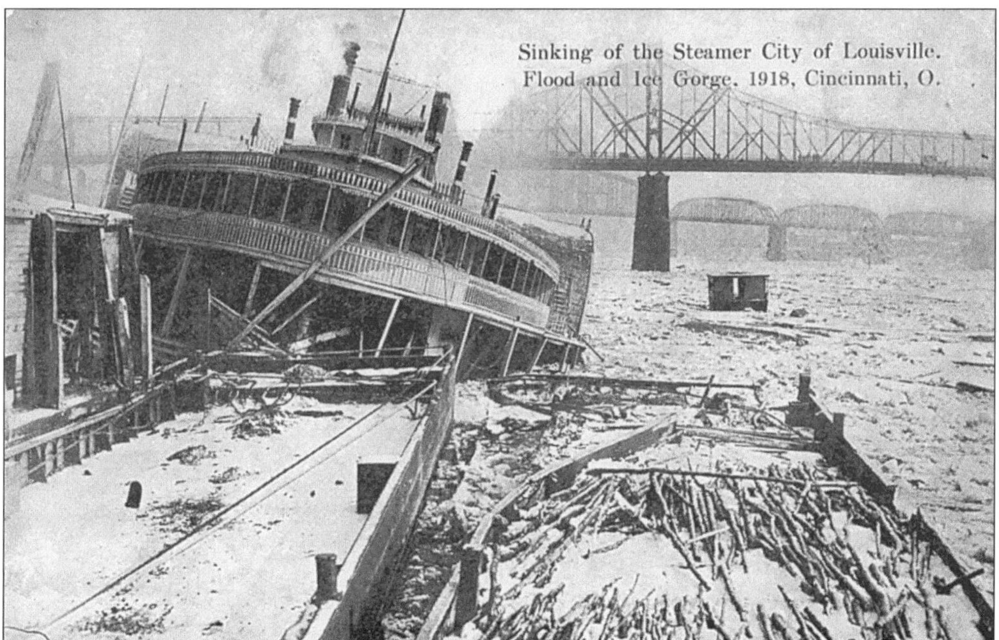

The end of the "big boat" at the Cincinnati Public Landing is shown on January 30, 1918.The *Str. City of Cincinnati* met a similar fate nearby. Wood-hulled boats and barges were not a match for the massive force of ice driven by rising water.

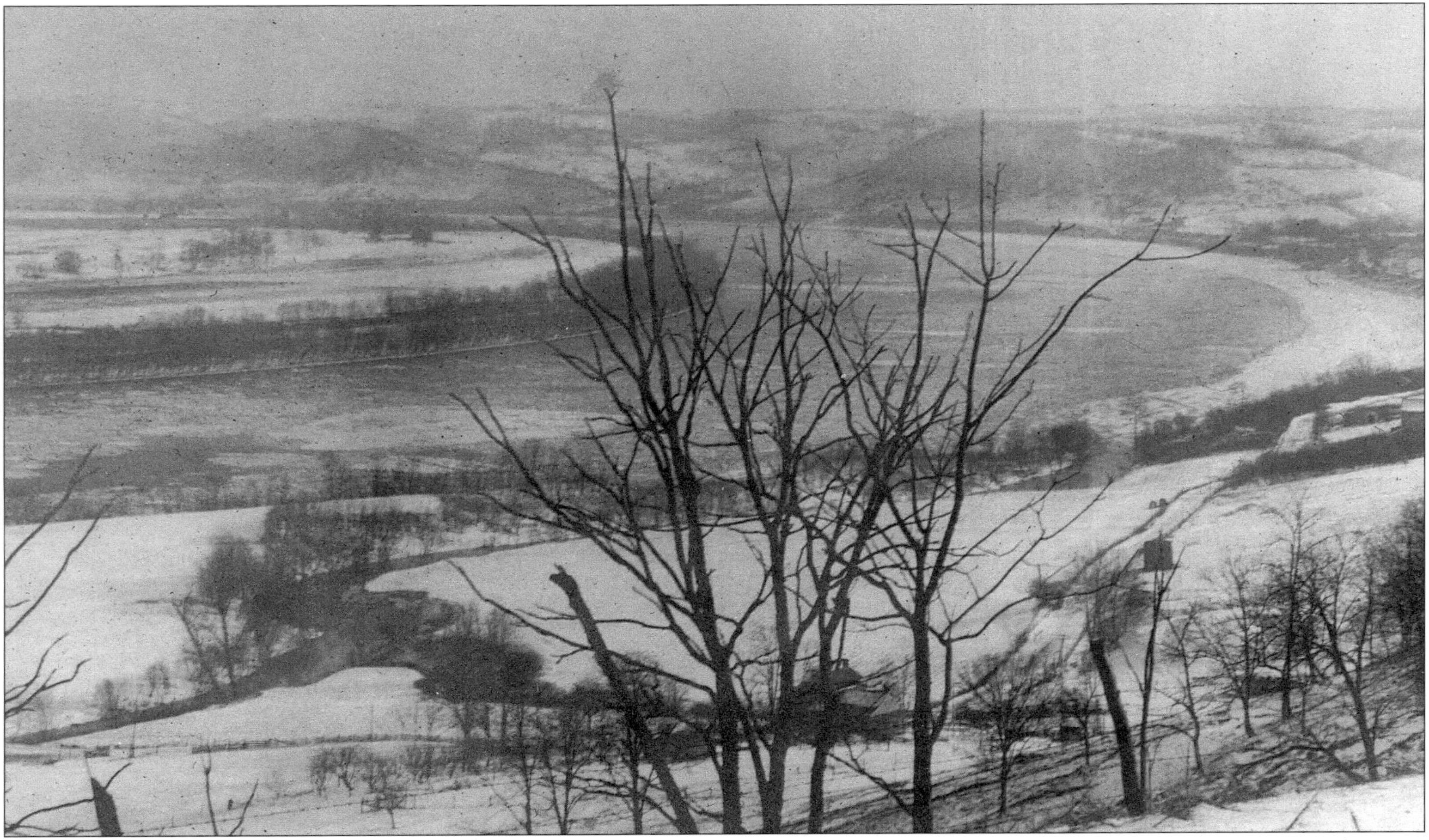

The beauty of ice and snow on the Ohio River Valley is seen below Rising Sun, Indiana, in the early 1900s. A thin skin of ice covers the river, with some open water still visible. Thicker ice, that would prevent boats from landing, has formed in the still water along the outside of the bend on the Indiana shore.

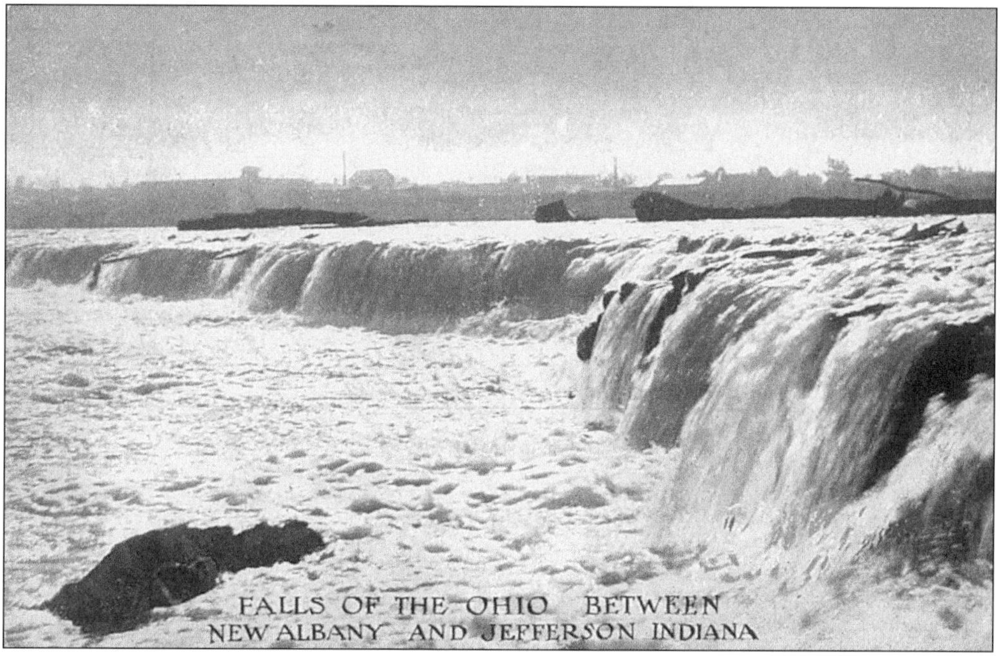

The beautiful Falls of the Ohio are stopped here by cold temperatures.

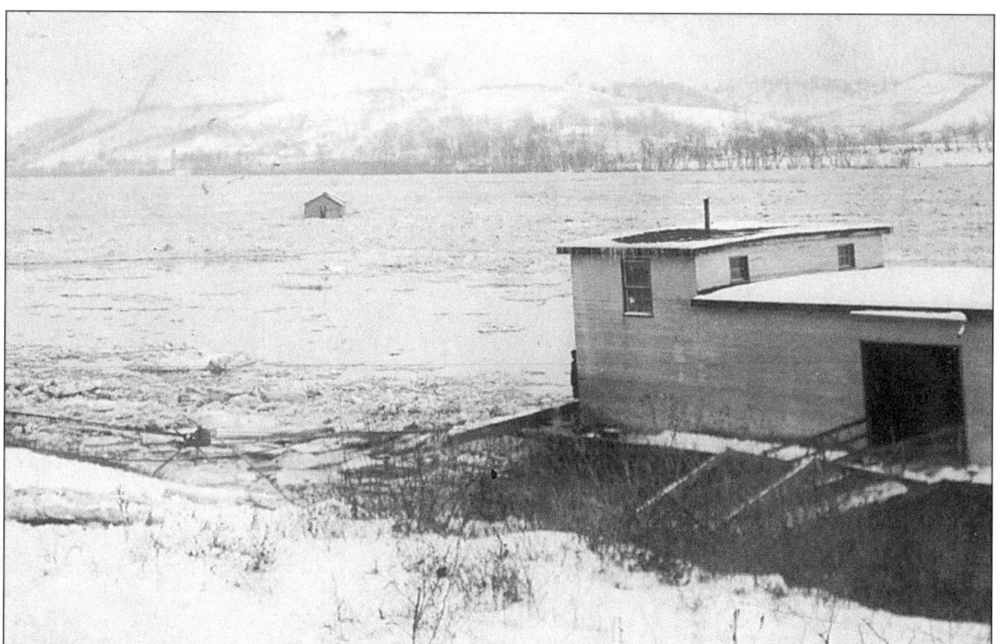

The ice of 1910 was not as thick or long lasting as that of the winter of 1917–1918. The weather broke with warm rains. The wharfboat at Vevay, Indiana, rides safely tied to shore as the river rises and the ice is flushed away. The building floating downstream was possibly lifted out of a tributary stream that was more solidly frozen, impeding the run-off of the thawing rain.

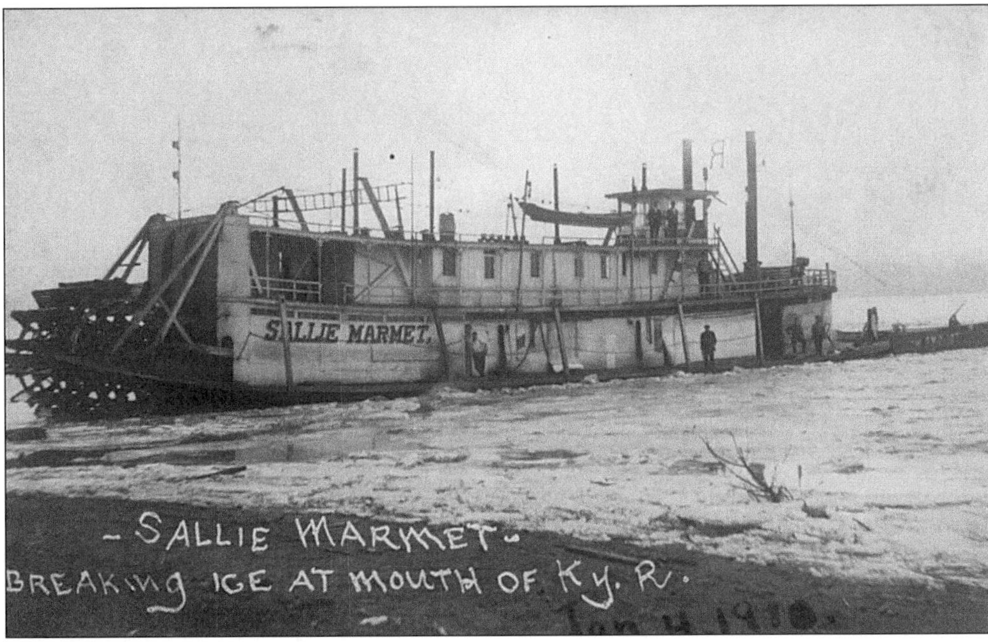

Steamboats were successfully used to keep ice broken up around boats and barges laid up in smaller tributaries during earlier river freezes, like here in 1910. This technique had only limited success in 1918. The rapid freezing of the low water level prevented some boats from seeking safer harbors. The depth to which all the tributaries froze eliminated some previously safe harbors.

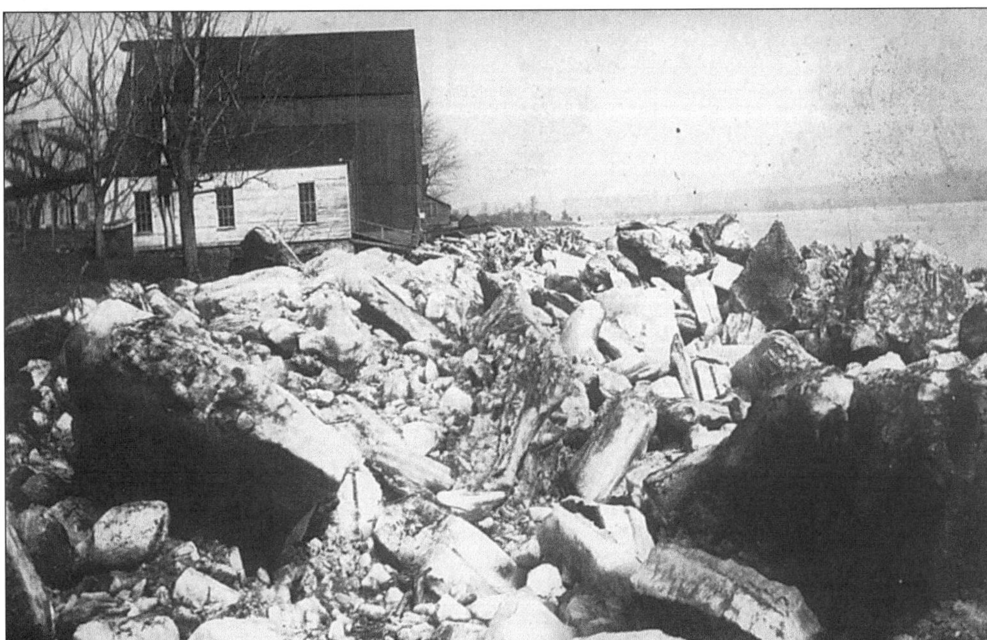

Shore ice is usually left behind when the river thaws. An old river saying was that "the river will come back to reclaim ice left on shore." Usually, this was correct. Warm rains and higher water accompanied most breakups of river ice, raising the river level and washing the ice away.

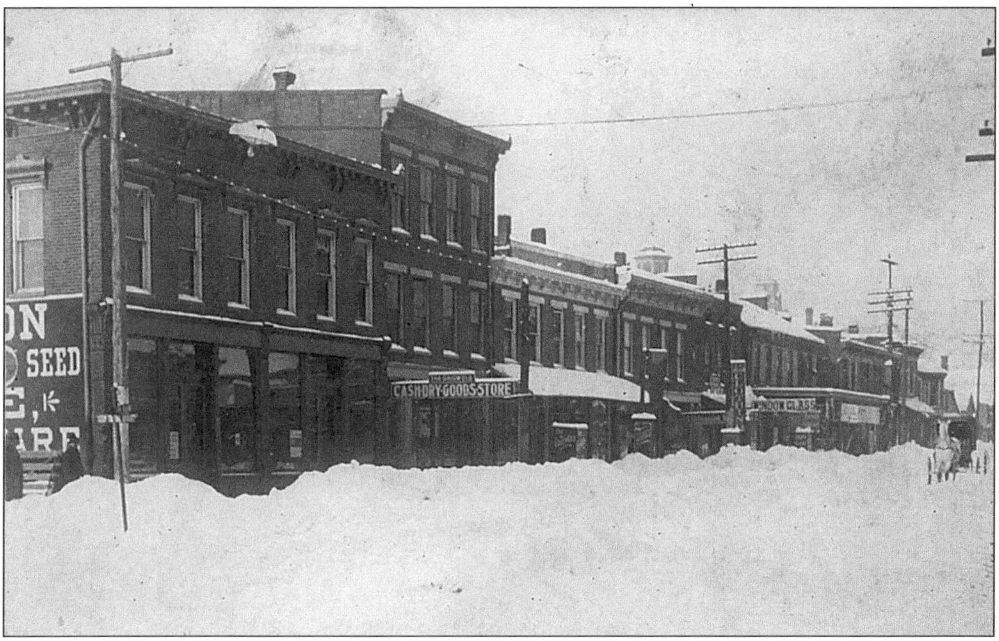

Rising Sun sleeps under a blanket of winter white in early January, 1918.

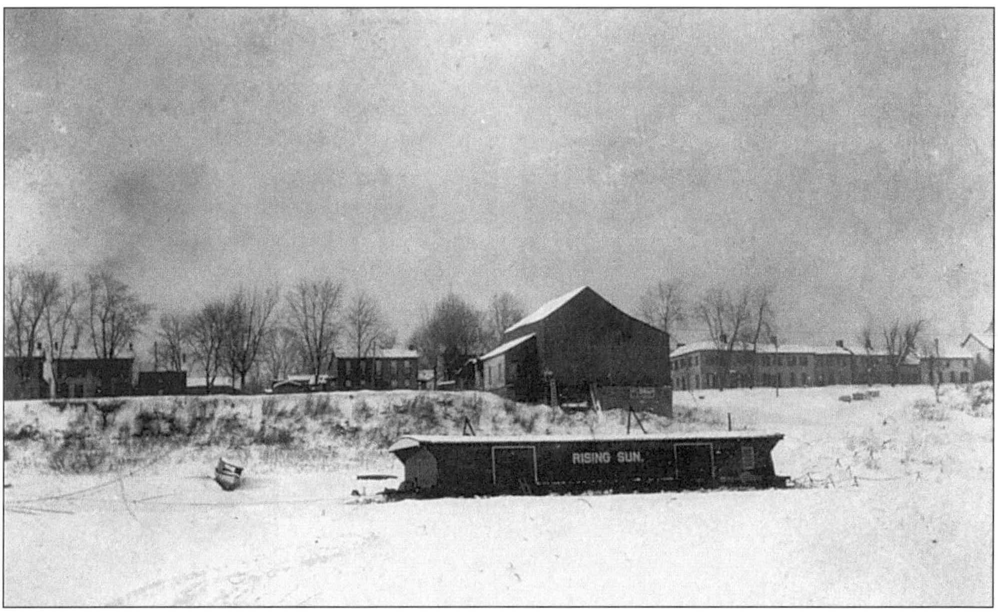

The wharfboat at Rising Sun, Indiana, froze tight in the winter cold early in 1918. The river level was low when the cold weather began. It froze through to the bottom in many spots, creating a tremendous amount of ice that would later block the flow of warm rains. Tracks on the ice in the lower left corner of this view are from people crossing the solid river to and from Rabbit Hash on the adjacent Kentucky shore. (North 34.)

Ray and Viola Bedgood posed standing on the ice pack at Rising Sun, Indiana, just as it began to buckle and rise into a gorge. An ice gorge is a natural dam created when accumulated ice blocks the flow of water. Ray was a riverman all of his life, and ran the local ferry until service was discontinued during World War II.

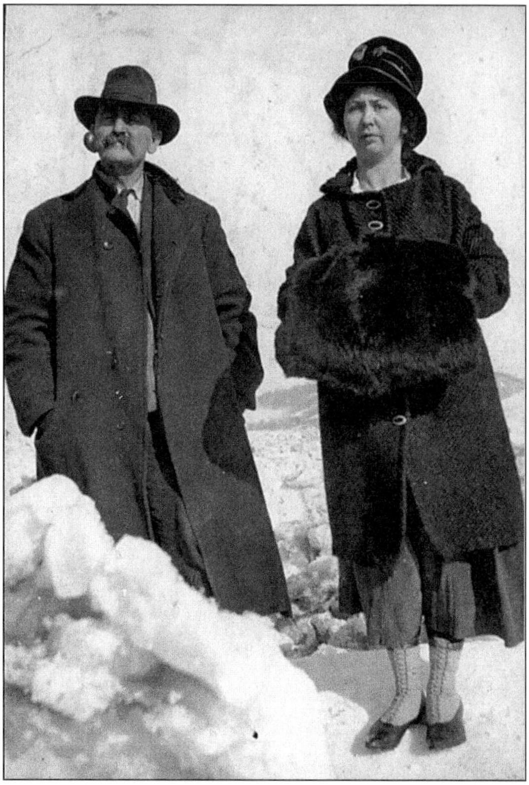

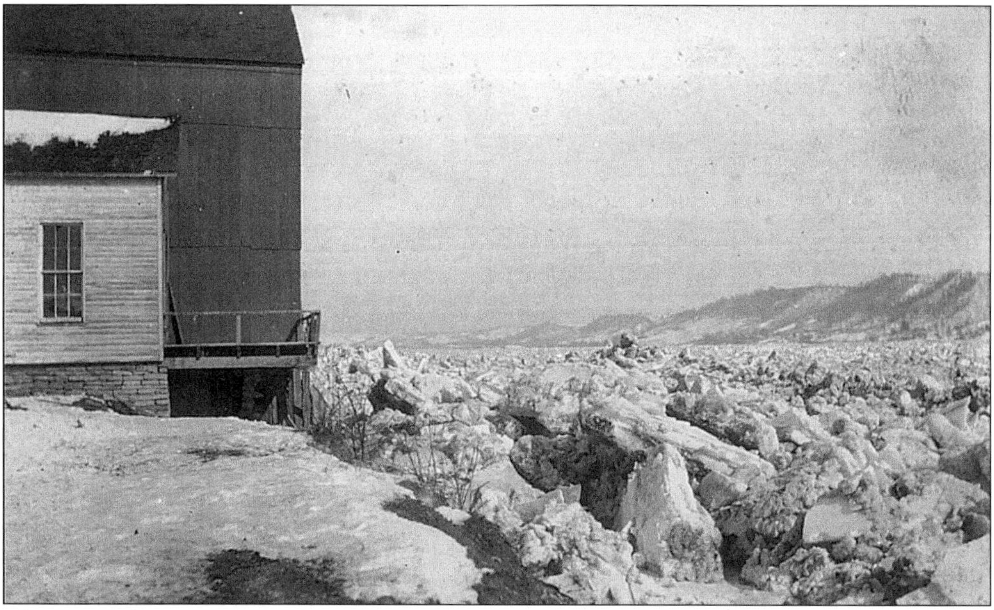

This is another view of ice building along the shore at Rising Sun, Indiana. The underlying water level had risen several feet since the river first froze. The rising water backed up behind huge piles of buckling ice, creating natural barriers that would soon unleash their destructive forces.

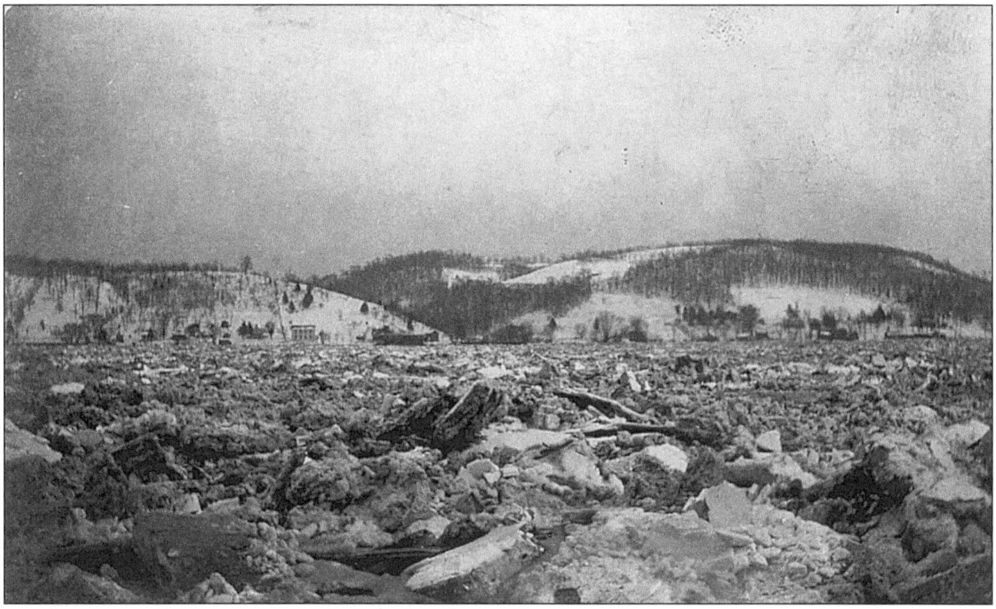

Ice builds adjacent to Rising Sun, Indiana, driven by floodwaters raising the river level. The smooth layer that had formed earlier buckled and heaved under tremendous pressure, creating a natural dam that held back additional ice from upriver. (North 35.)

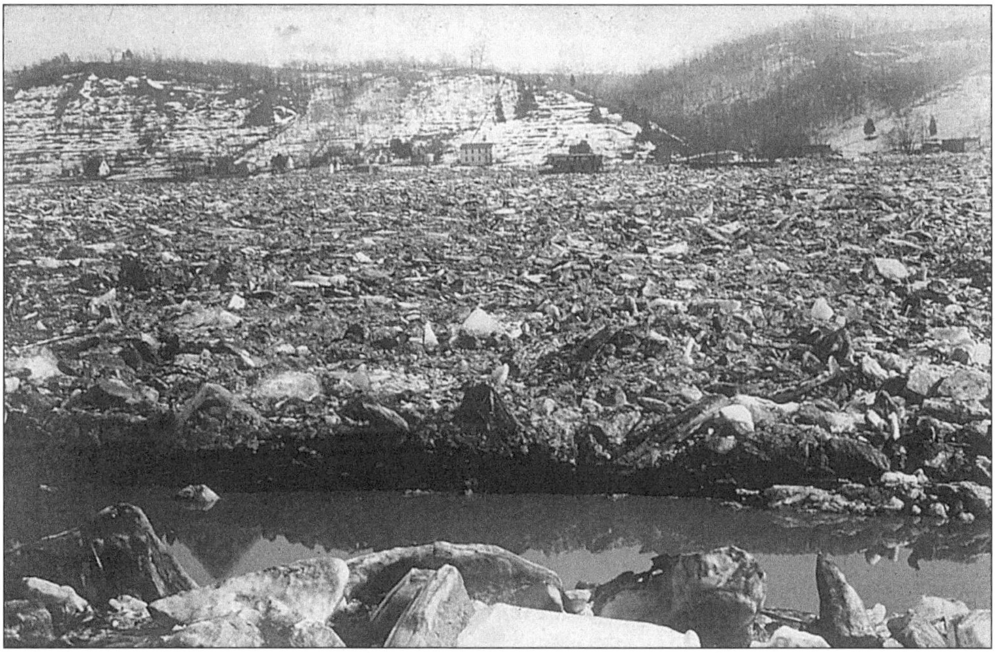

The picture above was taken a day or two later as the river continued to rise, further breaking the ice into smaller chunks. Free-flowing water is now visible in the foreground. Soon the ice dam would break under the increased strain.

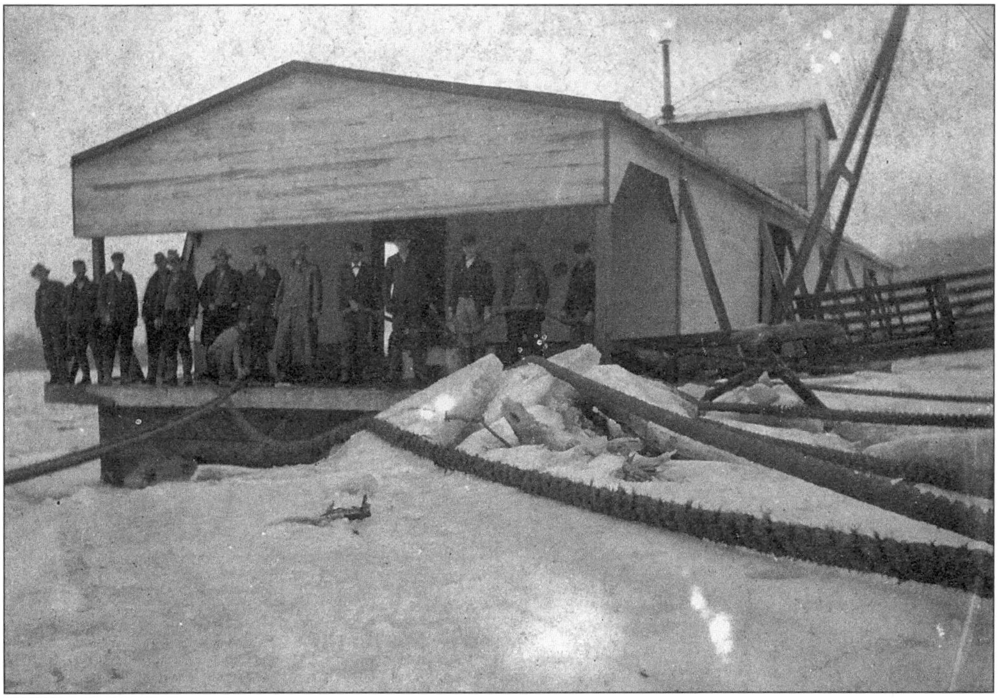

Here, the men of the North's Landing community survey the smooth, frozen river from the deck of the North's Landing wharfboat. The river was very low early in this big freeze. It was frozen down to its bottom. Extra lines run off towards the lower right to shore in hopes of keeping the wharfboat from breaking free.

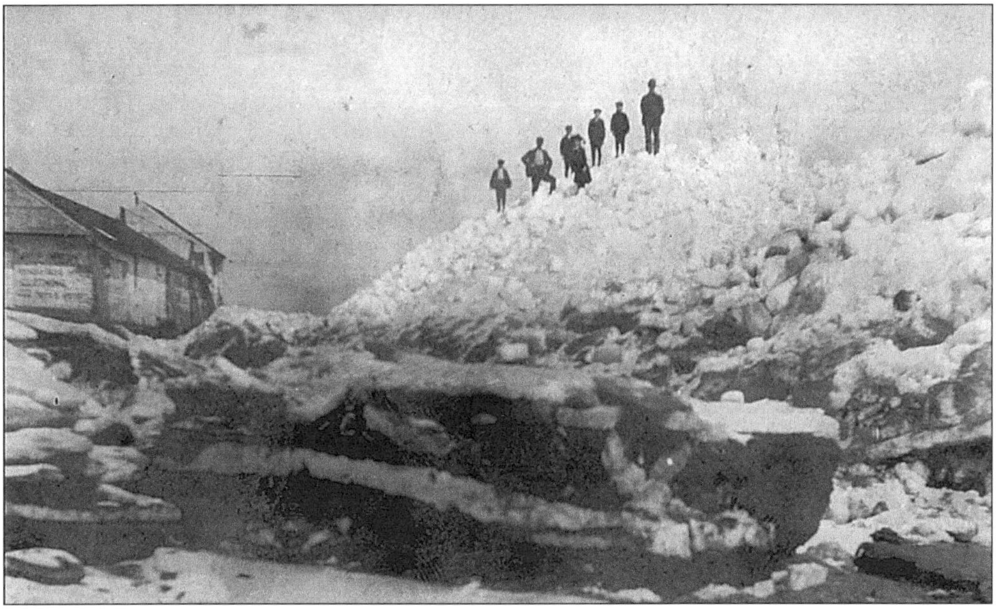

Ice continued to pile up along the Indiana shore, creating a natural dam that resisted the rising floodwaters arriving from upriver. When this ice gorge finally broke during the wee hours of early morning darkness, it created hours of loud cracking and grinding sounds that have not been heard since in the river valley.

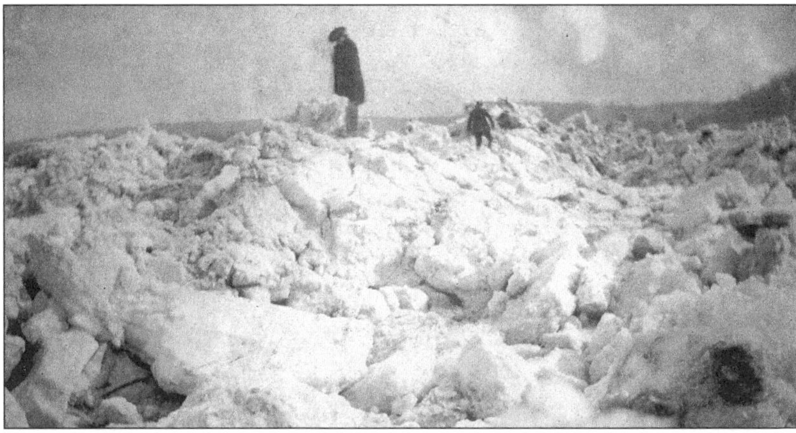

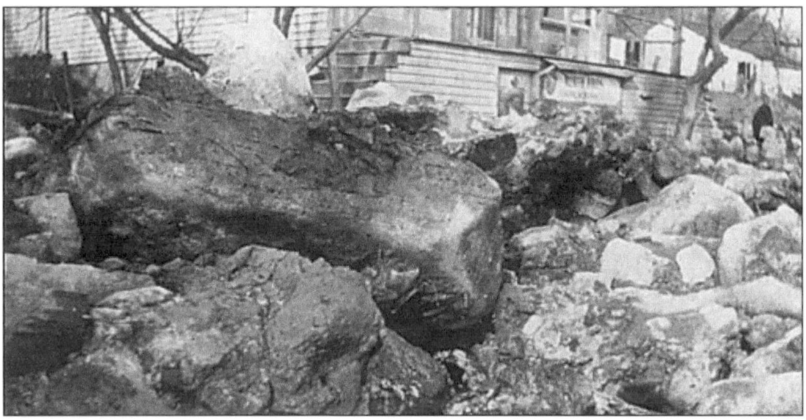

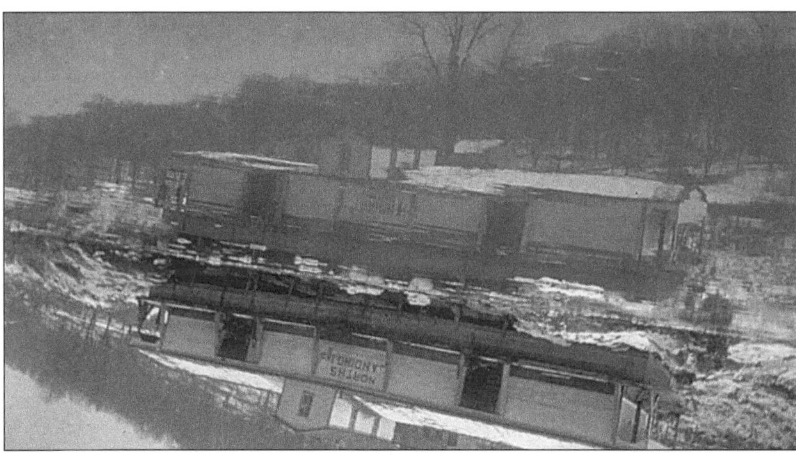

An unidentified man surveys the ice gorge above North's Landing just prior to its breaking. Ice was pushed up on shore next to the store. The wharfboat was pulled out onto shore near the flood crest. It later was dismantled due to severe hull damage. The North business closed the next year.

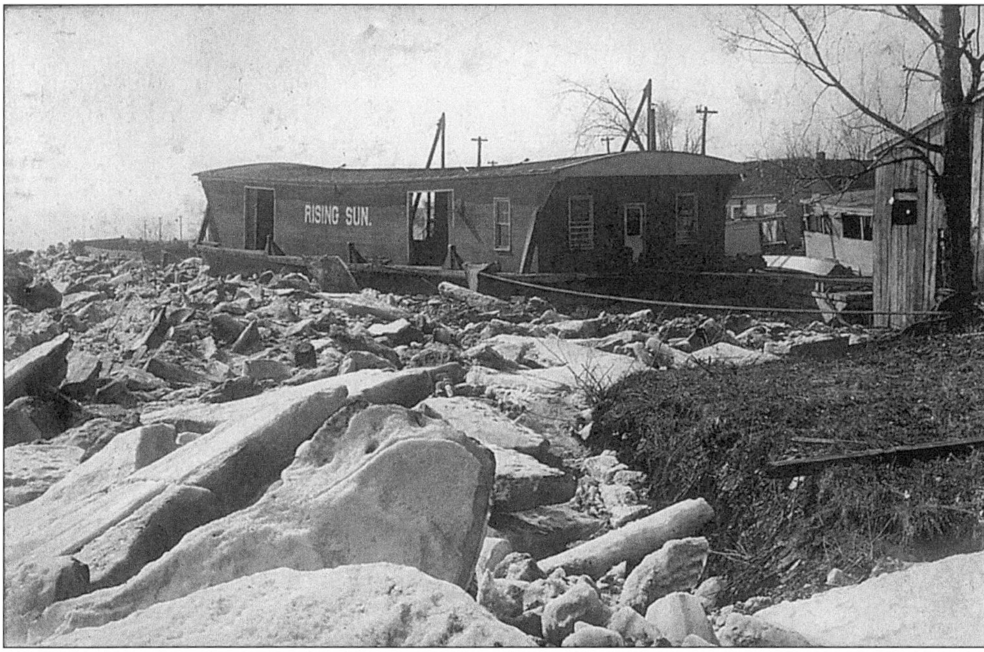

The wharfboat at Rising Sun, Indiana, was pushed to the top of the bank as ice flowed past on the flood crest. It was repaired and placed back in service.

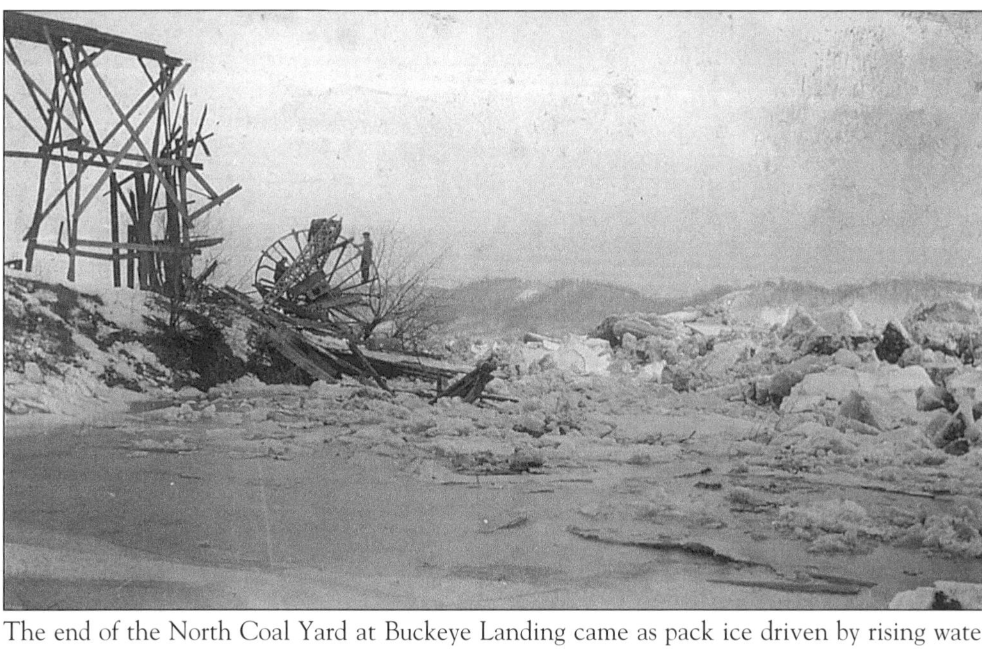

The end of the North Coal Yard at Buckeye Landing came as pack ice driven by rising water crushed the coal facility. The business was sold and moved to Rising Sun by its new owner later in 1918. This was the fate of many small river enterprises.

Seven
FLOODS

Flooding is the most frequently experienced natural disaster faced by those who live and work along a river. The annual rise caused by the thawing of accumulated winter snow, accompanied by spring rain, often reaches into towns and villages along the shore.

The gentle coming of spring, with a gradual warming accompanied by periodic light rains, lets the Ohio River carry water on its way to the Mississippi River, and then to the Gulf of Mexico without leaving its banks. Unfortunately, many spring seasons are marked by a rapid warming accompanied by heavy rains on the frozen ground. Water rapidly drains off the land. The smaller rivers and creeks that drain into the Ohio become large torrents of water. By the time the water from the east reaches the broad, flat, river valley below Cincinnati, it spreads out into the fields and towns along its banks.

Prior to the 1929 completion of the system of navigational dams on the Ohio River, the spring rise ran its course downriver without obstruction. These dams, although not specifically built for flood control, did provide some ability to manage the smaller spring rises. They were no match for the larger spring torrents of water.

The following images are from the floods of 1907 and 1913, before the dams were built. The flood of 1918 is covered in another chapter as a part of the story of the great ice of that year. Images from the greatest flood of 1937, well after the completion of the navigational dams in 1929 and the end of daily packet service, are also included because of their significance in the lives of those who lived along the river.

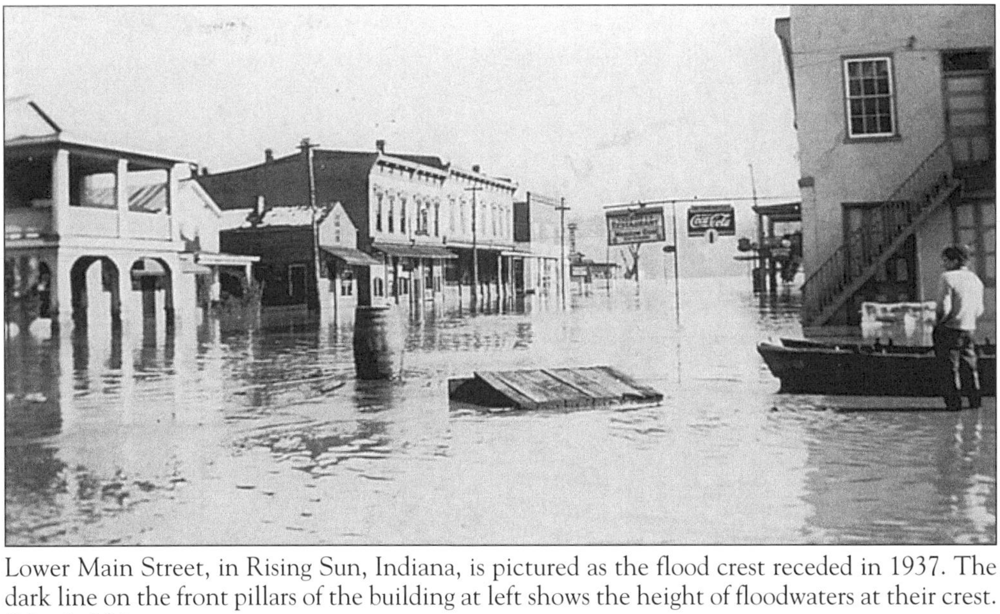

Lower Main Street, in Rising Sun, Indiana, is pictured as the flood crest receded in 1937. The dark line on the front pillars of the building at left shows the height of floodwaters at their crest. (North 36.)

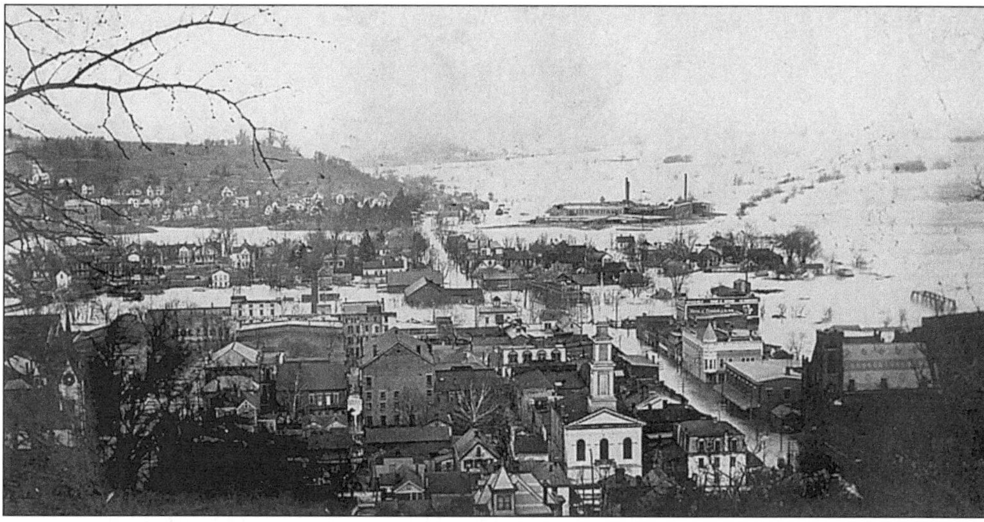

Aurora, Indiana, shows the dangers of being situated on low ground near the mouth of a creek during the flood in 1907. The water reached a depth of 62.1 feet on the Cincinnati, Ohio gauge.

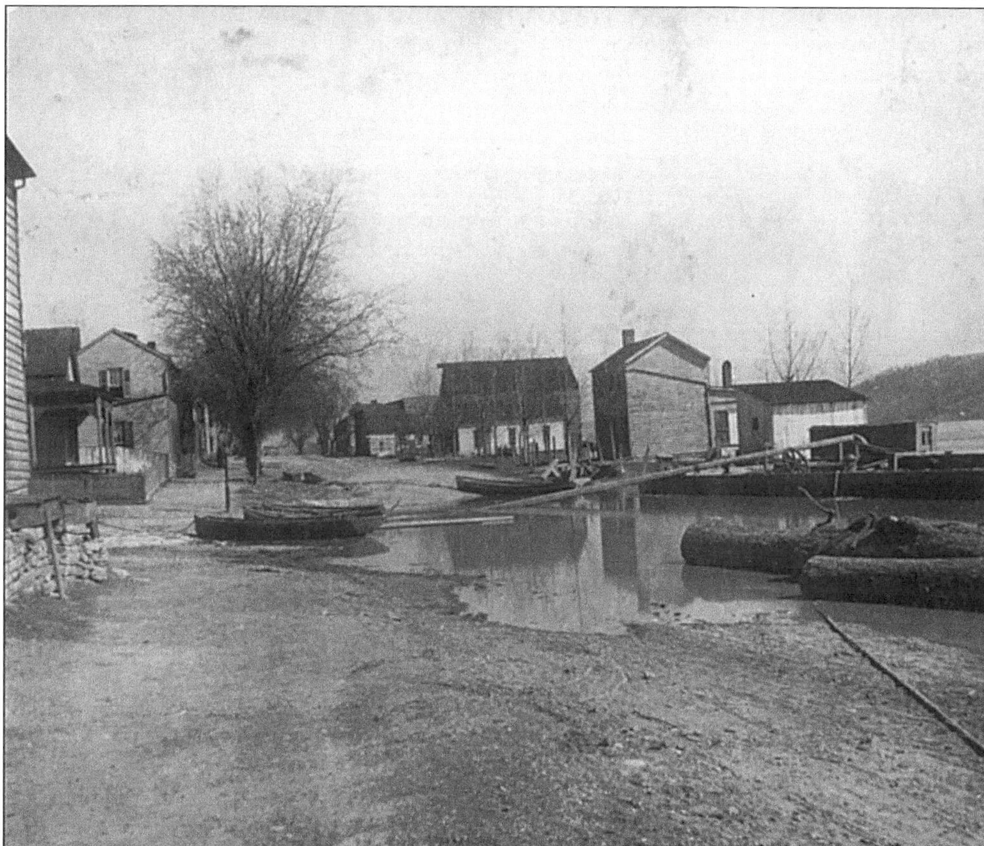

Rising Sun fared better in 1907, given its relatively high elevation above the normal or "pool" water level in the river. Water just began to creep onto Front Street, but for the most part stayed out of buildings.

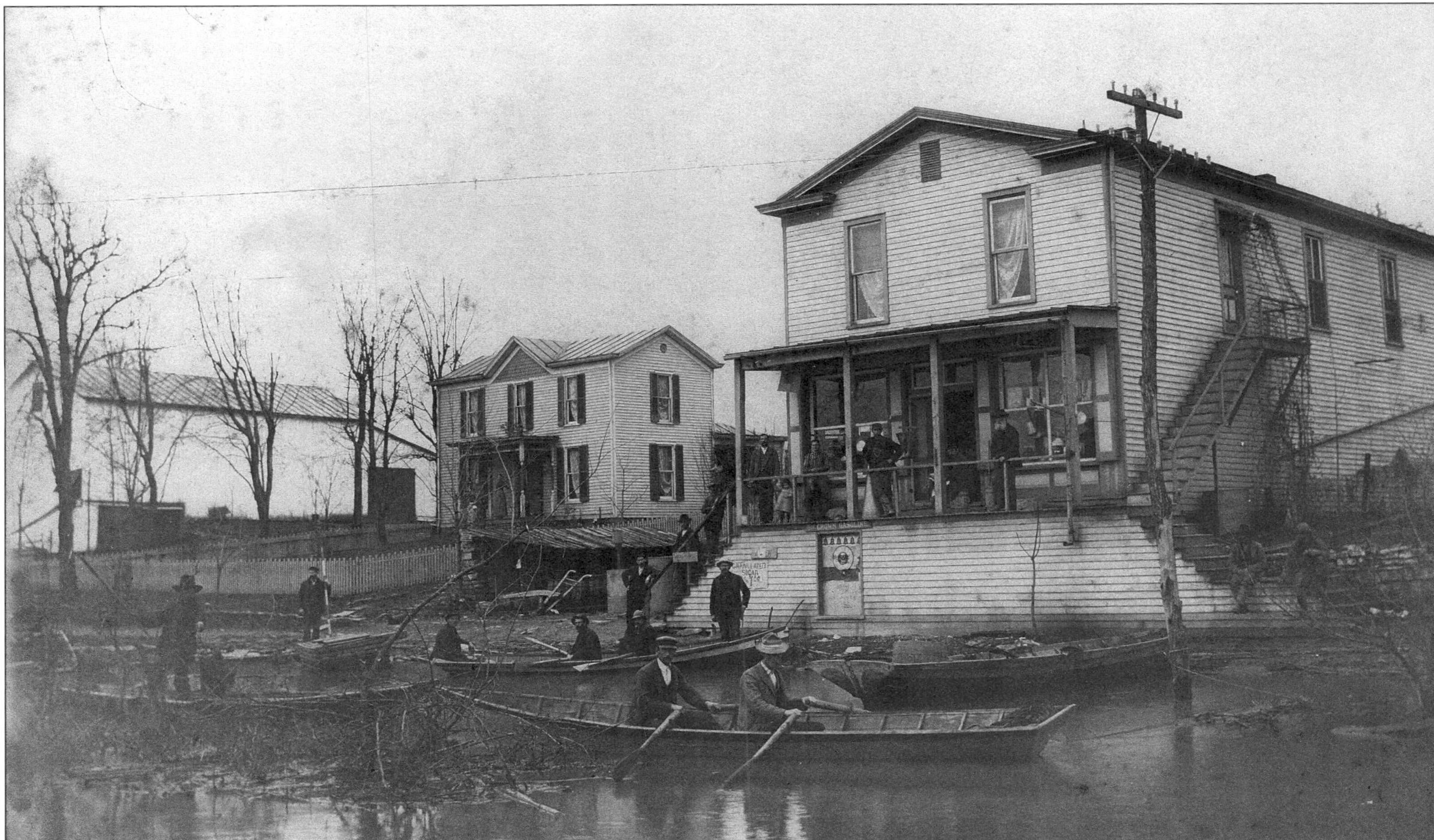

The floodwaters of 1907 reached the base of the North Store's front porch at North's Landing, Indiana. Benjamin Grant North is standing at the far left on the porch with six-year-old Pearl North (Stegemiller), the author's grandmother, peeking under the porch rail at his right. The other people in this view are unidentified, but some are probably additional members of the North family.

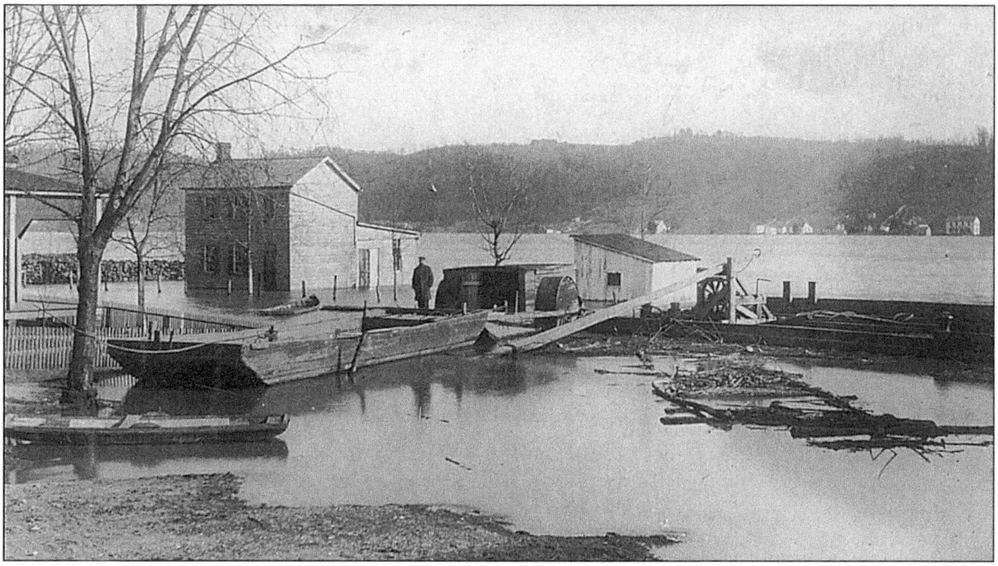

The flood of 1913 reached 69.9 feet on the Cincinnati gauge. Buildings on the river side of Front Street in Rising Sun, Indiana had water on their main floors for the first time. This was the highest recorded water level for the river up to that date.

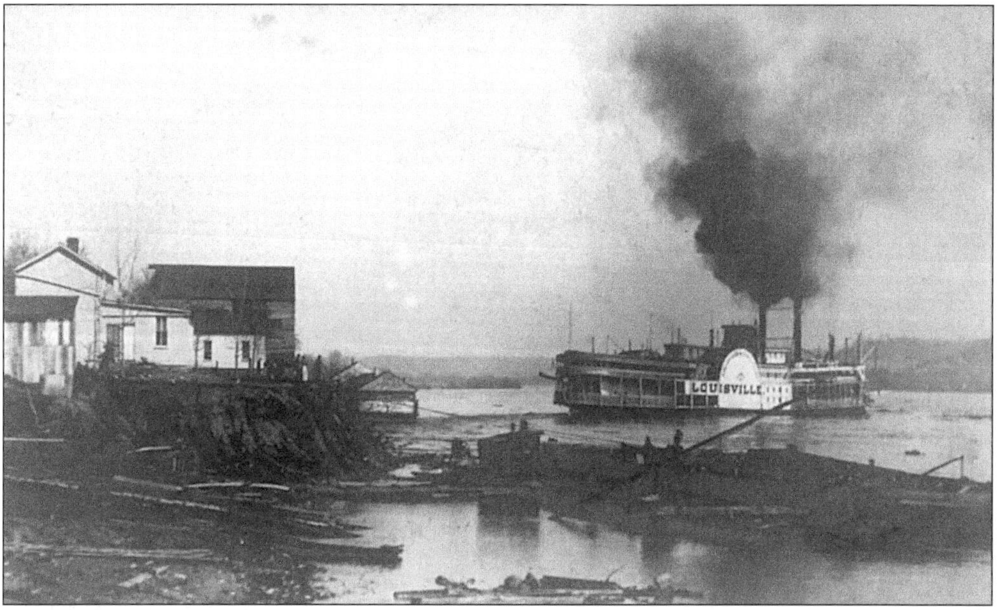

The *Str. City of Louisville* maintained service in the area during the flood of 1913. Above, she is carefully moving away from the wharfboat at Rising Sun, Indiana. Swift, high water filled with floating debris challenged the pilot's ability to control the boat. (North 37.)

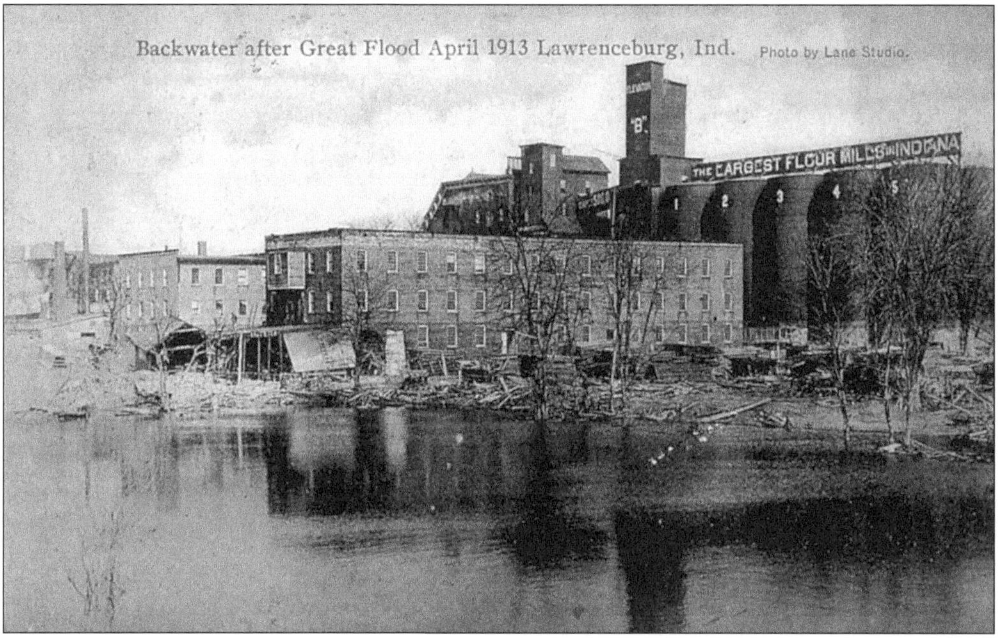

Lawrenceburg, Indiana, was again inundated by flood waters in 1913, causing extensive damage. A major flood control levee was constructed around Lawrenceburg in the 1920s. Usually, however, the river wins out over man. The levee was no match for the flood crest of 1937.

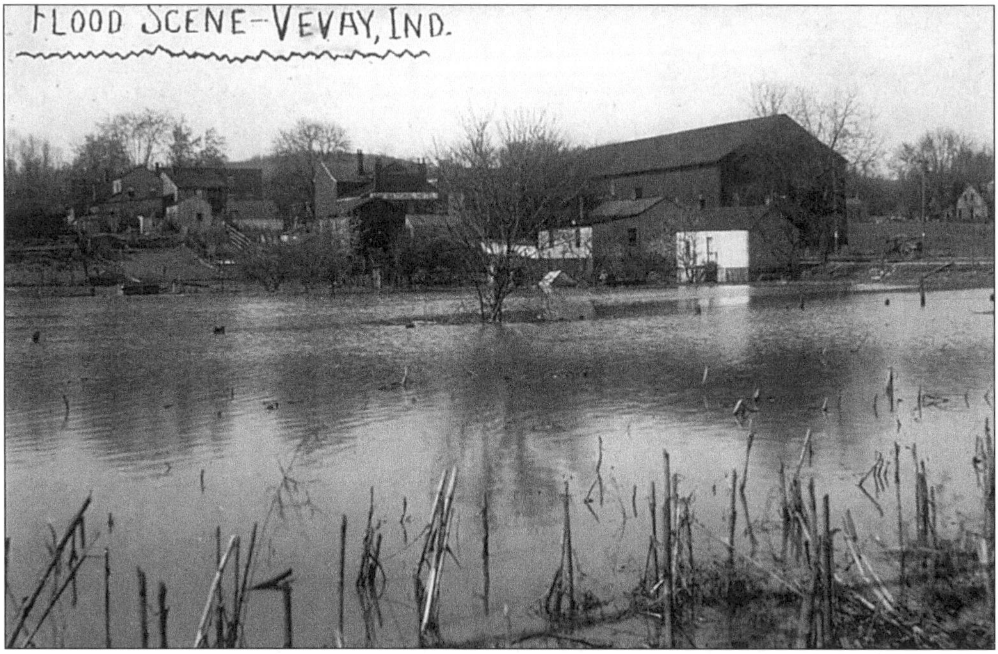

Vevay, Indiana, remained relatively secure from damage in 1913 because of its high elevation. However, farms and buildings on its outskirts were submerged.

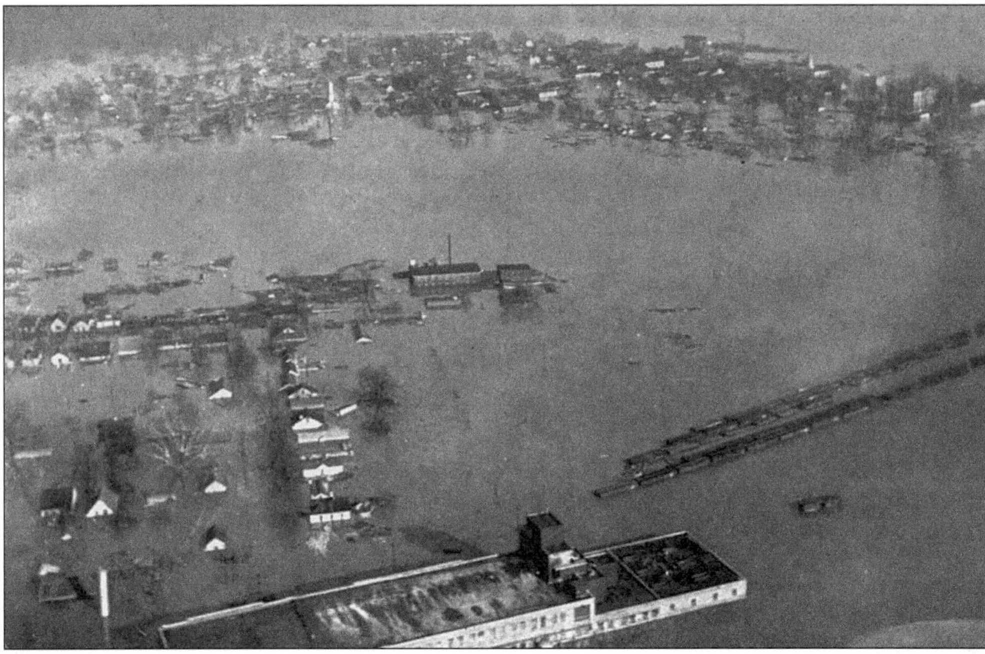

The great flood of 1937 crested on January 26th with 80 feet of water on the Cincinnati, Ohio gauge. The river has reached about seventy feet twice since then, but it has not returned to its 1937 level. The levee at Lawrenceburg was no match for the massive flood.

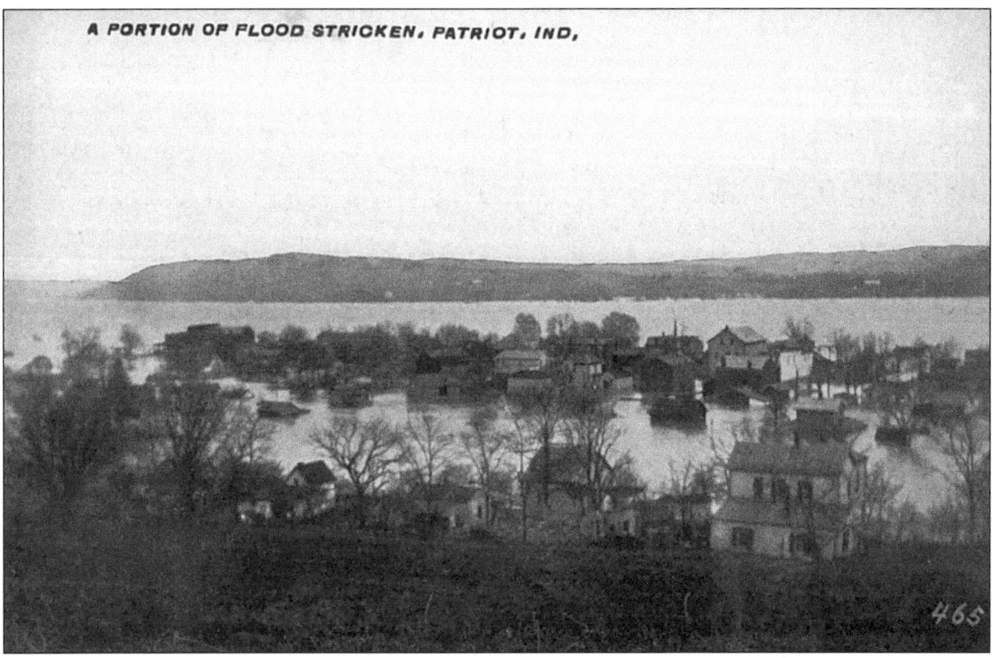

Floods always hit Patriot, Indiana, hard. Above, in 1937, almost the entire town was under water. Residents who lived through the flood of 1937 refer to it as the "great flood."

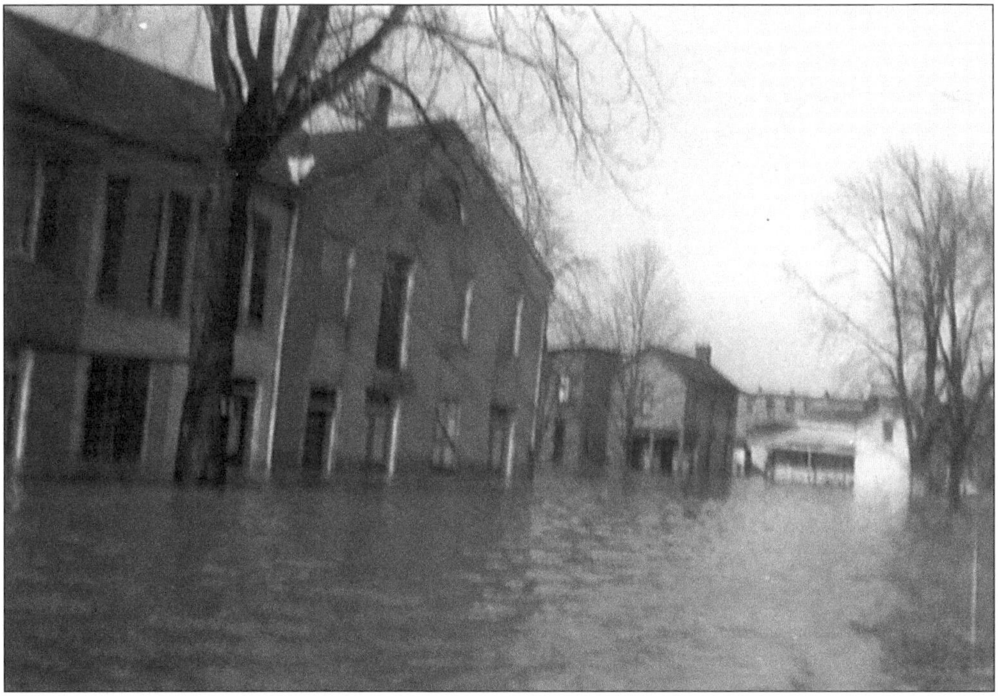

Upper Front Street in Rising Sun, Indiana, experienced water in the Hathaway Building at the corner of Main and Fourth Streets in 1937. Built prior to 1830 as a tavern and post office, it later became a private residence. Repaired after the flood, it is still in use today.

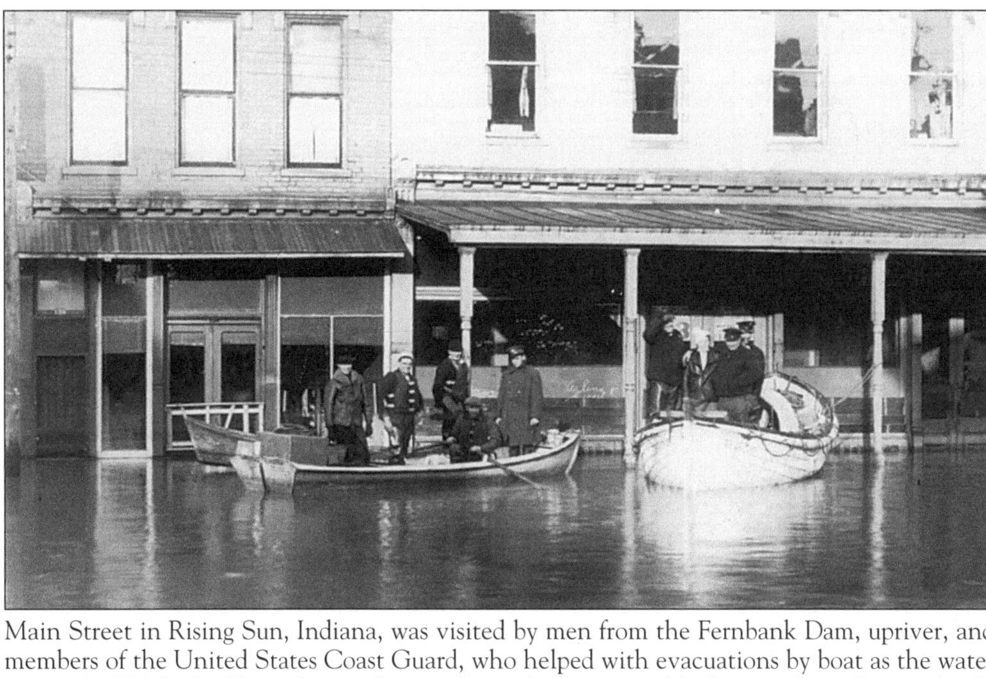

Main Street in Rising Sun, Indiana, was visited by men from the Fernbank Dam, upriver, and members of the United States Coast Guard, who helped with evacuations by boat as the water rose in 1937. The buildings shown above still stand, almost two blocks away from the riverbank. (North 38.)

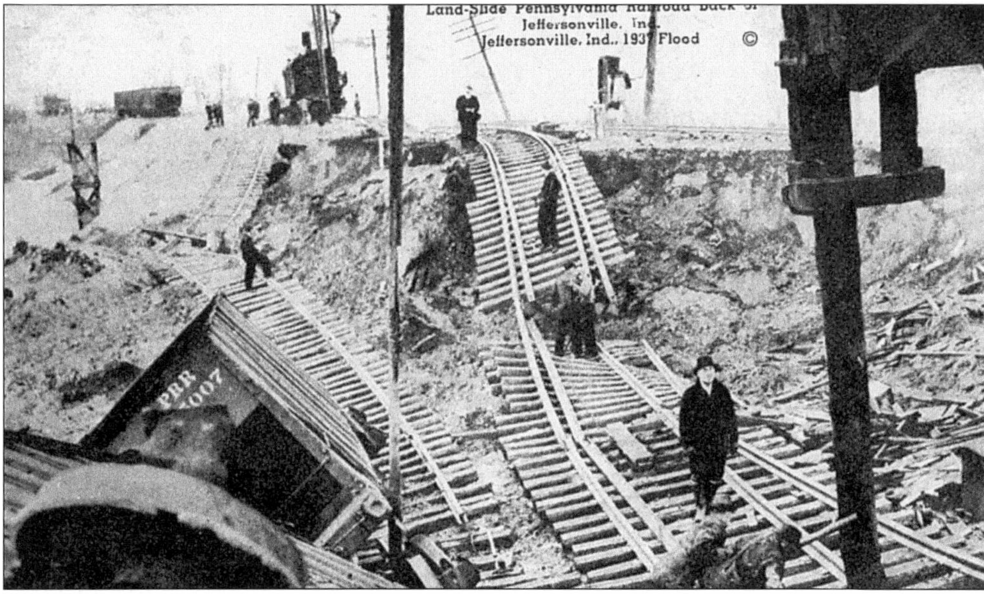

The power of floodwater is graphically illustrated above. The flood of 1937 left behind an estimated $65 million in damages throughout the river valley, back in the days when a dollar was worth something.

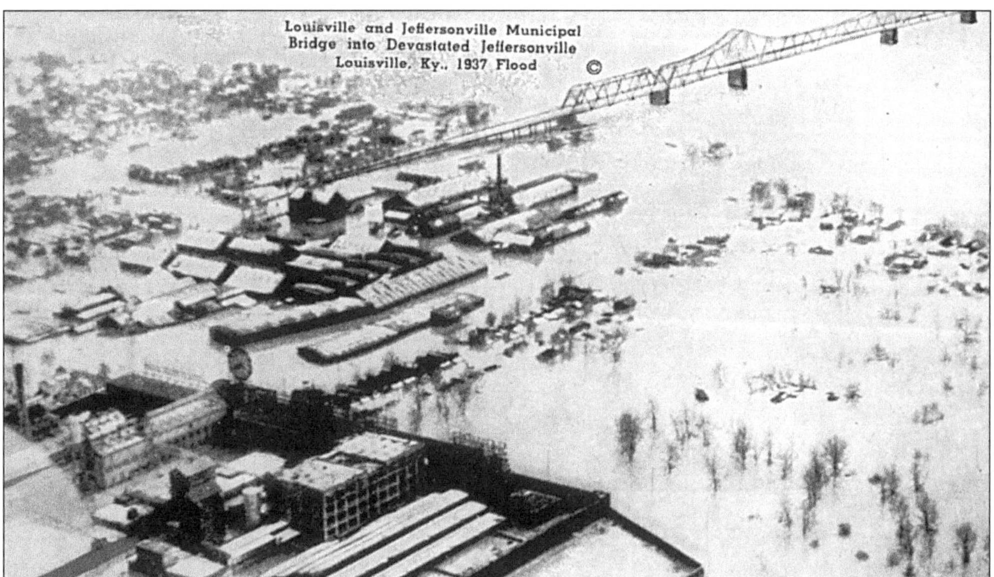

The above image of Louisville, Kentucky, says it all. Nineteen days of misery were followed by months of clean-up and repair. Flooding is the price you pay when you have a river in your life.

Eight

DAMS THAT TAMED THE RIVER

The Ohio River is the drainage system for the eastern parts of the Midwestern states. Until well into the twentieth century, water flowed uncontrolled down its valley towards the Mississippi River, and then to the Gulf of Mexico. Travelers had to plan their voyages around its winter ice, spring floods, and summer low water levels. Often, this meant not being able to consistently get people and goods where they were needed. As the number of people who settled along its shores increased, and the commerce carried on its waters became more important to the nation, the government began constructing dams and other aids to navigation.

The Falls of the Ohio in Louisville, Kentucky made up the biggest natural obstacle to navigation on the river. In 1830, the first canal and dam around this barrier were opened. These works were enlarged and expanded as the size and number of steamboats using the river increased.

The 1870s saw work begun on building dams on the upper Ohio River to provide a minimum water depth for navigation all year long. As a result, the river was finally controlled by a series of dams that provided a minimum of nine feet of navigable channels from Pittsburgh, Pennsylvania to Cairo, Illinois in 1929. Lock chambers at these dams were at least six hundred feet long and 110 feet wide. These dams, along with other channel improvements and markings, finally made year-round use of the river to haul large cargoes a reality.

The images in this chapter focus on the efforts to improve the flow of river traffic around the Falls of the Ohio in Louisville, and other dams built between that point and Cincinnati. They illustrate how these dams worked, and the development of better ways of moving cargo on the river.

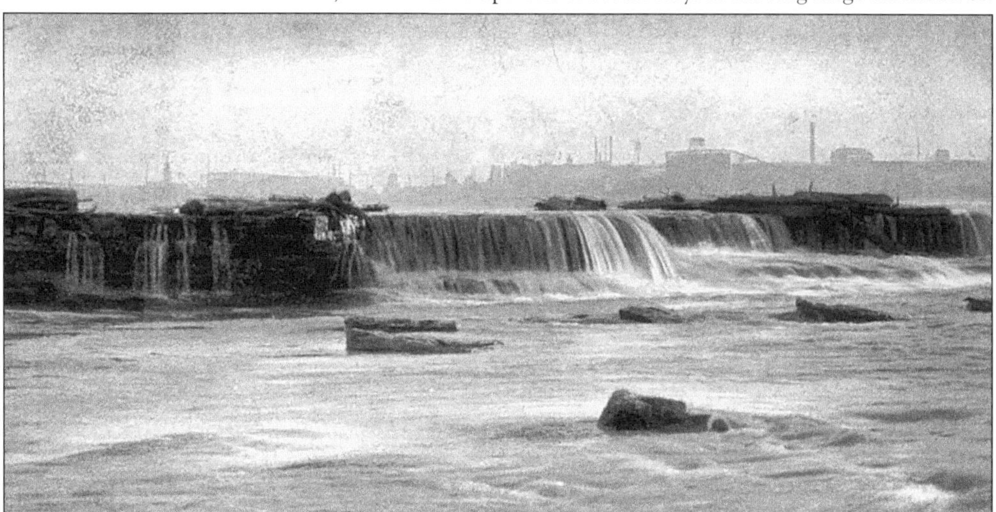

The Falls of the Ohio, adjacent to Louisville, Kentucky, are the largest natural obstacles to navigation on the Ohio River. The canal and dam that enabled passage around them are the earliest and most significant man-made aids to navigation on the river.

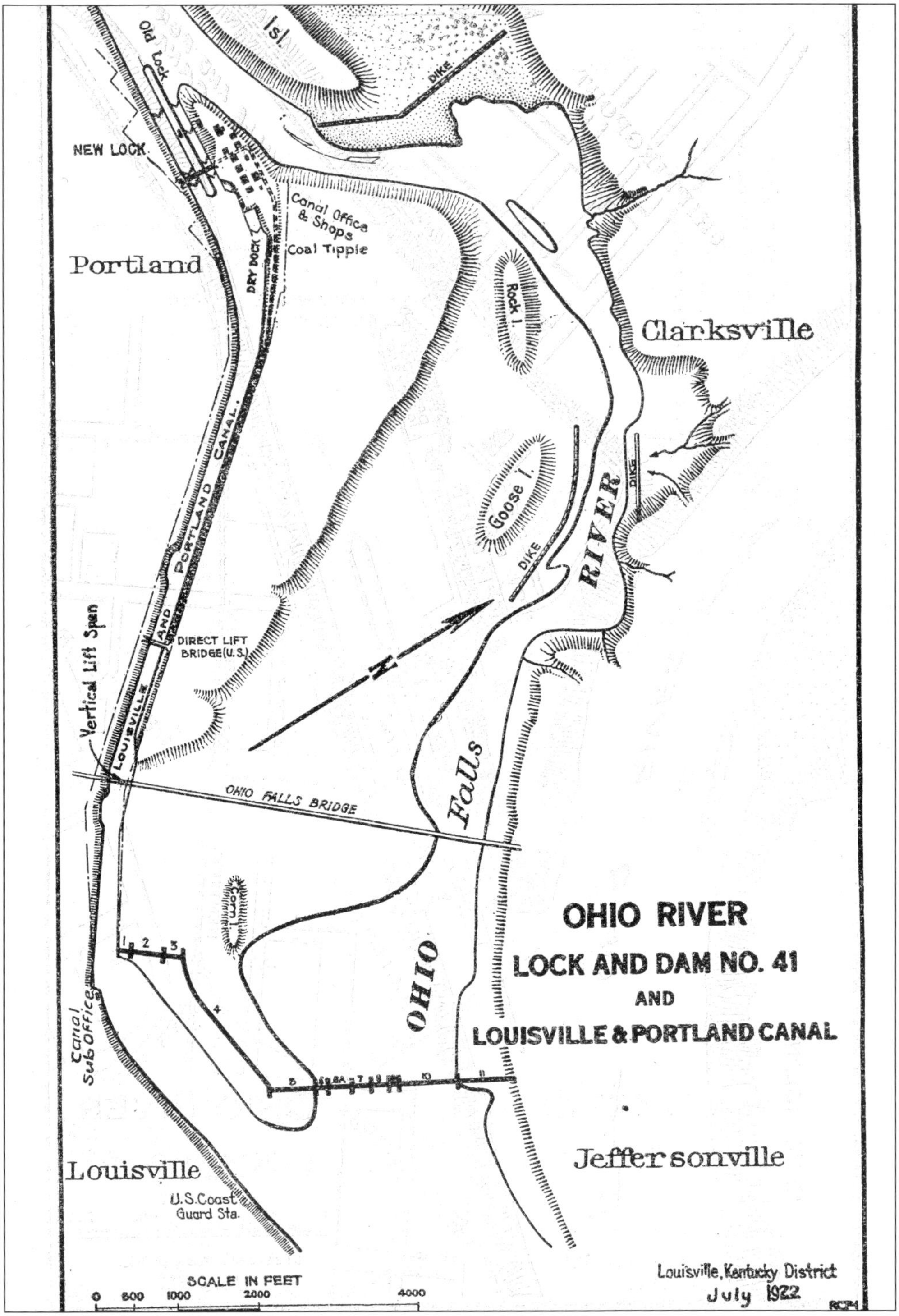

This diagram of the Portland Canal and Dam near Louisville, Kentucky, shows the major structures used to enable navigation around the Falls of the Ohio prior to 1922. The lock chambers built in 1870 were expanded to the new standard size in 1927.

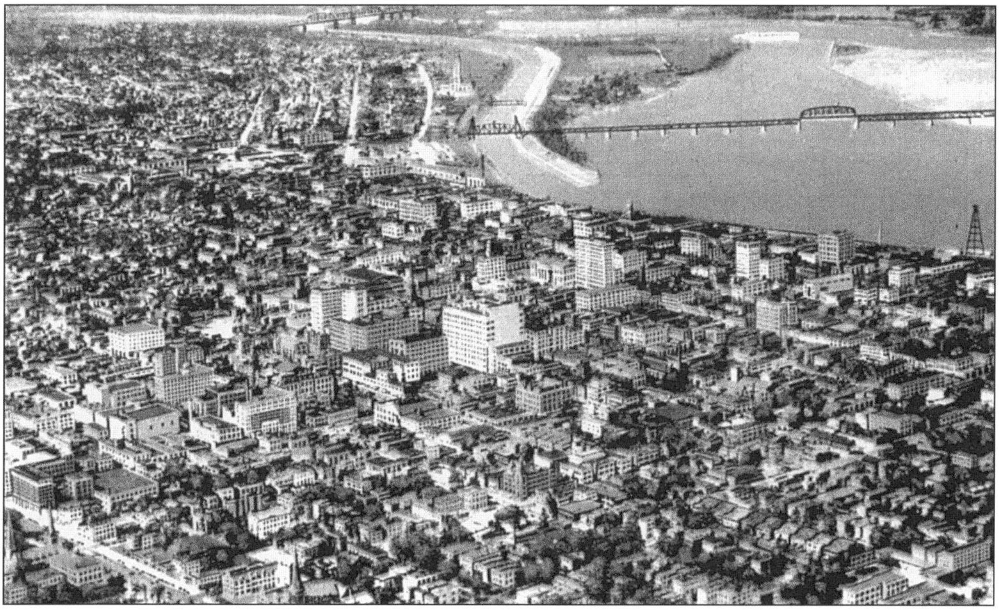

A later aerial view of Louisville shows the entrance to the Portland Canal with the hydroelectric power plant, built in 1927, in the upper left. The Pennsylvania Railroad Bridge crosses the river and the canal.

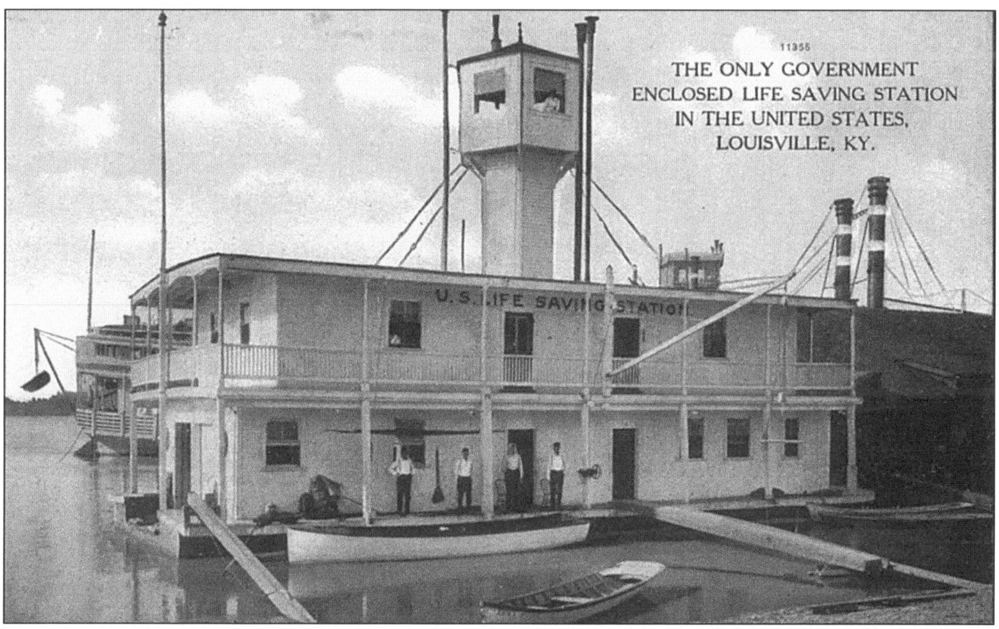

The unique design of the Louisville life saving station has been a fixture on the Louisville wharf since before 1900. Safety around the falls has been a concern ever since navigation began on the river.

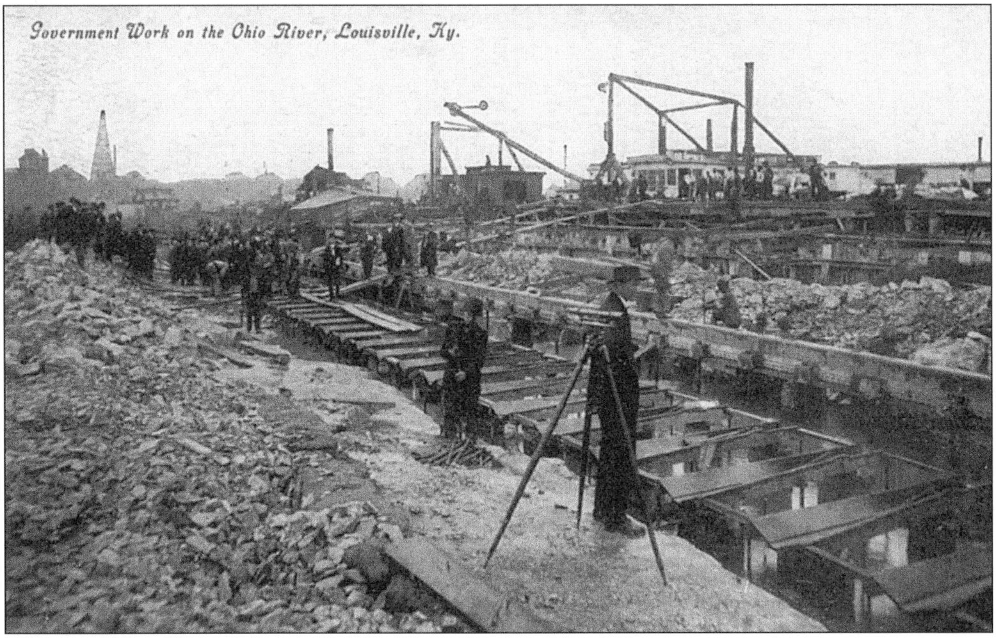

Gangs of men and steam cranes accomplished construction of the early dams. The rock-filled structure that runs diagonally towards the right is a temporary "coffer dam" used to hold back the river water, permitting the building of structures below water level.

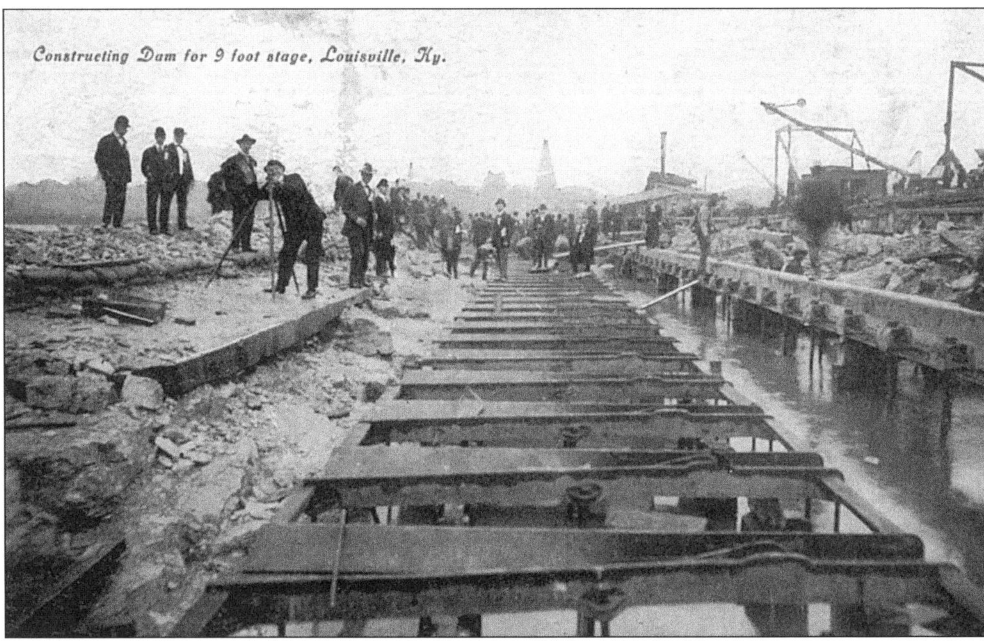

An engineer uses a surveying device to check the alignment of metal plates anchored to the river floor below water level. Wickets were added to this base, making a movable dam that could be raised and lowered to regulate the river level above Louisville as conditions warranted.

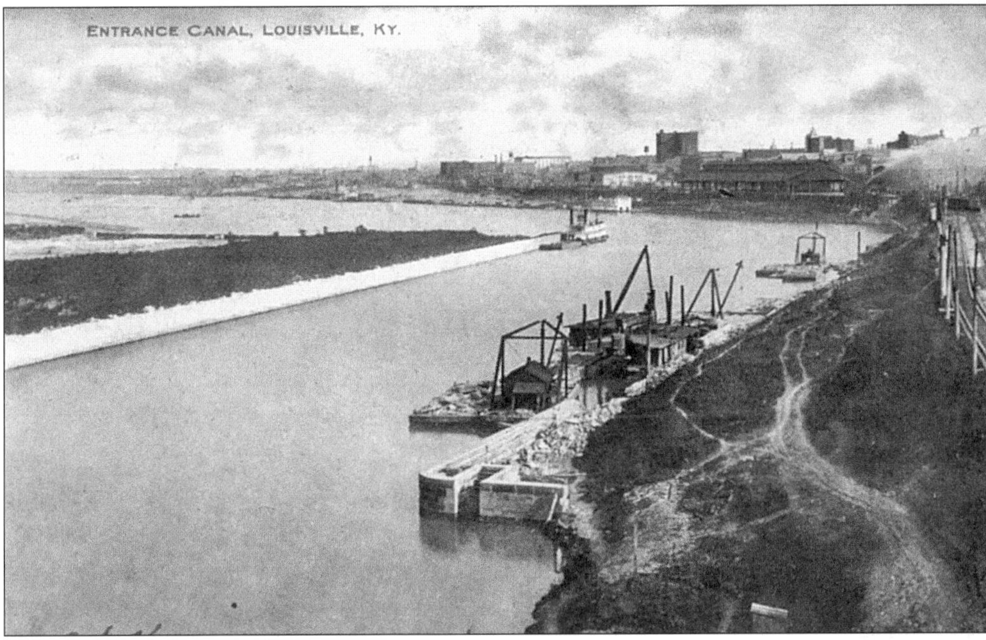

This view of the entrance to the Portland Canal, looking upriver towards Louisville, was taken in the early 1900s. The cranes on the barges were used to raise and lower the movable part of the dam.

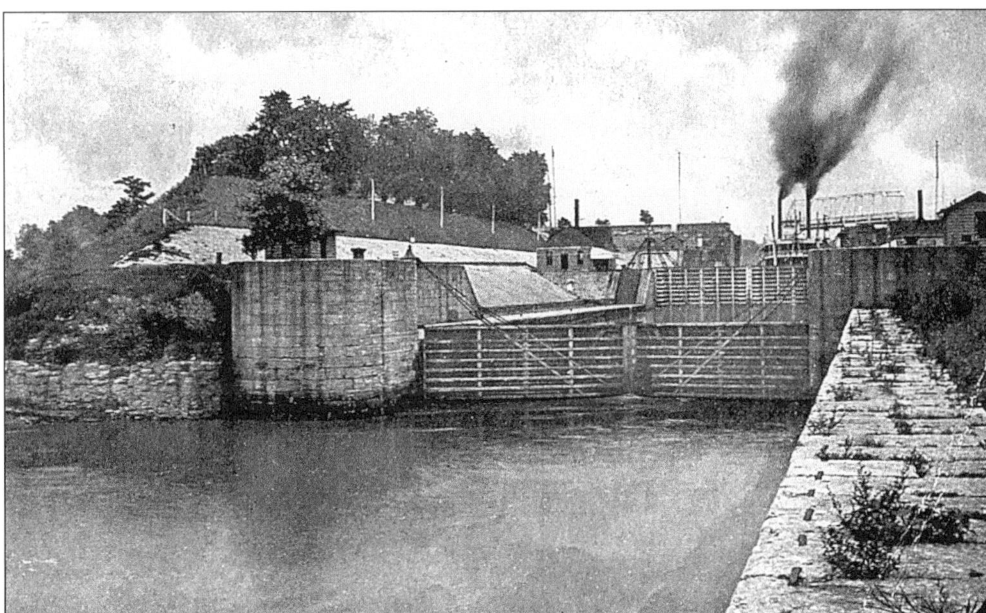

A steamer awaits the filling of the lock chamber at the end of the Portland Canal before "locking through" to move down. This chamber, constructed in 1879, was smaller than the minimum size required by the river-long system of locks and dams completed in 1929.

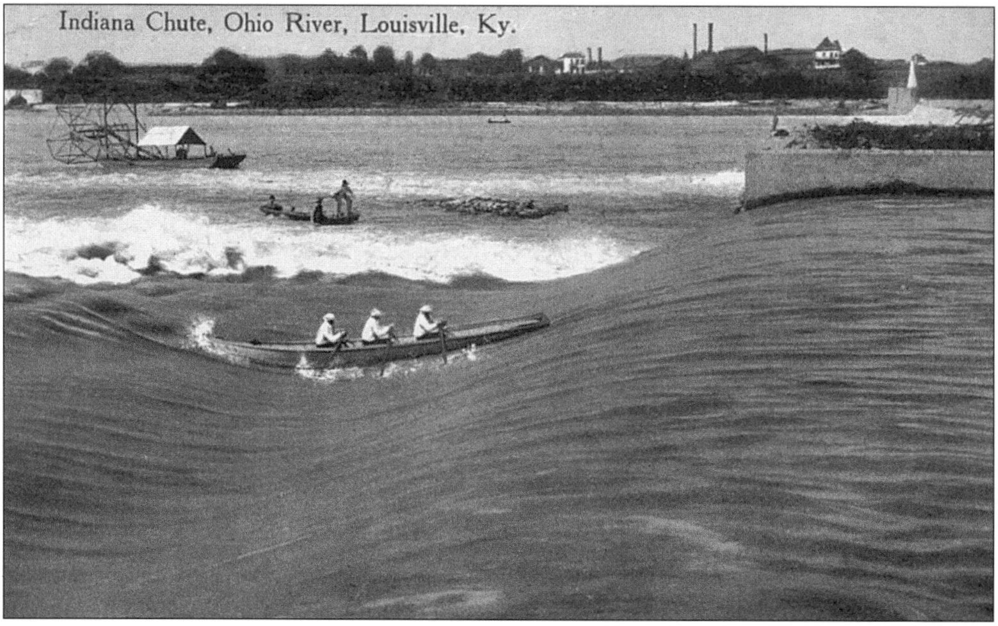

Water flowing over the top of the fixed dam built above the Falls of the Ohio provides a challenge for energetic rowers, and a thrilling ride.

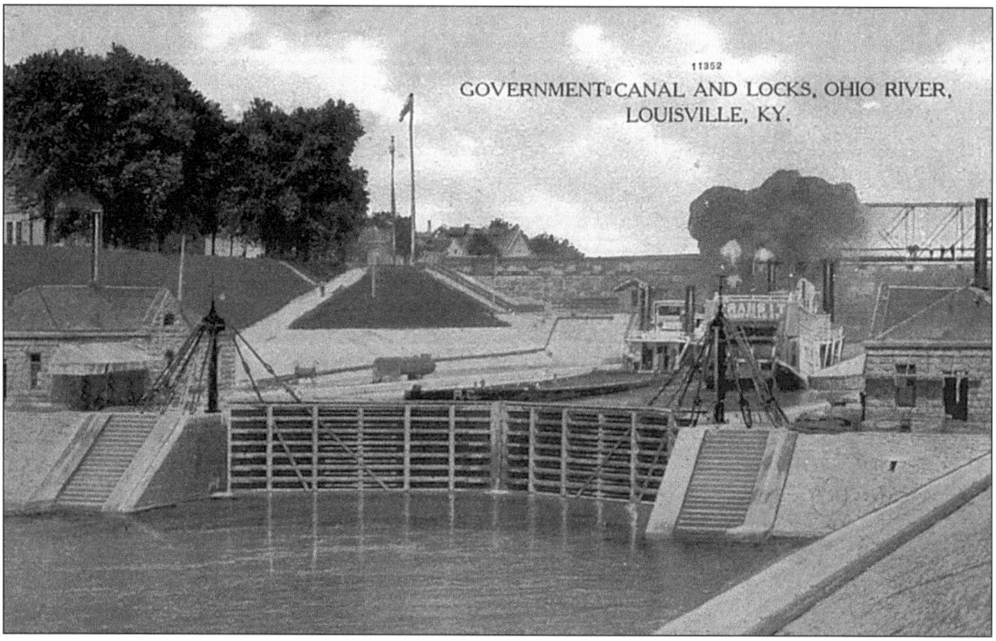

Two boats ride up on water flowing into the lock chamber from upriver in the enlarged lock chamber that was completed in 1927.

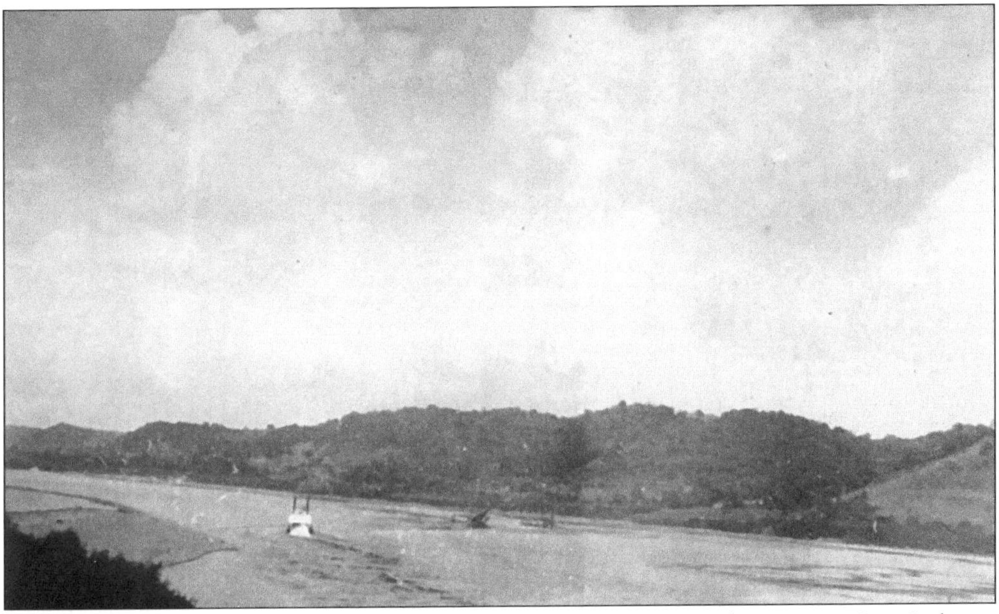

A steamboat carefully eases upriver around the bar and crib dike just above Rising Sun, Indiana, on very low summer water levels prior to 1920. The government dredge *Mallory* sits near the Kentucky shore trying to deepen the channel enough to permit navigation to continue. Congress would soon fund a series of dams the length of the river to alleviate the problem.

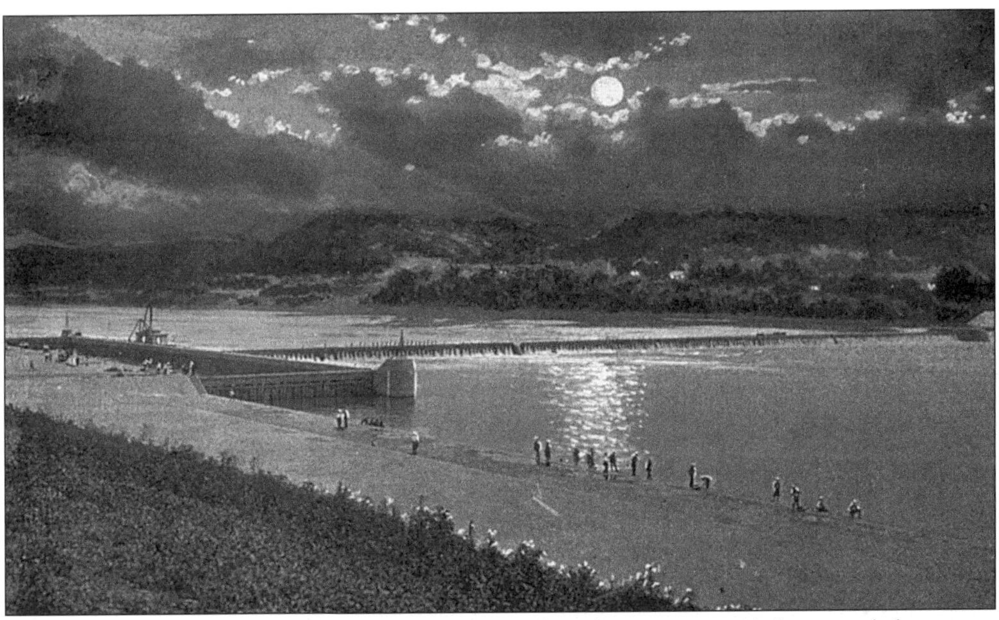

Congress appropriated $56 million in 1923 to complete the remaining 19 dams needed to create a minimum 9-foot navigable channel between Pittsburgh, Pennsylvania, and the Mississippi River at Cairo, Illinois. Locks at these dams were a minimum of 600-feet long and 110-feet wide. The project was completed and celebrated with a great parade of steamboats between those two ports in the fall of 1929. Above, the beauty of the river at Fernbank Dam below Cincinnati, Ohio, attracts visitors and fishermen to its lower guide wall.

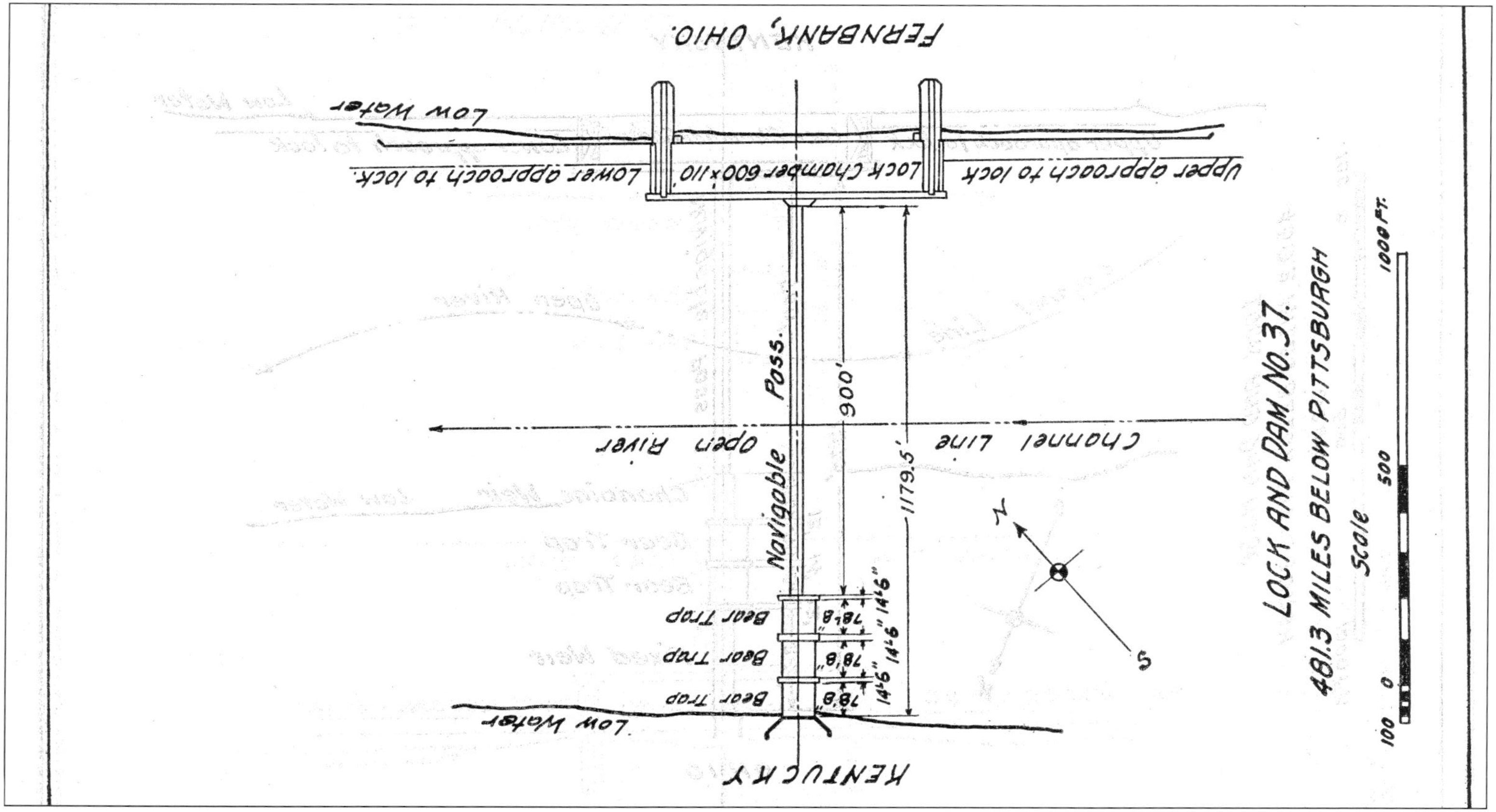

A diagram of Fernbank Dam below Cincinnati, Ohio shows its major structures. The "bear traps" are fixed structures along the opposite shore used to hold back water. Movable barriers called "wickets" close off the flow of water in the navigable pass. These can be raised or lowered depending upon river conditions. Fernbank opened for operations in 1911. Two additional, similar dams were constructed to maintain a minimum nine-foot channel depth from Cincinnati to Louisville. The Markland, Indiana dam opened in 1921. The McVille, Kentucky dam opened in 1924.

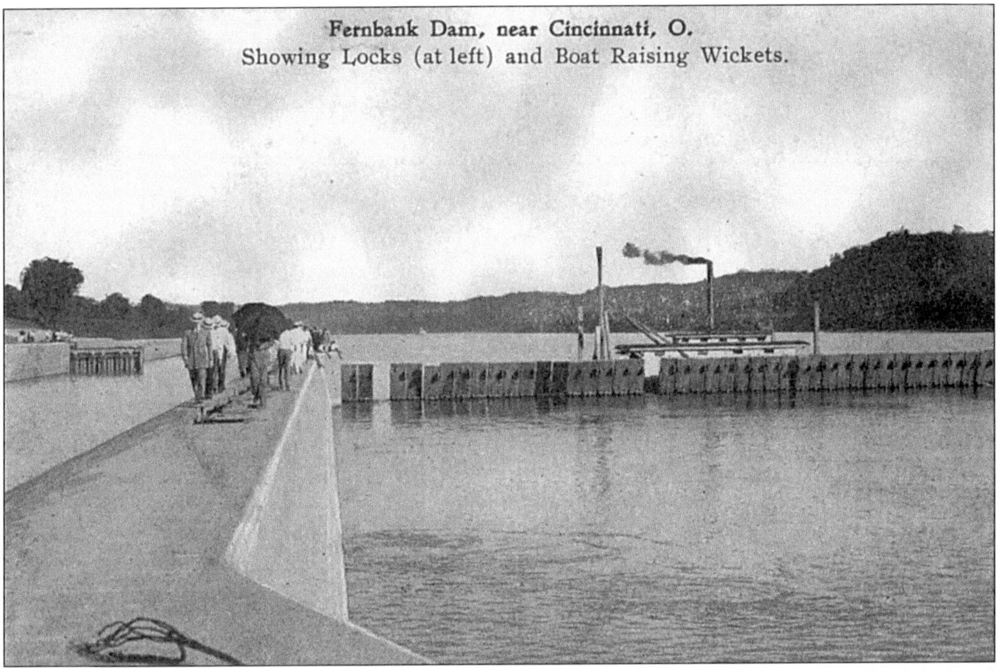

The wicket tender is in the process of raising the movable wickets that hold water back behind the dam. When the wickets are down, there is no difference between the water level in the river above and below the dam. Steamboats can pass outside of the lock chamber through the navigable channel.

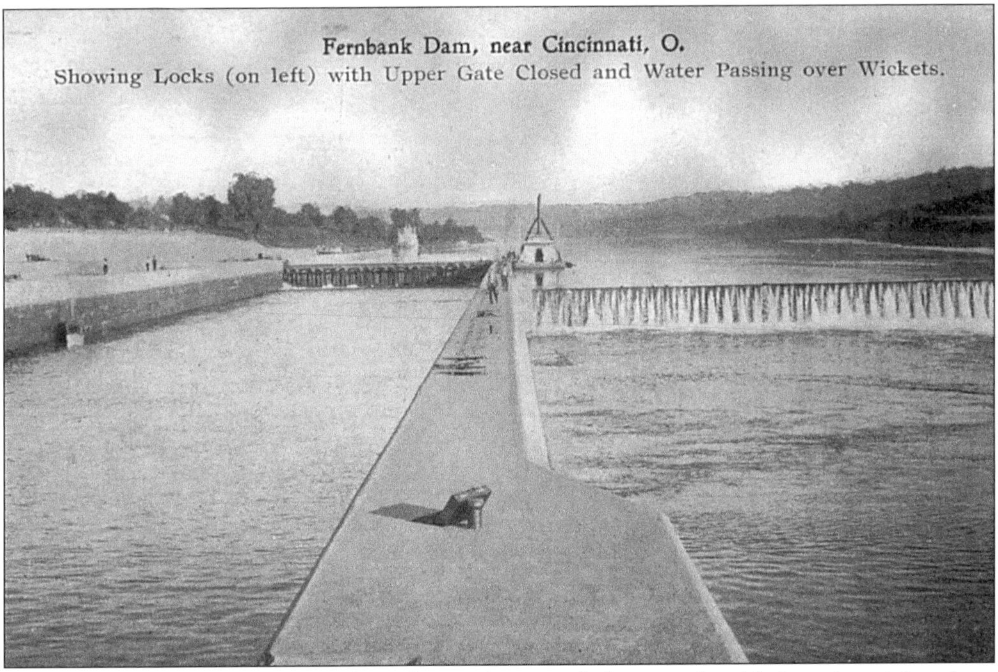

The water level in the lock has been lowered to equal the river level below the wicket dam. The wicket tender is tied against the upper lock guide wall where it was usually secured when idle.

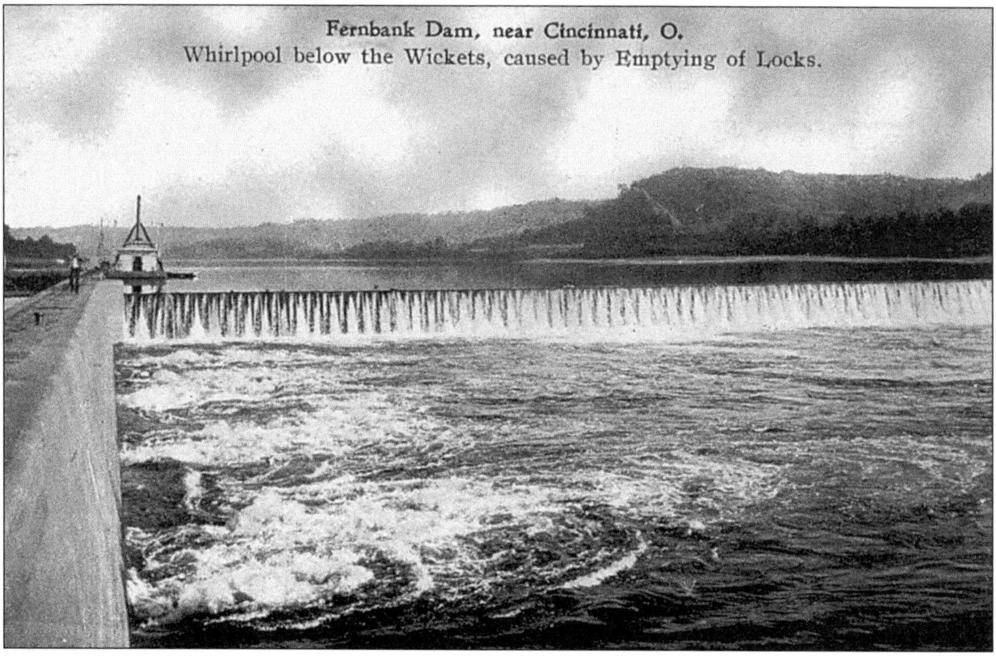

Water is moved in and out of the lock chamber by gravity through a series of pipes and valves. In this photo, taken looking upriver from the outer lock wall, the river appears to be near normal pool depth. The wickets at Fernbank dam raised the pool water level 7.8 feet.

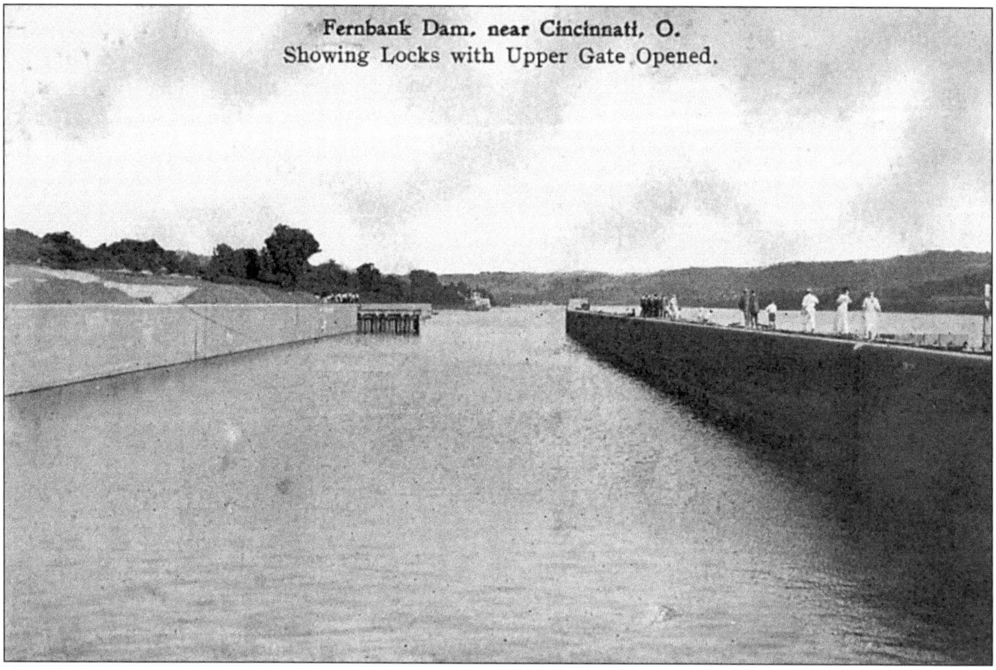

A pilot's-eye view is seen here departing upriver from the lock at Fernbank, Ohio. The completion of the system of locks and dams turned the river into a series of "pools" of slack water that were easier and safer to navigate. They also permitted the year-round operation of larger tows of barges.

Nine

After the Packets Were Gone

Traffic on the Ohio River continued to change after 1940. The development of better road and rail service to the towns along its banks reduced dependence on the river to meet basic daily needs. Navigation improvements led to larger boats and barges. These were made of steel, providing a safer, longer-lived vessel. Steam was replaced by more powerful and dependable diesel engines.

Other technologies and modes of travel replaced the river as the primary means of reaching the outside world from riverside towns and villages. The Cincinnati to Louisville trip that took a day by packet could now be made in a few hours at most at the convenience of the traveler. Trucks and trains took farm goods to market and returned with merchandise for business and homes in the river valley.

River transport moved along at about the same speed. But now it consisted of large diesel towboats that could push up to seventeen modern steel barges, and hold the equivalent of a season's cargo for one packet in a single trip.

The views that follow link the images of the past with the river of today. They do not tell the complete story of the river after the packets were gone; this would take at least one complete book in itself. They illustrate some of the sites shown in earlier chapters. If you are lucky enough to be sitting on the shore in a quiet place as one of the few steam-powered excursion or overnight passenger boats glides past, you experience—for a brief moment—the packet era and its transition to the world today.

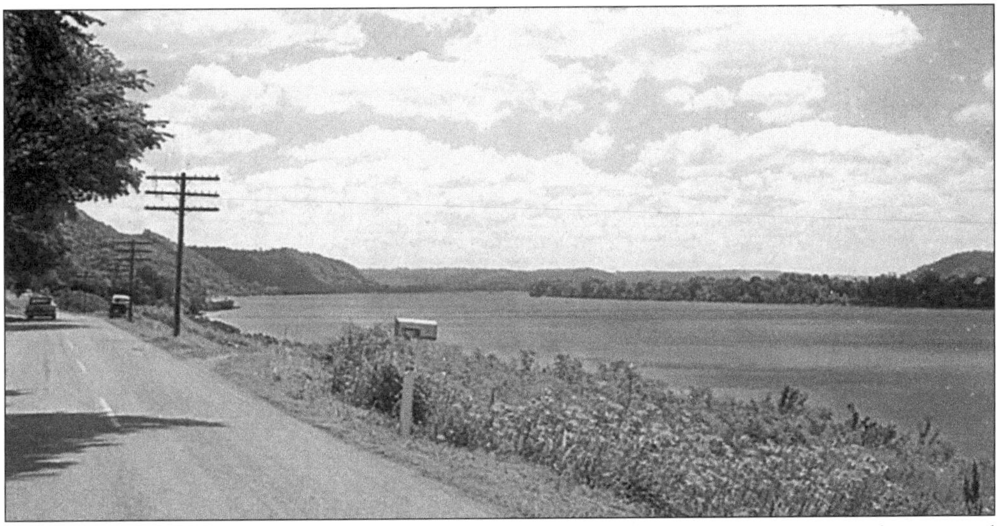

Larger, higher lift dams had replaced the dams completed in 1929. The broader river they created now had a minimum 12-foot, year-round navigable depth. The road, with its passenger car and accompanying telephone lines at left, replaced the packet as the primary way residents of towns along the river traveled and communicated between Patriot and Vevay, Indiana.

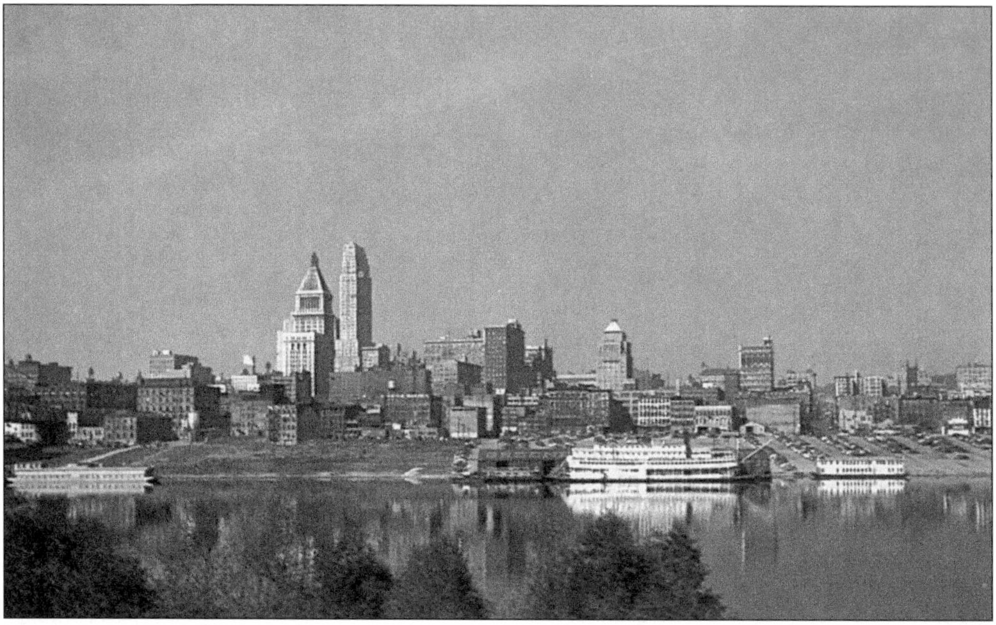

The Cincinnati Public Landing around 1940 shows the excursion *Str. Gordon C. Green* at the Green Line wharfboat. Captains Tom and Mary Green prospered by running overnight excursion boats after their packet trade dried up in the 1930s.

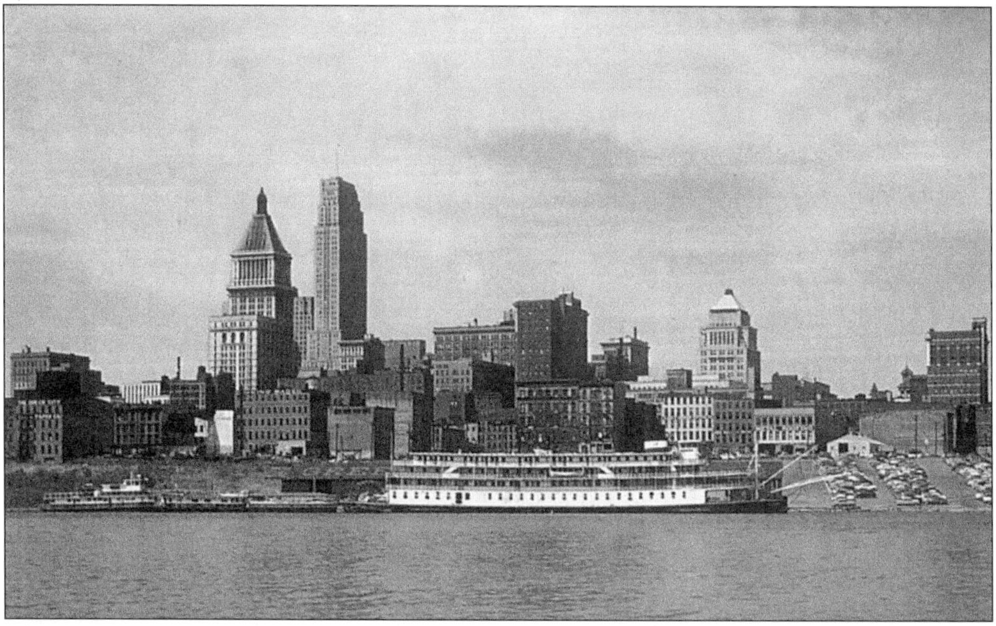

The Green Line *Str. Delta Queen* at the Cincinnati public landing is shown here sometime in the 1950s. Today, she cruises the Ohio, Mississippi, Tennessee, and other rivers with her two sisters, both steel-hulled, steam-powered sternwheelers designed specifically for overnight travel. They are the last of their breed. Unfortunately, the building of interstate highways, sports facilities, and other non-river related ventures finally drove their homeport out of Cincinnati to New Orleans in the late 1960s. All three boats visit the area regularly, but no overnight boats remain based in the area.

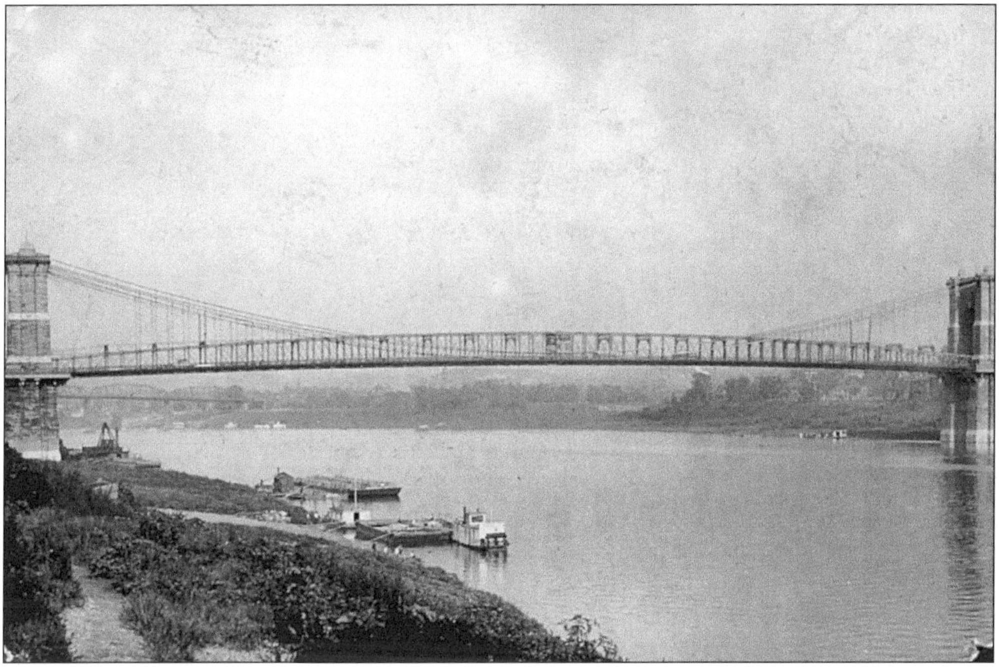

This is another 1930s view of the Cincinnati harbor on the Ohio shore below the suspension bridge. The steamboats are gone from the river. A few barges lie along shore. The summer water level is higher because of the dams now in place.

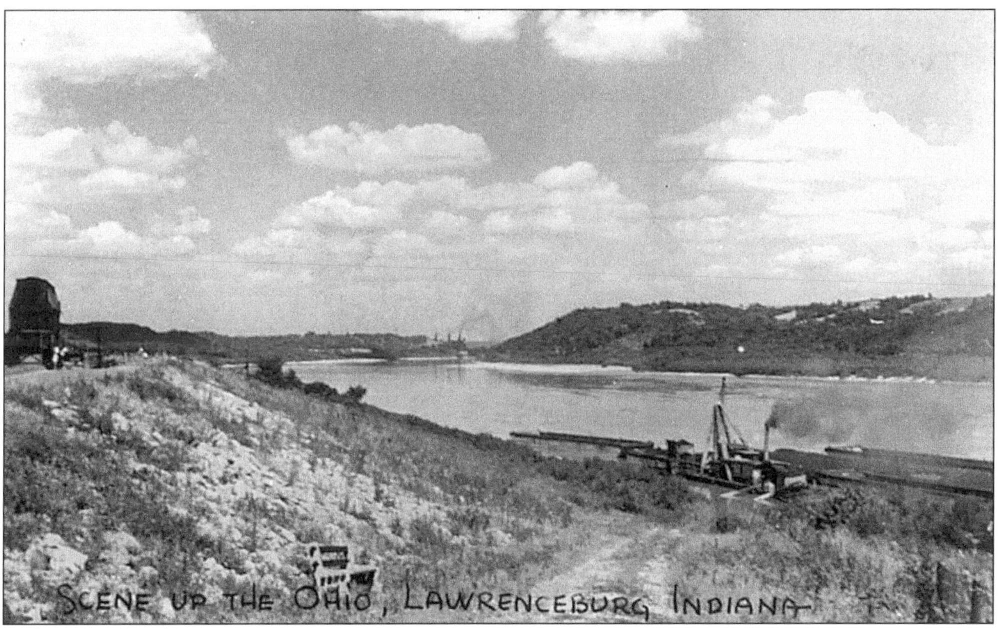

The landing area at Lawrenceburg, Indiana, sometime around 1950, shows the levee built in the 1920s to protect the town from flooding. A coal digger is unloading coal barges at the Peoples Coal Company. It was one of the last coal yards to survive.

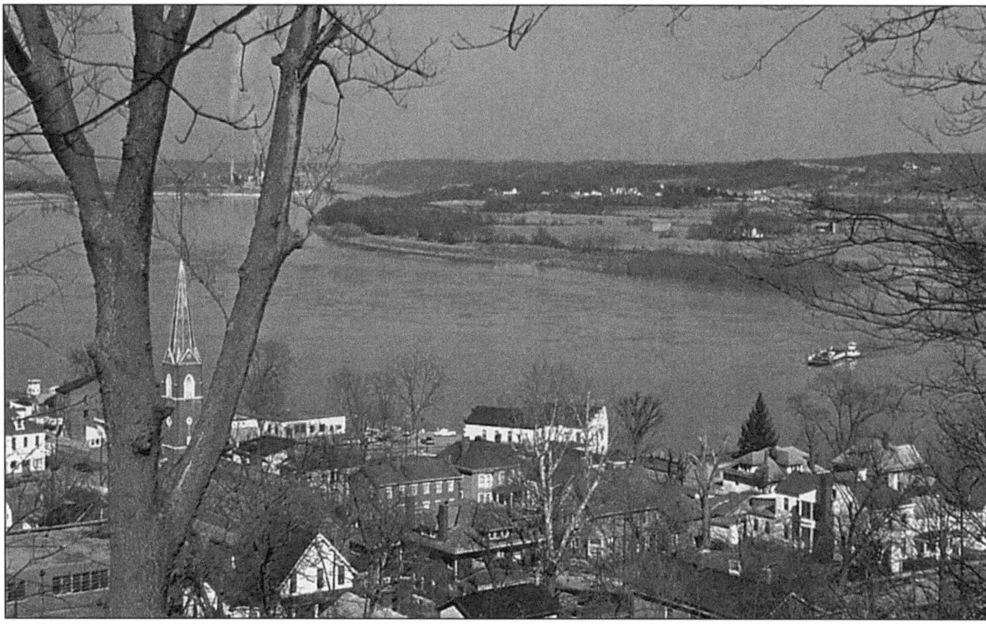

This view of Aurora, Indiana, from about 1970, still includes many buildings seen in the earlier 1907 flood view. The river now has a 26-foot pool depth thanks to the series of modern, high-lift roller dams completed in the 1960s. The diesel-powered *C.J.* can be seen pushing its steel ferry flat back towards Aurora from the Kentucky shore. The *C.J.*, and a ferry upriver at Anderson Ferry, Ohio, are the last two operating between Cincinnati and Louisville.

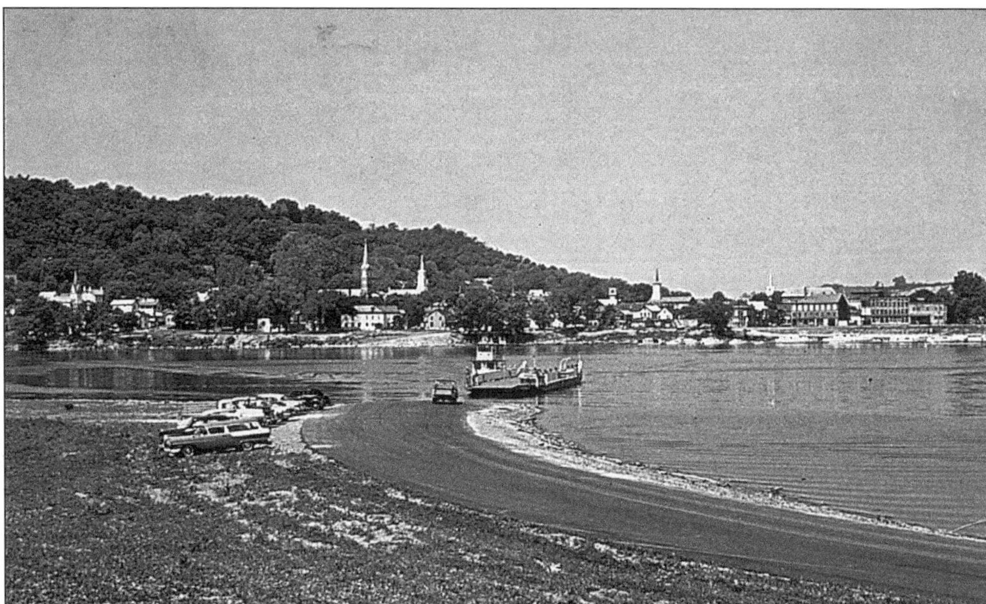

Here is an earlier picture of the Aurora ferry *C.J.* taken from the ferry landing on the Kentucky side of the river in the early 1960s. The ferry is now able to land level with what was once the top of the riverbank before the new dams raised the water level. The gravel road on the Kentucky side has been paved.

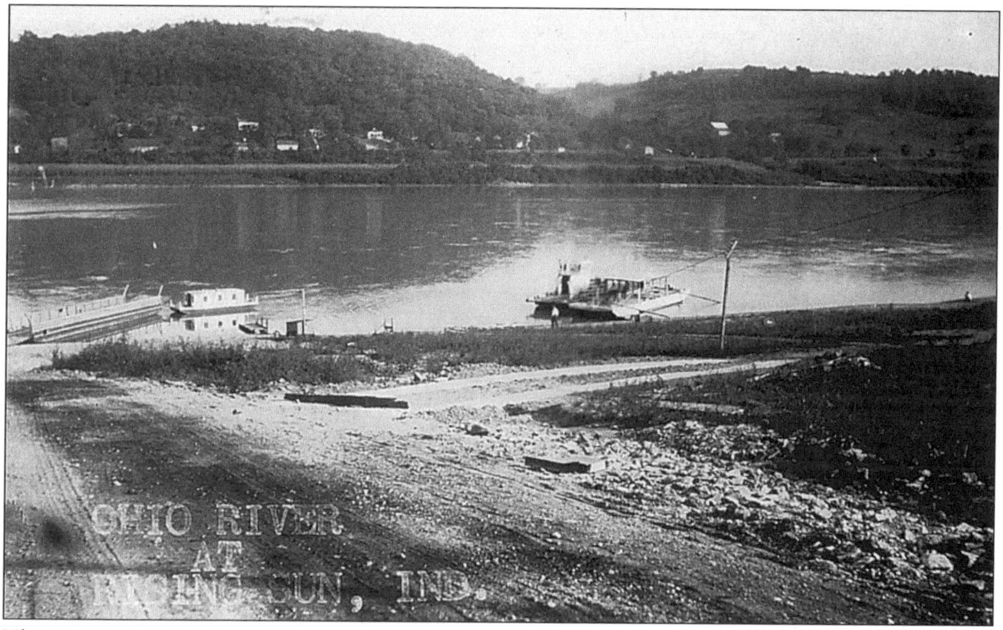

The river at Rising Sun, Indiana, shows very little activity in this picture from the late 1940s. Rabbit Hash, Kentucky, has changed little on the far shore.

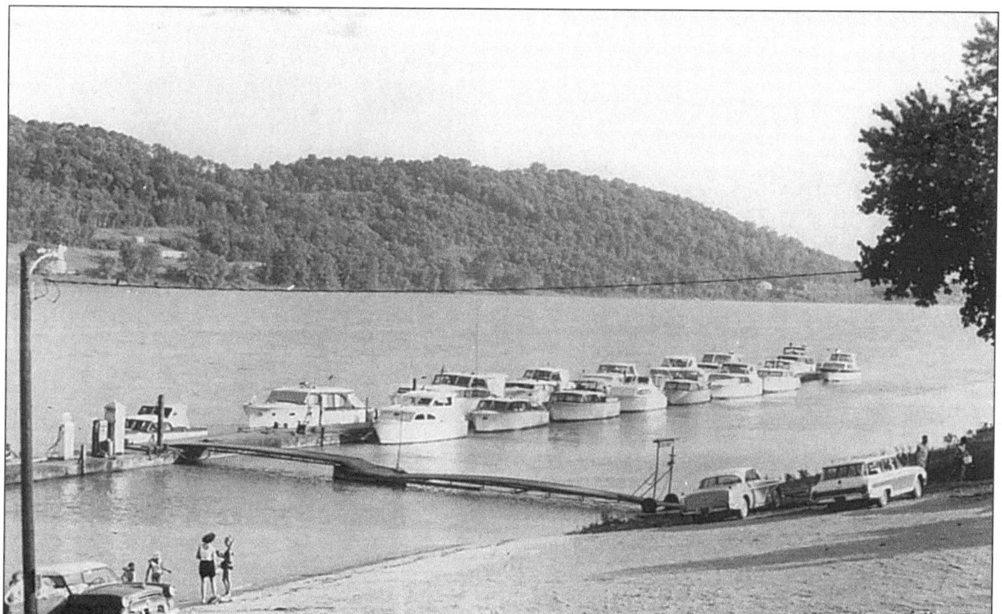
The author was fifteen when he snapped this picture of the boat dock at the former public landing site in Rising Sun, Indiana, in July, 1964. Pleasure boats are still plentiful today along the length of the river, especially in warm weather.

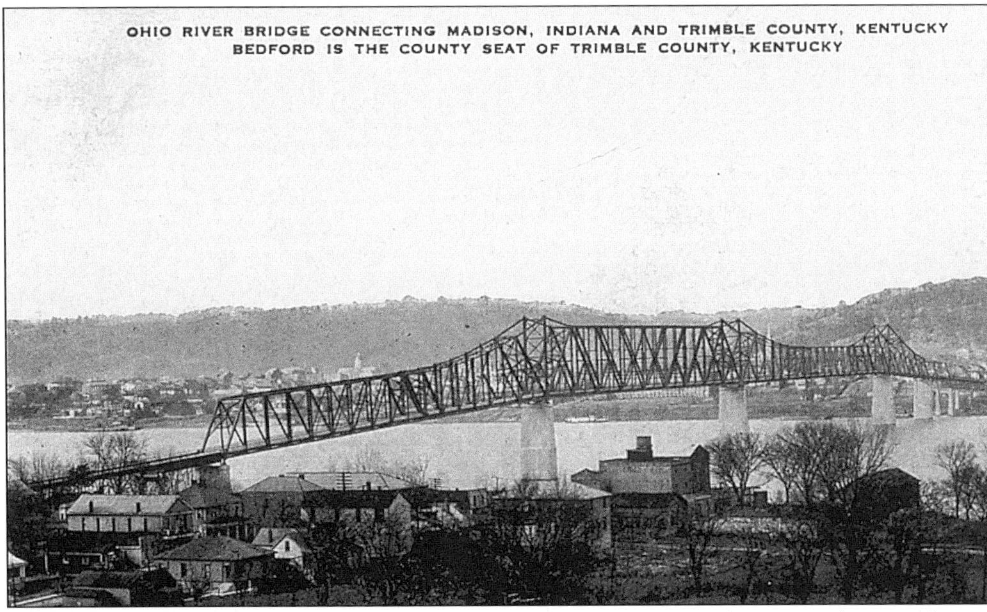

The highway bridge above was completed in Madison in 1929. Another opened across the top of the rebuilt dam at Markland, Indiana, in the late 1970s. Most ferries between Cincinnati and Louisville had already ceased operations as better roads made travel to the bridges practical and convenient.

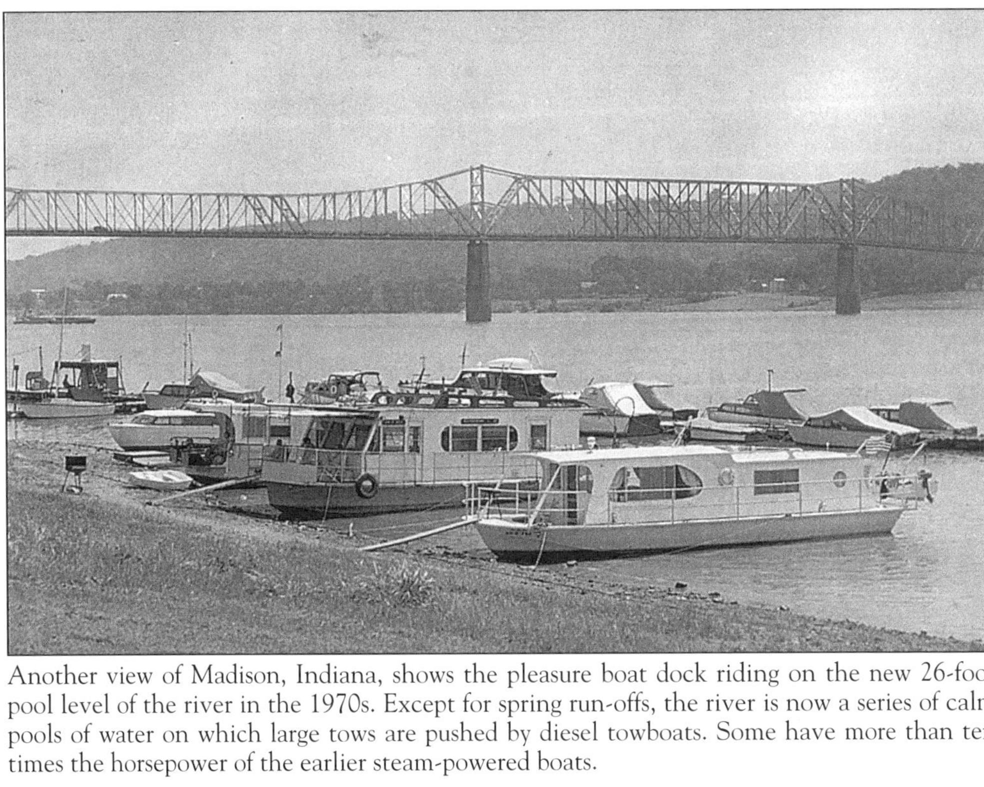

Another view of Madison, Indiana, shows the pleasure boat dock riding on the new 26-foot pool level of the river in the 1970s. Except for spring run-offs, the river is now a series of calm pools of water on which large tows are pushed by diesel towboats. Some have more than ten times the horsepower of the earlier steam-powered boats.

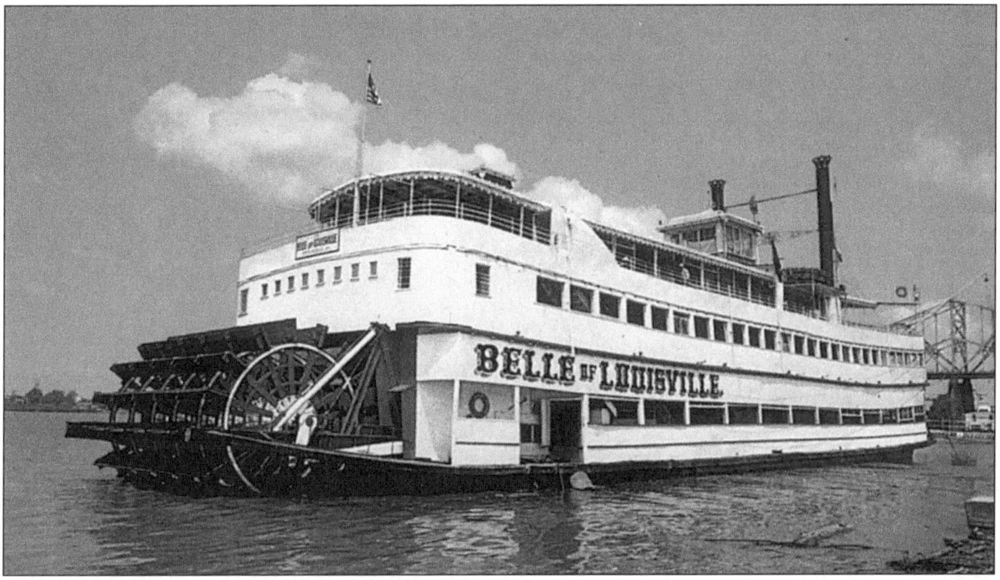

The excursion *Str. Belle of Louisville* operates area trips from the public landing at Louisville, Kentucky, to this day. Originally named *Idlewild*, she was built in 1914 for packet service. She was sold to Cincinnati and operated as the excursion *Str. Avalon* from 1948 to 1962. Sold "as is" in poor shape, she was purchased by Jefferson County, Kentucky. Renamed *Str. Belle of Louisville*, and extensively rebuilt in 1968, she is a fixture on the Louisville waterfront. Her fall cruises to Madison and into the Kentucky River below Carrollton are reminiscent of the "meet the boat trips" run by packets in an earlier time.

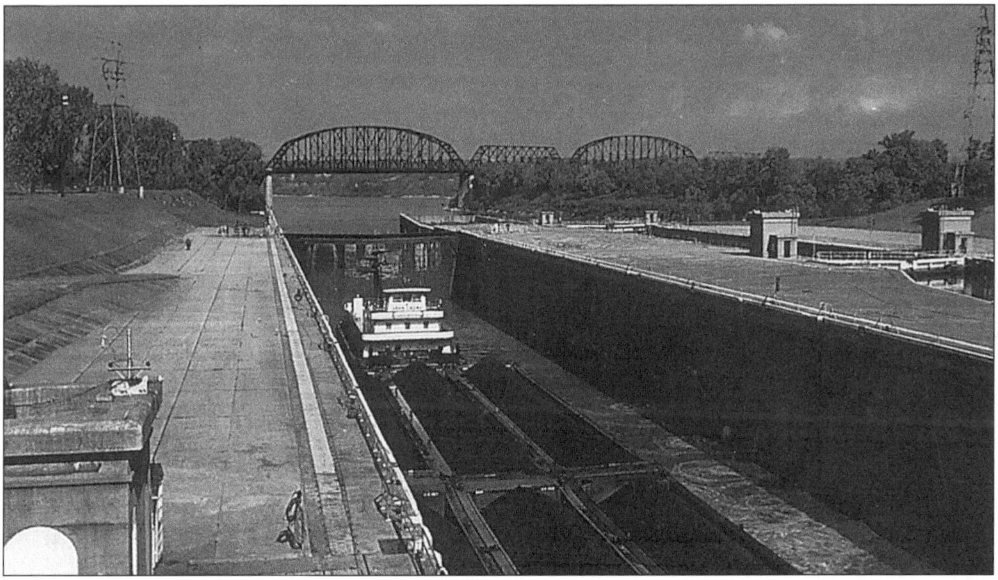

The diesel-powered, 3,240 horsepower M.V. *John J. Rowe* heads upriver towards Louisville, pushing a standard tow of fifteen 195-foot by 35-foot steel barges into the new, standard-size lock chamber that measured 1,200 feet by 110 feet at the lower end of the Portland Canal. An auxiliary lock of the old standard size, measuring 110 feet by 600 feet is on the right. Its predecessors were the wood-hulled, steam-powered, sternwheeled boats that struggled to control tows a fourth that size on high, spring river crests 70 years earlier.

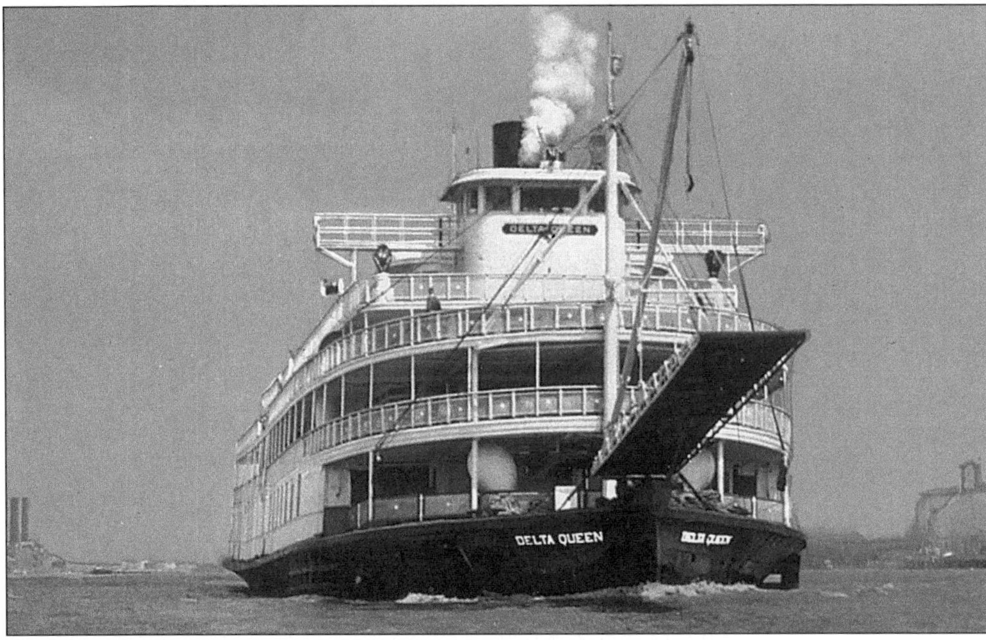

The *Str. Delta Queen* is headed downriver into the Portland Canal at Louisville. This card, signed by Captain Harry Louden, was a souvenir of the author's trips on the boat in the 1970s. Captain Harry was born on a farm in Rabbit Hash, Kentucky. A childhood friend of the author's family on both sides, he worked on the government dredge *Mallory* with the author's grandfather, Stanley Stegemiller, in the 1930s. He continued to pilot steam-powered government dredges until he retired and began working on the *Delta Queen*. He always blew the traditional greeting of one long and two short toots of her deep-throated whistle when passing Rabbit Hash.

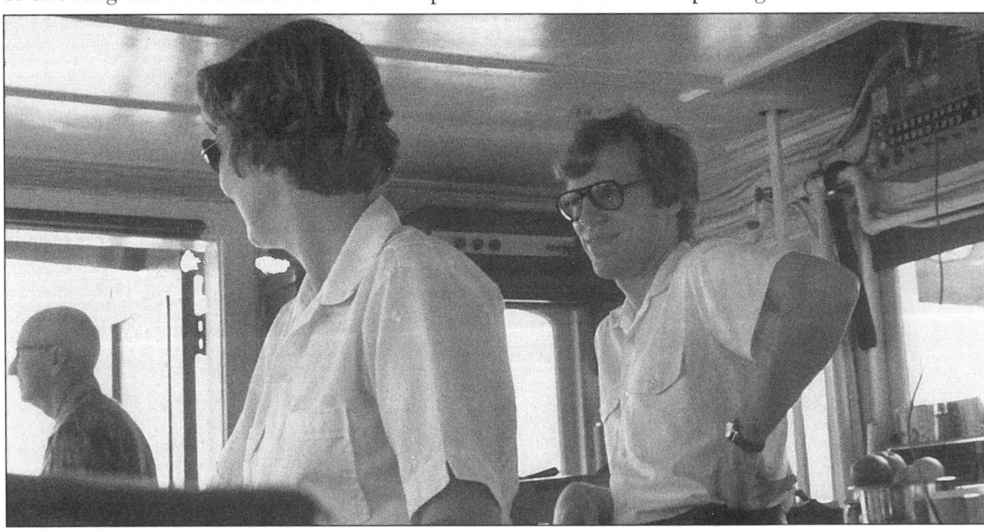

Captain Harry Louden is shown here at the door, and Captain Lexie Palmore is at the helm of the *Str. Delta Queen*. This photo was taken while cruising upriver towards Madison, Indiana in August, 1978. Calliope player and general hand Keith Norrington looks on. The author made two trips totaling twelve days on the Delta Queen between 1978 and 1979. Nights were spent seated on the bench at the back of the pilot house listening to Harry tell stories of the river, and to the quiet sounds of the boat gliding through the water.

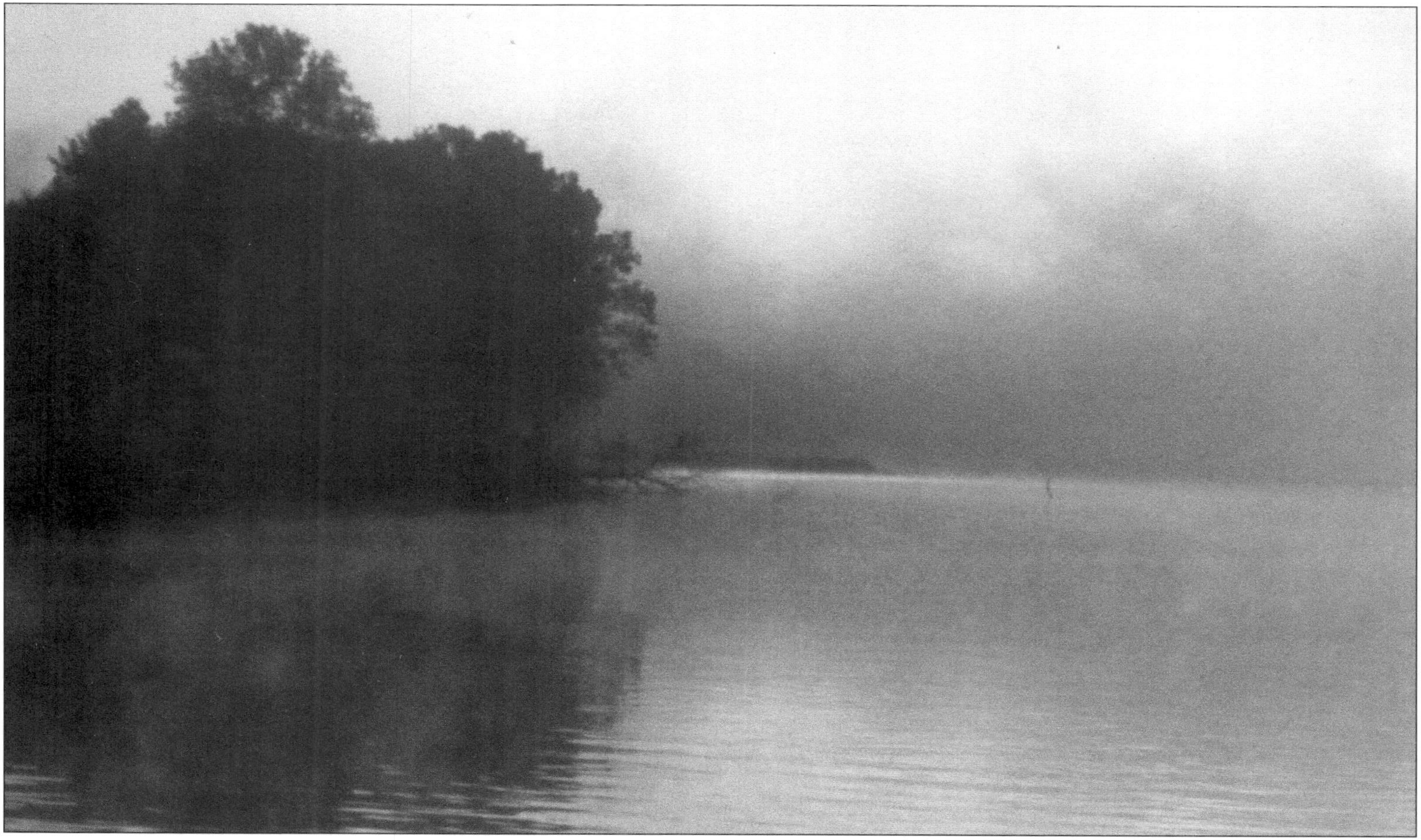

Sit on the deck of a steamboat safely nestled into the bank as the morning fog rises. Listen to the water flowing past, the birds and animals awakening to a new day on the bank, and the occasional splash of a big fish breaking the surface of the river and leaving behind concentric rings on its surface. Quietly reflect on your surroundings using all of your senses, and you will find peace.

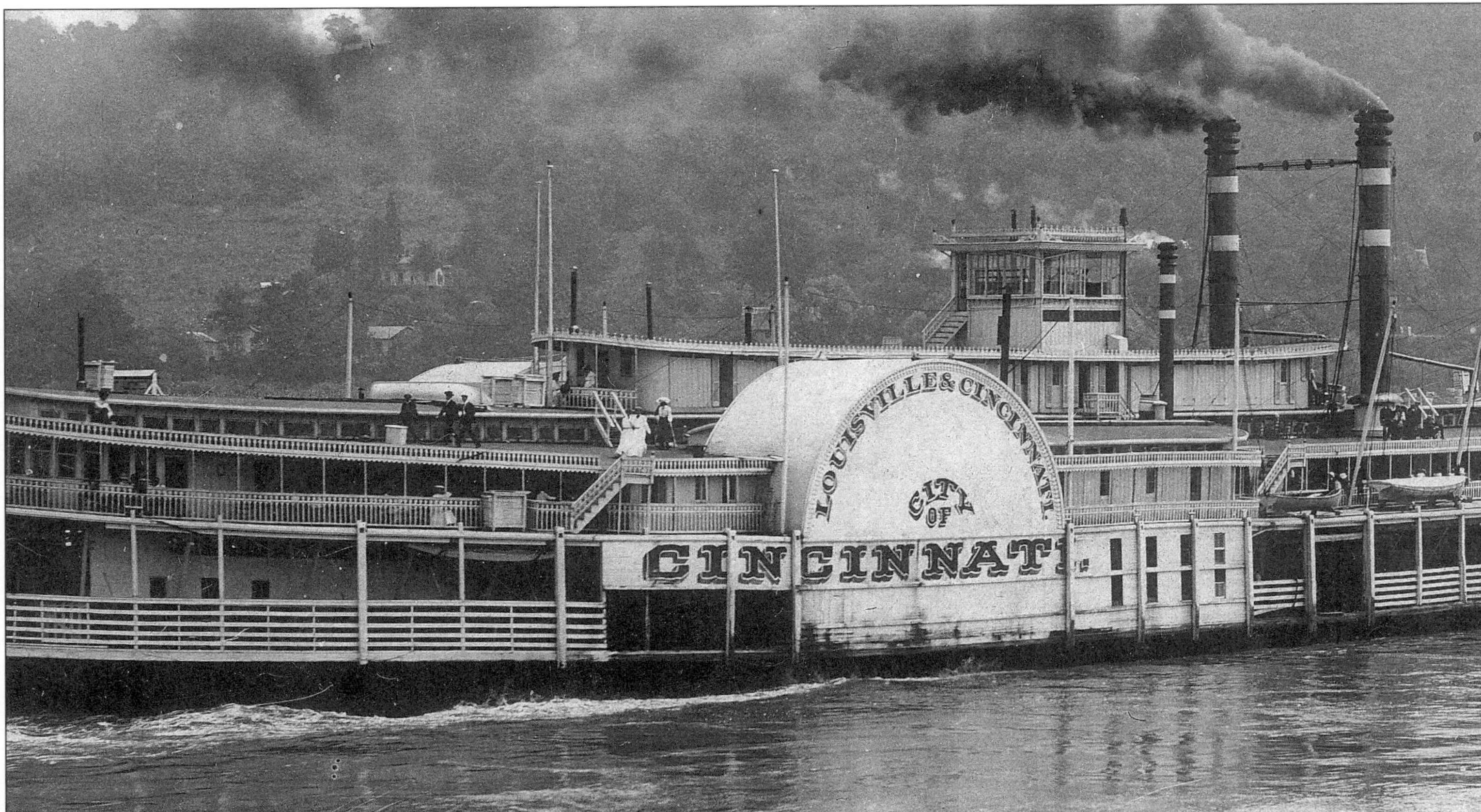

The *Str. City of Cincinnati* departing Rising Sun, Indiana on July 11, 1908, is another example of river and area photographs from the North family albums. Reprints of images in this book containing the (North) notation in their descriptions are available as post cards, or in a size suitable for framing. Please visit our web site at: www.theryles.com for ordering information and additional available items.

CONTRACT LAW IN THE USSR AND THE UNITED STATES

History And General Concept

Contract Law in the USSR and the United States

Vol. 1 E. Allan Farnsworth and Viktor P. Mozolin, The History and General Concept of Contract Law

Upcoming Volumes

Vol. 2 William T. Vukowich, Veniamin Yakovlev, and Margarita Shiminova, The Extent of the Power to Contract: Required Terms and Contracts of Adhesion (1988)

Vol. 3 Viktor P. Mozolin and Robert S. Summers, The Law of Sales (1990)

This series is produced under the auspices of the American Council of Learned Societies-Soviet Academy of Sciences Commission on the Humanities and Social Sciences. In the United States the work of the Commission is administered by the International Research and Exchanges Board (IREX). Preparation of the volumes is the joint responsibility of the International Law Institute and the Institute of State and Law, Academy of Sciences of the USSR.

CONTRACT LAW IN THE USSR AND THE UNITED STATES

History And General Concept

E. Allan Farnsworth
School of Law
Columbia University

Viktor P. Mozolin
Institute of State and Law
Academy of Sciences of the USSR

Volume 1

International Law Institute
in cooperation with
Parker School of Foreign and Comparative Law
Columbia University School of Law

International Law Institute
1330 Connecticut Avenue, N.W.
Washington, D.C. 20036
(202) 463-7979

Library of Congress Catalog No.: 87-80862

ISBN 0-935328-47-5

Printed and bound in the United States of America.

Table of Contents

INTRODUCTION

This is the first in a series of books entitled "Contract Law in the USSR and the United States." The series is a joint project of the International Law Institute and the Institute of State and Law, Academy of Sciences of the USSR. Each volume will be coauthored by American and Soviet legal authorities.

This initial volume not only establishes the perimeter of the concept and history of contract in both of our nations but also fixes the working methodology for the entire series. In our early planning, we first jointly determined the topic, then the outline, of the book. Allan Farnsworth, the American author, and Viktor Mozolin, the Soviet author, each prepared a draft of approximately half of the book, dealing with his country's approach to the topic at hand; this process included the exchange of early drafts between the authors. Thereafter discussions, questions, and cross-comment ensued through correspondence and in various meetings. The result was a book consisting of two distinct parts, each having benefitted by critical comments from the opposite perspective. Ultimately, the authors jointly prepared an afterword.

This approach is unusual in that it intentionally avoids a comparative work. Rather, each author has tried to be as true as possible to his understanding of his own system, bearing in mind that his work was being done in the context of a joint study that is to edify readers in both the United States and the Soviet Union, as well as in other countries. This kind of exchange of views has certainly sharpened the insights of each author; one learns much about one's own legal system when trying to explain it to people in a totally different system.

No one would deny that there are profound differences between the societies of the United States and the Soviet Union. Inevitably, therefore, the role of contracts in each country is different. Yet there are also similarities; a contract is a contract. A careful study of the contract law of the Soviet Union by an American, or of the contract law of the United

States by a Soviet citizen, will yield insights into the workings of the other's society. By focusing on contracts, with their attention to specific details of human interaction, the authors of the volumes in this series reveal the nuances of social and commercial life that may be overlooked in broader studies. It is our hope that this work and its companion volumes will clarify for readers in the United States and the Soviet Union the law of the other country, as well as the full significance of the law in the reader's own country. And for readers in other countries, this series of books may occasion reflections on the evolution of the law in their societies. We expect that the experience of our work on this series will lead to other collaborations, including the exchange of scholars, exchange of information in the nature of law reporters, conferences, and other work.

The series originated in correspondence between the coordinators of this project and Professor E. Allan Farnsworth. The actual decision to proceed and the planning of subsequent meetings resulted from a Soviet delegation's visit to the United States in April 1984, and the signing of a first protocol contemplating a series of books.

Publication is occurring in both countries, and the texts of the Russian and English editions will be as close as possible. The Russian-language edition of each volume in the series will be published by Nauka of the Soviet Academy of Sciences. The publisher of the English-language edition is the International Law Institute (ILI). This first book is also published in conjunction with the Parker School of Comparative and Foreign Law at Columbia University.

The second volume, now under preparation by Professors William T. Vukowich, of the United States, and Veniamin Yakovlev and Margarita Shiminova, of the Soviet Union, will deal with the extent of the power to contract. The third, to be prepared by Professor Robert Summers and Viktor Mozolin, will deal with sales contracts. Further volumes are contemplated.

Many organizations and individuals have contributed to this project. We would first like to thank the American Council of Learned Societies-Soviet Academy of Sciences Commission on the Humanities and Social Sciences for its sponsorship. The Commission's willingness to underwrite our approach enabled the authors of this volume to have the necessary contact to accomplish the goals of a shared book. At the inception of the project, Professor Leon Lipson of Yale University and Professor Konstantin Sheremet made valuable suggestions. In the United States the project is administered by the International Research and Exchanges Board (IREX); at IREX, Wesley Fisher and Arlen Hastings have provided unwavering support. Allan Farnsworth would like to thank Jeffrey P. Trout for his help with the manuscript and Brenda Fox for typing. Viktor Mozolin gratefully acknowledges the help of Frank Loftus, Arthur R. Bregman, and Vernita Greenfield of ILI, as well as Nancy White and Professor William T. Vukowich.

Don Wallace, Jr.
Director, International Law Institute
Georgetown University Law Center
Washington, D.C.

Viktor Pavlovich Mozolin
Head, Sector of Civil Law
Institute of State and Law
Academy of Sciences of the the U.S.S.R.
Moscow

May 1987

PART I

The History and Concept of Contract Law in the USSR

Viktor P. Mozolin

Chapter 1

The Concept of Contract

The concept of contract in Soviet civil law consists of two elements that are inseparably connected. One of these relates to the legal conception of contract, and the other to its social purposes. Only if both elements are taken into account can one understand a civil contract as a social phenomenon in Soviet society.[1] These elements are not merely of great theoretical

1. Such an approach is reflected, in particular, in the concept of the contract formulated by F.I. Gavze. "The contract and civil law in socialist society," he writes, "is the legal form of economic circulation in socialist society under the conditions of commodity production, and constitutes a general volitional act by the parties, directed by the planning and regulating measures of the state, establishing, modifying, or terminating obligations of civil law between them, with the aim of better satisfying the requirements of society and its individual members." F.I. Gavze, *Sotsialisticheskii grazhdansko-dogovor* [*The Socialist Contract in Civil Law*] (Moscow: Iuridecheskaia Literatura, 1972), pp. 6–7.

On the other hand, most works, including textbooks for postsecondary educational institutions, give a definition of the contract that is limited to purely legal characteristics. Here, a contract in civil law is understood as an agreement between the parties, directed toward the making, modification, or termination of relationships under civil law. See for example, I.B. Novitskii and L.A. Lunts, *Obshchee uchenie ob obiazatel'stve* [*The General Doctrine of Obligations*] (Moscow: Gosiurizdat, 1950), p. 95; *Sovetskoe grazhdanskoe pravo* [*Soviet Civil Law*], eds., V.T. Smirnov, Iu. K. Tolstoy, and A.K. Iurchenko (Leningrad: Leningrad State University Press, 1982), p. 328; *Sovetskoe grazhdansko pravo* [*Soviet Civil Law*], eds., V.F. Maslov and A.A. Pushkin (Kiev: Vyshchaia shkola, 1983), vol. I, p. 397.

importance. They also have the practical effect of determining the sphere of application and the basic functions of the contract in the USSR.

1.1 The Legal Conception of Contract

The legal conception of contract involves a system of interrelationships among various legal components that provide for the functioning of the contractual relationships between the parties. These components include the agreement between the parties and the procedure by which it is arrived at, the structure of the content of the contract including the rights and duties of the parties, the means of performance of the contract, and the extent of the responsibilities of the parties for nonperformance or improper performance of their duties.

The basic components of contract are usually made by legislation. In Soviet legislation, however, there is no single legal definition of a civil contract. The term *contract* is used in legislation in at least four senses—contract as an agreement, contract as a document, contract as a relationship between the parties, and contract as an integrated or comprehensive concept.

A. The Contract as an Agreement

The concept of contract as an agreement is the most widespread in scholarly literature and in textbooks.[2] It is based primarily on Article 34 of the Fundamentals of Civil Legislation of the USSR and the Union Republics, and the corresponding articles of the civil codes of the various republics.[3] The concept of the civil contract as an agreement has several important legal consequences.

First, the concept of contract is narrowed down to a legal fact. In and of itself, an agreement between the parties is not a contractual relationship, although it has the goal of establishing such a relationship. Being a mutual coincidence of the wills of the parties, directed toward achieving the indicated goal, the agreement defines the performance of the parties to the contractual relationship. This performance is obligatory for the parties because it is required by law and guaranteed by legal remedies.

---

2. *See supra* note 1.

3. Hereinafter the *Fundamentals of Civil Legislation of the USSR and the Union Republics* will be referred to as the *Fundamentals of Civil Legislation*; Civil Codes of the individual Union Republics will be denoted by "CC" plus the abbreviation of the relevant Union Republic.

Second, pursuant to Article 34 of the Fundamentals of Civil Legislation, a contract is made when an agreement between the parties on all the central points has been reached in the form required in each particular case. From the subsequent content of Article 34 it is clear that the legislators were referring to agreements, which involve contracts of a definite type (such as contracts involving purchase and sale, loans, or rental of residential premises, and the like) rather than separate rights and duties, which constitute only the elements of such contracts.

Soviet legislation applies the concept of a contract as an agreement only in regard to the making of a contract and not in connection with modification or termination. At the same time, the term *agreement* is used in a significantly broader sense. Thus, Article 233 of the Civil Code of the Russian Soviet Federal Socialist Republic (hereinafter referred to as the Civil Code of the RSFSR) speaks of the termination of the obligations of the parties by an agreement of the parties (but not by a contract). In the same way, the agreement of the parties to a contract of purchase and sale as to a change in the quantity of goods sold or to the establishment of a new price for them, may be classified as an agreement, but not as a contract. In Article 35 of the Fundamentals of Civil Legislation it is said that obligations, but not the separate rights and duties of the parties, arise from contracts. Thus, it may be said that every contract is an agreement, but not every agreement is a contract. It is therefore proper to understand by contract only that group of agreements that is directed toward the establishment of obligatory relationships at law. On the other hand, an agreement of the parties to modify or to terminate contractual relations that have already arisen (or of individual rights and duties) may be called an agreement but not a contract.

The law also provides the basis for an even broader concept of contract as a legal fact. This broader interpretation extends to all forms of agreements, including agreements for modification, or termination of rights and duties under civil law. Pursuant to Article 14 of the Fundamentals of Civil Legislation on transactions, the actions of individuals and organizations directed toward establishing, modifying, or terminating rights and duties under civil law are recognized as transactions.[4] Transactions may be unilateral, bilateral, or multilateral. Since both contracts and agreements

4. In civil legislation the term "organization" is used as a generic term, according to Article 11 of the *Fundamentals of Civil Legislation*. Enterprises, associations (in industry, agriculture, and other fields of the national economy), and institutions (in science, education, culture, medicine, etc.) are separate varieties of this notion.

are bilateral or multilateral transactions, these concepts are often identified with each other in the literature. This approach, however, is not supported by the rules for legislation on contracts or rules for definite types of contracts.

Third, under Soviet civil law, both agreements between parties calling for performance of duties in the future and agreements calling for performance at the time that the agreement is made, are recognized as contracts. The second category of agreements is directly provided for in general form by Article 43 of the Civil Code of the RSFSR, according to which transactions performed at the time that they are made can be concluded orally, if the legislation of the USSR or the RSFSR does not specify otherwise. Identical rules are contained in the Civil Codes of the other Union Republics. Among such agreements the law lists the contract of gift and the contract of retail cash purchases by individuals. The total number of contracts named in the general system of contracts at civil law is relatively small. This, however, does not change the essence of the matter, in as much as the concept of contract in the USSR, in contrast to the concept of contract as promise in Anglo-American legal systems, permits the existence of contracts that are executed when they are concluded.

In this connection, a question arises as to contracts that exist in Anglo-American legal systems that purport to transfer property rights and legitimize new property owners with respect to third parties. Soviet civil law does not recognize such a special category of contracts. Individual aspects of property relationships in connection with the transfer of property rights from one person to another are regulated by rules within the framework of contractual obligations. This is confirmed by Article 30 of the Fundamentals of Civil Legislation, according to which the right of ownership (the right of operative management) by contract arises at the moment of the transfer of the thing, if the law or the contract does not specify otherwise.

The established rule on the transfer of property rights, which is reminiscent in character of the system of delivery, is not exclusive, since Article 30 is a suppletive rule. In particular, Article 135 of the Civil Code of the RSFSR provides that if a contract for the alienation of a thing is subject to registration (as, for example, in the case of a contract for purchase and sale of a house) then the right to ownership by the person acquiring it arises not at the moment of transfer of the thing but at the moment of registration of the contract. Registration of the contract should not be confused with the registration of the property that is the subject of the contract. In the latter case, the rule of Article 30 of the Fundamentals of Civil Legislation applies, as is confirmed in judicial practice. For example, in the case of *Chernyshev v. Kolesov*, on the recognition of property rights in an automobile, a dispute arose out of the purchase by the plaintiff of an automobile through a commission store. The contract for sale was made on April 7, 1973, in accordance with the rules of the Commission of Trade for passenger cars, as confirmed by an order of the Minister of Trade of the RSFSR on September 22, 1971. After the contract was made and performed, however, the plaintiff did not have time to register the automobile with the State Automobile Inspectorate (GAI), as the law provided, and his right of ownership of the automobile was disputed by its former owner. The district court of the city of Saratov, which heard the case as the court of first instance, rejected the suit on the basis of Article 135 of the Civil Code of the RSFSR. The Presidium of the Saratov Oblast court, to which the case was appealed by the plaintiff, reversed the decision of the people's court. "The people's court," its decision said, "mistakenly declared that pursuant to Article 135 of the Civil Code of the RSFSR, the right of ownership of the automobile arises at the moment of the registration of the contract with GAI. In the given case what is subject to registration is not the contract, but the automobile, and the seller (the store), is under no obligation relative to the registration of the car with GAI."[5]

B. The Contract as a Document

The term *contract* is sometimes used to refer to the written form of the contractual relationship between the parties. Although such a concept does not appear in the Fundamentals of Civil Legislation and the Civil Codes, it is widely used in legal rules at lower levels and in practice. This is particularly true in the statutes on individual types of contracts between organizations, confirmed by the Council of Ministers of the USSR,[6] and in

5. *Biulleten' Verkhovnogo Suda RSFSR* [*Gazette of the RSFSR Supreme Soviet*], No. 30 (1974), 13–14.

6. See, for example, Point 3 of the Statute on Deliveries of Products for Industrial and Technical Purposes, adopted by the Decree of the Council of Ministers of the USSR on November 10, 1981, which states that, "the contract is the basic document that defines the rights and duties of the parties in the delivery of all forms of products, whether or not distributed in accordance with a plan." *Sobranie Postanovlenii Pravitel'stva SSSR* [*Collected Decrees of the Government of the USSR*] [hereinafter cited as *SP SSSR*], Nos. 9–10, item 62 (1981). *See also* Point 3 of the Statute on Deliveries of Commodities for Consumption by the Population, *Id.*; Point 3 of the Statute on Deliveries of Agricultural Equipment and other Material-Technical Means to Collective Farms and other Agricultural Enterprises and Organizations, adopted by the Decree of the Council of Ministers of the USSR on June 29, 1983 (with approximately the same wording.) *SP SSSR*, No. 17, item 90 (1983).

standard contracts for services to citizens, developed by the Union-wide and republic ministries and government bureaus.[7]

The documentary form of the contract records the agreement between the parties including their rights and duties thereunder. This form of the contract also serves to aid in problems of interpretation.

C. The Contract as a Relationship between the Parties

The concept of contract as a relationship between the parties arises immediately out of Article 33 of the Fundamentals of Civil Legislation. This article gives a legal definition of an obligation, and points to a contract as one of the major bases for the origin of obligations. The rule of Article 33 of the Fundamentals of Civil Legislation is implemented many times in civil legislation, in relation to the periods during which contracts remain in force and to modification and termination of contracts.[8] It is apparent that in such cases one is speaking not of a contract as an agreement (a legal fact), which has already been made at an earlier time (and which in this sense is not subject to changes over time), but of a contract as a continuing legal relationship between the parties.

The concept of the contract as a relationship between the parties makes it possible to establish the following qualitative characteristics:

---

7. See, for example, the Standard Contract for the Purchase of Excess Agricultural Products in the Personal Farming Operations of Individuals and Members of Garden Cooperatives of Workers and Employees, adopted by the April 7, 1981, Decree of the Central Union of Consumers' Cooperative Societies [hereinafter cited as the Tsentrosoivz], *Biulleten' normativnykh aktov ministerstv i vedomstr SSSR* [*Bulletin of Normative Acts of Ministries and Agencies of the USSR*] [hereinafter cited as "*Biulleten' normativnykh aktov ministerstv i vedomostr SSSR*"], No. 3 (1982), 33; The Standard Contract for the Rental to Citizens for Temporary Use of Household Items or Musical Instruments Other Than Upright and Grand Pianos, Sports Equipment, and other Property for Personal Use (i.e. household rentals), adopted by the Decree of the Council of Ministers of the RSFSR on February 1, 1965. *Sobranie Postanovlenii Pravitel'stva RSFSR* [*Collected Decrees of the Government of the Russian Socialist Federated Soviet Republic*] [hereinafter cited as *SP RSFSR*], No. 1, item 2 (1965), amended by *SP RSFSR*, No. 2 (1982), 4.

8. See, for example, Article 277 of the *Civil Code of the RSFSR* on the term of a contract for rental of property; Article 35 of the *Fundamentals of Civil Legislation* on the abolition and disposition of the contract for rental of dwellings, etc.

a. A contractual relationship between the parties arises by the will of the parties, on the basis of an agreement between them. In the case of a civil law obligation, neither party may have unfair bargaining power over the other. Otherwise, the fate of the civil contract itself is in jeopardy because unfair bargaining power in the hands of one of the parties may compel the other party to enter into the contract, or to submit to the other party's demands as to the content of the contract. The contract itself inevitably takes on a formal character. Contracts made between enterprises under the jurisdiction of government agencies and organs of the administration for the delivery of agricultural products, fully confirm the correctness of this assertion.[9] The only possible exception includes the contracts of administrative agencies and of organizations under their jurisdiction, which go outside the limits of superordinate-subordinate administrative relations. Such contracts include, for example, those made between a ministry on the one hand, and organizations under its jurisdiction, on the other, for the erection of buildings and structures needed by the ministry itself. In general, however, contracts and civil law are made between parties legally independent of each other.

b. A contractual obligation in civil law is considered a relative legal relationship (relation in personam) because it establishes legal ties only between the parties participating in the contract. An obligation to a third party is permitted in specific cases provided for by legislation, but the number of such cases is strictly limited. Even then, the relative character of the legal relationship is not changed. It is not transformed into an

9. Such contracts are encountered in the marketing of fruits grown on the state farms of the Crimean State Farm Wine Trust. In accordance with the existing structure of contractual relations, this trust delivers grapes to organizations operating on a Union-wide scale on the basis of delivery contracts. In order to perform its duties under such delivery contracts, the trust must then make production-and-supply contracts with state farms that grow the grapes. The established procedure for making production-and-supply contracts is commonly violated by the Crimean State Farm Wine Trust as is noted in the decision of the state Arbitration Board of the USSR in *Simerenko State Farm Winery v. The Moscow Interdistrict Fruit and Vegetable Base and the Petrozavodsk Fruit and Vegetable Combine*. See M.G. Masevich, "Spory voznikaiushchie iz dogovora kontraktatsil," *Komentarii arbitrazhnoi praktiki* ["Disputes Arising From the Production-and-Supply Contract," *Commentaries on Arbitration Practice*], Issue 17 (1984), 44–49. The author justly remarks that "one cannot help recognizing as ill-advised the entrusting of the functions of purchaser to the Crimean State Farm Wine Trust—the administrative organ to which the state farm is directly subordinate. *Id.*, p. 45.

absolute obligation (relation in rem) since only the individuals and organizations specified in the contract are recognized as third parties.

c. A contractual obligation is directed toward the achievement of particular legal results of interest to the parties and, in the cases permitted by law, also to third parties. These results may be the acquisition and the implementation of property rights over things (under contracts for purchase and sale), the construction of industrial, cultural, service, and residential buildings and structures (under contracts for capital construction), or the provision of consumer services (under contracts for services to consumers). An obligation arising out of a contract under civil law must not infringe upon the rights and legal interests of citizens and organizations not immediately participating in the contract.

d. A contractual obligation presupposes by its content the taking by the obligor of active measures to perform the duties undertaken by him, and the possession by the obligee of the right to demand performance. Along with obligations of a positive nature (the obligor's duty to perform a particular action), Article 33 of the Fundamentals of Civil Legislation provides in principle for the possibility of the creation of obligations of a negative nature, by virtue of which the obligor must refrain from a particular action. However, the rules in force and legal practice do not recognize any particular forms of civil contracts of this type. The legislation contains only individual elements of a negative nature in contractual obligations, which, on the whole, are of a positive nature.

Thus, for example, under Article 287 of the Civil Code of the RSFSR, the lessee in a contract for the rental of property assumes the duty of refraining from renting out the rented property on sublease without the consent of the lessor. But this duty of the lessee does not essentially change the positive nature of the contractual obligation as a whole. This positive nature is indicated by such basic duties of positive action in the contract as: 1) the duty of using the leased property in accordance with the terms of the contract and the type of property involved (Article 283 of the Civil Code of the RSFSR); and 2) the duty of making prompt payment for the use of the property (Article 286 of the Civil Code of the RSFSR). In the same way it is the duty of an author not to transfer, without consent of the other party to the contract, the work involved for use in the same way as is specified in the contract (Article 509 of the Civil Code of the RSFSR).

e. The contractual obligation has as its base a property character. Its major goal is to facilitate economic relations. In Soviet civil legislation, however, there are no rules limiting the content of the contractual obligations to actions connected in one way or another with property. Furthermore, by virtue of Article 1 of the Fundamentals of Civil Legislation, Soviet civil legislation regulates not only property relationships, but also the personal nonproperty relationships connected with them, as well as other personal nonproperty relationships in the cases provided for by law.[10] There is, therefore, every reason to assume that in its content a contractual obligation may also in principle be of a nonproperty character.[11] This is true both for obligations in which the nonproperty rights and duties make up only individual elements of the content of the obligation (obligations of this type are especially frequent in author's law), and also for obligations of an entirely nonproperty character. Thus, under a contract for retaining counsel (Article 396 of the Civil Code of the

---

10. In Soviet civil law, legal relations between persons, including organizations, are divided into two broad categories: property relations and non-property relations. The term *property relations* is used in a broad sense. It includes all kinds of relations between persons that involve either ownership or transfer of money or other valuable property. This transfer may, for example, result from a duty under a contract, a duty to make restitution, or a liability in tort for damages. Property relations can therefore be regulated not only by the law of ownership, but also by contract law, tort law, the law of copyright and invention, and other branches of civil law.

Non-property relations are in turn divided into two categories, depending upon whether they are connected with property relations. The first category has no intrinsic economic value, but relates to non-material items of a person's individuality, such as artistic creativity and inventiveness that are protected by law. Nevertheless, they may give rise to property relations, such as a right to royalties. The second category is purely non-economical. It does not give rise to property relations. Civil law deals with these relations only in those cases that are expressly mentioned by legislation, for example by Article 7 of the *Fundamentals of Civil Legislation* on the protection of honor and dignity.

11. There is no agreement on this question in the literature. Many scholars share the opinion that a contractual obligation can be of a non-property character. See, for example, I.B. Novitskii and L.A. Lunts, *Obshchee uchenie ob obiazatelstve* [*The General Doctrine of Obligations*], p. 59; I.A. Tanchuk, V.P. Efimochkin, and T.E. Abova, *Khoziaistvennye obiazatel'stva* [*Economic Obligations*] (Moscow: Iuridicheskaia Literatura, 1970), p. 10; *Sovetskoe grazhdanskoe pravo* [*Soviet Civil Law*], ed., V.A. Resentsev (Moscow: Iuridicheskaia Literatura, 1975), Vol. I, p. 427. Others deny the possibility of the existence of legal obligations of a non-property character, including contractual obligations. *See* M.M. Agarkov, *Obiazatel'stva po sovietskomu grazhdanskomu pravu* [*Obligations Under Soviet Civil Law*] (Moscow: Iurizdat, 1940), p. 34 *et seq.*. *See also* *Sovietskoe grazhdanskoe pravo* [*Soviet Civil Law*], eds., V.T. Smirnov, Iu. K. Tolstoy and A.K. Iurchenko, (1982), Vol. I, p. 321.

RSFSR), a lawyer is entitled to assume the duty to defend the interests of the accused in court without compensation. An obligation arising on the basis of such a contract will undoubtedly have a nonproperty character.

These characteristics of contractual obligations constitute the concept of the contract in civil law as distinguished from the other types of contracts (*e.g.*, administrative and constitutional contracts) known in Soviet law.

D. The Contract as an Integrative (Comprehensive) Concept

This concept of a contract is the broadest. It includes the agreement giving rise to a contractual obligation, the form in which the obligation is expressed, and, finally, the contractual obligation itself from the moment it begins to the moment it ceases to exist. It is in this sense, in particular, that the legislator uses the concept of a contract in grouping the legal rules, which individualize the various kinds of contracts in civil law including contracts for delivery, purchase and sale, rental of property, and small-scale or capital construction.

1.2 Social Purposes of a Contract

The social purposes of civil contracts are determined by the nature of the social relationships in the society in which the contract law is found. Under Article 10 of the Soviet Constitution, these relationships in the USSR are based on socialist ownership of the means of production in the form of ownership by the state (by the people as a whole) and by collective farms and cooperatives. In addition, the property of trade unions and other civic organizations is property of the state. Personal ownership by individuals, primarily of objects of consumption, is also important in the Soviet Union.

Public ownership of the means of production, in combination with personal ownership by the citizens, creates the economic infrastructure within the limits of which societal production is carried out in the country. The relationships with respect to the distribution and exchange of the results of labor and other forms of property values as they move in this sphere of consumption, for both personal and productive purposes, develop on the basis of this infrastructure. It is precisely these relationships, which have a commodity-and-money character, that constitute the field of contract law.

The concept of *commodity-and-money* relations is important in understanding how Soviet civil law fits into the Soviet economic system as a whole. In Marxist theory, economic relations in a socialist society are of two kinds: direct relations and commodity-and-money relations.

Direct relations involve the decisions taken by the state and its agencies with respect to things that do not have market value because there is no market at all. These decisions are made possible because of state ownership of the means of production, and they are implemented by the planning system on which the economy is based. The decisions involved in direct relations generally take the form of planning acts that concern the most important aspects of the economy, such as the division of national income for productive purposes and for consumption and savings, the defining of priorities in the development of different branches of the economy, the distribution of material and financial resources among union republics and other state units, the making of capital investments, the development of scientific and technological progress, and the use of labor.

Commodity-and-money relations, on the other hand, have a market nature. The parties to these relations are state enterprises and associations, public organizations including collective farms, individuals, and sometimes even the state itself. All of these parties hold various kinds of property and have bargaining power in making contracts.

Commodity-and-money relations nevertheless differ from relations found in market-oriented Western countries and have at least four distinctive features. First, labor is not regarded as a commodity. Second, major resources, such as land, water, timber, minerals in the ground, industry, and communications are excluded from commodity-and-money relations. Third, prices are in most cases fixed not by the contracting parties but by the state. Fourth, commodity-and-money relations are constrained by a planning system.

Direct relations and commodity-and-money relations are not independent of each other, since each exerts an influence on the other. In a socialist society, commodity-and-money relations are regarded as supplementary to direct relations and, indeed, because of the impact of planning on the economy they reflect many of the characteristics of direct relations.

Nevertheless, the state's power of decision in the field of direct relations is supposed to consider the cost-accounting approach to each problem, including wages, investments and the like. Indeed, the increasing role of commodity-and-money relations and contracts in the modern economy of the USSR was stressed in the decisions of the 27th Congress of the Communist Party of the Soviet Union in 1986.

By definition then, under commodity-and-money relations, marketability of certain items in the USSR is restricted. In accordance with Article 95 of the Fundamentals of Civil Legislation, property of the state may be granted to individuals only for purposes of use. This is done by administrative directives issued by state agencies having the authority to do this, according to procedures prescribed by law.[12] At the same time, the law establishes a legal regime for its use, which includes the possibility of the transfer of the use of the property to other persons both within organizations and outside them. For example, collective farms are entitled to transfer, within limits established by law, particular land parcels to their members for the latter's personal farming operations. Similarly, an individual who has as his personal property a dwelling is entitled to sell it to other persons and, in connection with this, to transfer but not to sell the rights of use of the corresponding land parcels to the new owner of the house. In this case, the land follows the house.

The Constitution of the USSR and other legislative documents do not contain an exhaustive list of all things that are the exclusive property of the state.[13] For this reason, other things, which at a particular period of development of the state are of special importance to society, may be found among them. For example, at the present time, railways and means of communication in general use are the exclusive property of the state.

In addition to the objects that are completely excluded from commercial markets, the law provides for a category of things that are limited in marketability. These things may be acquired only with special permission, and in a number of cases only by persons authorized by law. Limitations of

---

12. See The Fundamentals of Land Legislation of the USSR and the Union Republics, adopted by the Supreme Soviet of the USSR, December 13, 1968, *Vedomosti Verkhovnogo Soveta SSSR* [*Gazette of the USSR Supreme Soviet*] [hereinafter cited as "*Vedomosti Verkhovnogo Soveta SSSR*"] No. 51, item 485 (1968); *Fundamentals of Legislation of the USSR and the Union Republics on Mineral Resources*, adopted by the Supreme Soviet of the USSR, July 9, 1975, *Vedomosti Verkhovnogo Soveta SSSR*, No. 29, item 435 (1975); *Fundamentals of Water Legislation of the USSR and the Union Republics*, adopted by the Supreme Soviet of the USSR, December 10, 1970, *Vedomosti Verkhovnogo Soveta SSSR*, No. 50, item 556 (1970); and *Fundamentals of Forestry Legislation of the USSR and the Union Republics*, adopted by the Supreme Soviet of the USSR, June 17, 1977, *Vedomosti Verkhovnogo Soveta SSSR*, No. 25, item 388 (1977).

13. *See* the commentary on Article 95 of the *Civil Code of the RSFSR*, *Kommentarii k grazhdanskomu kodeksu RSFSR* [*Commentaries on the Civil Code of the RSFSR*], eds., S.N. Bratus and O.N. Sadikov (Moscow: Iuridicheskaia Literatura, 3d ed., 1982), p. 122.

this kind are based on the general importance of these things to the economy, on considerations of the security of the state or society, and on other reasons formulated by the legislature. Article 137 of the Civil Code of the RSFSR speaks of two groups of things with restricted marketability: a general group consisting of weapons, aircraft, and strong poisons; and a special group consisting of foreign currency.

The general group is not limited to objects named in Article 137. To this group can be added, in particular, military ammunition, explosives, radioactive substances, narcotics, and the like. Permission to acquire these things is issued by the agencies of the state whose activities include the satisfaction of particular interests specified in the law. Thus, the sale of hunting guns is conducted with the permission of the civil police and is limited to persons who belong to a voluntary hunting association. In addition, hunting guns must be registered with the civil police not later than one month after their purchase.[14] Even more rigorous requirements are established relative to the acquisition, use, and storage of other forms of firearms.

The special group of objects of limited marketability includes only foreign currency and certain precious metals. Article 137 of the Civil Code of the RSFSR includes among these: foreign currency (bank notes, treasury notes, coins); negotiable documents (checks, bills of exchange, letters of credit, and the like); negotiable bank documents (checks and others) made out in rubles that are receivable for and convertible into foreign currency; treasured metals—gold, silver, platinum, and metals of the platinum group in any form or state—and natural precious stones in raw or worked form. Pursuant to the November 30, 1976,[15] decree of the Presidium of the Supreme Soviet of the USSR entitled "On Transactions in Foreign Currency and Certain Precious Metals in the Territory of the USSR," this special group of limited marketability does not include articles of jewelry made of precious metals and stones produced either industrially or by hand, regardless of the assay marks on them, or fragments and waste from such articles. Gold leaf and disks of precious metals for dentistry are also not included in this special group. All other objects made for industrial or laboratory purposes, including half-finished products, component parts, and industrial waste, as well as coins made of

14. See the July 23, 1975 Decree of the Council of Ministers of the USSR, "Ob ustanvolenii edinogo poriadka priobreteniia, ucheta i khraneniia okhotnich'ikh ruzhei" ["On the Establishment of a United System for the Acquisition, Registration, and Safekeeping of Hunting Guns". *SP SSSR*, No. 18, item 11 (1975).

15. *Vedomosti Verkhovnogo Soveta SSSR*, No. 49, item 712 (1976).

precious metals (other than those circulating in Soviet territory) are to be considered in this group.[16]

The exclusive right to conduct operations for the purchase from organizations and citizens, and also the sale to them of foreign currency, belongs to the State Bank of the USSR, and, by delegation from it, to certain other organizations, such as the Foreign Trade Bank of the USSR. Individual cases, which do not fall under the above-mentioned rule, must be specified by law. These include, in particular, foreign-trade transactions. Article 175 of the Civil Code of the RSFSR also provides for the possibility, when this is permitted by a special law, of monetary obligations being expressed, and paid, in foreign currency. At the present time, this right is granted to the State Bank of the USSR, the Foreign Trade Bank of the USSR, and the International Bank of Economic Collaboration. Additionally, the right to sell goods for freely convertible foreign currency (both in cash and in travelers checks) is enjoyed by special stores.

Limitations of a different sort may be established with respect to the free marketability of a number of other things depending on their nature and purpose. For example, the basic means of production can be marketed only among organizations, and the sale of basic means of production to individuals is prohibited, with exceptions for small means of production.

The system for legal regulation of many categories of objects in the marketplace is strictly individualized. No general commodity market exists in the USSR. For this reason, the character of contractual relations is in many respects predetermined by the system of legal regulation that is established for individual forms of property.

The essence of relationships in society that are regulated by contract law is also manifested in the position of various categories of subjects. In a planned economy, in which public ownership of the means of production prevails, individuals, in the vast majority of cases, enter into contractual relationships as consumers of goods and services created by the society (as buyers, renters, passengers, patients, etc.). Their goal is to satisfy their material and intellectual needs. In turn, the society undertakes the duty of satisfying these needs. Socialist organizations and, rather more rarely, individuals appear in the role of parties to contracts directed toward the servicing of individuals.

The possibility of an individual appearing as a producer is an interesting subject. At present, along with the growth of the personal property of the

16. See the Guiding Instructions of the Plenum of the Supreme Court of the USSR of April 18, 1980, *Bulletin of the Supreme Court of the USSR*, No. 3 (1980), 7. *See also id.*, No. 4 (1978), 21–24.

individual as a consumer, the development of personal property of a productive character is being given prominent attention in the USSR. This development is intended not only to satisfy the personal requirements of the owners themselves and the members of their families, but also the requirements of other persons through the market. It is based upon Article 13 of the Constitution of the USSR (on the maintenance by citizens of personal farming operations, gardens, and orchards) and Article 17 of the Constitution of the USSR (on labor activity of individuals). Such individual production on the basis of personal property has great significance for society as a whole. This is suggested by the fact that at the beginning of the 1980's about 20 percent of the vegetables, 12 percent of the meat, and 8 percent of the milk sold on the market in the country was produced in personal farming operations.

After the 1977 Constitution of the USSR took effect, a number of rules were adopted that expanded individual rights of personal ownership. Among these was the September 8, 1981, Resolution of the Central Committee of the Communist Party of the Soviet Union (hereinafter referred to as the CC CPSU) and the Council of Ministers of the USSR entitled, "On Further Measures to Increase the Production of Agricultural Goods in the Personal Farming Operations of Citizens."[17] This resolution provided concrete measures to improve the conduct of personal farming operations by collective farm members, blue-collar and white-collar workers, and others. It also increased the incentive of collective farms, state farms and other agricultural enterprises, as well as consumer cooperative organizations, to make fuller use of the farming facilities of individuals so as to increase the production and sale of agricultural products, livestock and fowl. Today, because of this resolution, the supply of fodder to livestock and fowl in the personal farming operations of citizens is improving. Families are permitted to receive young livestock free of charge from the socialist farming organizations, and to receive help in the construction of personal farm buildings, provided the members of these families work on the farms involved. Also, state farms and other agricultural enterprises are permitted from their own funds to liquidate up to 50 percent of the credits issued to their workers.

The state undertakes the necessary measures to organize the sale of agricultural produce through the cooperative system and in the collective farm markets. Under the 1981 Resolution, the consumer cooperative is directed to expand the purchasing activity connected with the sale by individuals of produce received by them from their personal farming

17. *SP SSSR*, No. 6, item 37 (1981).

operations. The prices for this produce must be determined by agreement between the participants in the transaction. In accordance with the Standard Rules on the Collective Farm Markets, ratified by a decree of the Ministry of Trade of the USSR on November 14, 1978,[18] all persons who reach the age of 15 years are entitled to sell agricultural products. The establishment of maximum and minimum prices for produce sold by citizens in the collective farm markets is forbidden.

The legal position of socialist organizations, which enter into contractual relationships as legal persons,[19] also has some specific features. Under Article 12 of the Fundamentals of Civil Legislation, legal persons possess legal capacity consistent with the established goals of their activity. This is known in jurisprudence as the principle of special legal capacity of legal persons, and must not, however, be understood as a limitation. For example, arbitration boards, which consider disputes involving the legal capacities of organizations, proceed from a broad interpretation of their activity. In the case of *The Trade and Purchasing Base of the Krasnodar Administration of Workers' Supply of the Ministry of Forestry of the RSFSR v. The Taganrog Branch of the Rostov base of "Rosglavkoopkhoztorga,"* plaintiff sued defendant for damages for breach of contract. The case was heard by the State Arbitration Board of the Executive Committee of the Rostov Oblast Council of Working Peoples' Deputies in 1970. The plaintiff based its claim on a contract made with the defendant in the second quarter of 1970, for the delivery of housekeeping products valued at 4,485 rubles. The defendant did not supply the goods called for within the established time period, citing, among other reasons, the illegality of the contract. The defendant claimed that the contract was illegal because according to the statutes, the defendant was only empowered to sell goods wholesale to wholesale and retail consumer cooperatives. The plaintiff, on the other hand, was an organization of state trade, and therefore, the defendant asserted, the contract in question was made in violation of its established legal capacity. The decision of the arbitration board was for the plaintiff. The arbitration board pointed out that an economic organization is entitled to carry out, along with the transactions provided for in the statute governing it or in its charter, other transactions

18. *Biulleten' normativnoykh aktov ministerstv i vedmostr SSSR*, No. 8 (1979), 40.

19. Organizations that possess separate property may in their own names acquire property and personal non-property rights and have obligations. They may also act as plaintiffs and defendants before a court or private arbitrator. Such organizations are legal persons. Article 23 of the *Civil Code of the RSFSR*.

as well, which relate to its main activity. On these grounds the contract between the plaintiff and the defendant was found to be valid.[20]

By the aims of the legal person we usually understand, along with its basic manufacturing, economic, sociocultural, and other tasks, also subsidary operations necessary for the solution of the main tasks that are not expressly forbidden by law. Accordingly, in the charters and statutes on the basis of which socialist organizations function, there is never an exhaustive list of the actions that they are entitled to carry out. Such a broad approach to the special legal capacity of legal persons is especially important under modern conditions, where a country is expanding the economic autonomy of associations and enterprises. At the same time, it should be noted that under Article 50 of the Civil Code of the RSFSR and corresponding articles of the civil codes of the other Union republics, transactions carried out by associations and enterprises in contradiction to the goals indicated in their charters, in the statutes governing them, or in the general statutes concerning organizations of the same types, are declared invalid.

Further, the contract in civil law fulfills important organizational functions. In the course of the revolution in science and technology and of the intensification of processes of specialization and cooperative production, the contract provides the necessary technological connections between individual associations and enterprises for the production of various kinds of articles for the economy of the country. The significance of this function of contract is enhanced by the sectoral approach to management in the Soviet economy as conducted by various ministers and departments.

Finally, the substantive aspect of contract in civil law is predetermined to a considerable degree by the planned character of the commodity-and-money relationships regulated by law. This is manifested primarily in connection with the content of contracts. In Soviet society, the significance of contract is not limited to the interests of the parties themselves. Society as a whole has an interest in the proper organization of contractual ties. It may be said that in each civil contract, the interest of its participants and society are combined.

For this reason, the law approaches the formation of the content of the contract from the broad position of combining the interests of individuals and organizations, on the one hand, and those of society, on the other. The contract includes the agreement of the parties on all of its essential and

---

20. See *Nauchno-prakticheckii kommentarii arbitrazhnoi praktiki* [*Scholarly and Practical Commentary on Arbitration Practice*], ed., E.V. Anisimov (Moscow: Iuridicheskaia Literatura, 1973), Issue 6, pp. 158–160.

other terms, regardless of who introduced particular points. In all cases, these terms must pass through the conscience and the will of the parties to the contract, and be expressed externally in the form of an agreement. Otherwise, the contract cannot be said to have been made. Accordingly, the civil contract may consist of three groups of terms: terms established by law, terms formed under the influence of a plan, and terms established by the parties themselves.[21]

A. Terms Established By Law

As is noted in the literature, what is established by law is in most cases not the concrete content of the obligations, but the framework in which the terms of the contract are formed by the parties or by the planning agencies of the state.[22] For example, Article 162 of the Civil Code of the RSFSR establishes a rule for the making of a contract pursuant to a proposal that carries a deadline for an answer. The article does not, however, establish a specific deadline. This must be done by the parties within each case.

There are exceptions, however, where specific terms, which must be included by parties in their contracts, are established by law. These terms usually relate to the most important aspects of a contract, insofar as the public interest is primarily expressed in them. For the great majority of contracts, the price and quality of performance are such conditions.

1. Price

In general, prices for goods produced by associations and enterprises under the jurisdiction of the state or other public bodies, and also for work done and services provided, are established in a centralized fashion by the competent agencies of the state (the State Price Committee of the USSR, Ministries, Bureaus, and so forth). They are usually fixed in price lists, which have the force of legal rules. These lists contain the necessary data, including an indication of prices and various kinds of discounts and supplements applied to them, the procedures for determining them, and so forth, to permit the determination of prices of goods and services in each

21. V.G. Verdnikov, *Khoziaistvennye dogovery* [*Economic Contracts*] (Moscow: Publications of the USSR-wide Correspondence Institute of Law, 1965), p. 15.
22. See B.I. Puginskii, *Grazhdansko-pravovye sredstva v khoziaistvennykh otnosheniiakh* [*Civil Law Remedies in Economic Relations*] (Moscow: Iuridicheskaia Literatura, 1984), p. 114.

case. The prices set by the state are applicable mainly in contracts between socialist organizations and in contracts between socialist organizations and individuals.

In some contracts, such as those between organizations and individuals, the state may fix the order of payments. For example, Article 10 of the Edict of the Presidium of the Supreme Soviet of the USSR, "On the Strengthening of the Struggle Against the Extraction of Unearned Income," states that, "In the transactions between organizations and individuals, payments of sums exceeding 5,000 rubles should be made by written orders through the institutions of the State Bank or those of the State Labour Savings Bond."[23] In other contracts, such as those between socialist organizations, the state usually fixes the order of payment.

In particular cases, the law permits the establishment of prices by agreement between the parties to a contract. Associations and enterprises are permitted to do this in relation to various types of products, jobs or services, prices, and tariffs that are not required by law to be fixed by state agencies.[24] This includes, in particular, individualized goods, jobs, and services supplied to consumers on single orders.[25]

At the present time, prices set by agreement of the parties are being used increasingly in connection with goods provided to the population that are in especially great demand, and that are produced by associations and enterprises of light industry.[26] Agricultural enterprises are also permitted

---

23. *SP SSSR*, No. 21, item 20 (1986).

24. See, for example, Point 74 of the Statute of Socialist State Productive Enterprises, adopted by the Decree of the Council of Ministers of the USSR of October 4, 1965, *SP SSSR*, Nos. 19–20, item 155 (1965).

25. See Point 56 of the Statute on Deliveries of Products for Technical and Production Purposes, adopted by the Decree of the Council of Ministers of the USSR of April 10, 1981, *SP SSSR*, Nos. 9–10, item 62 (1981).

26. See the Statute on the System for Establishing Contractual Prices for the First Experimental Batches of Commodities and Especially Fashionable Articles, and for Differentiating Trade Discounts, adopted by the State Committee of the USSR on Prices on May 27, 1980, *Sovershenstovovanie hoziaistvennogo mekhanizma: Sbornik normativnykh dokumentov* [*The Improvement of the Economic Mechanism: A Collection of Normative Documents*] (Moscow: Pravda Publishing House, 2d ed., 1982), p. 298. *See also* the April 24, 1986, Decree of the Central Committee of the Communist Party of the Soviet Union (CC CPSU) and the Council of Ministers of the U.S.S.R., "Ob ulushchenii planirovaniia, ekonomicheskogo stimulirovaniia i sovershenstvovaniia upravleniia v legkoi promishlennosti" ["On the Improvement of Planning, Economic Incentives and Perfection of Management in Light Industry"], *SP SSSR*, No. 20, item 108 (1986).

to set prices by agreement for their products sold to organizations of the consumer cooperative system and in collective farm markets. With a view to fuller use of the resources of fruit and vegetable production, collective farms, state farms, and other agricultural enterprises are permitted to sell vegetables, melons, fruits, and berries to specific buyers at prices arrived at by agreement.[27] Agreed prices are also used in contracts between individuals,[28] and in contracts made by individuals with socialist organizations where individuals sell articles produced by them.[29]

2. *Quality*

The quality of performance of contractual obligations by the parties is also defined by law and is based chiefly on the application of standards and

27. See the August 5, 1982, Decree of the CC CPSU and the Council of Ministers of the USSR, "O dopolnitel'nykh merakh po rasshireniiu prodazhi kolkhozam, sovkhozam i drugimi sel'skokhoziaistvennymi predpriiatiiami plodoovoshchnoi produktsii organizatsiiam potrebitel'skoi kooperatsii i na kolkhoznykh rynkakh" ["On Further Measures for Expanding the Sales of Fruit and Vegetable Products by Collective Farms, State Farms, and other Agricultural Enterprises to Consumer Cooperative Organizations and Collective Farm Markets"], *SP SSSR*, No. 22, item 112 (1982). *See also* the March 20, 1986, Decree of the CC CPSU and the Council of Ministers of the U.S.S.R., "O dal'neishem soveshenstvovanii ekonomicheskogo mechanizma v agro-promishlennom komplexe strani" ["On Further Improvements of the Economic Mechanism of Management in Agro-Industrial Complexes of the Country"], *SP SSSR*, No. 17, item 90 (1986). This Decree states, "Collective farms, state farms and other agricultural enterprises have a right to sell to the organizations of consumers' co-operative societies and any person at a collective farm market an amount of particular products, not to exceed 30 percent of the volume of planned purchases of those products by the state. (The 30 percent limit applies to production that exceeds the plan, as well.) This production is considered a set-off for the fulfillment of the plan. The production relates to potatoes, vegetables, melons, fruits, berries, and table grapes. Prices are set by the parties to the contract." *Id.*

28. See, for example, the Standard Rules on Collective Farm Markets, adopted by a Normative Order of the Ministry of Trade of November 14, 1978, *Biulleten' normativinykh aktov ministerstv i vedomstr SSSR*, No. 8 (1979), 40.

29. See the January 9, 1981, Decree of the CC CPSU and the Council of Ministers of the USSR, "O dopolnitel'nykh merakh po uvecheniiu proizbodstva sel'skokhoziaistvennoi produktsii v lichnykh podcobnykh khoziaistvakh grazhdan" ["On Further Measures to Increase the Production of Agricultural Products in the Personal Subsidiary Farming Operations of Citizens"], *SP SSSR*, No. 6, item 37 (1981).

technical conditions. There is a state system of standards in the USSR, which functions on all levels of management of the economy. Supervision over the setting of standards is carried out by agencies of general competence (the higher agencies of state power and the agencies of state administration of the USSR, the Union and autonomous republics, and also the local Soviets of People's Deputies and their legislative committees), the State Committee on Standards of the Council of Ministers of the USSR as an agency of special competence,[30] and the agencies of competence in regard to sectors (ministries and agencies).

A standard establishes the requirements for designated products. From a legal point of view it is considered a rule of general application.[31] It specifies the technical and other characteristics applicable to the product. All industrial products, including the individual component parts and units, which are produced on a permanent basis by associations and enterprises, are subject to certification by standards.[32] Technological processes, methods of production, and other items are also subject to standardization.

Not subject to standardization are industrial products without preliminary processing (petroleum, coal, ore, gas, natural food products, and the like); thermal and electrical energy; industrial products prepared pursuant to single contractual orders; spare parts and components for industrial products that have been removed from production; drugs; books; works of art; articles of jewelry and other craft articles; experimental models (or experimental batches) of products; and certain other items.

Distinctions are made between state standards (GOST), adopted by agencies of the USSR (the Council of Ministers of the USSR, the State Committee on Standards of the USSR, and the State Committee on New

---

30. See the Statute of the State Committee on Standards of the Council of Ministers of the USSR of September 17, 1973, adopted by the Decree of the Council of Ministers of the USSR, *SP SSSR*, No. 21, item 117 (1973).

31. *See* V.M. Ogruzkov, *Osnovy pravovego regulirovaniia kachestva produktsii* [*Fundamentals of the Legal Regulations of the Quality of Goods*] (Moscow: Moscow Standards Publishing House, 2d ed., 1976), p. 76.

32. See the December 11, 1979, Decree of the Council of Ministers of the USSR, "O dal'neishem usilenii roli attestatsii promyshlennoi produktsii i povyshenii ee tekhnicheskogo urovniia i kachestva" ["On the Further Strengthening of the Role of Certification of Industrial Products and the Raising of Their Technical Level and Quality"], *SP SSSR*, No. 2, item 11 (1980). *See also* the May 12, 1986, Decree of the CC CPSU and the Council of Ministers of the USSR, "O merax po kornomu povisheniu kachestva produktsii" ["On Basic Measures of Raising the Quality of Production"], *SP SSSR*, No. 24, item 139 (1986).

Construction of the USSR); sectorial standards (OST), approved by ministries and agencies; republican standards (RST), approved by the Council of Ministers of the Union Republics and the state planning agencies of the Union republics; and, finally, standards of associations and enterprises (SP), approved by the managers of associations and enterprises.

In some situations, technical conditions are used instead of standards. Technical conditions have the same legal characteristics as standards and are used when approved standards for a given type of product are lacking. Technical conditions are also used where special requirements must be established for a product because of the peculiarities of its production and use. Objects of technical conditions may also include jobs and services. In such cases, the conditions specify the requirements for execution of the work and services (*i.e.*, the quality of repair of furniture, radio and television receivers, household appliances, and the like, and also for the quality of sewing and the external appearances of clothes, shoes, knitted goods, and so forth).[33]

The purpose of standards and technical conditions is to establish minimum requirements for quality of standardized goods and services. Associations and enterprises have no right to supply products that do not meet relevant standards or technical conditions. On the other hand, the production of higher quality goods is encouraged in every possible way (by elevated prices, etc.). For this, of course, the consent of the other parties to the contract must be obtained.

Rules establishing standards and technical conditions are usually mandatory. In recent years, however, use of suppletory rules has increased noticeably. This is reflected by the increasing role of the contract in the economy of the USSR.

Samples or models of goods approved by the competent state agencies for products that do not have standards or technical conditions, also play a significant role in defining the quality of production. In the absence of standards, technical conditions or samples for a given type of product, its level of quality is determined by agreement between the parties to the contract. In such cases, pursuant to Article 245 of the Civil Code of the RSFSR, the quality of the objects sold must correspond to the conditions of the contract, and in the absence of indications in the contract, to the requirements by custom and usage.

Where the health, welfare or safety of Soviet citizens is at issue, however, the articles and commodities sold on the basis of a contract are

33. V.M. Ogruzkov, *Osnovy pravovego regulirovaniia kachestva produktsii* [*Fundamentals of the Legal Regulations of the Quality of Goods*], pp. 74–75.

subject to special monitoring and verification by the State Inspectorate or other state agencies. This applies primarily to the sale of food products and medicine. When associations and enterprises fail to meet requirements of standards, technical conditions, samples or agreements in making goods and services, customers can sue the party to the contract upon which such goods and services were obtained. Courts (if the customer is an individual) and arbitration boards (if the customer is an organization) usually declare such contracts void and award a remedy to the plaintiff.

B. Other Terms

The terms of the contract laid down in the law are not limited to conditions as to price and quality, however. In certain types of contracts, other terms may be fixed as well. For example, in contracts between socialist organizations, the manner of payment for products (commodities) delivered, services provided, or work done, is usually established by law.

In these cases, however, parties to a contract are not to repeat the text of the applicable laws. Rather, they are to be incorporated by reference. Pursuant to the instructions of the State Board of Arbitration of the USSR, "On The Work of Arbitration Boards in the Settlement of Disputes Arising from the Making, Modification, and Termination of Contracts for the Supply of Products and Commodities," of October 31, 1975, the arbitration boards must exclude from the text of contracts terms not pertaining to delivery, and terms that repeat the text of the Statute on Deliveries, Special Conditions for Delivery, and other rules.[34] The requirements set forth apply equally to other types of contracts.

In general, the state determines the terms of the contract by law in those cases where the interests of society have a well-established and durable character. This law can be found in statutes and rules concerning individual types of contracts, price lists, standards, technical conditions, and the like, and in standard contracts, as well.

The process of standardization of terms of a contract has become widespread in the USSR both in relations between socialist organizations and in those involving individuals. The Fundamentals of Civil Legislation provides for a series of standard contracts, which must be approved by the

34. *Sistematizirovannyi sbornik instruktivnykh Ukazanii Gosudarstvennogo arbitrazha pri Sovete Ministrov SSSR* [*A Systematic Collection of Instructional Orders of the State Arbitration Board of the Council of Ministers of the USSR*] (Moscow: Iuridicheskaia Literatura, 1983), pp. 88–106.

authorized state agencies. These include standard contracts for construction (Article 52), for rental of household appliances (Article 55), for ordering of consumer services (Article 66), and for use of copyright material (Article 101). At the same time, the law usually contains, as applied to contracts involving individuals, a special stipulation guaranteeing their rights. Thus, under Article 101 of the Fundamentals of Civil Legislation, a provision in a contract made with an author, which adversely affects his position relative to the position established by law or in the standard contract, is invalid and is to be replaced by the conditions established by law or the standard contract. Standard contracts are approved by the Council of Ministers of the USSR, the Council of Ministers of the Union Republics, or, by delegation from these, by the Union and Republican Ministries and agencies, and have the effect of rules.[35]

C. Terms Formed under the Influence of a Plan

Terms of a contract formulated under the influence of a plan have a more dynamic character than do those fixed by law. They are intended to implement one of the most significant components of the organization and functioning of the Soviet economy—the planned management of the economy. Pursuant to Article 16 of the Constitution of the USSR, management of the economy is carried out on the basis of state plans for economic and social development, with consideration of the principles of sectoral

---

35. The following standard and specimen contracts may be cited as examples: 1) specimen contract for the organization of material and technical supply to a productive association, enterprise or organization, adopted by the December 30, 1981, Normative Order of the State Board of Supply, USSR, and the State Arbitration Board, USSR, *Biulleten' normativnykh aktov ministerstv i vedomstr SSSR*, No. 8 (1982), 39–46; 2) standard contract for the rental of grand and upright pianos to citizens for temporary use (household rentals), adopted by the February 1, 1965, Decree of the Council of Ministers of the RSFSR, *SP RSFSR*, No. 1, item 2 (1965); 3) standard contract for construction of a dwelling or nonresidential building (consumer-service order), adopted by the April 1, 1981, Decree of the Council of Ministers of the RSFSR, *SP RSFSR*, No. 18, item 71 (1981); and 4)standard publishing contract for literary works, adopted by the February 24, 1975, Order of the Chairman of the State Committee of the Council of Ministers, USSR on the Affairs of Publishing Houses, Printing Shops, and Book Trade, *Biulleten' normativnykh aktov ministerstv i vedomstr SSSR*, No. 7 (1975), 34–37.

and territorial control, and with a combination of centralized administration, economic autonomy, and initiative by the enterprises, integrated units,[36] and other organizations.

The effect of state plans of economic and social development of the country extends to all aspects of production in the public sector under socialism: the production of material and technical means and commodities consumed by the people, capital construction, distribution, economic circulation, transportation, services to citizens, and the like. There is a balanced system of planning based on a state plan of economic and social development of the country approved by the Supreme Soviet of the USSR.[37] The degree of influence of state plans on various aspects of the life of the country is not uniform. In relationships between socialist organizations, they achieve their most concentrated and imperative expression. Thus, in the area of deliveries of goods, capital construction, transportation, financing and credit, it is usually not only the type and quantity of products, services, and jobs, but also the makeup of contractual relations in terms of the parties that are the objects of the plan.

A special model of planning is applied to contracts for services between socialist organizations and individuals. Here, planning has a one-sided character, applying only to the organization. Individuals, on the other hand, who participate as consumers, feel the influence of state plans indirectly through the determination of total consumer demand in the country by the state. This indirect influence of the general system of state planning is felt even in relations between individuals when they make contracts in the collective farm markets. This influence primarily has an economic rather than legal effect.

The ways in which planning acts influence contractual relationships are extremely varied. Planning acts that are directly fixed in the terms of contracts are of most interest to jurists. Such contracts are primarily planning contracts made between socialist organizations. In the Soviet legal literature there are many publications devoted to the problems of the

36. Integrated units include every type of association, such as, productive associations, science-productive associations, and others.

37. See the July 12, 1979, Decree of the CC CPSU and the Council of Ministers of the USSR, "Ob uluchenii planirovaniia i usilenii vozdeistviia khoziaistvennogo mekhanizma na povyshenie effektivnosti proizvodstva i kachestva raboty" ["On the Improvement of Planning and the Strengthening of the Influence of the Economic Mechanism for Increasing the Efficiency of Production and Quality of Work"], *SP SSSR*, No. 18, item 118 (1979).

planned (economic) contract.[38] Along with other questions, the problem of the relationship between the plan[39] and the contract receives significant attention in these publications. This problem is treated on two levels: on a general theoretical level, and on a more practical level from the point of view of defining the basis on which contractual obligations arise.

1. Theoretical Analysis

Two basic approaches are applied on the general theoretical level at the present time. Under one approach, the contract is regarded chiefly as an

38. It is sufficient to mention such monographs as: M.M. Agarkov, *Obiazatel'stvo po sovetskomu grazhdanskomu pravu* [*Obligations Under Soviet Civil Law*] (Moscow: Iurizdat, 1940); S.N. Bratus' and L.A. Lunts, *Voprosy khoziaistvennogo dogovora* [*Questions of the Economic Contract*] (Moscow: Gosiurizdat, 1954); R.O. Khalfina, *Znachenie i sushchnost' dogovora v sovetskom sotsialisticheskom prave* [*The Significance and Nature of the Contract in Soviet Socialist Law*] (Moscow: Publishing House of the Academy of Sciences, USSR, 1954); R.O. Khalfina, *Pravovoe regulirovanie postavki produktsii v narodnom khoziaistve* [*The Legal Regulation of the Delivery of Goods in the Economy*] (Moscow: Publishing House of the Academy of Sciences, USSR, 1963); V.N. Mozheiko, *Khoziaistvennyi dogovor v SSSR* [*The Economic Contract in the USSR*] (Moscow: Gosiurizdat, 1962); M.I. Braginskii, *Obshchee uchenie o khoziaistvennykh dogovorakh* [*The General Doctrine of Economic Contracts*] (Minsk: Nauka and Technika Publishing House, 1967); I.A. Tanchuk, V.P. Efimochkin, and T.E. Abova, *Khoziaistvennye obiazatel'stva* [*Economic Obligations*] (Moscow: Iuridicheskaia Literature, 1970); A.G. Bykov, *Plan i khoziaistvennyi dogovor* [*The Plan and the Economic Contract*] (Moscow: Publishing House of Moscow State University, 1975); N.I. Klein, *Organizatsiia dogovorno-khoziaistvennykh sviazei* [*The Organization of Contractual-Economic Relations*] (Moscow: Iuridicheskaia Literatura, 1976); M.G. Braginskii and G.S. Shapkina, *Khoziaistvennye dogovory v material'no-tekhnicheskom snabzhenii* [*Economic Contracts in the Process of Material and Technical Supply*] (Moscow: Economica, 1976); A.K. Kravtsov, *Planovye obiazatel'stva* [*Planning Obligations*] (Voronezh: Publishing House of Voronezh University, 1980).

39. By the plan, we are referring to an administrative document that serves as the basis for making the contract (i.e. the plan of connecting customers to suppliers, or ordering the delivery of goods, and the like). This is not the same as a production plan of an integrated unit (or enterprise), which is formed on the basis of contracts made and orders received by the integrated unit (or enterprise) and affirmed by superordinate agencies. These plans are related, however, and they are coordinated by ministries, agencies, and other administrative organs, which carry out supervision of the integrated units and enterprises.

instrument of planning, conducted by the state. It is thereby regarded as one of the internal elements of the general system of planning in the economy. As such, the contract fulfills the function of making the plan concrete and precise and giving it form. It also serves as a criterion for evaluating the implementation by associations and enterprises of tasks set by the plan. The role of contract, as one of the most important components of commodity-and-money relationships themselves, retreats into the background.[40] Under the other approach the independent existence of the contract is taken as a point of departure and the emphasis is shifted to the interaction between the plan and the contract in which priority is given to the plan.[41] Accordingly, all functions of contract, including its use in the process of planning the management of the economy, are considered in light of this interaction.

The second approach to the evaluation of the relationship between the plan and the contract seems sounder. In a socialist society in which a planned commodity economy functions, both the plan and the contract, as legal instruments, are directed in the final analysis toward the achievement of one goal. They are called upon to provide for the realization of one of the basic economic laws of socialism—the law of the planned development of society, which acts under conditions of commodity production. As is noted in the economic literature, "the law of planned development does not in and of itself regulate any particular proportions or economic connections."[42] It determines only the main, prevailing mode of conduct-

---

40. See, for example, V.V. Laptev, "XXVI s'ezd KPSS i sovershenstvovanie regulirovaniia rukovodstva narodnym khoziaistvom," *XXVI s'ezd KPSS i pravovye voprosy sovershenstvovaniia khoziaistvennogo mekhanizma* ["The Twenty-Sixth Congress of the CPSU and the Improvement of the Regulation and the Supervision of the Economy," *The Twenty-Sixth Congress of the CPSU and Legal Questions of the Improvement of the Economic Mechanism*] (Moscow: Institute of Law and Government, Academy of Sciences, USSR, 1982), pp. 10–11.

41. See, for example, S.N. Bratus', "Grazhdansko-pravovoe regulirovanie imushchestvennykh otnoshenii mezhdu sotasialisticheskimi organizatisiami," *XXVI s'ezd KPSS i problemy ghrazhdanskogo i trudovogo pravam grazhdanskogo protsessa* ["The Regulation by Civil Law of Property Relationships Socialist Organizations," *The Twenty-Sixth Congress of the CPSU and Problems of Civil and Labor Law and Civil Procedure*] (Moscow: Institute of Law and Government, Academy of Sciences, USSR, 1982), p. 27; B.I. Puginskii, *Grazhdansko-pravovye sredstva v khoziaistvennykh otnosheniiakh* [*Civil Law Remedies in Economic Relations*] (Moscow: Iuridicheskaia Literatura, 1984), p. 115.

42. L.I. Abalkin, *Ekonomicheskie zakony sotsializma* [*The Economic Laws of Socialism*] (Moscow: Nauka Publishing House, 1971), p. 101.

ing the economy under socialism.[43] The proportions and connections, which have been indicated, are established by means of state plans of economic and social development and contracts. It would be a mistake, however, to think that the plan serves as the expression only of an economic law of planned development, and the contract as an expression of the economic law of value, which functions under socialism. Both the plan and the contract reflect in themselves the simultaneous operation of the economic law of planned development and the economic law of value. Under socialism, by its very essence, the economy can only be a planned one. The forms of planning are, however, of different kinds—direct, indirect, and so forth. For this reason, it is possible in principle to establish individual economic connections between enterprises without making a contract, on the basis of planning documents alone (for example, the supply of commodities to self-financing associations engaged in foreign trade for export). In the same way, contracts in which indirect methods of planning come into play are also possible. From the economic point of view, both of these fit completely into the framework of a unified planned economy.

Of course, both the plan and the contract have their own peculiarities. In its current form, the plan in the USSR is the directive that expresses primarily the interests of the state as a whole. The interests of individual associations and enterprises have a subordinate significance in it. In the contract, on the other hand, the interest of the state as a whole is refracted through the prism of individual interests of the associations and enterprises participating in it. The latter takes on an autonomous character.

2. *Practical Analysis*

The peculiarities of the plan and the contract, which have been mentioned, make it necessary for them to be applied together in the process of organizing economic relations among associations and enterprises. Since the plan reflects the general economic regularities and interests of society, while the contract reflects the localized interests of individual associations and enterprises, the plan, on the whole, takes precedence over the contract. On the other hand, the forms in which the plan and the contract interact are subject to constant change. They depend on the methods used by the state in the management of the economy, and they exert direct influence at the stage at which planning contracts are made. Three basic

43. *Id.*, p. 102.

positions have been expressed in legal literature concerning the bases on which contractual obligations subject to the plan arise.

The first position is that a contractual obligation arises immediately out of a plan as an administrative act. The contract only makes concrete the mutual obligations of the parties. The administrative act and not the contract is the legal fact that gives rise to the obligation.[44] This point of view was expressed immediately after the end of the Great Patriotic War (World War II), when the role of the contract in relations between socialist organizations was reduced. Even at that time, however, this view was criticized.[45] Today this view completely contradicts existing legislation, and for this reason is only of historical interest.[46]

The second position is based upon a combination of complex legal facts. Under this approach a contractual obligation arises from two legal facts—the plan and the contract. However, the character of interaction of these facts giving rise to the obligation does not coincide, according to some legal scholars. M.M. Agarkov, the originator of this position believed that the planning document gave rise to an obligation of the parties to make a contract, and to discharge this obligation if for some reason the making of the contract should be delayed.[47] Agarkov supported this approach by references to arbitration practice of the period 1938–1948. During this period, which was difficult for the country, deliveries of goods on the basis of planned assignments without contracts occurred. But after

44. N.G. Aleksandrov, "K voprosu o roli dogovora v pravovom regulirovanii obschchestvennykh otnosheniii," *Uchenye zapiski VIIuN* ["On the Question of the Role of the Contract in the Legal Regulations of Social Relationships," *The Scholarly Contributions of the all Union Institute of Legal Research*] (Moscow: Iurizdat, 1946), Issue 6, p. 75.

45. See V.I. Shkundin, *Obziatel'stvo postavki tovarov v sovetskom prave* [*The Obligation for the Delivery of Goods in Soviet Law*] (Moscow: Iruizdat, 1948), pp. 162–165.

46. For this reason it is difficult to agree with the opinions of A.K. Kravtsov, expressed as recently as 1980. In his words, obligations for delivery arise directly from a plan. "In accordance with the obligation arising from a plan," he writes, "the producer and the consumer are obliged not only to make a contract, but to carry out production, on the one hand, and to accept and pay for it, on the other. The planned contract constitutes a legal fact with which the law connects the developments of a single obligation arising from a plan." A.K. Kravtsov, *Planovye obiazatel'stvo* [*Planning Obligations*] (Voronezh: Publishing House of Voronezh University, 1980), p. 10.

47. M.M. Agarkov, *Obiazatel'stvo po sovetskomu grazhdanskomu pravu* [*Obligations Under Soviet Civil Law*], pp. 122–126.

the Council of Ministers of the USSR adopted the resolution of April 21, 1949 on economic contracts, which condemned the practice of non-contractual deliveries, Agarkov's theory lost its legal foundation to a considerable degree.

The legislation in force today requires the formalization, in contracts, of economic relations between socialist organizations, with the exception of cases specifically excluded by law.[48] This requirement prohibits making deliveries or doing work without a contract, prohibits the defense of claims arising out of non-contractual relationships, and requires corresponding organizations to make a contract when the parties have refused, without legal grounds, to do so.[49] Thus, from the bilateral task assigned by the plan, there arises an obligation on the part of associations and enterprises to make a contract in accordance with the provisions of the plan, which, however, can be modified in certain cases by the parties themselves. No other obligation arises directly from the plan. Exceptions relate to a very limited group of cases. In the realm of deliveries, the exceptions relate to goods produced for export, goods destined for the state reserves, or goods taken out of the state reserves for consumption. Essentially, the only case that falls under M.M. Agarkov's theory at the present time relates to the hauling of freight by railroad. On the basis of a monthly plan of freight shipments, senders are obliged to deliver goods for shipment in a timely fashion, before the making of a contract, and the railway is obliged to supply cars in the same way. The contract is then made for shipment of the goods to the appointed place.[50]

---

48. See the October 4, 1965, Decree of the CC CPSU and the Council of Ministers of the USSR, "O sovershenstvovanii planirovaniia i usilenii economicheskogo stimulirovaniia promyshlennogo proizvodtsva" ["On the Improvement of Planning and the Strengthening of Economic Stimulation of Industrial Production"], *SP SSSR*, Nos. 19–20, item 153 (1965); the May 28, 1969, Decree of the CC CPSU and the Council of Ministers of the USSR, "O sovershenstvovanii planivovania i ob stimulirovanii stroitel'nogo proizvodstva" ["On the Planning and Strengthening of Economic Stimulation of Construction Production"], *SP SSSR*, No. 15, item 83 (1969).
49. See the Letter of Instruction of the State Arbitration Board under the Council of Ministers of the USSR of May 31, 1975 (Point 20) in *Sistematizirovannyi sbornik gosudarstvennogo arbitrazha SSSR* [*A Systematic Collection of Instructional Orders of the State Arbitration Board of the Council of Ministers of the USSR*] (Moscow, 1975), p. 163.
50. See Points 18 and 37 of the Charter of the Railroad of the USSR of April 6, 1964, *SP SSSR*, No. 5, item 36 (1964).

In light of what has been said, present day supporters of this theory involving complex legal facts shift their emphasis to other aspects of the interaction of the plan with the contract. First, particular attention is on the impact of the plan on the contract after the contract is made. This is manifested in the possibility of modifying or terminating the contractual obligation before its expiration, through an order given in the plan. Second, supporters emphasize that in the planned contract the terms are determined by the planning directives and not by the parties themselves.[51] They therefore propose that the obligations themselves should be called planned-contractual.[52]

Regarding the first position, it should be noted that all changes introduced into the plan after the contract is made are included in the contract with the consent of the parties. Only with the consent of the parties can the contract be modified or terminated prior to its expiration (Point 31 of the Statutes on Deliveries of Goods for Industrial-Technical Use, and Point 26 of the Statutes on Deliveries for Consumption By the Population). The transformation of a contractual obligation through modification takes place not immediately on the basis of planning directives but rather with the supplementary agreement of the parties to the contract.

Nor is the second position, relating to the basis on which a contractual obligation is formed, convincing. Proponents of this position confuse the provisions of planning directives and the terms of the contract itself, and, in effect, restrict the content of a planned contract to those terms that can be determined by the parties themselves. This directly contradicts Article 34 of the Fundamentals of Civil Legislation. Under this article, planning directives are, in many cases, not automatically included in the contract, but are included by agreement of the parties. In the process of reaching such an agreement, individual directives of the plan may be subjected to modification, and in certain cases may even be rejected. Thus, the theory of complex legal facts does not solve the problems connected with the origin of planned contracts.

---

51. See Z.M. Zamangof, *Izmenenie i rasporiazhenie khoziaistvennykh dogovorov* [*The Modification and Termination of Economic Contracts*] (Moscow: Iuridicheskaia Literatura, 1967), p. 46; Iu. K. Kalmykov, *Pravovoe regulirovnia khoziaistvennykh otnoshenii* [*Legal Regulation of Economic Relationships*] (Saratov: Publishing House of Saratov University, 1982), pp. 135–142.

52. *See* G.S. Shapkina and M.M. Shestakova, *Plan i khoziaistvennyi dogovor* [*The Plan and the Economic Contract*] (Moscow: Znanie, 1981), pp. 32–41.

Today, interactions between the plan and the contract are more flexible and multifold than these arguments recognize. Although in the past the plan normally preceded the contract, today this system is in the process of changing, especially in the field of delivery of goods produced by associations, enterprises, and trade organizations.

Because the above positions do not reflect accurately contemporary contracting practices, a third position, which we can arbitrarily call *the theory of transformation*, seems preferable.[53] It originated at the beginning of the 1960's as a consequence of the increase in the role of the contract in the economy of the country. This theory reflects the development of current legislation on the interaction of the plan and the contract to a considerably greater degree than does the theory of complex legal facts. It is based on three elements.

First, the planning directive is considered a prerequisite for the making of a contract, but not as the immediate basis of the origin of contractual obligations. The directive contains an obligation on the part of socialist organizations to make a contract in accordance with its provisions.

Second, the contract made between socialist organizations is considered as the basis on which a contractual obligation arises between them. The provisions of the planning directives are transformed into the terms of the contract. The character of such transformations in various types of contracts is not identical. One can only say that at the present time, a stable tendency has developed toward broadening the rights of socialist organizations in regard to the possibility of adopting and amplifying the directives of a plan relating to the content of the contract. As an example, we may cite the contract for delivery. Pursuant to Point 16 of the Statute on Deliveries for Productive and Technical Processes, the customer is entitled to refuse all or part of the articles assigned to him and to reject the making of the contract for the delivery of such items. Furthermore, Point 15 of the Statute on Deliveries of Goods for Consumption by the Population empowers the customer to refuse in whole or in part excessive or unnecessary goods allotted to him and to refrain from making a contract for the

---

53. *See* R.O. Khalfina, *Pravovoe regulirovanie postavki produktsii v narodnom khoziaistve* [*The Legal Regulation of the Delivery of Goods in the Economy*], pp. 104–120; I.V. Feodorov, *Khoziaistvennye sviazi v SSSR voprosy teorii pravovogo regulirovaniia* [*Economic Connections in the USSR on Questions of the Theory of Legal Regulation*] (Tomsk: Tomsk University Publishing House, 1978), pp. 8, 109–126; A.G. Bykov, *Plan i khoziaistvennyi dogovor* [*The Plan and the Economic Contract*], pp. 31–36.

delivery of the goods. In practice, customer organizations frequently make use of these rights.[54]

Third, the directives of the plan remain in force throughout the entire period of the contract. However, its functions undergo specific changes in connection with the provisions of the plan included in the contract. At a particular stage the plan is transformed into a monitoring and directive document intended to promote the performance by the organizations of the contractual obligations that they have assumed. In addition, the plan performs the function of a mechanism to help the planning agencies carry out modifications of directives for contracts where necessary.

The theory of transformation, however, is inadequate to explain the new developments in modern contract law. Today, contracts made at whole-sale fairs provide the bases for which the production plans of associations and enterprises in light industry are created. Since January 1, 1987, only three elements contained in five-year and one-year plans must be approved by state agencies for associations and enterprises in light industry. These elements relate to: 1) the types of goods to be produced, 2) profits, and 3) making production facilities and facilities for socio-cultural purposes funded by state-centralized capital investments operational.[55] Associations and enterprises of other ministries and agencies have followed the example set by light industry concerning the free sale of goods. These associations and enterprises are free to purchase whatever products are necessary for industrial and technical purposes through wholesale trade. Long-term contracts with territorial organizations of the State Committee for supply of the USSR are made in this way.[56] In the future, associations and

---

54. "Postanovlenie glavnogo gosudarst vennogo arbitra Gruzinskoi SSR ob otkaze v ponuzhdenii pokupatelia k zaluchenia dogovora," *Khoziaistvo i pravo* ["Decision of the Main State Arbitor of the Georgian Soviet Socialist Republic to Refuse to Compel the Purchaser to Make a Contract." *Economy and Law*], No. 2 (1984), 89–90.

55. See the April 24, 1986, Decree of the CC CPSU and the Council of Ministers of the USSR, "Ob ulushchenii planirovaniia, ekonomicheskogo stimulirovaniia i sovershenstvovaniia upraveleniia v legkoi promishlennosti" ["On the Improvement of Planning, Economic Incentives and Perfection of Management in Light Industry"], *SP SSSR*, No. 20, item 108 (1986).

56. See the March 27, 1986, Decree of the CC CPSU and the Council of Ministers of the USSR, "O perevode ob'edinenii, predpriiatii i organizazii otdel'nix ministerstv i vedomstv na material'no—technicheskoe snabzhenie v poriadke optovoi torgovli" ["On the Transfer of Associations, Enterprises, and Organizations of Some Ministries and Agencies of Material—Technical Supplies in the Way of Wholesale Trade"], *SP SSSR*, No. 18, item 94 (1986).

enterprises of most other industries will also participate in wholesale trade. In light of this new relationship between the plan and the contract, it is perhaps more appropriate to speak of this as the theory of interaction of the plan and the contract rather than as the theory of transformation.

The terms of the contract formed under the influence of a plan occupy a prominent place in the relations between socialist organizations. As the analysis of individual types of contracts shows, these terms are most common in contracts for the transportation of freight, for capital construction, and for credit and accounting relations. The number of such terms decreases in contracts for agricultural products and becomes still lower in delivery contracts.[57]

However, an extreme variant is also possible, in which all the conditions of a contract are determined on the basis of a plan. Such is the case when a contract is made by the adoption of an order (Article 160 of the Civil Code of the RSFSR), which usually occurs during the delivery of products and goods. An order is a planned directive issued to suppliers and customers by the agencies of material and technical supplies, the Ministry of Trade or other ministries and agencies, on the basis of which a delivery contract is made. It specifies all the data needed for a delivery, including the types of products or commodities, the quantity, the assortment, and the means and price of delivery. The order is considered to have been accepted, and acquires the force of a contract, if within a ten day period after its receipt, neither of the parties makes a demand on the other that it agree to additional terms or declares its non-agreement to it. If one party responds with such a demand or declaration, then the usual procedure for making a contract is applied.[58] Most writers consider the order as a contract when it has been accepted for implementation.[59] This opinion is well founded, because as acceptance of the terms of the order depends in the final analysis, on the will of the parties to the contract.

---

57. See B.I. Puginskii, *Grazhdansko-pravovye sredstva v khoziaistvennykh otnosheniiakh* [*Civil Law Remedies in Economic Relations*], pp. 113–114.
58. See Pointe 23 of the Letter of Instruction of the State Arbitration Board of October 31, 1975, *Sistematizirovannyi sbornik gosudarstvennogo arbitrazha SSSR* [*A Systematic Collection of Instructional Orders of the State Arbitration Board of the Council of Minister of the USSR*], pp. 96–98.
59. See, for example, F.I. Gavze, *Sotsialisticheskii grazhdansko-pravovoi dogovor* [*The Socialist Contract in Civil Law*], p. 113. A contrary opinion is expressed by I.A. Tanchuk. "Without the effect and the accent," he writes, "there is not a contract in the precise sense of this word." I.A. Tanchuk, *Khoziaistvennoe pravo* [*Economic Law*] (Moscow: Iuridicheskaia Literatura, 1967), p. 328.

D. Terms Established by the Parties Themselves

The interests of individuals and organizations that are not reflected in the terms defined by rulemaking procedures and on the basis of planning directives, are manifested in the terms established by the parties. This method of contracting is broadest in relations between individuals. Not infrequently, parties determine all of the terms of their contract. It is applied less frequently in contracts for service to the population by socialist organizations, and becomes even more limited in relations among organizations. Even in the latter group of relations, however, contractual terms established by the parties occupy an important place. As is noted in the literature, the parties are entitled, at their own discretion, to include in the contract any terms that they think necessary, provided that the given terms are not assigned to the exclusive authority of state agencies and do not contravene the law.[60] That the parties are free to establish their own terms is firmly based on legislation. For example, pursuant to Point 4 of the Statute on Deliveries of Products for Industrial and Technical Purposes, ministries and departments are not permitted to include in the Special Conditions of Deliveries provisions that infringe upon the rights of the parties to establish the terms of such deliveries themselves.

In connection with the broadening of the economic autonomy of associations and enterprises and the reduction in the number of requirements set by the plan that define their activity in the fields of production and marketing, the rights of associations and enterprises in contracting are also being expanded. In particular, associations and enterprises are granted the right to alter the assortment of products to be delivered pursuant to a contract and the times and other terms of such deliveries.[61]

In addition, many terms determined by rulemaking procedures and on the basis of planning documents can be corrected in particular ways by associations and enterprises. In essence, such terms are transformed into mixed terms of a contract. They are combinations of prescriptions by the state derived from both legislation and other rules and tasks set by the

60. G.S. Shapkina, *Obsobye usloviia postavki produktsii proizvodstevenno-tekhnicheskogo naznacheniia* [*Special Conditions for the Delivery of Goods for Productive and Technical Purposes*] (Moscow: Iuridicheskaia Literatura, 1980), p. 33.

61. See Point 100 of the Statute on Productive Associations (Combines), adopted by the March 27, 1974, Decree of the Council of Ministers of the USSR, *SP SSSR*, No. 8, item 38 (1974); Pointe 67 of the Statute on Socialist State Productive Enterprises of October 4, 1965, *SP SSSR*, Nos. 19–20, item 155 (1965).

plan, and from decisions adopted by the parties. Legally speaking, this is often achieved by means of prescriptions that are suppletory.

The presence in the contract of the three types of terms—those laid down in law, those formulated under the influence of a plan, and those made by the parties themselves—may be different in each case depending upon the category to which a particular contract belongs (i.e whether the contract is between organizations, between organizations and individuals, or simply between individuals) and the method of management being applied to the industry involved in the contract. In the most important sections of the economy, a multi-structural system of terms of civil contracts is applied, which has as its main goal the harmonization of the interests of society and those of individual citizens and organizations. Beyond the limits of such a system, the contract cannot function under the conditions of socialist society.

In the past two years the significance of the civil law contract has grown considerably. This is particularly evident in the normative acts passed during this time.[62] These acts reflect a recent trend towards creating a new system for managing the national economy based mostly on economic methods.

1.3 The Distinction between the Contract as Civil Law and Other Forms of Contracts

Contract as a legal institution is widely used in other branches of Soviet law, as well as in international law. In each of these branches it has its own peculiarities. There is no general legal concept of contract suitable for all branches of law.

Along with the concept of the contract as a legal institution, the concept of contract as a pure theoretical model is also encountered in the literature.

62. See, for example, the June 5, 1986, Decree of the CP CPSU and the Council of Ministers of the USSR, "O povishenii otvetstvennosti ob'edinenii, predpriatii i organizazii za vipolnenie dogovorov postavki produkzii i tovarov" ["On Raising the Responsibilities of Enterprises and Organizations for Performance of Contracts of Delivery of Products and Goods"] *SP SSSR*, No. 25, item 140 (1986). See also the report given by N. Talizuen about the State Plan of economic and social development of the USSR in 1947 and the course of fulfillment of the plan in 1946, which states that, "Beginning in 1947, the criteria for industrial associations and enterprises would be to have 100 percent of their contractual obligations performed." *Izvestia*, November 18, 1986, p. 2, col. 2.

Whereas the concept of contract as a legal institution is embodied in the law, the concept of contract as a theoretical model is used for scholarly purposes.[63] The latter concept is very arbitrary in nature. It treats a contract as a general concept applicable to the establishment, modification, or termination of legal relationships in all branches of law.[64] This model, however, is of relatively little value. As has already been noted, the very concept of an agreement in only one branch of the law is itself ambiguous. For this reason, the use of the concept of an agreement in the definition of a contract raises more questions than it answers.

Descriptions of the content of contracts, which relate to various specific branches of law, are of considerably greater scholarly and practical importance. From the totality of legal characteristics, which are accumulated in the branch-by-branch concept of contract, there proceeds an individualization of one type of contract relative to another. This is necessary not only for their differentiation, but for the possibility of simultaneous use of various contracts in complex relationships regulated by the rules of several different branches of law.

The distinction between the contract as civil law and other types of contracts specific to particular branches does not involve any particular complexities. In some branches of the law, contracts are referred to by a different name. For example, in constitutional law, contracts are called treaties. Treaties are made between bodies of state, which extend beyond the limits of the status of legal person. The content of such treaties includes questions of the structure of national states and the execution of functions of political power in the political, economic, and social life of society. The most vivid example of this is the Treaty on the Formation of the USSR made in December of 1922. This treaty provided for the unification of four republics (the Russian Soviet Federated Socialist Republic, the Ukranian Soviet Socialist Republic, the Belorussian Soviet

---

63. M.K. Suleimenov, "Pravovoi institut v sisteme sovetskogo prava," *Izvestiian A.N. Kazakhskoi SSR* ["The Legal Institution in the System of Soviet Law," *Proceedings of the Academy of Sciences, Kazakh SSR*], No. 2 (1976), 78–79; I.A. Tanchuk, "O dogovornykh formakh i metodakh upravleniia narodnym khoziaistvom," *Dogovornye formy upravleniia: postanovka problemy i puti resheniia* (Materialy Moskovskovogo soveshchaniia VNII sistemnykh issledovanii) ["On Contractual Forms and Methods of Administration of the Economy," *Contractual Forms of Administration: Formulation of the Problem and Paths to a Solution* (Materials of the Moscow Meeting of the USSR-Wide Scientific Research Institute of Systems' Research)] (Moscow, 1981), p. 65.
64. *Id.*

Socialist Republic, and the Transcaucasian Soviet Federal Socialist Republic) into a single federated state—the Union of Soviet Socialist Republics.

There are also significant differences between the contract as civil law and the two basic contracts envisaged by labor legislation—the labor contract and the collective contract. As distinct from the civil contracts for construction, commissioning, and copyright, all of which can be compared with the labor contract, the labor contract is an agreement relating to a particular labor function of an employee. Under this agreement the employee loses his autonomy and becomes a member of a working collective of an enterprise, institution, or organization. In this capacity, he is subject to an internal labor regime.[65]In the civil contract, on the other hand, the parties retain their independent positions in discharging their duties. Other distinctions between the labor contract and the civil contract usually relate to the more comprehensive bargaining powers of the parties to a civil contract, including payments.

The collective contract, which is also provided for in labor legislation, is made by the factory, plant, or local committee of a trade union, in the name of a collective of blue-collar or white-collar workers, with the management of an enterprise or organization (Article 6 of the Fundamentals of Labor Legislation). This contract specifies the relationship between management and the working collective with regard to questions of labor, wages, the development of production, the satisfaction of the sociocultural and material needs of the workers, and other questions connected with the activity of the enterprise or organization. None of these terms are included in the civil law contract because civil legislation is not supposed to regulate such relations within the enterprise itself.

The civil law contract also differs from the administrative contract, whose fate has not yet been fully defined. Along with assertions that this type of contract should be recognized[66] one encounters doubts as to the

---

65. See Article 8 of the *Fundamentals of Legislation of the USSR and the Union Republics on Labor*, *Vedomosti Verkhovnogo Soveta SSSR*, No. 29, item 265 (1970).

66. See, for example, I.A. Iampolskaia, "O teorii administraivnogo dogovora," *Sovetskoe gosudarstva i pravo* ["On the Theory of the Administrative Contract," *Soviet Law and Government*], No. 10 (1966); V.I. Novoselov, "K voprosu ob administrativnogo dogovorakh," *Pravovedenie* ["On the Question of Administrative Contracts," *Jurisprudence*], No. 3 (1979).

correctness of such assertions.[67] This negativism in regard to the administrative (or, more broadly, management) type of contract hardly seems justified. As has been indicated in the literature, "their use to overcome barriers between branches and agencies, both on the level of the central organs of management, and on the middle and lower levels for rational organization of comprehensive territorial management, is especially significant at the present time."[68]

The content of an administrative contract usually consists of the cooperation of the agencies of state administration that supervise the activity of organizations under their jurisdiction. In a number of cases, this applies to individuals as well. In principle, the possibility of making administrative contracts along vertical lines, between superordinate and subordinate organs and organizations also is not excluded. As distinct from the civil law contract, which has as its goal the exchange of performances between the parties themselves relating to goods or services, the administrative contract has a different goal. Exchange of performance between the parties in such contracts means that each of the parties will bring into the action third persons, who are obligated to discharge duties mentioned in the contract.

In those cases where associations and enterprises involved in economic activity appear as third persons, the administrative contract fulfills organizational and planning functions in relation to civil contracts that will be made as a result of administrative contracts. This type of administrative contract is therefore called an organizational contract.

In recent years, the attention of scholars has been drawn to two administrative contracts. One is the contract specifying the interrelationship between the Union-wide supply-and-marketing agency under the State Board of Supply of the USSR, on the one hand, and the management of an integrated industrial unit or other self-supporting organ of industrial management on the other. This contract is used in connection with the supply-

---

67. See Iu. M. Kozlov, *Administrativnye pravootnosheniia* [*Administrative Legal Relationships*] (Moscow: Iuridicheskaia Literatura, 1976), p. 183.

68. B.P. Kurashvilli, "O poniatii administrativnogo dogovora," *Dogovornye formy upravleniia: postanovka problemy i puti resheniia* ["On the Concept of the Administrative Contract," *Contractual Forms of Administration: Formulation of the Problem and Paths to a Solution*] (Materials of the USSR-Wide Scientific Research, Institute of Systems' Research) (Moscow, 1981), p. 53.

ing of products to the economy for industrial and technical purposes.[69] The other is the contract between the main trade administration of the Ministry of Trade of the USSR (or the wholesale organization of the ministry of trade of a Union republic) and an integrated industrial unit (or the main management body of a ministry). This contract is used in connection with the organization of production, delivery, and sale of commodities for consumption by the population.[70] In their economic and legal nature both of these contracts belong to the category of organizational contracts. No performance relating to goods or services occurs within the framework of these contracts. Such performance is carried out by other contracts, such as delivery contracts.

The organizational nature of the contracts under consideration is reflected in their content. This can be seen for example, from individual provisions of a contract for supplying products to the economy for industrial and technical purposes. Pursuant to Point 2 of the Specimen Statute on this contract, the management of an integrated industrial unit (or other self-supporting organ of industrial administration) undertakes to provide for the procurement of products by its member enterprises, in quantities and in an assortment (or according to a list) agreed upon by the Union-wide supply-and-marketing agency. The latter then undertakes to sell these products and to supply to the member enterprises of the integrated units, in timely fashion, planning documents for the delivery of the raw and intermediate materials and equipment for which it issues such planning documents. Other obligations of the parties, of a specific, informational,

---

69. See the Specimen Contract on the Relationship of the USSR-wide Chief Supply-and-Marketing Agency Under the State Bureau of Supply of the USSR with the Management of an Integrated Industrial Unit and Other Self-Supporting Organs of Industrial Administration for the Organization of Supply of the Economy with Goods for Industrial and Technological Purposes, adopted by the December 28, 1981, Normative Order of the State Bureau of Supply of the USSR and the State Arbitration Board of the USSR, *Biulleten' normativnykh aktov ministerstv i vedomstr SSSR*, No. 9 (1982), 9.

70. See the Statute on Times and Procedures for the Conclusion of a Five Year Agreement Between the Main Administrations of the Ministry of Trade of the USSR (the wholesale organizations of the Ministries of Trade of the Union republics) and Integrated and Industrial Units (main administrations of ministries); and the Specimen Agreement on the Organization of Production, Delivery, and Marketing of Goods for Consumption by the Population, adopted by the May 12, 1981, Normative Order of the State Arbitration Board of the USSR, *Biulleten' normativnykh aktov ministerstv i vedomstr SSSR*, No. 10 (1981), 23.

and coordinational character, are formulated in accordance with the obligations set forth. Here, the management aspect of the activity of the parties in supervising the enterprises and organizations under their jursidiction lies at the basis of the contract itself. Liability, in the form of payment of damages for losses and the exaction of fines, is provided for in case of violation of the obligations assumed by the parties to the contract. In the literature, this liability is considered to be liability under civil law.[71]

The opinion of scholars is divided on the question of how such contracts[72] should be described in legal terms. At least four points of view exist, according to which the contract is considered as falling under civil law,[73] under economic law,[74] under administrative law (the evaluation of the contract as a tool of economic management approximates this view),[75]

---

71. See, for example, N.I. Klein, "Dogovory organov gosudarstvennogo upravleniia v sfere snabzheniia i sbyta," *Dogovornye formy upravleniia: postanovka problemy i puti resheniia* ["Contracts of the Organs of the State Administration in the Sphere of Supply and Marketing," *Contractual Forms of Administration: Formulation of the Problems and Paths to a Solution*] (Materials of the USSR-Wide Scentific Research, Institute of Systems' Research) (Moscow, 1981), p. 59; G.S. Gurevich, "Problema sanktsii v dogovore mezhdu organami gosudarstvennogo upravleniia v sfere narodinogo khoziaistva," ["The Problem of Sanctions in the Contracts Between Organs of State Administration in the Sphere of the Economy"], *Id.*, p. 104.

72. The positions set forth here apply in full to the contract of the main administration of the Ministry of Trade of the USSR (the wholesale organization of the Ministry of Trade of the Union republics) with organizations for production, delivery, and marketing of goods for consumption by the population.

73. V.F. Iakovleva, V.T. Smirnov, *Pravovye problemy perevozki i materialnotekhnicheskogo snabzheniia* [*Legal Problems of Transportation and Material-Technological Supply*] (Leningrad: Publishing House of Leningrad State University, 1978), p. 28.

74. A.G. Bykov, *Plan i khoziaistvennyi* [*The Plan and the Economic Contract*], pp. 76–77; V.V. Laptev, "Khoziaistvennyui mekhanizm i khoziaistvennoe pravo," *Kommunist* ["The Economic Mechanism and Economic Law," *The Communist*], No. 16 (1980), 51.

75. N.I. Klein, "Dogovory organov gosudarstvennogo upravleniia v sfere snabzheniia i sbyta," *Dogovornye formy upraveleniia: postanovka problemy i puti resheniia* ["Contracts of the Organs of the State Administration in the sphere of Supply and Marketing," *Contractual Forms of Administration: Formulation of the Problems and Paths to a Solution*], p. 60; I.A. Tanchuk, *Khoziaistvennow pravo. Obshchie polozheniia* [*Economic Law: General Provisions*], ed., V.V. Laptev (Moscow: Nauka Publishing House, 1983), pp. 210–213.

and as a compound phenomenon, uniting elements of administrative law and civil law.[76]

From the point of view of the legislation now in force, the contract between the Union-wide supply-and-marketing agency and the management of a combined industrial unit does not seem to be a contract under civil law. Parties to this contract are not supposed to exchange products for money,[77] and most important, the contractual relationship itself does not involve reciprocal legal relationships. Its basic goal is the exertion of legal influence on third persons, which are administratively subordinate to the enterprises under the jurisdiction of the management of the integrated unit or functionally dependent on the parties to the contract (the customers who receive orders from the Union-wide supply-and-marketing agency). In addition, the parties to the contract appear in the role of agencies of the administration of the economy, and not in the role of legal persons. This applies in equal measure to the impossibility of describing such contracts as relating to economic law, inasmuch as the economic contract constitutes one of the varieties of the contract as civil law.

As for the assertion that such contracts have a compound character, there cannot be any doubt. This is true because this contract, being organizational in its substance, has a liability provision that looks like a liability provision in a civil law contract. A liability provision in such a contract does not, however, change its organizational aspect.

For this reason, it seems preferable to describe such contracts as administrative contracts of a cooperative type.[78] They are intermediate organizational links in the system, which provide for interrelation between state plans and delivery contracts. Their basic goal is to organize the legal connections, pursuant to the plan, between suppliers and purchasers for large groups of products and commodities produced for both industrial and personal consumption.

---

76. M.I. Braginskii and G.S. Shapkina, *Khoziaistvennyi dogovory v material'no-tekhnicheskom snabzhenii i sbyta* [*Economic Contracts in the Process of Material and Technical Supply*], pp. 180–181.

77. Property sanctions do not enter into the content of the basic contractual obligation. They are a part of the secondary obligations, arising as a result of breaches of the contractual duties by the parties.

78. "Coordination is an inseparable element of almost any of the functions of administration, which fully corresponds to the coordinational nature of administrative activity." *Osnovyn upravleniia narodnym khoziaistvom* [*Fundamentals of the Administration of the Economy*], eds., M.M. Koslov, B.M. Lasarev, A.E. Lunev, M.I. Piskotin (Moscow: Iuridicheskaia Literatura, 1981), p. 101.

The effectiveness of these contracts depends to a considerable degree on the methods of planning which are applied. When there is detailed planning for associations and enterprises relating to the production and delivery of goods (quantity, assortment and so on), the significance of organizational contracts is reduced. It follows then, that as economic autonomy of associations and enterprises is broadened, the role of such contracts increases in the organization of deliveries of products and commodities for the economy and for the population of the country.

Chapter 2

History of Contract Law

The present-day concept of the contract is the result of seventy years of development of contract law in the USSR. It has involved the creation of a new type of contractual relationship in connection with the transition to a socialist organization of the economy, based on public forms of property and planned supervision of the economy. Previously unknown social elements and characteristics were introduced into the institution of contract. At the same time, the legal concept of contract retained its basic features, similar to those found in the legal systems of other countries.

As one of the basic institutions of civil law, contract law, in the course of its development, has been subject to the influence of the same socioeconomic and political factors as Soviet civil law in general. Its development has gone hand in hand with the development of those relationships in society that it has been called upon to regulate.

The history of the creation and development of socialism in the USSR can be divided into three major stages. These are: first, the stage of the construction of the foundations of socialism (the transitional period), occupying the first two decades after the Great October Socialist Revolution of 1917; second, the stage of the complete and final victory of socialism, from the mid-1930's to the end of the 1950's and early 1960's; and third, the stage of developed socialism. The country is now in the initial stage of developed socialism.[1]

1. In the CPSU Program (new edition) adopted by the 27th Party Congress, the modern period of the development of socialism is characterized by the systematic and comprehensive perfection of socialism and further progress of Soviet society towards communism on the basis of the acceleration of the socio-economic development of the country. ("Materials from the 27th Congress of the Communist Party of the Soviet Union," Moscow, Political Literature Publishers, 1986, p. 122).

These stages determine the basic stages in the development of Soviet law and government. In the history of civil law in general, and of contract law in particular, there were of course peculiar features determined by their own dates of reckoning, such as the dates of the adoption of legal codes and other major legislation. These landmarks, in the development of contract law, were in the last analysis indissolubly connected with the major socioeconomic and political events in the life of society as a whole.

2.1 Contract Law at the Stage of the Construction of the Foundations of Socialism

During the first stage, the foundations of Soviet contract law were laid. This took place under complex historical conditions. Foreign intervention and the civil war, the heterogeneous sectors of the economy during the transitional period from capitalism to socialism, and finally, the very novel nature of the tasks to be solved, not only complicated the legislative activity of the state in creating new laws, but also made the process of decision-making in this area highly tentative. In order to comprehend this, it is necessary to trace the development of contract law by individual periods, as is done in the literature.[2]

A. The Period of the Great October Socialist Revolution, the Foreign Intervention, and the Civil War (1917–1920)

The first period under discussion began with the Great October Socialist Revolution of 1917 and ended with the conclusion of the Civil War in 1920. The most characteristic feature of this period in the field of contract law was the spread of regulation by administrative law in many areas, which before the revolution, had been subject to the effect of civil law.

With the nationalization of major means of production and the formation of the institutions of socialist ownership, a significant number of prerevolutionary contractual relationships were abolished. This applied primarily to transactions in land. According to the "Decree on Land"

---

2. See, for example, I.B. Novitskii, *Istoriia sovetskogo grazhdanskogo prava* [*The History of Soviet Civil Law*] (Moscow: Gosiurizdat, 1957); F.I. Gavze, *Razvitie sotsialisticheskoi grazhdansko-pravovogo dogovora* [*Development of the Socialist Civil Contract*] (Minsk: Publishing House of Belorussian State University, 1959).

adopted by the First Congress of Soviets on October 26, 1917, and the "Peasant Mandate On The Land," on which it was based,[3] the right of private ownership of land, underground deposits, forests, and water, was abolished without compensation. These were declared to be the property of the whole people and passed into the exclusive use of the state. At the same time, the "Peasant Mandate On The Land" declared that land could not be bought or sold, rented, or mortgaged or alienated in any other way. The prohibitions applied equally to the underground deposits, forests, and water. By this act, contracts of purchase and sale, gift, rental, and mortgaging of land and other objects of the exclusive ownership of the state were placed outside the law. The transfer of the land to the use of the peasants was carried out by administrative acts.

After the adoption of the Resolution of the All-Union Central Executive Committee of December 14, 1917,[4] most bank transactions were not allowed. Stocks and bonds issued by banks were annulled. Only short term bonds and series of the State Treasury remained in force. All acts and transactions of any type involving the transfer of stocks and bonds were forbidden under penalty of a prison sentence of up to three years.

The state took a more cautious attitude with regard to the nationalization of industry and the limitation of transactions of private enterprises. In the original draft of the "April Theses," written prior to the Great October Socialist Revolution, Lenin envisaged "*not* the introduction of socialism *at once* but the systematic, step by step transition of the Soviets of Workers' Deputies, without undue delay to *control* production and distribution of products for the use of society as a whole."[5]

Events developed otherwise, however. The first half of this plan was implemented immediately after the accomplishment of the revolution. On November 14, 1917, the "Statute on Workers' Control" was adopted by the All-Union Central Executive Committee and the Council of People's Commissars. Pursuant to this statute, "control by the workers over the production, purchase, sale, and storage of products and raw materials, and also over the financial aspect of the enterprise, is instituted in all industrial, commercial, banking, agricultural, transportation, consumers' and producers' cooperatives, and other enterprises, which have hired workers

3. *Sobranie Uzakonenie RSFSR* [*Collection of Normative Rules adopted by the Central Execution Committee and/or the Council of the Peoples Commisars of RSFSR*] [hereinafter cited as *SU RSFSR*], No. 1, item 3 (1917).

4. *SU RSFSR*, No. 10, item 150 (1917).

5. V.I. Lenin, *Soch. izdanie 4-oe* [*Collected Works, 4th Edition*] (Moscow: Politicheskaia Literatura, 1950), Volume 31, p. 100.

or give out work to be done at home."[6] The organs of the worker's control received the right to establish the minimum quantity of products produced by the enterprise, to receive necessary information on the cost of production, and to exercise control over the business correspondence of the enterprise. For example, in 1918 the Raw Materials Commission under the Central Council of Factory and Plant Committees of Petrograd distributed raw material, regulated its delivery to the factories, gave permission for the shipping of commodities, reported to the Soviets at the receiving points the prices at which the commodity was bought, and arranged for the arriving commodity to be taken under control.[7]

In order to ensure the productive activity of the enterprises, their owners were permitted to make contracts for the purchase of materials, fuel, and equipment. These contracts were under the supervision of the organs of workers' control. There could, of course, be no question of any "freedom of contract" for the owners. At the same time, all transactions under civil law involving these enterprises themselves were limited or forbidden.[8]

The second part of the plan relating to the nationalization of private enterprise had to be implemented by the state at an accelerated pace because of sabotage and insubordination by owners of the enterprises.

---

6. *SU RSFSR*, No. 3, item 35 (1917).

7. See "Rabochii kontrol' i natsionalizatsiia promyshlennykh predpriiatii Petrograda v 1917–1919 gg." ["Workers' Control and the Nationalization of the Industrial Enterprises of Petrograd from 1917–1919"]. (From the statement of the Committee of Workers of the Nevka Spinning Factory on January 16, 1918, sent to the district and central council factories, enterprises, and the Committee of Petrograd for the permission of exchange of the lowest quality of cotton for the highest quality.) Document #306 (Leningrad, 1947), p. 327.

8. *See* the Decree of the Council of People's Commissars of the RSFSR of December 14, 1917, "O zapreshyenii sdelok po prodazhe, pokupke, zalogu i.t.p. vsex nedvizhemostei i zemej' v gorodax" ["On the Prohibition of Transactions for the Sale, Purchase, Mortgaging, etc., of All Real Estate and Land in Cities"], *SU RSFSR*, No. 10, item 154 (1917); Decree of the Council of People's Commissars of the RSFSR of April 20, 1918, "O zapreshyenii, bez osobogo v kazhdom otdel'nom sluchae razreshenia narkomata torgovli i promishlennosti, prodazhi, zdachi v arendu ili ustupki polnost'u ili chastichno torgovix i torgovo prozhishlennix predpriatii" ["On the Prohibition, Without Special Permission in each Individual Case from the People's Commissariat of Trade and Industry, of the Sale, the Leasing, or Mortgaging, Transfer, Transmission, or Concession, in Full or in Part, of Commercial and Commercial-Industrial Enterprises"], *SU RSFSR*, No. 32, item 425 (1918).

Originally only individual large enterprises were to be nationalized.[9] After the beginning of the foreign intervention and Civil War in the spring of 1918, however, the state was compelled to nationalize other enterprises. In 1920, medium-sized enterprises were nationalized.[10] Small enterprises remained unnationalized but were subject to registration and carried out their activity under the control of the state. In particular, the articles manufactured by them that were of interest to the state as a whole had to be delivered to state organs and cooperative organizations.

Other areas of activity, including insurance[11] and foreign trade,[12] were made subject to state monopoly. Wholesale and retail enterprises were nationalized.[13] At the end of this period the nationalization of basic means of production was completed. While this was occurring, however, the question of the management of the socialized sector, which was based on

---

9. See the Decrees of the Council of People's Commissars, "O nazionalizazii saxarnoi promishlennosti" ["On the Nationalization of Sugar"], *SU RSFSR*, No. 45, item 546 (1918);" O nazionalizazii torphianoi promishlennositi" ["On the Nationalization of the Peat Industry"], *SU RSFSR*, No. 34, item 457 (1918); "O nazionalizazii krupneishix predpriatii gornoi metalurgicheskoi metallo'obrabatuvaushyei tekstil'noi elektrotexnicheskoi, lesopil'noi, devevo'obrabativanshnyca tabacjpo. stelp'noi, keramicheskoi, kozhevennoi, zementnoi i prochix otraslei promishlennosti parovix mel'niz, predpriatii po mestnomu blagoustroistvu, predpriatii v oblasti zheleznodorzhnogo transporta" ["On the Nationalization of the Largest Enterprises in the Mining, Metallurgical, Metal-Working, Textile, Electrical Engineering, Lumbering, Woodworking, Tobacco, Glass, Ceramic, Leather, Cement, and Other Branches of Industry, Steam Mills, Public Utility Enterprises, and Enterprises in the Field of Railroad Transportation"], *SU RSFSR*, No. 47, item 559 and No. 61, item 672 (1918); "O nazionalizazii sudoxodnix predpriatii vladeushyix morskimi i rechnimi sudami" ["On the Nationalization of Shipping Enterprises Owning Ocean-going and River Vessels"], *SU RSFSR*, No. 19, item 290 (1918).

10. *See* the Decree of the Council of People's Commissars of September 7, 1920, "O regulirovanii kustarkix i nenazionalizirovannoi promishlennosti" ["On the Regulation of the Domestic Craft Industry and Non-Nationalized Industry"], *SU RSFSR*, No. 78, item 366 (1920); the Normative Order of the All Russian Economic Council of the National Economy of November 24, 1920, "O nazionalizazii predpriatii" ["On the Nationalization of Enterprises"], *SU RSFSR*, No. 93, item 512 (1920). An enterprise with more than five workers in the presence of power driven equipment, and with more than ten workers in the absence of such, was considered medium-sized.

11. *SU RSFSR*, No. 86, item 904 (1918).

12. *SU RSFSR*, No. 33, item 432 (1918).

13. *SU RSFSR*, No. 83, item 879 (1918).

nationalized enterprises, arose in very acute form. To this end, the Supreme Council of the Economy (hereinafter referred to as the VSNKh) was founded in December of 1917,[14] and given the task of developing general rules and plans for the regulation of the economic life of the country and supervising various sectors of the economy. Central committees (Centers) and main administrations (Glavki) were established within the VSNKh. This system of management of the state enterprises during the period of the foreign intervention and the Civil War became known historically as "Glavkism." The main consequence was that the economic connections among the state enterprises were arranged on the basis of administration dispositions by the Centers and the Glavki. Supplying enterprises with the material resources, which they needed for production, as well as marketing the product manufactured by them, was carried out by orders through the Centers and the Glavki without the help of contracts. The enterprises in essence had no economic autonomy. They received from the state everything necessary for production and returned to it all that they produced. Theoretically this was explained by the fact that the enterprises, which had passed into the ownership of the state, made up, in the final analysis, a single fund—"one big factory."[15]

The limited application of contracts, originally caused by the nationalization of the basic means of production, gradually began to spread to the other areas of life in the country. The severe food shortage, exacerbated by the antisocial action of petit-bourgeois elements and speculators of various kinds, compelled the state to take control of the trade in foodstuffs and certain other commodities of vital importance to the population. In the middle of 1918, the state imposed a monopoly over grain, agricultural machinery, matches, candles, rice, pepper and other spices, textiles, and various other kinds of commodities.[16] Direct barter of widely consumed articles manufactured in the cities (clothing, underwear, shoes, and the like) for grain and other forms of foodstuffs available in the countryside was introduced.[17] Set prices for foodstuffs and industrially produced goods were established.

14. See the December 2, 1917, Decree of the All-Russian Central Executive Committee and the Council of People's Commissars of the RSFSR, "O Visshem Sovete Narognovo Xoziastva" ["On the Superior Soviet National Economy"], *SU RSFSR*, No. 5, item 83 (1917).

15. M.I. Piskotin, *Sotsializm i gosudarstvennoe upravlenie* [*Socialism and State Management*] (Moscow: Nauka Publishing House, 1984), p. 60.

16. *SU RSFSR*, No. 16, item 232; No. 25, item 346; No. 29, item 385; No. 45, item 546; No. 54, item 599; No. 61, item 672 (1918).

17. *SU RSFSR*, No. 30, item 300 (1918).

Thus, even before the beginning of the Civil War, purchase and sale of a considerable portion of foodstuffs and industrial goods was replaced by exchange which, rather than falling under civil law, had an administrative character because it occurred with the permission of the foodstuff agencies of the state, which established the basic conditions of the transactions. After the situation in the country was exacerbated as a result of the foreign intervention and the Civil War, a system of state requisitioning of foodstuffs was introduced. Pursuant to the Decree of January 11, 1919, "On the Requisitioning of Grain and Forage Subject to Alienation in Favor of the State,"[18] all surplus grain and forage in the possession of peasants had to be given to the state at set prices. If it was not yielded voluntarily, it was to be taken by force and without recompense. At later times the requisitioning of foodstuffs was also extended to many other agricultural products including potatoes, butter, eggs, livestock, fowl, honey, and agricultural raw materials.[19]

This procurement was carried out by administrative methods. With regard to products falling under state monopoly, no contract of purchase and sale was made. In principle, only those products to which the state monopoly did not extend could be the subject matter of a contract. Even as to such products, however, the state set the terms of the contract, which included setting maximum and minimum prices, and determining the purchasers or organizations with which it was permitted to make contracts.

A considerable reduction in the use of contractual relationships also occurred in the supplying of the population with necessary goods and services. A forced transition took place from the system of trade to the system of distribution of the most important foodstuffs and industrial goods, and also of individual forms of services. This was originally done through a system of barter. After barter was replaced to a significant degree by the procurement of agricultural products through requisitioning of foodstuffs, a regulated system of supplying the population with foodstuffs and industrial goods at no charge was introduced. Payment for the use of housing, transportation, and means of communication was also abolished.[20] These measures became known as the policy of "war communism."

---

18. *SU RSFSR*, No. 1, item 10 (1919).

19. *SU RSFSR*, No. 64, item 579 (1919); *SU RSFSR*, No. 59, items 271 and 272 (1920); *SU RSFSR*, No. 13, items 81 and 82 (1920).

20. *SU RSFSR*, No. 93, item 505; No. 99, item 531; No. 100, item 539 (1920); *SU RSFSR*, No. 2, item 20; No. 6, items 45, 46, and 47; No. 9, item 60; No. 12, item 81; No. 32, item 178; No. 40, item 211; No. 48, item 237 (1921).

In view of the acute shortage of goods and services, however, this system of services free of charge proved to be inefficient. As V.I. Lenin noted in his article "On the Fourth Anniversary of the October Revolution," "We proposed without sufficient thought to organize state production and state distribution of products in a communist way, by direct order of a proletarian state, in a country of small peasants. Life has shown us our mistake."[21]

Even during those hard years, the use of the contract did not disappear completely. Everyday transactions (rental, construction contracts, and the like) were made between individuals. Contractual forms were also used for non-rationed goods. For example, articles made by craftsmen for the market were sold according to contracts legitimized by the state.[22] The private market continued officially to function, and state and cooperative organizations were permitted, in individual cases, to have recourse to that market. This was permitted when goods needed by an enterprise could not be obtained by order from the distributional organs of the state.[23]

The question thus arose as to what legal rules would regulate the contractual relationships, since disputes frequently arose, and judges had to decide them. From the beginning of November, 1920, to the end of April, 1921, 361 civil cases were appealed to the Council of People's Judges of the Belorussian SSR alone. Among them were cases on the payment of debts, restitution of losses, compensation for labor, non-performance of contracts, and the recovery of grain.[24] It appears that the state adopted no special rules pertaining to these relationships during this period.[25] General rules were considered adequate to guide the judges in

---

21. V.I. Lenin, *Soch. izdanis 4-oe* [*Collected Works, 4th Edition*], Volume 44, p. 151.

22. Decree of the Council of People's Commissars of the RSFSR of September 7, 1920, "O regulirovanii kustarnykh promyslov i nenatsionalizirovannoi promyshiennosti" ["On the Regulation of Handicraft Enterprises and Non-Nationalized Industry"], *SU RSFSR*, No. 78, item 306 (1920).

23. Decree of the Council of People's Commissars of the RSFSR of July 15, 1920, "O raschetnix operaziax" ["On Operations of Payment"], *SU RSFSR*, No. 67, item 305 (1920).

24. F.I. Gavze, *Razvitie sotsialisticheskoi grazhdansko-pravovogo dogovora* [*The Development of Socialist Civil Law Contracts*], p. 28.

25. G.M. Stepanenko, who made a special study of the question, found only one normative act published during this period. This was the Normative Order by the All Russian Economic Council of the National Economy on the Collection of Payment for the Net Weight of Commodities Issues, *SU RSFSR*, No. 17, item 185 (1919).

considering criminal and civil cases. Pursuant to "Decree Number One On The Courts" of November 22, 1917,[26] judges were permitted to be guided by the laws of the governments that had been overthrown to the extent that they had not been repealed by the revolution and did not contradict the revolutionary conscience and sense of law. This enabled judges to refer to the Collected Civil Laws of the Russian Empire of 1833. In practice, however, the new judges were reluctant to do this, and in the Statute of the People's Court of the RSFSR, published in November 1918, all references to the laws of the original governments were forbidden. The judges of the People's Court were directed to apply the decrees of the workers and peasants government. Where an applicable decree was absent or incomplete, they were to be guided by the revolutionary sense of law.[27]

Under these conditions, various theories, primarily psychological and sociological, (including Duguit's theory of social functions, which had nothing in common with the newly created law) came into wide use in the field of legal ideology. A.G. Goikhbarg, a well-known jurist of the early years of the Soviet regime, became enamored with such theories. In 1919, he wrote that if the legislature was the temple of bourgeois rule and the law was its fetish, then administration was the temple of the proletarian and socialist system.[28] Goikhbarg replaced the old law, which had been destroyed by the revolution, with the social law of the transitional period, which was characterized by administrative principles, and which left outside of the limits of its activity the "relationships under civil private

26. *SU RSFSR*, No. 4, item 50 (1917).

27. *SU RSFSR*, No. 85, item 889 (1918).

28. *See* A.G. Goikhbarg, *Proletariat i pravo (Sbornik statei)* [*The Proletariat and the Law. (A Collection of Essays)*] (Moscow: Publishing Division of the People's Commissariat of Justice, 1919), p. 12. Alexander Gregorievich Goikhbarg (1883–1962) was a famous Soviet jurist of the early years of the Soviet government. After the Great October Socialist Revolution he became a regional (*oblast*) commissar of justice in Siberia and was later a member of the College of the People's Commissariat of Justice of the RSFSR. At the same time he also became a member and chairman of the lower Soviet People's Committee (*Sovnarkom*).

From 1921–1924 he actively participated in the development of legislation and was in charge of work on the civil codes of the RSFSR of 1922. Later, for a long period of time he worked in the legal department of the People's Commissariat for Foreign Trade of the USSR.

He was the author of an entire collection of scientific works, the most important of which were: "Economic Law of the USSR" Vol. 1 (1923), "Essays on Economic Law" (1927), and "Comparative Family Law" (1927).

law."[29] These private relationships were considered bourgeois, and civil law itself was considered a dying branch of law.[30]

Along with such nihilistic attitudes toward civil law, there also developed a more correct understanding of law in general, and civil law in particular. This was reflected in the works of the well-known statesman and jurist, P. I. Stuchka. In the definition of law, which he gave in 1919, and in the articles that he published, he insistently emphasized the class character of any law, including Soviet law. "We," he wrote eight years later, "in 1919, were inclined toward the sociological—or more accurately, materialistic—interpretation of law as 'a system and organization of relationships in society (in the sense of relationships of production and exchange), corresponding to the interests of the ruling class, and defended by the class organization of the state'."[31] However, he mistakenly included law in the system of relationships of production (economic relationships) in society. Stuchka considered statutes as only one of the various forms in which law was fixed. He thereby admitted the possibility of the existence of law without statutes or other rules and therefore, the possibility of

---

29. A.G. Goikhbarg, *Proletariat i pravo (Sbornik statei)* [*The Proletariat and the Law (A Collection of Essays)]*, p. 16 *et seq*.

30. *See* L. Ia. Ginzburg, "Stanovlenie nauki grazhdanskogo prava v SSSR (1917–1920 gg.)," *Pravovedenie* ["The Development of the Science of Civil Law in the USSR, 1917–1920," *Jurisprudence*], No. 3 (1974), pp. 83–85.

31. P.I. Stuchka, *13 let bor'by za revolutsionno-marksistskuiu teoriiu prava* [*Thirteen Years of Struggle for a Revolutionary-Marxist Theory of Law*] (Moscow: State Law Publishing House, 1931), pp. 151–152. Peter Ivanovich Stuchka (1865–1932), a distinguished Soviet government and Party activist, was one of the founders of the Communist Party of Latvia. He was an active participant in the Great October Socialist Revolution, a member of the Central Committee of the People's Communist Party (Bolsheviks), and Chairman of the Soviet Government of Latvia from 1918–1919.

From 1923 to 1932 he was the Chairman of the Supreme Court of the RSFSR. He was a member of the All-Russian Central Executive Committee. He also held a number of responsible positions in the Government and Party Apparat.

Stuchka was the founder of the first Soviet legal scientific-research organization, and he was an outstanding representative of Marxist-Leninist theory of government and laws. He was the author of numerous works on the theory and history of government and law. These included: "A Course in Soviet Civil Law", Vols. 1–3 (1927–1931) and "Selections of Works on Marxist-Leninist Theory of Law" (1964). Under his direction the "Encyclopedia of Government and Law" Vols. 1–3 were prepared. (First printing 1925–1927, second printing 1929–1930).

carrying out judicial proceedings on the basis of a revolutionary sense of the law in the absence of rules.

This theory applied fully to contract law as well. Legal thought about a new type of contract law proved to be at a crossroad. The socialist conception of the contract as civil law had not yet been perfected in theory during those years, although in practice, the activity of the VSNKh and of the other agencies of the state that carried out the exchange of goods between the city and the countryside, had already begun to develop new approaches to the regulation of contractual relations. On the whole, the period 1917–1920, in the field of contract law, was destructive rather than constructive in character.

B. The Period of the Reconstruction of the Economy (1921–1925)

The period of the reconstruction of the economy began after the end of the Civil War. In the history of Soviet contract law, this period is remembered as one of the most creative. During a short period of only six years, many ideas, which later became integral parts of the contemporary concept of the contract as civil law, were formulated, laid down in legislation, and embodied in economic and law enforcement practice.

This was a consequence and an organic part of the great events that were taking place in the country. After the foreign intervention was repulsed and the civil war was successfully concluded, the task of restoring the economy, which had been destroyed by the war, confronted the young state in all its urgency. It was not possible to accomplish this complex task on the basis of the administrative methods of economic management, which had been applied in the years of the revolution and of "war communism". New solutions were demanded.

They were found and embodied in a system of measures that received the designation of the "New Economic Policy" (NEP). On the social level, the essence of the NEP, in Lenin's words, consisted of the strengthening of the alliance between the proletariat and the peasantry.[32] On the economic level, the NEP was directed toward reviving and developing the exchange of goods between the city and the countryside, toward involving state enterprises and permitting the participation of capitalist elements, and

32. V.I. Lenin, *Soch. izdanie 4-oe* [*Collected Works, 4th Edition*], Volume 44, p. 322.

toward the victory of the socialist sector of the economy over the capitalist sectors. The transition to the NEP was connected with the development of commodity-and-money relationships, and thereby with an immeasurably wider use of contract than in previous periods. The NEP was an important stage on the road to the creation of socialist methods of management of the economy in the USSR.

It began with the March 21, 1921, Decree of the All-Russian Central Executive Committee, RSFSR, "On the Replacement of the Requisitioning of Raw Materials by a Tax in Kind." This decree imposed a tax in kind on all peasants.[33] After paying the tax in kind, the peasants were permitted to exchange their surplus agricultural products for industrial and handicraft products, and to sell them later on the market. By the Decree of the Council of Commissars of the RSFSR of July 19, 1921, "On the Conduct of Trade,"[34] all citizens 16 years of age and older and all organized groups of citizens were permitted to trade in agricultural products, and in products of industry and handicrafts, except for commodities whose free-circulation was temporarily forbidden or made subject to a state monopoly. The number of items subject to state monopoly was constantly reduced, while those subject to private enterprise were broadened. Along with the contract of purchase and sale, the delivery and construction contract, and contracts for assignment and rental of property, and others became widespread. During 1922 and 1923, the private sector was responsible for 23 percent of wholesale circulation of goods and 57.7 percent of retail trade.[35]

The Soviet state also proceeded to involve foreign capital in the economy of the country. The making of concessionary contracts with foreign firms and individual enterprises,[36] and the creation on Soviet territory of

---

33. *SU RSFSR*, No. 26, item 147 (1921).

34. *SU RSFSR*, No. 57, item 356 (1921).

35. F.I. Gavze, *Razvitie sotsialisticheskogo grazhdansko-pravovogo dogovora* [*The Development of Socialist Civil Law Contract*], p. 68.

36. The Decree of the Council of People's Commissars of the RSFSR of March 23, 1920, "Ob obshyix ekonomicheskix i uridicheskix usloviax konzessii" ["On the General Economic and Legal Conditions of Concessions"], *SU RSFSR*, No. 91, item 481 (1920); the Decree of the Council of People's Commissars of the RSFSR of March 29, 1921, "Osnovnye printsipy kontsessionnykh dogovorov," *Dokumenty Vneshnei politiki SSSR* ["Basic Principles of Concessionary Agreements," *Documents of the Foreign Policy of the USSR*] (Moscow: Gospolitizdat, 1968), vol. 4, pp. 36–37. The statistics on concessions are of interest. In 1922, 300 proposals for concessions were received from foreign applicants. Of these, 14 concessionary agreements were made. In 1923, 600 proposals were received; 44

mixed companies in which foreign capital participated,[37] were permitted.

It is especially important to emphasize that the broad participation of state enterprises in the economic circulation exerted a decisive influence on the fate of the NEP itself. A year after its beginning, the retreat in the face of the private entrepreneur ended. The socialist features of the New Economic Policy began to manifest themselves in all the areas of the economy, including the socialization of the market. The contractual form spread to the relations between state enterprises. This became possible as a result of the transition of the state enterprises to a commercial (self-supporting) system of accounting. The introduction of self-support as a method of managing state enterprises was one of the major theoretical and practical discoveries in the political economy of socialism.[38]

The self-support system is based on the principle that a state enterprise should pay its own expenses, recouping the costs incurred in producing its products from the income received from their sale. The self-supporting activity of the enterprises is carried out on a planned basis. For this reason, one of the necessary elements of the system of self-support under the conditions of socialist society is the plan on which it is based. The self-support system presupposes the existence, for a state enterprise, of eco-

---

agreements were made. In 1924, 311 proposals were received; 30 agreements were made. In 1925, 253 proposals were received; 30 agreements were made (including the Lena Goldfield Ltd. concession and the Harriman concession for the Chiatura manganese deposit). *See Pravovye formy nauchno-tekhnicheskogo i promyshlenno-ekonomicheskogo sotrudnichestva SSSR* v *kapitalisticheskimi stranami* [*Legal Forms of Scientific-Technical and Industrial-Economic Collaboration of the USSR with Capitalist Countries*], ed., M.M. Boguslavskii (Moscow: Nauka Publishing House, 1980), p. 17.

The first concession in the country was proposed by the American United Company for Drugs and Chemicals, headed by Armand Hammer. On November 2, 1921, a concessionary agreement was made for the development of asbestos deposits in the Alapat'evsk region in the Urals for a period of twenty years. *Dokumenty Vneshnei Politiki SSSR* [*Documents of the Foreign Policy of the USSR*], Volume 4, pp. 465–471.

37. On January 1, 1925, 52 mixed companies existed in the country, of which 12 had foreign participation. *Pravovye formy nauchno-tekhnicheskogo i promyshlenno-ekonomicheskogo sotrudnichestva SSSR v kapitalisticheskimi stranami* [*Legal Forms of Scientific-Technical and Industrial-Economic Collaboration of the USSR with Capitalist Countries*], ed., M.M. Boguslavskii, p. 21.

38. See M.I. Piskotin, *Sotsializm i gosudarstvennoe upravlenie* [*Socialism and State Management*], pp. 83–84.

nomic autonomy and, of course, of the material and financial resources necessary for this.

It is obvious that during this period the self-supporting system of the state enterprises could not be highly developed. Suitable conditions for this did not exist. However, in and of itself, the fact of the transition of state enterprises to the commercial system of operation as the original form of self-support,[39] signified the transition to a new system of management of the economy oriented toward the future.

Within the framework of this system a new concept of a contract was created. This concept involved the trust, an industrial enterprise consisting of several small productive units. Under the Decree on Trusts of 1923, the trust was considered an autonomous subject of law in the field of circulation of goods. Its interrelationships with suppliers of raw and intermediate materials, fuel, equipment, and with consumers of the products manufactured by them, began to be implemented on the basis of contracts. The contract became the basic form of connection of the trust both with private contracting parties on the so-called free market, and—what is especially important—with other state enterprises.

At the same time, the sale of those products that were of the greatest interest to the socialist sector of the economy was subject to administrative regulation. The trust was obliged to supply such products, pursuant to orders issued by the VSNKh, to the state designated agencies and enterprises. The supplying of the goods ordered was carried out pursuant to

39. The transfer of state enterprises to a commercial method of operation began with the adoption of two acts: "Nakaza o provedenii v zhizn'nachal NEPa" ["Order for the Implementation of the Principles of the NEP], adopted by the Council of People's Commissars of the RSFSR on August 9, 1921, *SU RSFSR*, No. 59, item 403 (1921), and "Osnovnykh polozhenii o merakh k vosstanovleniiu krupnoi promyshlennosti i poniiatiiu i razvitiiu proizvodstva" ["Basic Positions on Measures for the Restoration of Large-scale Industry and the Promotion and Development of Production"], *SU RSFSR*, No. 62, item 462 (1921). For the publication of other such acts, see the Normative Order of the All Russian Economic Council of the National Economy of April 6, 1922, "O sniatii predpriiatii s gosudarstvennogo snabzheniia" ["On the Removal of Enterprises from the State Supply System"], *SU RSFSR*, No. 16, item 155 (1922). *See also* the April 23, 1923, Decree on Trusts, *SU RSFSR*, No. 29, item 336 (1923). This was one of the most significant normative rules in the field of legal provisions for the self-supporting operation of state enterprises. (A trust was in the position of an enterprise, and enjoyed the rights of a legal person).

contracts, at prices equal to their cost of production, with the addition of an average profit. This rule concerning the interaction of administrative regulation and the contract was one of the most significant innovations on which the contemporary conception of the contract as civil law was based.

The transition to new methods of management of the economy required the creation of a general system of civil legislation. Such legislation was also needed because of the lack of documents defining the rights of ownership of private persons and their relations both among themselves and with state enterprises.

On May 22, 1922, the law "On the Basic Rights of Private Ownership Recognized by the RSFSR, Protected by its Laws and Enforced by the Courts," was adopted.[40] Along with provisions relating to the right of private ownership by citizens of small industrial enterprises, commercial establishments, and structures, and the right of inheritance, it contained many rules concerning contracts. The making of all kinds of contracts not forbidden by law was permitted. A specimen list of such contracts was given, which included the formula of contracts applied in practice. At the same time, the law reserved to the state the right to control the legality of contracts made by private persons.

The adoption of the first civil codes in the history of the country—the Civil Code of the RSFSR and of the other Union republics—soon followed. The Civil Code of the RSFSR was confirmed by the session of the All-Russian Central Executive Committee on October 31, 1922, and put into effect on January 1, 1923.[41] After the adoption of the Civil Code of the RSFSR, the civil codes of the other Union republics, similar in content, were adopted (the Civil Code of the Ukrainian SSR at the end of 1922, the Civil Code of the Belorussian, Azerbaidzhani, and Georgian SSRs in 1923, the Civil Code of the Uzbek SSR in 1924, and the Civil Code of the Turkmen SSR in 1925).

The civil codes of the Union republics established the state as the leader in the field of the economy. At the same time, they gave rather wide latitude for the use of private initiative within the limits determined by the law. Under Article 1 of the Civil Code of the RSFSR, "Rights under the Code are protected by the law except in those cases where they are exercised in contradiction to their socioeconomic content." On the basis of this Article in the Civil Code, the Supreme Court of the RSFSR, in

---

40. *SU RSFSR*, No. 36, item 423 (1922).
41. *SU RSFSR*, No. 71, item 904 (1922).

1924, for example, found the sale of an orchard for timber contrary to good economic practice, and therefore impermissible.[42]

Along with general provisions on contracts, the Civil Code also contained many articles devoted to obligations arising from contracts, and to specific types of contracts, such as rental of property, purchase and sale, barter, loans, and private building contracts. The rules of the Civil Code extended to all contracts falling under civil law, including those between state enterprises.[43]

The Civil Code, however, lacked special rules regulating contractual relations between state enterprises. According to the application of Article 16 of the Civil Code of the RSFSR, the participation of state enterprises and institutions in civil law relations was defined by special rules. The state exercised strict control over the observance of contracts made between state institutions and enterprises. "The force of contracts," noted the Supreme Arbitration Commission Under the Council of Labor and Defense of October 20, 1923, in its decision in the case of the Mining Industry Trusts of the Don Council of the Economy, "must be protected; this is what the basic condition of the stability of the relations consists of."[44]

In the legal doctrine of the period under consideration, the emphasis began to shift from the consideration of the general nature of law toward the analysis of contracts made between state enterprises and the evaluation of the civil codes of the Union republics.

The works of P.I. Stuchka and E.B. Pashukanis were especially important for Soviet scholarship at that time. Pashukanis considered the problem of legal regulation of property relations between state enterprises from two points of view. First, he viewed the problem from the position of the immediate organizational and administrative connections. Second, he viewed the problem from the position of the legal forms in which these connections were clothed. In his opinion, the first position showed a

---

42. *Ezhenedl'nik sovetskoi iustitsii* [*Weekly of Soviet Justice*], No. 32 (1924), 765.
43. "The Civil Code was not made as a code for the oases," P.I. Stuchka noted, "But for the entire cycle, including the relations of state institutions and enterprises among themselves." P.I. Stuchka, *Vvedenie v teoriiu grazhdanskogo prava* [*Introduction to the Theory of Civil Law*] (Moscow: Publishing House of the Communist Academy, 2d ed., 1928), p. 121.
44. Vishaia arbitrazhnaia kommissia STO, *Reshenia vysshei arbitrazhnoi komissii* [*Collected Decisions of the Supreme Arbitration Committee*] (Moscow: Publishing House V.S.N.CH., 1924), vol. 3, Decision No. 215, p. 275–276.

tendency toward development, and the second a tendency toward dying out.[45] Pashukanis' conclusion was based on the mistaken theory propounded by him that law was to be identified with the market forms of property relations characteristic of the NEP. (He later recognized the incorrectness of this theory.)

Stuchka continued to develop persuasive ideas on the class character of Soviet law, which he had formulated in the previous period.[46] However, in his evaluation of the civil codes of the Union republics, other views were sounded. Stuchka held that the adoption of a civil code, in which many rules of bourgeois civil legislation and codes were included, was the result of a deviation. Furthermore, he called the Civil Code of the RSFSR a bourgeois code, applying primarily to contract law.[47] Stuchka used the term *bourgeois* to emphasize the fact that during the NEP period the Code

---

45. E.B. Pashukanis, *Obshchaia teoriia prava i marksizm: Opyt kritiki osnovnykh iuridicheskikh poniatii* [*The General Theory of Law and Marxism: An Expert Critique of the Basic Legal Concepts*] (Moscow: Socialist Academy, 1924), p. 94.

Evgeni Bronislavovich Pashukanis (1891–1937) was an outstanding Soviet scientist, jurist, professor, and participant in the Great October Socialist Revolution. From 1920 to 1930 he worked at the People's Commissariat for Foreign Affairs. In 1922 he and P.I. Stuchka organized the law section of the Communist Academy, one of the centers of scientific Marxist-Leninist thought in the USSR. In 1927 he became a full member of the Communist Academy, and later vice president. In 1931 he became the director of the Institute of Soviet Construction and Law of the Communist Academy. In 1936 he became Deputy of the People's Committee (Narkom) of Justice. He was the author of numerous scientific works of general legal theory, government and international law, philosophy, history and political science. Of these the most well known works are: "General Theory of Law and Marxism" (critical experience in the fundamentals of legal knowledge) (1927); "Imperialism and Colonial Policy" (1928); "The Soviet Government Apparatus in its Fight with Bureaucratism" (1929); "Teachings on Government and Law" (1932); and "Essays on International Law" (1935).

46. See P.I. Stuchka, *Klassovoe gosudarstvo i grazhdanskoe pravo* [*Class Society and Civil Law*] (Moscow: Socialist Academy, 1924), pp. 54 *et seq.*

47. "Our courts, which in their makeup are definitely class based on the working class, are obliged to implement and uphold law on which the bourgeois brand is visible. Not only the pseudo-bourgeois, but the true bourgeois GK (Civil Code), which is 9/10 borrowed from the best bourgeois civil codes of the West, is the basic guiding element for all the civil practice of our courts." P.I. Stuchka, "Proletarskii sud i burzhhauznoe pravo," *13 let bor'by za revolutsionno-marksistskyiu teoriiu prava* ["The Proletarian Court and Bourgeois Law," *Thirteen Years of Struggle for a Revolutionary Marxist Theory Law*], p. 106.

regulated relations that included the use of employed labor by private owners.[48]

Stuchka's position in evaluating the Civil Code of the RSFSR seemed to be unfounded. It ignored the fact that the individual provisions from the codes of Western countries, which had been included in the Civil Code, were filled with new socialist content and were used in the interests of the proletarian state. Stuchka tore the form of the legal rule from its content and social purpose and proceeded from a miscalculated evaluation of the commodity-and-money relationships during the period of transition from capitalism to socialism. In the contemporary doctrine of Soviet civil law, the civil legislation of this period, including the civil codes of the Union republics, is unanimously evaluated as socialist.[49]

In contrast to the works of Stuchka and Pashukanis on the theory of law in general, there were no fundamental studies in the general theory of contract law during the period from 1921–1925. The vast majority of works of that time were of a commentary and dogmatic character.[50]

---

48. *Id.* at 153.

49. See, for example, V.G. Verdnikov, *Istoriia sovetskogo grazhdanskogo prava* [*History of Soviet Civil Law*] (Moscow: VIuZi, 1956), p. 7; D.M. Genkin, I. B. Novitskii, and N.V. Rabinovich, *Istoriia sovetskogo grazhdanskogo prava 1917–1947 gg.* [*History of Soviet Civil Law 1917–1947*] (Moscow: Iurizdat, 1949), p. 7; S.N. Bratus', "O nekotorkyh chertakh istorii sovetskogo grazhdanskogo prava," *Sovetskoe gosudarstvo i pravo* ["On Some Features of the History of the Soviet Civil Law," *Soviet Society and Law*], No. 11 (1957), 87.

50. See, for example, *Grazhdansko kodeks RSFSR. Prakticheskii Kommentarii* [*The Civil Code of the RSFSR: A Practical Commentary*], eds., A.M. Vinaver and I.B. Novitskii (Moscow: Pravo i zhizn', 1925); I.S. Pereterskii, *Prinuditel'nye i disnozitivnye normy v obiazatel'stvennom prave grazhdanskogo kodeksa* [*Mandatory and Suppletory Rules in the Law of Legal Obligations of the Civil Code*] (Moscow: Soviet Law, 1924), No. 4, pp. 68–80; F.I. Gavze, "Dogovor po grazhdanskomu kodeksu," *Ezhenedel'nik sovetskoi iustitsii* ["The Contract Under the Civil Code," *Daily Soviet Justice*], No. 13 (1923), 290–292; F.I. Gavze, "O dogovornykh vzaimootnosheniiakh mezhdu gosudarstvom i chastnymi litsami," *Ezhenedel'nik sovetskoi iustitsii* ["On Contractual Interrelationships Between the State and Private Persons," *Daily Soviet Justice*], Nos. 46–47 (1922), 12–14; N.G. Vavin, *Forma i poriadok sovershenіia dogovoov po grazhdanskomu kodeksu* [*The Form and Procedure for Making a Contract Under the Civil Code*] (Moscow: Izdat. Sekzia vserokompoma, 1923); A.G. Goikhbarg, *Khoziaistvenno pravo RSFSR, t.1, Grazhdanskii kodeks, Rukovodtsvo dlia Vuzov* [*Economic Law of the RSFSR, Volume 1, The Civil Code, A Handbook for Post Secondary Institutions*] (Moscow: Gosizdat, 1923); F.I. Vol'fson, *Uchebnik grazhdanskogo prava RSFSR* [*A Textbook of Civil Law of the RSFSR*] (Moscow: Iurizdat, 1925).

C. The Period of Socialist Reconstruction of the Economy (1926–1935)

The years from 1926 to 1935 were devoted to socialist reconstruction of the economy. For contract law this was a period of further development and stabilization of the socialist elements in the conception of the civil contract. It took place under complex conditions, with sharp theoretical and practical discussions of a kind that had been absent in the previous period. The important question was the very essence of the new type of contract and the possibility of applying the contract to relationships between socialist organizations. The polarization of opinions about contracts reflected those major socioeconomic and political changes that were taking place in the country.

During the years under consideration, the economy and social structure of society were subjected to qualitative transformations. As a result of the industrialization of manufacturing and the collectivization of agriculture, the foundation of the socialist economy was laid. At the end of this period, socialist industry made up 99 percent of all the industry in the country and socialized agricultural production (collective and state farms) conducted on state owned land comprised 99 percent of the entire sown area. Elements of private enterprise were completely phased out of the field of trade. The economy of the country began to be conducted according a single state plan. Beginning in 1928, time was reckoned in five-year plans for the development of the economy of the USSR. Important changes took place in the social structure of society. At the beginning of the 1930's, the last class of private owners in the country, the kulaks (rich peasants who employed labor in cultivating land), ceased to exist.

All of this naturally changed the very character of those relationships in society that were mediated by contracts, and to a significant extent posed the question of the nature of the civil contract in a new light. During the preceding period all contracts (including the contracts between socialist enterprises, which were regulated by the state) could be validated by reference to the existence of a common market in which private entrepreneurial elements were present. From 1926–1935, however, the question of the nature of the civil contract had become pointless. With the disappearance from the economy of the holders of private or entrepreneurial interests, contracts involving these interests automatically ceased to be operative. Wholesale contracts made by private businessmen for the purchase of grain and other agricultural products disappeared, as did the contracts between entrepreneurs and merchants operating under the provisions of the NEP and between craftsmen not belonging to cooperatives. In 1928, the leasing of state enterprises to private persons was forbidden.[51] By a Decree of the Central Executive Committee and the Council of People's Commissars of the USSR of May 20, 1932, any private trade was made a criminally punishable act.[52] While the state had responsibility over the entire circulation of commodities in the country, the relationships that developed between socialist organizations significantly influenced the state in administering this responsibility.

Under these conditions, there was no question of the application of complete or partial "freedom" of contract, which had arisen from and were connected with private enterprise. At the same time, however, the concept of a civil contract continued to be associated with the "freedom" of contract among many theorists and practitioners. The planning contract was regarded as an innovation and made headway with great difficulty. This was despite the fact that its fundamentals had been formulated as early as the decrees of the early 1920's, and that since that time the legislation had, on the whole, continued to develop it. The state emphasized strengthening the planned supervision of economic relations between socialist organizations, and the development of self-support by enterprises entering as primary links into the field of industrial production. The strengthening of planned supervision of economic relations between organizations was clearly indicated in two pieces of legislation: the Statute on State Industrial Trusts of July 29, 1927,[53] and the Resolution of the Council of People's Commissars of the USSR of April 23, 1929, "On the Five Year Plan for the Economy, 1928/29–1932/33."[54]

The Statute on Trusts of 1927 emphasized the planned character of the economic activity of trusts and the enterprises that were parts of it. Article 2 defined a trust as an enterprise operating on the basis of commercial procedures in accordance with tasks assigned by the plan and approved by the agency having jurisdiction over the trust. The statute repealed the provision in the Decree on Trusts of 1923, which defined the extraction of profit as the goal of the trust's activity.

The state syndicates, which originally appeared in 1922 but which became widespread only at the end of the 1920s, were intended to

51. *Sobrenie Zakonov SSSR* [*Collection of Normative Rules adopted by the Central Executive Committee and/or the Council of the People's Commissars of the USSR*] [hereinafter cited as *SZ SSSR*], No. 9, item 80; No. 34, item 307 (1928). (Prior to the adoption of the 1937 Constitution, the name *SZ SSSR* was used instead of *SP SSSR*.)
52. *SZ SSSR*, No. 38, item 233 (1932).
53. *SZ SSSR*, No. 39, item 392 (1927).
54. *SZ SSSR*, No. 29, item 268 (1929).

strengthen the element of planning in the circulation of commodities in economic relations between socialist organizations. Under the Law on Syndicates of February 28, 1928,[55] syndicates were defined as integrated units made up of trusts for the purposes of selling the products manufactured by the trusts and supplying the trusts with fuel and raw and instrumental materials. In many sectors of industry (for example, textiles, metallurgy, and forest products), syndicates were responsible for the entire marketing and supplying operations of their member trusts.

The introduction into practice of the general contracts made between the Central Union of Consumers' Societies of the Country and the syndicates representing the individual sectors of industry[56] was also connected with the activity of the syndicates. These contracts had the basic goal of organizing the supplying of the cooperative organizations with industrial products and providing industry with raw materials procured through the cooperatives. On the basis of these contracts, annual and quarterly execution of contracts were made between the same subjects, but with the additional inclusion of subordinate cooperative organizations as shareholders brought in by the Central Union. In the history of contract law, the general contract was the precursor of the organizational contract used as a planning institution.

In accordance with the Resolution of the Central Committee of the All-Union Communist Party of December 5, 1929, "On the Reorganization of Industry,"[57] integrated units that supervised sectors of industry were created on the basis of the syndicate. Thus, for example, on the basis of the USSR-wide Metallurgical Syndicate and the Main Administration for Ferrous Metallurgy of the VSNKh, the steel integrated unit was formed. Such integrated units had two functions. First, the units supplied their trust members with material and equipment, and thus acted in an operational and economic capacity. Second, the units supervised their trust members, thus acting in a planning and administrative capacity. The integrated units proved to be too cumbersome and insufficiently efficient in coping with the tasks entrusted to them and, thus, most of them were liquidated by a

55. *SZ SSSR*, No. 16, item 129 (1928).

56. *See* Decree of August 18, 1926, "O vzaimnootnosheniiakh gosudarstvennoi promyshlennosti s potrebitel'skoi kooperatsiei," ["On the Interrelationships of State Industry with the Consumer Cooperative System"], *SZ SSSR*, No. 59, item 445 (1926).

57. See *Pravda*, December 14, 1929, p. 2, col. 1–4.

Resolution of the Council of People's Commissars of the USSR of October 8, 1932.[58]

Along with the measures for strengthening the planned supervision of the economic relations of the trusts, a process of self-support by the enterprises entering into the trusts was developed. The Resolution of the Central Committee of the All Union Communist Party of December 5, 1929, emphasized that the enterprises should become the basic link in the management of industry. They were to operate on a self-supporting basis, in strict adherence to the plans established for them.

As a result of this Resolution, the Resolution of the Council of People's Commissars of the USSR of March 20, 1931, "On the Change in the System of Credit, on the Strengthening of Credit Work, and on Achieving Self-Support in All Organs"[59] and the Resolution of the Council of Labor and Defense of July 23, 1931, "On the Circulating Funds of State Integrated Units, Trusts, and Other Economic Organizations,"[60] were adopted. They gave the enterprises, which had been incorporated into trusts, access to bank credit, and made it possible for them to have their own circulating funds. The enterprise that was incorporated into a trust thus acquired a limited civil legal capacity for making contracts. The enterprise had the right to make a contract in the name of the trust. At the same time, however, the enterprise was liable for nonperformance or improper performance. In arbitration practice the enterprise began to be considered an autonomous legal person.[61]

The result of the development of legislation in this way was that from 1928–1930 the trust began to lose its importance in the field of economic relations. It found itself caught between two organizations that were gaining strength. On the one hand (from above) the syndicates were active, followed by integrated units, to which the trusts transferred many of their marketing and supply functions. On the other hand (from below) the incorporated enterprises began to strengthen their positions. As a consequence of this, the immediate connections of the trusts with suppliers and consumers were lost. The trusts were preoccupied by processing documentation (presentation of claims, drawing up of forms, etc.). The situation was complicated by the fact that because of the rapid growth of industry and the increasing demand of the population, a shortage of many types of

58. *SZ SSSR*, No. 79, item 384 (1932).
59. *SZ SSSR*, No. 18, item 166 (1931).
60. *SZ SSSR*, No. 46, item 316 (1931).
61. I.B. Novitskii, *Istoriia sovetskogo grazhdanskogo prava* [*History of Soviet Civil Law*], p. 210.

raw and instrumental materials and industrial commodities arose in the country. This stimulated the development of tendencies toward administrative distribution in the activity of the state agencies that supervised the economy. In addition, a number of errors were made in the field of lending credit to enterprises and trusts. At first, credit was given under the plan without regard to the implementation of the contract entered into.

All this lead to a sharp decline in the role of the contract. At the First All-Union Conference of Staff Workers in Socialist Industry, held in February of 1931, the almost complete disappearance of contractual relations in the period preceeding the conference was noted.[62] The role of the contract as an instrument of the organization of planned economic relations between trusts and enterprises was further diminished by the practice of the arbitration commissions in those years. They took upon themselves the function of state agencies and supervised the trusts and enterprises. They solved questions of the economic desirability of implementing the contracts made and changed the content of contracts as they saw fit. The arbitration commissions ignored the fundamentals of the contract in general and of the planning contract in particular. A decision of the Supreme Arbitration Commission under the Council of Labor and Defense of October 14, 1929, indicated that in contracts made between state organizations on the basis of instructions by superior agencies, "the interests of the contracting parties not only recede into the background, but may not exist at all for a given party. In addition, such contracts are sometimes unprofitable for one or both parties."[63] This approach to the planning contract was in clear contradiction to the policy of the state in strengthening the self-support of the enterprises. It did not strengthen it but destroyed it.

The essence of the new planning-contractual relations between socialist organizations was miscalculated by many legal theorists. These included those who expressed antisocialist views[64] and those who were confused

62. F.I. Gavze, *Razvitie sotsialisticheskoi grazhdansko-pravovogo dogovora* [*Development of Socialist Civil Law Contracts*], p. 89.

63. "Ot Visshix Arbitrazhnix Komissii pri Sovete Truda i Oboroni, CCCP i EKOSO RSFSR," *Sudebnaia praktika* ["From the Supreme Arbitrage Commissions of the Council of Labor and Defense of the USSR and the EKOSO RSFSR." *Court Practice*], ed., P.I. Stuchka, No. 14 (1929), 16.

64. They included, in particular, A.M. Liberman, who believed that all of Soviet civil law, including contract law, being effectively similar to bourgeois civil law, would die out with the destruction of ownership by the kulaks. (Kulacks are rich peasants who employ laborers.) A.M. Liberman, "Poslednii etap NEPa i khoziaistvennoe pravo," ["The Last Stage of the NEP Period and Economic Law," *Problems of Socialism*] Nos. 5 and 6 (1931).

and proceeded from mistaken postulates in terms of general theory.[65] These views were criticized at the First USSR-wide Conference of Marxist Political Scientists in January of 1934.[66]

At this time, a sharp turn took place in the activity of state agencies of management with respect to the planning contract. By the Resolution of the Council of People's Commissars of the USSR of January 14, 1931[67] and of March 10, 1931,[68] it was forbidden to issue bank credit to economic organizations directly pursuant to a plan. Formalization of the economic relationships by contract, in addition to the plan, was to become, from this point on, an obligatory precondition for the receipt of credit. In accordance with the Resolution of the Central Executive Committee and the Soviet of Peoples' Commissars of the USSR of February 18, 1931,[69] all orders and deliveries by state agencies were to bc formalized with written contracts. In order to support and strengthen planning-and-contractual discipline, both state and agency arbitration commissions were established. Finally, the Council of People's Commissars adopted the Resolution on the Making of Contracts for 1934,[70] which was exceptionally significant in the development of the planning contract in the USSR. This resolution contained provisions that defined the plan as the basis of the contract among socialist organizations and formulated the most important terms of the contract concerning the type, quantity, and quality of product to be delivered, and the method and time of performance of the obligation. It also established requirements relating to the duties of the parties to enter into a contract and to the procedures of making a contract. In addition, the

---

65. P.I. Stuchka proved to be among these. In the theory of two-sector law, which he advanced in 1929, he asserted that civil law regulated the relation between private owners and between sectors, while economic-administrative law regulated relations within the socialist sector. The latter, which were based on subordination and planning, therefore excluded the application of the contract. P.I. Stuchka, "O sisteme i predelakh material'noi i osobennoi chasti grazhdanskogo kodeksa," *Revoliutsiia prava* ["On the System and the Limits of the Material and Special Parts of the Civil Code," *The Revolution of Law*], No. 5 (1929), p. 79; P.I. Stuchka, *Kurs sovetskogo grazhdanskogo prava* [*A Course in Soviet Civil Law*] (Moscow-Leningrad: Izdatel'stvo Kommoonisticheskoi Akademii, 1931), vol. 3, pp. 10–11.

66. See the Resolution of the Congress in *Sovetskoe gosudarstvo i revoliutsii prava* [*The Soviet State and the Revolution in Law*], No. 3 (1931), 143–153.

67. *SZ SSSR*, No. 4, item 52 (1931).

68. *SZ SSSR*, No. 18, item 166 (1931).

69. *SZ SSSR*, No. 10, item 109 (1931).

70. *SZ SSSR*, No. 73, item 455 (1931).

resolution required the settlement of precontract disputes by arbitration, required the application of the principle of specific performance, prohibited modification or termination of the contract in contravention of the law, and established liability for non-performance or improper performance of a contract. With the adoption of this resolution, the general problem of stabilizing the planning contract in the economy was settled. A special law of planning contracts was even proposed.[71]

During the same years, a new conception of general contracts, made between centers of economic systems and having a planning and organizational character, was introduced into contractual practice. On the basis of these, local contracts were made with the participation of enterprises and organizations under the jurisdiction of parties to a general contract. The principle of planning was widely introduced into forms of contracts other than those for delivery, such as production-and-supply contracts for agricultural products, contracts for capital construction, and contracts for the shipment of freight.

The new-found importance of the planning contract was reflected in scholarly investigations. Whereas earlier, the dominant position in the literature was occupied by textbooks and works of a dogmatic character,[72] now studies on concrete problems of the planning contract began to appear.[73]

---

71. See, for example, the Draft of the Statute on Contractual Relations Among State, Cooperative, and Public Institutions, Enterprises and Organizations, prepared in 1934 in the Appendix to the book by G. Amfiteatorov, *Osnovnye cherty zakonoproekta o dogovorakh* [*Basic Features of the Draft Law On Contracts*] (Moscow: Sovetskoe zakonodatel'stvo, 1934), pp. 51–62.

72. See, for example, F.I. Vol'fson, *Grazhdansko pravo (uchebnik)* [*Civil Law (A Textbook)*] (Moscow: Iurizdat, 2d ed., 1939); Ia. M. Magaziner, *Sovetskoe khoziaistvennogo pravo* [*Soviet Economic Law*] (Leningrad: Kassavzainopomoshi stoodentov Leningradskogo Instituta Narodnogo Khoziaistva im. F. Englel'sa, 1928); S. I. Raevich, *Osnovy knoziaistvennogo prava* [*Fundamentals of Economic Law*] (Moscow: Gosfinizdat, 1932–1933), Issues 1 & 2; P. I. Stuchka, *Kurs sovetskogo grazhdanskogo prava* [*A Course in Soviet Civil Law*] (Moscow-Leningrad: Communist Academy, 1927–1931), Vols. 1–3; K.A. Grave, *Torgovye ustanovleniia* [*Trading Regulations*] (Moscow: Finizdat, 1927).

73. See, for example, A.A. Karavaikin, *Ispolnenie dogovora* [*Performance of a Contract*] (Moscow: Sovetskoe zakonodatel'stvo, 1934); A. V. Venediktov, *Dogovornaia ditsiplina v promyshlennosti* [*Contractual Discipline in Industry*] (Leningrad: Izadtel'stvo Lenoblispolkoma i Lensoveta, 1935); M.O. Krasnosel'ski, *Praktika dogovorov v promkooperatsii* [*The Practice of Contracts in Industrial Cooperatives*] (Moscow-Leningrad: KOIZ, 1934).

2.2 Contract Law during the Stage of the Complete and Final Victory of Socialism

The stage of the complete and final victory of socialism lasted from 1936 to the early 1960s. The contract law of this phase developed in the direction of improving the legal rules adopted in the preceding periods. In legislation, practice, and doctrine, primary attention was paid to the general principles of the civil contract. The civil codes of the Union republics, adopted in the early period of the NEP, became obsolete. They were intended to regulate relationships in society under the conditions of a mixed economy, but a unified socialist economy now prevailed in the country. The special legislation in force was oriented toward a differential approach to the various groups of subjects of contractual relationships.

The preparation and adoption of unified rules for all forms of relationships of society regulated by civil law was urgently needed. The Civil Code of the USSR, the publication of which was envisaged by the Soviet Constitution of 1936, was intended to meet this need. The first All-Union Conference on questions of the science of Soviet law, held in 1938,[74] provided a theoretical approach for the unity of regulation of contractual relationships under the civil law.

These plans, however, were postponed because of the war against the USSR launched by Germany in 1941. Accordingly, it is necessary to divide the history of the stage of the complete and final victory of socialism into three periods: the one preceding the Great Patriotic War; the war period; and the postwar years, during which the construction of socialism was completed.

A. The Period from the Adoption of the Soviet Constitution to the Great Patriotic War (1936–1941)

The Soviet Constitution of 1936 fixed the basic socio-economic provisions for civil contracts under the conditions of socialist society. This was primarily reflected in Articles 4 and 11 of the Constitution. According to Article 4, "The economic foundation of the USSR is the socialist eco-

---

74. See *Materialy pervogo soveshchaniia nauchnykh rabotnikov prava* [*Papers of the First Congress of Scholarly Workers in Law*] (Moscow, 1938).

nomic system and the socialist ownership of all tools and means of production." Article 11 spoke of the planned character of the economy.

The Constitution envisaged the adoption of a Civil Code of the USSR, in addition to the separate civil codes of the various republics. Pending adoption of such a new code, unity in the legal regulation of contractual relations had to be provided for by the organs of law enforcement. The activity of the courts and the arbitration commissions in carrying out this difficult task is shown in the application of Articles 30 and 147 of the Civil Code of the RSFSR. Article 30 declared null and void all transactions carried out with an aim that ran counter to the law, that evaded the law, or that clearly disadvantaged the state. The consequences of these transactions being declared null and void were determined by Article 147. Neither of the parties to a contract was entitled to demand from the other the return of the proceeds of the contract, with a penalty for unfounded enrichment to be made to the state.

The Plenum of the Supreme Court of the RSFSR, in its decision of May 16, 1927, gave, without any adequate legal grounds for doing so, a restrictive interpretation of Article 147 of the Civil Code of the RSFSR. It indicated that Article 147 was inapplicable to cases in which both parties were state institutions, or in which one party was a state institution and the other a cooperative organization.[75] It is quite obvious that limiting the application of Article 147 of the Civil Code of the RSFSR solely to relations in which individuals participate was a direct reflection of the mistaken views as to the legal nature of relationships between socialist organizations that prevailed at the end of the 1920's.

This limitation was abolished in 1939. The State Arbitration Board under the Council of People's Commissars of the USSR and the Plenum of the Supreme Court of the USSR explained that the rules in Articles 30 and 147 of the Civil Code of the RSFSR and the analogous articles of the civil codes of the other Union republics were applicable not only to relationships in which citizens participated, but also to transactions to which state and public institutions and enterprises were parties.[76] Arbitration practice, in particular, recognized the applicability of the these articles of the Civil Code to contracts that violated the principles of state planning in material

75. *Civil Code of the RSFSR* (Moscow: Gosiurizdat, 1957) (Supplementary materials to Article 147).
76. *Id.*

and equipment supply, the granting of credit and financing, capital construction, transportation of goods, and the like.[77]

Along with providing for unity in the regulation of contractual relationships by civil law, much attention was paid to the development of legislation for various types of contracts. This legislation related both to contracts between socialist organizations, and to those in which individuals participated. For example, in the field of supply, there was a transition from the system of general and local contracts to one of direct contracts made between producers and consumers of products. In a number of cases, these contracts were made with marketing and supply organizations. This was promoted by such factors as the strengthening of the self-supporting status of productive enterprises, and the transition, in a number of sectors of industry, to the so-called two-tier system of management (consisting of the enterprise and the Glavk, or the People's Commissariat) with the abolition of the trust as an intermediate link. In the Resolution of the Council of People's Commissars of the USSR of March 15, 1936, "On the Making of Contracts for 1936,"[78] direct contracts were cited as the basic method of contracting.

Supervision of contractual relations between socialist organizations, primarily at the stage of the making of contracts, began to be exercised with the aid of Protocol Agreements and Basic Conditions of Delivery. Protocol Agreements were made between the main committees of the People's Commissariat, as suppliers, and the People's Commissariats as consumers, which as a rule were not run on a self-supporting basis. These Agreements called for a certain procedure in making supply contracts and, in the most general form, specified the conditions making up the content of these contracts. Protocol Agreements were not considered contracts under civil law. By their character, they fell into the category of administrative documents of a management type.

The Basic Conditions of Deliveries contained rather detailed descriptions for the most important elements in delivery contracts for specific types of products, such as procedures for making contracts, delivery deadlines, specifications of quantity and quality, prices, and the like. They were approved by the main committees of the People's Commissariats (or by the Commissariats directly), which were responsible for production, with the consent of the main committees of the People's Commissariats, which were responsible for the consumer-enterprises of these products. By

77. I.B. Novitskii, *Istoriia sovetskogo grazhdanskogo prava* [*History of Soviet Civil Law*], p. 229.
78. *SZ SSSR*, No. 3, item 27 (1936).

their legal nature, the Delivery Conditions were considered rules of law.[79] The development of the legal regulation of relationships involving the supply of products and commodities was promoted by the activity of the State Arbitration Board under the Council of People's Commissars of the USSR.[80]

The planned contract became the dominant method in economic law for the organization and implementation of economic ties and relationships among the socialist organizations—the dominant method, but not the only one. Along with it, in the pre-war years, there continued to exist (and in a number of cases to be expanded) non-contractual relationships in which deliveries were carried out pursuant to orders issued by state agencies.[81]

---

79. On these grounds, the State Arbitration Board under the Council of People's Commissars of the USSR in 1938 refused to grant the demand of the Main Trading Bureau of the People's Commissariat of Trade of the RSFSR that the Main Administration of the People's Commissariat of the textile industry pay a fine for supplying data on the group assortment late, which violated the procedure agreed upon by the parties, and established in the Basic Terms for Deliveries. *Arbitrazh* [*Arbitration*] [hereinafter cited as "*Arbitrazh*"], No. 8 (1938), 23. For a discussion on the normative character of the basic terms for deliveries, see Z.I. Shkundin, *Obiaztel'stvo postavki tovarov v sovetskom prave* [*Obligation for the Delivery of Goods in Soviet Law*], p. 79; See also, S.N. Bratus', L.A. Lunts, *Voprosy khoziastvennogo dogovora* [*Questions of Economic Contracts*], p. 37.

80. See, for example, the Decree of the Council of People's Commissars of August 29, 1939, "Ob utverzhdenii Instrukzii Gosudarstvennogo Arbitrazha pri Sovete Narodnix Komissarov SSSR i poriadko i srokax pred'iavlenia pretenzii pri postavke tovarov nenadlezhashyego kachestva odnimi gosudarstvennimi khoziastvennimi kooperativnimi i obshyestvennimi organizaziami drugim" ["On the Confirmation of the Instructions of the State Arbitration Board under the Council of People's Commissars of the USSR on the Procedure and Schedule for Submission of Claims for the Delivery of Goods of Adquate Quality by One State Economic, Cooperative, or Public Organization to Another"], *SP SSSR*, No. 51, item 428 (1939).

81. Beginning in 1935, deliveries of automotive vehicles were made by this procedure. *See* the Normative Order of the Council of Labor and Defense of April 7, 1935, *SZ SSSR*, No. 21, item 167 (1935). Beginning in 1938, the same was done for deliveries of ferrous metals. *See* "The General Conditions for Deliveries of Metal Products", confirmed by the Normative Order of the Economic Council of the Council of People's Commissars of the USSR of November 29, 1938; I.B. Novitskii, *Istoriia sovetskogo grazhdanskogo prava* [*History of Soviet Civil Law*], p. 235. For the delivery of goods for export, see the Decree of the Council of People's Commissars of the USSR of October 31, 1940, *SP SSSR*, No. 27, item 636 (1940).

During this period important changes were also introduced into the legal regulation of capital construction. The Resolution of the Council of People's Commissars of the USSR and the Central Committee of All-Union Communist Party on February 11, 1936, "On the Improvement of Construction and on Cheaper Methods of Building,"[82] recognized the construction contract as the most suitable method of contracting for work. The possibility of using the self-construction method (construction by the organization from its own resources) was limited to the building of small projects not requiring the use of industrial methods.

In the Resolution of the Council of People's Commissars of the USSR on February 26, 1936, "On the Improvement of the Planning and Budgeting Procedure and On the Systemization of the Financing of Construction,"[83] the Rules on Construction Contracts were approved. They established a clear system of relationships between the contractor and the client and defined the basic rights and duties of the parties to the contract.

The system of prime contracts was taken as the basis for construction-contracts. By this system, the client made one contract with a single organization as the general contractor for the entire extent of the construction work. The general contractor, in turn, made subcontracts with specialized organizations, for particular types of work, (including electric, plumbing, heating, etc.) while remaining responsible to the client for the entire project under the contract. These rules on building contracts played an important role in the legal regulation of capital construction in the USSR.

Among the contracts in which individuals participated, legislators paid the greatest attention to contracts on the use of housing. Such contracts affected the vast majority of individuals. On October 17, 1937, the Central Executive Committee and the Council of People's Commissars of the USSR adopted a special Resolution, "On the Preservation of the Housing Supply and the Improvement of Housing Maintenance in the Cities,"[84] which specified the rights of individuals to receive and use housing space in state and publicly owned buildings. The housing offices of the local Soviets of Working Peoples' Deputies authorized (through administrative dispositions) housing in these buildings for individuals in need. The right to use this housing was formalized through contracts made

82. *SZ SSSR*, No. 9, item 70 (1936).
83. *Izvestiia*, February 27, 1938, p. 1, col. 1–6.
84. *SZ SSSR*, No. 69, item 314 (1937).

by the tenants and the building manager for a period of five years. After the expiration of this period the tenants had a preemptive right to renew the contract. In practice, this meant that housing contracts were made for indefinite periods of time.

Application of the October 17, 1937 law was broadly reflected by the Resolution of The Plenum of the Supreme Court of the USSR of December 12, 1940.[85] This law created a new kind of civil contract differing from the contract for the rental of property.

The development of legislation on contracts discussed above has been appropriately reflected in scholarly literature. However, the vast majority of works continued to be commentaries.[86] The only exceptions were

---

85. See *Sbornik deistvuiushchikh postanovlenii Plenuma Verkhovnogo Suda SSSR za 1924–1951 gg.* [*Collection of Guiding Instructions in Force by the Plenum of the Supreme Court of the USSR for 1924–1951*] (Moscow: Gosiurizdat, 1952), pp. 125–135.

86. On the delivery contract, see, for example, V. Mal'tsman, "Iski ob ubytakh po dogovoru postavki (obzor praktiki)," ["Suits for Damages Under the Delivery Contract (A Survey of Practice),"] *Arbitrazh*, No. 16 (1937), 7–10; V.N. Mozheiko, "Spory o tsenakh v praktike vedomstvennogo arbitrazha" ["Disputes on Prices and the Practice of Interagency Arbitration,"] *Arbitrazh*, No. 5 (1939), 12–14; M. Rabinovich, "Preddogovornye spory po postavke tovarov shirokogo potrebleniia" ["Precontractual Disputes on the Delivery of Goods of Wide Consumption,"] *Arbitrazh*, No. 2 (1940), 8–10; Z.I. Shkundin, "O pravovom znachenii osnovnykh uslovii postavki" ["On the Legal Significance of the Basic Conditions of Delivery,"] *Arbitrazh*, No. 2 (1940), 19–23. On the capital construction contract, see Ia. Donde, "Nekotorye voprosy kapital'nogo stroitel'stva v praktike Leningradskogo Gosarbitrazha" ["Some Questions of Capital Construction in the Practice of the Leningrad State Arbitration Board,"] *Arbitrazh*, No. 17 (1937), 11–13; P. Liberman, "Vzaimootnesheniia zakazchika i podriadchika no stroike" ["Interrelations of the Client and the Contractor on the Building Site,"] *Arbitrazh*, No. 17 (1937), 4–6; B. Patushinskii, "Sistema dogovornykh sviazei v kapital'nom stroitel'stve" ["The System of Contractual Relations in Capital Construction,"] *Arbitrazh*, No. 6 (1939), 22–26. On the contract for rental of housing space, see B. Borisov, "O poriadke primeneniia zakona ot 17 oktobria 1937g.," *Sotsialisticheskaia zakonnost'* ["On the Procedure for Applying the Law of October 17, 1937," *Socialist Legality*], No. 2 (1939), 54–60. See also, S. Ginzburg, "Pervye itogi primeneniia novogo zhilishchnogo zakona," *Sovetskaia iustitsiia* ["First Results of the Application of the New Housing Law," *Soviet Justice*], No. 13, pp. 9–12 and No. 18, pp. 21–25 (1938); V.K. Khitev, *Zhilishchnye dela* [*Housing Cases*] (Moscow: Iurizdat, 1939).

certain fundamental works by M.M. Agarkov and other scholars.[87] The articles devoted to the preparation of the Civil Code of the USSR had a tentative character.[88] The war with Germany prevented the development of legal constructions that might have been embodied in specific articles of the Civil Code.

B. THE PERIOD OF THE GREAT PATRIOTIC WAR (1941–1945)

The contract law of the war years helped to solve the major tasks before the Soviet people—defense of the Motherland and repulsion of the troops of the aggressor that had invaded the country. Contract law promoted the mobilization of all of the materiel and manpower necessary for the victory over Germany, Italy, and Japan, while preserving the personal and property rights of individuals in wartime conditions.

The legislation on contracts adopted before 1941 continued in force, with minor corrections, during the war years. It was in effect in the territories temporarily occupied by the enemy. The Resolution of the Plenum of the Supreme Court of December 1, 1944, stated that any

87. See, for example, M.M. Agarkov, *Obiazatel'stva po sovietskomu grazhdanskomu pravu* [*Obligations Under Soviet Civil Law*]; S.I. Asknazii, *Sovetskoe zhilishchnoe pravo* [*Soviet Housing Law*] (Moscow: Iurizdat, 1940); A.D. Keilin, *Transportnoe pravo SSSR i kapitalisticheskikh stran* [*Transportation Law of the USSR and the Capitalist Countries*] (Moscow: Mezhdunarodnaia Kniga, 1938), Issue I. For a systematized exposition of the problems of contract law, see *Grazhdanskoe pravo* [*Civil Law*] (a textbook for legal post-secondary schools), eds., Ia. F. Mikolenko and P. E. Orlovskii (Moscow: Legal Publishing House of the People's Commissariat of Justice, 1938) vol. 2.

88. See, for example, G.N. Amfiteatrov, "Proekt Konstitutsii SSSR i Grazhdanskii kodeks sotsialisticheskogo obshchestva," *Sovetskoe gosudarstvo i pravo* ["The Draft Constitution of the USSR and the Civil Codes of a Socialist Society," *Soviet State and Law*], No. 4 (1936), 84–99; M.V. Gordon, "O sisteme budushchego Grazhdanskogo kodeksa Soiuza SSR," *Revoliutsionnoe pravo* ["On the System of the Future Civil Code of the USSR," *Revolution Law*], Nos. 5–6 (1938), 36–42; N. K. Krylenko, "Grazhdanskii kodeks sotsialisticheskogo obshchestva," *Problemy sotsialisticheskogo prava* ["The Civil Code of Socialist Society," *Problems of Socialist Law*], No. 2 (1937), 308; Ia. F. Mikolenko, "Osnovnye printsipy GK SSSR," *Trudy pervoi nauchnoi sessii Vsesoivznogo instituta iuridicheskikh nauk* ["Basic Principles of the Civil Code of the USSR," *The Papers of the First Scholarly Session of the All-Union Institute of Legal Science*] (Moscow, 1940), pp. 276–279, 313–337, 514–523.

transaction under civil law, involving any territory during its occupation by the enemy, was void and therefore did not give rise to any rights or duties,[89] if it did not comply with Soviet law. On the other hand, all contracts made during the period of occupation that were directed towards the implementation and protection of the rights of citizens and organizations were declared valid.

The state strove to support the stability of the contract. The contract continued to be considered the major means of organizing and implementing economic relations between socialist organizations. The war, in and of itself, was not a basis for excusing the parties from contractual obligations. The decisions rendered by the Civil Division of the Supreme Court of the USSR excused the parties from liability under a contract only in those cases where the impossibility of performance was brought about by specific circumstances caused by the war.[90]

At the same time, special attention was paid to the principle of specific performance of the contract by the parties. For example, the Civil Division of the Supreme Court of the USSR overruled the decision of a lower court in a suit brought by the Biisk office of Skotimport against the collective farm, Voroshilova, for damages in hay. (The Biisk office of Skotimport was responsible for the imposition of livestock.) The decision was overruled because the lower court awarded the plaintiff either specific performance or damages. The Civil Division indicated that the plaintiff should have been awarded only specific performance of the contract. The decision of the Civil Division was affirmed by the Plenum of the Supreme Court of the USSR.[91]

Under wartime conditions, the degree of centralized influence by the state on the economic relationships of enterprises and organizations increased. The planning of the supply of materiel and equipment and of the marketing activities of socialist organizations became more business-like and concrete. Plans for the supply of goods and commodities were approved once every quarter rather than once a year, as had been done previously. The practice of extending the term of contracts between organizations after the expiration of the original period became widespread. At

---

89. *See Sbornik deistvuiushchikh postanovlenii Plenuma Verkhovnogo Suda SSSR za 1924–1951 gg.* [*Collection of Guiding Instructions in the Plenum of the Supreme Court of the USSR for 1924–1951*], p. 123.

90. See *Sudebnaia praktika Verkhovnogo Suda SSSR* [*Judicial Practice of the Supreme Court of the USSR*], Issue 3 (1942), 33; *Id.*, Issue 3 (1943), 24.

91. See *Sudebnaia praktika Verkhovnogo Suda SSSR* [*Judicial Practice of the Supreme Court of the USSR*], Issue 1 (1942), 6–9.

the same time, contracts made before the war, if they did not correspond to the needs of defense, were terminated.

With regard to specific types of products of the extractive sectors of industry, a planning-and-administrative procedure for supply was introduced. For example, in accordance with the Resolution of the Council of People's Commissars of the USSR of December 17, 1943, "On Economic Contracts for 1943,"[92] the obligations to consumers of the State Coal Supply and Oil Marketing Bureaus under the Soviet of People's Commissars of the USSR were to be regulated in the future by the basic terms of supply and by orders, without contracts. These and other measures resembling them helped the state to supervise the war economy. Even under the extreme conditions that had developed, however, the management of the economy continued to be based on principles and provisions that had been developed in peacetime. The use of a contract served as a convincing confirmation of that.

Of the contracts in which individuals participated, the most significant, as in pre-war years, was the contract for rental of housing. The state was compelled to decide a multitude of complex questions connected with the rights of the members of the armed services and their families who were in the zone of military action or in areas seized by the enemy. A Resolution of the Council of People's Commissars of August 5,1941,[93] provided that for the duration of the war all persons serving in the ranks of the Red Army, the Navy, or the troops of the People's Commissariat of Internal Affairs, and also the members of their families, should retain the housing space occupied by them. At the same time, members of the armed services were completely exempted from payment for the housing space allotted to them, and the members of their families were to pay rent on privileged bases. If, after the return of the member of the military from service, his home space proved to be occupied by outsiders, it was to be immediately vacated by administrative procedures. Many other contracts in which individuals participated became widespread during the war, including the contract for storage. On the whole the legislation of the war period could not aspire to any goal of conceptual or structural development of contract law. This task arose immediately after the end of World War II. It was natural that during the period of the war there were no profound studies in the field of contract law. Many scholars were at the front, and those who remained behind the lines were occupied chiefly with practical activity and

92. *SP SSSR*, No. 11, item 191 (1942).

93. See *Sbornik postanovlenii, prikazov i instruktsii po finansovo-khoziaistvennym voprosam* [*Collection of Resolutions, Orders and Instructions on Questions of Finance and Economics*] (Moscow: Gosfinizdat, 1941), No. 10, p. 20.

teaching. Individual works and chapters in textbooks on contracts began to appear in the final years of the war and the postwar years.[94]

C. The Period of the Completion of the Construction of Socialism (1946–early 1960s)

In the history of contract law, the period between 1946 and the early 1960's occupies a very important place. During this period the most important pieces of civil legislation to date—the Fundamentals of Civil Legislation of the USSR and the Union Republics, and the civil codes of the Union republics—were prepared. This period also marked the intensive development of legislation on particular kinds of contracts and, in the doctrine of civil law, the creation of fundamental works on basic problems of Soviet contract law.

Drafting the Civil Code of the USSR, interrupted by the war, was resumed. After a short period of time, three drafts of the Code were prepared.[95] Contract law was a very important subject area in these drafts,

94. See P.E. Orlovskii, *Praktika Verkhovnogo Suda SSSR po grazhdanskim delam v usloviiakh Otechestvennoi voiny* [*Practice of the Supreme Court of the USSR on Civil Cases Under the Conditions of the Great Patriotic War*] (Moscow: Iurizdat, 1944); D.M. Genkin, "Velikaia Otechestvennia voina i voprosy grazhdanskogo prave," *Uchenye zapiski VIIuN* ["The Great Patriotic War and Questions of Civil Law," *The All-Union Institute of Legal Research*] (Moscow: Iurizdat, 1944), Issue 3; M. M. Agarkov, "K voprosu o dogovornoi otvetstvennosti," *Voprosy Sovetskogo grazhdanskogo prava* ["On the Question of Contractual Liability," *Questions of Soviet Civil Law*] (Moscow: Publishing House of the Academy of Sciences, 1945), Collection No. 1, pp. 132–144; *Grazhdanskoe pravo* [*Civil Law*] (Textbook for Institutes of Law), eds., M.M. Agarkov and D.M. Genkin (Moscow: Iurizdat, 1944), Volume 1; *Sovetskoe pravo v period Velikoi Otechestvennoi voiny* [*Soviet Law in the Period of the Great Patriotic War*], ed., I.T. Goliakov (Moscow: Iurizdat, 1948), Part 1.

95. *See Grazhdanskii kodeks Soiuza SSR. Proekt* [*The Civil Code of the USSR: A Draft*] (Moscow, 1947); *Ob'iasnitel'naia zapiska k proektu GK SSSR i tekst proekta priniatogo Komissiei po postanovlniiu proektov GK i GPK SSSR* [*An Explanatory Note to the Draft of the Civil Code of the USSR and the Text of the Draft Adopted by the Drafting Commission for the Civil Code and the Code of Civil Procedure of the USSR*]; *Grazhdanskii kodeks SSSR. Proekt* [*The Civil Code of the USSR: A Draft*] (Moscow, 1948) (Compiled by the Government Commission on the basis of a Decree of the Council of Ministers of the USSR of July 27, 1946); *Grazhdanskii kodeks SSSR. Proekt* [*The Civil Code of the USSR: A Draft*] (Moscow, 1951) (Compiled by the Government Commission on the basis of a Decree of the Council of Ministers of the USSR of November 26, 1948).

but none of them became law. This was explained by several reasons, including the inadequate degree of development of individual legal institutions, and, more important, the expansion of the powers of the Union republics in the various fields of life. On February 11, 1957, the Supreme Soviet of the USSR amended the 1936 Constitution, which had mandated that a Civil Code for the USSR be adopted.[96] This new law declared that the Fundamentals of Civil Legislation would be adopted instead. After the adoption of the Fundamentals of Civil Legislation, it was up to each Union republic to adopt its own civil code.

Three years later the draft of the Fundamentals of Civil Legislation was published for discussion,[97] and in 1959, the draft of the Civil Code of the RSFSR was prepared.[98] Thus, at the beginning of the 1960s the entire drafting of the Fundamentals of Civil Legislation and the Civil Codes of the Union Republics was completed.

Along with this, legislation on individual types of contracts was refined. As was to be expected, the delivery contract—one of the most widespread contracts in relations among socialist organizations—was the primary subject of revision. In the Resolution of the Council of Ministers of the USSR of April 21, 1949, "On the Making of Economic Contracts,"[99] which played an important role in the development of the planned contract in the postwar period, the practice of non-contractual deliveries was decisively condemned. The contract made by socialist organizations on the basis of a plan was essentially recognized as the single form of organization and implementation of economic relations. Instances of non-contractual deliveries were limited to cases of deliveries of commodities for export and one-time deliveries carried out in the execution of special resolutions by the government of the USSR. The State Arbitration Board under the Council of Ministers of the USSR also allowed suits for payment for products delivered according to the plan for the first quarter, if the loading of the products was carried out before the expiration of the deadline for the making of the contract.[100]

---

96. See *Izvestiia*, February 12, 1957, p. 1, col. 5.
97. See *Biulleten' Verkhovnogo Suda SSSR*, No. 4 (1960), 1–20; *Sovetskoe gosudarstvo i pravo* [*Soviet State and Law*], No. 4 (1960), 3–22; *Sotsialisticheskaia zakonnost'* [*Socialist Legality*], No. 8 (1960), 4–20; *Sovetskoe iustitsiia* [*Soviet Justice*], No. 7 (1960), Appendix pp. 1–16.
98. *Proekt Grazhdanskogo kodeksa RSFSR* [*Draft Civil Code of the RSFSR*] (Moscow: Ministry of Justice of the RSFSR, 1959).
99. *SP SSSR*, No. 9, item 68 (1949).
100. See I.B. Novitskii, *Istoriia sovetskogo grazhdanskogo prava* [*History of Soviet Civil Law*], p. 301.

In all other cases, suits involving the delivery of goods could be brought only on the basis of a contract. By the Resolution of the Council of Ministers of April 21, 1949, a system of general and local contracts was again introduced as the basic form. This time the legal competence of enterprises and organizations in making and performing local contracts was broader than it had been in the 1920's.

In 1957, in connection with a change in the management of industry and construction, direct contracts took the leading place in the organization of economic relations among enterprises and organizations. The strengthening of the role of the contract in the field of deliveries of goods was promoted by the Resolution of the Council of Ministers of the USSR and the Central Committee of the Communist Party of the Soviet Union of August 21, 1954, "On the Role and Tasks of the State Bank of the USSR."[101] This Resolution required suppliers to indicate, in payment requests that they sent to consumers through the bank, the date and number of the contract or order on which the delivery had been made. When this requirement was not complied with, the bank refused to accept the documents from the suppliers. An exception was made for deliveries carried out before the expiration of the deadline for the making of the contract, and for deliveries that by virtue of the law had a non-contractual character.

The Resolution of the Council of Ministers of the USSR of April 21, 1949, however, did not solve many problems in the field of deliveries of goods. This lacuna was filled by the Basic Terms for Deliveries for various types of products. In 1956-1957 more than 250 sets of Basic Terms for Deliveries, of an interagency character, were in effect, excluding the huge number of interagency Sets of Basic Terms.[102] Together with rules for the delivery of specific types of products, the Basic Terms for Deliveries also established without sufficient ground, rules for a differentiated approach to the regulation of a whole series of general terms for delivery contracts. It is clear that this complicated the action of the economic mechanism for deliveries in the country.

With the adoption of two Statutes on Deliveries (the Statute on Deliveries of Products for Industrial and Technical Purposes and the Statute on Deliveries of Commodities for Consumption by the Population)[103] by the

101. *Direktivy KPSS i Sovetskogo pravitel'stva po khoziaistvennym voprosam* [*Directives of the CPSU and the Soviet Government on Economic Questions*] (Moscow: Gospolitizdat, 1958), vol. 4, p. 290.

102. See R.O. Khalfina, *Pravovoe reglirovanie postavki produktsii* [*Legal Regulations of Delivery of Goods in the Economy*], p. 19.

103. *SP SSSR*, No. 11, item 68 (1959).

Council of Ministers of the USSR on May 22, 1959, the first codification of legal rules in this sphere of contractual relationships was introduced. Both Statutes proceeded from the principle of combining the contract with planning. A strengthening of the influence of a plan on contractual relationships proceeded along with measures taken by the state to strengthen the self-supporting qualities of state enterprises and organizations.[104] This was also reflected in the rules of the Statutes on Deliveries. In particular, the parties were granted the right to put into the contract terms (including significant ones) not envisaged by the Statutes on Deliveries.

These statutes included rules relating to the most significant terms of the delivery contract. At the same time, the possibility of adopting Special (but not Basic) Terms for Deliveries that should reflect the peculiarities of specific types of goods and commodities was envisaged. The duty of adopting the Special Conditions was entrusted to a single organ—the State Arbitration Board under the Council of Ministers of the USSR. Statutes on Deliveries of Goods and Commodities took a firm place in the legislative practice of the following years.

In the field of capital construction, the regulation of contractual relations under the plan underwent many changes in connection with the expanding scale of capital construction, the further improvement of the system for administering it, and the more intensive use of the scientific and technological advances made in this area.[105] The increased legislative activity

---

104. Decree of the Council of Ministers of the USSR of August 9, 1955, "O rasshirenii prav directorov predpriatii," *Postanovleniia TsK KPSS i Soveta Ministrov SSSR po voprosam promyshlennosti i stroitel'stva*, ["On the Expansion of the Rights of Directors of Enterprises," *Decrees of the CC CPSU and the Council of Ministers of the USSR on Questions of Industry and Construction*] (Moscow: Gospolitizdat, 1956), p. 91.

105. *See* the Decree of the CC CPSU and the Council of Ministers of the USSR of August 23, 1955, "O merakh po dal'neishei industrializatsii, ulushcheniiu kachestva i snizheniiu stoimosti stroitel'stva," *Postanovlenie TsK KPSS i Soveta Ministrov SSSR po voprosam stroitel'stva* ["On Measures for the Further Industrialization, the Improvement of Quality and the Reduction of the Cost of Construction," *The Decree of the CC CPSU and the Council of Ministers on Questions of Construction*] (Moscow, 1956), pp. 82–137; and the Decree of the Council of Ministers of the USSR of August 24, 1965, "Ob uporiadochenii planirovaniia, ukreplenii khoziaistvennogo rascheta, finansovoi ditsipliny i ululshchenii smezhnogo dela v stroitel'stve," ["On the Setting in Order of Planning, the Improvement of Accounting, Financial Discipline, and the Improvement of Estimates in Construction" (with appendices consisting of the Rules for the Financing of Construction by Long-Term Deposits by Banks, the Rules on Construction Contracts, and the Standard Construction Contract)], *Id.*

of the state also extended to contracts for transportation,[106] contracts for the production and supply of agricultural products,[107] and, more important, to contracts for housing, trade, and consumer services involving individuals.[108]

By the end of this period a quite broad and well-balanced system of legal regulation of various types of contracts had been developed. This was

---

The February 20, 1959, Resolution of the Council of Ministers of the USSR, "Ob ulushchenii proektnogo dela v stroitel'stve," ["On the Improvement of Estimates and Construction"], was also important. *SP SSSR*, No. 3, item 18 (1955). The State Arbitration Board under the Council of Ministers of the USSR adopted the Letter of Instruction of December 29, 1956, "O rassmotrenii sporov sviazannykh c kapital'nym stroitel'stovm," *Sbornik instruktivnykh ukazanii Gosarbitrazha pri Sovete Ministrov SSSR* ["On the Consideration of Disputes Connected with Capital Construction," *Collection of Letters of Instruction of the State Arbitration Board under the Council of Ministers of the USSR*] (Moscow: Gosiurizdat, 1957), Issue 4, pp. 57–84, which defined the major directions of arbitration practice for this category of cases.

106. See *Ustav zheleznkyh dorog SSSR* [*The Charter of Railroads of the USSR*], approved by the Council of Ministers of the USSR on December 8, 1954 (Moscow: Transzheldorizdat, 1955); *Ustav vnutrennego vodnogo transporta* [*The Charter of Internal Water Transportation*], approved by the Council of Ministers of the USSR on October 15, 1955 (Moscow: Rechnoi Transport, 1956).

107. *See* the Decree of the Council of Ministers of the USSR of June 30, 1958, "Ob otmene obiazatel'nykh postavok i naturoplaty za raboty MTS, o novom poriadke, tsenakh i usloviiakh zagotovki sel'skokhoziaistvennykh produktov" ["On the Abolition of Obligatory Deliveries and Payment in Kind for the Work of Machine Tractor Stations, and On a New Procedure and New Prices and Terms for the Supply of Agriculture Products"], *SP SSSR*, No. 11, item 92 (1958). Beginning in 1958, in accordance with this Decree, production and supply contracts, which had ceased their activity on the eve of the Great Patriotic War, were again introduced.

108. See the Decree of the Council of Ministers of the USSR of March 20, 1958, "O zhilishchnogo-stroitel'noi i davno-stroitel'noi kooperatsii" ["Housing Construction and Dacha Construction Cooperatives"], *SP SSSR*, No. 5, item 47 (1958); the Edict of the Presidium of the Supreme Soviet of the USSR of September 10, 1953, "Ob otmene administrativnogo vyseleniia iz domov gosudarstvennykh predpriiatii, uchrezhdenii i organizatsii rabochikh i sluzhashchikh, prekrativshikh trudovye otnosheniia" ["On the Abolition of Administrative Eviction from Housing of State Enterprises, Institutions, and Organizations, of Blue Collar and White Collar Workers who Have Ceased their Labor Relationship"], as presented in the February 28, 1957, Edict of the Presidium of the Supreme Soviet of the USSR, *Vedomosti Verkhovnogo Soveta SSSR*, No. 7, item 193 (1957). *See also* "Pravila pol'zovania i soderzhania zhilogo pomeshyenia" ["Rules for the

promoted by the doctrine of Soviet civil law. In contrast to previous periods, where the studies conducted by scholars were limited to commentaries on existing laws, during this period scholars also studied possible future developments in the law. They gave scientific recommendations for the preparation of the Fundamentals of Civil Legislation and the civil codes of the Union republics,[109] and concentrated on the most important problems of civil law, including contract law. Many works on the general theory of the civil contract and on individual problems of contract law appeared in these years—works that have retained their significance to the present time.[110]

Use and Maintenance of A Dwelling"], adopted by the Ministry of Municipal Facilities of the RSFSR on November 30, 1950, *Zhilishchnye zakony* [*Housing Laws*] (Moscow: Publishing House of the Ministry of Municipal Facilities of the RSFSR, 1958), p. 336; Decree of the CC CPSU and the Council of Ministers of the USSR of April 8, 1960, "O merakh po dal'neishemu ulushcheniiu torgovli" ["On Measures for the Further Improvement of Trade"], *SP SSSR*, No. 14, item 114 (1960); "Pravila obmena promishlennix tovarov kuplennix v roznichnoi torgovoi seti" ["Rules for the Exchange of Industrial Goods Bought From the Retail Trade Network"], ratified by the order of the Minister of Trade of the USSR of June 15, 1956, *Pravila raboty torgovykh predpriiatii. Pravila prodazhi tovarov. Sbornik normativnykh materialov* [*Rules for the Work of Trade Enterprises, Rules for the Sale of Goods: A Collection of Normative Materials*] (Moscow: Gostorgizdat, 1961), pp. 510–512; Decree of the CC CPSU and the Council of Ministers of the USSR of March 6, 1959, "O merakh po ulushcheniiu bytovogo obsluzhivaniia naseleniia" ["On Measures for the Improvement of Consumer Services to the Population"], *SP SSSR*, No. 5, item 30 *et seq*. (1959).

109. See *Sovetskoe grazhdanskoe pravo. Sovetskoe semeinoe pravo. Bibliografiia 1917–1960* [*Soviet Civil Law; Soviet Family Law: A Biblography 1917–1960*] (Moscow: Gosiurizdat, 1962), pp. 55–58, 63–70.

110. In addition to the monographs already mentioned on the planned nature of the contract, see N. I. Krasnov, *Real'noe ispolnenie dogovornykh obiazatel'stv mezhdy sotsialisticheskimi organizatsiiami* [*Specific Performance of Contractual Obligations Between Socialist Organizations*] (Moscow: Gosiurizdat, 1959); V.K. Reikher, *Pravovye voprosy dogovornoi ditsipliny v SSSR* [*Questions of Contractual Disciplines in the USSR*] (Leningrad: Leningrad University Publishing House, 1958); G.K. Matveev, *Vina v sovetskom grazhdanskom prave* [*Fault in Soviet Civil Law*] (Kiev: Kiev State University Publishing House, 1955); I.B. Novitskii, L. A. Lunts, *Obshchee uchenie ob obiazatel'stve* [*The General Doctrine of Obligations*]; *Otdel'nye vidy obiazatelstv* [*Individual Forms of Obligations*], eds., K.A. Grave and I. B. Novikskii (Moscow: Gosiurizdat, 1954); R. O. Khalfina, *Znachenie i sushchnost dogovora v sovetskom sotsialisticheskom grazhdandskom prave* [*The Significance and Nature of the Contract in Soviet Socialist Civil Law*] (Moscow: Academy of Sciences of the USSR, 1954).

Chapter 3

Sources of Contract Law

In Soviet literature, "sources of law" as used in the legal sense, refers to several different kinds of authoritative resources where legal rules can be found.[1] Such resources include not only statutes[2] and subordinate

1. See *Pravotvorchestvo v. SSSR* [*The Creation of Law in the USSR*], ed., A.V. Mitskevich (Moscow: Iuridicheskaia Literatura, 1974), p. 14; *Teoriia gosudarstva i prava* [*The Theory of State and Law*], eds., A.I. Korolev and L.S. Iavich (Leningrad: Leningrad University Publishing House, 1982), p. 241; S.S. Alekseev, *Obshchaia teoriia i prava* [*General Theory of Law*] (Moscow: Iuridicheskaia Literatura, 1981), vol. I, p. 314.

2. The USSR, which is a federated state, consists of 15 Union Republics. Each of them has its own legislative government, and republican legal system. Additionally, in a number of Union Republics (the RSFSR, the Uzbek SSR, the Georgian SSR, and the Azerbaidzhan SSR), there are Autonomous Republics (20 in all) with their own legislature and government.

Accordingly, in the USSR, the laws include statutes approved by the Supreme Soviet of the USSR and the Supreme Soviet of the Union and Autonomous Republics. It should also be noted that the Presidium of the Supreme Soviet of the USSR and the Presidium of the Supreme Soviets of the Union and Autonomous Republics, which carry out the functions of the supreme organs of state power within their own territories between sessions of the Soviets, are empowered to introduce changes into existing legislation with subsequent presentation of the decrees adopted by them for ratification at the sessions of the Soviets. These decrees have the force of statutes between sessions.

In a number of cases the term "statute" is given a meaning that includes not only "statute" in the strict sense of the word, but also the subordinate rules based upon it. For example, "statute" is used in this sense in Article 37 of the Constitution of the USSR, according to which foreign citizens and stateless persons located on the territory of the USSR are obliged to respect the Constitution of the USSR and observe Soviet laws.

rules,[3] but also, in exceptional cases specifically noted in the law, customs.[4] In relationships in which foreign individuals and enterprises participate, sources of law on the territory of the USSR may also include international treaties (Article 129 of the Fundamentals of Civil Legislation) and laws of foreign nations (Articles 123–128 of the Fundamentals of Civil Legislation). The practice of courts, arbitration commissions, and other bodies in applying legal rules is important. This practice, however, is not a source of law. This is true of contract law and of law in general.

3.1 Statute Law as a Source of Contract Law

The contract law now in effect is based on principles established in the basic laws of the state—the Constitution of the USSR and the constitutions of the Union and autonomous republics. The functioning of the contract system, which connects all the members of the economy beginning with production and ending with consumption by the individual, is provided for on the constitutional level by Articles 15 and 16 of the Constitution of the USSR and the corresponding articles of the constitutions of the Union and autonomous republics. These articles set forth the goals of production under socialism[5] and the conditions of the use of commodity-and-money relationships in a planned economy.[6]

---

3. Subordinate rules include the edicts of the Presidiums of the Supreme Soviet of the USSR and of the Union Republics (other than those listed in footnote 2) on questions directly assigned to their jurisdiction; decrees and ordinances of the Counsel of Ministers of the USSR and the Counsel of Ministers of the Union and Autonmous Republics; joint decrees of the CC CPSU and the Council of Ministers of the USSR adopted on the most important questions of life in the country; normative orders and instructions of the Ministries and agencies; normative decisions and orders of the local soviets of people's deputies and of their executive committees; and acts adopted by public organizations within their jurisdiction.
4. Legal customs in the USSR are usually only applied with regard to the transportation of freight by sea. See for example Articles 134, 135, and 149 of the Code of Merchant Shipping of the USSR, approved by the edict of the Presidium of the Supreme Soviet of the USSR on September 17, 1968, *Vedomosti Verkhovnogo Soveta SSSR*, No. 39, item 351 (1969).
5. "The supreme goal of public production under socialism," states Article 15 of the Constitution of the USSR, "is the fullest possible satisfaction of the growing material and spiritual needs of the citizens."
6. Under Article 16 of the Constitution of the USSR, "The economy of the USSR is a unified economic complex embracing all the phases of public production, distribution, and exchange in the territory of the country."

The most basic legislation on contracts made by individuals with socialist organizations consists of the provisions of Chapter 3 (particularly Articles 22 and 24) of the Constitution of the USSR that concern social development and culture and the provisions of Chapter 7 (particularly Article 44) of the Constitution of the USSR that are devoted to the basic rights, liberties, and duties of the citizens of the USSR. The most important rules concerning the application of the civil contract, its content, and the procedure for making, performing, and terminating the contract, as well as the regulation of particular kinds of contract are contained in the Fundamentals of Civil Legislation of the USSR and the Union republics and in the civil codes of the Union republics. The Fundamentals of Civil Legislation[7] prevails over the civil codes of the Union republics and all other rules of civil law.

In the field of contract law these rules include those on: the application of the civil contract (Articles 2–3); the civil (including contractual) legal capacity of Soviet citizens (Articles 8–9), foreign citizens and stateless persons (Articles 122, 123, and 1231), and Soviet (Articles 11–13) and foreign enterprises (Article 124); determining the law applicable in cases of conflict relating to transactions (Articles 125–126); transactions as the basis of origin of civil rights and duties (Article 4); the concept of the transaction, and the most important grounds and consequences for proving a transaction to be invalid (Article 14); the general prescriptions for a contract, which are a component part of the general provisions on legal disabilities (Articles 33–38); the specific varieties of contracts devoted to purchase and sale of goods, delivery of products and commodities between organizations, state procurement of agricultural products from state and collective farms and similar operations, rental of property and housing space, work and capital construction, transportation, state insurance, accounts and credits (Articles 39–87); and contracts with owners of literary property (Articles 101, 102) and patents (Article 112). Thus, of

---

The supervision of the economy is carried out on the basis of state plans for economic and social development, taking into account sectorial and territorial principles, and by combining centralized management with economic autonomy and initiative of enterprises, associations and other organizations. In this process, active use is made of accounting methods, profit, cost of production, and other economic levers and stimuli.

7. *The Fundamentals of Civil Legislation of the USSR and the Union Republics* was adopted by the Supreme Soviet of the USSR on December 8, 1961, and put into effect on May 1, 1962, *Vedomosti Verkhovnogo Soveta SSSR*, No. 50, item 525 (1961).

the 136 articles now included in the Fundamentals of Civil Legislation, 71, or more than half, are directly related to civil contracts. This does not include other articles connected less directly with civil contracts; for example, articles on property rights.

The legal regulation of the vast majority of relationships considered here falls under the exclusive competence of the USSR. According to Article 3 of the Fundamentals of Civil Legislation, "The civil legislation of the USSR regulates . . . relations among socialist organizations for the delivery of products and capital construction; relations involving the state's procurement of agricultural products from collective farms, state farms, and other operations; relations of organizations of railroad, river, air, pipeline transport, communications, and credit institutions with their clients and among themselves; relations involving state insurance; and also other relations, the regulation of which is authorized by the Constitution of the USSR, by the present Fundamentals and other legislative acts of the USSR under the jurisdiction of the USSR. On these relationships the legislatures of the Union republics may have jurisdiction only over those questions on which they are given jurisdiction by the legislation of the USSR."

Thus, Point 4 of the Statute on Deliveries of Products for Industrial and Technical Purposes provides that the Special Terms for Delivery of Products produced by integrated units, enterprises, and organizations under the jurisdiction of the republics and local authorities may be developed and approved by a procedure established by the Council of Ministers of the Union Republics. There are, for example, Special Terms for Deliveries of Local Building Materials.

The regulation of relationships involving foreign trade and other forms of economic relations with foreign countries are the exclusive jurisdiction of the USSR. In contrast to the regulation of other relationships, this regulation is based on the application of Special Legislation of the USSR and on the General Civil Legislation of the USSR and the Union Republics.

New civil codes of the Union republics, replacing the codes of the 1920's, were adopted and put into effect in the period 1963–1965.[8] As in the Fundamentals of Civil Legislation, a significant part is devoted to rules

---

8. *The Civil Code of the RSFSR* was adopted by the Supreme Soviet of the RSFSR on June 11, 1964, and put into effect on October 1, 1964, *Vedomosti Verkhovnogo Soveta RSFSR*, No. 24, item 406 (1964).

for contractual relationships. These rules may be divided into three groups.

The first group reproduces rules of legislation of the USSR. It includes rules of the Fundamentals of Civil Legislation on contracts on matters that fall under the exclusive jurisdiction of the USSR (*e.g.*, deliveries and capital construction). It also includes rules of legislation of the republics, which decide questions relating to the jurisdiction of the republics by reproducing legislation of the USSR (Article 3 of the Civil Code of the RSFSR and analogous articles of the civil codes of the Union republics).

The second group consists of rules envisaged by the Fundamentals of Civil Legislation for the regulation of contractual relationships. It includes both rules borrowed from the Fundamentals of Civil Legislation and rules of significance to the republics, all directed toward specifying and further developing the general requirements established in the Fundamentals of Civil Legislation. The rules of the Civil Code are much more detailed than those of the Fundamentals of Civil Legislation—particularly with respect to the participation of individuals. Thus, the Civil Code of the RSFSR contains 21 articles on transactions, where the Fundamentals of Civil Legislation contains only one; and 78 articles on general provisions for obligations instead of only six. On individual varieties of contracts, the Civil Code of the RSFR contains 18 articles on purchase and sale, in place of only five in the Fundamentals of Civil Legislation; 20 articles on the rental of property in place of only three; and 18 articles on construction contracts in place of only three. Naturally, the provisions introduced into the civil codes by the Supreme Soviets of the Union Republics must not contradict the rules of the Fundamentals of Civil Legislation or the other USSR-wide laws.

The third group includes rules not envisaged by the Fundamentals of Civil Legislation for the regulation of contractual relationships. These rules are devoted to such transactions as gifts, loans, use of property free of charge, commission, agency, storage, joint activity, and others.

The civil codes of the various Union republics are almost identical with respect to rules relating to the types of contracts mentioned. The differences are seen as insignificant. For example, the civil codes of the Kazakh and Tadzhik SSRs govern relationships arising out of activity without power of attorney. In the civil codes of the other Union republics there are no rules on this subject.

Because there are some differences among the various civil codes, a possibility of conflict exists whenever relationships involve two or more Union republics. Article 18 of the Fundamentals of Civil Legislation resolves such conflicts with rules for the application of civil legislation of one Union republic in the territory of another. In relation to contracts, these rules state that the legal capacity and legal ability of the parties is determined according to the place where the transaction is made (Article 18, Part 2). The law of the place where the transaction was made is also applied to the form of the transaction and to the obligations arising out of it, if the law, or the agreement between the parties, does not specify otherwise (Article 18, Part 3). Questions relating to statutes of limitations for suits are decided according to the law of the Union republic whose legislation regulates the relationship as a whole (Article 18, Part 6).

In addition to the Fundamentals of Civil Legislation and the Civil Codes of the Union Republics, other laws of the USSR and the various republics also provide sources of contract law. As a rule they determine questions relating to specific varieties of civil contracts. Most important, these laws usually have a compound character, including, in addition to rules of civil law, rules of other branches of law (administrative, financial, and the like). One of the most striking examples is the Fundamentals of Housing Legislation of the USSR and the Union Republics, adopted by the Supreme Soviet of the USSR on June 24, 1981, and put into effect on January 1, 1982,[9] and the housing codes of the Union republics.[10] At present, all of the basic rules on the contract for rental of housing space are concentrated in these laws.

3.2 Subordinate Rules

In regulating contractual relationships, wide use is made of subordinate rules. This name is given to rules that apply throughout the USSR or within a particular republic, locality, or agency. They are adopted by state agencies of government and administration (and in isolated cases by public organizations), having the power to do so, on the basis of and in further development of existing laws.

In a hierarchical sense, the highest rank among these rules is held by the edicts of the presidiums of the Supreme Soviet of the USSR and the Union and Autonomous Republics. In the field of contract law, we should

---

9. *Vedomosti Verkhovnogo Soveta RSFSR*, No. 26, items 834, 835 (1981).

10. *The Housing Code of the RSFSR* was adopted on June 24, 1983, and put into effect on January 1, 1984, *Vedomosti Verkhovnogo Soveta RSFSR*, No. 26, item 884 (1983).

mention first the Edict of the Presidium of the Supreme Soviet of the USSR of September 17, 1968, "On the Adoption of the Merchant Shipping Code of the USSR,"[11] and the Decree of the Supreme Soviet of the USSR of May 11, 1983, "On the Adoption of the Civil Aviation Code of the USSR.[12] Both of these codes are complex sets of rules. They include rules of administrative and other branches of law, together with rules of civil law. In relation to the rules of the Fundamentals of Civil Legislation, the rules of civil law contained in the these codes are special rules. It is stated, for example, in Article 18 of the Merchant Shipping Code that "the rules of civil, administrative, or other legislation of the USSR and the Union republics are applied respectively to citizens, ministries, and other legal relationships arising out of merchant shipping."

The next level among the subordinate rules is occupied by the Decrees and Ordinances of the Council of Ministers of the USSR and of the Union and Autonomous Republics. Among these, most important in the sphere of contract law and in the other fields of regulation by civil law, are the rules adopted by the Council of Ministers of the USSR. In many cases these rules are adopted in the form of charters and statutes.

Among the major sources of rules on particular varieties of contracts, of significant importance is the Railroad Charter of the USSR, adopted by the Decree of the Council of Ministers of the USSR of April 6, 1964;[13] the Charter of the Internal Water Transport, adopted on October 15, 1955;[14] the Statute on Deliveries of Products for Industrial and Technical Purposes and the Statute on Deliveries of Products for Consumption by the Population, adopted on February 10, 1981;[15] the Statute on Deliveries of Agricultural Equipment and other Material-Technical Means to Collective Farms, State Farms, and other Agricultural Enterprises and Organizations, adopted on June 29, 1983;[16] the Rules on Contracts for Capital Construction, adopted on December 24, 1967;[17] the Basic Statute on Accounting in

11. *Vedomosti Verkhovnogo Soveta SSSR*, No. 39, item 351 (1968).
12. *Vedomosti Verkhovnogo Soveta SSSR*, No. 20, item 303 (1983) (Appendix).
13. *SP SSSR*, No. 4, item 36 (1964).
14. *Ustav vnutrennego vodnogo transporta SSSR* [*Charter of Internal Water Transportation of the USSR*] (Moscow: "Transport," 1975).
15. *SP SSSR*, No. 9–10, item 62 (1981).
16. *SP SSSR*, No. 17, item 90 (1983).
17. *SP SSSR*, No. 2, item 11 (1968).

the Economy of the USSR, adopted on September 16, 1983;[18] the Basic Statutes on Bank Credit, adopted on November 11, 1982;[19] and others.

The most fundamental questions relating to the basic direction and character of the development of contracts in the economy, and to particular kinds of contracts (*e.g.*, economic contracts, and contracts for services to individual) are usually decided in joint decrees of the CC CPSU and the Council of Ministers of the USSR. Examples of such joint decrees include, the decree of the CC CPSU and the Council of Ministers of the USSR of July 12, 1979, "On the Improvement of the Planning and the Strengthening of the Impact of the Economic Mechanism to Further Accelerate the Effectiveness of Production and Quality of Work";[20] the Decree of July 14, 1983, "On Additional Measures to Expand the Rights of Production Units (Enterprises) in Industry, and in Planning and Economic Activity, and to Increase Their Responsibility for the Results of Their Work";[21] the Decree of February 2, 1984, "On Measures to Expand the Economic Autonomy and to Strengthen the Incentive of Production Units (Enterprises) in Consumer Services for a Fuller Satisfaction of the Demands of the Population for Services";[22] the Decree of April 29, 1984, "On the Improvement of the Planning, Organization, and Administration of Capital Construction";[23] the Decree of November 14, 1985, "On the Subsequent Improvement of the Management of Agro-Industrial Complexes";[24] the Decree of March 20, 1986, "On the Subsequent Improvement of the Economic Mechanism of Management in the Agro-Industrial Complexes of the Country";[25] the Decree of April 24, 1986, "On the Improvement of Planning and Economic Incentives and Management of the Production of Consumer Goods in Light Industry";[26] the Decree of March 13, 1986, "On the Additional Measures for the Improvement of Capital Construction for the Purpose of Accelerating the Scientific-Technical Progress in the National Economy of the Country."[27]

---

18. *SP SSSR*, No. 27, item 155 (1983).
19. *SP SSSR*, No. 32, item 160 (1982).
20. *SP SSSR*, No. 18, item 118 (1979).
21. *SP SSSR*, No. 20, item 109 (1983). This decree laid the foundation for a large scale experiment in improving management of the economy.
22. *SP SSSR*, No. 6, item 29 (1984).
23. *SP SSSR*, No. 15, item 91 (1984).
24. *SP SSSR*, No. 34, item 160 (1985).
25. *SP SSSR*, No. 17, item 90 (1986).
26. *SP SSSR*, No. 20, item 108 (1986).
27. *SP SSSR*, No. 11, item 67 (1986).

A large number of legal rules devoted to contracts—primarily contracts for services to individuals—are contained in Decrees of the Council of Ministers of the Union Republics. Such decrees of the Council of Ministers of the RSFSR include the "Instructions on the Procedure for Sale of Commodities on Credit" of March 9, 1965,[28] the "Standard Contract for Rental and Also Ordering of Consumer Services" of February 1, 1965,[29] the "Standard Contract for Construction of a Residential or Nonresidential Buildings" of April 1, 1982,[30] and the "Charter of Automobile Transportation of the RSFSR" of January 8, 1969.[31]

Among the subordinate rules on contract law, the Orders and Instructions of ministries and agencies of the USSR and the Union republics are also important. On the basis and in fulfillment of the laws, resolutions, and ordinances of the Council of Ministers of the USSR and the Union Republics, these orders and instructions approve many rules and standard (or model) contracts under various types of contractual relations. As examples, we may cite the "Basic Rule for the Work of a Store," approved by the Order of the Ministry of Trade of the USSR of May 18, 1973;[32] the "Standard Rules for the Exchange of Industrial Commodities Bought in the Retail Trade Network of State and Cooperative Trade," confirmed by the order of the Ministry of Trade of the USSR and the State Committee on Standards of the Council of Ministers of the USSR of February 1, 1974;[33] the "Standard Rules for Trade in the Collective Farm Markets," approved by an order of the Ministry of Trade of the USSR of November 14, 1978;[34] the "Specimen Contract for the Organization of Material and Equipment Supply to an Integrated Production Unit, Enterprise, or Organization," approved by a decree of the State Board of Supply of the USSR and the State Arbitration Board of the USSR on December 30, 1981;[35] the "Statute on the Procedure for Making and Performing Production and Supply Contracts for Agricultural Products," approved by the Ministries of Pro-

28. *SP RSFSR*, No. 4, item 19 (1965).
29. *SP RSFSR*, No. 1, item 2 (1965).
30. *SP RSFSR*, No. 11, item 71 (1981).
31. *SP RSFSR*, Nos. 2–3, item 8 (1969).
32. *Osnovnye pravila torgovli. Sbornik normativnykh mateialov* [*Basic Rules for Trade: A Collection of Normative Materials*], compiled by B.V. Pavlov, V.V. Smirnova, M.F. Kooz'menkov (Moscow: Ekonomika, 1981), pp. 48–67.
33. *Id.*, pp. 262–267.
34. *Biulleten' normativnykh aktov ministerstv i vedomstv SSSR*, No. 8 (1979).
35. *Biulleten' normativnykh aktov ministerstv i vedomstv SSSR*, No. 8 (1982).

curement and Agriculture of the USSR on November 15, 1983, with the agreement of the Ministries of Finance and Justice of the USSR, and the Supreme Court of the USSR, and the State Arbitration Board of the USSR;[36] the "Standard Contract for Rental of Non-Residential Premises (Buildings) in Houses Belonging to Local Soviets, State, Cooperative, and Public Organizations," approved by an Order of the Ministry of Municipal Economy of the RSFSR on October 9, 1965;[37] the "Rules for Voluntary Insurance of Domestic Property," approved by the Ministry of Finance of the USSR on November 26, 1980;[38] and the "Standard Permission Contract for Literary Work," approved by an Order of the State Committee of the Council of Ministers of the USSR on Publishing, Printing, and the Book Trade, on February 24, 1975.[39]

As can be seen from this list, standard contracts and rules have become widespread in the practice of making contracts. Specific contracts are made on the basis of them. In this connection, it is necessary to note two important points. First, standard contracts and rules, which have the force of law, are never formulated by the parties themselves. They are promulgated either by state agencies of general competence (the councils of ministers of the USSR and of the Union republics) or agencies of sectoral competence (ministries and agencies). Secondly, many rules included in standard contracts are merely suppletory in character. Within the framework of such rules, provisions formulated by the parties may be included in the contract. However, the Fundamentals of Civil Legislation and the civil codes of the Union republics do contain one significant qualification directed toward protecting the rights of individuals in contracts for services to the population and in authors' contracts. According to this qualification, deviations from the standard contracts that limit the rights of individuals are considered null and void (see, for example, Articles 55, 66, and 101 of the Fundamentals of Civil Legislation).

A special word should be said about the rulemaking activity of the State Arbitration Board of the USSR. According to the law, it is empowered to approve (together with other agencies or on its own) special terms for the

---

36. *Biulleten' normativnykh aktov ministerstv i vedomstv SSSR*, No. 4 (1984).
37. *Zakonodatel'stvo o zhilishchno-kommunal'nom khoziaistve* [*Legislation on Housing and Public Utilities*], compiled by S.U. Lisovor, V.N. Litovkin, A.G. Khasikov (Moscow: Iuridicheskaia Literatura, 1972), vol. I, p. 771.
38. *Sbornik normativnykh aktov po grazhdanskomu zakonodatel'stvu* [*Collection of Normative Acts of Civil Legislation*], ed., A.G. Bikov (Moscow: Iuridicheskaia Literatura, 1984), Part II, pp. 314–319.
39. *Biulleten' normativnykh aktov ministerstv i vedomstv SSSR*, No. 7 (1975).

delivery of products and commodities, instructions, procedures for receipt of material valuables in terms of quantity and quality, and standard contracts for the execution of particular jobs in connection with relations among socialist organizations.[40] These acts by the State Arbitration Board of the USSR are sources of contract law.

The legal rules relating to contracts for services to individuals are very often contained in decisions and ordinances of local Soviets of Working People's Deputies and their executive committees. Examples of such legal ordinances are the rules on registering individuals in need of improved housing conditions and the rules on providing housing space to individuals adopted by the executive committees of the Krai and Oblast Soviets of Working People's Deputies and those of the cities of Moscow and Leningrad.[41] These rules specify the conditions on the basis of which contracts for the rental of housing space in houses belonging to the state and public housing stock are made.

Finally, some subordinate rules are adopted by public organizations within the limits of the competence granted to them by the law. Such rules include, among others, the "Standard Contract for the Purchase of Surplus Agricultural Products in the Personal Subsidiary Farming Operations of Citizens and Members of Gardening Associations," confirmed by the Decree of the Board of Directors of the Central Cooperative Union of the USSR on April 7, 1981, by agreement with the State Bank of the USSR.[42]

3.3 Court and Arbitration Practice

Court and arbitration practice has an important place in the system of legal mechanisms that provides for the functioning of contractual relations in the

---

40. February 12, 1987 Edict of the Central Committee of the Communist Party of the USSR and the USSR Council of Ministers on the State Arbitration Board, published in *Pravda*, Feb. 28, 1987, p. 1.

41. See Article 29 of the Housing Code of the USSR. *See also* Point 2 of the July 31, 1984, Decree of the Council of Ministers of the RSFSR, "O poriadke ucheta grazhdan nuzhdauchikhsia v uluchshenii zhilishynix uslovii i predostavlenii zhilix pomeshyenii v RSFSR" ["On the Procedure for Registering Citizens in Need of Improved Housing, and for Providing Housing in the RSFSR"], *SP RSFSR*, No. 14, item 12 (1984). (This Decree includes an appendix of the Modern Rules for Registering Citizens.)

42. *Biulleten' normativnykh aktov ministerstv i vedomstv SSSR*, No. 3 (1982), 33.

USSR.[43] In considering civil and economic disputes, the courts and arbitration tribunals establish definite rules for the application of legislation in effect, which give this legislation a practical character. The courts and arbitration tribunals have an active, creative function in trying and deciding economic lawsuits. Their role is by no means reduced to the solution of a simple syllogism—a formal logical application of a general rule contained in a legal rule to the concrete circumstances of the case under consideration. In fact, the courts and the arbitration tribunals formulate a whole system of rules in the field of law enforcement practice. The nature of court and arbitration practice must be evaluated in terms of this function.

A. Court Practice

First we turn to court practice and what it involves. As the literature rightly notes, by no means are all decisions handed down by People's, City, Oblast, Krai, and Republic Courts. Nor can all decisions of judicial panels and individual guiding explanations of the Supreme Court of the USSR be considered court practice.[44] Many of them may be random, contradictory, or sometimes simply mistaken.

The concept of court practice has a narrower and more special meaning. It is limited to those decisions in which the steady practice of the courts in deciding a particular category of cases, or a particular question on the basis of a correct application of the law, is embodied. This practice may be laid down in judgments and in decisions of courts at all levels, from the People's Courts, to the Supreme Court of the USSR. Court practice is also found in the explanations issued as guides by the Plenums of the Supreme Court of the USSR and the Plenums of the Supreme Courts of the Union republics.

The first form of court practice is usually established by the fundamental decisions of the higher courts, although it often begins in judgments of People's Courts. An example is the decision of the Civil Judicial Panel of the Supreme Court of the RSFSR in a suit brought by Citizen P for damages caused by a fire in a purchased television set.[45] Citizen P bought

43. The present chapter does not consider the activity of the administrative organ of power in applying the rules of contract law. This will be done in part in chapter 5.

44. See *Sudebnaia praktika v sovetskoi pravovoi sisteme* [*Judicial Practice in the Soviet Legal System*], ed., S.N. Bratus' (Moscow: Iuridicheskaia Literatura, 1975), pp. 8–9.

45. *Biulleten' Verkhovnogo Suda RSFSR*, No. 3 (1982), 9–10.

a Rubin 714D television set manufactured by the Moscow Integrated Production Unit, Rubin, from the Moscow-Lenin Department Store. The following day, the television set caught fire causing much damage to Citizen P's property. The expert evaluation showed that manufacturing defects, for which the manufacturer was responsible, caused the fire. Citizen P brought suit against two defendants, the Moscow Integrated Production Unit, Rubin, as manufacturer of the set, and the Moscow-Lenin Department Store, as the seller. The People's Court, which heard the suit in the first instance, decided that the losses should be recovered from the Moscow-Lenin Department Store, and freed the Integrated Production Unit, Rubin, of liability.

The Civil Judicial Panel of the Supreme Court of the RSFSR, to which the case came on the appeal, affirmed the decision of the People's Court. The Judicial Panel reasoned that the television set was bought by the plaintiff through a contract of purchase and sale made with the Moscow-Lenin Department Store. The fire occurred before the expiration of the guarantee period, as a result of a manufacturing defect. Under these conditions, liability for the losses caused by the sale of a television set of improper quality must be borne by the Moscow-Lenin Department Store as a party to a contract of purchase and sale that did not perform the duties it had undertaken—to sell the plaintiff a television set of suitable quality. In this connection, the Judicial Panel cited Article 248 of the Civil Code of the RSFSR on guarantees against defects in articles sold with a warranty period, and Article 219 of the Civil Code of the RSFSR concerning the seller's duty to make good any losses. As for the possibility of the manufacturer being liable, the Judicial Panel pointed to the right of the Moscow-Lenin Department Store to bring a suit for recovery against it and concluded that this was sufficient to protect the plaintiff.

The reasoning of the Civil Judicial Panel of the Supreme Court of the RSFSR is of fundamental importance for the courts of the Russian Federation. It contains an interpretation of the law that excludes the possibility of suing the manufacturers of products for damages before the expiration of the guarantee period.[46] This decision, however, does not itself create a new legal rule. According to law and doctrine, the decisions of courts in

---

46. This interpretation of the law on the All-Union level was approved by the Plenum of the Supreme Court of the USSR in the guiding explanation of April 5, 1985. The Plenum of the Supreme Court of the USSR also said that after the expiration of the guarantee period the plaintiff can bring a suit for the recovery of damages against the producer for any harm caused by latent defects in the article purchased. *See Bulletin of the Supreme Court of the USSR*, No. 3 (1950), 17.

specific cases do not constitute the sources of law. Courts carry out the function of law enforcement, and not of legislative organs of the state. At the same time, as indicated above, their decisions create principles of judicial application to be followed in similar cases.[47] A special term applicable to such principles has even appeared in the literature as "a precedent in the interpretation of the legal rule."[48] It is important to emphasize, as distinct from a precedent as a source of law, an interpretative precedent does not lead to the creation of a new legal rule, but is intended to explain an already existing rule of law by establishing a definite rule for applying the rule of law in analogous cases.[49]

The second form of court practice is represented by the guiding explanations of the Plenum of the Supreme Court and the Plenums of the Supreme Courts of the Union republics. According to the Law on the Supreme Court of the USSR, adopted by the Supreme Soviet of the USSR on November 30, 1979,[50] the Supreme Court of the USSR studies and generalizes judicial practice, analyzes judicial statistics, and gives guiding explanations on the application of legislation arising during the consideration of court cases. The guiding explanations by the Plenums of the Supreme Courts of the Union republics have an analogous purpose. They give judicial explanations of the legal rules in effect, relative to particular categories of cases that are considered by the court. The guiding explanations of the Plenums of the Supreme Courts of the USSR and the Supreme Courts of the Union republics are binding on all courts involved in judicial business in the territory of the USSR or of individual Union republics respectively. This binding character is intended to give legal force to the

---

47. Such rules have received in the literature the name "provisions of law." *See Sudebnaia praktika v sovetskoi pravovoi sistem* [Judicial Practice in the Soviet Legal System], ed., S.N. Bratus' (Moscow: Iuridicheskaia Literatura, 1975), p. 26, *et seq*; S.S. Alekseev, *Obshchaia teoriia prava* [*General Theory of Law*], p. 352. This designation would not be objectionable if certain authors did not associate it with the "subordinate provisions of normative character" (S.N. Bratus') or as "interpretative acts containing normative provisions on the application of legal rules" (S.S. Alekseev). Such borrowing of terminology from the field of legislation is hardly justified.

48. A.B. Vengerov, "*O pretsedentnom tolkovanii pravoi normy*," *Uchenye zapiski VNIISZ* ["*On the Interpretation of a Legal Rule Through Precedent*," *The All-Union Institute of Legal Research*], No. 6 (1966), 3.

49. *Sudebnaia praktika v sovetskoi pravovoi sisteme* [*Judicial Practice in the Soviet Legal System*], p. 58.

50. *Vedomosti Verkhovnogo Soveta SSSR*, No. 49, item 842 (1979).

rules for the interpretation of the legislation in effect contained in the explanations.

Theoretical disputes with regard to the legal nature of the guiding explanations continue to be conducted in the literature up to the present time, even though it might seem that the Statute on the Supreme Court of the USSR gives an unambiguous answer. According to these Statute, these explanations are acts relating to law enforcement, and not the legislative activity of the courts.[51] The opposite opinion, which regards these explanations as sources of law,[52] is to a considerable degree based on the practice of the activity of the Plenum of the Supreme Court of the USSR during the 1940's and 1950's. During those years, certain specific explanations were in fact adopted, which went outside the boundaries of laws. This is explained primarily by the fact that the codified civil legislation for many fields at that time had become out-dated.[53]

---

51. See, for example, I.B. Novitskii, *Istochniki sovetskogo grazhdanskogo prava* [*The Sources of Soviet Civil Law*], p. 138, *et seq*.; O.P. Telushkin, "Tolokovanie zakona Plenuma Verkhovnogo suda SSSR," *Sovetskoe gosudarstvo i pravo* ["The Interpretation of Law by the Plenum of the Supreme Court of the USSR," *Soviet State and Law*], No. 12 (1976), 35; V.G. Verdinkov, A. Iu. Kabalkin, *Grazhdansko-pravovye formy tovarno-denezhnykh otnoshenii* [*Civil Law Forms of Commodity-and-Money Relations*] (Moscow: Iuridicheskaia Literatura, 1970), p. 39; S.S. Alekseev, *Obshchaia teoriia prava*, [*General Theory of Law*], pp. 350–352, 355; *Sudebnaia praktika v sovetskoi pravovoi sisteme* [*Judicial Practice in the Soviet Legal System*], p. 26.

52. S.I. Vil'nianskii, *Lektsii po sovetskomu grazhdanskomu pravu* [*Lectures on Soviet Civil Law*] (Khar'kov: Khar'kov University Publishing House, 1958), pp. 57, 60; S.I. Vil'nianskii, "Pravovye i inye sotsial'nye normy v period razvernutogo stroitel'stva kommunizma," *Pravovedenie* ["Legal and Other Social Rules in the Period of the Comprehensive Building of Communism," *Jurisprudence*], No. 4 (1962), 21; *Sovetskoe grazhdanskoe pravo* [*Soviet Civil Law*], eds., V.F. Maslov and A.A. Pushkin (Kiev: Vishcha shkola, 1983), vol. I, p. 51.

53. See, for example, Point 18 of the Guiding Instructions of the Plenum of the Supreme Court of the USSR, passed on December 12, 1940, "O sudebnoi praktike po primeneniiu postanovleniia TSIK i SNK SSSR ot 17 oktiabria 1937" ["On the Judicial Practice in the Application of the Decree of the Central Executive Committee and the Council of People's Commissars on October 17, 1937]"; "O sokhranenii zhilishcheh nogo fonda i uluchshenii zhilishchnogo khoziaistva v gorodakh," *Grazhdanskii Kodeks RSFSR* ["On the Preservation of the Housing Supply and the Improvement of Housing Available in Cities," *The Civil Code of the RSFSR*] (Moscow: Gosiurizdat, 1957), p. 186. (Supplementary Materials on Individual Articles).

In order to avoid judicial activities of this type, Article 113 of the Constitution of the USSR grants the Supreme Court of the USSR the right of legislative initiative, so that it can always go to the Supreme Soviet of the USSR, if necessary, with a proposal for the adoption of the required legal rules. If, despite this, the Plenum of the Supreme Court of the USSR, in issuing guiding explanations, still should exceed the powers granted to it, then these explanations can be annulled. Analogous rules are applied relative to the Supreme Courts of the Union republics. In the field of contract law, the existing guiding explanations of the Plenum of the Supreme Court of the USSR and the Plenums of the Supreme Courts of the Union republics answer questions of the application of legislation on particular types of contracts, including rental of housing, transportation, purchase of agricultural products from collective and state farms, and services to the population.

B. Arbitration Tribunals

The concept of arbitration practice rests, in general, on the same bases as the concept of judicial practice. In the process of considering economic disputes among enterprises, organizations, and institutions, state arbitration tribunals establish specific rules for the application of legislation. The State Board of Arbitration under the Council of Ministers of the USSR, and the State Board of Arbitration under the Council of Ministers of the Union Republics are also empowered by the Law on State Arbitration of the USSR of November 30, 1979,[54] to issue instructions on questions of the application of the legislation of the USSR and of the Union republics, respectively. Such instructions are obligatory for arbitration tribunals, ministries, state committees, agencies, enterprises, institutions, and organizations (Article 26). In addition, the state boards of the republics are entitled to issue to ministries, state committees and agencies, explanations

---

See *also* the Guiding Instructions of the Plenum of the Supreme Court of the USSR of September 17, 1960, "Po voprosu o merax vozdeistvia na s'emshyikov, narushaushyix uslovia dogovora naima zhiligo pomeshyenia," *Sbornik zhilishchnogo zakonodatel'stva* ["On the question of measures for influencing tenants who violate the terms of the housing rental contract," *Collection of Housing Legislation*], ed., V.I. Zamiatin (Moscow: Iuridicheskaia Literatura, 1963), p. 34.

54. *Vedomosti Verkhovnogo Soveta SSSR*, No. 49, item 844 (1979).

on the application of decisions of the councils of ministers of the USSR and decisions of the councils of ministers of the Union republics, respectively, regulating economic activity (Article 25).

The rules for the application of laws contained in the cited documents collectively form the body of arbitration practice. It should also be noted that a system of intra-agency arbitration is in effect in the USSR. Each intra-agency arbitration board considers economic disputes among enterprises, institutions, and organizations under the jurisdiction of a given ministry or agency, and in so doing contributes to the general body of arbitration practice.

In analyzing the sources of contract law in the USSR we must not neglect to consider the question of the rules of socialist common life and morality. Although these rules are not sources of law, they may emerge, according to the law, as criteria for the evaluation of the behavior of parties in contractual relationships. Article 5 of the Fundamentals of Civil Legislation states that, "in implementing the rights of fulfilling duties, citizens and organizations should respect the rules of socialist common life and the moral principles of a society that is building communism." For example, a court has the power to evict persons from apartments for gross misconduct.

3.4 Unity and Differentiation of the Legal Regulation of Contractual Relationships

Civil legislation in the Soviet Union assumes the unity of legal regulations of contractual relationships. In whatever sphere of the country's economy in which civil contracts are used (whether, for example, in relations among socialist organizations, or in the sphere of services to individuals), they are always under the direct influence of general principles established in the Fundamentals of Civil Legislation and in the civil codes of the Union republics. This makes it possible to unify all contracts into a single system of contracts, which aids in the functioning of a single economic complex in the country.

The unity of legal regulation of contractual relationships is provided for by Article 2 of the Fundamentals of Civil Legislation, which speaks of three inseparably connected groups of social relationships that make up the object of civil law. These are: first, the relationships among state, cooperative, and other public organizations; second, the relationships of citizens with state, cooperative, and other public organizations; and third, the relationships among citizens. A participant in relationships regulated by civil legislation may also include, in cases provided for by the law, other organizations—particularly religious ones—and also foreign companies and individuals.

In accordance with the articles cited, provisions of general application are established in the Fundamentals of Civil Legislation, whose effect extends to all types of civil contracts regardless of where they are applied. These provisions are conveyed in Article 4 (concerning the foundation from which rights under civil legislation and duties arise), Article 5 (concerning the implementation of rights under civil legislation and the performance of obligations), Article 6 (concerning the protection of rights under civil legislation), Article 14 (concerning transactions), Articles 15 and 16 (concerning statute of limitations), Articles 33–38 (concerning general provisions on liabilities), and a number of other articles. The unified legal rules relating to the contract are set forth in somewhat more detailed form in the civil codes of the Union republics—primarily in the chapters on transactions and the general provisions on obligations.

These principles of the unity of the regulation of contractual relationships by civil law are consistantly applied in practice. Arbitration practice is an example. Immediately after the adoption of the Fundamentals of Civil Legislation, the State Arbitration Board under the Council of Ministers of the USSR published a special Bulletin of Instructions, as of April 17, 1962, "On Some Questions Connected with the Application of the Fundamentals of Civil Legislation by the Arbitration Tribunals."[55] Point 1 of the Instructions says, "in settling disputes arising between enterprises, organizations, and institutions involving the making and performing of contracts, and on other grounds, the arbitration tribunals are obliged to be guided without deviation by the Fundamentals of Civil Legislation." In addition, references are made to other articles, including Articles 16–17 (concerning statutes of limitations), Article 34 (concerning the making of contracts), and Article 38 (concerning the imposition of liability on a third party). Subsequently, the State Arbitration Board adopted the Instructions

55. *Sistematizirovanii sbornik instruktivnykh ukazanii Gosudarstvennogo arbitrazha pri Sovete Ministrov SSSR* [*A Systematic Collection of Instructional Orders of the State Arbitration Board of the Council of Ministers of the USSR*], pp. 52–55.

on the Application by the Arbitration Tribunals of certain of the most important articles of the Fundamentals of Civil Legislation.[56]

The presence of general rules of civil law in the area of contractual relations creates a necessary base for the different approaches to the regulation of individual groups and kinds of contracts. Such differentiation is called forth by the need to take account of the peculiarities of the application of the contract in various spheres of the economy of the USSR. More than this, in connection with the further development of economic relations, the need for it continues to increase.

In this monograph, we can consider only the most general classifications of civil contracts, which are based on two major criteria: the character of the participants in contractual relations in terms of subjects of law, and the character of the relationships in society that are affected by the contracts (the sphere of their application).

In terms of this classification, the Fundamentals of Civil Legislation provides for three groups of civil contracts: 1) contracts between socialist organizations (Articles 34 [Parts 2–4], 35, 36 [Parts 5–6], 44–50, 51–52, 67–71, and others); 2) contracts between individuals and socialist organizations (Articles 41 [Part 3], 55, 66, and others); and 3) contracts between individuals (Article 350 and others). Export transactions are included in a special group (Section 8).[57] Each of the groups named has its own peculiar legal features in terms of procedures for making contracts, means of determining the content of contracts, and so on.

---

56. See in particular the Instructions of the State Arbitration Board of the USSR of May 27, 1963, "O primenenii organami arbitrazha st. 14 Osnov grazhdanskogo zakonodatel'stva (o sdel'kakh)," *Sistematizirovanii sbornik instruktivnykh ukazanii Gosudarstvennogo arbitrazha pri Sovete Ministrov SSSR* ["On the Application of Article 14 of the Fundamentals of Civil Legislation (on transactions) by the Arbitration Organs," *A Systematic Collection of Instructional Orders of the State Arbitration Board of the Council of Ministers of the USSR*], pp. 55–56; and of October 6, 1969, "O praktike primenenii arbitrazhami st. 37 Osnov grazhdanskogo zakonodatel'stva Soiuza SSR i soiuznykh respublik" ["On the Practice of the Application by the Arbitration Organs of Article 37 of the Fundamentals of Civil Legislation of the USSR and the Union Republics," (on fault as a condition for liability for breach of obligations)], *Id.*, pp. 59–62.

57. Export-Import Transactions cases are not considered in this monograph. *See* V.S. Pozdnyakov, O.N. Sadekov, *Pravovoe regulirovanie otnoshenii povneshnei torgovee USSR* [*Legal Regulation of Relationships in the Field of Foreign Trade of the USSR*] (Moscow: International Relations, 1985), Part I, pp. 106–183.

Among the contracts made between socialist organizations, the most prominent and significant place belongs to economic contracts. The term *economic contract* is not used in the Fundamentals of Civil Legislation or in the civil codes of the Union republics. It is, however, widely used in the rules on economic legislation,[58] which include rules of civil law, and rules of administrative, financial, and labor law, along with a number of other legal branches. Economic legislation is generally more complex than civil legislation.[59] In Soviet civil law scholarship, the economic contract is always considered a type of civil contract.[60] Some differences, however, are present in the approach to its definition.

---

58. See, for example the June 12, 1979, Decree of the CC CPSU and the Council of Ministers of the USSR, "Ob ulushchenii planirovaniia i usilenii vozdeistviia khoziaistvennogo mekhanizma na povyshenie effetktivnosti proizvodstva i kachestva raboty" ["On the Improvement of Planning and the Strengthening of the Influence of the Economic Mechanism on the Increased Efficiency of Production and Quality of Work"], *SP SSSR*, No. 18, item 118 (1979).

59. The basic purpose of economic legislation is defined in the June 25, 1975, Decree of the CC CPSU and the Council of Ministers of the USSR, "O merakh po dal'neishnemu sovershenstvovaniiu khoziaistvennogo zakonodatel'stva" ["On Measures for the Further Improvement of Economic Legislation"], *SP SSSR*, No. 16, item 98 (1975). "Economic legislation," we read, "is intended to promote the further growth of production in the public sector and the solution of the tasks of the building of communism in accordance with the requirements of the objective economic laws of socialism. It must provide for the clear cut function of all the links in the economic mechanism, and for a correct relationship between rights and responsibilities on all levels of the management of the economy, and for the universal development of initiative on the part of Ministries and agencies, as well as associations, enterprises, and other economic organizations, the broadening of self-support relationships, the increased role of economic contracts, and the further strengthening of the socialist rule of law and a state discipline." *Id.*

60. See, for example M.I. Braginskii, *Obshchee uchenie o khoziaistvennykh dogovorakh* [*General Doctrine of Economic Contracts*], pp. 10–11; V.G. Verdnikov, A. Iu. Kabalkin, *Grazhdansko-pravovye formy tovarno-denezhnykh otnoshenii* [*Civil Law Forms of Commodity-and-Money Relations*], p. 111; I.V. Fedorov, "Khoziaistvennyi dogovor—osobyi vid grazhdansko-pravovogo dogovora," *Trudy Tomskogo universiteta* ["The Economic Contract—A Special Kind of Civil Contract," *Papers of Tomsk University*] Vol. 219 (1971), 66–67 *et seq.*; A.A. Sobchak, *Pravovye problemy khozrascheta* [*Legal Problems of the Self-Support System*] (Leningrad: Leningrad University Publishing House, 1980), p. 165; Iu Kh. Kalmykov, *Pravovoe regulirovanie khoziaistvennykh otnoshenii* [*Legal Regulation of Economic Relationships*], p. 133; V.F. Iakovleva,

Three characteristics of economic contracts are of special importance:

1. Only socialist organizations, including collective farms and other public organizations, can be parties to an economic contract.

2. The economic contract pertains to commodity-and-money relations in the planned socialist economy. It applies to the basic production activity of organizations (the production of products and commodities, the performance of work, and the provisions of services). For this reason contracts for the acquisition of inventory in retail trade, and other one-time contracts not related to basic production are not included among economic contracts.

3. The economic contract has a planned character. Legal scholars are not in agreement, however, on the question of the precise nature of the planned character of the economic contract. For example, Yuri Kalmykov argues that only those economic contracts that are based upon the prescriptions of an administrative planning act that is binding on both parties should be called planned.[61] Others approach the explanation of the planned character of the contract more broadly. Thus, for example, A.G. Bykov defines the planned nature of an economic contract not by the presence of administrative planning documents addressed to the parties, but by the planned nature of the commodity-and-money relationships affected by the contract.[62] The second position seems more persuasive and corresponds more closely to the general tendencies of development of economic legislation.

These differences in approach to the nature of planned contracts do not, however, give rise to differences in result. The adherents of the first view include in their definition of economic contracts not only planned contracts but also some contracts that they regard as being unplanned but of the same nature as planned contracts in terms of the type of obligations

---

"Znachenie grazhdansko-pravovogo dogovora dlia ekonomiki razvitogo sotsializma," *Sbornik grazhdansko-pravovoi dogovor i ego funktsii* ["The Significance of the Contract Under Civil Law for the Economy of Developed Socialism," *Collection on the Contract as Civil Law and its Functions*], p. 25, N.I. Ovchinnikov, "Khoziaistvennyi dogovor kak raznovidnost' grazhdansko-pravovogo dogovora" ["The Economic Contract as a Variety of the Contract under Civil Law"], *Id.*, p. 31.

61. Iu. Kh. Kalmykov, *Pravovoe regulirovanie khoziaistvennykh otnoshenii* [*Legal Regulation of Economic Relationships*], p. 130.

62. A.G. Bykov, *Plan i khoziaistvennyi dogovor* [*The Plan and the Economic Contract*], p. 20.

they involve (for example, an unplanned delivery contract).[63] Those who support the second view include among economic contracts only those they consider to be planned contracts, but they include the same contracts as do the adherents of the first view because they use a broader interpretation of the concept of the plan.[64] Thus both groups consider the following to be economic contracts: delivery contracts, production and supply contracts, capital construction contracts, transportation contracts, and contracts connected with the organization and implementation of accounting and the extension of credit, and other contracts of a similar type.

In addition to the description of the economic contract from the point of view of civil law, the discipline of economic law uses another approach to define the nature of the economic contract.[65] Under this approach, the economic contract is viewed not as a variety of civil contract, but as an independent type of contract constituting a special part of economic law.[66] This is justified by the fact that the sphere of action of the economic contract is not limited to relationships of a commodity-and-money character. It extends to relationships involving the implementation of economic

63. Iu. Kh. Kalmykov, *Pravovoe regulirovanie khoziaistvennykh otnoshenii* [*Legal Regulation of Economic Relationships*], p. 131.

64. A.G. Bykov, *Plan i khoziaistvennyi dogovor* [*The Plan and the Economic Contract*], p. 20.

65. This scientific tendency gained noticeable popularity in the Soviet legal literature beginning with the second half of the 1950's. *See* L. Ia. Ginzburg, "K voprosu o khoziaistvennom prave," *Sovetskoe gosudarstvo i pravo* ["On the Question of Economic Law," *Soviet State and Law*], No. 8 (1956), 85–96; V.S. Tadevosian, "Nekotorye voprosy sistemy sovetskogo prava" ["Some Questions of the System of Soviet law"], *Id.*, pp. 99–8; V.V. Laptev, "O sovetksom khoziaistvennom prave" ["On Soviet Economic Law"], *Id.*, No. 4 (1959), 70–78. The proponants of economic law suggest that a special branch of law be created in the sphere of the regulation of the economic activity of state organs, enterprises, and associations. The rules and institutions of civil administrative law would be removed from the civil and administrative laws, and would be included in this special branch of law. At the same time, the proponants wish to limit the sphere of application of civil legislation only to those relationships in which citizens participate. *See Khoziaistvennoe pravo. Obshchie poiozheniia* [*Economic Law: General Provisions*], ed., V.V. Laptev, (Moscow: Navka, 1983), pp. 5–17. The conception of economic law set forth here is in contradiction to the legislation in effect, and to the Fundamentals of Civil Legislation and the Civil Codes of the Union Republics.

66. See, for example I.A. Tanchuk, V.P. Efimochkin, T.E. Abova, *Khoziaistvennye obiazatel'stva* [*Economic Obligations*], pp. 147–150.

supervision and also to internal economic relationships. The latter includes relationships within an enterprise. An example is a contractual relationship between the management and brigades of workers, who are in a situation called internal self-support.[67]

It seems preferable, however, not to isolate the economic contract from its economic base (commodity-and-money relationships) since only in connection with this base will it serve its basic function of assisting in the development of a planned socialist economy. In addition, management relations as a rule are not contractual in their nature, and in those rare cases where contracts are used to coordinate the activity of the state organs in supervising the integrated units and enterprises under their jurisdiction, it is an administrative, and not an economic, contract that is made. The contracts employed within integrated production units and enterprises are also of a subordinate character.

Contracts among individuals and socialist organizations are of many different types such as authors' contracts and contracts with agricultural enterprises for the raising and purchase of livestock and poultry. Beyond question, however, the leading examples are contracts for services (including supply of goods) to consumers. These contracts have not yet been reflected in generalized form in the Fundamentals of Civil Legislation and in the civil codes of the Union republics. Only individual types of such contracts are laid down in these laws, and then, as a rule, only in the form of citations of other rules.[68] Detailed regulations are given in subordinate rules. In scholarly literature, such contracts have been rather extensively discussed. They are described as agreements by specialized socialist organizations with individuals, by which the organization undertakes (for compensation, as a general rule) to carry out specified actions to satisfy the material and cultural needs of individuals.[69]

As for contracts among citizens, this application in the USSR is relatively narrower than that of economic contracts and contracts for services to consumers. Currently they are used chiefly in trade in collective farm

---

67. See *Khoziaistvennoe pravo. Obshchie polozheniia* [*Economic Law: General Provisions*], ed., V.V. Laptev, pp. 208– 215.

68. See Articles 41 and 43 of the *Fundamentals of Civil Legislation* on purchase and sale in the retail trade network; Article 55 on rental of household equipment; and Article 66 on the consumer service order, etc.

69. See A. Iu. Kabalkin, *Grazhdansko-pravovoi dogovor v sfere obsluzhivaniia* [*The Contract under Civil Law in the Sphere of Service*] (Moscow: Nauka, 1980), p. 53.

markets, purchase and sale of dwellings belonging to individuals by right of personal ownership, the provision of household services (frequently without compensation), and a number of other cases. On the whole there is thus a tendency toward differentiation of the regulation of contractual relationships by civil law.

Chapter 4

Characteristics and Organization of Contract Law

The civil contract creates a system of legal relations among the parties that effective within the limits of a defined period of time and is directed toward the achievement of a predetermined result. In legislation, these legal relations are dealt with under such topics as the conditions of a civil contract's validity, the procedure for making it, its performance and means of enforcement, and its modification and termination due to non-performance or improper performance. These topics are similar to those found in most countries of the world. At the same time, however, the contract in the Soviet Union has its own peculiarities, which will be shown below.

4.1 Conditions of Validity of a Contract

The law does not contain unified legal rules that set forth the conditions for the validity of a contract, as is done, for example, in Article 1108 of the French Civil Code. General provisions concerning such conditions are scattered over various articles of the Fundamentals of Civil Legislation and the civil codes of the Union republics, primarily in the chapters dealing with transactions.

In general they require: a) that there be agreement between the parties; b) that the content of the contract be lawful; c) that the parties be legally competent; and d) that the form of the contract provided for by law be observed (in those cases envisaged by the law). If any of these conditions is not observed, the contract is invalid.

A. The Agreement between the Parties

The requirement of an agreement flows from the very nature of a contract, since in law a contract is an agreement that is the result of direct action of the parties. This action must be mutually agreed upon and intended to create an obligatory relationship that is permitted by law. In the absence of such an intention the contract is considered to be illusory (for example, a contract for a loan involving no money) and of no effect. "A transaction is invalid," according to Article 53 of the Civil Code of the RSFSR, "if it is carried out merely for the sake of appearances, without an intention of creating legal consequences."

In giving legal force to an agreement, the legislator proceeds from the unity of subjective and objective factors: the expression of the will of the parties to the contract. The external actions of the parties in realizing their intentions in the form of reaching an agreement (expression of will) must correspond to the internal (psychological) intention of the parties to make a particular agreement (the volitional aspect).[1]

The application of these principles is provided for by a series of rules, including rules on illusory transactions. According to Article 53 of the Civil Code of the RSFSR, "if the transaction is carried out with the intention of concealing another transaction, then the rules relating to the transaction that the parties actually had in mind are applied." Usually, the illusory contract is made with the intention of concealing an illegal contract. Suppose, for example that the purchase and sale of a plot of land, which is the property of the state, is made to appear as a gift of a residential building. In this case, both the illusory and the concealed contract are invalid. However, the illusory contract may also serve to conceal a perfectly legal contract. Thus, in the case of the gift of a residential building, the purchase and sale of a house, and not of a plot of land, may be intended. The illusory contract is then invalid, and the concealed contract is valid. The parties are obliged to carry it out under the procedure provided for by law, if the circumstances call for this.

The principle of the unity of will and expression of will of the parties is the basis for the existence of an agreement. In the organization of contractual relationships in society, there can be such unity only if individuals and organizations have autonomy in making contracts.

---

1. On the various interpretations on the concept of will and the expression of will in Soviet legal scholarship, see V.A. Oigenzikht, *Volia i voleiz'iavlenie* [*Will and Expression of Will*] (Dushanbe: "Donitsa" Publishing House, 1983).

Naturally, in any society, the parties to a contract are not absolutely free to exercise their will. They are always restrained by the general conditions of life and their individual requirements. In making a contract, the individual or organization must be free from unlawful pressure from other persons. The parties will must be formed under the influence of the parties' own requirements and goals under conditions of full disclosure that allow them to make an objective judgment about the contract. The will of the parties to an agreement must be free from defects of will that lead to the invalidity of the contract. Such invalidity is explained not by the absence of unity between the will and expression of will, but by the defective character of the will.[2]

The civil codes of the Union republics envisage two types of such invalid contracts. One type includes contracts made as a result of mistake. The other includes contracts made under the influence of misrepresentation, duress, and combinations of unfavorable circumstances (see second monograph). Also included in this second type are agreements that result from the improper acts of the representative of one of the parties. The distinction between these two types of invalid contracts is based not only on the degree of severity of the defects of the will of the parties, but also on the character of the legal consequences that result from invalidity.

Under Article 57 of the Civil Code of the RSFSR, a contract made under the influence of a significant mistake can be declared invalid pursuant to a suit brought by the mistaken party. A significant mistake was defined by the Civil Panel of the Supreme Court of the RSFSR on February 12, 1970, in invalidating a contract for the exchange of living space in the case of *Bol'shkova v. Mikheev*, as "an idea not corresponding to reality about some circumstances essential to the given transaction, or ignorance of such circumstances."[3] These circumstances include primarily those relating to the legal character of the contract, its subjects and objects, or its content.[4] However, ignorance of the law or a miscalculation by the mistaken party is not considered to be a mistake. The cause of the mistake is also not relevant. If the contract is invalid for mistake, the

2. *Sovetskoe grazhdanskoe pravo* [*Soviet Civil Law*], ed., D.M. Genkin, p. 228; *Sovetskoe grazhdanskoe pravo* [*Soviet Civil Law*], ed., V.A. Riasentsev, pp. 209–212; N.V. Rabinovich, *Nedeistvitel'nost' sdelok i ee posledstviia* [*Invalidity of Transactions and the Consequences*] (Leningrad: Leningrad State University Press, 1960), p. 63.

3. *Biulleten' Verkhovnogo Suda RSFSR*, No. 1 (1971), 2–3.

4. *Biulleten' Verkhovnogo Suda RSFSR*, No. 3 (1973), 10; *Socialist Legality*, No. 7 (1968), 84.

parties are to be restored to their original positions in terms of property (bilateral restitution).

The causes of the mistake are significant only in cases where losses arise. "The party," Article 53 of the Civil Code of the RSFSR states, "by whose suit the transaction is declared invalid, is entitled to demand from the other party the restitution of expenditures, losses or damage to his property (positive damage), if it can prove that the mistake was caused by the fault of the other party."[5] If fault is not proved, then the party by whose suit the transaction is declared invalid is obliged to restore the above-mentioned losses to the other party.

As distinct from mistake, intervention with the formation of the will of the parties to the contract made under the influence of misrepresentation, duress, improper acts by the representative of one of the parties or combinations of unfavorable circumstances are more dangerous to the parties to the agreement and to society as well. (In the latter case, only individuals are considered to be damaged parties).[6] Conscious illegal influence on a contracting party intended to compel him to make a disadvantageous contract renders the contract invalid. When such contracts are declared invalid on the basis of the judgment of a court (or an arbitration tribunal) rendered pursuant to the suit of a damaged party or of a state, cooperative, or public organization, the law provides for unilateral restitution. Under unilateral restitution the victim recovers the benefits he conferred on the other party. (If it is impossible to restore the benfits in kind, their value is restored in money). If the victim received benefits under the contract from the other party, those benefits are given to the state. If, however, the victim did not receive any benefits under the contract from the other party, the other party must pay money, equal to the value of the performance to be rendered, to the state. In addition to this,

5. What is at issue here is fault in the form of negligence. Where there is intent, it becomes a matter of deception, in the presence of which, if the contract is declared invalid, other consequences occur.

6. The legal characterization of the conditions on which contracts can be declared invalid in Soviet civil law coincides, in its general outlines, with the characterizations given in the law of European countries. See I.B. Novitskii, *Sdelki. Iskovia davnost'* [*Transactions. Statute of Limitations*] (Moscow: Gosiurizdat, 1954), pp. 112–124; N.V. Rabinovitch, *Nedeistvitel'nost' sdelok i ee posledstviia* [*Invalidity of Transactions and the Consequences*], pp. 68–75; V.P. Shakhmatov, *Sostavy protivopravnkyh sdelok i obuslovlennye imi posledstviaa* [*The Contents of Illegal Transactions and The Consequences*] (Tomsk: Tomsk University Press, 1967), pp. 227–245; V. A. Oigenzikht, *Voila i voleiz'lavenie* [*Will and Expression of Will*], pp. 214–215.

the damaged party may recover from the other party the value of losses or damages incurred by his property (Article 58 of the Civil Code of the RSFSR). The effect of unilateral restitution, then, is to restore the damaged party to his position prior to his performance, and to punish the other party for his faults by forcing him to pay the value of his performance to the state.

Since the principle of the unity of will and the expression of will of the parties is provided for by law, scholarly discussion concerning the possibility of use of the subjective theory of will and the objective theory of the expression of will in Soviet law is essentially moot. Although such a discussion continued in the literature of the 1950s and early 1960s,[7] current authors are virtually unanimous in the position that will and the expression of will are one.[8]

This principle is applied in full in the interpretation of contracts, when the need arises to determine the meaning of words and expressions used in the contract. The task of interpretation consists of explaining the meaning of the expression of the will of the parties during the making of the contract.

Interpretation is a necessary stage in the process of application of the law, carried out by a court or arbitration tribunal in considering civil cases on contracts. Its foundations were established as long ago as the 1920's. They were most clearly expressed in 1923 in the Instructions of the Supreme Court of the RSFSR. Specifically, the Plenum of the Supreme Court of the RSFSR noted that, "The contract should be interpreted on the basis not of its letter or the name that the parties have given it, but of its content, and of the essence of the relations between the parties."[9]

This approach to the interpretation of a contract retains its significance in principle even now. At the present time it is based on the rule of Article 16 of the Fundamentals of Civil Legislation of the USSR and the Union

7. N.V. Rabinovich was considered to be one of the adherents of the theory of will. See *Nedeistvitel'nost' sdelok i ee posledstviia* [*Invalidity of Transactions and the Consequences*], p. 7. I.B. Novitskii was a proponent of the theory of expression of will. See *Sdelki. Iskovia davnost'* [*Transactions. Statute of Limitations*], p. 22.

8. See V.P. Shakhmatov, *Sostavy protivopravnykh sdelok i obuslovlennye imi posledstviaa* [*The Contents of Illegal Transactions and the Consequences*], p. 42–45; V.A. Oigenzhikht, *Volia i voleiz'iavlenie* [*Will and Expressor of Will*], p. 208; *Sovetskoe grazhdanskoe pravo* [*Soviet Civil Law*], eds., V.M. Smirnov, Iu. K. Tolstoi, and A.K. Iurchenko, p. 173.

9. *Sbornik opredelenii Verkhovnogo suda RSFSR* [*Collection of the Decisions by the Supreme Court of the RSFSR*], No. 93, Item 211 (1925).

Republics as of 1961.[10] "The court is obliged," this Article says, "to take all measures envisaged by the law toward a comprehensive, full, and objective explanation of the true circumstances of the case, and of the rights and obligations of the parties, without limiting itself to the data and explanations offered to it."

Unfortunately, special studies on the problem of interpreting contracts, in which generalizations are drawn from the existing practice of court proceedings and arbitration and general theoretical propositions are formulated, are lacking in the field of Soviet civil law. Among the available brief references contained on contracts and transactions, the positions formulated by I.V. Novitskii deserve attention. As an initial thesis, he correctly writes that in the process of interpretation, the parties must not have imposed on them the contents of a contract that they did not intend and that, on the contrary, it is necessary to establish the true intentions of the parties.[11]

B. The Contents of the Contract

The legality of the content of a contract is determined by three basic features: 1) the kind of contract; 2) the agreement between the parties; and 3) the aim of the contract. Each is considered from the point of view of its conformity to the law.

1. *Kinds of Contracts*

Soviet civil law takes the position that contracts are to be openly listed. Under Article 4 of the Fundamentals of Civil Legislation, rights and duties under civil legislation arise from transactions envisaged by the law and

10. *Vedomosti Verkhovnogo Soveta SSSR*, No. 50, item 526 (1961).

11. I.B. Novitskii, *Sdelki. Iskovaia davnost'* [*Transactions. Statute of Limitations*], pp. 128–136. On the question of interpreting contracts in foreign trade, see M.G. Rosenberg, "Tolkovanie dogovora v praktika Vneshne-torgovoi arbitrazhnoi komissii pri Torgovo-promishlennoi palate SSSR," *Vneshai torgovl'a* ["Interpretation of Contracts in the Practice of the All Union Trade Arbitration Commission Direct Industrial Chamber of the USSR," *Foreign Trade*], Nos. 2–3 (1981). See *also* V.S. Pozdnyakov, O.N. Sadikov, *Pravovoe regulirovanie otnoshenii poveneshnei torgovee SSSR* [*Legal Regulation of Relationships in the Field of Foreign Trade of the USSR*] (Moscow: International Relations, 1985), Part I, pp. 114–15.

also from transactions that, although not envisaged by the law, do not contradict it.

Transactions envisaged by the law include not only contracts regulated by the Fundamentals of Civil Legislation and the civil codes of the Union republics (contracts for delivery, purchase and sale, rental, and the like) but also contracts fixed by subordinate rules. Important contracts under the subordinate rules are contracts of mixed type, (nontypical) which unite individual elements of the traditional types of contracts, known to general civil legislation. With the development of Soviet society, the number of such contracts is constantly increasing. Contracts of mixed type include, in particular, contracts for the supply of materials and technology to an integrated industrial facility, an enterprise, or an organization;[12] contracts for the purchase of livestock and poultry by collective farms, state farms, and other agricultural enterprises from the personal farming operations of citizens;[13] and contracts for the performance of work in providing materials and equipment to collective farms, state farms, and other agricultural enterprises and organizations by raion (and interraion) integrated production units, and divisions of agricultural equipment.[14]

Contracts not provided for by subordinate rules are also considered enforceable if they do not contradict the law, but they are not often used. Nevertheless, judges and arbitration tribunals have to deal with them in a

---

12. See, for example the Specimen Contract for the Organization of Material and Technological Supply to an Industrial Unit, Enterprise and Organization, adopted by the State Bureau of Supply of the USSR and the State Arbitration Board of the USSR of December 30, 1981, *Biulleten' normativnykh aktov ministerstv i vedomstv SSSR*, No. 8 (1982).

13. See the Standard Contract for the Purchase of Livestock and Poultry by Collective Farms, State Farms, and other Agricultural Enterprises from the Personal Subsidiary Farming Operations of Citizens, adopted by the Ministry of Agriculture, the Ministry of Purchasing, the Ministry of Finance, and the Central Statistical Bureau of the USSR of March 12, 1981, *Sbornik normativnykh aktov po granzhdanskomu zakonodatel'stvu* [*Collection of Normative Acts in Civil Legislation*], Part 2, p. 105.

14. See the Statute on the Procedure of Making and Performing Contracts for Work in the Industrial and Technological Servicing of Collective Farms, State Farms, and Other Agricultural Enterprises and Organizations by Raion (Inter-Raion) Productive Associations and Divisions of the Agricultural Equipment Agency, confirmed by the State Committee on Agricultural Equipment and the Ministry of Agriculture of the USSR as of December 30, 1980, *Sbornik normativnykh aktov po granzhdanskomu zakonodatel'stvu* [*Collection of Normative Acts in Civil Legislation*], Part 2, p. 155.

in a number of cases. For example, a court recognized as enforceable an agreement under which a tenant and the members of the tenant's family obligated themselves to vacate a room occupied by them in a dwelling house belonging to the state in the event that they received another larger room.[15] The expression *noncontravention of the law by the contract* signifies the correspondence of the contract to the general principles and meaning of Soviet legislation (Article 12 of the Fundamentals of Civil Procedure).

It should be added that mixed contracts, like contracts not envisaged by the law, represent those legal forms of relations among the parties on which the development of new kinds of contracts in civil law are based. This was at one time the case with delivery contracts, contracts for capital construction, purchase and supply contracts, contracts for the rental of living space in housing belonging to state and public agencies, and other contracts, which afterwards acquired the status of autonomous types of contracts in general civil legislation. Contemporary legal practice is proceeding along the same path.

2. The Agreement between the Parties

Contractual relations are based on the parties reaching an agreement on the basic terms of the contract. "The contract," Article 34 of the Fundamentals of Civil Legislation states, "is held to be made when an agreement has been reached between the parties on all essential terms."

The content of the contract as an agreement is represented by its terms. The concept of a term includes two aspects—objective, and subjective. The objective aspect is concerned with such questions as the subject matter of the contract, the time of performance, the means of performance, and so forth. The subjective aspect is concerned with the definition of the rights and duties of the parties with regard to the objective aspects of the contract.

The list of essential terms is established by law according to the kind of contract in question, for example, contracts for purchase and sale, for rental of property, and so forth. The only essential term common to all contracts is the subject matter.

---

15. *Biulleten' Verkhovnogo Suda RSFSR*, No. 5 (1972), 12.

The law provides three ways of determining the essential terms. The essential terms of a contract are those that: 1) are recognized as such by the law, 2) are necessary for the particular kind of contract in question, and 3) are designated by the parties themselves.

The first two groups of essential terms that are recognized by law are similar to each other. In both cases they are established directly in the law. The only difference lies in the form in which they are established.

In the first case a system of direct listing of the essential terms of the contract is applied. Part 7, Point 25 of the Statute on Deliveries of Goods for Industrial and Technical Use provides that in the absence of terms specifying the price and the subject matter of delivery (description, quantity, nomenclature, assortment, and quality of goods) in a contract that is to run for a year or less, the contract will be held not to have been made. Similarly, the statute also provides that in the absence of provisions on the description, quantity and group nomenclature (assortment) of goods in a long-term contract for the delivery of goods according to direct and long-term economic relations, the contract will be held not to have been made. This system of direct listing of essential terms is usually applied in contracts made between socialist organizations.

In the second case, the list of essential terms of a contract is derived from the character of the particular type of contract. For example, in a contract for purchase and sale, these terms include the subject matter and the price (with appropriate specification of the rights and duties of the parties with regard to them). In a contract for the rental of property, the terms they include are those making the property available for temporary use, and those specifiying the amount of compensation for its use.

Regardless of whether the essential terms are established directly by the law or are derived from the character of some particular type of contract, their total number must be kept to a minimum. This number is limited solely to those terms without which the existence of the contract becomes impossible.

On the other hand, the essential terms in the third group, those established by the parties themselves, may in principle be numerous. These terms may relate to the means, time, and place of performance of the contractual obligation (Article 16 of the Civil Code of the RSFSR) and so forth. The only requirement is that they go beyond the bounds of those essential terms that are assigned by law to the first two groups.

In addition to the essential terms that directly influence the legal validity of a contract, the content of a contract may include other terms that do not have a similar force. In the literature, these are called usual and incidental terms. Usual terms are those that are intended to specify the essential terms of a contract defined by the law.[16] These terms are typical for the definite type contracts. They do not require agreement of the parties, and are included in the contract automatically by law if the parties do not formulate alternative terms in place of them. The usual terms of the contract are given in the form of general rules and suppletory terms of the law, but they may be contained in other sources as well, such as custom, business relationships developed in practice between the parties to the contract, and so forth. An example of a usual term defined by a suppletory rule is offered by the provision set forth in Part 1, Article 30 of the Fundamentals of Civil Legislation: "The right of ownership (right of operative management) of the purchaser of property by contract arises at the moment of transfer of the subject matter, unless otherwise provided by the law or by the contract."

Incidental terms are those that differ from the terms ordinarily used in the contractual practice. Therefore, their inclusion in the contract is obligatory. For example, through incidental terms the parties are entitled to specify a different moment of transfer of the right of ownership (right of operative management) than that which is envisaged in Part 1, Article 30 of the Fundamentals of Civil Legislation.

3. *The Aim of the Contract*

Two definitions of the aim of a contract[17] are given in the Soviet literature on civil law. The distinction between the definitions lies in the starting point of the analysis.

The first group conceives the contract as an agreement. They term the aim of the contract the *proximate aim*, and they believe that the proximate aim is understood as the immediate legal result toward which the parties

---

16. "Usual" terms must not be confused with "implied" terms, which are commonly found under U.S. contract law. "Usual" rules do not consider the unexpressed will or intent of the parties. They are taken from outside the parties to the contract, from statutes, customs, etc.

17. Under Soviet civil legislation there is a distinction between the terms "transaction" and "contract." "Transaction" is a broader term and includes not only contracts, but unilateral transactions, such as wills. In the majority of cases, the concepts of "transaction" and "contract" coincide. In this monograph, devoted to contract law, we will use the term "contract" when the terms "contract" and "transaction" have the same meaning.

strive in making the contract.[18] In a contract for purchase and sale, for example, this result is, for the seller, the receipt of the purchase price, and for the purchaser, the receipt of the item of property. The aim of the contract is thereby identified with the content of the obligation, arising out of the contract as an agreement.

The second group conceives of the contract in a broader sense that includes, in addition to the agreement, the obligation arising out of it. This group calls the aim of a contract the *ultimate aim*. "The aim of a transaction, in this understanding of it," writes V. P. Shakhmatov, "extends beyond the bounds of the legal relationship and refers to that final factual result for the sake of which the given transaction has established, modified, or terminated the legal relationship."[19] It would probably be more correct to speak not of a factual, but of a legal, result, which the parties strive to achieve by performance of the obligations arising out of the agreement. Thus, in the example of the contract for purchase and sale given above, the ultimate aim is the exchange by the owners of property sold for money. The ultimate aim of the contract connects the obligation with legal relationships in which third persons and society as a whole also participate. The concept of an ultimate aim permits one to define not only the legal means by which the results desired by the parties are achieved, but also to establish the legal compatibility of a particular contract with the law and order of the country.

Which of these two opinions of scholars corresponds more closely to the legislation in force? We believe it is the second. Control over the legality of the contract with the aid of the concept of proximate aim, which contract is to a considerable degree insignificant. This control is implemented by the use of other legal approaches. For example, the rights and duties of the parties to a contract are implemented on the basis of a general interpretation of the obligation laid down in Article 33 of the Fundamentals of Civil Legislation. Conformity to the requirements of the law of the rights and duties of the parties to a contract is assured by legal rules dealing with particular types of contracts by general provisions on obligations. The possibility of declaring a contract not to be in accordance with

18. The most consistent proponent of this point of view is V.A. Riasentsev. *See Sovetskoe grazhdanskoe pravo* [*Soviet Civil Law*], ed., V.A. Resentsev (Moscow: Iuridicheskaia Literatura, 1975), vol. I, p. 198.

19. V.P. Shakhmatov, *Sostav protivopravnykh sdelok i obuslovlennye imi posledstviia* [*The Contents of Illegal Transactions and Their Consequences*], pp. 74–75.

the requirements of the law and therefore to be invalid, is provided for by the rule of Part 3, Chapter 14 of the Fundamentals of Civil Legislation.

The only practical application of the concept of proximate aim is indicated by Article 49 (concerning the invalidity of a transaction made with an aim contrary to the interests of the state and of society)[20] and Article 50 (concerning the invalidity of a transaction by a legal person in contradiction to its goals)[21] of the Civil Code of the RSFSR and the corresponding articles of the civil codes of the other Union republics. Even in the cases indicated, however, the application of this concept frequently becomes insufficient, since the unlawful nature of these transactions may consist not in the violation of rules relating to the legal mechanisms of transactions, but in the receipt of an end result incompatible with the law and order of the country. Under such a regime, for example, unlawful contracts for the sale of land may be made under the pretext of purchase and sale of residential structures. For cases of this kind, the concept of the ultimate aim is more effective.

C. The Legal Capacity of the Parties to Contract[22]

Under the law of the Soviet Union, the concept of civil ability in the sense of the ability to acquire, by one's own actions, rights under civil legislation

---

20. Article 49 of the *Civil Code of the RSFSR* states, "If the transaction is made with an aim intentionally contrary to the interests of the socialist state and society, then in the presence of intent of both parties, where the transaction has been performed by both parties, all that was received as a result of the transaction is forfeited to the state. Where the transaction has been performed by only one party, the other party forfeits to the state all that it received and all future receipts from the first party in recompense for what has been received.

On the other hand, in the presence of intent by only one party, everything it has received through the transaction must be returned to the other party, and what the latter has received, as well as future receipts owed in recompense for the performance is forfeited to the state.

21. Article 50 of the *Civil Code of the RSFSR* states, "Any transaction is invalid, which is carried out by a legal person in contradiction of the aims set forth in its charter, in the statute concerning it, or in the general statutes on organizations of the particular type in question. The rules envisaged in Chapters 48 and 49 of the present code, are applied respectively to such transactions."

22. *The Fundamentals of Civil Legislation and the Civil Codes of the Union Republics* distinguish between "legal capacity" and "legal ability." "Legal capacity" under civil law is the ability to have rights and duties defined by civil

and to create for oneself duties under civil legislation (Article 8 of the Fundamentals of Civil Legislation) is applicable only to individuals. Relative to legal persons, civil ability is combined with the concept of legal capacity.

Legal persons have always possessed a constant capacity to perform legal actions through their agencies. Where there are obstacles to their activity, legal persons terminate their existence, but are not declared to be civilly incapable persons, or to have partial civil capacities. The concept of civil incapability or partial civil capacity is incompatible with the very essence of a legal person. The concept of civil capacity always presupposes the possibility (even if only in an abstract sense) of the corresponding person being declared a civilly incapable subject of law, or one having partial civil capacity.

In addition, the concept of capacity includes elements that are not at all applicable to legal persons. As is clear from Articles 15 and 56 of the Civil Code of the RSFSR, the legal concept of civil capacity of an individual is based upon the unity of activity of the rationale (the understanding of the actions performed by him) and the will (the control of his actions). The absence of any one of these qualities, either because the person has not reached legal age or suffers from some medical infirmity, makes the individual civilly incapable. It is clear that these qualities, connected with the biological factors that influence the activities of men and women, bear no relation to organizations.

Full civil capacity in the USSR begins with the attainment of legal age, which is 18 (Article 8 of the Fundamentals of Civil Legislation[23]). When the law permits marriage before reaching the age of 18, however, (as, for example, in the RSFSR and the Belorussian SSR, where the law permits marriage at age 16) a person acquires full legal capacity at the time of marriage.

Before reaching the age of full legal capacity a person's ability to conduct transactions is limited. This ability is dependent on the age group

---

legislation. "Legal ability" is the possibility of acquiring, by one's own actions, rights under civil legislation and to create for oneself duties under civil legislation. Article 8 of the *Fundamentals of Civil Legislation*. Under U.S. contract law, "legal capacity" includes both of these meanings. For this reason, this monograph will use only the term "legal capacity."

23. The law distinguishes between the concept of capability with regard to transactions and capability with regard to torts. Under Article 451 of the *Civil Code of the RSFSR* and the corresponding articles in the civil codes of the other Union Republics, the latter arises when a citizen reaches the age of 15.

to which the person belongs. The law provides for two such groups: one includes minors up to the age of 15 (the minimum age is not established by the legislation), and the other includes minors between the ages of 15 and 18.

Children up to the age of 15 (minors) are entitled to conduct transactions of two kinds: small household transactions and transactions connected with deposits in credit institutions (Article 14 of the Civil Code of the RSFSR). In all other cases, transactions in the name of minor children who have not reached the age of 15 are conducted by their biological or adoptive parents or guardians.

The concept of small household transactions is not defined in the law. In the civil code of some Union republics there are only isolated and very general provisions on this. For example, Article 13 of the Civil Code of the Tadzik SSR emphasizes that small household transactions must not cause harm to minors who conduct them. In practice, they are understood to include transactions directed toward the satisfaction of elementary material and cultural requirements characteristic of the minor's age. These may include the purchase of food, books, stationery, tickets to motion picture theatres, and the like.[24] The means for conducting such transactions include any funds that are legally in the minor's possession, and usually include those placed at his disposal by his parents or by other persons.

Transactions connected with deposits relate to money that the minor deposits in a credit institution in his own name and over which he has independent control.[25] The specific age of the minor is of decisive significance, of course, in the conduct of all such transactions.

Minors between the ages of 15 and 18 are also entitled to conduct small household transactions independently, and to deposit money in credit institutions in their own name. The definition of small household transactions is somewhat broader than that for minors under the age of fifteen, although the basic concept of a small household transaction remains the same. The character of transactions relating to deposits in credit institutions and to control over them, also shows no difference.

The civil capacity of minors between the ages of 15 and 18, however, has been expanded by two categories of transactions. First, these minors

---

24. See *Kommentarii GK RSFSR* [*Commentaries on the Civil Code of the RSFSR*], eds., S.N. Bratus' and O.N. Sadikov, pp. 32–33.

25. See Point 20 of the Charter of the State Labor Savings Banks of the USSR, adopted by the July 11, 1977, Decree of the Council of Ministers of the RSFSR, *SP RSFSR*, No. 21, item 131 (1977).

are permitted to dispose of earnings and stipends received by them, and second, they are allowed to exercise rights as authors or inventors (Article 13 of the Civil Code of the RSFSR). With regard to the disposition of earnings and stipends, under Article 74 of the Fundamentals of Labor Legislation of the USSR and the Union Republics of 1970,[26] minors who have reached the age of 16 (and in exceptional cases, by agreement with factory and plant committees and local trade union committees, persons of 15 years of age as well) may be hired for work and receive wages. Minors enrolled in trade-technical schools, other secondary institutions and courses, and also in post-secondary institutions and universities, receive stipends. Minors have independent control over such earnings.

The transactions conducted by them from such earnings may extend beyond the bounds of small household transactions. In this case, the character of transactions and their monetary ceiling are determined by the legislation regulating individual types of contracts (retail, purchase and sale, rental of goods and equipment, and the like). Thus, according to the Instructions on the Procedure for Sale of Goods on Credit confirmed by the Resolution of the Council of Ministers of the RSFSR on March 9, 1965,[27] the sale of goods on credit is permitted to all blue-collar and white-collar workers (regardless of age) upon their presentation of a certificate as to wages received. If the minor abuses the right granted to him, however, and spends the income he receives unwisely or in ways not permitted (for example, on alcohol, or the like), the organs of guardianship may, in accordance with Article 13 of the Civil Code of the RSFSR, deprive him of the right of independent control over his earnings or stipend.

With regard to the exercise of rights as authors or inventors, minors between the ages of 15 and 18 can contract for the transfer of their works for use, and so forth. All other transactions by minors between the ages of 15 and 18 must be carried out with the agreement of their biological or adoptive parents or guardians.

Persons may lose their civil capacity completely or in part for medical reasons. The law envisages three cases of this kind. The first case is connected with mental disease or deficiency of a person who cannot understand the meaning of his actions or control them. Such a person may be declared civilly incapable by the court (Article 15 of the Civil Code of the RSFSR). The obligation of conducting transactions in his name will

26. *Vedomosti Verkhovnogo Soveta SSSR*, No. 29, item 265 (1970).
27. *SP RSFSR*, No. 4, item 19 (1965).

thus be imposed on a guardian. In the event of recovery of a person who has been declared civilly incapable, or of significant improvement in his health, his civil capacity will be restored by a decision of the court.

The second case relates to the limitation of the civil capacity of individuals. "A citizen who, as a consequence of abuse of alcoholic beverages or narcotics," Article 16 of the Civil Code of the RSFSR states, "places his family in a difficult economic position, and may have his civil capacity limited. . . . A guardian is placed over him. He may conduct transactions relating to the management of his property, and also receive wages, a pension, or other forms of income under his personal control only with the permission of the guardian, with the exception of small household transactions." If the abuse ceases, the court may remove the limitations on his civil capacity.

The third case is more complex because the determination of the civil capacity of an individual is made retroactively, after a transaction has been conducted, and is applied to a very brief period of time. Under Article 56 of the Civil Code of the RSFSR, transactions conducted by an individual who, although possessing civil capacity, was at the moment of the transaction in a condition in which he could not understand the meaning of his actions or control them, are declared invalid by a court upon the legal application of the individual himself. The temporary condition of civil incapability at the moment of the individual's conducting the transaction may be explained by various circumstances, such as illness, nervous exhaustion, and in extreme cases, where this can be proved, extreme drunkenness, etc.

Transactions conducted by a person with a civil incapability (whether complete, partial, or temporary) for any of the above-mentioned reasons, are declared invalid by the court with the application of bilateral restitution (Articles 51, 52, 54, 55, and 56 of the Civil Code of the RSFSR). Furthermore, a party with civil capacity, if he knew or should have known about the incapacity of the other party, is obliged to pay actual damages.

D. The Form of a Contract

The observance of the form of a contract as a condition for its validity is applicable only to those cases specified in the law. "The contract is considered to have been made," Article 34 of the Fundamentals of Civil Legislation states, "when agreement has been reached between the parties on all of its essential terms *in the form required by the appropriate cases*" (emphasis added). This involves a rather limited number of contracts, primarily those that must be made in special written forms.[28] These contracts include notarized contracts, foreign trade contracts, and contracts relating to particular types of guaranteed obligations.

Notarization is obligatory for the following contracts: contracts between participants in joint ownership of a dwelling house as to the procedure for use of separate rooms (Article 124 of the Civil Code of the RSFSR); contracts for the mortgaging of a residence (Part 2 of Article 195 of the Civil Code of the RSFSR); contracts for the purchase and sale of a residence or part of it, or of a similar cottage located in a city or urban settlement (Parts 1 and 3 of Article 239 of the Civil Code of the RSFSR); contracts for the exchange of a house (Part 2 of Article 255 of the Civil Code of the RSFSR); contracts for the gift of a house (Part 3 of Article 257); and contracts for the gift of a sum of more than 500 rubles or of foreign currency in the amount of more than 50 rubles (Part 1 of Article 257 of the Civil Code of the RSFSR). Other types of contracts requiring notarization may be specified by the legislation and also by agreement between the parties.

Foreign trade contracts in which Soviet organizations participate must be made in a simple written form. A special procedure for signing them has been established, however, and is applied regardless of the place of making the contract. (Article 125 of the Fundamentals of Civil Legislation). Under the Resolution of the Council of Ministers of the RSFSR of February 14, 1978, "On the Procedure for Signing of Foreign Trade Transactions"[29] foreign trade contracts must be signed by two authorized persons. The names and surnames of such persons are listed in publications of the ministry, state committee, or agency involved.

---

28. The concept of the written form of a contract in Soviet civil law goes far beyond the limits of notarized form. The vast majority of contracts for which a written form is established are made in simple written form. They include, in particular, contracts of state, cooperative, and public organizations, among themselves, and with individuals, with the exception of those that are performed at the time they are made, and contracts between individuals for sums exceeding 100 rubles (Article 44 of the *Civil Code of the RSFSR*). Non-observance of the simple written form usually (unless the law specifies otherwise) does not lead to the invalidity of the contract. In this case, only the possibility of proving such a contract is made difficult. In case of a dispute, the law forbids reference to the evidence of witnesses in confirmation of the contract. Along with the written form, the possibility of making a contract in other forms, such as orally, by acts and by silence, are also envisaged (Article 42 of the *Civil Code of the RSFSR*).

29. *SP SSSR*, No. 6, item 35 (1978).

Other contracts whose validity is conditioned on the observance of a particular form include contracts of forfeiture (Article 188 of the Civil Code of the RSFSR), mortgages (Part 4 of Article 195 of the Civil Code of the RSFSR), and contracts for surety (Part 3 of Article 203 of the Civil Code of the RSFSR), which are executed in simple written form.

Nonobservance of the requirements of law as to the prescribed form in all the cases considered here results in the invalidity of the contract. The parties are then returned to their original positions through bilateral restitution.

4.2 The Procedure for Making a Contract

The law envisages a general procedure for making contracts, which applies to all contracts regardless of their subject matter and regardless of the parties. In addition, there are specific rules applicable to particular types of contracts.[30] These rules are most commonly used in the making of economic contracts.

The general procedure for making contracts is given by the rules of the civil codes of the Union republics. In the Civil Code of the RSFSR these rules are found in Articles 162–164. The procedure for making contracts consists of two basic steps. These are the proposal to make a contract (the offer) and the adoption of the proposal (the acceptance).

The offer must satisfy two requirements. It must contain all the essential terms of the proposed contract, and it must be addressed to an identifiable person, or to an unspecified group of persons, if it is possible to identify one or more of them, who desires to adopt the proposal. In the latter case, the proposal is a public offer, a type of proposal that is widely used in trade and in other areas of service to individuals.[31]

---

30. See, for example, the "Rules for the Sale of Passenger Automobiles and Motorcycles with Sidecars to the Population," confirmed by the Order of the Ministry of Trade of the USSR of December 22, 1977, *Osnovnye pravila torgovii* [*Basic Rules on Trade*] (Moscow: Ekonomika Publishing House, 2d ed., 1981), pp. 245–246.

31. This position does not cause doubt on the part of the vast majority of scholars. See I.B. Novitskii and L.A. Lunts, *Obshchee uchenie ob obiazatel'stve* [*The General Doctrine of Obligations*], p. 149; *Sovetskoe grazhdanskoe pravo* [*Soviet Civil Law*], eds., V.T. Smirnov, Iu. K. Tolstoy, and A.K. Iurchenko, p. 334; S.N. Bratus' and O.N. Sadikov, *Kommentarii k GK RSFSR* [*Commentaries on the Civil Code of RSFSR*], p. 205. Exceptions are R.O. Khalfina, *Znachenie i sushchnost' dogovora v sovetskom prave* [The Significance and Nature of the Contract in Soviet Law], p. 207; and F.I. Gavze, *Sotsialisticheskii grazhdansko-pravovoi dogovor* [*The Socialist Contract in Civil Law*], p. 92.

In the absence of any one of these requirements, there is no offer. Communications not having the force of offers are regarded as merely invitations to negotiate the making of a contract. This is the situation, in particular, with regard to various forms of advertising (booklets, catalogs, and the like), and with advertisements printed in newspapers and on street billboards. They do not impose any legal obligation on the person disseminating the information.

An offer, however, is binding on the person who makes it during its entire period of effect. The offeror becomes bound at the moment the offer reaches, or should reach, the person to whom it is addressed. Before this moment, the offeror is entitled to revoke his offer.

The question as to the duration of an offer is answered in the law in various ways. If the negotiations are oral or through immediate contact between the parties (in personal conversation, on the telephone, by teletype or radio, or the like), and there is no indication of a deadline for an answer, then, under Part 1 of Article 163 of the Civil Code of the RSFSR, the duration of the offer is determined by the length and character of the negotiations themselves.

If, on the other hand, the offer indicates a deadline for an answer (Article 162 of the Civil Code of the RSFSR), or is in written form, requiring a reasonable time for an answer (Part 1 of Article 163 of the Civil Code of the RSFSR), then the offer must remain open during the period designated.

If an offeror attempts to revoke the offer before the deadline, legal consequences follow. Unfortunately, the Fundamentals of Civil Legislation and the civil codes of the Union republics do not speak directly about these consequences. According to an opinion widespread in the literature, the offeror is obligated to pay to the person to whom the proposal was addressed damages equal to the losses connected with the preparation for the making of the contract that did not materialize—for example, the expenditures of a trip to inspect the subject matter of the contract.[32]

The legal nature of this liability does not fit into any of the most widespread forms of civil law liability, which include liability arising from contract, torts, and unjust enrichment. Instead, this liability arises from unilateral actions by the offeror, a liability that arises when he fails to wait for the offeree's answer. Under this approach, application of Article 219 of the Civil Code of the RSFSR on the payment of damages to the offeree is justifiable because of the offeror's nonperformance of an obligation.

---

32. See I.B. Novitskii and L.A. Lunts, *Obshchee uchenie ob obiazatel'stve* [*The General Doctrine of Obligations*], pp. 157–160; F. I. Gavze, *Sotsialisticheskii grazhdansko-pravovoi dogovor* [*The Socialist Contract in Civil Law*], p. 96.

Special rules relating to this question are established for economic contracts. The revocation of an offer in such a case is expressly forbidden by the law. Violation of this prohibition results in the application of sanctions. "For delaying the making of a contract or for unjustifiably refusing to make it," reads in Point 92 of the Statutes on Deliveries of Goods for Industrial and Technical Purposes, "the party at fault shall pay to the other party a fine in the amount of 100 rubles for each day's delay, but not more than 1000 rubles."

The acceptance is the second step necessary for the making of a contract. Acceptance is the consent of the offeree, given within an established period, to make a contract on the terms proposed by the offeror. Such consent to make a contract, sent by the offeree within the specified time but received by the offeror after a delay (which usually happens by the fault of third parties), also has the force of an acceptance, provided that the offeror did not notify the offeree immediately of the delayed receipt of the consent. If the offeror does not give such notice, such a delayed consent is transformed into a new offer.

The contents of the acceptance must respond to the terms in the offer. An answer expressing consent to make a contract on terms other than those proposed is a rejection of the proposal, and is considered to be a counteroffer (Article 165 of the Civil Code of the RSFSR). This rule does not apply to those contracts made between state, cooperative, and other public organizations, for which a special procedure for settling precontractual disputes is established.

In form, the acceptance may be either oral or written. In some cases the law also permits acceptance by silence or by acts. (For example, acceptance of a planning order for performance is implied if it is not expressly accepted within ten days.)[33]

During the making of a contract, the law makes no special distinction as to whether or not the parties are in the presence of each other. We cannot conclude from this, however, that such a distinction was altogether ignored by the legislation. For problems involving choice of law, account of this difference is taken in calculating the time necessary to receive a consent from the offeree to a written offer for determining the time and place of the making of the contract for problems involving choice of law.

The issue concerning the time and place of making a contract was addressed in legislation that was in force before the adoption of the Fundamentals of Civil Legislation and the present civil codes of the Union republics. "A contract with an absent person," Article 134 of the Civil

33. Part 3 of Article 160 of the *Civil Code of the RSFSR*.

Code of the RSFSR of 1922 states, "was considered to have been made at *the moment* of receipt of the consent by the offeror, provided that the meaning of the proposal did not imply something else" [emphasis added]. Accordingly, the place of the making of the contract was considered to be the place where the offeror was located.

In the civil codes of the Union republics now in force, there is no such categorical formulation. Article 162 of the Civil Code of the RSFSR provides that "when the proposal to make a contract includes a specified time period within which to answer, the contract is considered to be made *if* the offeror has received from the offeree an answer signifying acceptance of the proposal within this period" [emphasis added]. It is evident that the formulations contained in Article 134 of the Civil Code of the RSFSR of 1922 ("at the moment") and in Article 162 of the Civil Code of the RSFSR of 1964 ("if") are not identical. Article 162 of the Civil Code of the RSFSR may be interpreted in various ways. In legal literature, however, all authors speak in favor of the *receipt rule*, and not of the *mailbox rule*. The contract is considered to have been made from the moment the consent to the offer is received by the offeror and in the place where that consent is received.[34] Where acceptance occurs by silence or by acts, and in a few others cases specified in the law, the question of the time and place of the making of the contract is decided in other ways.

The rules as to the procedure for making economic contracts are special rules of law relative to the general rules of law set forth in the Fundamentals of Civil Legislation and in the civil codes of the Union republics. Only where there are gaps in these rules is the application of the general civil legislation permitted. Specific rules as to the procedure for making economic contracts proceed in four basic directions.

First, some general rules on the procedure for making contracts are expressly not applicable to economic contracts. Two such cases have already been noted: the prohibition of revocation of an offer when it is in force and the non-application of the rule of Article 165 of the Civil Code of

34. See *Kommentarii k GK RSFSR* [*Commentaries on the Civil Code of the RSFSR*], eds., S.N. Bratus' and O.N. Sadikov, p. 206; F.I. Gavze, *Sotsialisticheskii grazhdansko-pravovoi dogovor* [*The Socialist Contract in Civil Law*], p. 108; *Sovetskoe grazhdansko pravo* [*Soviet Civil Law*], eds., V.T. Smirnov, Iu. K. Tolstoy, and A.K. Iurchenko, p. 335. See also *Dogovornoe pravo stran-chlenov SEV i SFSU*, *Obshyie polozhenia Moskva Sovet Ekonomicheskoi vzaimopomoshyi* [*The Contract Law of Countries*, *Members of the Council of Economic Mutual Assistance*, *General Positions*] (Moscow: Council of Economic Mutual Assistance, 1986), p. 141.

the RSFSR on the making of a contract where there are changes in the terms of the offer. The rule of Part 1 of Article 163 of the Civil Code of the RSFSR as to the procedure for making oral contracts is also not applicable because transactions between public organizations must always be in writing.

Second, there is a system of state supervision over the actions of organizations that make economic contracts. Under Article 34 of the Fundamentals of Civil Legislation, disputes arising during the making of a contract based on planning directives binding both parties are settled by a court, if at least one of the parties is a collective farm, an organization, an integrated plant, an intercollective-farm enterprise, or farm enterprise in which both the state and the collective farm participate. An arbitration tribunal will settle such disputes if the parties are state, cooperative, or other public organizations (other than collective farms, intercollective-farms, state collective-farm enterprises, organizations, or integrated plants), provided that the law does not specify otherwise. Disputes among these organizations, arising during the making of a contract not based on planning directives binding on the parties, may be resolved by a court or by arbitration, if this is provided by law or by consent of the parties.

Third, the law contains many general provisions on the procedure for making contracts. In essence, a special and detailed legal procedure is established for making economic contracts, in accordance with their individual types. Relative to the contract for delivery of goods, for example, this procedure is set forth in the Statute on Delivery of Goods for Industrial and Technical Purposes.[35] In the absence of corresponding rules

---

35. This procedure is as follows: "In making contracts on the basis of planning documents for the delivery of goods, the supplier, not later than 20 days after receiving the planning document, sends the purchaser a signed draft of the contract in two copies, or a letter or telegram with a proposal for the establishment of contractual relations. . . . If technical specifications supplied by the purchaser or a detailed list (assortment) of goods are needed for the making of the contract, then such specifications must be sent by the purchaser to the supplier within a 10 day period after the receipt of the planning document for the delivery of the goods, provided that another deadline is not specified in the general terms for deliveries. The supplier is obliged to send the purchaser a draft contract within 10 days after the receipt of the above-mentioned specifications.

"Within not more than 10 days—and in cases of the receipt of a long-term contract, not less than 20 days after the receipt of the draft contract from the supplier—the purchaser signs the contract and returns a copy to the supplier. If a contractual relationship is established by way of the exchange of letters or

in the law on the procedure for making various types of economic contracts, the rules contained in the Statute on the Procedure for Presentation and Consideration of Claims by Enterprises, Organizations, and Their Institutions, and the Settlement of Disputes on Economic Contracts, confirmed by a Decree of the Council of Ministers of the USSR of October 17, 1973,[36] are applied. These rules are similar to those that are applied to delivery contracts.

Fourth, the law provides that if both parties adopt an order (Article 160 of the Civil Code of the RSFSR), there is no need for a two-step procedure for making the contract. The proposal to make a contract then proceeds not from the offeror but from the superior agency. This procedure is applied in deliveries of goods for both industrial and technical purposes and for consumption by the people.[37]

---

telegrams, the purchaser must reply to the letter or telegram of the supplier within ten-days. "Under special terms of delivery, it may be envisaged that the signed draft contract be sent by the purchaser to the supplier. . . ." (Point 26 of the Statute)

"If, on receipt of the contract, objections to its terms arise on the part of one of the parties, then that party, within a 10-day period—or in the case of a long-term contract, within a 20-day period after the receipt of the draft contract—draws up a list of the objections and sends two copies to the other party along with the signed contract, noting the presence of the objections in the contract.

"The party that has received the list of objections is obliged to consider it within a 20-day period (where necessary, in consultation with the other party . . .), and to include in the contract all the accepted suggestions, and to transfer the points still in dispute to the arbitration organ for settlement. . . .

"If the party that has received the list of objections . . . does not transfer the points of objection to the arbitration organ for settlement within the 20-day period, then the suggestions of the other party are considered to have been accepted. . . ." (Point 30 of the Statute).

36. *SP SSSR*, No. 23, item 128 (1973).

37. An example is the making of a contract of delivery through acceptance by the parties of an order for goods for industrial and technical use. "The order is considered to have been accepted for performance and to acquire the force of a contract," Point 29 of the Statute on Deliveries of Goods for Industrial and Technical Purposes states, "if, within 10 days after having received it, the interested party does not propose to the other party that they agree to other terms for delivery, or declare to the organ that issued the order (and in appropriate cases, to the holder of funds), and to the other party, its refusal to accept the order." In the presence of the proposals or declarations indicated here, the contract between the parties is made by the procedure common to the organizations involved.

4.3 The Performance of a Contract

The performance of a contract involves the implementation of the duties of the obligor and the realization of the rights of the obligee arising out of the agreement. This occurs within the context of the legal relationship arising out of the contract, and is subject to requirements established by law, by the terms of the contract, and in the case of planning contracts, also by the planning documents. These requirements are basically formulated at the time the contract is made (and in the case of requirements established by law or planning documents, significantly earlier). They may appear later, however, at the stage of its performance. The contract is a dynamic, not a static instrument. During its life, circumstances that cannot be ignored by the parties may arise.

For this reason, the law does not contain prohibitions of modifications in the terms of the contract at the performance stage, provided that this is done by mutual agreement of the parties. In economic contracts, the necessity for such modifications is usually made conditional on changes in the planning assignments imposed on both parties (Article 234 of the Civil Code of the RSFSR), and in the case of contracts on the delivery of goods for consumption by the population, also by changes in the supply and demand situation. At the same time, unilateral refusal to perform and unilateral modifications in the terms of the contract are forbidden, except in cases established by law (Article 169 of the Civil Code of the RSFSR).

The general requirements relating to performance are set forth in considerable detail in three principles established by law (Article 168 of the Civil Code of the RSFSR) and embodied in concrete rules of law. These principles are: 1) the principle of proper performance of the obligation; 2) the principle of economy; and 3) the principle of cooperation between the parties. The first of these principles is of a general character. It embraces all aspects of the performance of the contract, while the second and third principles extend only to certain parts of the legal relationships arising from the contract.

In Soviet legal literature there is a fourth principle—the principle of specific performance of obligations.[38] We believe that this opinion is not

---

38. See A.V. Venediktov, *Dogovornaia distsiplina v promyshlennosti* [*Contractual Discipline in Industry*] (Leningrad, 1935), p. 17; I.B. Novitskii, "Realnoe ispolnenie obiazatelstv," *Trudy nauchnoi sessii VIIuN 1–6 iiunia 1946 g.* ["Specific Performance of Obligations," *Papers of the Discussion of All-Union Institute of Legal Research June 1–6, 1946*] (Moscow: Iurizdat, 1948), pp. 145–153; V.K. Reikher, *Pravovye voprosy dogovornoi ditsipliny v SSSR* [*Legal*

entirely correct. In reality, specific performance is not a principle of performance of the contract, but a necessary prerequisite to the basic existence of the contractual obligation itself. It has meaning only at the stage when nonperformance occurs. For this reason, the rules concerning specific performance are included in the civil codes of the Union republics in the chapter on liability for breach. This approach in no way reduces the significance of the rules of specific performance in socialist society. Quite to the contrary, it gives it a more fundamental, and therefore more correct formulation.

A. The Principle of Proper Performance

The principle of proper performance of the contract is formulated in the civil codes of the Union republics. "Obligations," reads Article 168 of the Civil Code of the RSFSR, "must be performed in a proper manner, in the period stipulated, and in accordance with the directions of the law, the planning documents, and the contract, and, in the absence of such directions, in accordance with the usual requirements." Generally, this principle includes the performance of the rights and duties by the parties concerning all aspects of the legal relationships arising out of the contract: the subject of the performance, the subject matter of the performance, the time and place of the performance, and the means of the performance.

1. The Subject of the Performance

The definition of the proper subject of performance is very important. In the vast majority of cases, the parties who make the contract are at the same time the subjects of performance. Quite often, however, situations arise where third persons who did not participate in the making of the contract become involved in performance. Additionally, the problem of the proper subject of performance arises when there are several persons on the side of the obligor or of the obligee. Such cases may be divided into four groups.

Questions of Contractual Discipline in the USSR] (Leningrad: Leningrad University Press, 1958), p. 19; M.M. Agarkov, *Obiazatel'stvo po sovetskomu grazhdanskomu pravu* [*Obligations under Soviet Civil Law*], pp. 46–49; F.I. Gavze, *Sotsialisticheskii grazhdansko-pravovoi dogovor* [*The Socialist Contract in Civil Law*], p. 153; *Sovetskoe grazhdanskoe pravo* [*Soviet Civil Law*], eds., V.T. Smirnov, Iu. K. Tolstoy, and A.K. Iurchenko, pp. 349 *et seq*.

The first group comprises contracts in favor of third persons. These contracts are widely used in the field of insurance (for example, life insurance where the beneficiary to whom the face value of the insurance is to be paid on the death of the insured is named); credit relationships (for example, in cases of deposits by individuals in the name of a third person); transfers of freight addressed to consignees who are not parties to the transportation contract, and other cases. Under Article 167 of the Civil Code of the RSFSR, the performance of a contract for the benefit of a third person may be demanded either by the person who made the contract, or by the third person listed as the beneficiary of the performance, provided that the law or the contract does not specify otherwise and that nothing else is implied by the essence of the obligation. For example, in the case of life insurance, when the death of the insured occurs, a contract can only be performed by a third person. The binding of the third person by an obligation arising out of a contract for his benefit is unilateral in character. At any time he may waive his rights. If a third party waives his rights, such a contract, provided that this does not contradict its nature, is transformed into an ordinary contract with two parties.

The second group involves cases where the performance of the contractual obligation is imposed on a third person. "The performance of an obligation arising out of a contract," Article 171 of the Civil Code of the RSFSR states, "may be imposed in whole or in part on a third person, if this is envisaged by the established rules, and also if the third person is connected with one of the parties through administrative subordination, or by an appropriate contract." For example, it is an established rule that a transfer of freight in a direct mixed consignment, carried out on the basis of a contract of the consignor with a railroad, is also performed by other carriers, for example of marine and river transport, trucking, and air freight. The imposition of performance on an organization administratively subordinate to a party to the contract is usually done by integrated organizations relative to enterprises participating in them. Supplier organizations connected by contractual relationships with a marketing and procurement organization often appear in the role of actual performers of a delivery contract for products made by the marketing and procurement organization.

In contrast to the third persons named in contracts made for their benefit, the third persons considered here are not parties to the obligation. They are in the position of actual performers, and as a rule, the parties to the contract bear liability for their actions.

The performance of an obligation by a third person is possible both from the side of the obligor, and from the side of the obligee. The law envisages only one exception, relating to contracts that are to be performed by a particular person, for example, for the creation of works of art, the performance of unique tasks, and the like.

The actions of actual performers of a contract have legal force. "If the obligation of a particular individual to perform a contract himself does not follow from the law, from the contract, or from the nature of the circumstances, then the obligee is obliged to accept the performance offered by the obligor through another person" (Part 2 of Article 171 of the Civil Code of the RSFSR).

The third group involves replacement of the parties to the contract. In this case the obligee or the obligor drops entirely out of the obligation, and new persons appear in their places. The replacement of the obligee by another person is permitted in cases where this does not contravene the law or the contract, or where the requirement is not connected with the person of the obligee (Article 211 of the Civil Code of the RSFSR). On the other hand, the obligor's transfer to another person of his duty is possible only with the consent of the obligee (Article 215 of the Civil Code of the RSFSR). In connection with replacement of the parties to the contract, other problems in defining the proper subject of performance may arise. For example, if the obligor is not informed about the transfer of the rights, then there is a possibility that the obligor will perform his duties for the benefit of the original obligee. If this occurs then the performance is considered to have been made to the proper person. The replacement of the parties to the obligation in contractual relationships between socialist organizations must not violate the planning principles applied in such relationships. For this reason, it is more frequently encountered in relationships in which individuals participate—for example, in exchanges of apartments between individuals in buildings owned by the state or by public bodies.

The fourth group is associated with joint and several obligations. Under Article 180 of the Civil Code of the RSFSR, joint and several obligations arise under a contract or as established by law, particularly in cases where the subject matter of the obligation cannot be divided. In joint and several obligations, where there are numerous obligors, the proper obligor is determined by the will of the obligee. In cases where there are numerous obligees, the proper obligee is determined by an initiative procedure. Each obligee is entitled to make a demand on the obligor for full performance. Joint and several obligations are usually applied in relationships in which individuals participate, for example, in contractual relationships involving the rental of living space in buildings belonging to the state and to public organizations, in which all the members of the family of the tenant participate as joint tenants.

2. The Subject Matter of Performance

The subject matter of proper performance of the obligation is that article or other property or non-material value that is provided for by the contract. The subject matter of performance is supplied by the obligor to the obligee in the quantity and quality specified by the parties.[39] Deviation from the given requirements is considered to be improper performance.

The characterization of the subject matter of performance is set forth with adequate precision in the contract, and is prescribed for individual types of contracts in the corresponding rules and planning documents. For this reason, the civil legislation contains a limited number of general legal rules devoted to the subject matter of performance. For example, in the Civil Code of the RSFSR there are only three such rules. These are rules relating to the currency used in monetary obligations, to the rate of interest, and to the performance of alternative obligations.

Under Article 175 of the Civil Code of the RSFSR, monetary obligations must be expressed and paid in Soviet currency. This means that legal tender for debts and payments in the territory of the USSR can only be made with currency of the USSR. The expression and payment of monetary obligations in foreign currency is permitted only in the cases and by the procedure established by the legislation in force in the USSR.[40] Both the obligations in which currency appears as the sole subject matter of performance (for example, in contracts for loans) and obligations having as their subject matter other values in addition to money (for example, in a contract for purchase and sale) are considered to be monetary obligations.

A rule defining a generally negative attitude toward the possibility of charging interest on obligations is formulated in the civil codes of the Union republics. "Interest on monetary and other obligations," Article 176 of the Civil Code of the RSFSR states, "is not permitted with the exception of operations of credit institutions, obligations relating to foreign trade, and other cases specified in the law."

Credit is in principle granted on the basis of interest.[41] The amount of interest charged on loans is established by the Council of Ministers of the

39. *See* V.S. Tolstoy, *Ispolnenie obiazatel'stv* [*Performance of Obligations*] (Moscow: Iuridicheskaia Literatura Publishing House, 1973), pp. 86–125.

40. See pp. 21–24 of this text.

41. See, for example, the Basic Statutes on Bank Credit adopted by the November 11, 1982, Decree of the Council of Ministers of the SP SSSR, *SP SSSR*, No. 32, item 160 (1982); the Standard Charter for a Mutual Aid Fund, adopted by the Presidium of the USSR-wide Central Council of Trade Unions of November 23,

USSR, and in cases envisaged by the law, also by banks and other organizations empowered for this purpose by agreement with the Ministry of Finance of the USSR. By way of granting privileges to individual categories of citizens, credit may be offered without interest.[42]

The amount and procedure for calculating interest on obligations relating to foreign trade is established on the basis of a contract. Other cases specified in the law that provide for the charging of interest on obligations include the charging of interest by trading organizations on the sale of goods on credit.[43] Additionally, a debtor who has delayed the performance of a monetary obligation must pay 3 percent interest annually on the unpaid balance for the period of the delay, provided that the law or the contract does not specify another rate of interest (Article 225 of the Civil Code of the RSFSR).

The law permits the existence of alternative obligations with two or more subject matters of performance. In this case, the right of selection of the subject matter, as stated in Article 178 of the Civil Code of the RSFSR, is granted to the obligor if nothing else is specified in the law, in the contract, or by the nature of the obligation. An obligation concerning the sale of apples in several varieties with the customer having the right to choose the variety is as an example. Alternative obligations are rarely encountered in practice.

Contractual obligations with replacement of the performance are more common. As distinct from alternative obligations, in these cases the replacement of the subject matter of performance by others occurs by

---

1973, *Spravochnik profsoiuznogo rabotnika* [*Trade Union Staff Workers' Handbook*] (Moscow: "Profizdat," 1976), p. 321; Standard Charter for a Pawn Shop, adopted by the June 7, 1968, Decree of the Council of Ministers of the RSFSR, *SP RSFSR*, No. 10, item 54 (1968).

42. Thus, Point 6(b) of the January 22, 1981, Decree of the CC CPSU and the Council of Ministers of the SP SSSR, "O merakh po usileniiu gosudarstvennoi pomoshchi sem'iam, imeiushchim detei" ["On Measures to Increase State Aid to Families with Children"] permits enterprises, organizations, and collective farms to issue to one of the spouses under age 30 years, working at the given enterprise, organization, or collective farm for a period of not less than two years and who has given a good account of himself or herself on the job, an interest free loan for improvement of housing, or for the provision of household goods, in the amount of 1500 rubles, repayable within eight years. *SP SSSR*, No. 13, item 75 (1981).

43. See Point 11 of the Instruction on the Procedure for Sales of Goods on Credit, approved by the March 9, 1965, Decree of the Council of Ministers of the RSFSR, *SP RSFSR*, No. 7, item 19 (1965).

agreement between the parties after the making of the contract. For example, according to Point 13 of the Statute on the Procedure for the Making and the Performance of Production and Supply Contracts for Agricultural Goods,[44] the parties are entitled, by mutual agreement, in the course of the performance of the contract, to change the assortment of products purchased for an assortment not provided for by the purchase plan.

3. The Time of Performance

The time of performance of obligations is usually established in the contract, in the law, or in the case of economic obligations, in the planning document. The vast majority of contracts are limited in time. The period of time of performance is determined according to the type of contract and the circumstances surrounding its making. For this reason, there is, as a rule, no need to promulgate general legal rules, applying to all contracts as to the time of performance. The rules relating to the most stereotypical situations, which extend beyond the limits of the usual course of developments of contractual relationships, may be an exception to this rule. The Civil Code of the RSFSR contains three such rules. These rules relate to indeterminate times of performance of obligations,[45] performance of obligations before a deadline,[46] and the time of performance of a mutual obligation pursuant to a contract.[47] All of these are suppletory in character,

---

44. *Biulleten' Verkhovnogo Suda RSFSR*, No. 4 (1984).
45. "If the time for the performance of the obligation is not established or is determined by the moment when a demand is made," Article 132 of the *Civil Code of the RSFSR* states, "the obligee is entitled to demand performance and the obligor to carry out performance at any time.

"The obligor is obliged to perform such an obligation within a seven-day period from the time the obligee's demand is made, if immediate performance is not required by law, the contract, or the obligation."
46. "The obligor is entitled to perform the obligation before the time deadline," Article 17 of the *Civil Code of the RSFSR* reads, "if the law, the contract, or the essence of the obligation does not indicate otherwise. Performance of obligations between state cooperatives and state organizations before the deadline is permitted in those cases when this is envisaged by the law or the contract, and also with the agreement of the obligee."
47. "Reciprocal duties by contract," Article 177 of the *Civil Code of the RSFSR* provides, "are to be performed simultaneously, unless the law, the contract, or the essence of the obligation indicates otherwise."

and do not provide any fundamentally new answers relative to those that are known in world legislative practice.

A peculiarity is present only in rules devoted to the possibility of performance before a deadline in contracts between socialist organizations. In these cases, performance before the deadline is permitted with the consent of the obligee, when this is provided for by a special law or in the contract. In practice, however, performance of obligations before the deadline is frequently stimulated. As an example we may cite the legislation devoted to the contract for capital construction.[48]

The place of performance of obligations is treated in the Civil Code of the RSFSR in a single suppletory rule of law. The provisions contained in it are applied when the place of performance is not defined by the law, the contract, or the planning document, and does not follow from the nature of the obligation. In accordance with Article 174 of the Civil Code of the RSFSR "the performance must be carried out: 1) in an obligation to transfer a building—at the place where the building is located; 2) in a monetary obligation (besides the monetary obligations of socialist organizations)—at the obligee's place of residence; and 3) in all other obligations—at the obligor's place of residence." If the obligor is a legal person, then performance must be made at the place where the obligor is located.

4. *The Means of Performance*

The means of performance of the obligation is a complex concept. It includes various aspects of the relationships relating to the procedure for performance by the obligor of the obligation imposed on him. Many of these procedures are predetermined by the character of the contract. For example, a delivery contract presupposes extended relationships involving the delivery of the subject matter by means of some mode of transportation. On the other hand, in a contract made by an individual with a watch repair workshop, the performance has a one-time character and does not require any special procedure with regard to the performance by the obligor. For this reason, all the peculiarities of the means of performance of obligations, which differ in their nature, are usually reflected in contracts and legal rules relating to particular kinds of contracts. In economic

48. See Point 4 of the Rules for Financing Construction, approved by the October 8, 1965, Decree of the Council of Ministers of the USSR, *SP SSSR*, No. 21, item 156 (1965).

contracts, the means of performance of obligations are regulated by the corresponding planning documents as well.

In the general provisions on performance of obligations, contained in the civil code of the Union republics, the legislator proceeds on the basis of a narrow understanding of the means of performance limited to the extent of performance (i.e. whether performance will be made by a single act, or by a series of acts). A typical example of such obligations are those arising from a contract for a loan. Under Article 170 of the Civil Code of the RSFSR, the obligee is entitled not to accept performance in part (installments) unless the law, the planning document, or the contract, provides otherwise, or unless something else is implied by the nature of the obligation.

B. The Principle of Economy

The principle of economy supplements the principle of proper performance of obligations. Under Part 2 of Article 168 of the Civil Code of the RSFSR, each of the parties must perform his obligations in the manner that is most economical for the socialist economy of the country.

The performance of the obligation must be economical not only for the parties to the contract, but for the economy of the country as a whole. The significance of the principle of performance of the contract consists precisely in the latter. Where the parties have at their disposal several means of performing the obligation, they must choose the one that is the most economical from the point of view of the interests of the economy as a whole. This obligation has a legal character. Nonperformance of it may place the party at fault in the position of a defendant obliged to pay to the other party for the uneconomical performance.

As a rule, the concept of economy of performance for enterprises and individuals, on the one hand, and for the economy as a whole, on the other, coincides. As an example, we can cite the following case from arbitration practice. The "Gigant" Cement Plant was obliged, on the basis of a contract, to supply the Moscow Reinforced Concrete Article Plant with "500" brand cement. It instead delivered "600" brand cement at a higher price, resulting in an overpayment of 8651 rubles. The Moscow Reinforced Concrete Articles Plant brought suit against the "Gigant" Plant for the overpayment. The arbitration tribunal found for the plaintiff. In rejecting the defendants' application for a reconsideration of the decision, the Deputy Chief Arbitrator of the State Arbitration Board under the Council of Ministers of the RSFSR ruled that, through the fault of the cement plant, the customer was obliged to use the cement supplied, in order not to stop production. If production had stopped, the losses incurred would have caused the state greater damage than that represented by the difference in the prices of the cement.[49]

The principle of economy in the performance of obligations applies both in relationships in which organizations and individuals are involved.

C. The Principle of Cooperation

The principle of cooperation between the parties requires each party to extend to the other party all possible help in performing its obligation (Part 2 of Article 168 of the Civil Code of the RSFSR). It proceeds from the assumption that, in a contract, the parties should look upon each other as partners, and not antagonists, and that the performance of the obligations should be their common task.

The question arises as to how far this principle should extend in obligations. The opinion has been expressed in the literature that in planned-contractual relationships between socialist organizations the development of cooperation and mutual aid causes the obligation to grow into something quantitatively new, and even leads to a certain change in the status of the parties.[50]

We believe, however, that this is not the case. The character and depth of the influence of the principle of cooperation in the obligations between social organizations is higher than in other obligations. Even in this case, however, no transformation of the obligation takes place. The obligee remains an obligee, and the obligor, an obligor. As F.I. Gavze correctly writes, one must not underestimate the primary role of the obligor in performing the contractual obligation and his liability both to the state and to the obligee.[51]

---

49. *Nauchno-prakticheskii kommentarii arbitrazhnoi praktiki*, [*Scholarly and Practical Commentaries on Arbitration Practice*] (Moscow: Iuridicheskaia Literatura, 1968), No. 1, pp. 119–122.

50. See S.S. Alekseev, "Razvitie sotrudnichestva i vzaimopomoshchi mezhdu uchastnikami planovo-dogovornykh obiazatel'stv," *Sovetskoe gosudarstvo i pravo* ["The Development of Cooperation and Mutual Assistance Between Participants in Planning and Contractual Obligations," *Soviet State and Law*], No. 10 (1961), 110–111; I.B. Novitskii, L.A. Lunts, *Obshchee uchenie ob obiazatel'stve* [*The General Doctrine of Obligations*], p. 391; V.K. Reikher, *Pravovye voprosy dogovornoi distsipliny v SSSR* [*Legal Questions of Contractual Disciplines in the USSR*], p. 104.

51. F.I. Gavze, *Sotsialisticheskii grazhdansko-pravovoi dogovor* [*The Socialist Contract in Civil Law*], p. 130.

The principle of cooperation is expressed primarily by the obligee's help to the obligor in performing the obligations imposed on him. The principle of cooperation between the parties in performing the obligations extends to all contracts, including contracts in which individuals participate. In the legal sense, this cooperation is usually expressed in two ways: 1) in the acceptance by the obligee of the performance offered by the obligor, and 2) in the performance of other acts that facilitate the proper performance of the contractual obligation.

In accordance with the legislation in force, the acceptance of the performance properly tendered by the obligor is an obligation of the obligee.[52] The breach of this duty leads to consequences disadvantageous for the obligee, including the possibility of payment of damages to the obligor. Similarly, the obligor whose performance is not accepted by the obligee must not sit with his hands folded. He is obliged to do everything possible to reduce the losses caused by the refusal of the obligee to accept his performance.

The second way the principle of cooperation (expressed in the performance by the obligee of definite actions facilitating the proper performance by the obligor of contractual obligations) is applied is broader in its character. It reveals the primary significance and basic content of the principle of cooperation. Under this broad notion, acts encouraging coop-

52. "The obligee," Article 227 of the *Civil Code of the RSFSR* states, "is considered to be in delay if he has refused to accept the tender of proper performance made by the obligor or has not performed the actions prior to the completion of which the obligor could not perform his duties." The duty of the obligee, which is being considered here, is reflected in Article 185 of the *Civil Code of the RSFSR*, according to which, "in the event of the obligee's absence, and also in the event of his refusal to accept performance or of other delays on his part, as well as in the absence of an agent representing an obligee who lacks capacity, an obligor who is under a monetary obligation or under an obligation to transfer securities, has a right to deposit the money or securities due him at a notary's office, which notifies the obligee." Relating to third persons, it is directly stated in Article 171 of the *Civil Code of the RSFSR* that, "The obligee is obliged to accept performance tendered on behalf of the obligor by a third person." The question of the obligee's duty to accept performance of the contract is answered in the affirmative in the literature, as well. See M.M. Agarkov, *Obiazatel'stvo po sovetskomu grazhdanskomu pravu* [*Obligations Under Soviet Civil Law*], p. 65; I.B. Novitskii, "Uchastie kreditora v ispolnenii dogovornogo obiazatel'stva," *Sovetskoe gosudarstvo i pravo* ["Participation by the Obligee in the Performance of a Contractual Obligation," *Soviet State and Law*], No. 7 (1947), 29; V.K. Reikher, *Pravovye voprosy dogovornoi distsipliny v SSSR* [*Legal Questions of Contractual Disciplines in the USSR*], p. 89.

eration vary in character, from the creation of industrial-organizational conditions for the activity of the cooperating party, to the minimalization of losses in case of nonperformance or improper performance by the obligor of his duties. Such acts are formulated in rules relative to particular types of contracts, and, of course, by the parties themselves when they make the contract. The contract for capital construction is usually cited as the most vivid example of this. In accordance with the Rules on Contracts for Capital Construction, the client, in particular, is to extend to the contractor the necessary services in renting premises and buildings for use on the job, and in providing temporary living quarters and cultural and consumer services for the workers, etc.[53]

Securing the performance of obligations may be accompanied by the application of special methods established in the interests of the obligee. Article 35 of the Fundamentals of Civil Legislation provides five such methods: forfeits,[54] mortgages,[55] surety,[56] deposits,[57] and guarantees.[58] Forfeits, mortgages, and surety secure the performance of all obligations regardless of the parties. Deposits secure the performance of obligations in

---

53. See Points 28–36 of the Rules on Contracts for Capital Construction, approved by the December 24, 1969, Decree of the Council of Ministers of the USSR, *SP SSSR*, No. 2, item 11 (1970).

54. "A forfeit (by fine or monetary penalty) is recognized as the monetary sum set by law or by the contract, which the obligor is obliged to pay to the obligee in the event of non-performance or improper performance of the obligation, and in particular in the event of delays in performance." Article 187 of the *Civil Code of the RSFSR*.

55. "By virtue of a mortgage, the obligee (mortgage-holder) has a right, in the event of non-performance by the obligor of the obligation secured by the mortgage, to receive satisfaction from the value of the properties mortgaged, in preference to other obligees, with the exception provided for in the legislation of the USSR and in the *Code of Civil Procedure of the RSFSR*. . . . The mortgage arises by virtue of a contract or law." Article 192 of the *Civil Code of the RSFSR*.

56. "By a contract of surety, the surety-giver obligates himself, vis-à-vis the obligee of a third person, to be responsible for the performance by the latter of his obligation in full or in part." Article 203 of the *Civil Code of the RSFSR*.

57. "The deposit is the name given to the sum of money provided by one of the contracting parties out of the money owed by him to the other party pursuant to the contract, as proof of the making of the contract, and to secure its performance." Article 209 of the *Civil Code of the RSFSR*.

58. "The rules of Articles 203, 205, 207, and 208 of the present Code extend to the guarantees given by one organization to secure the liquidation of its indebtedness to another, unless the legislation of the USSR and the RSFSR provide otherwise." Article 210 of the *Civil Code of the RSFSR*. (The matter at issue concerns the rules relating to a surety).

which individuals participate, and guarantees secure the performance of obligations between socialist organizations. The forfeit is the most widespread means of security applied within the country. All the other means are applied more rarely and chiefly in relation to monetary obligations. Forfeits and mortgages may be established either on the basis of law or by virtue of a contract. Deposits, surety, and guarantees, however, may be established only by agreement of the parties.

In relation to the main contractual obligation, the securing obligations have a supplementary character. Their existence is fully dependent on the existence of the main obligation. In their legal nature, the securing obligations fall into the area of obligatory law. Therefore, the list of means of securing the performance of obligations provided by Article 35 of the Fundamentals of Civil Legislation is not regarded as exhaustive. This is confirmed, in particular, by the practice of the activity of foreign-trade, transport, and other Soviet organizations in their relations with foreign contracting parties.[59]

4.4 Liability for Breach of Contractual Obligations

Liability for breach of contractual obligations is one form of liability under civil law. In accordance with Article 36 of the Fundamentals of Civil Legislation, contractual liability is the compulsory means (through a property approach) by which a party who has failed to perform or has improperly performed obligations arising under the contract will redress and make whole the other party to the contract. Contractual liability ensues as a consequence of a violation of law through breach of a contract and has the goal of restoring the damaged property interests of the party that has suffered losses.

A characteristic feature of contractual liability is its property character. It is always expressed in the form of damages or in the form of a forfeit. It is unanimously noted in the literature that the obligor suffers disadvantageous consequences in terms of property.[60] It is difficult, however, to

59. See *Kommentarii k GK RSFSR* [*Commentaries on the Civil Code of the RSFSR*], eds., S.N. Bratus' and O.N. Sadikov, p. 229.

60. See, for example, S.S. Alekseev, *Obshchaia teoriia prava*, [*General Theories of Law*], pp. 276–277; *Sovetskoe grazhdanskoe pravo* [*Soviet Civil Law*], eds., V.T. Smirnov, Iu. K. Tolstoy, and A.K. Iurchenko, p. 362; N.S. Malein, *Pravonarushenie: poniatie, prichiny, otvetstvennost'* [*Violation of Law: Concept, Causes, Liability*] (Moscow: Iuridicheskaia Literatura, 1985), pp. 134–136.

agree with such an assertion, which is mistakenly associated with the obligor's being deprived of particular property values at the moment of compensation for the losses caused by him to the obligee. In fact, these values must be transferred to the obligee as part of his rights pursuant to the contract at a considerably earlier time—even before the question of liability arises. To leave them at the obligor's disposal would be tantamount to unjustly enriching him. The proposition that the property consequences should be disadvantageous to the obligor where liability arises would be meaningful only in one case—where the liability has the character of a fine, *e.g.*, where, in addition to the payment of damages, a supplemental sanction is also exacted from the obligor in the form of a fine. The legislation in force provides only one case of such liability. This is the liability of the supplier for supplying products (goods) of improper quality or products with parts missing (Point 504 of the Statute on Deliveries of Products for Industrial and Technical Purposes, and Point 104 of the Statute on Deliveries of Goods for Consumption by the People). If, in addition to these arguments we consider the fact that in practice contractual liability is limited, in the vast majority of cases, to the exaction of a forfeit, it is not difficult to draw the general conclusion that in fact, in the event of nonperformance of contractual obligations, the disadvantageous property consequences arise not for the obligor but for the obligee, and, certainly, for society as a whole.

The obligor is usually the party on whom liability is imposed. However, cases are also possible in which the obligee is liable in a contractual obligation (for example, in cases of delay beyond the time limit—Article 227 of the Civil Code of the RSFSR), and even in which a third person is liable. For example, a manufacturer, who is not a party to the contract, is liable for breach of a delivery contract relating to the quality of products (Point 72 of the Statute on Deliveries of Products for Industrial and Technical Purposes). It should be emphasized, however, that the third parties can be held liable only in exceptional cases, *e.g.*, when it is directly provided for by law. In accordance with the general rule, the liability for nonperformance or improper performance of obligations by third parties is borne by the obligor (Article 223 of the Civil Code of the RSFSR).

Contractual liability arises under one of two conditions: nonperformance or improper performance of the contract. In cases of nonperformance the function of liability is to replace the actual performance of the contract. In cases of improper performance the function of liability is supplementary, to promote the performance of the obligation arising under the contract. The legislation gives preference to the second method, if it can be applied. "The payment of a forfeit (fine or monetary penalty) established for delay beyond the deadline or other improper performance of an obligation, and compensation for losses caused by improper performance," Part 6 of Article 36 of the Fundamentals of Civil Legislation states, "do not free the obligor from the duty to perform the obligation in kind, except in cases where the planning document on which the obligation between socialist organizations is based, has lost its force."

In connection with this, it is understandable that great importance is attributed in Soviet civil legislation to the question of specific performance of contractual obligations. Under the conditions of a planned economy, and in the absence of a free market, the sums of money received by the obligee in place of performance of the contract, however imposing they might be, will not, as a rule, protect the property interests violated by the nonperformance of the contract. The obligee is not in a position to purchase elsewhere the goods that the obligor should have supplied pursuant to the contract. This applies primarily to socialist organizations.

In addition to the general provisions on the performance of obligations provided for by Part 6 of Article 36 of the Fundamentals of Civil Legislation, there are two special provisions in the civil codes of the Union republics. One of them relates to the individually specified articles. Under Article 217 of the Civil Code of the RSFSR, "in cases of non-performance of an obligation to transfer the ownership, operative control, or use of an individually specified article to the obligee, the obligee is entitled to demand the confiscation of this article from the obligor and its transfer to the obligee."

The second special provision relates to the performance of a specific task. "In case of non-performance by the obligor of an obligation to carry out a specific task," Article 218 of the Civil Code of the RSFSR states, "the obligee is entitled to carry out this task at the obligor's expense, unless otherwise provided for by law or the contract, or to demand damages."

It should be noted that the provision for specific performance of obligations is included in the Fundamentals of Civil Legislation and in the civil codes of the Union republics in the chapter on liability for breach of contract. This emphasizes two points. First, damages received in place of the performance of a contract are regarded as a type of performance of the obligation. Second, damages are awarded when and insofar as actual performance becomes impossible.

At the same time, the compulsory means provided for by law in relation to the taking of specific articles and the possibility of the obligee's performing particular tasks, should not be considered as among the forms of contractual liability. This is a question of performance by the obligor of his primary duties under the contract itself. Liability, on the other hand, presupposes an action of a secondary nature. This action is carried out within the context of a supplementary, protective legal relationship, arising as a result of nonperformance or improper performance of contractual obligations. An opposing point of view is expressed by S. N. Bratus, who extends the concept of legal liability to the limits of the compulsory means in relation to the performance of obligations at all stages of their existence, including specific performance.[61]

Like any legal construction, contractual liability is applied within the limits established by law. The question of liability arises at a particular stage of the existence of the contractual obligation (when it is not performed or is improperly performed) and has a strictly functional purpose: to compensate for the damage caused by the nonperformance of the contract. In connection with this, the remedies applied when a contract is invalid are not included in the concept of contractual liability. Similarly, remedies in the form of operative influence by one party on another, which are used in the course of performance, are not part of liability. These may include, for example, in a contract where the duties of the parties must be carried out simultaneously (Article 177 of the Civil Code of the RSFSR), the refusal by one party to carry out its duties before the performance of the corresponding duties by the other party; and in cases of persistent and unfounded refusal to accept a bill,[62] a change in the method of payment from a documentary collection to a letter of credit for a term of three months.

Some legal scholars have written that the concept of civil law liability should be limited to cases of harm or damage caused by fault.[63] This

---

61. See S.N. Bratus', *Iuridicheskaia otvetstvennost' i zakonnost* [*Legal Liability and Legality*] (Moscow: Iuridicheskaia Literatura, 1976], pp. 85, 90–95, 117.
62. See Point 173 of the Instructions of the State Bank of the USSR, of May 31, 1979, "O beznalichikh raschetakh v narodnom khoziaistve," *Zakonodatel'stvo v kapital'nom konstruktsii* ["On Non-Cash Transactions in the National Economy," *Legislation in Capital Construction*] (Moscow: Iuridicheskaia Literatura, 1981), Vol. I, Issue 7, pp. 488–562.
63. O.A. Krasavchikov, "Otvestvennost', mery zashchity i sanktsii v sovetskom grazhdanskom prave," *Problemy grazdanskopravovoi otvetstvennosti i zashcity grazhdanskikh prav* ["Liability, Defenses, and Sanctions in Soviet Civil law," *Problems of Civil Liability and the Defense of Civil Rights*], Issue 27 (1973), pp. 5–16; N.S. Malein, *Pravonarushenie: poniatie, prichiny, otvetstvennost'* [*Violation of Law: Concept, Clauses, Liability*], pp. 12–14.

opinion, however, is in contradiction to the legislation currently in effect. Under Article 37 of the Fundamentals of Civil Legislation, the person who does not perform an obligation or performs it improperly, is liable in terms of property only in cases of fault (either by intention or by negligence) except where the law or the contract provides otherwise. Such contractual liability without fault is expressly provided for by Part I of Article 427 of the Civil Code of the RSFSR, relative to professional custodians (for example, pawn shops). The possibility that civil law liability may arise without fault is also widely recognized in the literature.[64]

In evaluating the nature of contractual liability in civil law, one must consider its specific character. The basic premise of contractual liability lies in compensation, in terms of property, for the losses incurred by the obligee for the nonperformance or improper performance of an obligation. For this reason, from a subjective point of view, contractual liability can be expanded to the reasonable limits of the effective risks in relation to the parties to the contract, as is done in the legislation now in force.[65] This approach provides an incentive to the parties to take the necessary measures beforehand to prevent undesirable consequences from arising in connection with the breach of contractual obligations.

The conditions of liability are united by the composition of unlawful conduct under civil law committed by the obligor's nonperformance or improper performance of contractual obligations. The substance of this unlawful conduct is not the same in cases of awarding damages and exacting forfeits.

An award of damages usually requires that all the conditions of liability be satisfied: 1) the obligor's conduct must be of an unlawful nature; 2) the obligee must have incurred losses; 3) there must be a causal connection between the action (or inaction) of the obligor and the losses incurred by

64. See I.S. Samoshchenko and M. Kh. Farukshin, *Otvetstvennost' po sovetskomu zakonodatel'stvu* [*Liability Under Soviet Legislation*] (Moscow: Iuridicheskaia Literatura, 1971), p. 44. See *also* U.G. Basine, "Osnovania grazhdansko-pravovoi otvetstvennosti za xoziastvennie pravonarushenia," *Izvestia Akademii Naux Kazachskoi SSR, Seria obshyestvennix nauk* ["The Grounds of Civil Law Liability in Economic Relations," *Izvestia, Series of Social Sciences*] No. 1 (1986), p. 88.

65. V.A. Oigenzikht, *Problemy riska v grazhdanskom prave* [*Problems of Risk in Civil Law*] (Dushanbe: Ifron Publishing House, 1972), pp. 209–210; S.N. Bratus', *Iuridicheskaia otvetstvennost' i zakonnost'* [*Legal Liability and Legality*], p. 178.

the obligee; and 4) the obligor must be at fault. In the case of liability without fault an abbreviated list of requirements is applied, consisting only of the first three of the conditions mentioned above.

An exacting of forfeits requires that only two conditions of liability be satisfied: 1) the obligor's conduct must be unlawful, and 2) he must be at fault. In the case of liability without fault, composition of the unlawful conduct is limited to a single condition—the unlawful conduct of the obligor. By law, the exaction of a forfeit is carried out without regard to the presence of losses incurred by the obligee.

In either case, the unification of the conditions of liability with the composition of unlawful conduct has practical significance. This emphasizes the interconnections between the various conditions of liability.

The unlawful nature of the conduct of the obligor in a contractual obligation is manifested by his deviation from the terms of the contract—the nonperformance of the duties imposed upon him. This may be expressed in the form of inaction (in the case of nonperformance of the contract and of delay beyond the time limit) or of action not corresponding to requirements established by the contract (in the case of the improper performance of the obligation). In both cases, the conduct of the obligor goes outside the bounds of what is permitted by law. The violation of the obligee's subjective rights and, at the same time, of the law, takes place.

Conduct by the obligor that deviates from the terms of the contract is not considered unlawful conduct in cases specified in the law—for example, in connection with an officially declared moratorium (Part 1 [2] of Article 85 of the Civil Code of the RSFSR).

The size and type of damages to be compensated in cases of nonperformance or improper performance of contractual obligations are determined by Article 36 of the Fundamentals of Civil Legislation. These damages include:

1) expenses incurred by the obligee—for example, expenses in renting structures for storing equipment that was not delivered pursuant to the contract;

2) losses or injury to property—for example, demolition of structures on a site for construction of an enterprise that was not built by the fault of the contractor; and

3) income not received by the obligee. In relation to organizations, this is usually expressed in profit not received. As is said in Point 5 of the Instructions of the State Arbitration Board of the USSR of September 23, 1974, "Income not received by the plaintiff, in the form of shortfall in planned profit is subject to recovery, regardless of whether the plaintiff performed or over-performed plans for profit for the corresponding period,

through over-performance of the plan of production of other products."[66] Income not received, in the case of individuals, refers to income that is considered to have been earned through labor. Such income, in particular, is income in the form of payments not received for the use of dachas within the limits established by the law.[67]

The first two types of damages are represented by positive damage to the property of the obligee, while the third is a loss of income. Both cases, however, involve actual damages resulting from the circumstances of each contract. Soviet law does not divide damages into direct and consequential. For this reason, the division of losses into these types, which is sometimes encountered in the literature, has no legal force.[68]

In establishing the outer limits of damages the legislation proceeds on the assumption that the party that has suffered a loss must be placed in the conditions it would have been in had the contractual obligation been properly performed. By comparison with the legal systems prevailing in the majority of countries of the world, the maximum amount of contractual liability in the USSR, according to law, is greater. The concept of subjective foreseeability by the parties to the contract, in evaluating possible damages, is unknown in Soviet legislation. In the past few years, however, well-founded proposals have been made that this rule should be adopted.[69]

The causal connection between the obligor's unlawful conduct and the losses suffered by the obligee is regarded as an objective condition for contractual liability. For this reason, contemporary practice and doctrine does not accept such theories of causal connection as the theory of

---

66. *Sistematizirovannyi sbornik instruktivnykh ubazanii Gosudarstvennogo arbitrazha pri Sovete Ministrov SSSR* [*A Systematic Collection of Instructional Orders of the State Arbitration Board of the Council of Ministers of the USSR*], p. 84.

67. See *Kommentarii k GK RSFSR* [*Commentaries on the Civil Code of the RSFSR*], eds., S.N. Bratus' and O.N. Sadikov, p. 265.

68. See G.K. Matveev, *Osnovanie grazhdanskopravovoi otvetstvennosti* [*The Conditions of Civil Law Liability*] (Moscow: Iuridicheskaia Literatura, 1970), pp. 146–151; V.A. Oigenzikht, *Imushchestvennaia otvetstvennost' v khoziaistvennykh dogovorakh* [*Property Liability in Economic Contracts*] (Dushanbe: Tadzhik University Press, 1980), p. 28.

69. See O.N. Sadikov, "Grazhdanskoe pravo i ego otraslevye osobennosti," *Problemy sovershenstvovavniia sovetskogo zakonodatel'stva* ["Civil Law and its Branch Particularities," *Problems of the Improvement of Soviet Legislation*] (Paper No. 29 of the USSR-wide Research Institute for Soviet Legislation, Ministry of Justice, USSR) (Moscow, 1984), p. 22.

adequate causal connection[70] and the theory of necessary conditions (*conditio sine qua non*).[71] The most widespread theories in the Soviet legal literature are the theory of necessary causal connections and the theory of possible and actual causation. Both theories are based upon objective criteria for the understanding of causal connections.

Under the theory of necessary causal connections, one should distinguish between necessary and chance causal connections when analyzing civil law. The presence of necessary causal connections serves as a sufficient basis (along with other conditions) for civil liability to arise. Chance causal connections, on the other hand, exclude such liability.[72]

The theory of possible and actual causation proceeds from the assumption that in establishing causal connections, one may take into account only cases in which the defendant's unlawful actions create a concrete (actual) possibility that damage will arise or that turn such a possibility into reality.[73]

---

70. The theory of adequate causal connections recognizes as the actual cause of an unlawful result only those actions, which according to the concept that has developed, always lead to the given result. Thereby, the actually acting causally conditioned phenomena, which in every concrete case have an individual character, are replaced by typical connections, which are often products of the human consciousness. The best known and most recent proponent of this theory in the USSR was M.M. Agarkov. See M.M. Agarkov, *Grazhdanskoe pravo*, [*Civil Law*], p. 327.

71. The theory of the necessary condition is based on the principle of combining objective and subjective criteria. In the objective sense, any behavior by a person under an obligation, which directly or indirectly results in damage, is considered to be the cause of the damage that took place. The fault of the person who caused the damage appears as the subjective element. With the help of this factor, the final selection of the phenomenon, which is in direct causal connection with the damage, is made. *See* T.V. Tsereteli, *Puchinnaia sviaz' v ugolovnom prave* [*Causal Connection in Criminal Law*], Author's Abstract of Doctorate Dissertation, (Moscow, 1949).

72. See I.B. Novitskii and I.A. Lunts, *Obshchee uchenie ob obiazatel'stve* [*The General Doctrine of Obligations*], pp. 300–319; G.K. Matveev, *Osnovanie grazhdanskopravovoi otvetstvennosti* [*The Conditions of Civil Law Liability*], pp. 88–113; V.A. Tarkhov, *Otvetstvennost' po sovetskomu grazhdanskomu pravu* [*Liability Under Soviet Civil Law*] (Saratov: Saratov University Press, 1973), pp. 116–136.

73. The most consistent version of this theory is set forth by A.A. Sobchak in the textbook, *Sovetskoe grazhdanskoe pravo* [*Soviet Civil Law*], eds., V.T. Smirnov, Iu. K. Tolstoy, and A.K. Iurchenko, pp. 372–375.

These theories are based on philosophical approaches: in the first case, the categories of necessity and chance, and in the second case, those of possibility and actuality. In practice, one must have recourse to supplemental criteria, which flow directly out of the circumstances of each case considered by the court or arbitration tribunal. Additionally, the classification of causes as either necessary (and not accidental) or concretely possible (and not abstractly possible) is in itself often rather difficult. For this reason, dissatisfaction with these theories has been expressed with increasing frequency in the past few years.[74]

In establishing a causal connection as a condition of civil liability, one should proceed from the assumption that the consequence (the occurrence of damage) resulting from the action of the corresponding cause (the defendant's unlawful conduct) is inevitable. This cause must be the sole or the main cause (if there are several) leading to the occurrence of damage.

In the field of contractual liability, whether the question of establishing causal connections as a condition for liability on the obligor's part will arise, has a clearer answer than in the case of tort liability. This is explained to a considerable degree by the character of the connections existing between the parties.

Fault as a condition for liability in civil law is dominant in the vast majority of contractual obligations. It constitutes the psychological attitude of the person toward his unlawful conduct and its result. As a general rule, the degree and the form of fault exercise no influence on the conditions and amount of civil contractual liability. Applying mixed liability, where the damages arise by the fault of both parties to the contract, is an exception to this rule.[75]

Additionally, in certain cases specified in the law, liability arises not from just any form of fault, but only from actions involving intentional fault or gross negligence. Thus, a person who transfers property for use without compensation is liable for any defect of this property that he has

---

74. See, for example, *Sovetskoe grazhdansko pravo* [*Soviet Civil Law*], eds., V.F. Maslov and A.A. Pushkin, pp. 449–450.

75. "If the non-performance or improper performance of the obligation, took place through the fault of both parties, then the court, the arbitration commission or the arbitration court, reduces to an appropriate degree, the liability of the obligor. The court, the arbitration commission, or the arbitration court, also has the right to reduce, to an appropriate degree, the obligor's liability if the obligee intentionally or through negligence promoted an increase in the amount of damages caused by the non-performance or improper performance, or failed to take measures to reduce these damages." Article 254 of the *Civil Code of the RSFSR*.

failed, intentionally or through gross negligence, to specify at the time of transferring the property (Article 345 of the Civil Code of the RSFSR).

The civil law, however, does not give a legal definition of intentional fault or gross negligence. Therefore, in practice it is necessary to use by analogy the concepts that are established by the criminal legislation—taking account, of course, of the distinctive features of civil legal relationships. Intentional fault is present in those cases where the liable party foresees the harmful result of his unlawful conduct, and either desires or consciously permits it to occur. In the field of contractual liability, intentional fault is rarely encountered. Nonperformance or improper performance of obligations is mostly the result of negligent conduct by the obligor.

In cases of gross negligence, the obligor, while foreseeing the harmful consequences of his unlawful conduct or being aware of the possibility of such consequences, mistakenly believes that he has prevented them. In being at fault for gross negligence, the obligor violates the usual requirements (through wanton and reckless conduct) that are applied in the particular field of activity in question. Examples of this kind of violation are provided by the shipment of products by the supplier to the purchaser in packaging that is inadequate or in poor condition, the storage of perishable goods in spaces that are not temperature-controlled, and so forth.

In cases of minor negligence, the obligor does not foresee that harmful consequences will arise, although objectively he should connect his conduct with the possibility of their occurrence. In these cases, greater attention, prudence, and care are required than in the case of gross negligence. Thus, if a supplier manufactured standard equipment for a particular individual's use without informing the individual that no special provisions had been made to accomodate his particular needs, the supplier would be liable for minor negligence.

The provisions of the law concerning fault as a condition of contractual liability extend not only to individuals but, to an equal degree, to legal persons. This is shown by the Instructions of the State Arbitration Board of the USSR of October 6, 1969, "On the Application by the Arbitration Board of Article 37 of the Fundamentals of Civil Legislation of the USSR and the Union Republics."[76] At the same time, the concept of the fault of a legal person itself remains disputed in practice and in the literature.

---

76. *Sistematizirovannyi sbornik instruktivnykh ukazanii Gosudarstvennogo arbitrazha pri Sovete Ministrov SSSR* [*A Systematic Collection of Instructional Orders of the State Arbitration Board of the Council of Ministers of the USSR*], pp. 59–64.

It is a striking fact that in the field of tort liability, the category of fault of a legal person is set forth in the law itself. "An organization," Article 445 of the Civil Code of the RSFSR states, "is obliged to make compensation for the damage caused *by the fault of its workers*, in the execution of their labor (official) duties" (emphasis added). This is not done in the law in regard to contractual liability.

Here the fault of the legal person cannot be limited to the fault of individual workers. According to the prevailing opinion in the literature, the fault of a legal person may be manifested in the actions of persons who organize its activities. The fault of a legal person is not reducible to a simple arithmetical sum, composed of the fault of its individual workers. This is a qualitatively new phenomenon, formed on the basis of the activity of a working collective of a legal person.[77]

We should add that in practice there are very strict criteria for the concept of the fault of a legal person. "To answer the question of fault," it is emphasized in the Instructions of the State Board of Arbitration of October 6, 1969, "one must take into account all the circumstances of the case established in the sessions of the Arbitration Board, proceeding on the assumption that the enterprise, institution, and organization must, in the interests of the economy as a whole, apply all necessary measures for the unconditional and proper performance of their duties to the other party, taking full advantage, to this end, of the potentialities inherent in the Soviet economic system. . . . As a general rule, references by the defendants to failures by their suppliers to provide a means of transportation within the limits of the plan for transportation, to absence or flaws of equipment, labor, technical documentation and the like, are not circumstances that release the defendants from liability for breach of their obligations, inasmuch as, by the rules in effect, the removal of all of these causes is part of the obligation and liability of the supplier." This orientation on the part of the State Arbitration Board of the USSR, and also a contradictory approach to the settlement of specific cases by individual arbitration tribunals, has prompted a number of authors who are practical lawyers, to take the position that the action of the element of fault should

---

77. See G.K. Matveev, *Osnovanie grazhdanskopravovoi otvetstvennosti* [*The Conditions of Civil Law Liability*], pp. 218–233; V.S. Iakushev, *Iuridicheskaia lichnost' gosudarstvennogo proizvodstvennogo prepriiatiia* [*The Legal Personality of a State Production Enterprise*] (Sverdlovsk: Sredne-Ural'skoe knizhoe izdatel'stvo, 1973), p. 236; T.I. Illarionova, *Sistema grazhdansko-pravovykh okhranitel'nykh mer* [*The System of Safeguards in Civil Law*] (Tomsk: Tomsk University Press, 1982), pp. 143–147.

be weakened, or even that the principle of fault should be entirely abolished in economic relationships.[78] This position contradicts the legislation in effect.

Finally, the law calls for a presumption of fault on the part of the person responsible for nonperformance or improper performance of a contractual obligation. "Absence of fault," Article 37 of the Fundamentals of Civil Legislation states, "must be proved by the person who has breached the obligation."

The size of the damages subject to award must, as a rule, coincide with the amount of actual damages incurred by the obligee from the nonperformance or improper performance of the contract. This follows from the principle of awarding full damages for losses, set forth in Article 36 of the Fundamentals of Civil Legislation. In the absence of direct indicators to the contrary in the law or in the contract, this principle continues to operate even where, in accordance with the law or the contract, the obligee is entitled to demand from the obligor the payment of a forfeit. "If," Article 36 of the Fundamentals of Civil Legislation states, "a forfeit (fine or monetary penalty) is set for nonperformance or improper performance of the obligation, then the damages are awarded for that part not covered by the forfeit." This type of forfeit has been termed a *forfeit with deduction*.

The amount of damages subject to award must be precisely established by evidence supplied by the obligee. This requirement, as it applies to organizations, has been confirmed in the Instruction of the State Arbitration Board of the USSR of September 23, 1974, "On the Settlement Connected with the Award of Damages Resulting From the Breach of Obligations Arising from Delivery Contracts."[79] "In making a claim for the recovery of damages," Point 3 of the Instruction states, "the plaintiff must prove the amount of damages suffered by him in connection with the

78. See L.M. Shor, "Sovershenstvovanie dogovorno-pravovykh otnoshenii v sfere material'no-tekhnicheskogo snabzheniia," *Sovetskoe gosudarstvo i pravo* ["The Improvement of Relations of Contractual Law in the Field of Material and Technical Supplies," *Soviet State and Law*], No. 1 (1973), 48–49; B.I. Puginskii, *Pravovye sredstva obespecheniia effektivnosti proizvodstva* [*On Legal Means of Insuring the Efficiency of Production*] (Moscow: Iuridicheskaia Literatura, 1980), p. 30.

79. *Sistematizirovannyi sbornik instruktivnykh ukazanii Gosudarstvennogo arbitrazha pri Sovete Ministrov SSSR* [*A Systematic Collection of Instructional Orders of the State Arbitration Board of the Council of Ministers of the USSR*], pp. 83–86.

breach by the defendant of his obligations, and must present evidence concerning the causal connection between the nonperformance or improper performance of the obligation and the damages incurred." The recovery of income not received (future damages), in particular, can occur only on the basis of bookkeeping and other statistical documentation that indisputably confirms the real possibility that such income would have been received if the contractual obligation had not been breached by the obligor.

As an exception to the rule that full damages be awarded, the law sometimes permits limited liability for the breach of a contractual relationship (Part 4 of Article 36 of the Fundamentals of Civil Legislation). The legislation presently in effect allows such limited liability in three basic cases:

1) Actual positive damages suffered by the obligee in connection with the breach of obligations are awarded. Here, the plaintiff may not claim future damages from the defendant. This limitation applies to liability pursuant to a contract for the use of property without charge (Article 344 of the Civil Code of the RSFSR), to a contract for capital construction (Article 371 of the Civil Code of the RSFSR), to a contract for the shipment of goods and baggage by various means of transportation (Article 383 of the Civil Code of the RSFSR, and other documents), and to a storage contract (Article 428 of the Civil Code of the RSFSR).

2) Damages are awarded within the limits of the positive damages established by law. For example, in accordance with Article 165 of the Merchant Marine Code of the USSR, in the case of shipment of freight to foreign points under consignment, if the value of the freight was not declared and included in the bill of consignment, damages for a lost or injured piece of freight or conventional unit of freight must not exceed 250 rubles.

3) In specified cases, only the recovery of a forfeit is permitted, but not that of damages. Such a forfeit is termed exclusive. It is usually less in amount than the damages. Most frequently, the exclusive forfeit is applied where liability is imposed on banks, communications agencies, transportation organizations, and enterprises supplying the population and the economy as a whole with electricity, gas, and thermal energy.

In principle, the law does not prohibit the limitation of liability in contractual relationships in which individuals participate (in addition to the three cases specified above). However, in relationships among socialist organizations, agreements limiting liability are not permitted if the amount of the liability for the specific type of obligation is precisely determined by the law (Part 5 of Article 36 of the Fundamentals of Civil Legislation).

The legislation permits increased liability for the breach of contractual obligations, but it is applied in extremely rare cases. At the present time, only two such cases can be specified. One of these—the possibility of exaction of a forfeit in the form of a fine in addition to damages due to the delivery of products (goods) of inappropriate quality—was discussed above. The second case is connected with the application of the so-called multiple liability in certain contracts for the rental of household appliances and for the use of property without charge. Thus, in accordance with Point 10 of the Standard Contract for the Provision of Household Appliances, Musical Instruments (Except for Upright and Grand Pianos), Sports Equipment and Other Personal Property for Temporary Use, confirmed by the Decree of the Council of Ministers of the RSFSR of February 1, 1965,[80] if the lessee refuses to return part or portions of the object rented, he is required to pay one and one-half times the value of the parts missing, provided that further use of them is possible. In the legal literature, however, the possibility of claiming multiple damages is justly placed in doubt, as not being based directly on the rules of the Fundamentals of Civil Legislation and the civil codes of the Union republics.[81]

In evaluating the overall practical effectiveness of the legal rules currently in force on liability for breach of contractual obligations, primarily in the area of economic relationships, many authors note that when contracts are breached, the parties, as a rule, confine themselves to claiming a forfeit. The requirement that full damages be awarded is encountered relatively rarely in arbitration and judicial practice.[82] To a

---

80. *SP RSFSR*, No. 1, item 2 (1965); No. 2, item 4 (1982).

81. See A. Iu. Kabalkin, *Grazhdansko-pravovoi dogovor v sfere obsluzhivaniia* [*The Civil Law Contract in the Sphere of Service*] (Moscow: Nauka Publishing House, 1980), p. 202.

82. See N.S. Malein, *Imushchestvennaia otvetstvennost' v khoziaistvennykh dogovorakh* [*Property Liability in Economic Relationships*] (Moscow: Nauka Publishing House, 1968), pp. 114–115; A.A. Sobchak, [*Pravovoe regulirovanie khoziaistvennoi deiatel'nosti*] [*Legal Regulation of Economic Activity*] (Leningrad: Leningrad State University, 1981), pp. 161–162; *Effektivnost' grazhdanskogo zakonodatel'stva* [*The Effectiveness of Civil Legislation*], ed., V.P. Gribanov (Moscow: Moscow University Press, 1984), p. 78; E.V. Anisimov, "Problemy ukrepleniia planovoi i dogovornoi distsipliny v praktike gosarbitrazha i sviazi s iuridicheskoi naukoi," *Sovetskoe gosudarstvo i pravo* ["Problems of the Strengthening of Plan and Contractual Discipline in the Practice of State Arbitration in Connection with Legal Scholarship," *Soviet State and Law*], No. 4 (1985), 32.

large extent this is explained not by defects in the legal rules devoted to liability for nonperformance or improper performance of obligations, but by the imperfect conditions of the mechanisms that provide for the organization of contractual relations among various subjects of the law.

The improvement of the general system of management of the economy, which is now occuring in the USSR, will undoubtedly exercise a beneficial influence on these conditions.

4.5 Impossibility of Performance

The impossibility of performance is one of the bases on which contractual obligations can be terminated. "An obligation is terminated by the impossibility of performance" Article 235 of the Civil Code of the RSFSR states, "if this impossibility was called forth by a circumstance for which the obligor is not responsible." (Article 222). This formulation leads to the following conclusions about the concept and the limits of the application of impossibility of performance in Soviet civil law.

1) Impossibility of performance means the subsequent impossibility of performance, where circumstances that prevent the obligor from performing the obligations imposed on him occur after the making of the contract. Prior impossibility of performance (*i.e.*, impossibility that existed when the contractual obligation arose) renders the contract invalid.

2) The concept of impossibility of performance extends to the contractual obligation as a whole or to that part of it that makes the further existence of the obligation itself meaningless. This concept is inapplicable to all other cases that influence the content of the obligation that has already arisen. Thus, if during the time of a delivery contract, the state changes the prices for the goods being delivered, the contractual obligation retains its force even though in a changed form, and despite the fact that the newly established price may be burdensome for the customer. In legislation and in practice there is no rule relating to economic difficulties in the performance of contractual obligations. References to economic difficulties arising during the time of the contract are not, however, excluded in principle in the area of foreign economic relations.

3) Impossibility of performance may arise in two forms—actual and legal. Actual impossibility of performance occurs when the subject matter of the obligation (usually an individually specified object) ceases to exist, when the obligated party loses the ability to perform the service or the work, or when other physical forces of a natural or social character have an impact on the contractual obligations.

Special mention must be made of general property that is the subject matter of a contract and that is destroyed before the contract is performed. The Civil Code of the RSFSR of 1922 contained a rule (Part 1 of Article 119), according to which the impossibility of performance did not release the obligor from liability if the subject matter of the obligation was general property and delivery of the same kind of property had not become objectively impossible (*i.e.* the same kind of property could be easily obtained elsewhere). Essentially, what was at issue in this rule was not the impossibility of performance, but the obligation of the obligor to perform his obligation in accordance with the terms of the contract. This rule was applied in unconditional form only in the case of monetary obligations.[83] In all other cases, the application of the rules of Part 1 of Article 119 of the Civil Code was significantly restricted. This was especially true of contractual obligations in which socialist organizations participated. The planned character of their activity limited the applicability of these rules to articles that the socialist organizations themselves had produced. This practice retains its significance today, even though the legislation now in force does not contain a rule similar to that contained in Part 1 of Article 119 of the Civil Code of the RSFSR of 1922.

The legal impossibility of performance is usually connected with prohibitions issued by competent state agencies. These prohibitions extend to activities that make up the content of contractual obligations—for example, the prohibition of imports or exports of particular types of goods.[84]

Recently, the concept of legal impossibility of performance has been given a broader meaning in the legal literature. It is applied in all cases in which performance of the obligation contradicts any acts of state agencies, including the rules of law adopted during the time of the contract.[85] This

83. See the March 21, 1944, decision of the Civil Panel of the Supreme Court of the USSR on a claim of 7000 rubles in *"Polenoi" Rest Home of the Bolshoi Theatre of the USSR v. the Tula Oblast's Office of Gostbank. Sbornik postanovlenii Plenuma i opredelenii kollegii Verkhovnogo suda za 1944 g.* [*Collection of the Guiding Instructions of the Plenum and Decisions of the Judicial Panels of the Supreme Court of the USSR for 1944*], pp. 242–243.

84. See M.P. Bardina, *Otvetstvenost' khoziaistvennykh organizatsii—chlenov SEV po vneshnetorgovym sdelkam* [*Liability of Economic Organizations-Members of the Council of Economic Mutual Aid in Foreign Trade Transactions*] (Moscow: Mezhdunarodnaia otnosheniia, Moscow, 1981), p. 65.

85. See M.G. Masevich, "Nevozmozhnost' ispolneniia obiazatelstv," *Kommentarii arbitrazhnoi praktiki* ["Impossibility of Performance of Obligations," *Commentary on Arbitration Practice*], Issue 13 (1980), 37; MI. Braginskii, "Kategoriia iuridicheskoi nevozmozhnosti ispolneniia v khoziaistvennykh

concept includes, in particular, the impossibility of performance of economic contracts brought about by changes in the corresponding planning documents.[86]

This broad approach to the concept of impossibility is still the subject of debate from the point of view of the existing legislation, because in a number of cases problems of impossibility are covered by other rules of law.

Thus, in relation to the termination or modification of an obligation as a consequence of a change in the plan, there are special articles in the civil codes of the Union republics. "An obligation among socialist organizations," it is written in Article 234 of the Civil Code of the RSFSR, "is to be terminated or modified by the parties according to a set procedure in cases where measures in the planning of the national economy on which the obligation is based, are modified by a disposition that is obligatory for both parties." Thus, in this case the result of the impossibility of performance of the obligation in its original form, as distinct from the general rule of Article 235 of the Civil Code of the RSFSR, may be not only the modification of the obligation but also a termination of it. In addition, the modification or termination of a number of economic contracts (for example, of delivery contracts) when there is a change in the plan, does not take place automatically but by agreement between the parties ("by the established procedure").[87]

---

dogovorakh," *Problemy sovershenstvovaniia sovetskogo zakondatel'stva* ["The Category of Legal Impossibility in Performance of Economic Obligations," *Problems of the Improvement of Soviet Legislation*] (Paper No. 29 of the USSR-wide Research Institute for Soviet Legislation, Ministry of Justice, USSR) (Moscow, 1984), p. 135.

86. M.I. Braginskii, *op. cit.*, pp. 145–148.

87. See Point 31 of the Statute on Deliveries of Goods for Industrial and Technical Use; Point 26 of the Statute on Goods for Consumption by the Population; Point 7 of the Instructions of the State Arbitration Commission of the USSR of August 16, 1973, "O praktike razresheniia organami arbitrazha, sporov, sviazannykh s pros-roschkoi postavki, nedopostavkoi i nevyborkoi produktsii i tovarov," *Sistematizirovannyi sbornik instruktivnykh ukazanii Gosudarstvennogo arbitrazha pri Sovete Ministrov SSSR*, ["On the Practice of Settlement by the State Arbitration Tribunals of Disputes Connected with Late Deliveries, Inadequate Deliveries and Off-quality Goods and Commodities," *A Systematic Collection of Instructional Orders of the State Arbitration Board of the Council of Ministers of the USSR*], pp. 109–110.

Concerning rules of law that go into effect during the time of a contract that may cause the impossibility of performance of the obligation, one must note the existence in the civil law of a general rule forbidding retroactive law. Individual exceptions to this general rule, if there is an urgent need for them, are specified at the time when these laws go into effect. Therefore, the practical significance of the opinion that the performance of obligations becomes legally impossible in connection with the adoption of new rules of law is extremely problematic.

It is correct to conclude that together with the legal impossibility of performance of obligations provided by Article 235 of the Civil Code of the RSFSR, there is a need for a more generic concept of legal impossibility of performance of obligations based on this Article, and on other provisions of the law.

4) The concept of the impossibility of performance of obligations in Soviet civil law is interrelated to the action of a subjective factor. Article 235 of the Civil Code of the RSFSR contains a direct reference to Article 222 of the Civil Code of the RSFSR that is devoted to fault as a condition for liability arising from breach of obligations. From the point of view of the subjective aspect, the obligor's liability extends, as a general rule, to the limits of the action of accidents and rather more rarely, to the limits of force majeure. Where there is death or damage to the health of a passenger during the use of air transportation, the obligor's liability extends to intentional action on the part of the victim. (Article 96 of the Aviation Code of the USSR.) Beyond the above-mentioned limits lies a zone, in which obligations must be terminated by the impossibility of performing them.

In those cases when the boundaries of the zone are represented by force majeure, the delimitation of the concept of force majeure and of accidents takes on decisive significance (in all other cases, these concepts are joined into one from the point of view of the law). Accidents arise without fault and show the blamelessness of the obligor for the nonperformance or improper performance of the contractual obligation. In the case of accidents, the obligor did not, could not, and must not know of the possibility that his unlawful act could injure the obligee.[88]

The concept of accidents, which has been set forth here, and which is recognized in the legal literature, is rather broad. It includes everything

88. See E.A. Pavlodskii, *Sluchai i nepreodolimaia sila v grazhdanskom prave* [*Accident and Force Majeure in Civil Law*] (Moscow: Iuridicheskaia Literatura, 1978), pp. 33–34.

that is beyond the boundary of the fault of the obligor, including force majeure.

In order to formulate a definition of force majeure, it is necessary to isolate from the general concept of accidents a particular part of it that possesses special characteristics. Thereby, force majeure, while retaining the general characteristics of the concept of accidents, takes on a certain individuality. On the other hand, the remaining parts of the general concept become "accidents" in the narrow sense of the word. Accidents in the last sense and force majeure are concepts that are located in a single dimension. Therefore, they are in practice often called *simple* and *qualified* accidents.

The concept of force majeure as described above is provided by law. Under Article 85 of the Civil Code of the RSFSR, force majeure is considered to be an extraordinary event, the effects of which cannot be overcome under the given conditions.

Force majeure is always an event that can be identified with a phenomenon external to the conduct of the obligor.[89] This may be a natural phenomenon (an earthquake, a flood, an avalanche, or the like) or any phenomenon connected with the life of society—for example, a war. Many authors classify as force majeure the prohibitions by state agencies that make it impossible to perform obligations.[90] In the source from which it arises, and in the force of its action, the given event is extraordinary and unusual and is impossible to prevent by technical and other means present under the given conditions. The concept of force majeure has a relative character. The sphere and time of its actions, as the law states, are limited only to the given conditions. That which once could not be prevented may with the development of science and technology be placed under the control of society.

5) The concept of impossibility of performance as a general rule leads to the release of the obligor from liability under the obligation that has been terminated. The possible exceptions to this rule must be directly noted in the law. Thus, according to Article 225 of the Civil Code of the RSFSR, an obligor who has delayed performance is liable to the obligee for the damages caused by the delay and for the accidental impossibility of performance that occurred during the delay.

---

89. A simple accident can be either an event or circumstances connected with the behavior of the obligor himself—for example, an illness leading to the loss of the obligor's professional ability to perform the work that represents the subject matter of the contract.

90. See *Kommenarii k GK RSFSR* [*Commentaries on the Civil Code of the RSFSR*], eds., S.N. Bratus' and O.N. Sadikov, p. 110.

Chapter 5

Settlement of Contract Disputes

Under Article 6 of the Fundamentals of Civil Legislation, rights under civil legislation may be asserted in court or in arbitration. In exceptional cases, provided for by law, comrades courts, trade unions and other public organizations and administrative agencies are used to settle disputes. The interested parties attach great importance to the settlement of disputes by themselves before going to court or arbitration. Toward this end, an amendment was made in 1973 to Article 6 of the Fundamentals of Civil Legislation, to the effect that before a claim arising from relationships between organizations could be brought to court or arbitration, an attempt had to be made to settle the claim.[1] In practice, this provision has been extended to the settlement of disputes arising from contracts of other kinds as well.

5.1 Judicial Settlements of Contract Disputes

The main activity of courts is related to individuals and collective farms. The vast majority of contract disputes in which either individuals or collective farms are involved go to court rather than arbitration. Under Article 151 of the Constitution of the USSR, the court is the sole judicial organ of the state that administers the law in the USSR. The consideration of civil as well as criminal cases in all courts is carried out in a collegial

1. Edict of the Presidium of the Supreme Soviet of the USSR of October 31, 1973, *Vedomosti Verkhovnogo Soveta SSSR,* No. 45, item 637 (1973).

manner. In courts of first instance, People's Assessors, who enjoy all the rights of judges, participate in the trial together with a staff judge. In the consideration of cases on appeal or review, only staff judges participate.

The judicial system includes the courts of the USSR and of the Union republics. The court of the USSR in the field of civil jurisdiction is the Supreme Court of the USSR, in which civil cases are heard by the Civil Judicial Panel, and if they are complex, by the Plenum of the Court. The courts of the Union republics are: the Supreme Court of the Union Republics; the Supreme Courts of the Autonomous Republics; the Krai, Oblast, and City Courts; the Courts of the Autonomous Oblasts and Autonomous Okrugs; and the District (City) People's Courts.[2] In all of these courts, except the District (City) People's Courts, there are panels for civil cases, and plenums or presidiums. In the District (City) People's Courts, the law does not provide for such structural subdivisions. In these courts the judge is usually specialized in civil or criminal matters.

All judges in the USSR are elected. People's Judges in District (City) People's Courts are elected by the citizens of the district, city, and district within the city by secret ballot for a term of five years. People's Assessors of People's Courts are elected at meetings of citizens at their places of work or residence for terms of two-and-one-half years. The members of all other courts are elected by the appropriate Soviets of Peoples's Deputies, the Supreme Soviets of Autonomous and Union Republics, and the Supreme Soviet of the USSR for a five-year term.

Under Article 4 of the Fundamentals of Civil Procedure and the corresponding articles of the codes of civil Law of the Union republics, the courts have jurisdiction over: 1) disputes arising from legal relations between citizens or legal relations in which at least one of the parties to the dispute is an individual, a collective farm, or an agricultural organization, in which a collective farm participates, except in those rare cases where administrative settlement of disputes is provided; 2) disputes arising from the shipment of goods under international contracts in purely international rail or air traffic where the dispute is between a state enterprise, institution, or organization, and a rail or air carrier; and 3) disputes involving foreign citizens, stateless persons, or foreign enterprises or organizations.

Most civil cases, including contract disputes, heard by trial courts are considered by District (City) People's Courts. Under Article 113 of the Code of Civil Procedure of the RSFSR, any civil case that goes to court

---

2. *See* Point 19 of the Fundamentals of Legislation of the USSR and the Union Republics on Court Organizations in the USSR of June 25, 1980, *Vedomosti Verkhovnogo Soveta SSSR*, No. 27, item 545 (1980).

can be heard by a District (City) People's Court. The jurisdiction of all other courts is defined by an exclusionary method. In practice, the above-mentioned courts consider cases involving more specialized disputes. The Plenum of the Supreme Court of the USSR has recommended to Oblast and Krai Courts, and also to the Supreme Courts of the Autonomous and Union Republics that they take jurisdiction in the first instance over the most important and complex civil cases, given the fact that the consideration of these is of great importance for the practice of the lower courts.[3] These cases include those that have a broad significance for the life of society, those that were not correctly resolved after repeated consideration in the People's Courts, and those that were transferred for their consideration in the first instance after reversal of the decisions of the People's Court, by way of supervisory procedures.[4] The consideration of cases by higher courts is of great significance in achieving uniformity in the application of the law in practice.

The procedure for trying civil cases was established by the Foundations of Civil Procedure of the USSR and the Union Republics, approved by the Supreme Soviet of the USSR on December 8, 1961,[5] and the other laws of the USSR and the codes of civil procedure of the Union republics adopted in accordance with it. In the RSFSR, for example, the Code of Civil Procedure of 1964 is in effect.[6]

The administration of justice in civil cases is carried out along democratic lines. Every interested party is entitled to turn to the court to assert a right that has been violated or disputed or of an interest that is protected by law. Cases are heard in all courts, in open sessions, as a rule with observance of the complete equality of the parties from the point of view of participation in the process at all of its stages, including the right to use the services of an attorney. The procedural schedule for the hearing of civil

---

3. *See* Point 4 of the Guiding Instructions of the Plenum of the Supreme Court of the USSR of October 6, 1970, "O merakh po dal'neishemu deiatel'nosti sudebnykh kollegii po grazhdanskim delam Verkhovnykh sudov soiuznykh respublik," *Sbornik postanovlenii Plenuma Verkhovnogo suda SSSR* ["On Measures for the Further Improvement of the Activity of the Civil Judicial Panel of the Supreme Courts of the Union Republics," *Collection of the Guiding Instructions of the Supreme Court of the USSR*], p. 77.
4. See *Kommentarii k GPK RSFSR* [*Commentary to Article 115 of the Code of Civil Procedure of the RSFSR*] (Moscow: Iuridicheskaia Literatura, 1976), pp. 166–167.
5. *Vedomosti Verkhovonogo Soveta SSSR*, No. 50, item 526 (1962).
6. *Vedomosti Verkhovonogo Soveta SSSR*, No. 24, item 407, (1964).

cases is established by law. In suits arising from disputes on contracts, in courts of first instance, there must be no more than one month's delay between the receipt of the declaration of the suit and the time the case is heard. The legal expenses of the parties (the fee and the court expenses connected with the hearing of the case) are reduced to a minimum. Most of these costs are assumed by the state. In general, one must note the high efficiency of the judicial procedure for settling contract suits.[7]

Court decisions in civil cases are published in the Bulletin of the Supreme Court of the USSR and the Bulletins of the Supreme Courts of the Union republics. A "Commentary on Judicial Practice" is also published annually. These commentaries are prepared by the USSR-wide Research Institute on Soviet Legislation, and are published by the Iuridicheskaia Literatura Publishing House.

5.2 The Settlement of Contract Disputes by Arbitration

Contract disputes between organizations (with the exception of those under the jurisdiction of courts and in some cases of administrative agencies) are, as a general rule, heard in arbitration. "The settlement of economic disputes between enterprises, institutions, and organizations," Article 163 of the Constitution of the USSR states, "is carried out by the organs of state arbitration within the limits of their competence." On the basis of this Article of the Constitution of the USSR, the Supreme Soviet, on November 29, 1979, adopted the Law on State Arbitration in the USSR.[8] In 1980, as a development of this law, the Council of Ministers of the USSR adopted a statute on the State Arbitration Board under the Council of Ministers of the USSR.[9] In the Union republics, there are statutes on state arbitration boards adopted by the Councils of Ministers of

---

7. There is much scholarly and textbook literature on Soviet civil procedure. The most fundamental scholarly work that has recently appeared is a two-volume work edited by A. Melnikov, entitled, *Kurs sovetskogo grazhdanskogo protsessual'nogo prava. Teoreticheskie osnovy pravosudiia po grazhdanskim delam* [*A Study of Soviet Civil Procedural law: Theoretical Foundations of Jurisprudence for Civil Cases*] (Moscow: Nauka Publishing House, 1981).

8. February 12, 1987 Edict of the Central Committee of the Communist Party of the USSR and the USSR Council of Ministers on the State Arbitration Board, published in *Pravda*, Feb. 28, 1987, p. 1.

9. *SP SSSR*, Nos. 16–17, item 104 (1980).

these republics and statutes on lower state arbitration boards.[10] These laws determine the structure, tasks, and functions of the state arbitration in the USSR.

The state arbitration system in the USSR constitutes a unified system of organs of Union-wide and republican scope. The law provides the following structure for these organs: the State Arbitration Board of the USSR; state arbitration boards of the Union republics; state arbitration boards of the autonomous republics; and state arbitration boards of krai, oblast, city, autonomous oblast, and autonomous regions.

The arbitrators who are members of these organs of state arbitration are appointed and dismissed from office by the executive and management agencies of state power. But it should be stessed that the supervision over the legality and soundness of the decisions handed down by the arbitration boards does not come within the competence of those agencies. The arbitration boards are subordinate only to law.

The state arbitration system fulfills many tasks. In addition to resolving economic disputes, which is its basic task, it is expected to carry out preventive activity, aiding in the performance by enterprises and organizations of their planned assignments and contractual obligations; to lend assistance in improving work on contracts and claims in the economy; to secure uniform and proper application of the law in resolving economic disputes; and to work out proposals and implement measures for the improvement of the legal regulation of economic activity.

In carrying out these tasks, the arbitration boards are specifically empowered: 1) to consider precontractual disputes concerning the making and modification of economic contracts,[11] and disputes concerning the

---

10. The arbitration procedure for consideration of property disputes between state organizations has a rather lengthy history. It was established for the first time in 1922 when special arbitration boards were created, *SU RSFSR*, No. 60, item 769 (1922). In May of 1931 state arbitration boards as they are known today were formed. *See* Statute on the Central Executive Committee and the Council of People's Commissars of May 3, 1931, *SZ SSSR*, No. 26, item 203 (1931).

11. As an example of a before-the-agreement dispute, one can take item No. 157/I, which was considered by the Government court of arbitration in Ivanovskii Region in 1984. The crux of the dispute is as follows. The Ivanovskii Decorative Fabric Factory, named for worker Fedor Zinov'ev, sent a plan of agreement for the delivery in 1984 of filtering fabric to a buyer. The plan of agreement assumed the delivery of one year's volume of production during the third quarter, which corresponded to the production plan of the factory.

The buyer had drawn up a protocol of disagreement and specified a delivery date of the first quarter, motivated by the fact that the fabric was necessary for

performance of these contracts; 2) to familiarize itself, in ministries and agencies, enterprises and organizations, with legislation relating to the making and performance of contracts, and to hand down appropriate recommendations; 3) to study and draw conclusions from the practice of arbitration; and 4) to publish instructions and explanations on the application of legislation, and, when necessary, to go to the appropriate state agencies with proposals for the improvement of laws in force. The last of the functions listed above comes under the competency of the State Arbitration Board of the USSR and the state arbitration boards of the Union republics.

Economic disputes between enterprises and organizations belonging to a ministry or agency are removed from the jurisdiction of the State Arbitration Board. Such disputes are considered by organs for intra-agency arbitration—the appropriate arbitration boards of ministries and agencies.[12] The procedure for considering cases in the organs of state and intra-agency arbitration is determined by the Rules for the Consideration of Economic Disputes by State Arbitration Boards, confirmed by the Council of Ministers on June 5, 1980.[13] These rules regulate in considerable detail all stages of the consideration of cases by arbitration boards, including the review of decisions handed down by them in terms of supervisory procedure and execution. They are reminiscent in many respects of the rules applied in the field of civil judicial procedure. However, they also have many specific features shaped by the special position of the state and intra-agency arbitration system in the system of state agencies. These features include the active position of the arbitrator in the consideration of economic disputes, and the absence of formalization of many actions carried out by the arbitration system.

---

conducting experimental work included in the plan for the first quarter of 1984. In the plan statement (akt) for the delivery of this production, handed down on October 13, 1983, there was a directive for the establishment of dates for delivery of fabric by agreement of the consumer and the producer. State Aribitrazh (Gosarbitrazh) accepted this condition of agreement with the buyer's language. *Commentary on Arbritrational Practice*, ed., E.V. Anisimov (Moscow: "Furidicheskaia Literatura, 1986), Issue 19, p. 4.

12. Thus, the right of the ministries of the USSR to create arbitration commissions is provided for by the General Statute on the Ministries of the USSR, adopted by the July 10, 1967, Decree of the Council of Ministers of the USSR. *SP SSSR*, No. 17, item 1116 (1967).

13. *SP SSSR*, Nos. 16–17, item 104 (1980).

As a general rule, a case is considered by a single arbitrator, with the direct participation of the parties. In contrast to civil judicial procedure, the parties participate not only in the consideration, but also in the resolution of the dispute. In rendering a decision, the arbitrator attempts to get agreement between the parties, and in cases where this is not successful, renders his decision independently. The decision is rendered in the meeting hall and not in the separate conference chamber, as is the case in a court. The arbitrator is armed with broad powers in initiating and considering economic disputes. In particular he is entitled to bring cases on his own initiative when there is evidence of violation of planning and contractual discipline by enterprises and organizations, and to decide individual disputes without calling in the parties.

On the whole, a special procedure for the consideration of cases by arbitration boards, known as arbitration procedure, has developed in Soviet law. The legal nature of this procedure, however, remains in dispute.[14] Whatever point of view individual scholars may hold, it is

14. Scholars express four basic opinions regarding the nature of this procedure. Some authors classify the arbitration process as part of civil procedure. See, for example, N.B. Zeider, "Predmet v sisteme sovetskogo protsessu," *Pravovedenie* ["The Subject Matter in the System of Soviet Procedural Law," *Jurisprudence*], No. 3 (1962), 70–71; I.N. Zaitsev, *Xoziastvennii spor i arbitrazhnii prozess voprosi teorii* [*The Economic Dispute and the Arbitration Process: Questions of Theory*] (Saratov: Saratov University Publishing House, 1982), pp. 64–74; R.F. Kallistratova, "Khoziaistvennyi spor i arbitrazhnoi protsess," *Voprosy teorii* ["On the Concept of the Arbitration Process," *Problems of Modernization of Soviet Legislation*], (Paper No. 29 of the U.S.S.R.-wide Research Institute for Soviet Legislation, Ministry of Justice, U.S.S.R.) (Moscow, 1984), pp. 183–186. Others classify it as part of the administrative procedure. See, for example, D.M. Chechot, *Sub'ektivnoe pravo i formy ego zashchity* [*The Subjective Right and Forms of its Defense*] (Leningrad: Leningrad University Publishing House, 1968), p. 58; V. D. Sorokin, *Administrativno-protsessual'noe pravo* [*Administrative-Procedural Law*] (Moscow: Iuridicheskaia Literatura, 1972), p. 147.

A third group classifies the procedural law of arbitration as part of economic-procedural laws. See, for example, I.G. Pobirchenko, *Teoreticheskie problemy khoziaistevennogo prava* [*Theoretical Problems of Economic Law*] (Moscow: Nauka Publishing House, 1975), p. 312. Finally, a fourth group of authors considers this procedure an autonomous branch of law. See, for example, *Arbitrazhnyi protsess v SSSR* [*Arbitration Procedure in the USSR*], ed., A.A. Dobrovol'skii (Moscow: Moscow University Press, 1983), p. 23; T.E. Abova, *Arbitrazhnyi protsess v SSSR* [*Arbitration Procedure in the USSR*] (Moscow: Nauka Publishing House, 1985), pp. 75–77.

undisputed that the state and intra-agency arbitration boards, in accordance with the Constitution of the USSR, are not agencies of the administration of justice. The arbitration boards carry out the obligations entrusted to them in the field of law enforcement, functioning under the executive and management agencies of state power. Their existence is explained to a considerable degree by the planned character of management of the economy in the USSR. Accordingly, it is primarily contractual disputes based on planning measures that enter into the sphere of their activity. As a rule they deal successfully with the state functions entrusted to them in this capacity. True, there still exists in practice mutual amnesty between contracting parties, in which individual enterprises and organizations do not turn to the arbitration boards with suits for breach of contract and damages.[15] At the present time, the state is taking measures to eliminate this sort of undesirable phenomenon.

Arbitration decisions are regularly published in the journals *Economy and Law* and *The Economic Gazette*. Every year the Iuridicheskaia Izdatel'stvo Publishing House issues *Commentaries on Arbitration Practice* (complied by the USSR-wide Research Institute on Soviet Legislation). In addition, the State Arbitration Board under the Council of Ministers of the USSR periodically publishes the Instructions and Explanations adopted by them.

5.3 Other Means of Deciding Contractual Disputes

The law provides for arbitration courts, formed for the resolution of disputes among individuals and, separately, among organizations. Disputes between individuals, on the one hand, and organizations on the other, cannot be the subject of consideration by an arbitration court. According to the Statute on Arbitration Courts, which constitutes Appendix No. 3 to the Code of Civil Procedure of the RSFSR, individuals may transfer any dispute that has arisen among them to an arbitration court, with the exception of disputes arising from legal relationships relating to labor and to the family.

The arbitration court is set up by agreement between the parties for the sole purpose of settling a specific dispute, and consists of one or several

15. *Effektivnost' grazhdanskogo zakonodatel'stva* [*The Effectiveness of Civil Legislation*], ed., V.P. Gribanov (Moscow: Moscow University Publishing House, 1984), p. 78.

judges. The fundamental goal of an arbitration court consists in settling the dispute on the basis of an agreement between the parties. If this cannot be achieved, the court, in accordance with the legislation in effect, hands down a decision that can be put into compulsory effect on the basis of a writ of execution issued by a People's Court. The consideration of cases in arbitration courts is done without charge and without compensation to the judges chosen by the parties. In practice, the resolution of disputes between individuals by this method is extremely rare.

The procedure for the formation and activity of an arbitration court for the consideration of disputes among organizations is provided for by the Statute on Arbitration Courts for the Settlement of Economic Disputes Between Industrial Units, Enterprises, Organizations, and Institutions, confirmed by the Decree of the State Arbitration Board under the Council of Ministers of the USSR, of December 30, 1975.[16] In accordance with this Statute, economic disputes among industrial units, enterprises, organizations, and institutions may be transferred by mutual agreement of the parties, for consideration by an arbitration court chosen by them to consider that specific case. Arbitration courts consider disputes placed within the competence of arbitration boards, regardless of the affiliation or location of the disputing parties. At the same time, disputes may be transferred for the consideration of an arbitration court only after the parties have taken private measures towards settlement.

An arbitration court consisting of one or several judges (always an odd number) is chosen from among the directors of the units or enterprises, the executives of the organizations or institutions, the engineering and technical personnel or the personnel of the scientific research institutions, public organizations, and other persons competent to settle the dispute that has arisen. Decisions of the arbitration court are final and obligatory for execution by all organizations. If the defendant refuses to execute the decision, the plaintiff is entitled to apply to the state arbitration board in which the given case is on file for the issuance of an order for the compulsory execution of the decision. Practice shows that the consideration of cases by arbitration courts is highly effective even though recourse to their services by organizations is unfortunately not very frequent.

For the consideration of certain specialized types of disputes, two permanent arbitration courts, organized under the Chamber of Trade and Industry of the USSR, are in operation. These are the Foreign Trade

---

16. *Biulleten' normativnykh aktov ministerstv i vedomstv SSSR*, No. 6 (1976), 3.

Arbitration Commission[17] and the Marine Arbitration Commission.[18] The Foreign Trade Arbitration Commission settles contractual and other disputes that arise among subjects of law in different countries in implementing foreign-trade and other international contracts in the economic and scientific-technological fields. The Marine Arbitration Commission settles disputes of a contractual character and other disputes in civil law, arising from merchant shipping.

Comrades courts[19] are organs of independent public action by individuals established at their places of work or residence. In the settlement of contractual disputes, their competence is extremely limited. They are entitled to consider, with the agreement of individuals, disputes relating to property involving less than 50 rubles, and also disputes involving property and nonproperty relations arising from contracts for the rental of premises (payment of utilities, violation of the rules of conduct in apartment buildings, and the like).

Only disputes specifically listed in the law may be considered by administrative procedure as an exception to the general rule. In the field of contract law, only one such case is provided for at the present time. Under the Decree of the Presidium of the Supreme Soviet of March 14, 1955, disputes between state, cooperative (other than a collective farm), and other public organizations involving less than 100 rubles are to be settled by the agency directly superior to the defendant.[20]

These are the basic provisions of the legislation in effect relating to the settlement of contractual disputes.

---

17. The Statute on the Foreign Trade Arbitration Commission under the Chamber of Trade and Industry of the USSR adopted by the Edict of the Presidium of the Supreme Soviet of the USSR of April 16, 1975, *Vedomosti Verkhovnogo Soveta SSSR*, No. 17, item 269 (1975).

18. The Statute on the Marine Arbitration Commission under the Chamber of Trade and Industry of the USSR adopted by the Edict of the Presidium of the Supreme Soviet of the USSR of October 9, 1980. *Vedomosti Verkhovnogo Soveta SSSR*, No. 42, item 868 (1980).

19. The Statute on Comrades' Courts, adopted by the Edict of the Presidium of the Supreme Soviet of the RSFSR of March 11, 1977. *Vedomosti Verkhovnogo Soveta RSFSR*, No. 12, item 254 (1977); as amended, No. 49, item 1822 (1982).

20. *Vedomosti Verkhovnogo Soveta RSFSR*, No. 5, item 116 (1955).

PART II

The History and Concept of Contract Law in the United States

E. Allan Farnsworth

Chapter 6

The Concept of Contract

6.1 The Meaning of *Contract*

The word *contract* is used in different senses in American law. Sometimes it is used, as it is used in common speech, simply to refer to a writing containing terms on which the parties have agreed. Thus a party may say, "I have the contract on my desk." But often the term contract is used in a more technical sense to mean a promise, or a set of promises, that the law will enforce or at least recognize in some way.[1] Thus a court may say, "There is no contract because the offer was not accepted." The word *agreement* also has various senses but is generally used more broadly than "contract" to refer to any manifestation of assent on the part of two or more persons, regardless of whether or not it has legal consequences.[2] The two key words—*promise* and *enforce*—in the definition just given indicate two limitations on the scope of the law of contracts.

The first limitation is that the law of contracts is confined to promises that the law will enforce. It is therefore concerned primarily with *exchanges* because courts in the United States, as in other common law countries, have generally been unwilling to enforce a promise unless the

---

1. Restatement (Second) of Contracts (1981) § 1 defines a "contract" as a "promise or a set of promises for the breach of which the law gives a remedy, or the performance of which the law in some way recognizes a duty." For yet another use of the word "contract," see Uniform Commerical Code (hereinafter UCC) 1–201(11).

2. The Restatement (Second) of Contracts § 3 defines an "agreement" as a "manifestation of mutual assent on the part of two or more persons." For another definition, see UCC 1–201(3).

promisee has given the promisor something in return for it. The promisee may have given his own promise in return for the promisor's promise or may have rendered some performance in return for it. But, at least traditionally, a promisor's mere promise to do something—a "bare" or "naked" promise for which the promisee has given nothing in return—is not enforceable. So if nothing has been given in exchange for the promise, it has no legal consequences. There is no contract. The main concern of the law of contracts, then, is with exchanges.

The second limitation suggested by this definition is that the law of contracts is confined to promises. It is therefore concerned with exchanges that relate to the *future* because a promise is a commitment by a person to his future behavior.[3] One example of exchanges that does not include such a commitment (and so does not involve a contract in this sense) is the transaction of barter, in which the parties simply make a present exchange of, say, wheat for oil. Another example is the present, or *cash*, sale, in which the parties make a present exchange of, say, wheat for money. Because no promise is given in either of these exchanges, there is no contract.[4] No question of the law of contracts arises unless the dispute is open over a promise—a commitment as to future behavior.

An idea of what the word contract means in practice can be obtained from the cotton cases of 1973. That year saw a spectacular rise in the price of cotton in the American market. The causes were said to include large shipments to China, flooding and late planting because of heavy rains in the regions where cotton is grown, and the devaluation of the dollar. In the early months of each year, before planting, a cotton farmer makes a *forward* sales contract for delivery to the buyer of all cotton to be raised and harvested on a specified tract at a fixed price per pound. The farmer can then use this contract to finance raising the crop by borrowing money from a bank using the contract as security. Early in 1973, cotton farmers made such contracts to sell at a price roughly equal to the price on the market at that time, some 30 cents a pound. By the time the cotton had

3. Restatement (Second) of Contracts § 2(1) defines a "promise" as "a manifestation of intention to act or refrain from acting in a specified way, so made as to justify a promisee in understanding that a commitment has been made."

4. Such exchanges may give rise to interesting legal questions. For example, if the apples had been stolen by the seller from their rightful owner, a question might arise as to whether the buyer is entitled to keep them if the original owner claims them. But this is a question relating to conflicting rights of ownership of the apples themselves, and it is considered one for the law of property rather than as one for the law of contracts.

been raised and was ready for delivery, however, the market price had risen to about 80 cents a pound. The farmers felt, as one judge later expressed it, "sick as an old hound dog who ate a rotten skunk."[5] Many farmers refused to perform the contracts that they had made at the lower price, and dozens of lawsuits were brought against them. Not only were the farmers universally unsuccessful, but the decisions attracted little attention. One court put it simply, "The critical issue is whether . . . there was an enforceable promise to buy for each promise to sell. We believe there was."[6] The farmers were bound by contracts, that is by promises—to sell cotton—that the law would enforce.

6.2 The Role of Exchange

Exchange is the mainspring of any economic system that relies as heavily on free enterprise as does the American system. Such a system allocates resources largely by direct bilateral exchanges arranged by bargaining between private parties. In these exchanges each party gives something to the other party and receives in return something from the other party.

Of course it would be misleading to suggest that this is the only possible basis for an economic system. All contemporary developed societies rely to at least some extent on indirect exchanges that are channeled through the state. Some countries, such as the Soviet Union, place heavy reliance on such indirect exchanges. Even the United States relies on indirect exchanges in extensive programs for the construction of highways and for assistance to the poor. Furthermore, within large corporations and conglomerates the distribution of resources is arranged administratively by an internal hierarchy.

Consider, for example, a utility company that burns coal in order to generate electricity. (The electric power industry accounts for over 80 percent of domestic coal consumption in the United States.) The utility company can acquire the coal it requires in three ways. It can go into the "spot" market for coal and contract to buy coal in relatively small quantities for delivery within a short time (less than a year). It can go into the longer-term market for coal and make a contract for the delivery of a much larger quantity of coal over a period of from one to fifty years. Or it

5. Bolin Farms v. American Cotton Shippers Ass'n., 370 F. Supp. 1353, 1359 (W.D. La. 1974)

6. J. L. McEntire & Sons v. Hart Cotton Co., 256 Ark. 937, 943, 511 S.W.2d 179, 183 (1974).

may buy a coal mine which it will then own, perhaps as a subsidiary corporation, as a source of supply until the mine is exhausted. The first two ways, both of which involve the use of contracts and the resort to a market, account for about 85 percent of the coal used to generate electricity in the United States. The third way, which is called "vertical integration" and which eliminates the need for contract, accounts for only about 15 percent. Of the great bulk of coal that is supplied to electric utilities by means of contract, most—some 60 percent—is supplied under relatively long-term contracts (more than five years); the spot market is not of great importance. Of course, figures such as these will vary greatly from one industry to another. For example, the second most important use of coal in the United States is for the production of steel, and vertical integration accounts for 65 percent of all coal supplied for that purpose; there contract plays a lesser role.[7]

In the main, however, the American economy relies on direct bilateral exchanges between business entities. Even governments rely largely on private means of production and generally obtain goods and often also services by bilateral exchanges with business entities. The central assumption behind this reliance on bilateral exchanges was forcefully stated by the English economist Adam Smith in 1776. Man, he reasoned, cannot gain the help of his fellows by relying on their benevolence. He must "interest their self-love in his favour, and show them that it is for their own advantage to do for him what he requires of them." He does this by bargaining with his brethren in this way: "Give me that which I want, and you shall have this which you want." We thus obtain what we need from them by addressing ourselves "not to their humanity but to their self-love, and never talk to them of our own necessities but of their advantages."[8]

In a market economy, the terms of such bilateral exchanges are arrived at voluntarily by the parties themselves through this process of bargaining. Each party to an exchange seeks to maximize his own economic advantage on terms acceptable to the other party. Because of differences in value judgments and because of the division of labor, it is usually possible for each party to realize what is for himself a substantial advantage. "When the baker provides the dentist with bread and the dentist relieves the baker's toothache, neither the baker nor the dentist is harmed."[9]

---

7. See Joskow, Vertical Integration and Long Term Contracts: The Case of Coal Burning Electric Generating Plants, 1 J. L., Econ. & Org. 33 (1985).
8. A. Smith, An Inquiry into the Nature and Causes of the Wealth of Nations 19 (1811 ed.)
9. L. Von Mises, Human Action 666 (rev. ed. 1963).

6.3 The Role of Promise

The most primitive form of direct bilateral exchange in a market economy is barter, the immediate exchange of goods by both parties, with no promise on either side. One party delivers wheat to the other, and, in return, the other delivers oil to the first at the same time. When a society with a market economy comes to regard a particular form of wealth as money, there arises the present sale, in which goods are exchanged for money rather than for other goods, again with no promise on either side. A seller delivers wheat to a buyer, and, in return, the buyer pays money to the seller at the same time. But neither the transaction of barter nor that of present sale looks to the future—neither involves a promise. What role do promises play in a market economy?

The germ of promise was credit. The simplest form of credit transaction is the loan of money. From the loan, it was but a short step to the sale on credit, in which performance on one side is deferred, the buyer merely promising to pay while the seller immediately performs. A seller delivers wheat to a buyer and, in return, the buyer promises to pay the seller at the end of the month. Credit became even more significant when specialization of labor generated a demand for services. Services usually take time to perform, so an exchange of services for payment cannot be simultaneous—an extension of credit by one of the parties is inevitable. If a builder is to put a new roof on an owner's house, either the builder must work in reliance on the owner's promise to pay or the owner must pay in reliance on the builder's promise to do the work.

But the loan and other credit transactions still did not require a concept of promise, for the duty to which the loan gives rise was not generally regarded by primitive societies as arising out of the debtor's word alone. The debt was seen as recoverable, not because of the debtor's promise to pay, but because the debtor, having received money on request, would otherwise be unjustly enriched. It has even been suggested that a breach by the debtor is regarded as a wrong with respect to the creditor's property, so that the creditor's claim is founded not on what he is owed but on what he owns.

The credit transaction was thus a far cry from the purely executory exchange of promises, in which each party merely makes a promise looking to an exchange of performances at some later time. To conceive of enforcing such purely consensual transactions required a higher level of abstraction than that required for enforcing a debt arising out of the plaintiff's immediate performance.

Such purely executory exchanges of promises do not become practically important to a developing society until a relatively advanced level of economic development has been attained. As long as production and distribution remain in the hands of simple artisans and craftsmen, who themselves do all of the work required before consumption, there is little occasion for such transactions or for legal rules to support them. Indeed, a general theory of contract would be something of a luxury in a society concerned with basic protections of life and property. Eventually, however, producers' operations become more complex and, in a market economy, they begin buying raw materials from suppliers, employing others to work for them, and selling through distributors. Producers then see the need to plan for the future in order to compete with other producers. An exchange of promises looking to a future exchange of performances would give a producer the basis for predictable calculation.

From the perspective of a free enterprise society as a whole, the function of the law of contracts might have been seen as furthering the general economic good by encouraging parties to enter into such productive transactions. From the perspective of the parties themselves, the function might have been viewed more narrowly as aiding them in planning for the future by protecting their expectations. From either perspective, it was essential to provide a general basis for the enforcement of promises that included purely executory exchanges of promises. The development of such a general basis closely paralleled the specialization of labor and the development of competitive markets.

Consider the simple example of a contract for future delivery against future payment. A seller promises to deliver wheat to a buyer in six months, and in return the buyer promises to pay the seller $10,000 on delivery of the wheat. If the seller should fail to deliver the wheat in six months, the buyer will have to buy substitute wheat in replacement. If the purchase can still be made at the contract price of $10,000, the buyer's only loss is the inconvenience in arranging the substitute transaction, and the economic importance of the agreement to the buyer is minimal. If, however, the price of wheat has risen, so that the buyer must pay, say, $11,000 to have substitute wheat delivered at the date for delivery under the contract, the loss will be increased by $1,000, and the economic importance to the buyer is at least that amount. In making the contract, the buyer's expectation was that the transaction would provide protection against just such a rise in the market price. The seller, of course, had a comparable expectation of being protected against a falling market.

The decision to recognize purely executory exchanges of promises also allowed the parties to engage in more sophisticated planning for the future. They might extend the period to, say, five years; they might make the agreement cover many deliveries of wheat under a long term relationship; they might leave the quantity of wheat flexible in terms of all that the buyer might "require" to supply a flour factory; they might let the price vary according to a formula based on published market quotations. Furthermore, recognition of such exchanges permitted an entirely new form of economic activity—speculation. The same contract for future delivery, used by the producer to plan for the future, could be used by the speculator to gamble on the future course of the market.

From the standpoint of contract law, the decision to recognize purely executory exchanges of promises opened a Pandora's box of problems. What could the law do to ensure that the exchange of promises was followed by the exchange of performances expected by the parties. In the event of nonperformance by one party, how were the other party's disappointed expectations to be valued. Were any limits to be placed on the expectations for which recovery would be allowed. These and related questions will be examined in later chapters.

6.4 Impact of Government on the Bargaining Process

Despite the fact that the American economy is largely dependent upon bargained-for exchanges arranged by private parties without government intervention, the government often has an important impact on the bargaining process. In some instances this impact results from the power of courts to police bargains for unfairness. But to an important extent the impact results from legislation that determines the conditions in which bargaining takes place. The most pervasive legislation is found in the areas of trade regulation and labor law.

The field of trade regulation includes the law of antitrust, which is designed to encourage competition through the prevention of monopolization and the limitation of restraints of trade, and the law of unfair competition, which requires that competition meet acceptable standards of fairness. This body of law thus sets important limits both on the concentration of power in parties that bargain and on the way in which those parties bargain.

The principal source of law in this field is federal legislation, notably three major statutes enacted by Congress for the purpose of promoting competition. The first and most important is the Sherman Antitrust Act, enacted in 1890 during the period of industrial expansion and concentration of economic power that followed the Civil War.[10] It prohibits in general terms unreasonable restraints of trade and monopolization. The Clayton Act, which followed in 1914, is somewhat more specific. With some exceptions, it prohibits: first, exclusive dealing,[11] tying arrangements,[12] and similar restrictions on the distribution of goods; second, price discrimination (that is, differentiation) between purchasers, as well as some related discriminatory practices;[13] and third, acquisition by one corporation of stock or assets of another corporation—where the effect of any of these "may be substantially to lessen competition or to tend to create a monopoly." While the Sherman Act condemns only existing evils, the Clayton Act requires merely a reasonable probability that these evils will result. The third major statute, the Federal Trade Commission Act, also enacted in 1914, is directed generally at "unfair methods of competition." It created the Federal Trade Commission, which is empowered to enforce the Act. Together, these three statutes affect the horizontal relationship of a business with its competitors, the vertical relations of a business with its suppliers and customers, and in some cases the internal corporate relationship within the business enterprise itself.

A major characteristic of these statutes, and particularly of the Sherman Act, is that they are written in broader and more general terms than is usual for legislation in the United States. This calculated imprecision has given a decisive role to the judiciary, which has been responsible for interpreting the statutes and adapting them to the changing patterns of production and distribution that have evolved since their enactment. Rather than lay down precise and inflexible rules, the courts too have employed a general *rule of reason* (that is, standard of reasonableness) in implementing the Sherman Act. Its application has varied from time to time and from industry to industry according to the circumstances as judges have struggled with economic data and other considerations. There

10. The antitrust laws were named after the nineteenth-century "trust," a closely-knit business combination, composed of many corporations in a single industry such as oil or sugar, and held together by a trust agreement under unified management by a board of trustees.

11. An exclusive dealing arrangement is one in which one party is allowed to obtain the product of another on condition that it will not deal in the competing products of third parties.

12. A tying arrangement involves a sale or lease of a product on condition that some other product be purchased with it.

13. This second prohibition is contained in the Robinson-Patman Act of 1936, which amends and is now part of the Clayton Act.

is thus no absolute limit to the size of a business enterprise in the United States and size alone, or even dominance, is not of itself condemned, although these are among the circumstances to be evaluated. The courts are in agreement, however, that some practices, such as horizontal arrangements among competitors to affect prices or divide markets, are so offensive as to be *per se* (in themselves) unreasonable. Doctrines more similar to *per se* rules than to a rule of reason are also applied to exclusive dealing and tying arrangements under the Clayton Act and to most forms of price discrimination. As might be expected, there has been considerable controversy over the proper domain of the rule of reason and of *per se* unreasonableness under all of the antitrust statutes.[14]

Because virtually all of American business is privately owned and managed, the maintenance and control of competition is of the greatest importance. In some fields, however, Congress has departed from the ideal of free competition. Thus limited exemptions from the antitrust laws have been given to such industries as aviation, communications, railroads, trucking, and shipping, all of which are to varying degrees supervised by special regulatory agencies. Also exempted in most of their activities are labor unions and agricultural cooperatives, which have unique problems.

An entire branch of law has grown up to deal with disputes arising out of the activities of labor unions. It is this subject, sometimes called "labor relations," with which American labor law is chiefly concerned. Its modern development began in the 1930's. Prior to that time, the law of labor relations was largely case law, based on precedent and traditional principles. It was generally favorable to employers, who were able to obtain court injunctions forbidding many forms of union activity. In reaction to judicial excesses, the role of the courts was severely circumscribed by statute.

The Norris-LaGuardia Act of 1932 so curtailed the power of the federal courts to issue injunctions in labor disputes that it is now almost impossible for an employer to get an injunction against peaceful labor activity. The first comprehensive labor relations statute came soon afterward with the enactment in 1935 of the National Labor Relations Act, commonly known as the Wagner Act, to promote collective bargaining between

---

14. The government may proceed against violations of the antitrust laws in several ways, depending on the circumstances. These ways include a civil procedure to enjoin violations, a criminal prosecution, and administrative proceedings leading to a cease-and-desist order. Private parties also have remedies, notably an action for treble damages, in which the injured party may be awarded three times the amount of damages proved.

employers and unions. It assured employees of the right to organize into unions and to bargain collectively, and it prohibited a list of unfair labor practices by employers, including discrimination against employees because of their union activity and refusal to bargain with an authorized union. It created the National Labor Relations Board and gave it two tasks: first, to conduct elections in which employees can, if they choose, select representatives for bargaining purposes; and second, to hear and determine charges of unfair labor practices, subject to judicial review. In 1947, Congress enacted a statute more favorable to employers, the Labor Management Relations Act, popularly known as the Taft-Hartley Act. It prohibited unfair labor practices by unions and limited agreements between an employer and a union requiring or encouraging employees to be members of the union.[15]

In the half century that has passed since the first modern labor legislation in the United States, union membership has increased sixfold. Although it still makes up only about one-third of the non-agricultural work force, leaving most industrial firms without union representation, many of the characteristics of American labor law can be ascribed to the distinctive features of organized labor. Organized labor's chief goals have been higher wages and better working conditions rather than general political or social reform. It has achieved these objectives primarily through collectively negotiated agreements with employers rather than by comprehensive legislation.[16] These agreements both supplement minimum statutory benefits relating to wages, hours, and pensions, and add benefits such as paid vacations, sick leave, seniority, severance pay, and employee participation in the settlement of grievances. The peculiar significance of the collective bargaining agreement is symptomatic of the overall importance of voluntary private procedures for the settlement of labor problems in the United States.

---

15. The Labor-Management Reporting and Disclosure Act of 1959, also known as the Landrum-Griffin Act, amends the two earlier acts and provides for the regulation of internal union affairs to ensure honesty and fairness to individual members.

16. There are, however, many state and federal statutes providing, for example, for minimum wages and maximum hours beyond which additional compensation for overtime is payable. Recent decades have seen particularly significant federal legislation assuring safe and healthful working conditions, facilitating and improving employee pension plans, and prohibiting discrimination on grounds of race, color, religion, sex, national origin, or age.

The labor relations laws themselves provide no significant governmental machinery for the settlement of disputes over employment conditions but attempt only to compel bargaining in good faith between the employer and the elected union representatives, who are the exclusive bargaining agents for the employees. If the union is unable to negotiate a satisfactory collective bargaining agreement, the employees are free to strike on the termination of any prior collective bargaining agreement, and it is this weapon that makes the bargaining process effective.[17] In order to avoid and shorten strikes, both federal and state governments provide mediation and conciliation facilities, but they cannot force terms on the parties. Whether a strike occurs or not, the end result of bargaining is a lengthy and detailed collective bargaining agreement between the employer and the union for a period, commonly of two years, during which the union ordinarily agrees not to strike. For the most part, though this collective bargaining agreement is a legally enforceable contract, it provides for the settlement of disputes by arbitration rather than by courts.

17. The percentage of hours lost annually because of strikes is nevertheless very small, usually well under one quarter of one percent.

Chapter 7

History of Contract Law

7.1 Significance of History

No legal system can be understood without some understanding of its history. This is particularly true of a common law system like that in the United States. The history of the common law has been unbroken by the sweeping codifications that have been characteristic of civil law countries. Even the American Revolution produced no great rupture of America's connection with the English common law tradition. Many of the aspects of modern American contract law are therefore as much the product of history as they are the product of reason.

This chapter begins with an examination of early English history in connection with two questions: What is the general basis for the enforcement of promises? How are promises to be enforced? It then turns to the manner in which English law found its way into the American colonies, was received by the states after the American Revolution, and developed in nineteenth century America. This process is then illustrated in the context of two particular aspects of contract law: the requirement of a writing and the transferability of contract rights. The chapter closes with a discussion of developments in the twentieth century, including a description of contemporary currents in contract scholarship.

7.2 The Enforcement of Promises in Early English Law

How did the common law develop a general basis for the enforcement of promises. Curiously, the common law began at a less advanced stage than that attained by Roman law. Although Roman law notions of contract were known in England, their influence there faded with the break-up of the Roman political system, and contract law had to be painfully reconstructed by English courts during the Middle Ages. That they succeeded in doing so was all the more remarkable in view of the fact that, when they began, the English law of contracts was little more advanced than that of many primitive societies. "Surely," it has been written, "it would be hard to find a better illustration of the flexibility and power of self-development of the Common Law."[1]

No legal system has ever been reckless enough to make all promises enforceable. As a distinguished American legal philosopher expressed it, some freedom to change one's mind is essential "for free intercourse between those who lack omniscience." Most of us "would shudder at the idea of being bound by every promise, no matter how foolish, without any chance of letting increased wisdom undo past foolishness."[2] In framing a basis for enforcing promises, however, one can approach the goal from two opposite extremes. One can begin with the assumption that promises are generally enforceable, and then create exceptions for promises considered undesirable to enforce. Or one can begin with the assumption that promises are generally unenforceable, and then create exceptions for promises thought desirable to enforce.

The common law courts chose this latter assumption: a mere promise does not give rise to an action. Their choice was scarcely surprising. It accorded well with the procedural technicalities of common law courts, where recovery could not be had unless the claim could be fitted within one of the established forms of action. It also suited the status-oriented society of the Middle Ages, which was not receptive to the development of promise. Furthermore, no great pressure existed for enforceability of promises, because contracts were not yet a significant part of the business of the common law courts. At the end of the twelfth century, a writer apologized for the scanty treatment of the subject in his treatise on English common law with the remark that "it is not the custom of the court of the lord king to protect private agreements."[3]

Competing jurisdictions, however, were more hospitable to actions for breach of promise. Under the law merchant, the courts in the medieval fairs and markets entertained actions, as commerce required, on promises

---

1. Ames, The History of Assumpsit, 2 Harv. L. Rev. 252, 260 (1888).
2. Cohen, The Basis of Contract, 46 Harv. L. Rev. 553, 573 (1932).
3. R. de Glanville, Treatise on the Laws and Customs of the Realm of England, bk. 10, ch. 18 (G. Hall ed. 1965); see also bk. 10 ch. 8.

made by merchants. Under canon law, the Church courts regarded a sworn promise as enforceable and its breach as a sin subject to ecclesiastical censures, including excommunication, and there was support for the position that even an unsworn promise was sacred and therefore enforceable. And in equity, the Chancellor held that because a man was "damaged by the non-performance of the promise, he shall have a remedy."[4]

The general theory for enforcing promises that was ultimately fashioned by the common law courts succeeded less on its intrinsic merits than as an incident of the victories of those courts in their struggles to expand their own jurisdiction at the expense of their rivals. These victories were complete by the close of the sixteenth century. By that time the common law courts had so far succeeded in wresting jurisdiction from the commercial courts as to stifle the law merchant's view that promises made by merchants in commerce should be enforced. Although the Church courts had continued to enforce promises in the face of the prohibition of the Constitution of Clarendon of 1164, this business also dried up in the sixteenth century when the common law courts provided a forum for such causes. And since, in equity, the Chancellor often intervened if he found the common law to be wanting, it is a tribute to the ingenuity and flexibility of the common law judges that they succeeded in moving fast enough to hold off action by the Chancellor. Credit for the development of the general basis for enforcing promises that we know today is therefore theirs and theirs alone. The challenge faced and met by the common law courts in the fifteenth and sixteenth centuries was to develop a general basis for enforcing promises within the framework of the forms of action.

After the Norman conquest of England in 1066, the central king's courts began to administer a law that was "common" to all of England, rather than peculiar to a particular locality. This *common law* system was based on writs. A plaintiff who sought relief in the common law courts had to state his case in accordance with one of a limited number of standard forms known as writs. According to one memorable description, "English law knows a certain number of forms of action, each with its own . . . name. . . . The choice is not merely a choice between a number of queer technical terms, it is a choice between methods of procedure adapted to cases of different kinds. . . . The forms of action we have buried, but they still rule us from their graves."[5] The process by which the common law

4. Anon., Y.B. Pasch. 8 Edw. 4, f.4, pl. 11 (1468)(1640 ed.).
5. F. Maitland, The Forms of Action at Common Law 2 (1962).

courts fashioned a general basis for the enforcement of promises was first by developing a series of exceptional cases where promises were enforceable and then by fashioning those exceptions into a general basis for enforcing promises, including purely executory exchanges of promises. How did they do this?

One possible vehicle for the development of a general basis for enforcing promises might have been a formal acknowledgment of liability. The common law action known as *covenant* that grew up in England near the end of the twelfth century became associated with such a formal acknowledgment in the form of a wax seal. Had the trend then been toward the relaxation of formalities, the action of covenant might have developed into a general contractual remedy. This possibility was foreclosed, however, by the middle of the fourteenth century, when it became settled that an action of covenant could not be maintained unless the plaintiff produced a sealed writing. With this turn of events, any hope that covenant might serve as a general ground for contractual liability vanished, since a sealed writing was not suited to an informal exchange of promises.

Another possible avenue of evolution was through the concept of loan. By the end of the twelfth century, this concept had given rise to the common law action known as *debt*, which would lie to recover a sum certain in money. But the defendant's liability in debt was not seen as based on a mere promise. It depended instead on his having received what he had asked for—called a *quid pro quo* in imitation of the Romans—in the form of the loan. It was therefore thought to be unjust to allow him to retain it without paying for it. The debtor's wrong was more in the nature of misfeasance than of nonfeasance. Following this rationale, courts finally broadened the action of debt to allow recovery by anyone who had conferred a substantial benefit on the defendant, including one who had furnished personal services.

Suppose that an owner paid a builder $10,000 in return for the builder's promise to do specified work on the owner's house. If the builder failed to do the work, the action of debt was adequate to allow the owner to recover from the builder. Since the promisor, the builder, had received a benefit in the amount of $10,000, recovery prevented the unjust enrichment of the promisor.

But it was clear that, for there to be a *quid pro quo*, the benefit must have been actually conferred—a mere promise to confer it would not suffice. Therefore the action of debt was poorly suited to the enforcement of a mere exchange of promises, such as a promise to deliver wheat in the future in return for a promise to pay the price in the future. Moreover, the action of debt was subject to the further inconvenience—difficult for the modern mind to comprehend—that the defendant might "wage his law," that is, avoid liability by denying the debt under oath accompanied by a number of persons who swore that he was telling the truth. How was the common law to break out of this mold?

7.3 The Development of a General Basis for Enforcing Promises

The common law courts found the answer to this question in the law of torts. They had already recognized that liability in tort arose when a person undertook to perform a duty and then performed it in such a way as to cause harm to the obligee. The obligee could sue on the variety of the common law action of "trespass on the case" that came to be known as *assumpsit* (from the Latin word meaning "he undertook"). At the beginning of the fifteenth century it was available only if there had been misfeasance in the performance of the undertaking.

This example was given in 1436: "If a carpenter makes a [promise to] me to make me a house good and strong and of a certain form, and he makes me a house which is weak and bad and of another form, I shall have an action of trespass on my case."[6] Such a case of misfeasance cried out for recovery. The promisee, who had a worthless house on his land, had been harmed because he relied on the promise. Justice could be done by requiring the promisor to compensate him in an amount sufficient to put the promisee in as good a position as he would have been in had the promise never been made. The promisee's claim to recovery based on his reliance interest was less compelling than that based on his restitution interest, since the reliance interest did not depend on any benefit received by the promisor (i.e., it was not founded on the concept of unjust enrichment). Nevertheless, his right to recovery seemed clear on principles developed in tort cases.

But might not a remedy lie when there had merely been nonfeasance, a failure by the promisor to perform his undertaking. At first the answer was no. In 1409 it was said: "Certainly it would lie [if the carpenter had built the house badly], because he would then answer for the wrong which he had done, but when a man makes a promise and does nothing under that promise, how can you have an action against him without a writing under seal."[7] Nevertheless, by the second half of the fifteenth century there was

6. Y.B. 14 Hy. 6 [1679 ed.]. p. 18, pl. 58 (1436), 3 W. Holdsworth, History of English Law 430 (3d ed. 1927).
7. Y.B. Mich. 11 Hy. 4 [1605 ed.], f.33, pl. 60 (1409), 3 W. Holdsworth, supra note 1, at 433–434.

a growing inclination among common law judges, conscious of their rival jurisdictions, to make a major extension in the action of assumpsit by enforcing such promises, even where there had been only nonfeasance. But some limits had to be placed on which promises would be enforced, for the judges were not about to allow "that one shall have trespass for any breach of covenant in the world."[8] The courts were therefore forced to find a test to distinguish instances in which nonfeasance was actionable from those in which it was not.

Since the misfeasance cases that had originally given rise to the action in assumpsit were characterized by a detriment incurred by the promisee in reliance on the promise, it was natural to formulate an analogous test and to allow enforcement if the promisee had changed his position on the faith of the promise and had been consequently damaged by its nonperformance. Doing nothing can make things worse. Suppose, for instance, that a builder promised to do specified work on an owner's house in return for the owner's promise to pay the builder $10,000 on its completion, and, in reliance on the builder's promise, the owner rented and moved to another house to permit the builder to do the work. If the builder failed to do the work, the law could justify protecting the owner because of the detriment sustained by him. To the extent that the promisee incurred expenses in preparing to perform or suffered loss by foregoing other opportunities, a broken promise resulted in a waste. But the loss was purely economic, as contrasted with cases of misfeasance that had resulted in loss to person or property, and so the claim to recovery may have seemed less compelling. But in a society that depended on promises for cooperation, there was reason to protect those who relied on promises by placing the cost of that waste on those who broke them.

This first major extension of the action of assumpsit fell short, however, of recognizing claims based on purely executory exchanges of promises, in which there had been no reliance at all by the claimant. As the sixteenth century drew to a close, the common law courts made a second and dramatic extension of the action of assumpsit by allowing such claims. It was held that a party who had given only a promise in exchange for the other's promise had, nonetheless, suffered a detriment by having his freedom of action fettered, since he was in turn bound by his own promise. Suppose again that the builder promised to do specified work on the owner's house, and, in return, the owner promised to pay the builder

8. Y.B. Hil. 3 Hy. 6 [1679 ed.], p. 36, pl. 33 (1425), 3 W. Holdsworth, supra note 1, at 435.

$10,000. On this reasoning, if the builder repudiated the bargain before the owner had done anything in reliance on the builder's promise, the owner would have a claim for breach of contract. The reasoning is, of course, circular, since the conclusion that there was a detriment to the promisee, in this case the owner, assumed that he was in turn bound by his own promise, even though nothing but a promise had been given for it. Nevertheless, by the end of the sixteenth century the common law courts were enforcing exchanges of promises where no performance had been rendered on either side.

This extension of the action of assumpsit had important implications for the measure of recovery in damages for nonperformance of a promise. Because the promisee had neither conferred a benefit upon the promisor nor incurred any detriment in reliance on the promisor's promise, recovery could not be measured by either benefit or detriment. Almost inevitably, courts protected the promisee by requiring the promisor to compensate him for his disappointed expectation, that is to say, for the advantages that he would have received had the promise been performed.

Why, merely because the parties have exchanged promises, should the law protect one party's ephemeral expectation if the other repudiates before there has been any actual reliance on his promise. It has been contended that this protection of expectation has "a quasi-criminal aspect, its purpose being not so much to compensate the promisee as to penalize breach of promise by the promisor."[9] One explanation is that it is justified as the most effective way of protecting reliance. Unless agreements can be relied upon, they are of little use. A rule of law that only protected a promisee who had actually relied upon a promise would, in practice, tend to discourage reliance. The difficulties in proving and valuing reliance are such that a person in business would hesitate to rely on a promise if the legal sanction were important to him. These difficulties are especially acute when a party has relied by foregoing other opportunities, as in the

9. Fuller & Perdue, The Reliance Interest in Contract Damages (pt. 1), 46 Yale L.J. 52, 61 (1936). As the authors point out, "the force of argument will depend entirely upon the existing economic environment. It would be most forceful in a hypothetical society in which all values were available on the market and where all markets were 'perfect' in the economic sense. In such a society there would be no difference between the reliance interest and the expectation interest. The plaintiff's loss in foregoing to enter another contract would be identical with the expectation value of the contract he did make. The argument that granting the value of the expectancy merely compensates for that loss, loses force to the extent that actual conditions depart from those of such a hypothetical society." Id. at 62.

case of the buyer who contracts with a seller for the future delivery of wheat and who would have made arrangements to get them from another source had the seller not promised to deliver them. "To encourage reliance we must . . . dispense with its proof." Promises must be enforceable without regard to a showing of reliance "both in the sense that in some cases the promise is enforced although not relied upon . . . and in the sense that recovery is not limited to the detriment incurred in reliance."[10] The extension of the action of assumpsit to include the mere exchange of promise can be rationalized in this way. The result probably reflects the sense of justice of the average American in business.

The action of assumpsit was still subject to one important restriction. It had been held that where the action of debt was available, the action of assumpsit was not. This proved a disadvantage to creditors, since in assumpsit the plaintiff was entitled to a jury trial, while in debt the defendant could resort to wager of law. The next important step in the common law's development of a law of contract was therefore to permit assumpsit to supplant debt. By the middle of the sixteenth century, it had been recognized that an action in assumpsit could be brought against a defendant who, being already indebted (indebitatus), expressly undertook (assumpsit) to pay a particular sum. This action in *indebitatus assumpsit* was also described as *general assumpsit*, to distinguish it from the older action of assumpsit, which was known as *special assumpsit* because of the specifics that had to be pleaded. (Only special and not general assumpsit could be used for the enforcement of a purely executory contract, in which there had been an exchange of promises but no performance on either side.) Toward the end of the century, it began to be held that a debt alone, without a subsequent express promise, would support such an action of general assumpsit. The final triumph of this view came in 1602 in *Slade's Case*, in which the plaintiff sued for the price of a crop sold and delivered to the defendant. On a jury finding that "there was no other promise or assumption, but only the said bargain," it was decided by all of the common law judges assembled to pass upon this important matter that every such bargain "imports in itself an assumpsit."[11] The creditor could sue in assumpsit as an alternative to debt, even though there was no

10. Id. at 62.

11. Slade's Case, 4 Co. Rep. 92b, 94a, 76 Eng. Rep. 1074, 1077 (1602). This landmark decision was handed down by all the judges of the central courts assembled in a special chamber, after argument by Sir Edward Coke, then Attorney General, for the plaintiff, and Sir Francis Bacon, Coke's bitter rival, for the defendant.

subsequent promise. The creditor was at last assured of the benefits of jury trial in place of wager of law.

Over the course of the fifteenth and sixteenth centuries, the common law courts had thus succeeded in developing the action of assumpsit into a general basis for enforcing promises, including purely executory exchanges of promises. During the sixteenth century, the word consideration, which had earlier been used without technical significance, came to be used as a word of art to express the sum of the conditions necessary for an action in assumpsit to lie. It was therefore a tautology that a promise, at least if not under seal, was enforceable only if there was *consideration*, for this was to say no more than that it was enforceable only under those circumstances in which the action of assumpsit was allowed. In this way, however, the word *consideration* came to be applied to the test of enforceability of a promise and to be used to distinguish those promises that in the eyes of the common law were of sufficient significance to society to justify the legal sanctions of assumpsit for their enforcement.

It was, not surprisingly, neither a simple nor a logical test. Bound up in it were several elements. Most importantly, from the *quid pro quo* of debt, by way of the later extension of general assumpsit, came the notion that there must be a benefit to the promisor. From the reliance of special assumpsit came the notion that there must be a detriment to the promisee.

The requirement of such an exchange found easy acceptance in a society entering a commercial age. The doctrine of consideration took care of the bulk of economically vital commercial agreements, even if it afforded no ground for the enforceability of gratuitous promises, for which nothing was given in exchange. "The large commercial interests of the new age sought a general sanction not for charitable gifts but for business enterprise. In such an environment it is not surprising that the judges should have required some material inducement to the defendant's undertaking."[12]

As a cornerstone for the law of contract, the doctrine of consideration has been widely criticized. It would be foolhardy to attempt to defend it by an exercise in logic, for it must be viewed in the light of its history and of the society that produced it. Nevertheless, in view of the difficulty that other societies have had in developing a general basis for enforcing promises, it is perhaps less remarkable that the basis developed by the common law is logically flawed than that the common law succeeded in developing any basis at all.

12. C. Fifoot, History and Sources of the Common Law: Tort and Contract 399 (1949).

The development of a general basis for enforcing promises did not, however, dispose of the further question of how promises were to be enforced. In order to understand how this question was resolved, some understanding of the history of the distinction between law and equity is needed.

7.4 The Division Between Law and Equity

Under the writ system used by the early common law, it will be recalled, a plaintiff had to fit his case within one of a limited number of forms of action for which writs were available. The variety of writs available, and consequently the jurisdiction of the king's courts, expanded until the late thirteenth century. Then, under pressure from the nobles, who were especially fearful of radical change in land law, the power to issue writs was circumscribed, the jurisdiction of the king's courts was limited, and the flexibility of the common law was diminished. Nevertheless, there was a residual power in the king and his council to do justice in special cases, and the king began to refer petitions for redress to the Chancellor who, as the chief law member of the council, might give relief as a matter of "grace" or of "conscience" in cases in which relief at law was inadequate.

From these beginnings there grew up a supplementary system, known as *equity*, in which by the early fifteenth century justice was administered through a separate court, the Court of Chancery. The law courts were forced to accept this system after a notorious struggle that ended in the early seventeenth century, when limits were placed on the Chancellor's power as the result of the efforts of Sir Edward Coke, chief justice of two of the courts of King James I.[13]

Among the distinctive features of a suit in equity as opposed to an action at law were the absence of a jury, a more flexible procedure, and a wider

13. Edward Coke (pronounced "Cook") (1552–1634) rose to Attorney General in 1593 after serving as Solicitor General and Speaker of the House of Commons. He came to hold a favorable position in the court of James I and became Chief Justice of the Common Pleas in 1606 and Chief Justice of the King's Bench in 1613. He championed the cause of the common law in its struggle against the encroachments of royal prerogatives, including equity jurisdiction. His bitter rival, Sir Francis Bacon, helped to engineer his dismissal in 1616; but Coke got himself back on the Privy Council, and in 1620 was again elected to Parliament, where he was a leader of the opposition to James I and Charles I.

scope of review on appeal. While the law courts were generally restricted to the award of money damages as relief, equity operated on the person of the defendant, and the court could, for example, issue an injunction, forbidding a particular breach of promise of an obligation, or it could decree specific performance, ordering performance of the obligation. A defendant who disobeyed could be punished by fine or imprisonment for contempt of court until compliance. But because these equitable remedies were considered to be extraordinary, they were only available when the remedy at law could be shown to be inadequate, and money damages remained the standard kind of relief.

A claim for breach of an obligation to pay money was an obvious example of a case in which the remedy at law was adequate. Money damages were also held to be adequate in most cases of breach of an obligation to deliver goods, since it was supposed that the obligee could purchase equivalent goods with the sum awarded. Specific performance was, however, allowed for breach of an obligation to convey land, since each piece of land was regarded as unique, so that even with money damages the obligee could not buy a substitute.[14]

How did the English law of contract—including both law and equity—take hold in the American colonies and how was it received in the newly independent states after the American Revolution?

7.5 Reception of English Law in the United States

Although the English settlers who came to the American colonies, beginning in the early seventeenth century, came from the common law tradition, English law was not unhesitatingly accepted in the colonies. Not all of the colonists were English; there were also pockets of Dutch, French, German, Irish, Scots, and Swedes. And even among the English settlers there were several impediments to the immediate acceptance of English law during the early colonial period.

One impediment was the dissatisfaction with some aspects of English justice on the part of many of the colonists who had migrated to the New World in order to escape from what they regarded as intolerable conditions in the mother country. This was particularly true for those who had come in search of religious, political, or economic freedom. A second and more significant impediment was the lack of trained lawyers, which continued

14. For further discussion of this, see § 4.19 infra.

to retard the development of American law throughout the seventeenth century. The difficult life in the colonies had little attraction for English lawyers. English law books were not readily available, and few among the early settlers had any legal training. A third impediment was the disparity of the conditions in the two lands. Particularly in the beginning, life was more primitive in the colonies, and familiar English institutions that were copied often produced rough copies at best. Indeed, the fact that equity found its way from England into most of the colonies was somewhat surprising in view of the close relationship that equity had to the king.[15] The early settlers did not carry English law in its entirety with them when they came, and the process by which it was absorbed in the face of these impediments was not a simple one.

The extent to which English case law, as distinguished from statute law, was in effect, either in theory or in practice, during the early history of the colonies is not free from dispute. It is clear that though the British Parliament had legislative power over the colonies, it was not fully exercised. Although acts passed prior to the initial settlement of a colony, if adapted to the circumstances, were generally regarded as being in force in that colony as well as in England, acts passed after initial settlement did not extend to the colonies unless expressly provided. Power to legislate had been conferred upon the colonies themselves, and each had its own legislature with at least one elective branch and with considerable control over internal affairs. Codification was common in the early stages of some of the colonies partly because of the absence of law books and the lack of a trained bar, and partly because of colonial notions of law reform. Colonial legislation was reviewed by administrative authorities in the mother country and might be set aside if it was "contrary" or "repugnant" to the laws or commercial policy of England. Colonial legislation was also subject to judicial review and might be held to be void when appeals from judgments of colonial courts were taken to England. But no systematic control was exercised until the end of the seventeenth century.

During the seventeenth century the justice that was administered was often lacking in technicalities and was sometimes based on a general sense of right as derived from the Bible and the law of nature. Court procedure, at least outside of the superior courts, was tailored to suit American needs and was marked by an informality of proceedings and a simplicity of pleadings befitting a less technical system in which the judges were, for the most part, untutored in the law. The model may have been the local

15. On the subsequent merger of law and equity, see § 5.3 infra.

courts in England which would have been familiar to many of the colonists. Substantive law, as well as procedure, began to respond to colonial needs. In England the feudal policy in favor of keeping estates in land intact had resulted in the rule of primogeniture, the exclusive right of the eldest son to inherit the land of the father. In America, however, this rule was rejected in favor of equal distribution among all children, subject to varying rights of a surviving spouse. This practice began in the northern colonies, was confirmed there by statute, and had spread southward by legislation to all of the states by the end of the eighteenth century.

The beginning of the eighteenth century saw considerable refinement of colonial law and a concurrent increase in the influence of English case law. Review of colonial legislation had become more thorough. With the growth of trade and the increase in population—to some three hundred thousand in 1700—the ranks of trained lawyers were swelled and the courts of review began to be manned by professionals. Some were English lawyers who had immigrated, while others were native lawyers who had studied in London or as apprentices in law offices in the colonies. English law books had become increasingly available and it has been said that by the time of the Revolution William Blackstone's[16] widely read *Commentaries on the Laws of England*, which first appeared between 1765 and 1769, had sold nearly as many copies in America as in England. Interest in English law was stimulated by the necessity of dealing in commercial matters with English merchants trained in its ways and by the desirability of reliance upon its principles to support the colonists' grievances against the Crown. By the time of the Revolution English law had come to be generally well regarded and each colony had a bar of trained, able, and respected professionals, capable of working with a refined and technical system. The colonial legal profession, especially in the cities, had achieved both social standing and economic success. It was also politically active: 25 of the 56 signers of the Declaration of Independence were lawyers.

It is therefore not surprising that most of the thirteen original states formally "received," that is adopted, by constitution or statute some part of the law of England along with their own colonial enactments. The

16. William Blackstone (1723–1780), an English barrister, began the first university lectures on the common law in England at Oxford in 1753. In 1758 he was appointed to the first professorship of English law at that university. He is remembered chiefly for his *Commentaries*, which went through eight editions in his lifetime.

formulas varied, but a typical reception provision might include that part of English law that "together did form the law of said colony" prior to such a specific date as 1607 or 1776. In other states the reception of English law was achieved by judicial decision alone. As additional states were carved out of the western territories, similar procedures were followed with regard to reception. While the details of the reception of English law differ considerably from state to state, it is clear that the changes and developments in English law after the date of reception for a particular state have no binding force at all in that state.

The Revolution resulted in a setback to the influence of English law in some of the new states because of political antipathy. In a few, anti-British sentiment was implemented by statutes prohibiting the citation of English decisions handed down after independence. A common toast of the time is said to have been: "The Common Law of England: may wholesome statutes soon root out this engine of oppression from America."

At the same time the quality of the practicing bar as a whole declined. Some lawyers, who had been loyalists, had left the country before the end of the war; others, seizing the opportunity for leadership, accepted political or judicial posts under the new government. The standards and repute of the remainder deteriorated in many communities. The era of the lay judge was not entirely over and during the early nineteenth century the state of Rhode Island had a farmer as chief justice and a blacksmith as a member of its highest court. There was not even an adequate body of American case law that could be used by those judges who had the ability and inclination to do so. Although reports of cases began to be published at the end of the eighteenth century, they were few in number. The opportunity for broadening the base of American law was considerable. There was some inclination to look to French and Roman law, and European writers were cited, particularly in the fields of commercial law and conflict of laws where English treatises were inadequate. But few judges were versed in modern foreign languages and, while English treatises and reports were available, the *Code Napoleon* did not appear until after the beginning of the nineteenth century. Blackstone's *Commentaries*, which had been published in an American edition in 1803, remained particularly influential.

During the first part of the nineteenth century, agriculture and trade dominated the economy as energies went into the westward expansion and the production of staples for European markets. Judges labored to shape English legal materials to fit the conditions of their particular jurisdictions. They examined the pre-Revolutionary English law to determine its applicability to American conditions and laid the foundations of such fields as contracts. Sometimes the law grew out of local usages or needs. The customs of western farmers and gold miners formed the basis for water and mining law in some of the western states. Some of the prairie states where cattle-raising was the means of livelihood and wood for fences was scarce, changed the English rule that the owner of cattle is liable without fault for damage that they may cause to a neighboring crop-owner. But it was also an era of great "national" treatises such as James Kent's[17] *Commentaries on American Law* published from 1826 to 1830, and nine works by Joseph Story[18] published from 1832 to 1845. These treatises, which went through many revisions, played an important role in promoting uniformity by helping to counter the forces which contributed to diversity.

These treatises, however, paid relatively little attention to the law of contract, for the development of the doctrine of consideration as a basis for enforcing promises did not of itself give contract law any special impetus. The growth of contract law was a slow growth during the seventeenth and eighteenth centuries. True, the seventeenth and eighteenth centuries saw such developments as the requirement of a writing for some kinds of contracts and the recognition of the transferability of contract rights as a kind of property—both of which will be discussed shortly. But it was not until the nineteenth century that the law of contract came into its own.

7.6 Contract in Nineteenth-Century America

In 1861 the Englishman Sir Henry Maine assured himself of immortality by declaring that "the movement of the progressive societies has hitherto

---

17. James Kent (1763–1847) became the first professor of law at Columbia College in 1793. He resigned in 1798 to go on the New York Supreme Court and was appointed Chancellor of the state in 1814. Upon his retirement in 1823 he returned to Columbia, and during this period he published his *Commentaries on American Law*, a collection of his lectures dealing with nearly all phases of contemporary substantive law.

18. Joseph Story (1779–1845) was appointed to the United States Supreme Court in 1811. In 1829, while retaining his seat on the Court, he became a professor of law at the Harvard Law School, where he reorganized the curriculum and revitalized the school. His nine commentaries developed from his lectures on subjects ranging from the Constitution to conflict of laws.

been a movement from Status to Contract."[19] In the nineteenth century, economic conditions in America led contract law to its apogee, as the legal underpinning of a dynamic and expanding free enterprise system. A modern legal historian concluded that in America the years from 1800 to 1875 were, "above all else, the years of contract."[20] Contract showed "energetic self-interest," and the law that governed it expressed "the nature of contract by insisting that men assert their interests, push them, and fight for them, if they were to have the help of the state."[21]

This period, interrupted by the Civil War, 1861–1865, saw a rapid increase in population and its concentration in the cities. It witnessed the growth of large scale industry, transportation, and communication, with attendant complexities in the corporate form of organization. From 1850 to 1860 the population of the state of Minnesota increased from 6,000 to 172,000. In 1790 only about three percent of the people in the United States lived in the six cities which had 8,000 or more inhabitants; by 1890 about one of three Americans lived in a city of 4,000 or more. From 1869 to 1900 railway mileage grew from 30,000 to 166,000 miles. In 1876 the first telephone message was sent and in 1883 Edison's electric power plant began operation in New York City.

It was generally supposed during this period that freedom of contract—freedom to make enforceable bargains—would encourage individual entrepreneurial activity. Lawmaking devoted much of its energy to creating the conditions for a market on which such bargains could be made. By the end of the century, the bargain theory of consideration had taken shape and the objective theory of contract was in its ascendency. "The market took on legal definition mainly in the law of contract, and quite naturally in the temper of the time the law of contract dominated the nineteenth century legal order."[22] From a utilitarian point of view, freedom to contract maximized the welfare of the parties and therefore the good of society as a whole. From a libertarian point of view, it accorded to individuals a sphere of influence in which they could act freely.

---

19. H. Maine, Ancient Law 170 (1861).
20. Hurst, Law and the Conditions of Freedom in the Nineteenth Century United States 18 (1956). See also L. Friedman, History of American Law 244 (1973)("The 19th century was the golden age of the law of contract. As late as Blackstone [1765], contract occupied only a tiny corner of the temple of common law, Blackstone devoted a whole volume to land law, but a few pages at most to informal, freely negotiated bargains.").
21. J. Hurst, Law and Economic Growth 301 (1964).
22. J. Hurst, supra note 3, at 285.

In this rapidly expanding industrial society the creation of a stable system of law took on increased importance. Development continued in such fields as corporations, public service companies, railroads, and insurance. But during the final quarter of the century much of the law of the formative era began to crystallize and the role of the judge became one of systematizing rather than of creating. As the volume of case law increased, the uncertainty that had been inevitable in earlier years became unpopular and efforts turned toward a search for predictability. The principal achievements of the courts were the ordering of the system and the logical development of details. It is significant that the treatises of this period were more specialized than those of the first half of the century. Some creative activity was to be found in the legislatures, which had been more active than the judiciary until the Civil War, but popular esteem for the courts was at its height and aggressive judges asserted their judicial authority in holding legislation to constitutional standards.

By the turn of the century, however, the methodical accretion of rules, case by case, had begun to lose some of its popular appeal. The watchword of the courts was still stability, but they had failed to keep pace with the demands of the rapidly changing political and economic order. The shape of things to come might have been foretold from the organization in 1886 of the American Federation of Labor, the first of the great national labor unions; from the creation in 1887 of the Interstate Commerce Commission, the first of the great national regulatory agencies; and from the enactment in 1890 of the Sherman Act, the first of the great federal antitrust statutes. And so the present century ushered in a new era of change and creativity in law, marked by an increased pace of legislation, particularly social legislation, and by greater reliance upon administrative agencies instead of courts. During the second decade of the twentieth century most of the state workers' compensation laws were enacted. At about the same time, modern administrative power began to take its present shape, both in the nation and in the states.

Although contract provided opportunities for the realization of human wants, it did not shape those wants. "The cautious sense that contract alone was not a sufficient organizing principle for society never quite deserted us."[23] With the advent of the twentieth century, the tide in favor of freedom of contract began to be reversed. A contracts scholar has characterized the individualism of our rules of contract law, epitomized in the notion of freedom of contract, as "closely tied up with the ethics of free enterprise capitalism and the ideals of justice of a mobile society of

23. J. Hurst, supra note 2, at 76.

small enterprisers, individual merchants and independent craftsmen." As competitive capitalism has drifted toward monopoly and the free enterprise system has declined, "the meaning of contract has changed radically."[24] It has been suggested that "the question is not so much one of status and contract as it is of a broader classification that embraces these concepts: standardized relations and individualized relations" and that in this sense there is now a "distinct veering back to status."[25]

The influence of English law in America had virtually ended by the time of the Civil War and is negligible today. Only infrequently are the more recent English cases cited in contemporary American judicial opinions and even more rarely will a question arise that turns on the reception of English law. Yet the fundamental approach, much of the vocabulary, and many of the principles and concepts of the common law are as familiar in the United States as in England. English cases, though in relatively small numbers, are still part of the "taught tradition" in American law schools. And while American lawyers and judges may commonly ignore English authorities, they are nevertheless conditioned by English ideas that were imported into American law over a century and a half ago.

Before we consider contemporary thinking about contracts in the United States, it will be useful to trace two representative developments from their beginning in English law, through their incorporation into American law, to their modification in nineteenth-century America. They are: first, the requirement of a writing for some kinds of contracts; and second, the recognition of the transfer of contract rights as a kind of property.

7.7 History of the Requirement of a Writing

It would be difficult to imagine a question more important to a person expecting to make agreements in an unfamiliar legal system than this: when is a writing required to make an agreement enforceable. The answer

24. Kessler, Contracts of Adhesion—Some Thoughts about Freedom of Contract, 43 Colum. L. Rev. 629, 640 (1943). Furthermore, as Fuller and Perdue point out, "The enormous growth of the corporation . . . has meant a further decrease in the importance of contract as an organizing force, since the corporation and vertical integration tend to substitute for an organization resting on contract one resting on the relation of superior and inferior." Fuller & Perdue, The Reliance Interest in Contract Damages (pt. 1), 46 Yale L.J. 52, n. 13 (1936).
25. Isaacs, The Standardizing of Contracts, 27 Yale L.J. 34, 39–40 (1917).

will determine both his insistence that the other party put the undertaking in writing and his own willingness to give unwritten assurances. This question of the necessity of a writing in order that an agreement be enforceable is governed in the United States by *statutes of frauds*, patterned after the English Statute of Frauds of more than three centuries ago.

With the development of the action of general assumpsit[26] by the beginning of the seventeenth century, informal contracts had become generally enforceable. In contrast to formal contracts, such as those under seal, informal contracts might be oral. However, the trial of an action based on an oral contract raised problems: parties were not permitted to testify, jurors might rely on their own knowledge of the facts, and judges had no effective mechanism to control arbitrary jury verdicts. These circumstances tempted plaintiffs to give false testimony, so that in 1677, to prohibit those "many fraudulent practices, which are commonly endeavoured to be upheld by perjury and subornation of perjury,"[27] Parliament enacted "An Act for Prevention of Frauds and Perjuries,"[28] commonly known as the Statute of Frauds.

Section 4 of the act listed five classes of contracts on which "no action shall be brought . . . unless the agreement . . ., or some memorandum or note thereof, shall be in writing, and signed by the party to be charged therewith, or some other person . . . by him lawfully authorized." Included were contracts: (1) "to charge any executor or administrator upon any special promise to answer damages out of his own estate" (the executor-administrator provision); (2) "to charge the defendant upon any special promise to answer for the debt, default or miscarriages of another person" (the suretyship provision); (3) "to charge any person upon any agreement made upon consideration of marriage" (the marriage provision); (4) for the "sale of lands . . . or any interest in or concerning them"

---

26. The development of the action of general assumpsit is discussed in § 2.3 supra. On formal contracts, see § 2.2 supra, text following note 5.

27. These words are from the introductory clause. It is also said that "the confusion attending the rapid succession of Civil War, Cromwellian dictatorship and Restoration had encouraged unscrupulous litigants to pursue false or groundless claims with the help of manufactured evidence." G. Cheshire & C. Fifoot, Law of Contract 175 (9th ed. 1976).

28. Stat. 29 Car. 2, c.3. The Statute attempted to prevent fraud in the proof of many different kinds of transactions. It dealt with such matters as deeds, wills, trusts in land, and leaseholds in addition to contracts, but it is remembered for its provisions on contracts.

(the land contract provision); (5) "not to be performed within the space of one year from the making thereof" (the one-year provision). Section 17 contained special provisions applicable to contracts in a sixth class, those for the sale of goods (the sale of goods provision).

The Statute of Frauds was not part of the English common law that was received in the United States, but virtually all states have enacted their own versions of the Statute. Most of the American statutes of frauds impose, in varying formulations, writing requirements for all six of the classes of contracts that were covered by the English Statute and often add other classes as well.

In 1954, after 277 years, Parliament repealed most of the Statute of Frauds.[29] Only the suretyship provision and the land contract provision were retained. Among the reasons given by the English Law Reform Committee for repeal were these: the classes of contracts within the Statute "seem to be arbitrarily selected and to exhibit no relevant common quality"; the requirement of a writing is "out of accord with the way in which business is normally done" and "promotes more frauds than it prevents"; and the Statute was the product of a time when "essential kinds of evidence were excluded (e.g., the parties themselves could not give evidence), and objectionable types of evidence were admitted (e.g., juries were still in theory entitled to act on their own knowledge of the facts in dispute)" and has become "an anachronism" now that the parties can freely testify.[30]

There has been no serious movement to abolish the statutes of frauds in this country, though they have had many critics. During the period when England was moving to abolish most of its Statute, including the sale of goods provision, the drafters of the Uniform Commercial Code were deciding to retain that part of the statute, though in a less rigorous form. The different attitude toward the Statute in England may reflect differences in trial practice. In England, trial by jury in contract actions is within the discretion of the judge, which makes it possible to keep from the jury cases formerly within the Statute. Furthermore, in England counsel fees are included in the costs assessed against the losing party, which made it more likely that the technicalities and uncertainties of the Statute would discourage litigants from suing on otherwise meritorious claims.

---

29. Law Reform (Enforcement of Contracts) Act, 1954, 2 & 3 Eliz. 2, c.34.
30. Report of the (English) Law Revision Committee on the Statute of Frauds and the Doctrine of Consideration 6–7 (Sixth Interim Report, Cmd. 5449, 1937).

During its long life, the statute has occasioned an enormous amount of litigation.[31] Critics, however, are divided on how well it has served its purposes. One English jurist believed that the statute "promotes fraud rather than prevents it,"[32] and another thought that had it "been always carried into execution according to the letter, it would have done ten times more mischief than it has done good, by protecting, rather than by preventing, frauds."[33] An American critic agreed that the statute's provisions "are no longer preventing fraud, if they ever did, but rather are a cause of fraud."[34] On the other side, it has been argued that "after two centuries and a half the statute stands, in essence better adapted to our needs than when it first was passed."[35] Another observer suggested that the statute was justified by "the thousands of uncontested current transactions where misunderstanding and controversy are avoided by the presence of a writing which the statute at least indirectly aided to procure."[36] After three centuries, the statute still receives mixed reviews.

Attempts at justifying the statute of frauds in the United States stress the functions of a formality such as a writing. Such a formality may perform an *evidentiary* function, a *cautionary* function, and a *channeling* function.[37] It performs an evidentiary function by providing some proof of the fact that the promisor made the alleged promise. It performs a cautionary function by bringing home to the promisor the significance of his act and

---

31. Corbin and Williston each devote the equivalent of a volume to the statute. See 2 A. Corbin, Contracts (1950); 3 & 4 S. Williston, Contracts (3d ed. 1960, 1961).
32. Marvin v. Wallis, 6 El. & Bl. 726, 736, 119 Eng. Rep. 1035, 1038 (1956).
33. Simon v. Metivier, 1 Black. W. 599, 601, 96 Eng. Rep. 347, 348 (1766). But see Chaplin v. Rogers, 1 East 192, 194, 102 Eng. Rep. 75, 76 (1800)("One of the wisest laws in our Statute Books"). Lord Notingham, one of those responsible for the Statute, claimed that "every line was worth a subsidy." R. North, The Life of the Right Honourable Francis North 109 (1742). A learned lawyer replied, nearly two centuries later, that "every line has *cost* a subsidy." J.W. Smith, Lectures on the Law of Contract 29 (1847).
34. Willis, The Statute of Frauds—A Legal Anachronism (pt. 2), 3 Ind. L.J. 528, 541 (1928).
35. Llewellyn, What Price Contract?—An Essay in Perspective, 40 Yale L.J. 704, 747 (1931).
36. Vold, The Application of the Statute of Frauds under the Uniform Sales Act, 15 Minn. L. Rev. 391, 394 (1931).
37. See Fuller, Consideration and Form, 41 Colum. L. Rev. 799, 800–806 (1941).

preventing ill-considered and impulsive promises. It performs a channeling function by furnishing a simple test of enforceability to mark off enforceable agreements from unforceable ones. It is noteworthy that the more durable and well-regarded of the statute's provisions are those, such as the suretyship and land contract provisions, that fulfill more than just the evidentiary function.[38]

The sale-of-goods provision has always been regarded as distinct from the other provisions of the statute of frauds. In the English Statute it was set out in a separate section. Furthermore, all of its various versions have been unique in expressly permitting satisfaction not only by a memorandum but by part performance as well.

Although the sale of goods provision of the English Statute has been repealed, the drafters of the Uniform Commercial Code concluded that the provision should be retained in the United States because "the spread of literacy, the rise of metropolitan living, the drive toward internal records, and the Code's removal of those unwise interpretations which so largely influenced the English decision, leave reasonable room for some statute of frauds in the sales areas."[39] The present version of the provision is contained in Section 2-201 of the Uniform Commercial Code, which applies to contracts "for the sale of goods for the price of $500 or more."

UCC 2-201 applies to both a contract under which ownership of goods passes immediately to the buyer and also to a contract under which ownership is to pass at some future time. It applies regardless of whether the goods are in existence at the time the contract is made. If the contract is a mixed one, involving the sale of both goods and services, a court will classify the contract according to the dominant element as one for goods, falling within the provision, or as one for services, not falling within the provision.

Although the statute of frauds is not likely to be repealed in the United States, it has been the subject of constant erosion. Courts have long been receptive to pleas that the statute should be narrowly interpreted so as not to apply to the contract in question, and, if the statute does apply to the contract, an informal writing bearing only initials will satisfy it. Courts

38. suretyship provision performs a cautionary function in addition to an evidentiary function, warning the prospective surety of the seriousness of his promise. The land contract provision performs a channeling function in addition to an evidentiary one, furnishing a simple test to mark off unenforceable agreements from enforceable ones.

39. Supp. No. 1 to the 1952 Official Draft of Text and Comments of the Uniform Commercial Code 98 (1955).

have recently begun to entertain the argument that, even if the statute covers the contract in question, the claimant's reliance on the contract dispenses with the requirement of a writing.[40] This process of erosion promises to continue in the future.

7.8 History of the Transferability of Contract Rights

Today, in the United States, most contract rights are freely transferable. Were the law otherwise, the modern American credit economy could not exist.[41] Consider a seller who assigns his right to the price of goods that he has sold on credit. He might occasionally have the means to grant credit, even if he could not transfer the resulting right to future payment, but he would have to rely on his own resources to do so. Once his right to future payment becomes transferable, however, he can enlist the resources of a financial institution, either by selling to it his right to future payment in return for a price payable immediately, or by transferring to it that right as security for a loan. In effect, the financial institution, not the seller, gives the buyer credit. If the seller's right to payment were not transferable to the financial institution, the buyer would have little chance to buy from the seller on credit.[42]

It may therefore seem surprising that the common law began with the rule that many intangible rights, including contract rights, were not transferable. A rule that a debt was "personal" to the creditor was defensible in a society where sanctions against a defaulting debtor were severe and credit played only a minor role. For the atypical situation in which the transfer of choses in action was important to facilitate credit, special commercial courts were available. As long as common law recognition of the transfer of contract rights served no apparent function, common law

---

40. See Restatement (Second) of Contracts § 139.

41. See 1 H. Macleod, Principles of Economical Philosophy 481 (2d ed. 1872)("If we were asked—Who made the discovery which has most deeply affected the fortunes of the human race? We think, after full consideration, we might safely answer—the man who first discovered that a Debt is a Saleable Commodity.").

42. Of course, the buyer may be able to get a loan directly from a financing institution and pay the seller with the proceeds of the loan. Such a direct loan is an alternative to the transaction described in the text.

judges inevitably viewed such transfers with suspicion.[43] An attempted assignment of a contract right came to be regarded as maintenance—as tending to encourage litigation—much as an attempted assignment of a claim for slander or some other tort is still viewed. In Lord Coke's opinion, to allow the assignment of contract rights "would be the occasion of multiplying contentions and suits."[44]

But by the start of the seventeenth century, when the action of general assumpsit had fully developed, the common law courts had made a first grudging concession to the growing importance of credit. Although an assignor's (B's) attempt to assign to an assignee (C) a contract right that he held against an obligor (A) was still not effective as an assignment, the courts viewed it as giving the assignee (C) a power of attorney to sue the obligor (A) in the name of the assignor (B). At first this concession was made only if the assignor's (B's) purported assignment was to pay a debt that he owed the assignee (C). If the assignor (B) simply sold his claim to the assignee (C), this was still considered maintenance until the end of the seventeenth century, when the courts finally allowed the assignee (C) to sue in the assignor's (B's) name. However, the assignee's (C's) right was a fragile one, since the assignor's (B's) revocation, death, or bankruptcy would destroy it. These infirmities were eliminated at law largely through the competition of equity.[45]

---

43. It has also been suggested that the common-law mind had difficulty in abstractions and could not conceive of the transfer of an intangible contract right from one person to another. However, it has been argued that "the incapacity of early lawyers to corporealize the incorporeal has been greatly over-stressed by modern writers. Medieval lawyers were perfectly capable of visualizing ownership of disembodied interests—ownership of an office, the right to appoint a person to a particular church, rights to labor [or] services in homes or in fields, rights to be paid annuities, to collect tolls from passerby, or to occupy a front seat at the king's coronation." J. Dawson, W. Harvey, & S. Henderson, Cases and Comment on Contracts 908 (4th ed. 1982).

44. Lampet's Case, 10 Coke's Rep. 46b, 48a, 77 Eng. Rep. 994 (K.B. 1613). See J. Dawson, W. Harvey, & S. Henderson, supra note 3, at 909 ("[O]ne must imagine a society in which central governments were weak and power was dispersed through an aristocracy that was often turbulent. The favor and support of great men and their armed retainers were much sought after, especially by those who quarrelled with their neighbors. Maintenance . . . was a constant threat to the administration of justice, especially during the civil wars of the fifteenth century.").

45. Another factor was the absorption into the common law of the rules of the law merchant during the seventeenth century. The law merchant recognized free transferability of contract rights that were embodied in bills of exchange. Such

During the seventeenth century, assignees began to forsake the courts of common law for chancery in their efforts to enforce their claims. Chancery did not share the antipathy of the common law courts toward assignment and afforded the assignee broad protection, treating him as the owner of the claim, not merely as the assignor's agent. Thus, in equity, the right of an assignee who had given value was not defeated by the assignor's revocation, death, or bankruptcy. The common law judges were not insensitive to this threat to their business. Near the end of the eighteenth century, the Court of King's Bench held that an assignee whose assignor had become bankrupt was entitled to the assigned right as against his assignor's trustees in bankruptcy. One of the judges wryly observed that it had "been found productive of great expense to send the parties to the other side of the hall," meaning to chancery, and concluded that while it was "certainly true that a chose in action cannot strictly be assigned," the common law courts could nevertheless "take notice" of the assignee's right in equity by according him the same rights that he would have if he had gone "to the other side of the Hall."[46] Henceforth, the common law courts too would treat him as the owner of the claim though, true to the rhetoric of this decision, he would have to observe the formality of suing in the name of assignor.

The American states received the English law of assignments as part of the common law. Included were both seventeenth-century precedents, making it a mere formality. The anachronistic requirement that the assignor sue in the name of the assignee was finally abolished in most states in the nineteenth century in connection with procedural reforms. Statutes or rules of court directed against the institution of nominal or fictitious plaintiffs required that suits be brought in the name of the "real party in interest." The triumph of free assignability was complete.

The most recent major development in the law of assignments came with the enactment of the Uniform Commercial Code. The impact of the Code on the law of assignments is much greater than might at first be supposed, because rules on assignment are not limited to Article 2, which

developments made it increasingly awkward for the common law courts to maintain that an ordinary contract right, especially a right to money, was not transferable.

46. Term. Rep. at 622–623, 99 Eng. Rep. at 1286. See 1 G. Gilmore, Security Interests in Personal Property § 7.3 (1965) ("by the typically muddle-headed process of thinking known as the genius of the common law, assignments of intangibles were made effective in fact while basic theory still proclaimed them to be legal impossibilities").

applies only to the sale of goods, but are also found in Article 9. Though Article 9 is concerned primarily with secured transactions, it governs many outright sales of contract rights as well.[47] It applies generally to transfers for value of *accounts*, a term that refers broadly to most rights "to payment for goods sold or leased or for services rendered . . . whether or not . . . earned by performance."[48]

However, Article 9 applies only to the transfer of rights to payment and not to the transfer of rights to goods or services. It does not apply at all to the transfer of rights arising out of contracts for the sale of land. In addition, a few kinds of assignments are excluded from the scope of Article 9 and left to the common law and perhaps to other statutes.[49] Despite these exceptions, the Code leaves relatively little to the common law, and even there it can be expected to have an impact by analogy. Some of the most important types of transactions that are made possible because of the assignability of contract rights are suggested by the following illustrations.

The first situation is that of a retailer who sells to consumers on credit. If the retailer (B) has sold a $1,000 stereo on credit to a consumer (A), the retailer (B) may need cash to finance his business until he has been paid. He may therefore assign his right to payment to a financial institution (C) (usually a bank or finance company) in return for the immediate payment by it of $1,000, less a discount to compensate the financial institution for the loss of the use of the $1,000 until it can collect the money from the consumer (A). The financial institution (C) will then own the right that the retailer (B) previously had against the consumer (A) and will collect the $1,000 from him.

The second situation is that of a wholesaler who sells to retailers on credit. If the wholesaler (B) has sold $10,000 worth of carpets on credit to a retailer (A), the wholesaler (B) may need cash to finance his business until he has been paid. He may therefore assign his right to payment by the retailer (A), which is known as an *account receivable*, to a financial institution (C) (again, usually a bank or finance company). However, in contrast to the situation just described, in which a retailer assigns a

---

47. UCC 9–102 (with stated exceptions, "this Article applies . . . to any sale of accounts").

48. UCC 9–106.

49. Examples are assignments of wage claims, excluded by UCC 9–104(d), assignments of bank deposits, excluded by UCC 9–104(1), and assignments of rights under insurance policies, excluded by UCC 9–104(g).

consumer debt, the wholesaler (B) engages in what is known as *accounts receivable financing* and assigns his accounts in bulk, rather than individually, so that the total of all accounts assigned might be, say, $1,000,000. Furthermore, he does not assign them outright but only as security for a loan for, say, $800,000 (somewhat less than the value of the collateral). In what is called *non-notification financing*, it is understood that the wholesaler (B), not the financial institution (C), will collect from the retailer (A) and that the wholesaler (B) will repay the loan out of the proceeds when the retailer has paid him for the goods. The financial institution's (C's) compensation is the interest on the secured loan.

The third situation is that of the builder who makes construction contracts. If the builder (B) has contracted with an owner (A) to build a building for $10,000,000, payable as the work progresses, he may need funds immediately to begin work. He may therefore assign his right to payment from the owner (A) to a financial institution (C) (usually a bank) in return for a loan to help finance the construction. Here, in contrast to the wholesaler's account receivable in the situation just described, the builder's (B's) right to payment has not yet been earned, since it is constructively conditioned on his performance of the contract. As he performs and the progress payments become due, he collects them and repays the loan.

The fourth and most complex situation is that of an owner of a business that furnishes goods or services to other businesses. If the owner (B) wants to sell his business to a buyer (C) as a going concern, the parties may also plan to transfer long-term contracts with, say, a supplier (A) and a customer (A'). With respect to both the supplier (A) and the customer (A'), such a transfer involves not only assignment but delegation. The seller (B) wants both to assign to the buyer (C) his rights against both the supplier (A) and the customer (A'), and also to delegate to the buyer (C) the performances that he owes to both of them. There are, therefore, two significant problems not present in the three earlier situations. The first is that, with respect to his supplier (A), the right that the seller (B) wishes to assign is a right to a performance other than the payment of money. The second is that, with respect to both his supplier (A) and his customer (A'), the seller (B) wishes not only to assign his rights but also to delegate performance of his duties, the duty of paying the supplier (A) for what he supplies and the duty of furnishing his customer (A') with goods or services. If the seller (B) can overcome these problems and transfer these contracts, the buyer (C) will have both a right to be supplied by the supplier (A) in return for paying him and a right to be paid by the customer (A') in return for furnishing him goods or services.

7.9 Contemporary Thinking about Contracts

As we have seen,[50] eighteenth and early nineteenth century treatises on law, such as those of Blackstone, Kent, and Story, paid relatively little attention to the law of contracts. It was not until the middle of the nineteenth century that contract law began to be regarded as a subject worthy of the serious attention of American treatise writers.[51] The first treatises, however, tended to place little emphasis on general principles of contract law and concentrated instead on specific categories of contracts, such as those of agents, or brokers, and those for the sale of land or personal property.

This began to change at the end of the nineteenth century, when a revolutionary new method of instruction began to be introduced in American law schools. Instead of lecturing to a passive audience, professors began to question their students, by what came to be called "Socratic method," about cases that the students were required to read before class. This method of instruction was introduced by Christopher Columbus Langdell[52] through the publication in 1871 of his casebook on contracts. Langdell expected that by this method of examining cases his students would learn the general principles of the law of contracts "considered as a science."[53] The same period saw the publication in 1881 by Oliver Wendell Holmes,[54] one of America's most eminent judges, of a series of lectures called *The Common Law*, which contained an influential discussion of general principles of contract law.

---

50. See § 2.5 supra.
51. See, e.g., T. Parsons, The Law of Contracts (1853); W. Story, A Treatise on the Law of Contracts Not Under Seal (1844).
52. Christopher Columbus Langdell (1826–1906) was a New York lawyer who became professor of law at Harvard Law School in 1870. His principal achievement as professor and later dean was the introduction of the case method of instruction. He believed that instruction should be of such a character that the students "might at least derive a greater advantage from attending it than from devoting the time to private study."
53. Preface to Langdell's 1871 edition.
54. Oliver Wendell Holmes (1841–1935) practiced law in Boston, served briefly as professor of law at Harvard, and then for 20 years was Justice and later Chief Justice of the Supreme Judicial Court of Massachusetts. In 1902 he was appointed an Associate Justice of the United States Supreme Court, where the quality of his dissenting opinions won him the title "the Great Dissenter." He resigned because of age in 1932. His most famous work is The Common Law (1881), based on a series of lectures. His judicial opinions and other writings did much to shape the law of contracts at the turn of the century.

This process of generalization came to a climax in 1920 when Samuel W. Williston[55] published his *Treatise on the Law of Contracts*, in which he sought "to treat the subject of contracts as a whole, and to show the wide range of application of its principles."[56] Williston's later service as Reporter for the first Restatement of Contracts gave additional support to his views.

Williston and other traditionalists viewed contract law as composed of a relatively small number of rules that could be extracted from the cases in which judges had applied them. The process by which a legal scholar found the law in cases was thought of as similar to the process by which a scientist discovers a law of nature. Not all contracts scholars shared Williston's emphasis on doctrine, however. Arthur Linton Corbin,[57] the other giant in the field of contract law, studied cases not so much for their doctrinal statements but for their essential facts, from which the great variety of applications of contract law could be seen.

In the 1920's and 1930's the assumptions of the traditionalists such as Williston were challenged by a group of academics who came to be known as "legal realists."[58] This peculiarly American movement took the view that legal rules bore no resemblance to laws of the natural sciences. The realists viewed with great skepticism the case law on which the traditionalists based their analysis. The judicial opinions that remained the staple of law teaching and scholarship were to be read as efforts by the judge who wrote the opinion to put the action of the court in the most favorable light possible. Language, on which lawyers and judges depend for communication, was regarded as an imperfect medium. And lawyers and judges themselves were seen to have human failings in understanding as well as in communication. Coupled with this skepticism of the legal

55. Samuel W. Williston (1861–1963) joined the faculty of Harvard Law School in 1890, after practicing law for a short period in Boston, and taught there until his retirement in 1938. His principal fields were contracts and sales. He was the drafter of several uniform acts, including the Uniform Sales Act, the predecessor of the sales article of the Uniform Commercial Code, and was Reporter for the Restatement of Contracts. His treatise on contracts is a classic.

56. Preface to Williston's 1920 edition.

57. Arthur Linton Corbin (1874–1967) practiced law in Colorado for four years after his graduation from law school in 1899. He taught law, notably contracts, at the Yale Law School from 1903 until his retirement in 1943. He was Special Adviser and Reporter for the Chapter on Remedies of the Restatement of Contracts. His treatise on contracts is, like Williston's, a classic.

58. See generally W. Twining, Karl Llewellyn and the Realist Movement (1973); Schlegel, American Legal Realism and Empirical Social Science: From the Yale Experience, 28 Buffalo L. Rev. 459 (1979).

profession was a new faith that help could be had from other disciplines. While the traditionalists had found an analogy in the natural sciences, the legal realists saw an even more direct connection to the social sciences, notably economics and sociology.

The direct achievements of the legal realists were disappointing. They mounted a number of empirical studies, for example, that had little or no effect on the legal system. But because the legal realists were based in the law schools, they succeeded in working a profound transformation of the way that American lawyers and judges think about law. Much of the skepticism of the legal realists is widely shared by the American legal profession today. In the field of contracts, the impact of the legal realists is particularly evident in the work of Karl N. Llewellyn,[59] a follower of Corbin and the principal architect of the Uniform Commercial Code.

In the last decade, few if any fields of American law have attracted as much interest and produced as much ferment as contract law. Contemporary contracts scholars have been attracted—as the legal realists were—by the relation between contract law and other disciplines. They have looked to history and argued that it was not until the late eighteenth and early nineteenth centuries that the spread of markets forced jurists to attack "ancient precepts of morality and equity" as inimical to modern contract principles.[60] They have looked to sociology and concluded, on the basis of a study of the use of standard forms by businesses, that businesses have relatively little concern in planning their transactions so as to result in legally enforceable contracts.[61] They have looked to philosophy and posited that contract law is rooted in right and wrong and so is "a ramifying system of moral judgments working out the entailments of a few primitive principles" that are "the laws of freedom."[62] But most often they have looked to economics.

---

59. Karl Nickerson Llewellyn (1893–1962) practiced law in New York for two years and taught law at Yale for several years before becoming a member of the law faculty at Columbia in 1925. He remained there until 1951, when he joined the law faculty in Chicago. He was well known for his contributions to the field of jurisprudence, as a leader of the school of "legal realists," as well as to the fields of contracts and commercial law. Soia Mentschikoff, Llewellyn's wife, served as Associate Chief Reporter of the Code.

60. Horwitz, The Historical Foundations of Modern Contract Law, 87 Harv. L. Rev. 917, 956 (1974).

61. Macaulay, Non-Contractual Relations in Business: A Preliminary Study, 28 American Sociological Rev. 55 (1963).

62. C. Fried, Contract as Promise 132 (1981). For another philosophical treatment of contract law, see Kronman, Contract Law and Distributive Justice, 89 Yale L.J. 472 (1980). See also I. Macneil, The New Social Contract (1980).

Economic analysis of contract law has arrived at some conclusions that might startle the uninitiated. Suppose that a party, after having made a contract, discovers that it is less advantageous to him than he had supposed and considers breaking it. To what extent, if at all, should the law attempt to discourage him from doing so?

From a competitive or free enterprise model, the economist has derived a set of decisional rules to enable individual economic units to make optimal allocations of their own resources. Economists have also derived a set of normative rules to guide society in the allocation of its resources. The economist's goal in formulating normative rules is that of "efficiency." The allocation of resources in a society is considered to be "efficient" if no alteration in that allocation will make some economic unit better off without making some other unit worse off. (Such an allocation is often called "Pareto optimal," after the noted economist Vilfredo Pareto.) In order to determine whether a unit is "better" or "worse" off, however, account must be taken of the preferences of that unit. The determination of these preferences is not a task for the economist. But given a set of individual preferences, the normative rules formulated by the economist will help society to achieve an efficient allocation of its resources in terms of those preferences.

Furthermore, the economist insists that, for the good of society, its resources be allocated efficiently at every point in time. It is therefore in the interest of society that each economic unit shift its resources whenever this would lead to an efficient allocation. But what if that unit is bound by a contract not to shift its resources? Should it break the contract and reallocate them?

The answer for each party to a contract is, of course, affected not only by his preferences but by the legal consequences that would follow from a breach of contract. (For present purposes, we will assume, somewhat unrealistically, that available legal remedies are always exacted and that they are the only sanctions for breach.) The law could, for example, provide such a large measure of recovery for breach that reallocation through breach would seldom be advantageous to a party. Or it could provide such a small measure of recovery that reallocation through breach would usually be advantageous to him. Normative economics suggests, however, that the measure of recovery should be the diminution in value to the injured party. Why?

Lowering the measure of recovery below the diminution in value caused him by the breach would not put him at the same level of satisfaction of his preferences that he expected and would fail to protect his expectations and preserve his planned allocation of resources. Raising the measure of damages above this level would discourage the breaking of contracts when society would want them broken and impair the efficient allocation of its resources. For it is in society's interest that each individual reallocate his resources whenever it makes him better off without making some other unit worse off. Since reallocation through breach will not make the injured party worse off if his expectations are protected by preserving his planned allocation of resources, and will, by hypothesis, make the party in breach better off, it is in society's interest that the contract be broken and the resources reallocated.

To take a concrete example, suppose that a seller contracts to sell goods to a buyer for $100. If the seller then finds a second buyer who is willing to pay $110 for the goods, it will be efficient for the seller to break the contract and sell the goods to the second buyer, as long as the original buyer's damages based on his expectation are less than the $10 additional that the second buyer is willing to pay.[63]

An answer to this reasoning can be made if it is assumed that there are no transaction costs, that is, that it costs nothing to perform such tasks as acquiring information and negotiating. On this assumption, even if the law gave the original buyer a right to specific performance of the contract, that buyer and the seller would, without cost, negotiate a release from the contract so that the seller could sell the goods to the second buyer. And even if the contract were performed and the goods delivered to the original buyer, that buyer would, without cost, locate the second buyer and sell the goods to him. In either case, the goods would end up in the hands of the second buyer, who valued them more than the original buyer, and this would be the efficient result.[64] (It is important to understand that the economist is not concerned, as such, with the question of how the $10 is divided between the seller and the original buyer.) In actuality, however, transaction costs are not zero, and any realistic analysis of contract problems in terms of economics must take account of such costs, as recent examples of law and economics analysis attempt to do.[65]

---

63. See M. Polinsky, An Introduction to Law and Economics ch. 5 (1983); R. Posner, Economic Analysis of Law ch. 4 (2d ed. 1977).

64. This is the result of the Coase theorem, elaborated in Coase, The Problem of Social Cost, 3 J.L. & Econ. 1 (1960).

65. See M. Polinsky, supra note 14, ch. 8; Macneil, Efficient Breach of Contract: Circles in the Sky, 68 Va. L. Rev. 947 (1982).

Chapter 8

Sources of Contract Law

8.1 Sources in General

Contract law in the United States is largely case law rather than statute law. It is traditionally derived primarily from the published opinions of courts. Published opinions include state appellate courts and federal trial as well as appellate courts.

The legal effect of these cases is governed by the common law doctrine of precedent or *stare decisis* (from the Latin *stare decisis et non quieta movere*—to stand by the decisions and not disturb settled points). The essence of the doctrine is that each decided case establishes a precedent so that a like case arising in the future is to be decided in the same way. The first case is often said to be "binding" on the court that hears the later case.

The doctrine of precedent developed early in English law and was received in the United States as part of the tradition of the common law. As a tradition, it has not been reduced to a written rule.

The justifications commonly given for the doctrine may be summarized in four words: equality, predictability, economy, and respect. The first argument is that the application of the same rule to successive similar cases results in equality of treatment for all who come before the courts. The second is that consistent following of precedents contributes to predictability in future disputes. The third is that the use of established criteria to settle new cases saves time and energy. The fourth is that adherence to earlier decisions shows due respect for the wisdom and experience of prior generations of judges.

For several reasons the doctrine of precedent has never enjoyed in the United States the absolute authority that it attained in England. The great volume of decisions, with conflicting precedents in different jurisdictions, has detracted from the authority of individual decisions. The rapidity of change has often weakened the applicability of precedents to later cases that have arisen after social and economic conditions have changed with the passage of years. Nevertheless the doctrine of precedent, though less rigidly applied then in England, is still firmly established in the United States.

The doctrine only operates, however, within a single jurisdiction. Cases from the highest court of one state are precedents in that court and in lower courts of the same state. However, they are not precedents in the courts of another state. If the jurisdiction of a federal court is based on the circumstance that the two parties come from different states, the federal court must apply the law of whatever state a state court located in the same place as the federal court would apply.[1] This means that cases decided in the courts of the state whose law applies are precedents in the federal court.

A case that is not a precedent because it is from another jurisdiction may nevertheless be "persuasive" although not "binding." Thus in contract cases American courts frequently cite cases from other states. English cases, often from the nineteenth century, are also occasionally cited.

Although contract law remains primarily case law, an increasing number of statutes, both state and federal, deal with particular problems. Thus the Uniform Commercial Code, enacted by virtually all the states, contains important provisions dealing with contracts for the sale of goods. State and federal statutes regulate many aspects of contracts involving consumers. And by another federal statute, the Tucker Act, the federal government has waived its sovereign immunity in contract actions by consenting to suit in the federal courts. To the extent that such statutes apply, they are binding on courts and supercede case law.

Administrative regulations play a relatively minor role in contract law. There are, however, a few exceptional kinds of contracts for which administrative regulations have great importance—notably contracts of insurance and contracts between private parties and the government.

Contract law is largely a matter of state rather than federal law. Although Congress has the power to enact legislation concerning interstate commerce, it has been reluctant to exercise this power in this sphere of

1. This the rule of Erie v. Tompkins, 304 U.S. 64 (1938), for cases in which the federal courts have jurisdiction based on diversity of citizenship.

private law. Nevertheless there is considerable uniformity among the states in contract law.

Where case law is still dominant, uniformity has been furthered by the influence of treatises and of the Restatements of Contracts produced by the American Law Institute, a private organization. These sources, though persuasive only, have had a considerable impact on contract law. Where uniform legislation has been thought desirable, it has generally been prepared by the National Conference of Commissioners on Uniform State Laws, a body that has the power to draft and recommend legislation to the individual states but no power to enact it. Its most important achievement has been the Uniform Commercial Code.

We turn now to treatises and the Restatement and to the Uniform Commercial Code as sources of contract law.

8.2 Treatises and the Restatement

Contract law in England developed much later than did property law. Contract law in the United States did not become the subject of important treatises until the nineteenth century. Contracts scholars then struggled to fashion an orderly body of doctrine from the great amount of new case law. By the middle of the twentieth century, however, the subject of contract law had been blessed by the publication of two of the most influential treatises to appear in any field of American law, first that of Samuel W. Williston[2] and later that of Arthur L. Corbin.[3]

Nineteenth-century treatises had devoted considerable attention to specific types of contracts, such as insurance, but had treated many of them as outside the scope of general contract law. When Williston published his first edition in 1920, he criticized the tendency to exclude such contracts and sought to "treat the subject of contracts as a whole, and to show the wide range of application of its principles." Contracts scholars, seeking organizing principles in their field, thus came to focus their attention on general principles common to most contracts, rather than on aspects peculiar to a few.

Moreover, since the creative forces of contract law had traditionally been judicial rather than legislative, scholars tended to regard contract law as essentially case law and to seek these general principles in judicial decisions. In the accepted division of labor between judges and legislators,

2. S. Williston, Treatise on the Law of Contracts (1st Ed. 1920).
3. A. Corbin, Corbin on Contracts (1950–1960) (in 13 volumes).

the former were seen as responsible for the declaration of general principles and the latter as responsible for specialized exceptions. It was not entirely by accident that the first of the casebooks that were to revolutionize the method of teaching law was one on contracts.[4]

This emphasis on case law was reinforced by the American Law Institute. Formed in 1923 with a select membership of practitioners, judges, and law professors (now grown to over 1500), the Institute undertook to reduce the mass of case law to a body of readily accessible rules in the form of a Restatement of the Law, made up of nine subjects. Contracts was one of the first subjects on which the Institute began work, and the Restatement of Contracts was completed in 1932. Williston acted as Reporter, with responsibility for preparing drafts. Corbin served as Special Adviser and Reporter for the chapter on Remedies. Other experts in the subject were formed into a Committee of Advisers, who conferred with the Reporter in producing drafts for submission to the Council of the Institute. These drafts, after discussion and revision by the Council, were then submitted as tentative drafts to the annual meetings of the Institute. Publication required approval of the text by both the Council and a meeting of Institute members. The textual ("black-letter") statements of general principles are accompanied by comments and illustrations. An initial plan for supplementing the Restatement by treatises citing and discussing case authority was dropped when experience proved that group production of such volumes was not feasible. The original Restatement of Contracts is characterized by what has been described as a "staccato" style,[5] which seemed suitable when its authors thought that it would be orchestrated by accompanying treatises.

In 1952, the American Law Institute began the process of revising the Restatement to produce a Restatement Second, and in 1962 it started such a revision of the Restatement of Contracts.[6] The Restatement Second of Contracts was published in 1981. Its major changes in substance include an increased recognition of a party's reliance on the contract and the introduction of a number of innovations by analogy to the Uniform Commercial Code. In style, its fuller elaboration in text and comment contrasts with the style of its predecessor.

---

4. C. Langdell, A Selection of Cases on the Law of Contracts (1871).

5. Wechsler, Foreword to Restatement (Second) of Contracts (Tentative Draft No. 1, 1964).

6. Professor Robert Braucher of the Harvard Law School served as Reporter until his appointment to the Supreme Judicial Court of Massachusetts, when he was replaced by the author of this monograph.

What measure of deference will the Restatement be given by the courts? This general question can have only a general answer. There is agreement, among those who applaud the Restatement and those who deprecate it, about the persuasiveness of an ideal restatement of the law. "A restatement, then, can have no other authority than as the product of men learned in the subject who have studied and deliberated over it. It needs no other and what could be higher."[7] A former director of the Institute explained that if a court declines to follow the Restatement, "it will do so with the knowledge that the rule which it rejects has been written by the people who by training and reputation are supposed to be eminently learned in the particular subject and that the specialist's conclusions have been discussed and defended before a body of very able critics." He called the Restatement "common law 'persuasive authority' with a high degree of persuasion."[8]

A continuing controversy centers on the desirability of departing in the Restatement from rules derived from existing precedents, in the interest of a more just regime of law. A notable example of such a departure from precedent in the original Restatement of Contracts was the creative formulation in § 90 of the doctrine that is sometimes known as *promissory estoppel*, under which a promise made without consideration can be enforced if it has been relied upon. To some extent the expanded role of comments, to permit criticism as well as explanation, has helped to provide a vehicle for the expression of idealism.

A more fundamental controversy relates to the vitality of the enterprise itself. One of the reporters for the Restatement Second has claimed that "the effort to restate the law of contracts in modern terms highlights the resilience of private autonomy in an era of expanding government activity. . . . Freedom of contract, refined and redefined in response to social change, has power as it always had."[9] But it has been argued by some that it is not useful to restate case law at a time when large tracts of the subject have been recently occupied by legislation. Some insights into the validity of this argument can be gained from the most important single piece of such legislation—the Uniform Commercial Code.

---

7. Clark, The Restatement of the Law of Contracts, 42 Yale L.J. 643, 655 (1933).
8. Goodrich, Restatement and Codification, in A. Reppy (ed.), David Dudley Field Centenary Essays 241, 244–245 (1949).
9. Braucher, Freedom of Contract and the Second Restatement, 78 Yale L.J. 598 (1969).

8.3 Uniform Commercial Code

The origins of the Uniform Commercial Code lie in the *law merchant*, a specialized body of usages (or customs) that governed contracts dealing with commercial matters until the seventeenth century. The law merchant was applied by courts composed of merchants convened to pass on disputes that arose at the fairs that were the centers for much of early trade. Large amounts of this law were carried into the English common law of negotiable instruments and insurance. This was due in substantial part to Lord Mansfield, one of England's most noted judges, who became Chief Justice of the King's Bench in 1756.[10] In controversies between merchants, he made it a point to ascertain and apply the usages of the trade, sometimes using a special jury of merchants to advise him on commercial practices. But the influence of the law merchant on the common law relating to the sale of goods was limited, and a complex body of case law developed in this field in Britain.

This law was reduced to statutory form by the British Sale of Goods Act in 1893. The National Conference of Commissioners on Uniform State Laws entrusted to Williston the task of producing a similar statute for the American states. His draft of a Uniform Sales Act was approved by the Commissioners in 1906 and was eventually adopted by over 30 states. Like its British cousin, however, it had little to say about contractual problems arising out of the sale of goods, and these remained largely governed by case law.

At the close of the Second World War, the Commissioners joined forces with the American Law Institute in preparing a comprehensive Uniform Commercial Code, to replace not only the Uniform Sales Act but also other uniform acts dealing with commercial matters. Karl Llewellyn was named as Chief Reporter. A final Official Draft, with extensive comments, was approved by the two sponsoring organizations in 1952 and was promptly enacted in Pennsylvania, effective in 1954. In response to criticisms made in a study by the New York Law Revision Commission, the sponsors of the Code produced a revised text with comments in 1958.

---

10. William Murray (1705–1793), a Scot and the first Earl of Mansfield, was a rival of the elder Pitt in school, in Parliament, and in politics. He favored strict measures with the American rebels. He achieved greatness as a judge, being Lord Chief Justice from 1756 to 1788. In one important decision, he disapproved slaveholding in England, but he is remembered primarily because of his influence on commercial law.

By 1961, 13 states, including Pennsylvania, had adopted this text. In 1962, New York adopted it, effective in 1964, and the complete success of the Code was assured. A number of states, however, made changes in the 1958 Official Text, and, in order to curb this tendency away from uniformity, a Permanent Editorial Board for the Code was established in 1961. The Board passed upon the amendments made or proposed by each state, and those it approved were incorporated in a 1962 Official Text. Substantial revisions were later made in connection with secured transactions and investment securities, and these are incorporated in the latest version of the Code, the 1978 Official Text. Some version of the Code has been enacted in every state except Louisiana, which because of its French civil law tradition has adopted only a part of the Code, not including that on sales.

The Code is divided into nine substantive articles: Article 1, General Provisions; Article 2, Sales; Article 3, Commercial Paper; Article 4, Bank Deposits and Collections; Article 5, Letters of Credit; Article 6, Bulk Transfers; Article 7, Warehouse Receipts, Bills of Lading and Other Documents of Title; Article 8, Investment Securities; Article 9, Secured Transactions, Sales of Accounts and Chattel Paper. The concern in this monograph is almost exclusively with Articles 1 and 2, and with a few provisions of Article 9 that govern the assignment of contract rights and the delegation of performance.

The Code makes much less of an attempt than did the earlier codifications in Britain and the United States to follow existing formulations of the law. Very little of the language of the Uniform Sales Act is retained. The Code shows the influence of the legal realists and, in some respects, takes an entirely new approach to the law. Many of its provisions are designed to change prior law where that law was regarded as undesirable. Williston, who had drafted the Uniform Sales Act, found some of the changes in that area to be "not only iconoclastic but open to criticisms that I regard so fundamental as to preclude the desirability of enacting [the Sales Article] of the proposed Code." Corbin was among those who took a different view.[11] One of the most important of the Code's innovations is its reduction to statutory form of many of the rules of contract law relating to the sale of goods that had previously been left to case law.

One important question in working with the Code is to what extent recourse to prior drafts may be had to aid interpretation. The 1952 edition

11. Compare Williston, The Law of Sales in the Proposed Uniform Commercial Code, 63 Harv. L. Rev. 561 (1950), with Corbin, The Uniform Commercial Code—Sales; Should it be Enacted. 59 Yale L.J. 821 (1950).

of the Code attempted to close the door on such legislative history by providing that "Prior drafts of text and comments may not be used to ascertain legislative intent." The comment to this provision explained that the reason for the prohibition was that the changes might be misleading, because matters were often "omitted as being implicit without statement and language has been changed or added solely for clarity."[12] The provision was deleted in the 1958 Official Text "because the changes from the text enacted in Pennsylvania in 1953 are clearly legitimate legislative history." Courts have not, however, limited their inquiry to changes subsequent to the 1952 edition adopted in Pennsylvania; they have used drafts prior to that one when relevant. Nor have courts shown much concern with the extent to which changes made by a drafting group, unconnected with any legislature, should be regarded as legitimate legislative history.

A similar question is to what extent recourse should be had, in interpreting the Code, to the drafter's comments that follow each section. The question arises because the comments, though called "official," have not been enacted into law by the state legislatures that have enacted the text, and in many states it is doubtful that they were even put before the legislators in the form of a committee report. Yet the comments, written in an explanatory style, are easier to read than the text and often amplify it. The 1952 text of the Code addressed itself to the problem of the force of the comments by providing that they "may be consulted in the construction and application of this Act but, if text and comment conflict, text controls."[13] This provision was deleted in the 1958 version, but for reasons unrelated to its substance. The sponsors of the Code explain that to aid in uniform construction the comments "set forth the purpose of various provisions of this Act to promote uniformity, to aid in viewing the Act as an integrated whole, and to safeguard against misconstruction."[14] In practice, courts have given considerable weight to the comments—more than that ordinarily accorded an authoritative treatise or article but less than that accorded the text itself. If the statutory provisions adopted by the legislature contradict the comments, the comments must clearly be rejected. The more difficult problem arises where the comments make assertions as to matters on which the text is silent, and here also courts have often rejected the comments.

---

12. UCC 1–102(3)(g), Comment 2 (1952 ed.).
13. UCC 1–102(3)(f) (1952 ed.).
14. General Comment at p. ix of 1972 edition.

What lessons does the Code offer with regard to the continued vitality of general principles of contract law in the face of the twentieth-century tendency toward specialization?

8.4 The Code and the Adaptability of Contract Law

There is an endless variety of contracts in the United States. There are building contracts, employment contracts, contracts for the sale of land, contracts for the sale of goods, loan agreements, franchise agreements, collective bargaining agreements, insurance policies, theater tickets, and so on. They may involve small merchants or large corporations, governments or consumers. They may be short-term contracts for a single performance in the near future or long-term contracts under which a multitude of separate transactions are to take place. They may be negotiated face to face, over the telephone, or by mail. They may be made in writing, orally, or even by gesture.

How can a general body of contract law adapt itself to so many different types of transactions. In some instances the answer is that it has not succeeded in doing so and, as a result, separate fields such as insurance law and labor law have emerged. Indeed, one critic has denigrated the residuum of general contract law as "abstraction—what is left in the law relating to agreements when all particularities of person and subject matter are removed."[15] In many instances, however, the general rules of contract law have been successfully accommodated to the peculiarities of particular transactions, thus avoiding fragmentation into separate branches of law.

Often the parties themselves make this accommodation by express provision at the time of their agreement, creating their own body of specialized rules for their particular situation. In other cases they have accomplished much the same result by tacitly subjecting themselves to a body of usages that can be shown to be regularly observed in transactions of that particular sort and that then serve as a body of specialized rules for the transaction at hand.

It is important to understand in this connection that nearly all of the general rules of contract law are subject to contrary provision by the parties. European legal systems have terms of art to distinguish between rules of law that the parties can vary by express provision or usage and

---

15. L. Friedman, Contract Law in America 20 (1965).

rules of law that are beyond their power to modify. The most satisfactory English equivalent terms are *suppletory*, for those that are subject to contrary agreement, and *mandatory*, for those that are not. In this sense, then, we are speaking of rules of contract law that are suppletory rather than mandatory.

The suppletory character of most of its rules has been a source of both strength and weakness for contract law. To the extent that its general rules have admitted of departure, they have had an adaptability and a resilience that have enabled them to survive in an age when specialization has made it increasingly difficult to formulate such rules categorically. Many courts have approved and applied some general proposition of contract law explaining that, had the parties not desired its application, they could have provided to the contrary. At the same time, the fact that the parties frequently exercise their power to depart from these general rules has plainly undermined the significance of the rules themselves. Many are more honored in the exception than in the application. An important result of the combination of the suppletory character of most rules of contract law along with the propensity of the parties to vary them by agreement is the heightened significance of the process of interpretation, by which the scope of the parties' agreement is determined.

In addition to the efforts of the parties themselves to shape the general rules of contract law to their particular needs, legislatures have in recent years played an important role in shaping these rules to fit the peculiarities of the transaction. Notable examples have been the formulation of special rules for transactions involving merchants and for those involving consumers.

Although some of the European civil law systems have traditionally singled out for special treatment transactions involving those professionals called "merchants," the common law tradition has been to formulate general rules of contract law, applicable by their terms to businessmen as well as to others. The notion of special rules for merchants remained foreign to the American lawyer until the advent of the Uniform Commercial Code.

Not only did the drafters of the Code lay down special rules applicable only to contracts for the sale of goods, as opposed to other kinds of contracts, but they formulated special rules imposing higher standards on merchants than on other sorts of parties. Some of these rules apply if there is a "transaction between merchants,"[16] and others apply if only one party

---

16. See e.g., UCC 2–201(2), providing that a failure to object to a confirmation within a fixed period satisfies the requirement of a writing under the statute of frauds in a transaction "between merchants."

is a "merchant."[17] One is a merchant under UCC 2-104(1) if one is "a person who deals in goods of the kind or otherwise by his occupation holds himself out as having knowledge or skill peculiar to the practices or goods involved in the transaction. . . ." Under this provision, the required professional status may be based on specialized knowledge of either the goods or the practices involved. An ordinary businessman's knowledge of business "practices . . . involved in the transaction" is enough to make him a "merchant," even though he has no special familiarity with the goods involved. However, a few of the Code sections that lay down special rules for merchants do so only if the party is a merchant with respect to "goods of the kind" involved in the transaction, and under these sections knowledge of business practices alone would not suffice.[18]

It would be easy to imagine that the introduction of a definition of *merchant* would pose problems by requiring subtle distinctions at the borderline. For example, the UCC comments tell us that a person is a merchant only when acting in a professional capacity: "banks or even universities . . . well may be 'merchants'" but "a lawyer or bank president buying fishing tackle for his own use is not a merchant."[19] Judging from the litigation that has arisen from the definition, however, these distinctions have not often been the cause of controversy in practice. Such litigation has been largely devoted to determining the circumstances in which a farmer is a "merchant" under the Code.

Just as the general rules of contract law have traditionally applied to merchants as well as others, so too have they applied to consumers as well as others. Recently, however, legislation has begun to lay down special rules for transactions involving consumers. This legislation varies widely from one jurisdiction to the next, but the Uniform Consumer Credit Code is typical. Under it, consumer transactions are limited to those in which a person acquires goods, services, or land "primarily for a personal, family, household, or agricultural purpose" of "a person other than an organization."[20] As in the case of the Uniform Commercial Code's use of *merchant*, this attempt at marking off an area worthy of special rules appears not to have occasioned much controversy with respect to its borderline.

---

17. See, e.g., UCC 2–205, under which "an offer by a merchant" is firm (that is, irrevocable) in specified circumstances.

18. See, e.g., UCC 2–314, under which "a warranty that the goods shall be merchantable is implied in a contract for their sale if the seller is a merchant with respect to goods of that kind."

19. UCC 2–104, Comment 2.

20. Uniform Consumer Credit Code 2.104(1)(b), (c). This definition is derived from the definition of "consumer goods" in UCC 9–109(1).

Even where special rules have evolved for particular types of contracts, it would be a mistake to suppose that they bear no relation to the general body of contract law. For example, the provisions of the Uniform Commercial Code on sales are generally limited to "transactions in goods"[21] and do not apply to, say, contracts dealing with land or services. Courts have, nonetheless, used these provisions as a basis for the application of similar rules in analogous cases, such as contracts for the leasing of goods or for the sale of services. The comments themselves invite such use, citing with approval cases in which courts "have recognized the policies embodied in an act as applicable in reason to subject matter which was not expressly included in the language of the act."[22] The Restatement Second also encourages courts to do this in specific instances, by formulating general principles of contract law derived from, or at least supported by, rules found in the Code—for example, the provisions on *good faith* and on *unconscionability*.[23]

An important aspect of the Code's relation to general contract law appears from an important section under which: "Unless displaced by the particular provisions of this Act, the principles of law and equity . . . shall supplement its provisions."[24] If, therefore, no provision of the Code—even liberally construed[25]—applies to a case, the general body of contract law governs. This integration of rules from a specialized field of contract law into the body of general contract principles suggests the continuing vitality of those principles in spite of the twentieth-century tendency towards specialization.

21. UCC 2–102.
22. UCC 1–102, Comment 1.
23. On "good faith," compare UCC 1–203 with Restatement Second § 205. On "unconscionability," compare UCC 2–302 with Restatement Second § 208.
24. UCC 1–103.
25. UCC 1–102(1) principles that the Code "shall be liberally construed and applied to promote its underlying purposes and policies."

Chapter 9

Characteristics and Organization of Contract Law

9.1 Place of Contract Law in the Legal System

What is the place of contract law in the overall scheme of American law? Several features of American law make classification particularly difficult.

First, American law has no comprehensive plan of codification from which to derive a scheme of classification. Second, the common law case-oriented approach is more pragmatic than theoretical and does not lend itself to generalization. The American lawyer does not see the broad general categories that are perceived in civil law countries.[1] Third, the common methods that pervade all branches of law tend to inhibit the development of autonomous fields. This is due in part to the absence of special courts, like those found in some civil law countries, for such major branches as public and commercial law.

In spite of these difficulties, there are some well recognized distinctions that are perpetuated through the content of law school courses and casebooks, through the titles of treatises and the Restatement, and through the topic headings of digests and encyclopedias. Two of these distinctions are that between substantive law and procedural law and that between private law and public law.

---

1. The fragmentation of American law is most acute in the field of private law, where it was encouraged by the multifarious forms of action in the law courts before the procedural reforms of the nineteenth century. Thus the area of private law known in civil law countries as "civil law" is thought of by the American lawyer as such separate subjects as contracts, torts, property, and family law, and the field of torts, for example, is divided into such distinct torts as assault, battery, and trespass.

The distinction between substance and procedure is familiar to all legal systems. In the United States the subject of procedure may be regarded broadly as including civil and criminal procedure, evidence, and conflict of laws. It has taken on special importance, not only because of the creative role accorded the courts in all common law countries, but also because of such indigenous factors as the professional emphasis of law study and the complexities of the federal system. Although contract law is, of course, substantive rather than procedural, disputes arising out of contracts often raise issues that involve civil procedure, evidence, and conflict of laws.

The distinction between private and public law, though well recognized in civil law countries, is of more questionable utility in a common law country like the United States. As the Supreme Court of the United States has said, "It is often convenient to describe particular claims as invoking public or private rights, and this handy classification is doubtless valid for some purposes. But usually the real significance of each term will depend upon its context and the nature of the interests it is involved to distinguish."[2]

Whatever the merits or nature of the distinction, all American lawyers would include in public law the fields of constitutional law and administrative law. Other subjects for inclusion are labor law, which is concerned more with governmental control over labor relations than it is with employment contracts, and trade regulation, which is primarily concerned with government control over business activity including aspects of making contracts, along with criminal law and tax law.

Private law is more fragmented than it is in civil law countries. What is known in civil law countries as *civil law* is broken down into separate fields, notably contracts, torts, property law, and family law. The law of negotiable instruments, sales, and secured transactions have only in recent years, under the influence of the Uniform Commercial Code, been recognized as parts of a whole called *commercial law*. And the subjects of agency, corporations, and partnerships are only occasionally grouped together under the heading of business enterprises.

9.2 Scope and Related Fields

The scope of contract law includes capacity of the parties, formalities, offer and acceptance, consideration, mistake and misrepresentation, du-

2. Garner v. Teamsters Union, 346 U.S. 485, 494 (1953).

ress and unconscionability, unenforceability on grounds of public policy, interpretation and construction, performance and conditions of performance, frustration of purpose and impracticability of performance, discharge, rights of assignees and contract beneficiaries, and remedies. Contract law has, to a considerable extent, preserved its unitary quality, resisting fundamental distinctions between different classes of contracts according to either the subject of the agreement or the nature of the parties. Accordingly, with some important exceptions, its general principles are applicable to agreements on subjects as varied as employment and sale of land, and to parties as diverse as individuals, business organizations, and governmental entities. (Among the important exceptions are consumer contracts and insurance contracts.) Contracts for the sale of goods are somewhat exceptional, since they are governed by a statute, Article 2 of the Uniform Commercial Code, which has already been discussed.[3]

One of the most important bodies of law that is closely related to contract law is that of restitution. Indeed, restitution problems are often inseparable from contract problems. Suppose, for example, that two parties negotiate but never reach agreement. Can one recover from the other for benefits conferred in the course of those negotiations? Or suppose that the parties do reach agreement, but that the agreement is unenforceable. Can one recover from the other for benefits conferred under the agreement if it is unenforceable because it is too indefinite? Because one party lacked capacity? Because one or both of the parties was mistaken? Because the agreement is not evidenced by a writing as required by the statute of frauds? Because it offends public policy? Or suppose that the negotiations do result in a contract. Can one party recover from the other for benefits conferred under that contract if his recovery on that basis would exceed his recovery if he sued on the contract itself? If he is barred from recovery on the contract itself because of his own breach? If the duties of both parties to render any further performance have been discharged because it has become impracticable for one party to perform?

Since these claims for the redress of unjust enrichment do not fit comfortably into either the category of contract or that of tort, they have come to be regarded as falling within the distinct field of restitution. Restitution is the subject of a separate Restatement, the Restatement of Restitution. Restatement (Second) of Restitution § 1 states:

> A person who receives a benefit by reason of an infringement of another person's interest, or of loss suffered by the other,

3. See §§ 3.3 and 3.4 supra.

> owes restitution to him in the manner and amount necessary to prevent unjust enrichment.

The following discussion of contract law will include references to restitution where relevant.

The discussion that follows is in four parts. It begins with contract formation, taking up first the doctrine of consideration, peculiar to the common law, along with its alternatives, and the rules of offer and acceptance. There follows a treatment of the rules of contract interpretation, beginning with the use of the parol evidence rule to determine what is to be interpreted and concluding with the filling of gaps in the contract. The discussion then turns to problems of performance. It then takes up excuse from performance. Finally, it deals with remedies for breach of contract. (There is no discussion of the important ways in which courts police contracts for unfairness—including the rules governing misrepresentation, duress, and unconscionability—because these matters are covered in a future volume in this series.)

9.3 Formation: Consideration and its Alternatives

By the early seventeenth century, as we have seen,[4] the English courts recognized two bases for the enforcement of promises, the seal and consideration. The seal was a piece of wax affixed to a document and bearing an impression identifying the promisor. At first its use was confined to the nobility, but later it spread to common persons. With the growth of literacy and the use of the personal signature as a means of authentication, the required formality became so eroded that a seal could consist of any written or printed symbol, as long as it was intended by the promisor to serve as a seal. The promisor did not have to affix the seal himself, but could "adopt" a seal already printed on the instrument.

With the erosion of the solemnity of the seal, its effect was abolished or at least seriously curtailed throughout the United States. The most recent of these assaults on the seal came in the Uniform Commercial Code which, as its commentary explains, "makes it clear that every effect of the seal which relates to 'sealed instruments' as such is wiped out insofar as contracts for sale [of goods] are concerned."[5]

The abolition of the seal left consideration as the sole traditional basis for the enforcement of contracts. We have already seen how consideration

---

4. See §§ 2.2, 2.3 supra.
5. UCC 2–203, Comment.

evolved out of the common law action of assumpsit and how its core came to be that the promisee must give something in exchange for the promise that is either a detriment to himself or a benefit to the promisor.[6] But by the end of the nineteenth century, at least in the United States, the traditional requirement that the consideration be either a benefit to the promisor or a detriment to the promisee had begun to give way to a requirement that the consideration be "bargained for." When the Restatement of Contracts was promulgated in 1933, it defined *consideration* exclusively in terms of something that was "bargained for," with no mention of benefit or detriment. The Restatement Second does the same and adds a definition of "bargained for."[7] Something is said to be bargained for "if it is sought by the promisor in exchange for his promise and is given by the promisee in exchange for that promise."[8] The rise of this *bargain theory* of consideration had two consequences.

First, to the extent that it imposed a new requirement, that of bargain, the theory made some promises unenforceable that might previously have been enforceable. Bargain might well be lacking in transactions taking place outside or on the periphery of the marketplace. Exchanges in a family setting, for example, are often not arrived at by bargain, and promises made in such settings often turned out to be unenforceable under the bargain theory. This result is scarcely startling, given nineteenth-century America's concern with the marketplace. New doctrines would have to be devised if such promises were to result in liability.

Second, to the extent that the theory eliminated any requirement of benefit or detriment, it made some promises enforceable that might previously have been unenforceable. It shifted the concern of judges away from the fairness of the exchange; their sole inquiry was into the process by which the parties had arrived at that exchange. A promise that had been exchanged as a result of the process of bargain satisfied the fundamental test of enforceability. This development accorded well with the prevailing mood of nineteenth-century America, which placed its trust in free enterprise and in the dignity and creativity of the individual. New doctrines would also have to be developed if judges were to inquire into fairness. (These doctrines will not be dealt with in this monograph.)

---

6. See § 2.3 supra.

7. Restatement (Second) of Contracts § 71. Section 75 defines "bargain" to require that the consideration both be "sought by the promisor" and be "given by the promisor in exchange for his promise." See also § 79, which provides that if the requirement of consideration is met, there is no further requirement of "a . . . benefit to the promisor or a . . . detriment to the promisee."

8. Restatement (Second) of Contracts § 71(2). See also § 3 (defining "bargain").

Under the bargain theory, virtually anything that anyone would bargain for in exchange for a promise can be consideration for that promise. Usually the consideration is a return promise, as when a seller promises to deliver goods at a later time in return for a buyer's promise to pay at that time. Such contracts are often called *bilateral* contracts because promises are made on both sides. It is contracts of this sort that make up the bulk of economically significant promises in the United States today. Sometimes, however, the consideration is not a return promise but some performance by the promisee, as when a seller delivers goods in return for a buyer's promise to pay at the end of the month. Such contracts are often called *unilateral* contracts because a promise is made on only one side. They are less common and economically less significant than bilateral contracts.

A party's promise or a performance can be consideration even though it is relatively insignificant in value when compared to what the other party is giving in exchange for it. This fact has given rise to the hyperbole that even a peppercorn—symbolic of something trifling in value—can be consideration as long as it is bargained for, and this notion has been dignified, sometimes derisively, as the "peppercorn theory" of consideration. But even under the bargain theory, there are important situations in which a promise will be held to be unenforceable for lack of consideration.

The most significant class of promises unenforceable for lack of consideration is made up of purely gratuitous (or gift) promises—promises for which there has been no exchange at all. Suppose that an employer promises an employee that he will give him a gold watch as a present, but then reconsiders and refuses to deliver the watch. The employer's promise is not supported by consideration since there was no exchange—the employer received nothing in return. It is therefore not enforceable unless there is some alternative basis for enforceability, as there was in the case of a gratuitous promise under seal before the seal was deprived of its effect.

A gift (a present transfer of an interest in property) stands on a footing different from that of a promise to make a gift. Suppose that the employer, instead of merely making a promise, actually gives the employee the watch as a present, but then changes his mind and seeks the return of the watch. Here, because the employee's assertion of his right does not involve enforcement of a promise, the problem is not for the law of contracts. It is, instead, one for the law of property. Under that law, once the gift has been completed by the donor's delivery of the watch, with the intent to make a gift the transfer is irrevocable and the donor cannot recover it.

Why should the employer be able to revoke a promise to make a gift but not the gift itself? Why should delivery make a difference? One possible justification for the difference is that denial of relief in both instances evidences a policy of leaving parties to gratuitous transactions where they stand. Providing the legal machinery to dispense justice is costly, and it may not be warranted in the absence of the sort of exchange based on bargain that tends to enhance a society's total wealth. Furthermore the requirement of delivery performs an *evidentiary* function by providing some proof of the fact that the donor intended to make a gift and of the fact that a gift was actually made. And it performs a *cautionary* function, by bringing home to the donor the significance of his act and preventing ill-considered and impulsive gifts.[9]

Whatever its justification, the distinction remains. It accounts for the most important type of promise that lacks consideration, the purely gratuitous promise—the promise for which there has been no exchange at all.

Since the doctrine of consideration has been more the product of history than of logic, it is not surprising that it has been the object of criticism and of proposals for reform. Contemporary critics of the doctrine claim to trace their lineage back to the great English judge, Lord Mansfield, who mounted a memorable, if short-lived, attack on the doctrine in 1765. He advanced the heresy "that the ancient notion about the want of consideration was for the sake of evidence only: for when it is reduced into writing, there was no objection to the want of consideration."[10] Only three years later, Mansfield's heresy was extirpated from the common law by the House of Lords, which declared that if contracts "be merely written" and not under seal "a consideration must be proved."[11] But Mansfield's heresy did not remain quiescent. The view that the formality of putting a promise in writing should operate as an alternative to consideration continued to have appeal, and it gained new vitality when the abolition of the seal gave the doctrine of consideration even greater prominence.

In 1937 the English Law Revision Committee recommended the enactment of a statute making a signed written promise enforceable without regard to consideration. Although this recommendation has not been followed, a few of the American states have enacted legislation along similar lines. Pennsylvania has the most sweeping statute, under which any promise, even a purely gratuitous one, is not "unenforceable for lack of consideration, if the writing also contains an additional express state-

9. For discussion of the functions of formalities, see Fuller, Consideration and Form, 41 Colum. L. Rev. 799, 800-806 (1941).

10. Pilans & Rose v. Van Mierop & Hopkins, 3 Burr. 1663, 97 Eng. Rep. 1035 (K.B. 1765). In the same case, he said, "In commercial cases amongst merchants, the want of consideration is not an objection."

11. Rann v. Hughes, 7 T.R. 350n., 101 Eng. Rep. 1014n (1778).

ment, in any form of language, that the signer intends to be legally bound."[12] A more common variety of legislation, found in over a dozen states including California, makes a writing "presumptive evidence of consideration."[13] New York has enacted statutes making a writing a substitute for consideration in a limited number of situations.[14]

The limited success of efforts to reform the doctrine may be attributable more to the fact that it has met with complacency than to the fact that it has found universal approval. There are only a few instances of commercial promises in which the requirement of consideration is not met. For the most part, the doctrine works well enough in those areas of commercial life that are important to economic vitality. Furthermore, to the extent that it may enforce too few promises, it has been supplemented by reliance as an alternative ground for enforcement.

Under the bargain theory of consideration, the promisee's unsolicited reliance is not consideration because it is not bargained for. Suppose that an employer promises to pay an employee a pension of $500 a month upon retirement. Relying on the promise, the employee retires at an age when other employment is unavailable. If the employer then refuses to pay the pension, is the employee without recourse because the employer did not bargain for (did not seek to induce) the employee's retirement and therefore the employer's promise lacked consideration? Today, most courts would allow the employee to enforce the promise on the ground of reliance. Suppose that a debtor is in default on a debt, and his friend makes a gratuitous promise to the creditor to pay it. Relying on the promise, the creditor forbears from proceeding against the debtor for a time during which the debtor becomes insolvent. If the friend refuses to pay the debt, is the creditor without recourse because the friend did not bargain for (did not seek to induce) the creditor's forbearance and therefore the friend's promise lacked consideration? Today, there is authority that the creditor can enforce the promise on the ground of reliance.

---

12. 33 Pa. Stat. Ann. tit. 33, § 6. This was originally promulgated as the Uniform Written Obligations Act by the National Conference of Commissioners on Uniform State Laws. But it was adopted only by Pennsylvania and Utah, and then repealed by Utah, after which it was renamed the Model Written Obligations Act. With respect to the sufficiency of the statement of intention, see Fredun v. Mike's Cafe, 204 Pa. Super. 356, 204 A.2d 776 (1964), aff'd, 419 Pa. 607, 213 A.2d 638 (1965). New Mexico has a somewhat similar statute under which "Every contract in writing . . . shall import a consideration in the same manner and as fully as sealed instruments have heretofore done." N.M. Stat. Ann. § 20-2-8.

13. Cal. Civ. Code § 1614.

14. N.Y. General Obligations Law §§ 5-1103, 5-1105, 5-1107, 5-1109.

But it was not until the twentieth century that a generalized theory of recovery based on reliance developed. During the nineteenth century, reliance on a gratuitous promise had come to be recognized as a basis for recovery in a few categories of cases. In 1933, on the authority of such cases, the American Law Institute promulgated § 90 of the first Restatement of Contracts, which was destined to become its most notable and influential rule. It states, in terms generally applicable to all promises, the principle that courts had applied to a few categories of cases. This principle, as it appears in § 90 of the Restatement Second is:

> A promise which the promisor should reasonably expect to induce action or forbearance on the part of the promisee . . . and which does induce such action is binding if injustice can be avoided only by enforcement of the promise. . . .

Section 90 was the first contract Restatement's most significant departure from its stated policy of following precedents. It has been the fountainhead of recovery based on reliance in the United States. Such recovery has not displaced the doctrine of consideration but has supplemented it, by affording promisees an additional ground for recovery.

9.4 Formation: Offer and Acceptance

What requirements must the bargaining process meet in order to form a contract? Courts have had two concerns. First, did both parties *assent* to be bound? Second, is their agreement *definite* enough to be enforceable?

The first requirement, that of assent, is implicit in the principle that contractual liability is consensual. Since it is difficult for a workable system of contract law to take account of assent unless there has been an overt expression of it, courts have required that assent to the formation of a contract be manifested in some way, by words or other conduct, if it is to be effective.[15]

The second requirement, that of definiteness, is implicit in the principle that contract law protects the promisee's expectation interest. According to the Uniform Commercial Code, "a contract for sale does not fail for indefiniteness if . . . there is a reasonably certain basis for giving an

15. The bargain theory of consideration goes on to insist that the parties' manifestations have reference to each other, i.e., that they be reciprocal. Not only must the promisor seek the promise or performance that is the consideration in exchange for his promise, but the promisee must give it in exchange for that promise.

appropriate remedy."[16] In calculating the damages that will put the promisee in the position in which he would have been had the promise been performed, a court must determine the scope of that promise with some precision. In the less usual case in which the court orders specific performance or enjoins a threatened breach, it must know the scope of the promise with even greater precision in order to frame a decree, since failure to obey the decree will subject the promisor to the court's contempt power. The rest of the discussion here will be devoted to the requirement of assent.

What is meant by "assent"? When a court determines whether a party has assented to an agreement, is it the party's actual or his apparent intention that matters? This question provoked one of the most significant doctrinal struggles in the development of contract law, that between the subjective and objective theories.

The subjectivists looked to the actual or subjective intentions of the parties. Actual assent to the agreement on the part of both parties was necessary; without it there could be no contract.[17] As it was often expressed, there had to be a "meeting of the minds."

The objectivists, on the other hand, looked to the external or objective appearance of the parties' intentions as manifested by their actions. One of the most influential objectivists, Judge Learned Hand, wrote in a memorable passage that a contract "has, strictly speaking, nothing to do with the personal, or individual, intent of the parties" but "is an obligation attached by the mere force of law to certain acts of the parties, usually words, which ordinarily accompany and represent a known intent."[18] According to the objectivists, a party's mental assent was not necessary to make a contract. If his actions, judged by a standard of reasonableness, manifested an intention to agree, the real but unexpressed state of his mind was

---

16. UCC 2–204(3)

17. The subjectivists did not go so far as to advocate that subjective assent alone was sufficient to make a contract. Even under the subjective theory there had to be some manifestation of assent.

18. Hotchkiss v. National City Bank, 200 F. 287, 293 (S.D.N.Y. 1911), aff'd, 201 F. 664 (2d Cir. 1912), aff'd, 1231 U.S. 50 (1913). Learned Hand (1872-1961) was admitted to the practice of law in New York in 1897 and appointed to the United States District Court for the Southern District of New York in 1909 and to the United States Court of Appeals for the Second Circuit in 1924. He retired in 1951, after having sat on the federal bench longer than any other judge. Justice Cardozo called him "the greatest living American jurist" and he was so regarded by many of his contemporaries. His extra-judicial utterances may be sampled in The Spirit of Liberty (1952) and The Bill of Rights (1958).

irrelevant. By the end of the nineteenth century, the objective theory had become ascendant and courts generally accept it today.

The resulting rules accord well with practice. Parties to agreements, especially routine ones, often fail to consider the legal consequences of the actions by which they manifest their assent. The fact that a party gives the matter no thought does not impair the effectiveness of his assent, for there is no requirement that a party intend or even understand the legal consequences of signing it. This rule, making a party's intention to be legally bound irrelevant, has the salutary effects of generally relieving each party to a dispute of the burden of showing the other's state of mind in that regard and of helping to uphold routine agreements.[19]

The effect of assent is instantaneous. According to the orthodox catechism, there is a definite moment in time when a party becomes contractually bound on his promise as a result of the manifestation of assent. At that moment there is an abrupt transition from no liability to liability. Until that moment comes, both parties are free to withdraw from the negotiations.

The commentary to the Code points out that the facts may "not disclose the exact point at which the deal was closed" even though "the actions of the parties indicate that a binding obligation has been undertaken."[20] This is particularly likely if the dispute arises after performance is well under way. This does not mean that it is always necessary to determine that moment. As the Code puts it, "An agreement sufficient to constitute a contract of sale may be found even though the moment of its making is undetermined."[21] But it does mean that if a party has become contractually bound by his promise, there must have been some moment before which he was not bound and after which he was.

At least in principle, the contract is made at the moment of the acceptance of the offer. The question of the time and place a contract is made is sometimes important in applying tax and regulatory laws, choice of law rules, and rules of jurisdiction and procedure. Such cases often turn on policies different from those applicable to contract law in general. To the extent that they follow the rules of contract law, however, a contract is made at the time and in the place that the acceptance takes effect, which is

19. A different rule applies, however, in those unusual instances in which a party intends that his assent have no legal consequences. Under the objective theory, a court will honor that intention if the other party has reason to know it. And it will honor it if the other party actually knows it.

20. UCC 2–204, Comment.

21. UCC 2–204(2).

generally the time when and the place where the acceptance is put out of the offeree's possession.[22]

The orthodox catechism also holds that if both parties make promises, the moment when each becomes bound must be the same—unless both are bound, neither is bound. This principle of *mutuality of obligation* serves the needs of the marketplace, where prices fluctuate according to supply and demand, for it eliminates the possibility that one party will be able to speculate on such changes at the expense of the other. Suppose that a seller and buyer are negotiating a contract for the future delivery of goods at a fixed price. As long as neither is bound, the seller stands to lose if the market falls and to gain if it rises, while the buyer stands to gain if the market falls and to lose if it rises. As soon as both are bound, the reverse is true. It is the buyer who stands to lose if the market falls and to gain if it rises, and it is the seller who stands to gain if the market falls and to lose if it rises. In each case the risks are symmetrical.

If there is a period of time, however, during which one party is bound while the other party is not, the party not bound has, in effect, an option and can speculate at the expense of the party who is bound. If, for example, there is a period during which the seller is bound to sell the goods at $100 but the buyer is not bound to buy them, the buyer has an option to buy at $100 during that period. If the market price rises to $110 during that period, the buyer can take the advantage of the lower price at which the seller is bound under the option and insist upon delivery of the goods for $100. But if the market price falls to $90 during the period, the buyer can ignore the option and take advantage of the lower market price by buying the goods elsewhere, leaving the seller to sell his goods on the depressed market. The party who is not bound has the opportunity of speculating on market changes at the expense of the party who is bound. The unfairness of giving this advantage to one of the parties, at least if the other party has not agreed to it, suggests that neither party should be bound until both are bound. Traditional analysis of the agreement process attaches great importance to the principle of mutuality of obligation as a means of avoiding such opportunities for speculation.

By what means do the parties manifest their assent to a contract? The outward appearance of the agreement process varies widely according to the circumstances. It may, for example, involve face-to-face negotiations, an exchange of letters or telegrams, or merely the perfunctory signing of a

---

22. See Restatement (Second) of Contracts § 63 and Comment d. The rule that the acceptance takes effect when it is put out of the offeree's possession is often referred to as the "mailbox" rule, because in contracts by correspondence the acceptance takes place when it is put in the mailbox.

printed form supplied by the other party. Whatever the outward appearance, it is common to analyze the process in terms of two distinct steps: first, a manifestation of assent that is called an *offer*, made by one person (who is called the *offeror*) to another (who is called the *offeree*); and second, a manifestation of assent that is called an *acceptance*, made by the offeree to the offeror.

What is an "offer"? It can be defined as a manifestation of assent to enter into a bargain, made by the offeror to the offeree, conditional on a manifestation of assent in the form of some action (promise or performance) by the offeree. The offer confers upon the offeree the power to create a contract by that manifestation. An offer is nearly always a promise and, in a sense, the action on which the offeror conditions the promise is the "price" of its becoming enforceable. *Offer*, then, is the name given to a promise that is conditional on some action by the promisee if the legal effect of the promisee's taking that action is to make the promise enforceable. An offer puts it within the promisee's power to take action that will make the promise enforceable.

What is an "acceptance"? It can be defined as the action (promise or performance) by the offeree that creates a contract (i.e., makes the offeror's promise enforceable). *Acceptance*, then, is the name given to the offeree's action if the legal effect of that action is to make the offeror's promise enforceable. An acceptance is action by the promisee that makes the promise enforceable.[23]

---

23. Traditional analysis of the bargaining process recognizes a dichotomy between "bilateral" and "unilateral" contracts. In forming a bilateral contract each party makes a promise: the offeror makes the promise contained in the offer, and the offeree makes a promise in return as acceptance. For example, a buyer offers to pay the price 30 days after delivery in return for a seller's promise to deliver wheat. In forming a unilateral contract only one party makes a promise: the offeror makes the promise contained in the offer, and the offeree renders some performance as acceptance. For example, a buyer offers to pay the price 30 days after delivery in return for a seller's delivery of wheat. Thus in a bilateral contract there are promises on both sides (the buyer's promise to pay and the seller's promise to deliver); there are duties on both sides (the buyer's duty to pay and the seller's duty to deliver) and rights on both sides (the seller's right to payment and the buyer's right to delivery). In a unilateral contract, however, there is a promise on only one side (the buyer's promise to pay); there is is a duty on only one side (the buyer's duty to pay) and a right on the other side (the seller's right to payment).

Most economically significant contracts are bilateral not unilateral, and the discussion here is confined to bilateral contracts. For criticism of the distinction between bilateral and unilateral contracts, see Reporter's Note to Restatement (Second) of Contracts § 1.

Traditional analysis, in terms of an offer followed by an acceptance, may adequately describe the agreement process in simple transactions in which, for example, one person presents a printed form for the other to sign or both exchange letters or telegrams. But some contemporary observers have had difficulty accepting this model as representative of the complex negotiations typical of substantial transactions. Such negotiations commonly involve several parties, each represented by a number of businessmen and lawyers. They are often begun by the businessmen, who may refrain from making offers because they want the terms of the deal to be formulated by the lawyers before it becomes legally enforceable. Once these original negotiators decide that they have settled those aspects of the transaction that seem important from a business point of view, they turn matters over to the lawyers, with instructions to produce a document that all the parties will sign. The lawyers then prepare a succession of drafts. These are not offers either, since, among other reasons, the lawyers have no authority to make offers on behalf of their clients. When a text is finally agreed upon, the contract is made by the virtually simultaneous execution of the document or documents by all parties at a more or less ceremonial meeting.

One observer has suggested that the traditional analysis does not fit such negotiations because there is no offer and no acceptance.[24] But in defense of traditional analysis, it can still be said that the party who signs first is the offeror. Nevertheless, the requirement of assent is unlikely to cause trouble, at least as long as the parties are careful to make it clear that their negotiations are preliminary only and that the deal is not binding until it is finally closed. If this is done, problems of assent can be effectively eliminated. We now turn to problems arising out of traditional analysis in terms of offer and acceptance.

As we have seen, an offer is the penultimate communication in the making of a contract. It can be defined as a manifestation of assent that is made by the offeror to the offeree in the form of a promise that is conditional on a manifestation of assent in the form of some action by the offeree and that confers upon the offeree the power to create a contract by taking that action.[25] A simple example is: "I promise to deliver these goods if you promise to pay me $100."

---

24. 2 R. Schlesinger (ed.), Formation of Contracts: A Study of the Common Core of Legal Systems 1585 (1968).

25. According to Restatement (Second) of Contracts § 24, an offer is a "manifestation of willingness to enter into a bargain, so made as to justify another person in understanding that his assent to that bargain is invited and will conclude it."

No formalities are generally required for an offer.[26] It may be made by spoken or written words or by other conduct. Sometimes a contract that results from words is described as *express*, while one that results from conduct is described as *implied in fact*, but the distinction as such has no legal consequences. Conduct may amount to an offer if it would lead a reasonable person in the other party's position to infer a promise in return for a performance or a promise. One who holds out goods may be taken to be offering them for sale. One who begins to perform services for another in apparent expectation of payment may be taken to be offering to furnish them for reasonable compensation. Whether a reasonable person in the position of the other party would understand that the services were intended to be paid for and were not gratuitous is often a difficult question of fact when the parties are members of the same family.

An offer is not effective until it reaches the offeree. This requirement has been reinforced by the insistence of the bargain theory of consideration that the acceptance be made in response to the offer. The offer, however, need not be communicated directly by the offeror to the offeree. For example, it may be enough in the case of an offer of a reward that the offeree hears from a third person that a reward has been offered. But until the offer reaches the offeree, it is not effective and the offeror can withdraw it.

Whether a particular proposal amounts to an offer is a question of intention. The question most commonly arises when the maker of the proposal asserts that he did not intend to make an offer, while the one to whom the proposal was made asserts that he believed that it was intended as an offer. Under the objective theory the issue then becomes whether the one to whom the proposal was made had reason to believe that it was intended as an offer. A court will look first to the language of the particular proposal. It will then take account of any prior communications between the parties. It will also consider such circumstances as the completeness of the suggested bargain and the number of persons to whom the proposal is addressed. For example, the fact that a proposal is very detailed suggests that it is an offer, while omission of many terms suggests that it is not. "The more terms the parties leave open, the less likely it is that they have intended to conclude a binding agreement. . . ."[27]

Taken as a whole, such decisions show a reluctance, in doubtful cases, to characterize a proposal as an offer and to hold its maker to a contract. Courts have reason for caution, since to hold the maker of a proposal to a

26. As to the formalities imposed by the statute of frauds, see § 7.7 supra.
27. UCC 2–204, Comment.

contract exposes the maker to liability based on the recipient's expectation interest, even in the absence of any reliance.

A proposal will not usually be interpreted as an offer if such an interpretation would expose its maker to the risk of liability for performance far beyond his means. Suppose, for example, that a seller of goods makes a proposal to sell goods without specifying an upper limit on the quantity, as in a catalog or price list. The proposal will not be taken to be an offer for it would then be possible for the offeree to accept in a quantity that the seller could not supply. This rationale does not apply, however, if the proposal eliminates the risk by specifying a range or an upper limit within which the recipient may make a selection, or if such a restriction can be read in from usage, course of dealing, or under a standard of reasonableness.

A similar situation occurs when a proposal for a limited quantity has been sent to more persons than its maker could accommodate. One who receives, from an owner interested in selling a tract of land, a proposal stating that "this is a form letter" or "I am writing to several people" would not usually have reason to believe that its author intended to expose himself to the risk of several acceptances resulting in several contracts for the single tract. This rationale does not, however, apply if the proposal eliminates that risk by stating that it is "subject to prior sale." The same rationale extends to proposals made to the public through advertisements, posters, circulars, and the like, and these are generally held not to be offers.

What is an acceptance? We have seen that an offer is a manifestation of assent by the offeror in the form of a promise that is conditional on a manifestation of assent in the form of some action by the offeree. It confers upon the offeree the power to create a contract by taking action. If the offeree exercises this power, he is said to "accept" the offer. This acceptance is the final step in the making of a contract. Upon acceptance, the offeror is bound by the promise embodied in the offer.

The offeror is described as "the master of his offer" in the sense that, since by his offer he confers on the offeree the power of acceptance, the offeror has control over the extent of that power and over how it can be exercised. The bargain theory of consideration supports this conclusion. The offeror enjoys a "freedom *from* contract" except on his own conditions. It is the offeree's acceptance that furnishes the consideration for the promise embodied in the offer. Under the bargain theory, that consideration must have been sought by the offeror in exchange for his promise. What the offeror receives by way of acceptance of the offer must therefore be what the offeror sought in making the offer. (Under the objective theory, however, the question is not what the offeror actually seeks, but what the offeree has reason to believe the offeror seeks or, to express it more succinctly if less precisely, what the offer seeks.)

Typically, the offeror seeks not merely performance but a commitment from the offeree in the form of a promise in advance of performance. Perhaps the offeree's performance is to take place far enough in the future that the offeror is unwilling to rely (by performing, preparing to perform, or foregoing other opportunities) without such a commitment. The owner of land who makes an offer to pay a builder for putting up a building seeks the builder's promise to perform in order to be assured that the builder will undertake performance and will be responsible for its completion and for any deficiencies. Even if the offeree's performance is to take place soon after the offer is made, the offeror seeks a promise from the offeree to assure himself that the offeree will be responsible for any deficiency in the performance that is rendered.

If the offer seeks a promise, what will suffice as acceptance by a promise? Acceptance by a promise may be inferred from words or other conduct, including, in some circumstances, beginning performance and even preparing for performance.[28] Under the objective theory, the offeree's undisclosed intention is irrelevant, as long as the offeree's conduct gives the offeror reason to believe that the offeree intends to accept by making a promise. An offeree who signs and returns a written contract cannot avoid liability by testifying that he did so "for some other less binding purpose."[29]

The language or other conduct that will suffice as acceptance by a promise depends on the circumstances, and cases tend to turn on their special facts. When in doubt, courts may be somewhat more willing to find that an offeree has accepted an offer than that an offer has been made in the first place. Three general requirements for an acceptance by a promise can be identified.[30]

First, there must be an expression of commitment. A mere acknowledgement of receipt of the offer or an expression of interest in it is not

---

28. For an example, see UCC 2–206(1)(b), under which shipment of goods in response to an order may amount to a promise to supply conforming goods.
29. Gendzier v. Bielecki, 97 So.2d 604, 609 (Fla. 1957).
30. In addition to these three requirements, which courts have deduced from the nature of an acceptance, the offeror as the master of his offer may impose further requirements. If, for example, the offer invites the offeree to make a specification of terms, the offeree must do so. And if the offer insists that the offeree accept by words rather than other conduct, the offeree must do so.

enough. Second, the commitment must not be conditional on any further act by either party. Since an acceptance is the ultimate step in making a contract, the commitment cannot be conditional on some final step to be taken by either the offeror or the offeree. Third, at least according to traditional contract doctrine, the commitment must be one on the terms proposed by the offer without the slightest variation. The offeror, as the master of his offer, enjoys freedom from contract except on his own terms. An attempt to add to or change the terms of the offer changes the offeree's response from an acceptance into a counteroffer and a rejection of the offer.

This third requirement is sometimes called the "mirror image" rule because it requires that an acceptance be the mirror image of the offer. Courts have, however, developed techniques to mitigate the harshness of the mirror image rule. One technique is to interpret the offeree's varying language as a "mere suggestion," which the offeror might accept or reject, and to find an acceptance on the offeror's terms coupled with a further offer by the original offeree to modify that contract. Another technique is to read the offer as already containing by implication the apparent variation made by the offeree and to find an acceptance of a contract on the offeree's terms, which are also regarded as those of the offeror. Even as mitigated by these techniques, however, the impact of the mirror image rule has caused concern, particularly in connection with the sale of goods where routine negotiations are commonly carried on by the use of standard forms.

A buyer, after consulting a seller's catalog or price list, will send the seller a purchase order on the buyer's standard form. The seller will send back an acknowledgment indicating acceptance on the seller's standard form. Each form will have printed terms on the reverse side, and these will inevitably differ. Does the exchange of forms result in a contract. The answer under the mirror image rule is that it does not. If either party wishes to back out of the deal, that party can use the mirror image rule as a justification.

The Uniform Commercial Code made a significant change in the mirror image rule as it applies to the sale of goods. UCC 2-207 provides that an expression of acceptance is effective as an acceptance "even though it states terms additional to or different from those offered."[31] The offeree is regarded as having accepted a contract on the offeror's terms and as having

31. The offeree can, however, avoid this result by making the acceptance "expressly . . . conditional on assent to the additional or different terms." UCC 2–207(1).

made his own offer to modify the contract by incorporating the additional or different terms. These terms will only be incorporated in the contract if they are accepted by the original offeror. (In some circumstances, the original offeror's silence may amount to acceptance of terms that do not "materially alter" the contract.[32]) UCC 2-207 is one of the more controversial sections of the Code and has provoked considerable litigation.[33]

It is a fundamental tenet of the common law that an offer is generally freely revocable and can be countermanded by the offeror at any time before it has been accepted by the offeree. It is sometimes erroneously supposed that this principle of free revocability is a corollary of the doctrine of consideration. However, the principle of revocability is more properly regarded as a corollary of the principle of mutuality of obligation. For if the offeror were not free to revoke the offer, he would be bound—though the offeree would not be bound—and this would subject the offeror to the risk that the offeree might speculate in a fluctuating market.

What sort of manifestation of the offeror's intention suffices as a revocation of the offer? Just as the offeror need not say "offer" to offer, so too he need not say "revoke" to revoke. It is enough that the offeror indicate an intention not to make the proposed contract. Action without words suffices if the action is inconsistent with an intention to make the contract. Judicial reluctance to force an agreement on parties whose assent is not clearly shown produces a tendency to resolve doubtful cases in favor of finding revocations, a tendency analogous to the tendency to resolve doubtful cases against finding offers. The revocation is not effective, however, until it is received by the offeree. In keeping with the objective theory, an uncommunicated change of mind does not suffice. It is, however, generally accepted that the offeree's power of acceptance is terminated if the offeror dies before the offer has been accepted, regardless of whether the offeree has notice of death.

An offeror can make an irrevocable offer by agreeing that it shall be irrevocable (or "firm"), but traditionally such an agreement must be supported by consideration in order to be effective. Thus if the offeree pays something—even as little as a dollar—for the offeror's agreement not to revoke, the result is what is commonly called an *option* or *option contract*, an irrevocable offer. Under UCC 2-205, a merchant can make an irrevocable offer for the sale or purchase of goods by means of a signed writing, even if there is no consideration.

---

32. UCC 2–207(2).

33. See E. Farnsworth, Contracts § 3.21 (1982).

In recent decades, there has been a significant trend toward treating an offer as irrevocable if the offeree has justifiably relied upon the offer. Of course in most circumstances the offeree can be expected to accept the offer before relying. Sometimes, however, the offeror should reasonably expect the offeree to rely before accepting, and in such circumstances courts have increasingly protected the offeree who has relied even though, absent reliance, the offer would be revocable. The most common case is one in which a subcontractor makes an offer (or "bid") to a contractor, who is in turn bidding to do construction work for an owner. The contractor must rely on the subcontractor's offer by incorporating it in the contractor's own offer (or "bid") to the owner. Were the subcontractor to be allowed to revoke his offer once the contractor's offer had been accepted, the contractor would be obliged to find another, perhaps more costly, subcontractor. It has therefore been held that when the contractor relies on the subcontractor's offer by incorporating it in the contractor's offer and submitting it to the owner, the subcontractor's offer becomes irrevocable until, after the owner has accepted the contractor's offer, the contractor has had time to accept the subcontractor's offer.[34]

9.5 Interpretation: What Is to be Interpreted

The most common kind of contract dispute is one over the meaning of the contract. At the threshold of such a dispute is a question of what is to be interpreted. In particular, what role, if any, is to be given to negotiations between the parties that preceded or followed the making of the contract?

The parties to a contract often reduce to writing part or all of their agreement, following negotiations during which they have given assurances, made promises, and reached understandings. They do this in order to provide trustworthy evidence of the fact and terms of their agreement and to avoid reliance on uncertain memory. However, should litigation ensue, one party may seek to introduce evidence of the earlier negotiations in an effort to show that the terms of the agreement are other than as shown on the face of the writing. The party will be met with a rule known as the *parol evidence rule*, which may bar the use of such extrinsic evidence to contradict or perhaps merely to supplement the writing.[35]

---

34. The leading case is Drennan v. Star Paving Co., 51 Cal.2d 409, 333 P.2d 757 (1958), followed in Restatement (Second) of Contracts § 87(2).

35. The function of the parol evidence rule, which may bar extrinsic evidence if there is a writing, should not be confused with that of the statute of frauds, which may make a contract unenforceable if there is no writing.

The parol evidence rule is universally recognized and is embodied in the Uniform Commercial Code in UCC 2-202, a statutory formula applicable to contracts for the sale of goods. If kept within sensible limits, the rule has much to commend it. Certainly the rule is curiously christened for, as will be seen, it is not limited to "parol"—in the sense of "oral"—negotiations, nor is it, properly speaking, a rule of evidence. It may help to avoid confusion if the rule is thought of as applicable to prior negotiations rather than to parol evidence.

That the rule is not limited to oral negotiations is clear. A host of cases have applied the so-called "parol" evidence rule to exclude such writings as letters, telegrams, memoranda, and preliminary drafts exchanged by the parties before execution of a final written agreement.

That the rule is not one of evidence is affirmed by courts and scholars, specialists in the field of evidence, who assure us that the rule is one of substantive law. Rules of evidence bar some methods of proof to show a fact but permit that fact to be shown in a different way. In contrast, the parol evidence rule bars a showing of the fact itself—the fact that the terms of the agreement are other than those in the writing. The most satisfactory basis of the rule is that the subsequent agreement has, in accordance with the understanding of the parties, displaced what came before.[36] Viewed in this way, the rule simply affirms the primacy of a subsequent agreement over prior negotiations and even prior agreements.

The rule is amply justified if it is seen as fulfilling this purpose. There are many instances in which the parties, after concluding their negotiations, want to simplify the administration of the resulting contract and to facilitate the resolution of possible disputes by excluding from the scope of their agreement those matters that were raised and dropped or even agreed upon and superseded during the negotiations. It is often useful to be able to replace the negotiations of yesterday with an authoritative agreement of today.

It is this purpose that the parol evidence rule ought to serve—giving legal effect to whatever intention the parties may have had to make their writing a complete expression of the agreement that they reached, to the exclusion of all prior negotiations, whether oral or written. If the parties had such an intention, the agreement is said to be *integrated*, and the parol evidence rule bars evidence of prior negotiations for at least some purposes. If the parties had no such intention, the agreement is said to be *unintegrated*, and the parol evidence rule does not apply.

---

36. 3 A. Corbin, Contracts § 574 (1960). Restatement (Second) of Contracts § 213 expresses this thought by stating that the later written agreement "discharges prior agreements."

If an agreement is integrated, it is considered *partially integrated* or *completely integrated* according to the degree to which the parties intended the writing to express their agreement. If they intended the writing to be a final expression of the terms it contains, but not a complete expression of all the terms agreed upon—some terms remaining unwritten—the agreement is partially integrated. If the parties intended the writing to be a complete expression of all the terms agreed upon, as well as a final expression of the terms it contains, the agreement is completely integrated.

The legal effect of a determination that the agreement is integrated, according to the Restatement Second, is that "evidence of prior or contemporaneous agreements or negotiations is not admissible to contradict a term of the writing."[37] If the agreement is only partially integrated, however, evidence of prior agreements or negotiations is admissible to supplement the writing though not to contradict it.[38] If the agreement is completely integrated, not even evidence of "a consistent additional term" is admissible to explain the writing.[39]

In applying the parol evidence rule, therefore, agreements can be classified as unintegrated, partially integrated, or completely integrated. This can be done by asking two questions. First: is the agreement integrated? Second: if it is integrated, is it completely or only partially integrated?

Although there is general agreement on this analysis, controversy arises as to its application. Those who favor broad application of the rule have a spokesman in Williston, and those who favor a narrow application have a champion in Corbin. The trend in recent decisions has favored Corbin's view. The Code reflects this view, and the Restatement Second has been influenced by both Corbin and the Code.

We turn to the first question: Is the agreement integrated? The answer turns on whether the parties intended the writing as a final expression of

37. Restatement (Second) of Contracts § 215. The Code language is similar. UCC 2–202 ("may not be contradicted by evidence of any prior agreement").

38. Restatement (Second) of Contracts §§ 210(2), 215. See also UCC 2–202, Comment 3 ("consistent additional terms, not reduced to writing, may be proved unless the court finds that the writing was intended by both parties as a complete and exclusive statement of all the terms").

39. Restatement (Second) of Contracts § 216(1). The Code language is again similar. UCC 2–202 ("explained or supplemented . . . by evidence of conditional additional terms").

the terms it contains, even if it was not intended as a complete and exclusive statement of all terms on which agreement was reached.[40] No particular form is required for an integrated agreement, and the writing need not be signed by either party. Although preliminary written proposals exchanged by the parties are not ordinarily intended as final expressions of the terms they contain, they may later be assented to as such—orally, in writing, or by other conduct.[41] The character of the writing itself is often persuasive as to the intention of the parties. Indeed, it has been held that if a writing appears, in view of its thoroughness and specificity, to embody a final agreement on the terms that it contains, the agreement is to be taken conclusively as an integrated one with respect to those terms. However, the Restatement Second reflects the prevailing view that other evidence, including evidence of prior negotiations, is still admissible to show that the writing was not intended as a final expression of the terms it contains.[42] Thus the intention of the parties is determined from all the circumstances, including their language and other conduct, just as intention is determined for any other purpose.

If an agreement is only partially integrated, it must then be determined whether the evidence of prior negotiations sought to be introduced would contradict one or more of the terms of the writing or whether it would merely explain or supplement the writing. In the latter case it is admissible but in the former it is not. As might be expected, the outcome in borderline cases often depends on whether the court is sympathetic to the parol evidence rule itself.

We turn now to the second question: assuming that the agreement is integrated, is it completely, as distinguished from only partially, integrated? The answer depends on whether the parties intended the writing as

---

40. Restatement (Second) of Contracts § 209(1) (a writing "constituting a final expression of one or more terms of an agreement"); UCC 2-202 ("a writing intended by the parties as a final expression of their agreement with respect to such terms as are included therein").

41. See Restatement (Second) of Contracts § 209, Comment b ("A letter, telegram or other informal document written by one party may be orally assented to by the other as a final expression of some or all of the terms of their agreement.").

42. Restatement (Second) of Contracts § 209(3) ("where the parties reduce an agreement to a writing which in view of its completeness and specificity reasonably appears to be a complete agreement, it is taken to be an integrated agreement unless it is established by other evidence that the writing did not constitute a final expression.").

a complete and exclusive expression of all terms on which agreement was reached, as distinguished from merely a final expression of the terms that it contains.[43] The sharpest disagreement in connection with the parol evidence rule has been over the application of this test. It is one thing to accept that what is written cannot be contradicted; it is quite another to accept that what is written cannot be supplemented even by consistent terms. It is generally agreed that the mere fact that the agreement is integrated does not give rise to a presumption that it is completely integrated. The commentary to the Code concurs in rejecting "any assumption that because a writing has been worked out which is final on some matters, it is to be taken as including all the matters agreed upon."[44]

The point in dispute is whether the fact that the writing appears on its face to be a complete and exclusive statement of the terms of the agreement establishes conclusively that the agreement is completely integrated. In Williston's view, it does. "It is generally held that the contract must appear on its face to be incomplete in order to permit parol evidence of additional terms."[45] Many courts, particularly in cases decided in the first half of this century, have agreed that the issue is to be resolved by first inspecting the writing alone. If, on its face, the agreement appears to be completely integrated, the court should simply accept that this is so. Some courts have recognized the futility of trying to tell whether the writing is completely integrated without looking beyond the four corners of the writing and so have softened the test. These courts read the writing in the light of surrounding circumstances—excluding, however, the most vital circumstance of all, the evidence of the prior negotiations themselves.

The opposing camp, led by Corbin, rejects even this exclusion. According to Corbin, account should always be taken of all circumstances, including evidence of prior negotiations, since the completeness and exclusivity of the writing cannot be determined except in the light of those circumstances. "The writing cannot prove its own completeness and accuracy."[46] The trend clearly favors Corbin. The Restatement Second commentary agrees that "a writing cannot of itself prove its own com-

43. Restatement (Second) of Contracts § 210(1) ("an integrated agreement adopted by the parties as a complete and exclusive statement of the terms of the agreement"); UCC 2–202(b) ("intended also as a complete and exclusive statement of all the terms").

44. UCC 2–202, Comment 1.

45. 4 S. Williston, Contracts § 633 (3d ed. 1961).

46. Corbin, The Parol Evidence Rule, 53 Yale L.J. 603, 630 (1944), reprinted in 3 A. Corbin, Contracts § 582 (1960).

pleteness, and wide latitude must be allowed for inquiry into circumstances bearing on the intention of the parties."[47]

In the face of this controversy, the contract drafter is wise to recite that his agreement is completely integrated if he wishes it to be so regarded. He can do this by what is commonly known as a *merger clause*, which "merges" prior negotiations into the writing. A typical clause reads: "This writing contains the entire agreement of the parties and there are no promises, understandings, or agreements of any kind pertaining to this contract other than stated herein." Because integration depends on the parties' intention, courts have with very few exceptions treated such clauses as conclusive in determining whether the agreement is completely integrated.

In understanding the parol evidence rule, it is as important to know what kinds of evidence it does not exclude as it is to know what kinds it does exclude. First, since it applies only to evidence of prior—and, as is sometimes said, contemporaneous[48]—negotiations, it does not exclude evidence of negotiations that took place after the written agreement was made. Second, since the rule assumes a valid written agreement, it does not exclude evidence to show that there was not agreement or that the agreement was invalid. Third, since the rule excludes evidence only if it contradicts a term of the writing—or, if the integration is complete, if the evidence supplements the writing—the rule does not exclude evidence offered to help interpret the language of the writing.

Because the parol evidence rule applies only to pre-contractual negotiations, it does not bar evidence of subsequent negotiations to show modification of the contract. Even a completely integrated agreement can therefore be modified or rescinded orally, subject, of course, to the doctrine of consideration and the statute of frauds. In a few states, legislation requires a writing for the modification or rescission of a written agreement.

Parties to a written agreement sometimes insert a specific provision precluding modification in an attempt to make their contract immune to oral modification. Such no-oral-modification clauses are particularly common in commercial construction contracts, where they are inserted to protect the owner from claims that his project superintendent orally modi-

---

47. Restatement (Second) of Contracts § 210, Comment b. See also UCC 2–202, Comment 3 (test is whether "additional terms are such that, if agreed upon, they would certainly have been included in the document").

48. UCC 2–202 ("may not be contradicted by evidence of any prior agreement or of a contemporaneous oral agreement").

fied the contract so as to have the builder do extra work. A typical clause reads: "No extra work or changes from plans and specifications under this contract will be recognized or paid for, unless agreed to in writing before the extra work is started or the change made."[49] A party may also attempt to achieve this kind of protection by a clause limiting the authority of his representative to contract on his behalf, but the effectiveness of such clauses turns on the law of agency and will not be dealt with here.

Can the parties, by inserting a no-oral-modification clause, effectively erect a kind of private statute of frauds that will permit only written modifications? The common law answer has been that they cannot. In some cases courts have reasoned that any prior agreement, including the no-oral-modification clause itself, can be modified by a later agreement. In most cases, however, the party who seeks to escape the effect of the no-oral-modification clause has relied on the oral modification. As the Supreme Court of Pennsylvania concluded in one such case, "when an owner requests a builder to do extra work, promises to pay for it and watches it performed knowing that it is not authorized in writing, he cannot refuse to pay on the ground that there was no written change order."[50] Many cases have proclaimed the ineffectiveness of no-oral modification clauses more broadly than this, without regard to reliance. Nevertheless, these cases fall short of holding that an oral modification is enforceable, despite such a clause, if there has been no reliance.

Furthermore, the common law rule has been subjected to important statutory inroads. A New York statute gives effect to provisions in written agreements that prohibit oral modification or termination,[51] and the Uniform Commercial Code follows New York in this respect. Under UCC 2-209(2), "A signed agreement which excludes modification or rescission except by a signed writing cannot be otherwise modified or re-

---

49. This language is taken from the clause in Wagner v. Graziano, 390 Pa. 445, 136 A.2d 82 (1957). For a more general provision, see F. Hart and W. Willier, Forms and Procedures under the Uniform Commercial Code (5 Bender's Uniform Commercial Code Service) § 21.07[3] (1974) ("This contract may be modified or rescinded only by a writing signed by both of the parties or their duly authorized agents.").

50. Universal Builders v. Moon Motor Lodge, 430 Pa. 550, 560, 244 A.2d 10, 16 (1968).

51. N.Y. Gen. Oblig. L. § 15-301(1) ("written agreement . . . which contains a provision to the effect that it cannot be changed orally, cannot be changed by an executory agreement unless such executory agreement is in writing and signed").

scinded. . . ."[52] Such a complete reversal of the common law rule would be severely tested in a case in which one party had relied on the oral modification. The drafters therefore softened the reversal by adding that "an attempt at modification or rescission . . . can operate as a waiver" even though it is not in writing as required by the clause,[53] but "a waiver affecting an executory portion of the contract" may be retracted "unless the retraction would be unjust in view of a material change of position in reliance on the waiver."[54]

9.6 Interpretation: Meaning of Language

How do courts in the United States resolve disputes over the meaning of contract language? In such a dispute each party claims that the language should be given the meaning that he attaches to it at the time of the dispute. However, the resolution of the dispute begins, not with these meanings, but with the meanings attached by each party at the time the contract was made. Since a contract involves two parties, the search for meaning begins with the meaning attached by both parties to the contract language; each needs the other's assent.

The possible combinations of these two meanings can be analyzed through a series of hypotheticals based on the celebrated case of *Raffles* v. *Wichelhaus*.[55] The parties had agreed upon the sale of cotton to be sent to the buyer on the ship *Peerless* from Bombay. There happened, however, to be two ships named *Peerless* leaving Bombay at different times, one in October, the other in December. The buyer argued that *Peerless* should be interpreted to require October shipment, while the seller argued that it should be interpreted to require December shipment.

First, a seemingly simple case can be disposed of. Suppose it is shown that, when the parties made the contract, both had in mind the same ship,

---

52. This provision enables the parties to require a writing even when the statute of frauds (UCC 2–201) does not apply to the modification. UCC 2–209(2) takes on special importance in view of the fact that UCC 2–209(1) removes the requirement of consideration for a modification. UCC 2–209(2) goes on to say that "except as between merchants such a requirement on a form supplied by the merchant must be separately signed by the other party."

53. UCC 2–209(4).

54. UCC 2–209(5).

55. 2 H. & C. 906, 159 Eng. Rep. 375 (1864).

say the December *Peerless*. In practice, only rarely can one party show that the meaning that he asserts at the time of the dispute was shared by both parties at the time the contract was made. Nevertheless, if he does show this, should he not prevail? Surely, if one party shows that the other party attached the same meaning that he did, the other party should not be able to avoid that meaning by showing that a reasonable person would have attached a different one.

This, however, is one of the areas in which judicial attitudes have differed markedly in the United States. Here the controversy between the objective and subjective theories of assent, discussed earlier,[56] flared up again. The objectivists refused to concede the primacy of a common meaning, shared by both parties. They maintained that an objective standard of reasonableness should always be applied to determine the meaning of *Peerless*. If under that standard the word *Peerless* would have referred to the October *Peerless*, that should be the meaning of *Peerless*, even though both parties had the other ship in mind. But this reasoning sacrifices the actual expectations of the contracting parties to a supposed objective meaning. Fortunately, it is easier to find statements of his approach than it is to find instances in which the approach has clearly carried the day. Instead, such authority as there is in the United States supports giving effect to a common meaning shared by both parties in preference to an objective meaning.

The usual case, however, is not one of a common meaning, shared by both parties, but one that is best described as a "misunderstanding." Suppose that, when the contract was made, the buyer had the October *Peerless* in mind and the seller had the December one in mind. If the subjective theory were followed here—if a contract really required a "meeting of the minds"—there would be no contract. Nor would there be a contract in any of the many cases in which, in spite of apparent assent, ambiguity or vagueness masks hidden dissent. Unless no contract is to result whenever the parties have attached different meanings to the contract language, some basis must be found to tip the scales in favor of one meaning or the other.

In some cases, one party (and only one party) actually knows that the other party has attached another meaning and knows what that meaning is. Suppose, for example, that the buyer has in mind the October *Peerless* and the seller the December one, but the buyer knows, perhaps from something that the seller has said, that the seller has in mind the December one.

56. See § 4.4 supra.

In that case, any court would conclude that there is a contract on the seller's terms—for shipment on the December *Peerless*.[57] As in the situation in which the buyer actually knows that the seller attaches another meaning, the result can be rationalized on the ground that the buyer is at fault, but here it is a more attenuated kind of fault. The advantages in terms of predictability and certainty of this use of an objective standard are obvious and are much appreciated by courts.

A practical illustration of this reasoning is *Frigaliment Importing Co.* v. *International Sales Corp.*,[58] which involved the meaning of the word *chicken* in a contract of sale by an American exporter to a Swiss importer. When the seller shipped stewing chicken, the buyer, after accepting it, sued on the ground that *chicken* meant a young chicken, suitable for broiling or frying. The seller maintained that the word was used in a broader sense and included stewing chicken. The court assumed that, when the contract was made, each party attached the meaning that it asserted and that therefore a misunderstanding had arisen. It resolved the misunderstanding in favor of the seller. Although the buyer may have attached the narrower meaning to the word *chicken*, it did not appear that the seller had reason to know this. The court reasoned that the buyer had "the burden of showing that 'chicken' was used in the narrower rather than the broader sense, and this it has not sustained."[59]

In the situations discussed thus far, it has been assumed that each party attached a meaning to the language in question at the time the contract was made. In many disputes arising out of contemporary business transactions, however, the parties gave little or no thought to the impact of their words on the case that later arose. Perhaps the contract is embodied in a printed form that neither party prepared; perhaps its clauses have been lifted from a form book; perhaps the deal is a routine one struck by minor functionaries. For these and many other reasons the analysis suggested earlier may be unsuitable. The court will then have no choice but to look solely to a standard of reasonableness. Interpretation cannot turn on meanings that the parties attached if they attached none, but must turn on the meaning that reasonable persons in the positions of the parties would have attached if they had given the matter thought. If the contract is on a widely used standard form, the use of this purely objective test has the advantage of

57. Restatement (Second) § 201(2).
58. 190 F. Supp. 116 (S.D.N.Y. 1960).
59. Id. at 121.

promoting uniform interpretation, without regard to the chance circumstances of the parties.

In conclusion, one must look with some skepticism on the common judicial statement that in interpreting a contract the court merely carries out "the intentions of the parties." The court does indeed carry out their intentions in those relatively rare cases in which the parties attached the same meaning to the language in question. But if the parties attached different meanings to that language, the court's task is the more complex one of applying a standard of reasonableness to determine which party's intention is to be carried out at the expense of the other's. And if the parties attached no meaning to that language, its task is to find by a standard of reasonableness a meaning that does not accord with any intention at all. What principles guide a court in these tasks?

At the time the contract was made, a party may have attached a particular meaning to the language that is later in dispute or may not have considered its meaning. If he attached a meaning to the language, he at least has his own testimony to show this at trial. However, he is likely to have difficulty establishing that the other party should reasonably have been aware of this at the time of agreement. If, instead, he did not consider the meaning of the language when contracting, he is likely to have difficulty showing that the meaning he asserts at trial was the more reasonable meaning at the time of agreement. In either case, the court must apply a standard of reasonableness in interpreting the contract language. What principles guide the court in doing this?

The overarching principle of contract interpretation in the United States is that the court is free to look to all the relevant circumstances surrounding the transaction. This includes all writings, oral statements, and other conduct by which the parties manifested their assent, together with any prior negotiations between them and any applicable course of dealing, course of performance, or usage. The entire agreement, including all writings, will be read together in the light of all the circumstances, even though the effect of this may be to subordinate minor points of grammar or punctuation to the sense of the agreement as a whole. Since the purpose of this inquiry is to ascertain the meaning to be given to the language, there should be no requirement that the language be unclear before the inquiry is undertaken.

Indeed, it is questionable whether a word has a meaning at all when divorced from the circumstances in which it is used. Dictionary definitions may be of help in showing the general use of words, but they are not necessarily dispositive. In Judge Learned Hand's words, "it is one of the surest indexes of a mature and developed jurisprudence not to make a fortress out of the dictionary."[60] Parties do not always use words in accordance with their dictionary definitions, so that the meaning attached to a word by the parties must be gleaned from its context, including all the circumstances of the transaction. Sometimes the nature of either the parties or the subject matter shows that the contract was made with reference to a specialized vocabulary of technical terms or other words of art. And sometimes it can be demonstrated that the parties contracted with respect to a usage in their trade or even with respect to a restricted private convention or understanding.

The significance of surrounding circumstances in interpreting contract language is reflected in a judicial emphasis on *purpose interpretation*. According to the Restatement Second, "if the principal purpose of the parties is ascertainable it is given great weight."[61] Such purpose interpretation has a secure place in the field of statutory interpretation.[62] The analogy to contracts, however, is less than perfect because, although a legislature may be said in a sense to have but one collective purpose, the two parties to a contract often have different purposes. Nevertheless, each party may have an understanding of the purposes that the other expects the contract to serve. It seems proper to regard one party's assent to the agreement with knowledge of the other party's general purposes as a ground for resolving doubts in favor of a meaning that will further those ends, rather than a meaning that will frustrate them.

Sometimes, in the case of a written contract, the court need not look outside the writing to discern the parties' purpose. It may find a helpful statement of the purpose set forth in the writing itself in the form of a recital. It is not uncommon for written contracts to begin with a series of such recitals of the surrounding circumstances and of the objectives of the parties. Traditionally prefixed by the word *whereas*, contract recitals are not ordinarily drafted as promises or conditions. Although their proper role in the interpretation of the main body of the contract has sometimes been unclear, it is plain that they are frequently intended to, and often do, shed light on the circumstances the parties wish to have considered in the interpretation of the contract.

Although a court may look at all the circumstances in the process of interpreting contract language, the language itself imposes a limit on how far the court will go in that process. Learned Hand suggested somewhat

---

60. Cabell v. Markham, 148 F.2d 737, 739 (2d Cir.), aff'd, 326 U.S. 404 (1945).
61. Restatement (Second) of Contracts § 202(1).
62. See Heydon's Case, 3 Coke's Rep. 7a, Eng. Rep. 637 (Ex. 1584).

less flexibility when he wrote that "there is a critical breaking point . . . beyond which no language can be forced."[63] Most judges would probably agree, but just where that critical point comes in an actual case will turn on the language of the contract, along with other relevant facts and also on the attitude of the particular court toward the authority of words. But even though judicial attitudes differ considerably, some generally accepted rules in aid of interpretation can be distilled from the collective attitudes of judges as a body.

When interpreting contract language, courts start with the assumption that the parties have used it in the way that reasonable persons ordinarily do. Some of the assumptions that courts make as to normal habits in the use of language are so widely shared and so frequently articulated that they have come to be regarded as rules of contract interpretation. Some of these rules have been encapsulated in Latin maxims. One illustration is the assumption that parties who list specific items, without any more general or inclusive term, intend to exclude unlisted items, even though they are similar to those listed. From this assumption comes the maxim *expresso unius est exclusio alterius* ("the expression of one thing is the exclusion of another"). Another illustration is the assumption that parties who list specific items, followed by a more general or inclusive term, intend to include under the latter only things that are like the specific ones. From this assumption comes the *ejusdem generis* ("of the same kind") rule.

Other assumptions relate more specifically to the way in which reasonable persons ordinarily use language during the agreement process. Thus there is the assumption that the parties intend every part of the agreement to mean something, although not necessarily to be legally binding. Therefore, an interpretation that gives meaning to the entire agreement is favored over one that makes some part of it mere surplusage. Where, however, two provisions so clearly conflict that both cannot be given full effect, it is assumed that the more specific the provision, the more likely it is to reflect the parties' intention. Accordingly, a specific provision controls a general one and may operate as an exception to it.

Besides such rules of interpretation, which are designed to ascertain the meaning that the parties might reasonably have attached to their language, there are other rules that have, at least in part, a different purpose. An example is the assumption that the bargaining process results in a fair bargain, so that, between an interpretation that would yield such a bargain

63. Eustis Mining Co. v. Beer, Sondheimer & Co., 239 F. 976, 982 (S.D.N.Y. 1917).

as a reasonable person would have made and one that would not, the former is preferred. Furthermore, if language supplied by one party is reasonably susceptible to two interpretations, one of which favors each party, the one that is less favorable to the party who supplied the language is preferred. Such interpretation *contra proferentem* ("against the profferer") is much favored in the interpretation of standard form contracts, and often operates against a party who is at a distinct advantage in bargaining.

A particularly interesting rule is found in the Restatement Second in connection with the interpretation of standardized agreements: "Such a writing is interpreted whenever reasonable as treating alike all those similarly situated, without regard to their knowledge or understanding of the standard terms of the writing."[64] Under this rule, the meaning that an individual party may have attached to the contract language is plainly subordinated to the goal of equality of treatment for parties who are similarly situated.

The rules discussed so far have made use of intrinsic aids, derived from the contract itself and not dependent on outside circumstances. To what extent will a court also look to extrinsic aids for guidance in interpreting contract language?

We have already seen that in interpreting a contract, an American court will look to all the relevant circumstances surrounding the transaction. A court may, for instance, consider prior negotiations, even if they show that both parties attached to the contract language a meaning different from the one that would ordinarily be given to it. All courts agree that the parol evidence rule permits them to do this even though the language is contained in an integrated agreement, as long as the language itself is unclear. Not all courts agree, however, that the parol evidence rule permits them to do this even though the language is clear.

Although judicial attitudes differ, the better view is that the parol evidence rule does not exclude evidence of prior negotiations to interpret contract language that is clear on its face. Even advocates of this view must admit, however, that the concept of a "plain meaning" of language appears to have retained some vitality in the field of contract interpretation, perhaps because of judicial skepticism as to the authenticity of proffered evidence of prior negotiations.

Under the older, more restrictive view, held by Williston and the first Restatement, evidence of prior negotiations may be used for the purpose of

64. Restatement (Second) of Contracts § 211(2).

interpretation only if the language in the writing is unclear, in the sense of being ambiguous or vague.[65] Under this restrictive view, the decision to admit extrinsic evidence involves two steps: first, the court must decide as a question of law whether the language is unclear; second, if it concludes that the language is unclear, it then admits evidence of prior negotiations for the sole purpose of resolving that lack of clarity. Courts following this view have insisted that a party seeking to introduce such extrinsic evidence be specific in pointing to the lack of clarity that he claims.

Under the newer, more liberal view, championed by Corbin and followed by the Restatement Second, the parol evidence rule does not apply at all to matters of interpretation.[66] Integrated and unintegrated agreements are treated alike, and extrinsic evidence of prior negotiations is always admissible as long as it is used for the purpose of interpretation. The court need not first determine that the language is unclear, as it must do under the restrictive view. In Corbin's words, "No parol evidence that is offered can be said to vary or contradict a writing until by process of interpretation the meaning of the writing is determined."[67] Although under this liberal view it is unnecessary to determine whether the language of an integrated writing is "clear," it is still necessary to determine that what is involved is merely "interpreting" the writing and not "contradicting" it or, in the case of a complete integration, "adding to" it. Because interpretation ends with the resolution of problems that involve the meaning of language, even under the liberal view, extrinsic evidence is admissible only where the question is what language means.

The two views come into conflict when a party offers extrinsic evidence to resolve a claimed ambiguity or vagueness that is not apparent from the face of the document. Should evidence of prior negotiations be admissible to show that the parties attached to their language a meaning that differs from the one that reasonable persons would have attached, at least as long as that meaning does not exceed the "critical breaking point . . . beyond which no language can be forced"? The difference between the two views in practice is less than might be supposed because, though occasionally the two views lead to different results, in most instances they will lead to the same result. For example, sometimes evidence rejected by courts that

65. See 1 S. Williston, Contracts § 95 (3d ed. 1957).

66. A. Corbin, Contracts § 572B (Supp. 1971); Restatement Second § 212 and Comment b.

67. Corbin, The Parol Evidence Rule, 53 Yale L.J. 603, 622 (1944), adapted in 3 A. Corbin, Contracts § 579 (1960).

have adopted the restrictive view would not be admitted by courts adhering to the liberal view either, since the evidence is not offered for the purpose of interpretation at all. And in some of the cases in which courts have purported to have accepted the liberal view, the extrinsic evidence admitted would have been admitted even under the restrictive view because the language was characterized by the court as vague and ambiguous.

With a decline in the judicial reverence for the written word and with a growing recognition that the meaning of language may vary greatly according to the circumstances, it has become increasingly difficult to defend the restrictive view, even though that view may tend to shorten the judicial process. If it is recognized that all language is infected with uncertainty and that even language that seems on its face to have only one possible meaning may take on a different meaning when the circumstances are disclosed, it makes little sense for a court to ask whether language is on its face "unclear" as opposed to "clear." Nevertheless, it does make sense for a court to ask whether evidence is offered for the purpose of resolving a question of the meaning of language. In this way the liberal rule can be so applied as to keep the trial of issues of interpretation within manageable bounds.

Having considered the admissibility of extrinsic evidence of prior negotiations, we turn next to the admissibility of other kinds of extrinsic evidence, notably evidence of course of dealing, usage, and course of performance.

9.7 Course of Dealing, Usage, and Course of Performance

Sometimes one of the parties to an agreement contends that it is to be read in the light of a prior course of dealing between the parties or a usage current in a trade, vocation, or place involved in the transaction. Such contentions are especially common in disputes over commercial contracts, and the Uniform Commercial Code contains an important provision on course of dealing and usage of trade.[68]

The Code describes a course of dealing as "a sequence of previous conduct between the parties to a particular transaction which is fairly to be

---

68. UCC 1–205. Because this section is in Article 1, General Provisions, it applies to all commercial contracts, not only those for the sale goods. Its principles extend by analogy to noncommercial contracts as well.

regarded as establishing a common basis of understanding for interpreting their expressions and other conduct."[69] The concept of a course of dealing, therefore, is relevant only when the parties to an agreement have dealt with each other in similar transactions on previous occasions. A sequence of conduct by the parties in their earlier transactions is said by the Code to "give particular meaning to and supplement or qualify" the terms of their later agreement.[70] The words *supplement* or *qualify* make it clear that conduct may have an effect beyond mere interpretation of those terms. Although the term *course of dealing* has been popularized by the Code, the underlying idea that an agreement is to bc read in the light of the parties' previous dealings is not novel and has force even in situations to which the Code is not literally applicable.[71]

The Code describes a usage of trade as a "practice or method of dealing having such regularity of observance in a place, vocation or trade as to justify an expectation that it will be observed with respect to the transaction in question."[72] A usage may be limited to a particular geographical area or to a particular kind of activity, or it may be limited in both ways. Under the Code "any usage of trade in the vocation or trade in which [the parties] are engaged or of which they are or should be aware" is said, just like a course of dealing, to "give particular meaning to and supplement or qualify terms of an agreement."[73] The term *usage of trade* is relatively new and favored by the Code over the more traditional and narrower term *custom*. However, the underlying principle, which is that an agreement is to be read in the light of a common practice or method of dealing, is an old one. This principle extends to "usages" generally, even though they may not be "of trade" and therefore not subject to the Code.[74] As in the case of a course of dealing, the Code's use of the words *supplement or qualify* makes clear that more may be involved than merely interpretation of contract language, although many cases involve no more than that.

Reliance on usages to supplement the terms of an agreement has sometimes been criticized as an unwarranted encroachment on the general

69. UCC 1–205(1).

70. UCC 1–205(3).

71. See Restatement Second § 223, which states an analogous rule.

72. UCC 1–205(2). As Comment 7 makes clear, "usages may be either general to trade or particular to a special branch of trade."

73. UCC 1–205(3).

74. See Restatement (Second) of Contracts §§ 219-222, which state analogous rules.

rules of law that would otherwise be used to perform this task. The Code commentary, however, rejects "those cases which see evidence of 'custom' as representing an effort to displace or negate 'established rules of law'" and asserts that usages "are the framework of common understanding controlling any general rules of law which hold only where there is no such understanding."[75]

Whether a usage exists is a matter of fact rather than law. "The existence and scope of . . . a usage," the Code provides, "are to be proved as facts."[76] A party commonly shows a usage by producing expert witnesses who are familiar with the activity or place in which the usage is observed.[77] Their testimony must establish that the practice or method of dealing has "such regularity in a place, vocation or trade as to justify an expectation that it will be observed with respect to the transaction in question."

Once a party has proved a usage, he must also prove that the other party is chargeable with knowledge of it. He may do this by showing that at the time the contract was made the other party either was actually aware of the usage or should have been aware of it. Under the Code, if a party is engaged in the vocation or trade in question, he is presumed to have the requisite knowledge.[78] A party who enters a vocation or trade, therefore, subjects himself to usages of which he may not in fact be aware.

To what extent is a party precluded from showing a course of dealing or a usage by the fact that the agreement in question is a written one? Under the Code's formulation of the parol evidence rule, a writing may be "explained or supplemented" by evidence of course of dealing or usage of trade even if it is a complete integration.[79] But under the Code's specific provisions on course of dealing and usage, however, evidence will only be admitted to show a course of dealing or usage of trade that is "consistent" with the express terms of the contract; otherwise the terms alone will

75. UCC 1–205, Comment 4.
76. UCC 1–205(2). The Code does not require the party who seeks to show a usage to plead it, but, under UCC 1–205(6), the party offering evidence of a usage must give the other party notice "sufficient to prevent unfair surprise."
77. For example, in Frigaliment Importing Co. v. B.N.S. Intl. Sales Corp. 190 F. Supp. 116 (S.D.N.Y. 1960), discussed in § 9.6 supra, text at note 58 (operator of a chicken eviscerating plant and an employee of a publisher of a market report on the poultry trade testified as to the meaning of "chicken.")
78. UCC 1–205(3)(3) subjects the parties to "any usage of trade in the vocation or trade in which they are engaged."
79. UCC 2–202.

control.[80] The question is then what is meant by "consistent"? If the evidence is offered merely for the purpose of interpretation, the Code commentary suggests that it will be admissible unless the course of dealing or usage of trade is "carefully negated" by the writing.[81] But the controversial cases under the Code are those in which the evidence is introduced to "supplement or qualify terms of an agreement."[82] In these cases courts have differed as to whether the evidence is admissible.

Both course of dealing and usage are based on facts existing at the time the contract was made. Sometimes the conduct of the parties after the contract is made indicates the meaning that they attach to the contract language subsequently in dispute. Such "practical construction" is given great weight by the courts. Conduct bearing on interpretation usually occurs during the course of performance of the contract. The Code says that if "the contract for sale involves repeated occasions for performance . . . any course of performance accepted or acquiesced in" shall be relevant in interpreting the contract.[83] The concept of a course of performance is not limited to the sale of goods and has long been applied to contracts of all kinds. It is sometimes difficult to draw the line between conduct that is the basis for a course of performance, on the one hand, and conduct that is the basis for waiver or modification, on the other,[84] but a "single occasion of conduct" cannot amount to a course of performance, although it may result in waiver or modification. In case of conflict, the provisions of the agreement prevail over course of performance but, at

80. UCC 1–205(4). In Comment 5 to UCC 1–205, reference is made to the incorporation of "trade code," presumably in writing, as usages. If such "trade codes" are incorporated by agreement, however, they would appear to qualify as express terms.

81. UCC 2–202, Comment 2.

82. It is not clear what the Code means by "qualify" or how a usage could "qualify" terms of an agreement under UCC 1–205(3) and still be "consistent" with them. The word "qualify" is not used elsewhere in this context. Under UCC 2–202, terms of an integrated agreement may be "explained or supplemented," but presumably not "contradicted" by usage. Comment 1 to UCC 1–205 speaks only of the instance in which the "commercial context . . . may explain and supplement" a writing.

83. UCC 2–208(1). Unlike the provisions on course of dealing and usage of trade, this provision is placed in the sales rather than in the general article.

84. See UCC 2–208, Comment 4 ("A single occasion of conduct does not fall within the language of this section but other sections such as the ones on silence after acceptance and failure to specify particular defects can affect the parties' rights on a single occasion.").

least according to the Code, course of performance controls both course of dealing and usage of trade.[85]

9.8 Interpretation: Filling of Gaps

Up to this point, our concern has been with disputes over the meaning of contract language as applied to particular situations. Courts resolve such disputes over *expression* by interpretation of the relevant contract language. Sometimes, however, disputes arise because there is no contract language that is relevant to the situation that has arisen. It is then up to the court to supply a term to deal with the omitted case. Such terms are called *implied* terms. Courts must resolve such disputes arising from *omission* by a process that is sometimes described as "gap-filling."

Interpretation is necessarily the first step in that process, since a court will supply a term only after it has determined that the language of the agreement does not cover the case at hand. It follows that any term that a court would supply can be derogated from by agreement of the parties, either explicitly or by necessary inference. Such terms are therefore suppletory rather than mandatory.

The process of interpretation used in determining whether there is an omitted case is essentially the same as that used for vague and ambiguous language. Courts rely on common practices in the use of language in deciding what parties might be expected to say in the circumstances. The more detailed and comprehensive the agreement, the less likely it is that the court will conclude that the case before it was omitted.

In interpreting the agreement, the court will also consider the foreseeability of the situation. If the court is convinced that the parties could not have foreseen it, and therefore could not have intended their agreement to cover it, the court may refuse to apply the contract language, despite its apparent applicability, and may find that the case before it is an omitted one. This result is particularly likely under long-term contracts, where unforeseeability is endemic. In the converse case, in which the court believes that the situation was foreseeable, it may conclude that the parties intended their apparently applicable language to cover the case. The problem with this reasoning is that a party may have foreseen the situation in question, yet not have intended the contract language to cover it. The party may have intentionally failed to raise it to avoid delay, the break-

85. UCC 2–208(2).

down of negotiations, or the inclusion of an unfavorable provision. As the commentary to the Restatement Second notes, "Factors such as the practical difficulty of reaching agreement on the myriad of conceivable terms of a complex agreement may excuse a failure to deal with improbable contingencies."[86] If this is the case, the court should recognize that it is faced with an omitted case, even though the dispute was foreseeable.

Once the court has determined through interpretation that it is faced with an omitted case, it must supply a term to deal with that case. The process by which a court supplies a term is often called *implication*. This process may have two bases.

The first basis for implication is the actual expectations of the parties. If the court is persuaded that the parties shared a common expectation with respect to the omitted case, the court will give effect to that expectation, even though the parties did not reduce it to words. However, if the parties' expectations were significantly different or if one party had no expectation, the court will substitute for the subjective test of shared expectation an objective test of whether one party should reasonably have known of the other's expectation. Expectation can sometimes be gleaned from the agreement itself. Thus a recital or a provision dealing with a related case may suggest the parties' intention with respect to the omitted case. Their intention may also be deduced from a course of performance, course of dealing, or usage, or from the negotiations that led up to the agreement if the parol evidence rule permits. In many cases, however, no reliable indication of expectation can be found. The court must then seek some other basis for implication.

It is sometimes suggested that if a court cannot determine the actual expectations of the parties, it should implement the expectations that it believes they would have had if they had considered the matter, thereby remedying "the shortsightedness of individuals, by doing for them what they would have done for themselves if their imagination had anticipated the march of nature."[87] However, this reasoning is out of place if the parties foresaw the situation but failed to provide for it. Furthermore, even if the parties did not foresee the situation, it is often naive to assume that a court can determine how the parties would have dealt with it had they foreseen it. And even if a court could determine this, it might find that the

86. Restatement Second § 261, Comment c.

87. J. Bentham, A General View of a Complete Code of Laws, in 3 Works of Jeremy Bentham 191 (J. Bowring ed. 1843).

term the parties would have chosen would be unjust for a court to supply because of the greater bargaining power of one of the parties.

In such situations, it should not be hypothetical expectations or fictitious intentions, but basic principles of justice that guide a court in extrapolating from the situations for which the parties provided to the one for which they did not. Where do courts find these basic principles of justice? Often they look to the idea of fairness in the exchange. In searching for what Lord Mansfield called "the essence of the agreement,"[88] a court seeks a fair bargain. It may, for example, justify the term it supplies on the ground that the term prevents one party from being in a position of "economic servility" and "completely at the mercy" of the other.[89] It is likely to supply a term that is suitable for a particular market or other segment of society or even for society in general. Furthermore, if the situation is a recurring one, a court will try to resolve the omitted case in a way that yields a convenient rule or that promotes certainty.

Courts are also influenced in deciding whether to supply a term by what might be called the "burden of expression." Although the parties can by express provision derogate from any term that the court would supply, the party who would do this bears the burden of having the provision added to the agreement. A court may therefore consider the realities of the negotiating and drafting processes and supply a term that will put the burden of expression on the party who can better cope with it because of bargaining power and drafting skill.

The parol evidence rule plays only a limited role in the process by which a court supplies a term to govern an omitted case. Its role in the initial step of interpretation has already been discussed. It may play no role at all in the second step of implication, because it is often unnecessary to resort to extrinsic evidence: the court's solution is based on circumstances that appear on the face of the contract. If it is necessary to resort to extrinsic evidence, the rule should not bar such evidence for the limited purpose of showing the circumstances on which a court must rely in deciding whether to supply a term. Evidence should be admissible for this purpose even if the agreement is completely integrated. But if the agreement is completely integrated, the parol evidence rule will bar extrinsic evidence for the purpose of showing additional promises or agreements of the parties, even if that evidence would enable the court to avoid having to supply a term.

---

88. Kingston v. Preston, Lofft 194, 198, 98 Eng. Rep. 606, 608, 2 Doug. 689, 691, 99 Eng. Rep. 437, 438 (1773).

89. Perkins v. Standard Oil Co., 235 Or. 7, 16, 17, 383 P.2d 107, 112 (1963).

Courts have been called upon to supply many different kinds of terms. We now consider two kinds of terms representative of the process described above: terms imposing a duty of good faith and terms imposing a duty of best efforts.

In recent years, courts have often supplied a term requiring both parties to a contract to exercise what is called *good faith* or sometimes *good faith and fair dealing*. This duty is based on fundamental notions of fairness, and its scope necessarily varies according to the nature of the agreement. Some conduct, such as subterfuge and evasion, clearly violates the duty. However, the duty may not only proscribe undesirable conduct, but may require affirmative action as well. A party may thus be under a duty not only to refrain from hindering or preventing the performance of the other party's duty, but also to take some affirmative steps to cooperate by helping the other party perform. Courts have often supplied a term requiring a party to exercise good faith when that party has been given a discretionary power over one of the terms of the contract. Output and requirements contracts are leading examples of this.

Under an output contract, the seller's duty to deliver is determined by his output, as to which he has some discretion; and under a requirements contract, the buyer's duty to purchase is determined by his requirements, as to which he has some discretion. Unless the parties have provided otherwise, the court will define the obligation to maintain output or requirements in terms of good faith. Any reduction in output or requirements, including the extreme case of complete cessation on going out of business, must be in good faith.[90] Any increase must also be in good faith, so that, for example, a buyer under a requirements contract has no right to goods for the purpose of stockpiling or speculation. However, this limitation on increases is usually less significant than that on reductions because an estimate, prior dealings, or other factors usually fix a ceiling on increases.

Another term that courts often supply is one imposing a duty of "best" or "reasonable" efforts. Such a duty requires a party to make such efforts as are reasonable in the light of his ability and the means at his disposal and of the other party's justifiable expectations. The duty of best efforts is thus more onerous than that of good faith. Courts have often supplied a term calling for best efforts under exclusive dealing agreements and under percentage leases.

---

90. UCC 2–306(1) ("such actual output or requirements as may occur in good faith").

9.9 Performance: Generally

When parties negotiate agreements, they usually assume that they will perform their obligations. Therefore they devote more attention to spelling out the required performances than to detailing what is to happen if those performances are not forthcoming. Frequently, then, it is left to the courts to determine the consequences of any nonperformance. Our focus here is on the rules courts fashion to deal with the nonperformance of bilateral contracts.[91]

When parties make a bilateral contract, they exchange promises in the expectation of a subsequent exchange of performances. Although the consideration for each party's promise is the other party's return promise, each party enters into the transaction only because he expects that the return promise will be performed. The principal goal of the rules applicable to the performance stage of such contracts is to protect that expectation against a possible failure of the other party to perform. It would be possible, of course, to leave a party who has not received the expected performance to pursue a claim for damages. But the injured party bargained for performance rather than for a lawsuit. Therefore courts have developed rules to give him, in addition to any claim for damages, the right to suspend his own performance and ultimately to refuse to perform if the other party fails to perform.[92]

9.10 Performance: Conditions

In developing these rules, courts have relied on the concept of a *condition*, an event that must occur before performance of a contractual duty becomes due.[93] In general, a party whose duty is conditioned on such an event is not required to perform unless the event has occurred.

---

91. Our concentration on bilateral contracts is only partly because they are economically more significant than unilateral contracts. Under the typical unilateral contract, the rules of offer and acceptance give the offeror the kind of security that must be achieved in a more complex way under a bilateral contract, and the offeree cannot avoid the risk inherent in performing first.

92. The terms "failure to perform" and "nonperformance" are used interchangeably here. They are used to include a defective performance as well as an absence of performance.

93. Restatement (Second) of Contracts § 224 defines a condition as "an event, not certain to occur, which must occur, unless occurrence is excused, before performance under a contract becomes due."

If language in a contract makes an event a condition of a duty of one party (the *obligor*), there are two effects if the condition does not occur. First, the obligor is entitled to suspend his performance on the ground that it is not due as long as the condition has not occurred. Second, if a time comes when it is too late for the condition to occur, the obligor is entitled to treat his duty as discharged and the contract as terminated.

Allowing the obligor to suspend his performance follows from the very definition of a condition. If a home buyer conditions his duty to close the deal on the bank's approval of his mortgage application, he is under no duty to take the deed and pay for the house if the bank has not approved his application. He may, if he chooses, suspend his performance on the ground that the condition has not occurred.

Allowing the obligor to treat his duty as discharged follows because ordinarily the suspension cannot last indefinitely. There is usually some period of time within which the condition must occur if it is to occur at all. This may be stated in a provision of the agreement or it may be a reasonable time under an implied term. Once the period has passed, it is too late for the condition to occur, and the party whose duty was originally conditional may, if he chooses, treat his duty as discharged. If the bank does not approve the home buyer's mortgage application within the appropriate period of time, he may treat his duty to take the deed and pay for the house as discharged. Furthermore, he is entitled to restitution of any down payment or part payment that he has made.

If the occurrence of a condition is required by the agreement of the parties, rather than as a matter of law, a rule of strict compliance traditionally applies. Williston wrote: "Since an express condition . . . depends for its validity on the manifested intention of the parties, it has the same sanctity as the promise itself. Though the court may regret the harshness of such a condition, as it may regret the harshness of a promise, it must, nevertheless, generally enforce the will of the parties. . . ."[94]

These effects do not follow, however, if the condition has been excused. Even if a duty is conditional at the time the contract is made, subsequent events may cause the performance to become due, even though the condition has not occurred at all or has not occurred within the required time. The occurrence of the condition, or its occurrence within the required time, is then said to be *excused*. Either waiver or breach may result in excuse.

94. 5 S. Williston, Contracts § 669 (3d ed. 1961).

A common ground for excuse of a condition is that, after the contract was made, the obligor promised to perform his duty despite the nonoccurrence of the condition or despite a delay in its occurrence. A promise of this kind is generally termed a *waiver*. A waiver results in the excuse of the nonoccurrence or of a delay in the occurrence of a condition of a duty. If a party, without consideration, has waived a condition that is within the other party's control before the time for occurrence of the condition has expired, he can retract the waiver and reinstate the condition unless the other party has relied to such an extent that retraction would be unjust. The retracting party must either give notice while there is still a reasonable time to permit the other party to cause the condition to occur or must give an extension of time.

An obligor may also excuse a condition of his duty by committing a breach that causes the nonoccurrence of the condition. When the condition is excused, the obligor's duty becomes absolute. The breach may take the form of nonperformance, either by prevention or by failure to cooperate, or it may take the form of a repudiation.

9.11 Performance: Duties

We turn now from conditions to duties. If a duty is fully performed, it is discharged. The converse is equally clear. Nothing less than full performance operates as a discharge. This is true even if the defect is insubstantial, even if it is neither willful nor negligent, and even if the party in breach is unaware of it. Courts occasionally ignore trifling defects under the principle *de minimis non curat le* ("the law does not concern itself with trifles"). Even so, courts usually render lip service to the requirement of full performance by concluding that, properly read, the contract itself tolerates such trifling defects. A court may rest a decision that the party in breach has performed, despite apparent defects, on the ground that the variance was within the range allowed by the specifications.

However, nonperformance does not always amount to a breach. Full performance may not yet be due, either because a required period of time has not yet passed or a condition has not yet occurred. Or the duty may already have been discharged, on a ground such as impracticability of performance or frustration of purpose. In these situations, the nonperformance is said to be "justified."

A party's nonperformance may, however, have even more dramatic consequences than that of making him liable for breach of contract. If the only consequence of a party's nonperformance were liability for breach of contract, a party to a bilateral contract would have little assurance of receiving the promised return performance. If the other party failed to render that performance, the injured party would still be bound to render his own performance. The injured party would have a remedy for breach, but this remedy might be no more than a claim for damages, collectible only after much delay. Were the injured party to refuse to perform in response to the other party's breach, the injured party would expose himself to a claim for damages that might exceed his own claim.

Courts have dealt with this situation by drawing an analogy to the concept of a condition and developing a concept of a constructive (*e.g.*, an implied) condition of exchange. To the extent practicable, a court will supply terms under which a party's duties are conditioned on the performance to be given in return. A party whose duty is in this way impliedly conditional on the other party's performance is afforded the security of not having to perform unless the other party has performed. Suppose that a house painter promises to paint a house in return for the homeowner's promise to pay $1,000. Even though the language of the contract does not make the homeowner's promise to pay conditional on the painter's performance, it is impliedly conditional on his performance. If the painter paints the house, payment becomes due; if he does not paint it, payment does not become due.[95]

In effect, the court supplies a term making each party's promise conditional on the other party's performance of the return promise. If the other party does not perform the return promise, this has the same two effects as the non-occurrence of any condition does. First, the first party's duty is suspended and he has no duty to perform unless the other party does. Second, after the time for performance by the other party has passed, the first party may treat his duty as discharged by the delay and therefore may terminate the contract. The rules of law applicable to such situations were first shaped by Lord Mansfield in the great English case of *Kingston* v. *Preston*, decided in 1773.[96]

---

95. Although the problems dealt with here most often arise if the failure of performance amounts to a breach, they may also arise if the failure is justified on a ground such as impracticability or frustration. A buyer is no less reluctant to pay for goods that the seller has failed to deliver if delivery was impracticable than if the failure was a breach. In both situations, the buyer is usually entitled to refuse to pay for goods that have not been delivered. However, the buyer has a right to recover damages from the seller only if the failure is a breach and not if it is justified.

96. 2 Dougl. 689, 99 Eng. Rep. 437 (K.B. 1773).

The timing of the parties' performances imposes some limits on the use of constructive conditions. If one party is to perform first and the other is to pay later, the law can afford the second party security by conditioning his duty to pay on performance by the first party, but it cannot afford the first party comparable security. Thus the order in which parties are to perform under a bilateral contract takes on an enhanced importance because of its relation to constructive conditions of exchange.

Sometimes the parties themselves fix the order of performance by the language of their agreement. If they do not, the situation may dictate that order. And over the years courts have developed some fairly simple rules to determine the order of performance under a bilateral contract if neither language nor circumstances indicates the order.

One of the most important of these rules is that, insofar as the agreement permits return performances to be rendered simultaneously, they are due simultaneously. This rule applies not only if no time is fixed for performance of either party, but also if a time is fixed for the performance of only one of the parties, or if one period is fixed within which both parties are to perform. It applies whether the performances that can be rendered simultaneously are whole or part performances. Thus, the law favors an order of performances that results in what are called *concurrent conditions of exchange*.[97] The Uniform Commercial Code reflects this preference in its general rule that delivery of the goods and payment of the price are to be simultaneous, so that tender of performance by each party is a condition of the other party's duty to perform.[98] The general rule for sales of land is the same. In addition to giving the parties symmetrical security, the rule avoids placing on either party the burden of financing the other party before the other has performed.

The judicial preference for simultaneous performances yields to the intention of the parties, as shown by their agreement or other circumstances. A common example of an agreement under which performances are not to be simultaneous is a contract for delivery of goods to the buyer on credit. In agreeing to such terms, the buyer loses none of the security that he would have had under a simultaneous exchange, since his duty to pay is conditional on the seller's delivery of the goods. The seller, in

97. See Restatement Second 234(1).

98. UCC 2–507(1) ("Tender of delivery is a condition to the buyer's duty to accept the goods and, unless otherwise agreed, to his duty to pay for them."); UCC 2–511(1) ("Unless otherwise agreed tender of payment is a condition to the seller's duty to tender and complete any delivery.").

contrast, loses the security that he would have had, since his duty to deliver the goods is no longer conditional on the buyer's tender of the price. A seller on credit who is unwilling to run this risk may take a security interest in the goods sold, but such transactions are beyond the scope of this discussion.

Often it is impossible for the parties to perform simultaneously. Sometimes, as in the case of a construction contract, the performance of one party will take time and that of the other will not. One of the parties must go first, forgoing the security that simultaneous performance would afford and bearing the burden of financing the transaction until the other party performs. Centuries ago the rule evolved that if one party is to do work and the other party is to pay, the performance of the work is to precede payment. This rule has its greatest impact on contracts of service, such as employment and construction contracts, but it also affects contracts to supply goods over a period of time. It has been suggested that the rule grew up in connection with employment contracts "and reflects a conviction that employers as a class are more likely to be responsible than are workmen paid in advance."[99]

The effect of the rule on employment contracts has been significantly diminished by the widespread enactment of statutes that give the employee a right to frequent periodic payment of wages. Furthermore, its effect on construction contracts has been reduced by express provisions that progress payments are to be made at stated intervals as work proceeds. The rule remains as a residual one from which the parties can depart if they choose. After all, it would not be feasible for courts to devise rules for progress payments in the wide variety of cases in which the parties have failed to do so, and the established rule is at least as fair as the opposite one would be.

9.12 Performance: Strict or Substantial

No sooner had Lord Mansfield conceived of what we now call constructive conditions of exchange than the need arose to mitigate the harsh effects of the rules traditionally applied to express conditions. By involving the

---

99. Restatement Second § 234, Comment e. See also Patterson, Constructive Conditions in Contracts, 42 Colum. L. Rev. 903, 919 (1942) ("The practice may be ascribed to the influence of employers as a dominant class, and to judicial inertia which allows an outmoded rule to continue unchanged. . . . That colleges and theatres ordinarily require payment in advance for the services which they furnish merely exemplifies the operation of the principle.").

concept of a condition to secure the expectations of one party, he exposed the other party to the risk of forfeiture. If strict performance were regarded as a condition of the duty to pay, the slightest breach would deprive a party of all right to payment under the contract. Lord Mansfield faced this problem only four years after he had decided *Kingston* v. *Preston*.[100]

In modern terms, his solution was that if one party's performance is a constructive condition of the other party's duty, only *substantial* performance is required of the first party before he can recover under the contract. This flexible requirement of substantial performance stands in sharp contrast to the requirement of strict compliance that protects a party who has taken the precaution of making his duty expressly conditional. Courts have applied the doctrine mainly to contracts for services, particularly construction contracts. If a builder can meet the test of substantial performance, he can recover on the contract the full price, minus any damages to which the owner is entitled because of the breach. These damages are based sometimes on the loss in value to the owner and sometimes on the cost to him to remedy the defect. Most courts have put on the owner the burden of showing the amount of his damages.

Whether performance is substantial is a question of fact that depends on the particular circumstances of the case. In Cardozo's words, "Where the line is to be drawn between the important and the trivial cannot be settled by a formula. . . . The question is one of degree, to be answered, if there is doubt, by the triers of the facts. . . ."[101]

The doctrine of substantial performance has not found universal favor. Courts generally have not applied it to a seller's claim against a buyer who has rejected property under a contract of sale. In this situation, the seller can often avoid forfeiture by selling the rejected property elsewhere at a reasonable price. In the words of Learned Hand, "There is no room in commercial contracts for the doctrine of substantial performance."[102] In the case of contracts for the sale of land, courts have also applied a rule of

100. Boone v. Eyre, 1 H. Bl. 273, note, 126 Eng. Rep. 160(a) (K.B. 1777).
101. Jacob & Youngs v. Kent, 230 N.Y. 239, 243, 129 N.E. 889, 891 (1921). Benjamin Nathan Cardozo (1870–1938) practiced in New York City after graduation from law school. He served as Judge and later Chief Judge of the Court of Appeals of New York and was appointed Associate Justice of the Supreme Court of the United States in 1932 to fill the vacancy left by Holmes. His judicial technique was characterized by careful working with both facts and rules of law to produce change that was evolutionary rather than revolutionary.
102. Mitsubishi Goshi Kaisha v. J. Aron & Co., 16 F.2d 185, 186 (2d Cir. 1926) (seller of soy bean oil, to be shipped "f.o.b. . . . Pacific Coast" and paid for against documents presented documents showing shipment from Dallas).

strict performance when the injured party brings an action at law for damages but have been more indulgent when he sues in equity for specific performance.

Although the Uniform Commercial Code adopts a rule of strict performance for the sale of goods,[103] a number of related sections soften the rule's impact. Among the most significant are those that subject a buyer who has accepted goods to a standard of substantial performance if he chooses to revoke his acceptance;[104] that subject a buyer under an installment contract to a similar standard if he chooses to reject an installment;[105] and that grant a seller the right to "cure" after the buyer has rejected the goods.[106]

In recent years, courts have tended to grant restitution to the party in breach. Thus, a party who is precluded from recovering on the contract because he has not substantially performed can at least recover for any benefit he has conferred, less damages for which he is liable because of his breach.[107] Granting restitution has become one of the principal means of mitigating the potentially harsh results of the concept of constructive conditions of exchange. In this respect, restitution plays a role similar to that of the doctrine of substantial performance.

Courts developed the doctrine of substantial performance to deal with the relatively simple case in which the party in breach had finished performing and the injured party refused to pay the price because the performance was defective or incomplete. Often the dispute arises at a much earlier stage of performance, however, and the question is whether a breach justified the injured party in refusing to render some performance that was then due. The injured party may be the defendant, seeking to justify his nonperformance in an action brought by the other party. Or he may be the plaintiff, seeking to justify his nonperformance in an action for damages against the other party.[108]

---

103. UCC 2–601 (buyer can reject "if the goods or the tender of delivery fail in any respect to conform to the contract").

104. UCC 2–608.

105. UCC 2–612.

106. UCC 2–508.

107. See Restatement (Second) of Contracts § 374, which states in the Reporter's Note that it "is more liberal in allowing recovery" than the first Restatement of Contracts § 357.

108. For the sake of clarity, this discussion is confined to claims for damages. However, a party who has a claim for damages for total breach may, as an alternative, have a claim for restitution based on the benefit that he has conferred by his own performance. What is said here applies to both types of claims. Somewhat different rules may apply to actions for specific performance.

Suppose that in breach of a construction contract the owner has delayed making a required progress payment, and the builder, after first refusing to go forward with the work, has finally terminated the contract, leaving the building unfinished.[109] Has the builder a defense if he is sued by the owner? Has the builder a claim against the owner for his breach? Under the concept of constructive conditions of exchange, the owner's payment of progress payments is an implied condition of the builder's duty to continue to work. Therefore, the owner's breach in failing to make a progress payment may have two effects on the builder's duty. First, further performance will not become due, so the builder will be justified in suspending performance. Second, after an appropriate period of time, the builder can choose to treat his remaining duties of performance under the contract as discharged and can terminate the contract. Two distinct issues are therefore raised. First, was the owner's breach in failing to make the progress payments significant enough to justify the builder's suspending performance? Second, did the owner's breach continue long enough to justify the builder's terminating the contract? If the answer to both questions is yes, the builder was entitled to terminate the contract and claim damages against the owner for breach. But if the answer to either is no, the builder's action was precipitous and unjustified, itself amounting to a breach that gave the owner a right to terminate and claim damages.

This sensible two-step analysis is carefully articulated in the Restatement Second.[110] It is in society's interest to accord each party to a contract reasonable security for the protection of his justified expectations. But it is not in society's interest to permit a party to abuse this protection by using an insignificant breach as a pretext for avoiding his contractual obligations. If the other party relied on the agreement, by performance or otherwise, "keeping the deal together" avoids the risk of forfeiture. Courts encourage this course as long as it will not seriously disappoint justified expectations. They do this by allowing the injured party to suspend performance only if the breach is *material*, that is, sufficiently serious to warrant this response. They curb abuse of this power to suspend by denying the injured party the power to exercise it if the breach is

---

109. The Uniform Commercial Code uses cancellation to refer to a party's act in putting "an end to the contract otherwise than for its breach." UCC 2–106. The word termination is used broadly in this book to refer to both kinds of acts. Although courts sometimes use rescission instead of termination, this usage is undesirable because it suggests avoidance of the contract, which would leave the injured party with no remedy other than restitution.

110. See Restatement (Second) of Contracts § 237 and Comment a.

immaterial, so that minor breaches will not disrupt performance. Courts also encourage the parties to keep the deal together by allowing the injured party to terminate the contract only after an appropriate length of time has passed. They restrain abuse of this power to terminate by denying the injured party the power to exercise it hastily, so that not all delays will bring the contract to an end, and the party in breach will be afforded some time to cure his breach. Both in choosing to suspend and in electing to terminate, the injured party takes precipitous action at his own risk. According to one court, his decision "is fraught with peril, for should such determination, as viewed by a later court in the calm of its contemplation, be unwarranted, the repudiator himself will have been guilty of material breach and himself have become the aggressor, not an innocent victim."[111]

If the injured party chooses to terminate the contract, he is said to treat the breach as *total*. His claim for damages for total breach takes the place of his remaining substantive rights under the contract.[112] It is calculated on the assumption that neither party will render any further performance. It therefore compensates him for the loss that he will suffer as a result of being deprived of the balance of the other party's performance, minus the amount of any saving that resulted from his not having to render his own performance.

If the injured party does not terminate the contract, either because he has no right to or does not choose to, he is said to treat the breach as *partial*. He has a claim for damages for partial breach, in addition to his remaining substantive rights under the contract.[113] It is calculated on the assumption that both parties will continue to perform in spite of the breach. It therefore compensates him only for the loss suffered as the result of the delay or other defect in performance that constituted the breach, not for the loss of the balance of the return performance. Since he is not relieved from performing, there is no saving to him to be subtracted.[114]

---

111. Walker & Co. v. Harrison, 347 Mich. 630, 635, 81 N.W.2d 352, 355 (1957).

112. See Restatement (Second) of Contracts § 236(1) ("A claim for damages for total breach is one for damages based on all of the injured party's remaining rights to performance.").

113. See Restatement § Second 236(2) ("A claim for damages for partial breach is one for damages based on only part of the injured party's remaining rights to performance.").

114. Under the Uniform Commercial Code, the buyer, on notifying the seller, may deduct damages for partial breach from the balance due on the price. UCC 2–717.

Suppose that the builder under a construction contract is in breach because of delay. If the breach is immaterial, the owner has no choice but to treat it as partial and continue his own performance. His only remedy is to claim damages for partial breach to compensate him for the loss caused by the delay. Similarly, if the breach is material, but the builder has cured it in time, the owner must continue his performance and claim damages for partial breach. If the breach is material and an appropriate length of time has passed, however, the owner can treat the breach as total and terminate the contract. The duties of both parties to perform are discharged, and the owner has a claim for damages for total breach in place of his substantive rights under the contract. In calculating the amount of this claim, the court will subtract the amount the owner saved, by not having to pay the balance of the price, from the owner's loss resulting from the builder's failure to complete the building.

Sometimes, when a dispute arises during the course of performance of a contract, both parties stop performing, and each claims that he was justified in terminating the contract because of the other's breach. The builder who has not received a progress payment may suspend and later terminate on the ground of nonpayment. On the other hand, the owner who has failed to pay may contend that his nonpayment was not a breach because the builder had already committed a material breach by failing to follow specifications, and the owner may terminate on that ground. In resolving such disputes, courts apply the principles discussed in this section. Often these principles lead a court to impose liability on the party who committed the *first material breach*. If the owner is correct in asserting that the builder committed the first material breach, that breach justified suspension by the owner, and the builder is liable for damages for total breach for his wrongful termination. Indeed, even if the owner had terminated and ordered the builder off the site because of his breach in not following specifications, the builder might be liable in damages for total breach if the owner had waited an appropriate time for the builder to cure his breach. But if the owner had not waited long enough before ordering the builder off the site, the owner's precipitous action would render him liable to the builder in damages for total breach of contract. This would be the result even though the builder was first to commit a material breach.

The breach on which an injured party relies in cases like these need not be of a duty that is stated in the agreement itself. Often the duty is an implied one, such as the duty of good faith that is generally imposed on a party to a contract. A party whose performance is hindered or prevented by the other party in violation of the duty of good faith may not be limited to a claim for damages for the other party's breach. If the breach is material, the injured party can suspend his performance and, should the breach continue too long, he can terminate. The same results may follow from a breach of an implied duty to take affirmative steps to cooperate.

9.13 Excuse: Impossibility at Common Law

In general, the early common law was not receptive to claims of excuse based on events occurring after the making of the contract. It held to the strict view that impossibility of performance was not an excuse. To this view, it admitted three important exceptions that are still recognized today.

Under the first of these exceptions, if supervening governmental action prevents a party's performance by prohibiting it or imposing requirements that make it impossible, that party is excused. The supervening governmental action need not be a statute; it may, for example, be an administrative or judicial order. The fact that the party can still perform if he is willing to break the law and take the consequences does not prevent his discharge, nor does the fact that the governmental action may prove to be invalid, as long as the party who claims discharge acts in good faith.[115] The action must, however, directly affect that party's performance, so that he cannot both comply with it and perform; it is not enough for the action merely to make performance somewhat more difficult by, for example, aggravating a shortage of supply.

Under the second exception, if a particular person's existence is necessary for performance of a duty, and performance is prevented by that person's death or disability, the duty is discharged. The person in question is usually the one who owes the duty, but he may also be the one to whom the duty is owed or a third person. However, the typical bilateral contract does not require the existence of the party who is to receive the performance. "The promise of a painter to paint a landscape is discharged by his physical inability to paint, but the death or illness of one who has contracted to buy the painting will not free his estate from liability."[116] If a party can delegate his duty to perform to someone else, his own death or incapacity will not excuse him.

Under the third exception, if the existence of a particular thing is necessary for a party's performance, the party is excused if the destruction

115. UCC 2–615(a) ("compliance in good faith with any applicable foreign or domestic governmental regulation or order whether or not it later proves to be invalid").

116. 18 S. Williston, Contracts § 1941 (3d ed. 1978).

or deterioration of that thing prevents performance.[117] This rule was confirmed and elaborated in the celebrated case of *Taylor* v. *Caldwell*,[118] the fountainhead of the modern law of impossibility.

That case arose out of a contract under which Taylor was to have the use of Caldwell's music hall for performances on four days, in return for payment of a fixed sum at the close of each day. When the hall was accidentally destroyed by fire less than a week before the first performance, Taylor sued Caldwell for breach of contract, claiming as damages the expenses he had incurred in preparing for the performances. The Court of King's Bench held, however, that Caldwell was excused because, "looking at the whole contract, we find that the parties contracted on the basis of the continued existence of the Music Hall at the time when the concerts were to be given; that being essential to their performance."[119] Whether a particular thing is necessary for performance is a question much like whether a particular person is necessary for performance, and the answer depends on all the circumstances. A clear case is dealt with in the Uniform Commercial Code, which excuses the seller from his duty to deliver if "the contract requires for its performance goods identified before the contract is made, and the goods suffer casualty without fault of either party before the risk of loss passes to the buyer."[120]

9.14 Excuse: Impracticability Under the Code

The common law development described above is synthesized in UCC 2-615, Excuse by Failure of Presupposed Conditions:

> Except so far as a seller may have assumed a greater obligation . . ., [d]elay in delivery or non-delivery in whole or in part

117. See Restatement (Second) of Contracts § 263.
118. 3 B. & S. 826, 122 Eng. Rep. 309 (K.B. 1863).
119. 3 B. & S. at 839, 122 Eng. Rep. at 314.
120. UCC 2–613. Once the risk of loss passes to the buyer, he must pay the price, even though the goods have been destroyed. UCC 2–709(a). Consequently, if goods are identified when the contract is made and are destroyed before risk passes, the seller is not liable in damages for breach of contract because he is excused, but he cannot recover the price; if the goods are destroyed after risk passes, the seller is not liable in damages because he has performed, and he can recover the price. Risk passes at a time determined by UCC 2–509, 2–510—most commonly at the receipt of the goods by the buyer.

> . . . is not a breach of his duty under a contract of sale if performance as agreed has been made impracticable by the occurrence of a contingency the non-occurrence of which was a basic assumption on which the contract was made. . . .

This synthesis, designed for the sale of goods, promises to have a substantial influence on the law of contract generally and has been adopted by the Restatement Second.[121]

The basis of the new synthesis is far removed from the reasoning in *Taylor* v. *Caldwell*. As a federal judge has pointed out, "The doctrine of impossibility of performance has gradually been freed from the earlier fictional and unrealistic strictures of such tests as the 'implied term' and the parties' 'contemplation.'"[122] The new synthesis candidly recognizes that the judicial function is to determine whether, in the light of exceptional circumstances, justice requires a departure from the general rule that a promisor bears the risk of increased difficulty of performance. However, the Code formulation does not include the word *risk*, and one judge has faulted its language as a "somewhat complicated way of putting Professor Corbin's question of how much risk the promisor assumed."[123] Nevertheless, the Code formulation is preferable to the alternative, facetiously suggested by Corbin, of praying for the "wisdom of Solomon."[124]

Under the new synthesis, the party who claims that a supervening event or "contingency" prevented his performance must meet four requirements.[125] First, the event must have made "performance as agreed . . . impracticable." Second, the nonoccurrence of the event must have been "a basic assumption on which the contract was made." Third, the impracticability must have resulted without the fault of the party seeking to be

---

121. Restatement (Second) of Contracts § 261.

122. Transatlantic Fin. Corp. v. United States, 363 F.2d 312, 315 (D.C. Cir. 1966).

123. United States v. Wegematic Corp., 360 F.2d 674, 676 (2d Cir. 1966).

124. 6 A. Corbin, Contracts § 1333 (1962), quoted in American Trading & Prod. Corp. v. Shell Intl. Marine, 453 F.2d 939, 944 (2d Cir. 1972).

125. Comment 4 to UCC 2–615, quoted in text at note 128 infra, suggests that the seller must be able to point to a particular "contingency" that has caused the impracticability. Restatement (Second) of Contracts § 261 speaks of an "event," while UCC 2–615 speaks of a "contingency," but no difference in meaning seems to have been intended. No event is required for existing, as distinguished from supervening, impracticability.

excused.[126] Fourth, that party must not have assumed a greater obligation than the law imposes.[127]

The first requirement for excuse is that the occurrence of the event must have made "performance as agreed . . . impracticable." The use of *impracticable*, rather than *impossible*, to describe that burden is not an innovation of the Code; courts did not insist on strict impossibility even under the traditional analysis. They recognized, for example, that a party's mere apprehension of illness, unaccompanied by actual disability, might excuse him from rendering personal services, and that a party's fear of exposing other persons or property to danger might excuse him from performing. Of course, a party is expected to exert reasonable efforts to eliminate the impediment to his performance.

Does this mean that a court may excuse a party merely because his performance has become more expensive? The Code commentary gives an ambivalent answer:

> Increased cost alone does not excuse performance unless the rise in cost is due to some unforeseen contingency which alters the essential nature of the performance. Neither is a rise or a collapse in the market in itself a justification, for that is exactly the type of business risk which business contracts made at fixed prices are intended to cover. But a severe shortage of raw materials or of supplies due to a contingency such as war, embargo, local crop failure, unforeseen shutdown of major sources of supply or the like, which either causes a marked increase in cost or altogether prevents the seller from securing supplies necessary to his performance, is within the contemplation of this section.[128]

Thus far, courts have only rarely held that a duty is discharged on the ground of mere increase in the expense of performing it. They have

---

126. This rather obvious requirement appears in Restatement Second 261 but not in UCC 2–615, although presumably it should be read in. It appears in UCC 2–613, which requires that "the goods suffer casualty without fault of either party."

127. Restatement (Second) of Contracts § 261 expresses this with the phrase "unless the language or the circumstances indicate the contrary."

128. UCC 2–615, Comment 4; see also Restatement (Second) of Contracts § 261, Commend d.

generally concluded that the additional expense, even if traceable to an identifiable supervening event, does not rise to the level of impracticability.

For example, in a series of cases in the federal courts, manufacturers who have contracted with the government to produce a product by means of a technological breakthrough have been unsuccessful in arguing that they are excused when technological difficulties have resulted in unexpectedly heavy costs. The federal courts have repeatedly held that the additional expense does not make performance impracticable. Similarly, in the Suez cases, ocean carriers were unsuccessful in arguing that they were excused by the closing of the Suez Canal, which forced them to use the longer and more costly route around the Cape of Good Hope. Courts consistently concluded that the additional expense did not make performance impracticable.

Courts have also been reluctant to excuse a party when, in the language of the Code commentary, the "impossibility of performance arises in connection with an incidental matter [and does not go] to the very heart of the agreement."[129] In such a case, a party is usually expected to take advantage of whatever substitute arrangements are available for performance by, for example, finding other means for loading, carrying, or delivering the goods.[130]

It is important to bear in mind that it is a party's "performance as agreed" that must become impracticable before he will be excused. Therefore, if the agreement gives a party a choice between alternative ways of performing, the fact that one of these alternatives becomes impracticable will not excuse him if another remains open. It was, for example, the courts' conclusion in the Suez cases that carriage through the Suez Canal and carriage around the Cape of Good Hope were alternative ways of performing. However, courts do not apply this principle if a party is given an alternative that is not "performance." For example, a party who undertakes to perform or pay liquidated damages is not regarded as having a choice between alternative performances.

---

129. UCC 2–614, Comment 1.

130. UCC 2–614(1) (if "the agreed berthing, loading or unloading facilities fail or an agreed type of carrier becomes unavailable or the agreed manner of delivery otherwise becomes commercially impracticable but a commercially reasonable substitute is available, such substitute performance must be tendered and accepted").

The second requirement for excuse is that the nonoccurrence of the event must have been "a basic assumption on which the contract was made." The commentary to the Restatement Second amplifies this:

> Determining whether the non-occurrence of a particular event was or was not a basic assumption involves a judgment as to which party assumed the risk of its occurrence. In contracting for the manufacture and delivery of goods at a price fixed in the contract, for example, the seller assumes the risk of increased costs within the normal range. If, however, a disaster results in an abrupt tenfold increase in cost to the seller, a court might determine that the seller did not assume this risk by concluding that the non-occurrence of the disaster was a 'basic assumption' on which the contract was made.[131]

The assumption may be tacit; a party may be said to have an assumption even though he is not conscious of alternatives, as one who walks into a room may assume that it has a floor without giving thought to the matter. But the assumption must be shared by both parties; no account is taken of one party's purely private assumptions.

Cases in which courts have traditionally excused promisors on grounds of impracticability can be grouped into three categories according to the basic assumptions involved.[132] First, parties ordinarily assume that the government will not directly intervene and prevent performance. Second, they ordinarily assume that a person who is necessary for performance will neither die nor be deprived of the necessary capacity before the time for performance. Third, they ordinarily assume that a thing that is necessary for performance will remain in existence and in such condition that performance can take place. Nearly all of the cases of impracticability that have arisen can be placed in one of these three traditional categories. However, other assumptions may also be considered "basic," in line with the tendency toward liberality in excusing promisors on the occurrence of extraordinary events.[133]

---

131. Restatement (Second) of Contracts, Chapter 11, Introductory Note.

132. In the Restatement (Second) of Contracts, a general statement of the rule on impracticability (§ 261) is followed by sections of each of these three categories (§§ 262, 263, 264).

133. The situation in which a labor dispute makes performance impracticable is one in which the basic assumption does not seem to fit within any of the three categories. See note 136 infra.

In determining what assumptions the parties made, a court should look at all relevant circumstances. Some courts have held that if the agreement is completely integrated, the parol evidence rule bars extrinsic evidence to show the assumptions of the parties. However, as already noted, there is no reason why such evidence should not be admitted for the limited purpose of showing circumstances that would justify the court in supplying a term. The better view allows such evidence to show, for example, an assumption that a particular source of supply would be in existence at the time for performance.

The third requirement for excuse is that the impracticability must have resulted without the fault of the party seeking to be excused. For example, a seller who is unable to deliver goods because they have been destroyed due to his negligence is not excused.[134] Neither is a party excused who is unable to perform personal services because of a disability resulting from his own misconduct; however, since it is often difficult to foresee the effect of a party's conduct on his ability to perform, the fault must be clear if it is to prevent excuse.

The fourth requirement for excuse is that the party must not have assumed a greater obligation than the law imposes. If a party expressly undertakes to perform, even though performance becomes impracticable, impracticability will not excuse him, and he will be liable for damages if he fails to perform. Even absent an express assumption of a greater obligation, a court may find, by negative implication from a clause excusing a party on the occurrence of some specified events, that he assumed the risk of some other event. Furthermore, the surrounding circumstances will sometimes justify an inference that a party assumed the risk of impracticability. For example, a manufacturer who has contracted with the government to produce a product by means of a technological breakthrough has generally been held to have assumed the risk that achieving it may be impracticable. If a product is to be manufactured in accordance with specifications furnished by the government, however, courts usually hold the government to an implied warranty that a satisfactory product will result if the specifications are followed. In that case the manufacturer is not liable if his failure is caused by a shortcoming in the specifications.

---

134. UCC 2–613 and Comment 1 ("'Fault' is intended to include negligence and not merely wilful wrong.").

It is sometimes said that if an event is foreseeable, a party who makes an unqualified promise to perform necessarily assumes an obligation to perform, even if the occurrence of the event makes performance impracticable. Admittedly there are cases, as the Code commentary explains, "when the contingency in question is sufficiently foreshadowed at the time of contracting to be included among the business risks which are fairly to be regarded as part of the dickered terms."[135] For example, if governmental approval is required for a party's performance, the party may be taken to assume the risk that approval will be denied if he fails to include a provision excusing him in that event. This reasoning may also explain why courts hesitate to excuse a party for impracticability resulting from labor disputes in the absence of an express provision to that effect.[136] But, as already suggested, a party may fail to provide for a risk, even though it is foreseeable, because he does not consider it to be significant enough to make it a subject of bargaining or because he regards his bargaining position as too weak to risk broaching the subject. Although the foreseeability of the event will often be a factor that suggests that a promisor assumed the risk of its occurrence, it should not be conclusive on that issue.[137] A court may also conclude that a party has assumed the risk of the occurrence of an event if he could have shifted this risk to a third party by contract. On this reasoning, a party may be held to have assumed a risk against which he could readily have protected himself by procuring insurance.

It is sometimes said that, while a party may be excused on the ground of *objective impossibility* ("the thing cannot be done"), he will not be excused on the ground of *subjective impossibility* ("I cannot do it"). Financial inability is commonly cited as an example of subjective impossibility. Under the new synthesis, however, it seems preferable to say that such risks as these are generally considered to be sufficiently within the control of one party that they are assumed by him.

---

135. UCC 2–615, Comment 8.

136. For an interesting discussion of foreseeability in this context, see Mishara Constr. Co. v. Transit-Mixed Concrete Corp., 365 Mass. 122, 310 N.E. 2d 363 (1974) ("Certainly, in general, labor disputes cannot be considered extraordinary in the course of modern commerce. . . . Much must depend on the facts known to the parties at the time of contracting. . . . Where the probability of a labor dispute appears to be practically nil, and where the occurrence of such a dispute provides unusual difficulty, the excuse of impracticability might well be applicable.").

137. See Restatement (Second) of Contracts, Chapter 11, Introductory Note.

9.15 Excuse: Frustration of Purpose

From impracticability of performance we turn to the closely related doctrine of frustration of purpose. The fountainhead of this doctrine is the English case of *Krell* v. *Henry*.[138] In 1902, when King Edward VII succeeded Queen Victoria, Britons awaited their first coronation in more than 60 years. Henry saw in the window of Krell's flat an announcement of windows to be let to view the coronation processions. He arranged with Krell's housekeeper to take a suite for the daytime of June 26 and 27 for a fixed sum, of which a part was paid in advance. On June 22, the House of Commons was informed that the King had been required to undergo an operation for appendicitis, and the coronation was indefinitely postponed. Henry refused to pay the balance, and Krell sued in what became the most noted of the coronation cases. The Court of Appeal held for Henry on the ground that his duty to pay had been discharged because "the coronation procession was the foundation of this contract, and . . . the object of the contract was frustrated by the non-happening of the coronation and its procession on the days proclaimed."[139]

The doctrine announced in *Krell* v. *Henry* has come to be known as that of frustration of purpose. Cancellation of the procession did not make performance by either party impracticable; it did not prevent Krell from letting Henry use his rooms or Henry from paying Krell the balance. Rather, its effect was to deprive one party entirely of the benefit he expected from the other's performance, since it made the use of Krell's rooms during the period for which they were let virtually worthless to Henry. In general, the doctrine of impracticability of performance operates to the advantage of those who are bound to furnish goods, land, services, or some similar performance, while the doctrine of frustration of purpose operates to the advantage of those who are to pay money in return for those performances.

The doctrine of frustration has been generally accepted by American courts. Although the doctrine is not explicitly recognized by the Uniform Commercial Code, there is little doubt that it is applicable to contracts for

---

138. [1903] 2 K.B. 740 (C.A.). Other noted coronation cases that arose out of the hiring of rooms are Chandler v. Webster, [1904] 1 K.B. 493, and Griffith v. Brymer, 19 T.L.R. 434 (K.B. 1903).
139. Id. at 751, 754.

the sale of goods.[140] It has been incorporated in both the first and second Restatements.[141]

The Restatement Second synthesis of the doctrine of frustration of purpose is strikingly similar to that of the doctrine of impracticability of performance.[142] The party who claims that a supervening event frustrated his purpose must meet four requirements, only the first of which is different from those for impracticability. First the event must have "substantially frustrated" his "principal purpose." Second, it must have been "a basic assumption on which the contract was made" that the event would not occur. Third, the frustration must have resulted without the fault of the party seeking to be excused. Fourth, that party must not have assumed a greater obligation than the law imposes.[143] Despite the similarity of the requirements for the two doctrines, courts have been much more reluctant to hold that a party has been excused on the ground of frustration than on the ground of impracticability. Parties seeking excuse on this ground have found the first and fourth requirements particularly troublesome, and we shall consider only these two.

Under the first requirement, a party must show that his principal purpose in contracting has been substantially frustrated. Courts have raised two obstacles to his doing so. First, they have viewed the affected party's principal purpose in broad terms. The mere fact that some exceptional event has prevented a party from taking advantage of the transaction in the particular way expected may not suffice to satisfy the requirement of substantial frustration if he can turn the bargain to his advantage in some other way. Second, courts have insisted that the frustration be nearly total. The mere fact that what was expected to be a profitable transaction has turned out to be a losing one is not enough. These two obstacles are illustrated by a Third Circuit case in which an American buyer of lamb pelts that were to be delivered in Toronto by a Canadian seller unsuccessfully urged frustration as an excuse when his planned importation of the pelts into the United States was prevented by the issuance of stricter import regulations. Although the contract itself indicated the buyer's

140. See UCC 1–103 ("Unless displaced by the particular provisions of this Act, the principles of law and equity . . . shall supplement its provisions.").

141. Restatement (Second) of Contracts § 288; Restatement (Second) of Contracts § 265.

142. Compare Restatement (Second) of Contracts § 265 with § 261.

143. Restatement (Second) of Contracts § 265 expresses this by the phrase "unless the language or the circumstances indicate the contrary."

intention to ship the pelts to Philadelphia, the court viewed the purpose of the agreement in much broader terms. According to the court, "the rest of the world was free to the buyer, so far as we know, as destination for the shipment."[144] Viewing the buyer's purpose as that of making any commercial disposition of the pelts, the court concluded that this purpose was not substantially frustrated, even though the buyer's "expectation of a profitable transaction was disappointed."[145]

Under the fourth requirement, the party seeking to be excused on the ground of frustration must not have assumed a greater obligation than the law would impose. Even if a party can show that his principal purpose has been substantially frustrated, a court may hold that he is not excused because the frustrating event was foreseeable at the time of agreement and he therefore assumed the risk of its occurrence. For the reasons already advanced, however, it seems preferable to follow what one court called "the now more widely accepted view that foreseeability of the frustrating event is not alone enough to bar [relief] if it appears that the parties did not intend the promisor to assume the risk of its occurrence."[146]

9.16 Remedies: Purposes and Types

The system of remedies for breach of contract in common law countries differs significantly from that of civil law countries and especially from that in civil law countries with planned economies. For the most part, the common law system of remedies for breach of contract rights rejects compulsion of the promisor as a goal. It does not impose criminal penalties on one who refuses to perform his promise, nor does it generally require him to pay punitive damages. The common law system of contract remedies is not directed at *compulsion of promisors to prevent* breach; it is aimed, instead, at *relief to promisees to redress* breach. Its preoccupation

144. Swift Canadian Co. v. Banet, 224 F.2d 36, 38 (3d Cir. 1955). Accord: Amtorg Trading Corp. v. Michel Printing Press & Mfg. Co., 206 F.2d 103 (2d Cir. 1953)(duty of buyer under contract for sale of printing presses not discharged when government regulations prohibited their export to Soviet Union, even though buyer was Soviet-owned corporation organized for export to that country).
145. 224 F.2d at 38.
146. West Los Angeles Inst. for Cancer Research v. Mayer, 366 F.2d 220, 225 (9th Cir. 1966).

is not with the question of how promisors can be made to keep their promises. Its concern is with a different question: How can people be encouraged to deal with those who make promises? The result may sometimes be to compel a promisor to keep his promise, but this is only the incidental effect of a system designed to serve other ends. It is more consistent with a market economy to promote the use of contract by encouraging promisees to rely on the promises of others rather than by compelling promisors to perform their promises. Along with the celebrated freedom to make contracts goes a considerable freedom to break them as well.

How do common law courts encourage promisees to rely on promises? Ordinarily they do so by protecting the expectation that the injured party had when he made the contract, by attempting to put him in as good a position as he would have been in had the contract been performed, that is, had there been no breach. The interest measured in this way is called the *expectation interest* and is said to give the injured party the "benefit of the bargain."[147] The expectation interest is based not on the injured party's hopes at the time he made the contract, but on the actual value that the contract would have had to him had it been performed. The expectation of the foolishly optimistic landowner who contracted to have an oil well dug on his property is not the gusher that he hoped for but the well that actually would have resulted. Since the circumstances at the time for performance, rather than those at the time of making of the contract, are determinative, changes adverse to the promisee that occur in the market between the time of making and the time for performance diminish his expectation interest.

At times, a court will enforce a promise by protecting the promisee's reliance instead of his expectation. The injured party may, for example, have changed his position in reliance on the contract by incurring expenses in preparation or in performance. In that case, the court may attempt to put him back in the position in which he would have been had the contract not been made. The interest measured in this way is called the *reliance interest*. It is useful to distinguish two kinds of reliance. Reliance that consists of preparation for and performance under the contract in question

147. For a statement of the expectation interest, see UCC 1–106(1) ("remedies provided by this Act shall be liberally administered to the end that the aggrieved party may be put in as good a position as if the other party had fully performed"). The seminal article on the expectation, reliance, and restitution interests is Fuller & Perdue, The Reliance Interest in Contract Damages (pts. 1, 2), 46 Yale L.J. 52, 373 (1936, 1937). See also Restatement (Second) of Contracts § 344.

has been called *essential* reliance. It includes whatever is, in a sense, the "price" that a party must pay for what he is to receive under the contract. Reliance may, however, also consist of preparations for collateral transactions that a party plans to carry out when the contract in question is performed. Reliance of this kind has been called "incidental" reliance. Consider a contract to build a store. If the owner repudiates after the builder has spent money on architect's drawings, labor, and materials, these expenditures are essential reliance. In either case the reliance interest is ordinarily smaller than the expectation interest because, while the expectation interest takes account of the injured party's lost profit as well as his reliance, the reliance interest includes nothing for his lost profit. Yet another kind of reliance consists in forgoing opportunities to make other contracts. In the example given, the builder may have passed up another job, and the owner may have passed up the possibility of hiring another builder in reliance on their contract. But the difficulties of proving this are obvious, and courts have not been receptive to claims based on this kind of reliance.

Sometimes a court will recognize a third interest in cases of breach of contract by granting restitution to the injured party. However, the object of restitution is not the enforcement of a promise, but rather the prevention of unjust enrichment. The focus is on the party in breach rather than on the injured party, and the attempt is to put the party in breach back in the position in which he would have been had the contract not been made. The party in breach is required to disgorge what he has received in money or services by, for example, returning the benefit to the injured party who conferred it on him. The interest of the injured party that is measured in this way is called the *restitution interest*. It is ordinarily smaller than either the expectation interest or the reliance interest. Although recovery measured by either of those interests takes account of cost incurred in conferring a benefit on the party in breach, the restitution interest includes neither the injured party's lost profit nor the part of his expenditures in reliance that conferred no benefit on the party in breach.

For a simple illustration of the three interests—expectation, reliance, and restitution—consider a contract by a builder to build a building on an owner's land for $100,000. If it would have cost the builder $90,000 to build the building, and the owner repudiates the contract before the builder has done anything in reliance on it, the builder's only loss is the $10,000 profit that he would have made. This is his expectation interest, since payment to him of $10,000 will put him in as good a position as he would have been in had the contract been performed. Since the builder has done nothing in reliance and the owner has had no benefit conferred on him, the builder's reliance and restitution interests are both zero. If, however, the owner does not repudiate until the builder has spent $60,000 of the $90,000 it would have cost him to build it, the builder's expectation interest is now $70,000, for this is the amount it will take to put him in as good a position as he would have been in had the contract been performed.[148] The builder's reliance interest is now $60,000, the amount that he has spent. And if the benefit to the owner of the partly furnished building is, say $40,000, the builder's restitution interest is now $40,000.

The judicial remedies available to protect these interests in cases of breach of contract can be characterized as *specific* or *substitutional*. Relief is said to be specific when it is intended to give the injured party the very performance that was promised, as when the court orders a defaulting seller of goods to deliver them to the buyer. Relief is said to be "substitutional" when it is intended to give the promisee something in substitution for the promised performance, as when the court awards a buyer of goods money damages instead of the goods.

In common law systems, judicial remedies for breach of contract can also be characterized as either *legal* or *equitable*, depending on whether, before the merger of law and equity, they were available in the common law courts or in courts of equity. Thus in the United States, the principal legal remedy to enforce a promise is a judgment awarding a sum of money. This is usually substitutional relief, as when the sum is damages to compensate the injured party for breach; but it may also be specific, as when the sum is an amount due under the contract. And in the United States, the principal equitable remedy to enforce a contract is an order requiring specific performance of the contract or enjoining its nonperformance. This is *specific relief*.

Other remedies in contract cases include replevin of a chattel, cancellation or reformation of a writing, and issuance of a declaratory judgment. Arbitration, a nonjudicial remedy, may also be available. Moreover, in some circumstances a party to a contract is empowered to protect himself or to obtain satisfaction by methods not involving recourse to a court, such as retaking goods or foreclosing on security.

Economic theory is a useful adjunct to legal analysis in the field of contract remedies. The important role that contracts play in the economy has inspired much economic analysis, which tends, to a large extent, to confirm the choices that common law judges made without the benefit of such insights.

---

148. This assumes that no part of the price has been paid to the builder and that the builder cannot salvage any part of what he has paid $60,000 for.

According to traditional economic theory, the mechanism of bargained-for exchange plays a vital part in the voluntary reallocation of goods, labor, and other resources in a socially desirable manner. The basic notion is that an economy will operate *efficiently* only to the extent that available goods and resources are utilized in their most productive manner. Ideally, each good must be consumed by the person who values it most highly, and each factor of production must be employed in the way that produces the most valued output. However, actual allocations of wealth rarely meet this test of efficiency, since assets are often owned by persons who place lower values on them than do others. Through voluntary agreements, in which individuals exchange assets that they own for others that they value more, society progresses toward the goal of economic efficiency. A bargained-for exchange from which both parties benefit is socially desirable in the sense that it results in a gain in efficiency by moving the assets that are exchanged to higher valued uses.

Economic theory presupposes people who are rational and who strive to maximize their own welfare. Such a person will not freely enter into an agreement that is detrimental to his own interests. Absent some impediment, such as mistake, misrepresentation, or duress, each party will place a value on the other's performance that is greater than the anticipated cost to him of his own performance. At the time the agreement is made, each party has reason to suppose that it will be profitable for him. A party may, however, err in calculating the net benefit to be anticipated from performance of the agreement, or circumstances may change so as to disappoint his initial hopes. A contract that he once thought would be profitable for him may turn out to be unprofitable. If it is still profitable for the other party, should the reluctant party be compelled to perform?

If nonperformance of the agreement would result in a gain by the reluctant party at the expense of a loss by the other party, the result of nonperformance is economically efficient only if the value of the gain to the reluctant party is greater than the value of the loss to the other party. However, since individuals differ in their value judgments, the gain and the loss cannot be simply compared in absolute terms. One of the principles that has been developed to overcome this difficulty states that a redistribution of wealth is desirable if the party who benefits values his gains more than the loser values his losses. This principle can be applied to the redistribution of wealth that follows from a breach of contract and to the payment of damages for that breach. The party in breach may gain enough from the breach to have a net benefit, even though he compensates the injured party for his resulting loss, calculated according to the subjective preferences of the injured party. If this is so, nonperformance and the consequent reallocation of resources is socially desirable, and economic theory not only sanctions but encourages breach. To prevent breach by compelling performance would result in an undesirable wealth distribution, since the party in breach would lose more than the injured party would gain.[149]

This conclusion accords remarkably with the common law's traditional assumptions of the law of contract remedies. The principal interest protected by that law is the expectation interest, measured by the amount of money required to put the injured party in as good a position as he would have been in had the contract been performed. This amount is the counterpart of the compensation that economic analysis suggests. The effect is to give the reluctant party an incentive to break the contract if, but only if, he gains enough from the breach that he can compensate the injured party for his losses yet still retain some of the benefits from the breach. Since the goal is compensation and not compulsion, the promisor who could have performed, but chose not to for financial reasons, should not be dealt with harshly. Punitive damages should not be awarded for breach of contract because they will encourage performance when breach would be socially more desirable. "Willful" breaches should not be distinguished from other breaches. And specific performance should generally not be required, at least where compensation in damages is an adequate substitute for the injured party. All of these conclusions accord well with traditional contract doctrine.

This economic analysis is not, however, without its critics. Suppose, for example, that there are no transaction costs, so that both parties can obtain information and negotiate without cost.[150] On this assumption, a rule of specific performance would be as economically efficient as a rule of damages. Under a rule of specific performance, a party who found it advantageous not to perform a contract would negotiate (without cost, it is assumed) a settlement with the other party under which the reluctant party would be relieved from the contract duty to perform in return for a payment of money in an agreed sum. If performance of the contract would be inefficient, it will be to both parties' advantage to reach such a settlement, and therefore in that situation even a rule of specific performance would not result in performance.

---

149. For an argument that in this situation "breach would be value maximizing and should be encouraged," see R. Posner, Economic Analysis of Law 89–90 (2d ed. 1977).

150. This is known as the "Coase theorem," elaborated in Coase, The Problem of Social Cost, 3 J.L. & Econ. 1 (1960).

Another criticism of economic analysis is that it supposes an ability to measure value with a certainty that is often not possible in the judicial process. And its focus on the relative pecuniary advantages that flow from breach leaves no place for notions of the sanctity of contract and the moral obligation to honor one's promises. Nevertheless, economic analysis exercises a strong influence on contemporary thought in the United States with regard to remedies for breach of contract.

9.17 Remedies: Damages

The award of damages is the common form of relief for breach of contract. Virtually any breach gives the injured party a claim for damages. Even if the breach caused no loss or if the amount of loss is not proved with sufficient certainty, the injured party can recover as nominal damages a small sum, commonly six cents on a dollar, fixed without regard to the amount of the loss. In most cases where a breach of contract is shown, however, substantial damages are awarded.

The basic principle for the measurement of those damages is that of compensation based on the injured party's expectation. He is entitled to recover an amount that will put him in as good a position as he would have been in had the contract been performed.[151] At least in principle, a party's expectation is measured by the actual worth that performance of the contract would have had to him, not the worth that it might have had to some hypothetical reasonable person. Damages based on expectation should therefore take account of any circumstances peculiar to the situation of the injured party, including his own needs and opportunities, his personal values, and even his idiosyncracies. It has been pointed out that to allow this generous measure of recovery is to "'compensate' the plaintiff by giving him something he never had. This seems on the face of things a queer kind of compensation."[152]

This generous measure of expectation is, however, severely qualified by rules that grew out of the attempts by judges during the industrial expansion of the nineteenth century to control the award of damages by juries. Prior to the nineteenth century, the common law courts paid little attention to this problem. At first they were intent on expanding their influence and,

---

151. However, the injured party cannot generally recover his lawyer's fees.

152. Fuller & Perdue, The Reliance Interests in Contract Damages (pt. 1), 46 Yale L.J. 52, 52–53 (1936).

since trial by jury was a means of attracting litigants who might otherwise have gone elsewhere, they followed the popular course of leaving the assessment of damages in the hands of the jury. Gradually, however, the common law developed procedures for the control of the jury, including those by which the trial judge ruled on the admissibility of evidence, instructed the jurors on the law, and might set aside the jury's verdict after trial and grant a new trial before another jury. It was the last of these that was the most significant. Since the trial judge could order a new trial on the ground that the jury had disregarded his advice by awarding excessive damages, he gained added assurance that his instructions would be given proper weight. From this it was only a short step to more direct control over the assessment of damages by specific instructions to the jury as to the amount to be allowed should there be recovery. Most important, the ruling of the trial judge on a motion for a new trial was a matter of law, which could be considered on appeal by a higher court. It was out of appeals from these rulings that common law courts, toward the end of the eighteenth century, finally began to limit the body of principles that were to govern the award of damages for breach of contract. To the general principle of recovery based on the promisee's expectation there emerged three important limitations that now serve as a basis not merely for instructing jurors, but for passing on the admissibility of evidence and for withdrawing some elements of damage from the jury's consideration altogether.

One of these limitations is that the injured party cannot recover damages for loss that he could have avoided if he had taken appropriate steps to mitigate that loss. To take an obvious case, the builder who stubbornly continues work after the owner has repudiated the contract cannot recover for his expenditures in doing work after the repudiation. A second limitation denies the injured party recovery for loss that the party in breach did not have reason to foresee as a probable result of the breach at the time the contract was made. The classic, if apocryphal, case is that in which "a man going to be married to an heiress, his horse having cast a shoe on the journey, employed a blacksmith to replace it, who did the work so unskillfully that the horse was lamed, and, the rider not arriving in time, the lady married another"—the blacksmith would not be liable for the loss of the marriage. The third limitation is that the injured party cannot recover damages for loss beyond the amount that he proves with reasonable certainty. The operation of this requirement of certainty within the framework of the procedure for new trial is said to have caused the body of rules for damages to develop more rapidly in contract than in tort. The effect of these three limitations is to reduce the amount of damages recoverable under the general principle that the law protects the injured party's expectation.

Furthermore, no matter how reprehensible the breach, damages that are punitive, in the sense of being in excess of those required to compensate the injured party for his lost expectation, are not ordinarily awarded for breach of contract. It is a fundamental tenet of the law of contract remedies that, regardless of the character of the breach, an injured party should not be put in a better position than he would have been in had the contract been performed. As Holmes said, "If a contract is broken the measure of damages generally is the same, whatever the cause of the breach."[153] Contract law is, in its essential design, a law of strict liability, and the accompanying system of remedies operates, in theory at least, without regard to fault. Punitive damages may, however, be awarded in tort actions,[154] and a number of courts have awarded them for a breach of contract that is in some respect tortious.

9.18 Remedies: Liquidated Damages and Penalties

So strong is the common law's antipathy toward the award of punitive damages for breach of contract that contracting parties are denied the power to stipulate in the contract a sum of money that will operate as a "penalty" for breach. Surprisingly, in view of the extensive power that contracting parties have to bargain over their substantive rights, their power to bargain over their remedial rights is severely limited.

The advantages of stipulating damages in advance are manifold. For both parties, it may facilitate the calculation of risks and reduce the cost of proof. For the injured party, it may afford the only possibility of compensation for loss that is not susceptible of proof with sufficient certainty. For society as a whole, it may save the time of judges, juries, and witnesses, as well as the parties, and may cut the expense of litigation. These advantages are of special significance when the amount in controversy is small.

If, however, the stipulated sum is significantly larger than the amount required to compensate the injured party for his loss, the stipulation may

153. Globe Refining Co. v. Landa Cotton Oil Co., 190 U.S. 540, 544 (1930).

154. See Restatement (Second) of Torts § 908 ("Punitive damages are damages, other than compensatory or nominal damages, awarded against a person to punish him for his outrageous conduct and to deter him and others like him from similar conduct in the future.").

have quite a different advantage to him—an *in terrorem* effect on the other party that will deter breach by compelling him to perform. A simple example of such a provision is one that adds a stipulated sum to the injured party's actual damages. Enforcement of such a provision would allow the parties to depart from the fundamental principle that the law's goal on breach of contract is not to deter breach by compelling the promisor to perform, but rather to redress breach by compensating the promisee. It is this departure that is proscribed when a court characterizes such a provision as a penalty.

The common law's hostility toward penalties can be traced back to the development in the seventeenth century of equitable relief in cases involving penal bonds, which were used to secure performance under contracts. A distinction grew up between provisions characterized as *penalties*, and therefore condemned, and those characterized as *liquidated damages*, and therefore permitted. If a provision is condemned as a penalty, it is unenforceable, but the rest of the agreement stands, and the injured party is remitted to his conventional damage remedy for breach of that agreement. If the provision is sustained as one for liquidated damages, both parties are bound by it, and it displaces the conventional damage remedy for breach.

Once a distinction between penalties and liquidated damages had been recognized, there remained the considerable task of drawing the line between the two. The question is one of law for the court. The conditions for enforcement of a clause as one for liquidated damages have been said to be: "(1) the damages to be anticipated as resulting from the breach must be uncertain in amount or difficult to prove; (2) there must have been an intent on the part of the parties to liquidate them in advance; and (3) the amount stipulated must be a reasonable one, that is to say, not greatly disproportionate to the presumable loss or injury."[155] In recent years the emphasis is shifted to the last of these three conditions, and the trend has been to favor freedom of contract by enforcing such clauses as long as they do not clearly disregard the principle of compensation or, as it is often put, as long as the stipulated sum is "a reasonable one" in the light of the "presumed loss." The time as of which the forecast of loss must be judged to be reasonable has traditionally been regarded as the time when the contract was made, not the time when the breach occurred. The injured party does not have to show his actual loss and, indeed, that loss is irrelevant except to help show what loss was anticipated.

155. Banta v. Stamford Motor Co., 89 Conn. 51, 55, 92 A. 665, 667 (1914).

The Uniform Commercial Code makes a slight shift from the traditional stress on anticipated, rather than actual, loss by requiring only that the stipulated amount be "reasonable in the light of the anticipated *or actual* harm caused by the breach."[156] However, this says only that a stipulation might be upheld as one for liquidated damages on the ground that the sum was reasonable in the light of the actual loss, even though it was not reasonable in the light of the anticipated loss. It does not say that the stipulation might be stricken as one for a penalty on the ground that the sum was unreasonable in the light of the actual loss, even though it was not unreasonable in the light of the anticipated loss. Thus a court should look to the actual loss to sustain provisions that might otherwise be unenforceable, but not to strike down provisions that would otherwise be enforceable. In this respect, the Code follows the trend favoring enforcement.

9.19 Remedies: Specific Relief

Although in some cases damages will permit the injured party to arrange an adequate substitute for the expected performance, specific relief is plainly better suited to the objective of putting the promisee in the position in which he would have been had the promise been performed. There are, however, some situations in which specific relief is simply not possible. The promise may, for example, have been one to deliver particular goods that are defective, destroyed, or owned by a third person. Even if specific relief is possible, performance will usually be delayed, and the passage of time may reduce its effectiveness. But there remain many instances in which specific relief will be both feasible and timely.

The common law courts did not, however, generally grant specific relief for breach of contract. The usual form of relief at common law was substitutional, and the typical judgment declared that the plaintiff recover from the defendant a sum of money. This, in effect, imposed a new obligation on the defendant for the breach of the old. This new obligation could be enforced even without cooperation on the defendant's part. If the sum was not paid, a writ of execution was issued, empowering the sheriff to seize and sell so much of the defendant's property as was required to pay the plaintiff.

Promises were enforced in equity in a very different way. Prior to the development of assumpsit by the common law courts in the sixteenth

---

156. UCC 2–718(1). The same language is carried over into Restatement (Second) of Contracts § 356.

century, most of the cases brought before the chancellor were based on promises that would not have been enforceable at common law, and the question was whether they would nevertheless be enforced in equity.[157] After the development of assumpsit, equity accepted the doctrine of consideration, the test for enforcement that had been developed by the rival common law courts. To this extent, the jurisdiction of equity in contract cases became concurrent with that of the common law courts, and its concern shifted from the enforceability of promises to the nature of their enforcement. Claimants now sought relief from the chancellor as an alternative to the judgment for damages to which they were entitled at common law. Under the influence of canon law—for the early chancellors were usually clerics—decrees in equity came to take the form of the chancellor's personal command to the defendant to do or not to do something. If the defendant disobeyed, he could be punished not only for criminal contempt, at the instance of the court, but also for civil contempt, at the instance of the plaintiff. This put into the plaintiff's hands the extreme sanction of imprisonment, which might be supplemented by fines payable to the plaintiff and by sequestration of the defendant's goods. So it was said that equity acted *in personam*, against the person of the defendant, while the law acted *in rem*, against his property. But it did not follow that the chancellor stood ready to order every defaulting promisor to perform his promise. Equitable relief was confined to special cases by both historical and practical limitations.

The most important historical limitation grew out of the circumstance that the chancellor had originally granted equitable relief in order to supply the deficiencies of the common law. Equitable remedies were therefore readily characterized as "extraordinary." When, during the long jurisdictional struggle between the two systems of courts, some means of accommodation was needed, an adequacy test was developed to prevent the chancellor from encroaching on the powers of the common law judges. Equity would stay its hand if the remedy of an award of damages at law was "adequate." To this test was added the gloss that damages were ordinarily adequate—a gloss encouraged by the philosophy of free enterprise with its confidence that a market economy ought to enable the injured party to arrange a substitute transaction. As one writer put it:

> The law, concerning itself more and more with merchandise bought or sold for money, with things having a definite and calculable exchange value, came to conceive that the money

157. See generally § 7.4 supra.

> compensation, which was an entirely adequate remedy in the common case, and in many cases the only possible one when once the wrong complained of had been committed, was [generally] the only remedy available for their use. . . .[158]

So English courts came to regard money damages as the norm and specific relief as the deviation. Only for land, which English courts regarded with particular esteem, was a general exception made, on the ground that each parcel of land was unique, so money damages were inadequate. This strong preference of English courts for substitutional relief stands in sharp contrast to the preference of civil law systems (those derived from the Roman law) for specific relief.

A second historical limitation, or group of limitations, is based on the concept that equitable relief is discretionary. Since the chancellor was to act according to "conscience" (which prompted the notorious charge that his conscience might vary with the length of his foot[159]), he might withhold relief if considerations of fairness or morality dictated. Gradually these equitable restrictions became more precise and hardened into rules. Some of the most renowned are embodied in equity's colorful maxims: "he who seeks equity must do equity"; "he who comes into equity must come with clean hands"; and "equity aids the vigilant." One of the most troublesome of these rules was the now discredited "mutuality of remedy" rule, under which the injured party's right to specific relief depended on whether it would have been available to the other party, had the breach been on the other side.

The practical limitations on specific relief in equity grew out of the problems inherent in coercing the defendant to perform his promise. In some cases, of course, specific relief does not require the defaulting promisor's cooperation. If, for example, the promise is to convey land, the court can transfer the title by virtue of its own decree, or it can be transferred by a deed executed by an officer of the court. But there is no such simple solution if the performance is personal in nature, and courts have bridled at coercing such performances. They will not, for example, compel a singer to sing, although they have been willing to order the

158. C. Huston, The Enforcement of Decrees in Equity 74 (1915).

159. "'Tis all one, as if they should make his foot the standard for the measure we call a Chancellor's foot; what an uncertain measure this would be'. One Chancellor has a long foot, another a short foot, a third an indifferent foot; 'tis the same thing in the Chancellor's conscience." J. Selden, Table Talk, as quoted in Gee v. Pritchard, 2 Swanst. 402, 414, 36 Eng. Rep. 670, 679 (Ch. 1818).

singer not to act inconsistently with his promise, by enjoining him from singing elsewhere. Courts have also been reluctant to order performance if difficulties of supervision or enforcement are foreseen, as may be the case under a building contract, especially if the absence of clear standards may lead to conflict and unfairness. Moreover, the practical demands of drafting decrees to guide future conduct under the threat of the severe sanctions available for contempt have moved courts to require that contract terms be expressed with greater certainty if specific relief is to be ordered than if damages are to be awarded.

Thus it came to be that, although the injured party can always claim damages for breach of contract, his right to specific relief as an alternative is much more limited. The historical development of parallel systems of law and equity may afford an adequate explanation for the reluctance of our courts to grant specific relief more widely, but it is scant justification for it. A more rational basis can today be found in the severity of the sanctions available for enforcement of equitable orders.

The most direct form of equitable relief for breach of contract is specific performance. By ordering the promisor to render the promised performance, the court attempts to produce, as nearly as is practicable, the same effect as if the contract had been performed. A court will not order a performance that has become impossible, unreasonably burdensome, or unlawful, nor will it issue an order that can be frustrated by the defendant through exercise of a power of termination or otherwise. Specific performance may be granted after there has been a breach of contract by either nonperformance or repudiation.

Instead of ordering specific performance, a court may, by injunction, direct a party to refrain from doing a specified act. If the performance due under the contract consists simply of forbearance, the effect of an injunction is to order specific performance. Often, however, an injunction is used as an indirect means of enforcing a duty to act. Instead of ordering that the act be done, as a court would in granting specific performance, the court orders forbearance from inconsistent action. This is done most often in cases in which specific performance is objectionable on some ground that can be avoided by the use of an injunction. Difficulties in supervising compliance with the order may, for example, be fewer if an injunction is issued than if specific performance is ordered.

In framing an order of specific performance or an injunction, the court can mold it to do justice as fully as is practicable. Along with any equitable relief by specific performance or injunction, a court may also award damages and grant other relief. Because an order granting equitable relief seldom results in performance within the time required by the contract, damages for delay are often appropriate. A court may grant a preliminary injunction to prevent an undesirable change in the situation before trial and may, in granting preliminary or final relief, require an indemnity against future harm. A claimant who sues for specific performance or an injunction and is denied that relief may be awarded damages or restitution in the same proceeding.

As we have seen, it came to be recognized that equitable relief would not be granted if the legal remedy of damages was adequate to protect the injured party, and this historical limitation has persisted in spite of the merger of law and equity.[160] The tendency is, however, to liberalize the granting of specific performance and injunction by enlarging the classes of cases in which damages are regarded as an inadequate remedy. The contemporary approach is to compare remedies to determine which is more effective in affording suitable protection to the injured party's legally recognized interest, which is usually his expectation interest. The concept of adequacy has thus tended to become relative, and the comparison more often leads to granting equitable relief than was historically the case. A provision for liquidated damages does not preclude the grant of specific performance or an injunction instead of the award of such damages.

Damages will not be adequate to protect the injured party's expectation if the loss caused him by the breach cannot be estimated with sufficient certainty. His damages may then be nominal only, and they will not, in any case, give him full compensation for his loss. If the subject of the contract involves matters of taste or sentiment, as in contracts for the sale of works of art or heirlooms, it may be impossible to value the injured party's expectation in money. This may be so even in the case of contracts of a more commercial character. The breach of a contract to transfer shares of stock may deprive the buyer of control over the corporation that cannot be accurately valued in money. The breach of a contract to sell a business may leave the buyer unable to prove damages based on his prospective profits. The breach of a requirements contract may cut off a vital supply of raw materials of inestimable worth.[161] If the breach occurs when the contract still has many years to run, it may not be possible at the time of the trial to forecast the loss that will result in the future. In such situations equitable relief has often been granted.

---

160. See § 10.3 infra.

161. See UCC 2–716, Comment 2 ("Output and requirements contracts involving a particular or peculiarly available source or market present today the typical commercial specific performance situation. . . .").

A critical factor in determining whether damages are an adequate remedy is whether money can buy a substitute for the promised performance. If a substitute can readily be obtained, the damage remedy is ordinarily regarded as adequate. Because entering into a substitute transaction is a more efficient way of preventing further injury than is specific performance or an injunction, there is good reason to limit the injured party to damages in such a case. Furthermore, it is ordinarily in the interest of the injured party, as well as of the party in breach, to find a substitute. Damages will be awarded to compensate the injured party for any additional cost in arranging the substitute transaction, and interest will be allowed to compensate him for any additional burden in financing the transaction. In some situations, however, no substitute is available, or its procurement would be unreasonably difficult or inconvenient or would impose serious financial burdens or risks on the injured party. If the performance consists of forbearance, as under a contract not to compete, no substitute is possible. Patents and copyrights are unique so that there is no substitute. Shares of stock in a corporation may not be obtainable elsewhere.

Specific performance is rarely allowed under contracts for the sale of goods. In a market economy it is generally supposed that, with rare exceptions for such *unique* items as heirlooms and objects of art, substantially similar goods are available elsewhere. The trend, however, has been to relax this restriction on the availability of specific performance. The commentary to the Uniform Commercial Code explains that it "seeks to further a more liberal attitude than some courts have shown in connection with the specific performance of contracts of sale."[162] It asserts that the buyer's "inability to cover is strong evidence of" the propriety of granting specific performance and that "where the unavailability of a market price is caused by a scarcity of goods of the type involved, a good case is normally made for specific performance under this Article."[163] But the text of the Code is more circumspect, stating only, "Specific performance may be decreed where the goods are unique or in other proper circumstances."[164] The Code does not reject the adequacy test, and specific performance remains the exception rather than the rule under contracts for

162. UCC 2–716, Comment 1.
163. UCC 2–713, Comment 3.
164. UCC 2–716(1). See also UCC 1-106(1) ("The remedies provided by this Act shall be liberally administered to the end that the aggrieved party may be put in as good a position as if the other party had fully performed. . . .").

the sale of goods. If the seller fails to deliver the goods, the typical buyer must still content himself with money as a substitute.

Even if damages are adequate in other respects, they are not an effective remedy if they cannot be collected. If the injured party has already performed, and the party in breach is insolvent, specific performance may be against public policy because it would result in a transfer that would give the injured party a preference over other creditors of the party in breach. But if the contract is unperformed on both sides and provides for a fair exchange, performance of the contract will not result in a preferential transfer and may even benefit other creditors of the party in breach by improving his financial condition. In such cases, some courts have granted specific performance on the ground of the defendant's insolvency.

Because the restraints on the availability of equitable relief have traditionally been viewed as a matter of jurisdiction, it is generally supposed that the parties cannot enlarge the availability of specific performance or injunction by dispensing with the adequacy test or with the other criteria for such relief. This limitation on the power of the parties does not apply if they wish to reduce the availability of equitable relief, and it is therefore open to them to eliminate the possibility of specific performance or injunction by providing for the payment of a sum of money as an alternative, as long as they make clear their intention to do so.

Chapter 10

Settlement of Contract Disputes

10.1 Methods of Settlement

Countless contract disputes arise in the United States every year. The great majority are settled informally by the parties themselves, perhaps with the aid of lawyers, but without the intervention of judges, arbitrators, or others. Some disputes are resolved by what has come to be called *alternative dispute resolution* (sometimes ADR). These alternatives include most notably arbitration, but also such other methods as mediation and conciliation, fact finding, and mini-trials. No public records are kept of such settlements, and no statistics concerning them are available.

A much smaller number of contract disputes are the subject of legal actions in court. Each year nearly 15 million civil actions of all kinds are filed in the state courts and about a quarter of a million civil actions are filed in federal courts. Most of these court actions—over 90 percent—are resolved before trial. Some actions are dropped, some are dismissed by the court, and some are settled. Often the settlement comes before trial, though sometimes it does not come until after a decision of a court of first instance, when the case is on appeal.

Frequently the source of the rules that apply to the settlement of contract disputes is the contract itself rather than the general body of the law including the Uniform Commercial Code and case law. It is important to understand that in the United States lawyers are sometimes involved in important business transactions beginning at the negotiation and drafting stages. Contract documents are characteristically detailed and prolix. They are sometimes compounded of standard clauses, popularly known as "boilerplate," taken from other agreements kept on file or from form books. Even when a lawyer is not directly involved in drafting, the parties may use or incorporate by reference a standard printed form that has been drafted by a lawyer, perhaps for a particular enterprise, perhaps for an association of enterprises, or perhaps for sale to the general public. This attention to detail may be due to a number of causes in addition to the involvement of lawyers, including the standardization of routine transactions, the inclination to use language that has been tested in previous controversies, and the desire to avoid uncertainty when the law of more than one state is involved. All of these add to the general disposition of the American lawyer to provide expressly for specific disputes that have arisen in the past or might be foreseen in the future.

It will be helpful at the outset to consider the background of the legally trained professionals who are involved in the drafting of contracts and the settlement of contract disputes.

10.2 Lawyers and Judges

The typical American lawyer has had seven years of university education—four years in a college and three years in a law school. He has also passed an examination for admission to the bar.[1] The examination is given by the state in which the lawyer will practice, because in the United States the regulation of the legal profession is primarily the concern of the states.[2] In all, more than forty thousand persons succeed in being admitted to the bar each year.

A lawyer may not only practice law, but is permitted to engage in any activity that is open to other citizens. It is not uncommon for the practicing lawyer to serve on boards of directors of corporate clients, to engage in business, and to participate actively in public affairs. A lawyer remains a member of the bar even after becoming a judge, an employee of the government or of a private business concern, or a law teacher, and may return to private practice from these other activities. A relatively small

1. Originally the "bar" was a partition in the courtroom separating the general public from the judges, lawyers and others involved in the proceeding. The term is now used to refer generally to the legal profession.

2. A lawyer may, however, be admitted in more than one state, and one may by special permission be permitted to appear before a court in a state where one is not admitted. A law firm may have offices in more than one state.

number of lawyers give up practice for executive positions in commerce and industry.

There is no formal division among lawyers according to function. The distinction between barristers and solicitors found in England did not take root in the United States, and there is not a branch of the profession that has a special or exclusive right to appear in court, nor is there a branch that specializes in the preparation of legal instruments. The American lawyer's domain includes advocacy, counselling, and drafting. Furthermore, within the sphere broadly defined as the "practice of law," the domain is exclusive and is not open to others.[3] Because of the wide range of activities open to lawyers in the United States, the number of persons admitted to practice is large, over 600,000. Out of every 20, approximately 15 are in private practice, two are employed by private business concerns, two are in government service, and one is a member of the judiciary or the teaching profession.

Among these fifteen lawyers in practice, nine, a clear majority, are single practitioners. The remaining six practice in law firms, which are generally organized as partnerships. Four or five of these six are partners and the others are associates, a term applied to salaried lawyers employed by a firm or another lawyer. This trend toward group practice is of relatively recent origin. Throughout most of the nineteenth century law practice was general rather than specialized, its chief ingredient was advocacy rather than counselling and drafting, and the prototype of the American lawyer was the single practitioner. Marked specialization began in the latter part of that century in the large cities near the financial centers. With the growth of business, government, and organized labor, the work of the lawyer accommodated itself to the needs of clients for expert counselling and drafting to prevent as well as to settle disputes. The best lawyers were attracted to this work, and leadership of the bar gravitated to persons who rarely if ever appeared in court and who were sought after as advisors, planners, and negotiators. Today the lawyer regards it as sound practice to be continuously familiar with clients' business problems and to participate at all steps in the shaping of their policies. Major business transactions are rarely undertaken without advice of counsel.

---

3. The office of notary or notary public is a minor state office with power to perform such routine functions as the attestation of writings and the administration of oaths. It requires no legal training, is often held as a part-time post by a clerk or secretary, and cannot be compared with professions bearing similar names in other legal systems.

The breadth of vision required has been suggested by one American judge: "The modern lawyer almost invariably advises his client upon not only what is permissible but also what is desirable. . . . His duty to society as well as to his client involves many relevant social, economic, political and philosophical considerations."[4] Often the challenge cannot be met by one person alone. The complexity of American law and the flexible and malleable character of American business organizations make a specialized knowledge of many fields as well as a substantial library increasingly necessary.

Today large law firms can be found in many cities. The firm may have a total complement of over a hundred lawyers, some of whom are partners but more of whom are salaried associates.[5] Although generally speaking each client looks to one particular partner, there are partners specializing in such fields as taxation, corporation law, antitrust law, real estate transactions, and litigation. Such firms claim most of the business of the major American corporations, whose problems seem to call for the cooperation of specialists, and each year they hire many of the top graduates of the leading law schools. These young men and women do much of the painstaking legal research,[6] and while they hope for partnership, they know that, in any case, after five or six years of experience as an associate in such a firm, other attractive opportunities will be open to them. Even outside of the relatively small number of such large firms, specialization is becoming more common, with lawyers whose practice consists largely or exclusively, for example, of personal injury cases, criminal cases, tax matters, or labor cases.

These same changes have brought about an increase in the number of lawyers engaged as house (or corporate) counsel. Out of every 20 lawyers, two are employed by private business concerns, such as industrial corporations, insurance companies, and banks, usually as house counsel in the concern's legal department. The growth of corporations, the complexity of business, and the multitude of problems posed by government regulation

4. Judge Wyzanski in United States v. United States Shoe Machiney Corp., 89 F.Supp. 357, 359 (D. Mass. 1950).

5. Law firms have traditionally been organized as partnerships, but in recent years a new form of organization known as the professional service corporation has been used increasingly.

6. In large law firms routine work is sometimes done by persons, called "legal assistants" or "paralegals," who have not had the legal training that a lawyer has and who are not admitted to the bar.

make it desirable for such firms to have in their employ persons with legal training who, at the same time, are intimately familiar with the particular problems and conditions of the firm. In large corporations the legal department may number one hundred or more. The general counsel, who heads the office, is usually an officer of the company and may serve on important policymaking committees and perhaps even on the board of directors. House counsel remain members of the bar and are entitled to appear in court, though an outside lawyer is often retained for litigation. However, it is the house counsel's skill as advisor rather than as advocate that is a valued asset. Constantly in touch with the employer's problems, house counsel is ideally situated to practice preventive law and may also be called upon to advise the company on its broader obligation to the public and the nation.

A parallel development has taken place in government, and two out of 20 lawyers are now employees of the federal, state, county, and municipal governments, exclusive of the judiciary. Many of those entering public service are recent law graduates who find government salaries sufficiently attractive at this stage of their careers and seek the training that such service may offer as a prelude to private practice. Most serve by appointment in the legal departments of a variety of federal and state agencies and local entities. As a rule, lawyers in government are directly engaged in legal work, since law training is infrequently sought as preparation for general government service.

Fewer than one in 20 of those admitted to practice law is a federal, state, county, or municipal court judge. Except for some lower courts, judges are generally required to be admitted to practice but do not practice while on the bench. There is so little uniformity that it is difficult to generalize further than to point out three salient characteristics that relate to the ranks from which judges are drawn, to the method of their selection, and to their tenure.

Judges are drawn from the practicing bar and less frequently from government service or the teaching profession. There is in the United States no career judiciary like that found in many other countries and there is no prescribed route for the young law graduate who aspires to be a judge, no apprenticeship that must be served, no service that must be entered. While it is not uncommon for a vacancy on a higher court to be filled by a judge from a lower court, even this cannot be said to be the rule. The legal profession generally believes that the advantages of a career judiciary are outweighed by the experience and independence which American lawyers bring to the bench. Many of the outstanding judges of the country's highest courts have had no prior judicial experience. Criticism has centered instead on the prevalent method of selection of judges.

State court judges are usually elected, commonly by popular vote, but occasionally by the legislature.[7] Popular election has been the subject of much disapproval on the ground that the public lacks interest in and information on candidates for judicial office and that therefore the outcome is too often controlled by leaders of political parties. The situation has been somewhat improved since many local bar associations have undertaken to evaluate the qualifications of candidates and to support or oppose them on this basis. A system under which the governor appoints judges from a list submitted by a special nominating board and the judge then periodically stands unopposed for reelection by popular vote on the basis of his or her record is now in effect, for at least some judges, in a substantial minority of states. In a small group of states, judges are appointed by the governor subject to legislative confirmation. This is also the method of selection of federal judges, who are appointed by the President subject to confirmation by the Senate. Judges commonly serve for a term of years rather than for life, though even where selection is by popular election, it is customary to return to office sitting judges whose service has been satisfactory. In a few state courts and in the federal courts the judges sit for life. The prestige of the judicial office is high, and the bench has been able to attract many of the country's ablest legal minds. The great names in American law are in large part the names of its great judges.

10.3 The Court System

One of the results of the particular form of federalism which has grown up in the United States is a judicial structure in which a nationwide system of federal courts functions alongside the state courts. Contract disputes are heard in both state and federal courts.

---

7. It has not always been so. The first state constitution generally provided for selection of judges either by the legislature or by the governor, or both, and for life tenure. This system was swept away during the wave of Jacksonian democracy in the middle of the nineteenth century and the change was made to popular vote and short judicial terms.

As we have seen, the great bulk of such disputes come before the state courts.[8] Each state by constitution and statute has established its own system, and the lack of uniformity makes it impossible to give a detailed description to fit all states. A trend toward multiplication of courts and decentralization of the court system has persisted until modern times, though in recent years considerable progress has been made in the simplification of state court systems and the improvement of judicial administration.

In each state there is a trial court of general jurisdiction where a single judge presides, whether there is a jury or not, and is competent to hear most cases, including contract disputes. In the United States there are no special commercial courts like those that exist in some countries. Nor are there separate courts for law and equity like those inherited from England.[9] By the middle of the nineteenth century there was a demand for the merger of law and equity. During the latter half of the nineteenth and the early part of the twentieth century practically all of the states abolished the distinction between law and equity, so that a single civil action is now brought in a single court.[10] But the term *equity* is still used, not as a synonym for "fairness" or "justice" but to refer to a particular body of rules that originated in a special system of courts and that still exist, though courts of equity have disappeared. At the top of the state judicial system is the highest appellate court of that state. In most states it is called simply the supreme court; in some it is known by another name, such as the court of appeals in New York and in several other states. The number of judges is most commonly seven, including a chief justice and associate justices. In over half the states there are intermediate appellate courts, between the courts of general jurisdiction and the highest court.

---

8. See § 10.1 supra. In the decade 1970–1980, state appellate court decisions filled nearly one thousand volumes in the regional unofficial reports while federal appellate court opinions filled over two hundred volumes.

9. See §§ 7.4, 7.5 supra.

10. Law and equity procedure were united in the federal courts as recently as 1938. The merger of law and equity cannot be fully realized, however, because the right to a jury trial under federal and state constitutions generally extends only to cases formerly triable at law and not to those formerly triable in equity. Thus, for historical reasons the distinction between law and equity must be observed for this purpose. Where there are both legal and equitable issues in a jury trial, the legal issues of fact are decided by the jury while the equitable issues are decided by the judge.

The federal judicial system has three principal levels: the district courts, the courts of appeals, and the Supreme Court. There are also special courts of limited jurisdiction, including the Claims Court, which has jurisdiction over contract claims against the United States government. The district courts are the trial courts of general jurisdiction for both civil and criminal matters, including contract disputes. There are 90 district courts located throughout the 50 states and one for the District of Columbia. Although a judicial district has a number of judges, a single judge presides over both jury and non-jury cases.

Appeals from a district court are generally heard in the court of appeals for the circuit in which the district is located. There are 12 such circuits, 11 comprising geographical divisions of the states and including a number of districts, and a twelfth for the District of Columbia. These are the intermediary appellate courts in the federal system, but because of the limitations on review by the Supreme Court they are, in fact, the courts of last resort for most federal cases that arise out of contract disputes. The number of judges in each circuit varies, but the judges ordinarily hear appeals in panels of three.

Appellate review of the decisions of the courts of appeals is in the hands of the Supreme Court, which since 1869 has consisted of nine members—one chief justice and eight associate justices—who sit as a body and not in panels. As will be explained shortly, it is not only the highest appellate court of the federal system, but also has a limited power of review over the state courts. However, the proportion of cases in which either sort of review occurs is very small.

The determination of the jurisdiction of the state and federal courts is a part of the more general problem of the distribution of state and federal power. Most of the civil business of the federal courts is of three kinds: first, cases in which the United States is a party; second, cases between private parties involving federal laws, under the so-called "federal question" jurisdiction; and third, cases between citizens of different states, under the so-called "diversity" jurisdiction. Most of the contract disputes that come before the federal courts are of this third kind.

Diversity jurisdiction includes cases where the dispute is between citizens of different states, including foreign states, and the amount in controversy exceeds $10,000.[11] The conventional explanation of this

---

11. For the purpose of determining whether there is diversity, a corporation is regarded as a citizen not only of the state where it has been incorporated but also of the state where it has its principal place of business.

ground of jurisdiction is that the framers of the Constitution sought to avoid the partiality that might result if, for example, a New York creditor were obliged to try a contract claim against a Massachusetts debtor before a Massachusetts state court. Today litigants' preference for the federal courts comes less from a fear of prejudice than a belief that the court, the procedure, or the court calendar is more favorable.

The federal and state courts have concurrent jurisdiction in diversity cases. Thus a plaintiff in a diversity case involving a contract dispute can bring suit in either a federal or a state court. Where jurisdiction is concurrent and suit has been brought in the state court, however, the defendant usually has the right to have the case removed to the federal district court. In these cases of concurrent jurisdiction, either party may select the federal courts; the plaintiff by the original choice of forum and the defendant by removal.[12]

The Supreme Court's jurisdiction is mainly appellate and is determined, within constitutional limits, by Congress. The mechanism of review is designed to limit those cases decided on the merits with full consideration to a relatively small and manageable number, which are usually of some concern to the public at large as well as to the litigants. Thus while the Court may dispose of more than four thousand cases a year, it decides less than ten percent of them on the merits and roughly one-half of this smaller number with full opinions. In most cases review may be had, if at all, only upon a *writ of certiorari*, a command issued from the Supreme Court to the lower federal court or to the state court of last resort requiring it to certify and return the record of the proceedings in the case. Even in a proper case, the issuance of such a writ is within the discretion of the Court; certiorari will only be granted for "special and important reasons" and the fact that the decision below is erroneous is not such a reason. The Supreme Court hears very few cases involving contract disputes.

An especially troublesome question that arises in diversity cases concerns what law the federal court is to apply. Over nearly a century, until 1938, the federal courts developed a "federal common law," binding on the federal courts but not on the state courts. During this period, the outcome of a contract dispute might have depended on which court, state or federal, heard the case. But in 1938, the Supreme Court held in *Erie Railroad Co.* v. *Tompkins*[13] that state case law was binding on the federal

12. There are some exceptions. A resident defendant who is sued in a state court by a non-resident plaintiff cannot remove on the ground of diversity.
13. 304 U.S. 64 (1938).

courts in diversity cases. Thus a federal court deciding a contract dispute in a diversity case is to apply state law so as to arrive at substantially the same outcome as would a court of the state in which the federal court sits.

10.4 Court Procedure in Civil Cases

The procedure followed in an American court in a civil case such as an action for breach of contract has been greatly influenced by two factors. First, the adversarial rather than inquisitorial character of litigation has encouraged the opposing lawyers to act as zealous partisans in presenting their cases, and has contributed to a tradition of surprise and proprietorship over witnesses and information. It has accorded a relatively passive role to the judge, who, in spite of some recent changes that make the judge more active, often acts only as arbiter and undertakes no independent investigation. Second, the institution of the jury has tended to compress the trial, has given it a dramatic flavor, and has resulted in elaborate rules to separate the functions of the jury from those of the judge and to control the jury. In spite of these similarities in approach to procedural problems, each state court system, as well as the federal court system, operates under its own law of civil procedure, so that the law of civil procedure is far from uniform.

Civil procedure varies not only with the jurisdiction but also with the remedy sought by the plaintiff. Most contract cases involve claims for compensatory money damages. Money damages are the standard remedy unless it is shown that compensatory relief will be inadequate so that equitable relief, such as a decree of specific performance or an injunction, may be granted. The discussion in this monograph is necessarily both general and simplified and is limited to the most common sort of case, an action *in personam* (that is, a personal action against the defendant) for compensatory money damages. The object of such an action is to determine the rights of the parties with respect to the controversy and to impose liability.

There is a sharp distinction between the proceedings that precede the trial and the trial itself. At the trial the issues of fact will be heard and determined. In the pre-trial proceedings these issues must be defined and the adversaries must be given adequate notice to prevent their surprise at the trial. This is of special importance because the trial, owing to the influence of the jury system, is normally concentrated in one continuous hearing in open court. Any rulings before trial are made, often after argument, by a judge without a jury.[14]

An action is commenced by two writings, a *complaint* and a *summons*. The complaint is a statement setting out the nature of the plaintiff's claim and a demand for relief. The summons is a notice informing the defendant that an action is being brought and calling upon the defendant to answer the complaint. In order to meet the constitutional requirement of due process, service of the summons must be by a means that is reasonably designed to give the defendant actual notice. Ordinarily it is delivered to the defendant personally or left with an appropriate person at the defendant's residence or place of business within the geographical jurisdiction of the court. In special cases service may be accomplished by mail, by publication, or by some other means. The defendant then commonly enters an appearance by filing a paper, known as an *answer*, that is responsive to the complaint; if the defendant does not appear, a default judgment may be entered against the defendant. The plaintiff's complaint, the defendant's answer and any reply the plaintiff may file, make up the pleadings. In a proper case the plaintiff may also use provisional remedies to ensure that the action, if successful, will not have been futile. For example, the plaintiff may be able through an attachment to have the defendant's property seized and held as security for any judgment, or to obtain a temporary injunction or restraining order to prevent the defendant from taking action to frustrate the plaintiff's suit.

Modern American systems of civil procedure are based on what is called *notice pleading*. The premise is that the function of the pleadings is merely to give the parties notice of the nature of their contentions; if further information is needed, other more efficient means of obtaining it are available. Thus the complaint need contain only a short and plain statement of the claim showing that that plaintiff is entitled to relief; allegations may be general and even inconsistent; and protection against surprise at trial is afforded by important new pre-trial procedures. The opportunities to learn about an opponent's case include, for example, the

---

14. Parties to litigation need not be, but almost invariably are, represented by lawyers, who undertake the preparation of the necessary papers and appear in court. The steps taken by the parties in the description that follows are, therefore, ordinarily taken by their lawyers in their clients' behalf. Judges in the United States wear black robes, but no wigs or caps. Lawyers wear business suits and jurors wear street dress.

right to interrogate the other party, to take the deposition of any person, and to inspect documents and property. In addition, the judge may call a pre-trial conference, a hearing at which both sides are present, in order to limit the issues and obtain admissions that will avoid unnecessary proof. Important by-products of the pre-trial conference are said to be the settlement of many cases without trial and the shortening of trials through concessions, limitation of issues, and better preparation.

Pre-trial procedure will occasionally result in a decision by the court that there should be no trial at all. The defendant may attack the legal basis of the plaintiff's case by a motion to dismiss the complaint on the ground that it fails to state a legally sufficient cause of action or claim for relief. The judge will grant the defendant's motion only if, assuming the truth of all the allegations of the complaint, the plaintiff would still have no right to relief. Such motions, however, rarely end the litigation. If the complaint is found to be insufficient, the plaintiff will ordinarily be allowed to amend it; if it is found to be sufficient, the defendant will usually interpose an answer that raises an issue of fact. This the defendant may do in two ways, either by denying some or all of the plaintiff's allegations or by alleging additional facts that constitute a defense. Under modern pre-trial procedure, however, it is sometimes possible to resolve even an issue of fact before trial. The judge may grant a motion for summary judgment in favor of either party if the judge determines, on the basis of affidavits and other documents, that there is no genuine issue of fact justifying a trial. The defendant may also make a variety of motions that do not go to the merits of the controversy. They range from a motion to dismiss the complaint because the court does not have jurisdiction to a motion to require the plaintiff to make the complaint more definite and certain or to give further particulars on some matter.

The great bulk of cases are settled or otherwise terminated before the trial stage. In the federal courts, for example, only about one out of every 20 cases commenced actually goes to trial, and judges often take an active—even aggressive—role in encouraging settlements. But if the plaintiff's complaint has withstood the defendant's tactics and if the case is not one of the great majority settled before the trial, the plaintiff will request the clerk of the court to put the case on a list, called a calendar or docket, to await trial. Because of the number of litigants, the plaintiff may have to wait for a substantial period of time, well over a year in some congested courts, before the case comes to trial.

Although modern pre-trial procedure has done much to counter the tradition of surprise and proprietorship over proof, it is still a basic tenet that the parties themselves can most effectively present their own cases and, after each case has been subjected to attack by an adversary, the truth can then be determined by an impartial tribunal. The trial is held before a single judge, who may sit with or without a jury. It may last for a matter of hours, days, or even weeks, and, particularly where a jury is involved, it is customarily a single continuous process without prolonged adjournment. Where the plaintiff seeks compensatory money damages, there is generally a right to jury trial, although this right may be waived. Jurors are not noted for their skill in coping with complex and involved transactions and, for this or for other reasons, both parties may prefer to put their case solely in the hands of a judge.

Assuming, however, that trial is to be by jury, the jurors are selected by lot from a larger group of qualified citizens, a cross section of the community, who have been summoned for jury duty. Traditionally there were 12 jurors, but many states now provide for a smaller number, ranging down to six. Jurors sit for a single case only and are paid a modest amount to cover expenses. They must meet minimum requirements relating to such matters as citizenship, eligibility to vote, age, general health, and impartiality. Prospective jurors are subjected to questioning on their qualifications and may be challenged for cause by either party and excluded if they are not qualified. In addition, each party has a number of peremptory challenges that may be used to exclude a juror without any stated reason. After the jurors have been sworn to try the issues, they are seated in the jury box, and the trial begins. It is the task of the jury, at least in theory, to decide issues of fact, and that of the judge to decide issues of law. The dividing line between the two is often a shadowy one, and, for example, whether the jury's decision on an issue of "fact" has been reasonable is itself an issue of "law."

The plaintiff has the initial burden of presenting evidence. First, both parties make opening statements in which they explain their side of the case to the jury so that it will be better able to follow the proof. (In some jurisdictions, however, the defendant's opening is not made until just before the defendant's proof.) The plaintiff then proceeds with proof. This is done by the introduction of both oral and written evidence. Documentation may be voluminous in large cases where business records are involved. The initiative is on the parties rather than the judge to develop the evidence. The parties bear the sole responsibility for producing the proof, and witnesses are generally called on behalf of the parties themselves and not on behalf of the court. The court may, by subpeona, order a person who is within the court's territorial jurisdiction to appear and give testimony or to produce a writing or object, if the witness will not do so voluntarily. The parties themselves are generally allowed to testify.

The first witness for the plaintiff is called to the witness stand for direct examination and is sworn to tell the truth.[15] The witness's testimony is elicited by questions posed by the plaintiff's lawyer. It is the practice of lawyers in the United States to discuss with their clients' witnesses their testimony in advance of trial in order to prevent waste of time and surprise at trial. It is, of course, improper for a lawyer to use this occasion to manipulate the testimony of the witness. After direct examination, the defendant's lawyer is permitted to cross-examine the witness to show additional facts or inconsistencies or to attack the witness's credibility. Because the witness has been called on behalf of the plaintiff, the right to cross-examination is an important one. There may then be redirect and recross-examination. The judge may also question the witness, but the burden of examination is on the opposing lawyers. Other witnesses are then called and documents and physical objects may be presented. These are subject to the rules of evidence, however, and, for example, the results of the pre-trial procedure, such as depositions and documents, are not necessarily admissible at the trial. A party is expected to make prompt objection if an improper question is asked or if an inadmissible item is proferred; failure to do so is ordinarily a waiver of the objection.

At this point the plaintiff must have introduced enough evidence on all issues as to which the plaintiff has the burden of proof to justify a favorable jury verdict. The defendant may test whether the plaintiff has done so by a motion that the action be dismissed. The issue raised is only whether a reasonable jury could, on the basis of the plaintiff's evidence, reach a verdict for the plaintiff. This is therefore regarded as an issue of law rather than one of fact, and the judge alone passes upon the motion. If it is granted, the dismissal ends the trial and operates as a judgment on the merits for the defendant. If it is denied, the defendant must proceed with proof.

The defendant will present evidence in the same manner as did the plaintiff. This time the latter will have the right of cross-examination. At the conclusion of the defendant's case, the plaintiff may offer proof in rebuttal. At the close of all the evidence either party may move for a directed verdict on the ground that a reasonable jury could only return a verdict in favor of the moving party. This motion is also considered to raise

15. A witness who has religious scruples about taking an oath can make an affirmation.

a question of law rather than one of fact. If the judge grants the motion, the trial will end and judgment will be entered for the moving party. Under modern practice the judge no longer actually goes through the formality of directing the jury to bring in the appropriate verdict. If the judge denies the motion, the trial will proceed to its conclusion.

Both parties will then make their closing arguments to the jury. In some jurisdictions the plaintiff's closing is first, followed by the defendant's closing, and then by the plaintiff's rebuttal. In others the defendant's closing is first, followed by the plaintiff's closing. Arguments must be confined to the evidence that has been presented, and each side will attempt, by analysis of the proof, to persuade the jury that it should decide the case in its favor.

The judge will then charge the jury by instructing it in the rules of law under which it is to reach its decision. Before closing argument, both sides may submit to the judge instructions that they propose that the judge give, and the judge will then disclose to them the instructions that will be given so that they can frame their argument accordingly. In some jurisdictions, however, the charge is given before the closing argument. The authority of the judge was reduced during the nineteenth century as a result of confidence in the average juror's abilities and of unpleasant recollections of arbitrary and absolute judges who were supposed to have represented crown control during colonial times. The narrower role of the judge has resulted in a wider one for the jury, and indirectly for the opposing lawyers. One symptom of this is the rule in a number of states that the charge must not contain any comment on the weight of the evidence or the credibility of the witnesses, but must be confined to the rules of law to be applied. In some states the judge is not even permitted to summarize the evidence and in some he may not charge the jury orally but must do so in writing. These limitations have been much criticized by the organized bar, however, and the trend is now toward an expansion of the judge's role. Where the trial has been without a jury there is, of course, no charge.

After the charge, the jurors retire to the jury room where they deliberate in secret for a matter of hours and sometimes days, until they reach their verdict. In a civil case the jury must be persuaded "by a preponderance of the evidence," or, in other words, that the existence of the contested fact is more probable than not. Historically the verdict of the jurors had to be unanimous, but this rule has often been altered by constitution or statute. In some jurisdictions, however, less than a unanimous verdict is possible only with the consent of the parties. The "hung" jury, one unable to reach a decision by the required majority, is nevertheless highly unusual. The jury may be polled by asking each juror in open court whether he or she agrees with the verdict in order to make certain that the required number of jurors consent. No record is kept of their deliberations and rules severely restrict jurors from testifying to impeach their own verdict. The jury's verdict may be simply a general one, finding for one side with an assessment of damages; or the jury may be required to answer specific questions of fact put to it by the judge.[16] In some places the verdict is given orally. In others a written verdict signed by the foreman is returned and the jury gives oral assent when it is read in court.

After receiving the verdict, the judge discharges the jury, and the trial is ended. If there has been no jury the judge makes findings of fact and conclusions of law. The judge may also write an opinion.

After the jury verdict, the losing party may move for a new trial on a variety of grounds, including prejudicial error by the judge in ruling on the admissibility of evidence or in instructing the jury, or a verdict that is against the weight of the evidence. If the judge concludes that the damages awarded by the jury are unreasonably high, the judge may by a device known as *remittitur* subtract an appropriate amount and order a new trial if the change is not accepted by the parties. The losing party may also make a motion for judgment notwithstanding the verdict in order to permit the judge to give a favorable judgment on the merits where the judge had denied an earlier motion to direct a verdict in favor of the losing party. The grounds of the earlier and the later motions are the same. The judge may be more willing to grant a motion to give judgment as a matter of law after the jury has reached its verdict because, should the granting of the motion be reversed on appeal, there is then a verdict upon which the appellate court can enter judgment and it will save the time and expense of a new trial. The judge will also have had more time to deliberate before passing on a motion for judgment notwithstanding the verdict.

Finally, assuming that all motions made after the verdict was rendered have been denied, judgment will be entered on the verdict. The judgment will ordinarily require the losing party to pay the costs of the successful party. These include such fees as those paid to the court by the successful party but generally do not include lawyers' fees. If the losing party refuses to pay a money judgment, a number of procedures are available by way of

---

16. Traditionally the answers to specific questions were given in the form of a special, as distinguished from a general, verdict. Today a more common procedure is to ask the jury for a general verdict together with the answers to questions known as interrogatories.

execution. For example, that party's property may be seized by a court officer and sold at a public sale to pay the judgment.

After the trial, a party may appeal from the judgment, claiming error on the part of the trial judge. During the appeal, execution of judgment can be suspended upon the posting of a bond by the appellant. Ordinarily the appellant must have taken appropriate steps during the trial, by making or opposing a motion, by raising an objection, or otherwise bringing the matter to the attention of the judge. By the end of the trial the judge will have ruled on a variety of such contested points—motions attacking pleadings, objections to the admission or exclusion of evidence, motions for a directed verdict, and so on. The appeal will usually be based on one or more of these rulings. Whether the losing party may appeal from interlocutory rulings that are not finally dispositive of the case will vary from state to state.

There is no new trial, no jury, no witnesses, in the appellate court. The judges' knowledge of the case is derived solely from the record, a stenographic transcript of the proceedings in the lower court that shows the asserted errors of the trial judge. The appellate court is aided by detailed written briefs prepared by the parties in support of their cases. When the question on appeal is of importance beyond the immediate parties themselves, the court may also have before it a brief *amicus curiae*, one by a "friend of the court" such as the government or an interested private group. Oral proceedings are limited to questions of law, and the parties will urge upon the court those precedents and other authorities that they regard as controlling. The court will not intrude upon the province of the jury as trier of issues of fact, but it may determine that the jury exceeded the bounds of reasonableness in reaching its verdict if this issue has been raised by a proper motion before the trial judge. The appellate court will be reluctant to reach such a conclusion, however, where the judge and jury have had the opportunity of observing key witnesses when they testified.

The decision of the court, usually accompanied by a written opinion, may not be handed down for weeks or even months while the judges study the briefs and confer among themselves. If the court finds that there was no error (or if there was error that it was "harmless" and probably did not affect the outcome) it will affirm the judgment below. If it finds reversible error, it will reverse the judgment and remand the case either for entry of judgment for the appellant or for a new trial, depending on the circumstances. If the case is remanded, the lower court is bound to follow the instructions of the appellate court. The costs of the appeal, which again fall short of actual expenses, are borne by the losing party, and the expense of appeals tends to limit the number of litigants who seek review.

10.5 Arbitration

Although the United States has no special courts for commercial matters, like those that exist in some countries, it does have a well established tradition of arbitration of commercial disputes. One of the advantages of arbitration is that arbitrators, unlike judges, can be chosen for their experience and expertise in the field involved in the dispute. Other advantages are said to include speed, economy, informality, and privacy.[17]

In the United States, arbitration commonly is a voluntary system created by the agreement of the parties. The existence and scope of an arbitrator's powers are based on contract; arbitration is available only if and to the extent that the parties have agreed on it. The agreement may take the form of an agreement submitting to arbitration of an existing dispute, but more often it takes the form of an agreement to arbitrate future disputes. In addition, there is a growing tendency in the United States to use alternate dispute resolution as auxiliary proceedings in courts, with the litigants required to participate but free to return to the regular court processes if dissatisfied with the outcome.

Common law judges were initially hostile to agreements to arbitrate; judges in England and the United States regarded such agreements as "ousting" the courts of jurisdiction. This judicial attitude was met by the enactment of state and federal arbitration laws that make agreements to arbitrate both present and future disputes enforceable and provide for court enforcement of both arbitration agreements and awards. In addition, the United States is a party to the United Nations (New York) Convention on the Recognition and Enforcement of Arbitral Awards. Today, courts generally regard arbitration with approval rather than hostility.

The arbitration agreement need not refer to any set of arbitration rules or appointing agency. It is common, however, to specify both the arbitration rules and the appointing agency. The largest and most important agency in the United States that administers commercial arbitration is the American Arbitration Association (AAA). It is a private nonprofit organization, founded in 1926, with headquarters in New York City and offices throughout the country. It both serves as an appointing agency and promulgates rules for the conduct of commercial arbitration.

If the parties do not name the arbitrators or specify how they are to be selected, the AAA will select either one or three arbitrators from extensive

17. See generally Domke on Commercial Arbitration (rev. ed. G. Wilner, looseleaf).

lists of tens of thousands of arbitrators from all over the country that it keeps on file. Some of these persons are lawyers, but many are non-lawyers who have expertise in particular fields. Commercial arbitrators often serve without fee, as a public service.

Arbitration has long been especially common in the textile industry. The General Arbitration Council of the Textile Industry, now part of the AAA, administers textile arbitrations. Arbitration is also popular in the construction industry. Clauses providing for AAA arbitration under the Construction Industry Arbitration Rules are found in hundreds of thousands of building contracts, and several thousand construction cases go to arbitration every year. Arbitration is, of course, also in regular use in international transactions, where the International Chamber of Commerce is often designated as the administering agency.

Under AAA rules, each party has the right to be represented by a lawyer at the hearing, and in complex commercial disputes lawyers usually represent both parties. But the proceedings are less formal than courtroom proceedings. The parties sit on opposite sides of a conference table and the usual rules of evidence are relaxed. Evidence is, however, still often presented by the direct testimony of witnesses, who are subject to cross-examination.

In granting relief, an arbitrator has broad powers comparable to those of a judge. The award in an arbitration proceeding is binding and cannot be appealed. It can, however, be challenged in court on a very limited number of grounds. Thus a court may vacate an award if, for example, it was procured by fraud or the arbitrator exceeded his powers, but the court will not review the award on its merits. (Arbitrators in commercial cases do not usually write opinions explaining their awards, so it is often difficult to tell whether an arbitrator has exceeded his powers.) Because there is no appeal on the merits, the time and expense that might otherwise be spent on appellate litigation is avoided.

10.6 Other Alternate Dispute Resolution Techniques

In recent years, the United States has experienced what some have called a "litigation explosion," a dramatic increase in recourse to the court system. At the same time, American businesses have become increasingly aware of the costs in time, energy, and of money going to court. Many American business executives have an uneasy sense that if they go to court they lose control of the situation to their lawyers. The result has been a heightened interest in the resolution of disputes, such as those arising out of contracts, by informal techniques of alternate dispute resolution that will avoid the courts and may also lessen the influence of lawyers.

In addition to the traditional technique of arbitration, other alternatives to the court system include *mediation and conciliation*, *fact-finding*, and *mini-trial*. These other alternatives differ from arbitration in that they are generally non-binding and are intended to induce the parties to agree to settle their dispute. Such a settlement may, of course, occur without the use of any of these techniques—and it has already been pointed out that many court cases are settled during the pre-trial stage, without a trial.[18] The advocates of alternative dispute resolution, however, urge that the other alternatives mentioned here be used at a much earlier time, before any recourse has been had to the judicial system.

Mediation and conciliation are techniques for encouraging the parties to settle their dispute through the help of a neutral third party in whom both parties have confidence. These techniques are well-established in connection with disputes between labor unions and management, but are relatively new in connection with disputes between businesses. Sometimes the term *mediation* is used when the role of the third party (or mediator) is limited to encouraging dialogue between the parties, while the term *conciliation* is reserved for the situation where the third party (or conciliator) plays a more active role and may make specific proposals for settlement; sometimes the two terms are used interchangeably. In any case, the role of the third party—perhaps a retired judge—is not, in contrast to that of an arbitrator, that of resolving the dispute. If the parties cannot settle the dispute themselves, they can then go to court or to arbitration. Several organizations, including the American Arbitration Association, have promulgated mediation or conciliation rules.

Fact-finding is another technique for encouraging the parties to settle their dispute that is useful if difficult—and particularly technical—issues of fact are at the center of the dispute. The parties agree on the appointment of an independent third party who investigates the circumstances that gave rise to the dispute and makes findings of fact. The third party may have expertise that a judge would not have and may work more rapidly than a judge could. The findings are then used as the basis for settlement negotiations by the parties. (Occasionally, the parties agree to be bound by the findings.)

---

18. See § 10.1 supra.

The newest form of alternative dispute resolution is the mini-trial, an informal, confidential, and non-binding technique that has grown in popularity during the 1980's. It is thought to be particularly well-suited to complex disputes involving mixed questions of law and fact. The mini-trial involves two stages: first, exchange of information about a dispute and, second, negotiation in an attempt to settle the dispute. The exchange of information is achieved by having lawyers for both sides make summary presentations of their cases to senior executives of both sides who have authority to reach a settlement of the dispute. A neutral adviser chosen by the parties—for example a retired judge—may also be present. These presentations, which may take a day or two, are followed by negotiations between the executives, who meet without their lawyers, in an attempt to reach a practical settlement in the light of their knowledge of the business situation.

The so called "mini-trial" is not, of course, a trial at all. The executives who hear their lawyers present their cases do not reach a binding decision in the manner of judges or arbitrators. The object of the hearing is to give the executives a clear and balanced idea of the positions of both parties, including both strengths and weaknesses. This exchange of information plays an especially important role if, as is often the case, the lawyers and executives for each side have convinced themselves of the righteousness of their cause and have become overly optimistic as to their chances of success in court or arbitration. The purpose is to convert what has become a "lawyer's dispute" back into a "business person's problem."

Because the mini-trial is a voluntary technique, like all forms of alternate dispute resolution, its use depends on agreement by the parties. Usually the agreement results from one party's proposal to submit an existing dispute to a mini-trial, though it is also possible to provide in the contract itself that any disputes that may arise shall go to a mini-trial. Since the mini-trial is a new type of alternate dispute resolution it is still in its formative stage and the procedure for each mini-trial must be worked out by the parties in advance. (The parties may, for example, provide for a neutral third party who will render an advisory opinion if the parties are deadlocked.) Recently, however, some guidelines for mini-trials have been promulgated by organizations connected with dispute resolution.[19] The efficacy of the mini-trial is still to be determined and it is not yet clear whether it will meet with widespread acceptance.

---

19. The American Arbitration Association has promulgated Mini-Trial Procedures and the Center for Public Resources has issued a model mini-trial agreement that contains rules.

AFTERWORD

This monograph is composed of two separate accounts—one by an American author, the other by a Soviet author—of the contract law of their respective countries. There are, to be sure, some disadvantages to this method. Each of us is a product of his own system and cannot entirely escape the parochialism of his own background. Each has, however, to the best of his ability, presented a fair account of the law of his land as he understands it. At the outset, we agreed on the subjects to be treated in the five chapters and on the general scope of each chapter. By the end, we were giving each other editorial assistance. Our collaboration was facilitated by Viktor Mozolin's ability to work in both languages. The close contact that our work occasioned has been a source of great personal satisfaction to us both.

The reader who has reached this point in our monograph will be aware that it has two major limitations: it is essentially doctrinal, and it is not comparative. Its doctrinal character was more or less inevitable given our backgrounds and the nature of the enterprise. While each of us has the training and the means to discuss the legal rules that affect contracts in his own country, neither of us is equipped to describe how these rules actually work in practice. When it has seemed appropriate to do so, we have tried to point out how particular rules are affected by the society for which they were designed. We do not, however, pretend that we have given an account of how the institution of contract actually functions in either the Soviet Union or the United States. Thus we have not attempted to amass statistics on the relative role of contractual autonomy as opposed to state planning in the Soviet Union or on the relative importance of contract as compared to vertical integration of business in the United States. Our legal systems have a wealth of rules, and it is those rules that we have emphasized. Indeed, Allan Farnsworth found it of interest that these rules are as elaborate as they are in Soviet contract law.

The fact that our monograph is not comparative is scarcely surprising in view of the fact that neither of us is a comparatist. Viktor Mozolin has studied American law in the United States, Allan Farnsworth has worked with lawyers from civil-law countries, and both have had extensive contacts with law students from many other legal systems. Each author has therefore written with some appreciation for the difficulties faced when the law of his land is confronted by one trained in another law. Nevertheless, it was not our intention to compare contract law in our two countries. When we began the project, however, we did hope that we might be able to write a common part—some pages dealing with contract law both in the Soviet Union and in the United States—to which we could both subscribe.

In these shared pages we would prefer to emphasize what we see as similarities, rather than to stress differences. The latter course would be an easy one, given the geographical distance between our two countries, the gulf between our two social systems, and our very different national histories. We would rather, however, leave that course to others. While we have not ignored contradictions and differences, we have tried to find similarities and analogies when they exist. This is the first of what we expect to be a series of monographs, and the identification of similarities at this early stage may help to open a path for subsequent authors.

Although the two legal systems are enough alike to invite an attempt to compare them, finding similarities has not always been easy. When we looked at the contract law of our two countries, we too were first struck by the apparent contradictions and differences. In the Soviet Union, the legal tradition is one of civil law, derived from Roman law, with a theoretical deductive approach and a heavy emphasis on legislative sources. In the United States, the legal tradition is one of common law, based on English law, with a pragmatic inductive approach and a dependence on cases and precedent. These two traditions have even produced different definitions of the word *contract*. In the Soviet Union the term is taken to refer not only to promises of future performance but also to present performances under, for example, a cash sale. In the United States, however, the word is commonly used to refer only to promises and not, for example, to a cash sale. Furthermore, in the Soviet Union, as in most Continental countries, the subject of contracts is considered a part of the law of obligations, which is in turn a part of civil law. In the United States, on the other hand, the subject of contracts is thought of as a separate one, distinct, for example, from the law of torts.

In the Soviet Union the economic system is one of planned economy, with state ownership of the basic means of production and state involvement in distribution. In the United States the economic system is one of market economy, with private ownership of means of production and no state involvement in distribution. Thus specific performance is a routine type of relief, and liquidated damage and penalty clauses are a familiar feature of many varieties of contracts in the Soviet Union, where they provide the desired effect of reenforcing the obligation to perform in a system in which alternative sources of performance are not generally available and the principal object of contract remedies is to induce performance. But specific relief is generally unavailable and penalty clauses are unenforceable in the United States, where the injured party is traditionally expected to find an alternative source of performance and the principal object of contract remedies is merely to encourage parties to rely on exchanges of promises.

Furthermore, in some matters we found differences that seemed to have no explanation based on either legal tradition or economic system. Thus, while there is a general similarity in the rules relating to contract formation, with both legal systems relying on traditional notions of offer and acceptance, there is a tendency in American law to overlook minor discrepancies between offer and acceptance, a tendency that appears to have no counterpart in Soviet law. And in matters of contract interpretation, American law now uses an "objective" standard based on reasonable expectation, a notion that is not as well accepted in Soviet law, except in connection with foreign trade arbitration.

The histories of our two nations have been very different. Nevertheless, with respect to historical background, we perceive a few analogies. First, there is the "reception" of law. Because both legal systems were born—or reborn—after revolutions, both countries faced a question as to how much of the old law was to be "received" after the revolution. In the United States, where the old law was the law of England, a colonial power, the question was resolved by the adoption of statutes "receiving" a substantial part of the English law of the time until more suitable American rules could be put into operation. In the Soviet Union shortly after the Great October Revolution, pre-revolutionary law was abolished by statute. But during the first codification of civil law in 1922-1925, some legal rules of European—mostly German—origin suitable to the Soviet Union in the first years of the NEP were included in the civil codes of Union republics. This "reception," however, was limited to relations among individuals and lasted for only a short period of time. We find it interesting, though not surprising, that, at the time of reception, contract law was an area in which the old bodies of law seemed to be particularly tenacious in both countries.

Second, there is the matter of unification. Because each country is a union of political units that have the power to enact laws dealing with contracts, a question arises under each legal system as to whether it is desirable and feasible to unify contract law throughout the country. The

United States has unified contract law, notably that related to the sale of goods, by a process of state-by-state ratification of the Uniform Commercial Code, supplemented by a curiously private and nonbinding series of Restatements. Although this process strikes the Soviet author as cumbersome, it has been reasonably successful. The Soviet Union has unified contract law related to most kinds of contracts and particularly to economic contracts—a step that suggests the value of contracts in practice. Yet the Soviet Union has had what Allan Farnsworth considers to be surprising difficulty in producing a codified version of contract law centrally enacted for the entire nation, and has instead enacted a more general set of legal rules embodied in the Fundamentals of Civil Legislation. We think it noteworthy that both legal systems have had some problems defining the role that the central government should play, at least in principle, to produce uniformity in the field of contract law.

When we looked at the distinctions that have grown out of differences in the economic systems of the two countries, we found it more difficult to perceive similarities and analogies. The unfettered autonomy that is traditionally allowed parties to commercial contracts in the United States is necessarily limited in the Soviet Union, where commercial contracts are expected to comport with the system of state planning. In view of this, we find it somewhat anomalous that American courts, like other common-law courts, have refused to give parties unfettered autonomy where penalties for breach are involved. The Soviet Union takes a quite different approach in this respect.

The differences produced by the two economic systems, considerable as they are, may not be as great as they seem at first sight. Contracts play an important role in the planned economy of the Soviet Union as well as in the market economy of the United States. Furthermore, the unique features that each country has given to the institution of contract are not found uniformly throughout the system. In Soviet law, the peculiarities of a planned economy are not universal and do not extend to relations among individuals, who are governed by legal rules similar to those in countries without planned economies. In American law, the peculiarities characteristic of a market economy are likewise not universal and do not extend, for example, to government contracts, collective bargaining agreements, or agreements between public utilities and their customers. Each system contains extremes of contractual autonomy and of planning and has elaborate rules for both extremes, though the mix is very different in the two systems—a theme that will be developed in the second monograph in this series.

It is of interest that both legal systems show a tendency toward fragmentation of contract law. In the Soviet Union this is especially evident in distinctions among economic contracts, contracts between organizations and the individuals that they serve, and contracts between individuals. A similar tendency in the United States has produced distinctions depending on whether merchants or consumers are parties and on whether the subject of the contract is, for example, goods or insurance. Both systems have felt a need in the interests of society as a whole and in the interests of protection for individuals to give special treatment to consumers, tenants, and others. The presence of a market system in the United States has, however, given this tendency an urgency not felt in the Soviet Union, a matter that will be explored in the second mongraph in this series.

Certainly, if one were to compare contract law in America in the latter part of the nineteenth century, when freedom of contract was at its apogee, and contract law in the Soviet Union before the NEP period of the 1920s, when reliance on contract was at its nadir, one would see the greatest possible contrast. Since those two points in time, however, the two contract systems have tended to become more alike under the influence of such factors as greater complexity in human relationships and increasing economic demands of society.

Of what importance is it, the reader may ask, if contract law in the two countries shows a tendency to move closer, to diverge, or to do neither? To answer this question we must distinguish contract law from, for example, family law or criminal law, which primarily affect the internal affairs of nations. Contract law, by contrast, plays an important role in international trade. To the extent that contract law throughout the world shows a tendency to harmonize, this cannot but facilitate that trade.

In this regard, we note with interest that representatives of our two countries were among the most active participants in the drafting by the United Nations Commission on International Trade Law of a Convention on the International Sale of Goods, a convention that has already been ratified by the United States. This convention has as a premise that there is a common set of fundamental principles governing the sale of goods, principles that are either shared by nations throughout the world or can be accepted by those nations regardless of historical background or economic system. The acceptance that the Convention has thus far received encourages us to emphasize similarities and analogies rather than differences and contradictions in our systems of contract law.

As the world grows smaller and as occasions for international intercourse increase, the need to find some middle ground among widely differing legal systems will become more urgent. We hope that tendencies in our two countries will facilitate this commonality. And we hope further that our monograph will have in some small way encouraged this beneficial development.

E. Allan Farnsworth
Viktor P. Mozolin

INDEX